THIS IS DOUG HALL

THIS IS DOUG HALL

A Memoir

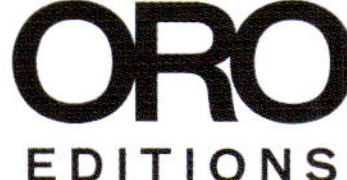

ORO EDITIONS

I feel there is much to be said for the Celtic belief that the souls of those whom we have lost are held captive in some inferior being, in an animal, in a plant, in some inanimate object, and are effectively lost to us until the day (which to many never comes) when we happen to pass by the tree or to obtain possession of the object which forms their prison. Then they start and tremble, they call us by our name, and as soon as we have recognized their voice the spell is broken. We have delivered them: they have overcome death and return to share our life.

—Marcel Proust, *Swann's Way*, "Overture"

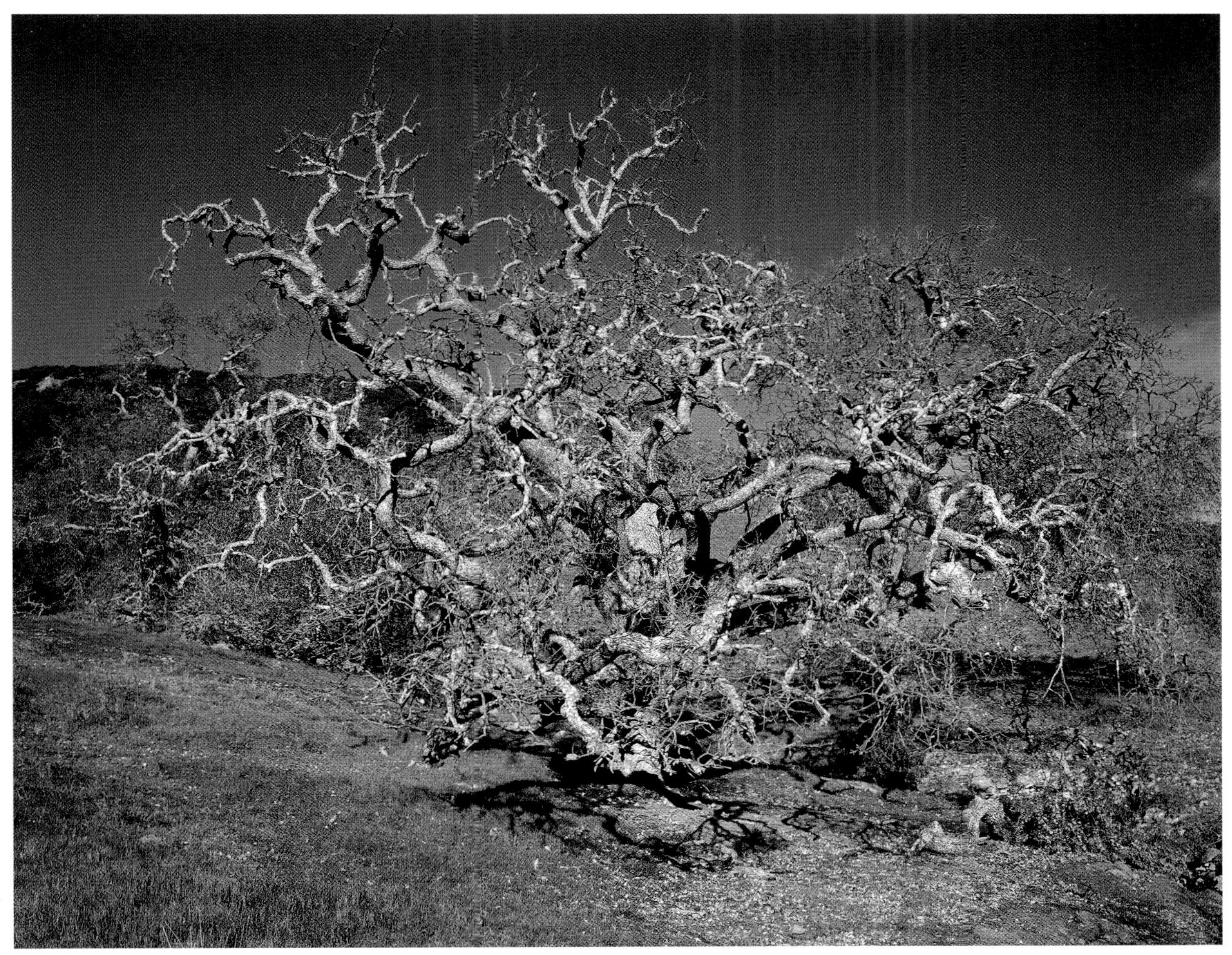

Doug Hall, *Olompali Valley Oak I*, 2023. Pigment print, 48 × 60 in. (121.9 × 152.4 cm)

For

Diane
Gannon
Atticus
Augustin

In solidarity

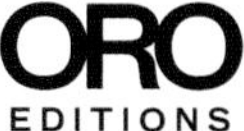

ORO Editions
Publishers of Architecture, Art, and Design
Gordon Goff: Publisher

www.oroeditions.com
info@oroeditions.com

Published by ORO Editions

Author: Doug Hall
Book Design: Miko McGinty, Inc.
Project Manager: Jake Anderson

10 9 8 7 6 5 4 3 2 1 First Edition

ISBN: 978-1-961856-11-0

Prepress and Print work by ORO Editions Inc
Printed in China

ORO Editions makes a continuous effort to minimize the overall carbon footprint of its publications. As part of this goal, ORO, in association with Global ReLeaf, arranges to plant trees to replace those used in the manufacturing of the paper produced for its books. Global ReLeaf is an international campaign run by American Forests, one of the world's oldest nonprofit conservation organizations. Global ReLeaf is American Forests' education and action program that helps individuals, organizations, agencies, and corporations improve the local and global environment by planting and caring for trees.

Contents

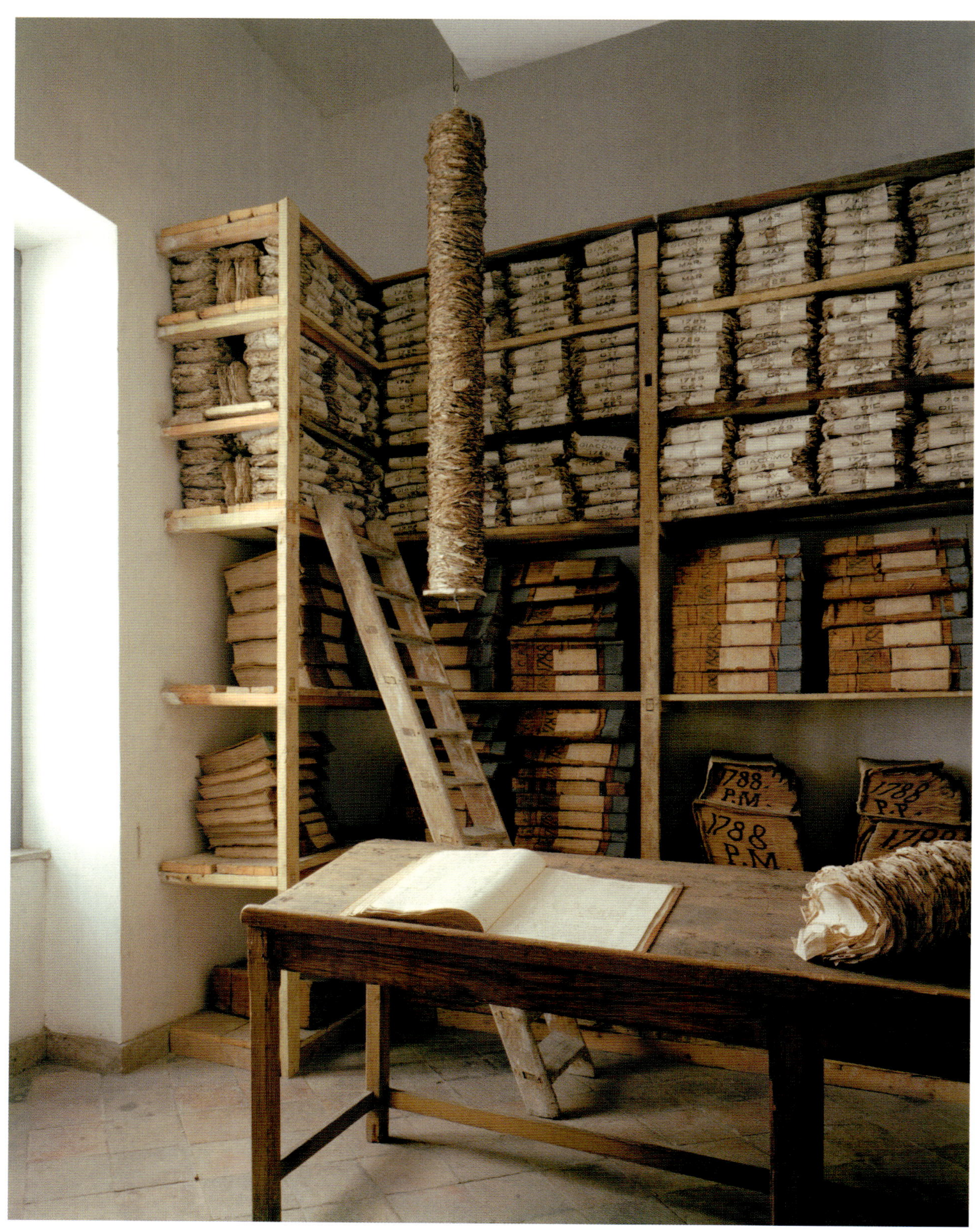

Doug Hall, *Archive of the Bank of Naples, 1780s Room*, 1996. Pigment print, 61 × 48 in. (154 × 121.9 cm)

Acknowledgments

Memory is such a strange thing. We think it accurately represents what happened, but in my memory-harvesting for this book, what surfaced was far from photographically accurate. Memory is corrupted by time and influences of which we are barely conscious. I think of this distortion as being somewhat like the game of telephone we played as children, when, by the tenth person in line, the whispered phrase that started out as "I love caramel ice cream" might become "The dove and the camel dream." In an email exchange with my son, Gannon, about the nature of memory, he wrote, "When we think about the past our cognitive machinations create a 'memory' which is nothing like a recording of what happened. It is a retelling of what happened as filtered through our processing of emotion, regret, joy, etc." In that way, our memories are true enough in that they represent our sense of self—a foundation from which we can begin to reflect on our lives. It is with this understanding that I offer my recollections and thoughts—my memories—in this book. My twofold intention is that my remembrances accurately portray the tone of the times in which I emerged as an artist and the events that sent me on my particular path, and that they reflect honest insight into the *who* of *what* I am as revealed over the trajectory of my life.

What started as a modest project of self-study, intended for an audience of one, me, grew over the two years of its writing into a more expansive exploration of my thoughts about teaching, the relationship between theory and practice, critical language, urban space, political spectacle, allegory, and the sublime, to name some of the topics most central to my eclectic interests. I was of course aided by diary entries, numerous published and unpublished essays, notes for realized and unrealized projects, photos, and assorted memorabilia, all of which I accessed in gathering material for what became this book. That these disparate resources eventually coalesced into something was largely due to the encouragement I received from a few trusted friends and family members who read my manuscript at various stages. I am indebted to two of the earliest readers: my wife, Diane Andrews Hall, and sister Lyn Hejinian, who encouraged me to forge onward without premature self-criticism, an unhealthy tendency to which I am susceptible—one that can undermine any creative act before it has a chance. Architect, author, and educator Nicholas de Monchaux helped me understand the world of book publishing, noting the importance of perseverance in the face of likely rejection.

As the words multiplied and the pages accumulated into a full manuscript, I needed additional feedback. For this I turned to screenwriter and actor Richard Marcus, and to author Alexandra Zapruder, whose books include *Twenty-Six Seconds: A Personal History of the Zapruder Film*, her fascinating account of her grandfather's "home movie" that had an impact on my own life. After further refinement, curator and author Steve Seid, media artist Jeanne C. Finley, and art collector Robin Wright read the entire manuscript and gave me invaluable criticism. Thank you all.

I am hugely indebted to Kathryn Moll, best known as an architect and partner with Nicholas de Monchaux in the interdisciplinary design practice Modem, for developmental editing that helped turn my thoughts and stories into a comprehensible narrative. Judy Bloch provided line and copy editing. She approached the task with rigor, humor, and a keen understanding of what I was trying to accomplish, making a potentially contentious phase of the project fun and interesting.

I have been fortunate to work with Miko McGinty Design. My deepest gratitude to Miko, Tina Henderson, Rita Jules, and Eleanor Morgan for their beautiful work. They understood the aesthetic I wanted to bring to the project and implemented it—no, vastly improved on it—in ways that I could not have imagined. Thank you also Sasha Wizansky, owner of Bartlett Books, who offered early design consultancy; and artist Jim Campbell, who helped solve more than one technical problem as I prepared the photographs for publication.

This is an unusual book, a memoir that wants to be visually stunning while remaining readable. Not a coffee table book but one that you lift from your bedside table in the evening to read before going to sleep. It required a unique publisher. It was a revelation to discover ORO Editions, whose main office is in Marin County, my backyard. I am indebted to owner Gordon Goff and his colleague Ashley Simone, who were immediately enthusiastic about the project and, understanding what I was after, committed to its publication. I am grateful to ORO's chief operating officer, Jake Anderson, who oversaw production with great care and attention. And thank you, Cathy Simon, who originally put me in touch with Ashley.

The great advantage of working with a fine art publisher like ORO is that one gets a level of image quality and overall feel to the book that is impossible with more mainstream, including academic, publications. The downside is that the author or supporting institution must cover some of the production costs, and they are significant. I appreciate the fiscal sponsorship that BAVC Media, San Francisco, granted me for this project. This book never would have been published without the generous help of Rena Bransten, Laurie Cohen, Eric Fischl, April Gornik, Diane Andrews Hall, Lyn Hejinian, Paull Hejinian, Ree Katrak, Teresa Metcalf, Jim Newman, Steve and Nancy Oliver, Laurie Plant, Pamela Helena Wilson, and Robin Wright. Thank you, also, Rachel Smith and Renee Bovenzi at Benrubi Gallery, and Rena and Trish Bransten, Jenny Baie, China Langford, and Kira Lyons at Rena Bransten Gallery for your support for this and many other projects over the years.

I must acknowledge all those who have supported and challenged me over the years—friends, colleagues, curators, students (particularly students), and scholars too numerous to name. My life would have been very different had I not known you.

Finally, a special tribute to my sister, Lyn Hejinian (1941–2024), who passed away as I was doing the final edits on this manuscript. As a writer, thinker, and loving comrade she inspired me, as she did countless others.

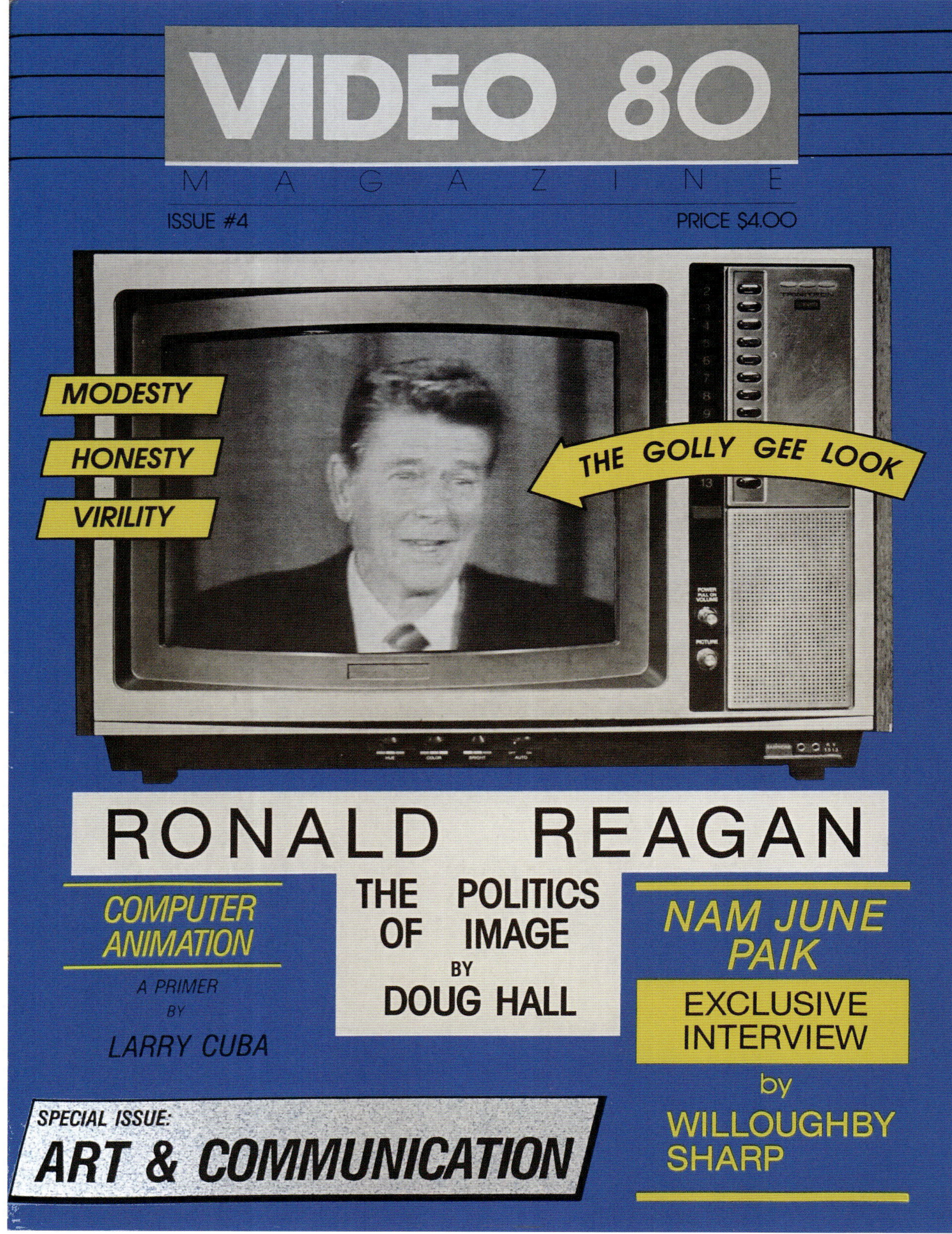

Video 80, No. 4, Spring/Summer, 1982. Published by the San Francisco International Video Festival. Cover article, "Ronald Reagan: The Politics of Image," by Doug Hall

The Terrible Uncertainty: An Introduction by Steve Seid

I met Doug Hall during a pivotal moment in his artistic endeavors. This demanding and insightful artist with a philosopher's stoned bearing was temporarily stymied. Having stepped away from T. R. Uthco, a decade-long performative collaboration with Jody Procter and Diane Andrews Hall, Doug was between two worlds: one dying, one yet unborn. Nevertheless, Hall would not waste this hiatus as he subtly reconfigured his aesthetic outlook, casting about for a new medium of expression. The platform he selected to fill this temporary gulf was single-channel video, again. Doug had helped orchestrate two seminal videoworks, gracing both with his searing "Artist-President" impersonations: *Media Burn* (1975) as a guest operative with Ant Farm, and more impactfully, *The Eternal Frame* (1976) with Ant Farm and T. R. Uthco as co-equal partners. These efforts were anything but solo, their logistics, resources, and inspiration being necessarily collective.

But this time, it was definitely solo. Well, almost. *The Amarillo News Tapes* (1980), staged at a functioning news station in Texas, was transitional, engaging Procter and Ant Farmer Chip Lord in a last hurrah. Here, the artists dissected the construction of the news, its embedded bias, its spectacular requirements (in the Debordian sense). Doug, posing as an anchorman, utters the remarkable one-liner, "People came and went on surfaces made for that purpose." What more could you ask for? The banality of observation made plain, the condescension exquisite.

Then on January 20, 1981, Ronald Reagan was sworn in as president. Over the next two years, Hall honed a half-dozen purposefully crude videoworks, each decimating some aspect of image domination, a practice Ronnie Raygun excelled at. To revisit these works, gathered in proximity to his *Songs of the 80s*, is to be startled by Doug's prescience. What he denounced then, the insidious politics of persuasion, has come back to us with a vengeance, now powered by a pack of feral media outlets and unscrupulous communicators, i.e., the Trumpian juggernaut.

If you detect the lack of weighted attention to these sirenic songs in Doug's meticulous memoir, don't assume he himself doesn't fully recognize their acute but deflating critique. There was just a lot to come. Yet, here I am praising them and their slightly knotty, haranguing nature—their sudden relevance. *The Speech* (1982), *This Is the Truth* (1982), and *These Are the Rules* (1983) find Hall jettisoning the prim enunciation of his Artist-President, a conjuring of JFK with all his tragic associations, for a roughneck autocrat of blunt explication. Through this despotic figure, we get a morphology of the moving image, the echoing acoustics, the autocratic clichés, the deadpan insistence, and the disciplined gestures. Power, expressed through media institutions, could quietly colonize the global reception of encountered and ingested images, prodding advantageous behaviors and social controls. "Smile when you meet a stranger, don't be negative, keep your clothes neat and clean, don't be jealous of your neighbor," demands Doug's televisual tyrant, pounding a red-gloved fist on a reverberant podium.

Summarizing this stark critique of power relations concealed within the circulation of banal images, Hall mounted an early but significant video installation, first at 80 Langton Street, titling it *The Tyrant's Last Dream* (1983), then a more refined version for the Whitney Museum of American Art, *Machinery for the Reeducation of a Delinquent Dictator* (1983). Upon entering a dim gallery space, the unwitting spectator activates an industrial fan that then unfurls a limp flag, snapping it forward, almost ensnaring the patron. The militaristic pageantry, the unexpected and aggressive gesture, the surrounding monitors issuing tyrannical demands—if Hall were a political campaign designer in 2023, there'd be an ironic dollar to be made.

Luckily, Hall is anything but. And lest I lose my way, I should remind the reader that this shudder of relevance, this keen awareness that Hall was on to something way back in 1983—a timely forty years ago—sits inside a memoir that recounts a much more formidable project, a life's work, if you will, one wrapped around an accreting sense of ethical and philosophical matters.

But, I request your patience for one more journey back. In 1986, Hall completed his grandest single-channel videowork, *Storm and Stress* (1986). The most exacting photographically, this majestic endeavor tracks big weather in all its fierce manifestations: tornados curling, storm clouds roiling, seas gone asunder. And to this array of natural phenomena set astray, Hall pairs, metaphorically, their technologic equivalents: wind tunnels, Tesla coils, and hydroelectric plants. There's a bit of Henry Adams here, in his 1907 essay "The Virgin and the Dynamo," surmising that the passion and reverence once reserved for the Virgin (Mary) had been waylaid by the newly invented electrical transformer and its equally uncanny power. But Hall's real quarry is the catastrophic sublime, that nineteenth-century Romantic ethos of lurking terror even in God's creations. One might be tempted to accuse Doug of being an early climate activist, of equating man's fixation with the technologic to the vengeful upheaval of nature. But please don't. What he is doing, if I may be so bold, is foregrounding a concealed aesthetic of power that occupies the tempestuous storm cloud, the oily brushstroke, and all between. In other words, that popular contemporary trope of a structural infiltration by the forces of colonization—injustice, inequality, and instability being just some of the insurgents. Old news to Doug.

Now I must disclose my own naiveté: once again returning to the thoughtful text of Doug's memoir, I suddenly realize that his pursuit was always power masquerading beneath image, architecture, and nature itself. We see it in his compelling installations *The Terrible Uncertainty of the Thing Described*

(1987), *People in Buildings* (1989/90), *Song of Ourselves (After Walt Whitman)* (2018), and—not to overlook his considerable preoccupation with photography, yes, large-format still photography, over the last few decades—*The GDR Project* (1992), *University* (1993), *Some Cities* (2004), and *American Landscapes* (2003–5). The heartless architecture, the landscapes bereft of occupation, the cities as sites of confinement, and through it all, a coursing sense of power applied but barely felt, concealed in the man-made, seeping slowly to conscious recognition. Could this be what Doug once declared "the insidious triumph of form over content"?

(The answer to the above question may be found within these pages.)

A final word: decades on, there was another Doug Hall. You could say wiser. But no, an informed caution might be a more apt term of description. Wary of the seduction of images, he threw their time-based tenacity to the wind and, instead, grappled with language itself: words and phrases wafting through a dry hillside, a choral ensemble of soft, curling voices with a sense of optimism even in their "poignant lament" to the limits of language. Based on Ludwig Wittgenstein's weighty *Tractatus* (1921), the multichannel audio work *Wittgenstein's Garden* (2017) sits in a glen while an oaky must fills the air alongside the dulcet voices of the San Francisco Girls Chorus. The sylvan installation conjures "the reflective repose that hides within our urges to action," as Hall was wont to say. The *Sturm und Drang* of earlier years dissipated in the delicious breeze. And for just a moment, the bullies, tyrants, and despots had lost.

How did Doug Hall get to this Edenic garden? That's what you're about to find out.

I

I Was Born Very Young and Had Everything to Look Forward To

Suddenly the Door Opened . . .

Those who accept the compulsion to become artists do so for reasons that can range from preternatural talent to existential need; that is, we become artists because we must, not because we want to. The overpowering necessity to make art can be more like an addiction or obsession than a rational aspiration. This is the story of my obsession, born of existential need, and the forces that led me to where I am today.

Rather than start at the beginning, I drop us into the main studio at the Rinehart School of Sculpture at the Maryland Institute College of Art where, in May 1969, I performed the *Inner Space Simulation Module*, the work I completed for my MFA degree. This event is pivotal in my imagination because it is where I began to think and speak as an artist. Later, I will fill in the blanks that brought me to this place and beyond.

"Ground Control to Hall. All looking good from our vantage point. We have thirty minutes until touchdown. All systems go. How you feeling?" I am listening to the voice of Sam Scott, a fellow graduate student, one of the eight flight controllers who have been on twenty-four-hour rotating shifts to make sure I remain safe during the seven-day performance. His voice reaches me through two speakers above the command console in front of me.

The *Inner Space Simulation Module* (ISSM) is an elaborate environment whose interior looks like a cross between Flash Gordon's spaceship and a technological torture chamber a teenage sadist might have thrown together

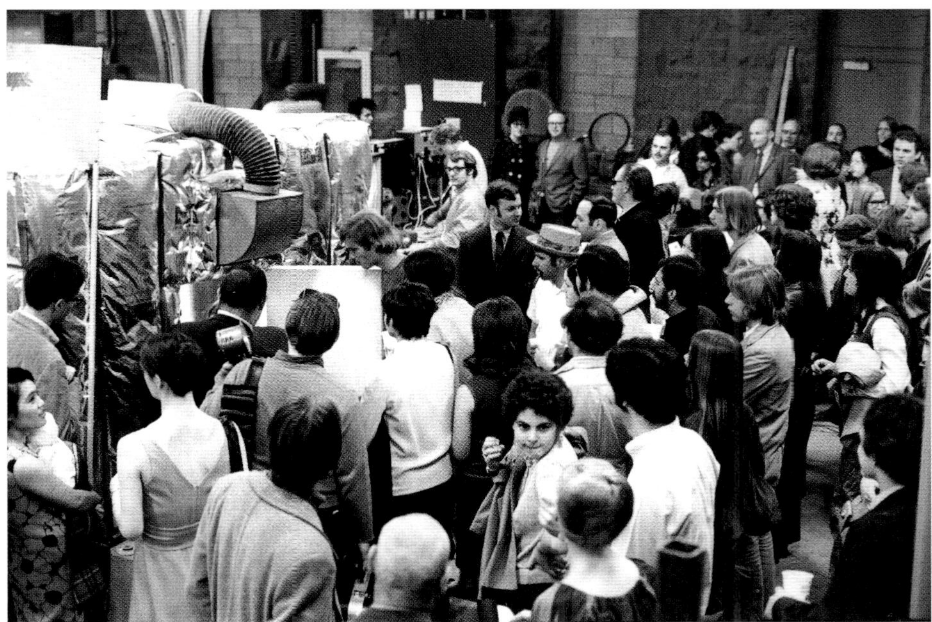

Inner Space Simulation Module—final preflight preparations
Photographer unknown

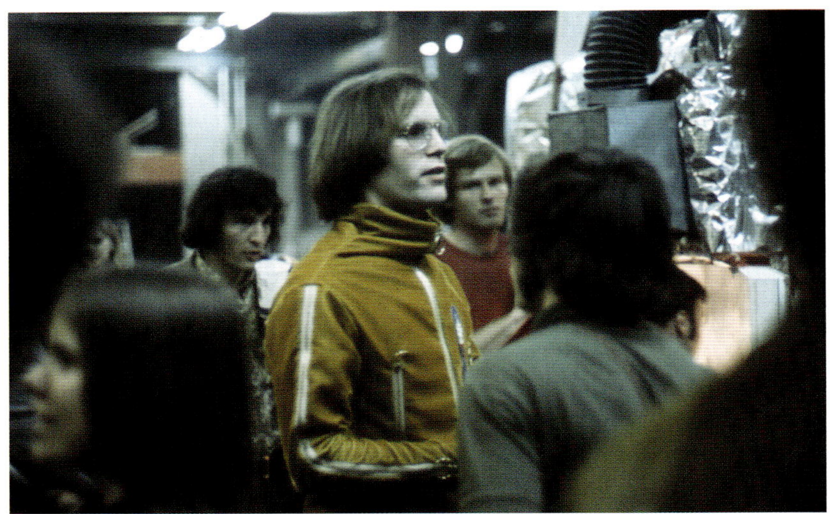

Checking last-minute details before entering the ISSM
Photograph by Diane Andrews Hall

from abandoned airplane parts and other mechanical castaways. The interior is festooned with lights and dials, some there for effect, others that work to signal information between me and the ground controllers. We are in the last few minutes of the week-long performance during which I have been secluded in a cramped, media-intensive environment. My connection to the exterior world has been through the flight controllers, who decide what kind of audio and visual data will be sent to me via electronics and a 16mm film rear-screen projection system.

"I'm feeling a little shaky right now. A little disoriented," I respond, my voice emotional and hesitant. I don't say this, but the experience is a bit like the tail end of an LSD trip. Less physical and without the colors, but my sense of time has become distorted, and I feel as if I've lost contact with my body. My world has become contained within this electronic box with its blinking lights and its random input of information generated by the whims of the ground controllers. As part of an experiment in the effects of an intense media bombardment over a sustained period, they have been given permission to blast me with information that includes bright flood lights that line the ceiling above me. Without a clock, I can only guess if it's day or night; the ground controllers on the outside keep a log of my waking and sleeping hours as part of the study, overseen by a Johns Hopkins University psychologist who is collecting data on the psychological and physical effects on me. Fortunately, there is not a sadist among the ground crew and, as they noticed around the fifth day that the experience was becoming increasingly difficult for me, they refrained from aggressively suffusing me with too many intrusive sounds or images.

"Doug." It's Sam again. "Diane is here and wants to say something."

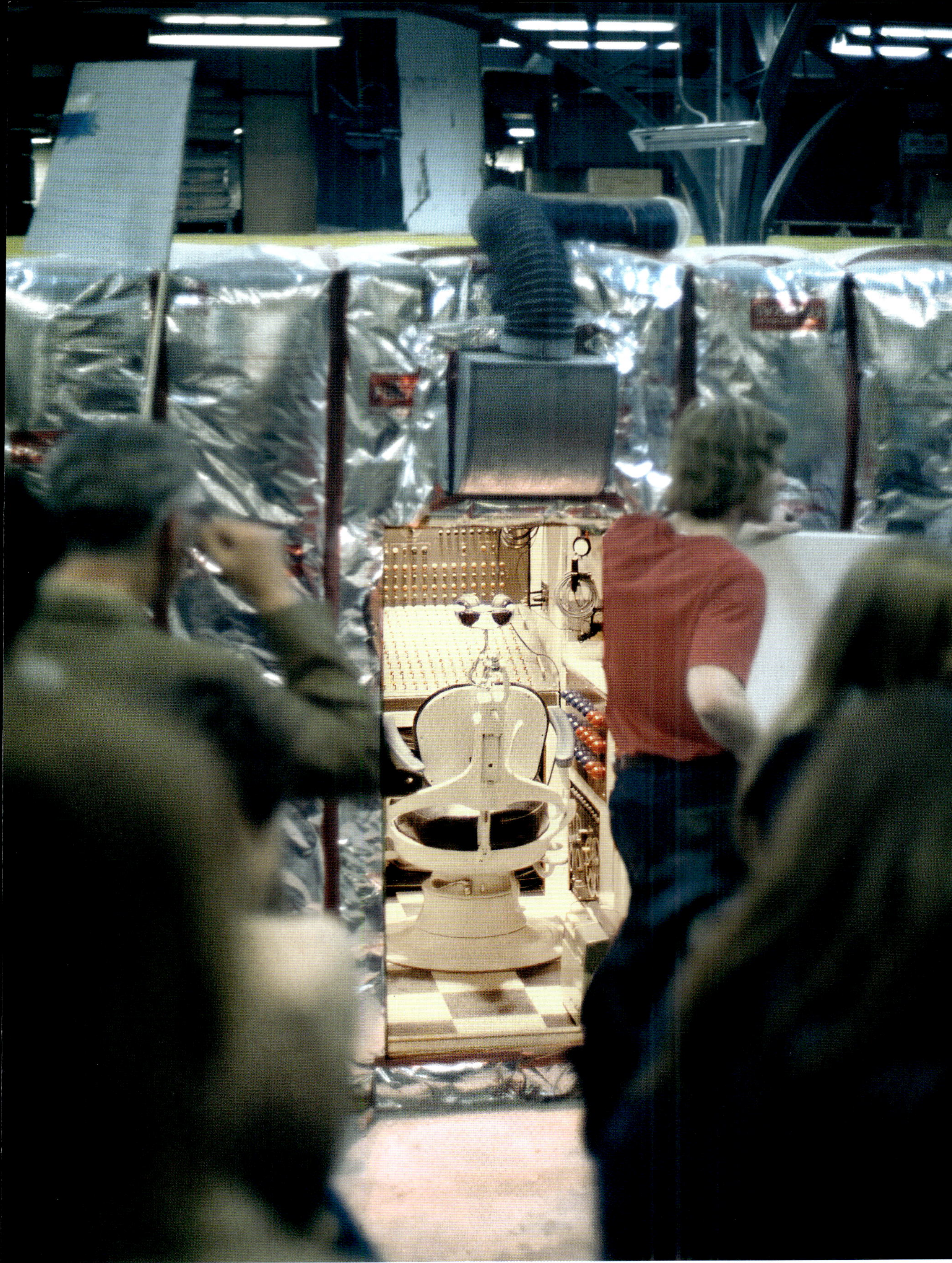

Flight attendant waiting for me to enter the ISSM
Photograph by Diane Andrews Hall

Diane Andrews (now Hall) and I married in December 1967, at a ceremony in Dallas, where she lived with her family before moving to New Orleans for college. We met that summer at the Skowhegan School of Painting and Sculpture in Maine, and after knowing each other for a few months, decided to get married. My art school friends thought I was crazy. I knew I was the luckiest person in the world. Diane transferred from Boston University—where she had started graduate study with painter Walter Murch (father of Walter Murch Jr., film sound designer)—to the Hoffberger School of Painting under Grace Hartigan at the Maryland Institute. This put us in the same city and on a schedule to graduate at the same time.

"Hi, Doug. There are a lot of people out here looking forward to seeing you. Me included. Your mom is here, too."

"Okay," is all I can muster. I am definitely starting to freak out.

The *Inner Space Simulation Module* had begun taking shape more than a year earlier, inspired by my interest in NASA's Apollo program, a staggering triumph of technology over the forces of gravity. That, and my experiences with psychedelics, which, although diminished since my undergraduate years, had convinced me that consciousness, too, was expansive, capable of defying its own gravity.

I had spent my first two years of graduate school trying to figure things out. Arriving in Baltimore with what I thought was a clear idea of what I could do as an artist, like many beginners, the more exposed I was to the possibilities, the more confused I became. I tried making sculptural objects in various styles, from the West Coast funk that my friend and roommate John Hillding embraced to the more formal and intellectualized approach that fellow MFA candidates Peter Richards, Bruce Colvin, and Bruce's partner, Mary Miss, pursued. None of my stylistic forays felt honest or consistent with what I was trying to get at. Part of the problem was that I couldn't fully articulate what that was. The activities that felt most sincere to me were those that many around me wouldn't consider to be art at all, being more related to performance, or just fooling around.

During the previous spring, I had set up a twelve-foot-high cone-shaped structure in a field that I wrapped in black plastic sheeting so that it looked somewhat like a synthetic volcano—perhaps a middle school science project on steroids. On command from a remote ignition switch, smoke and flames erupted from a concoction of flammable chemicals I had placed in a container at its top. All of this I filmed with the help of my former roommates, Mike Zelenka and Hillding, and my current roommate, Diane. Probably not great art, but it was getting at some things that mattered to me.

What were these things that mattered? First, objects involved in the volcano and similar actions weren't made with a particular aesthetic in mind. They didn't need to conform to any of the work I saw around me that fulfilled a kind of aesthetic predictability I found oppressive and reactionary. Rather than validating themselves as unique objects, frozen in time to be experienced in the moment, they existed as part of an operation. They were actors in a production, just as my friends and I were, our bodies directly involved. What interested me was the whole thing experienced over time, even if the undertaking resulted in an absurd outcome. Of course, this idea of placing a structure in the landscape that attempts, in a crude and impossible way, to emulate an actual volcano bubbles over with pathos and absurdity, which was consistent with my interests at the time.

As humans, we have a need to extend our minds and bodies into the spaces around us, the wilder and more distant the better. These gestures can be grand and heroic, like Ernest Shackleton's explorations of the Antarctic aboard *Endurance* or NASA's ventures to the moon. Or they can be simple, even silly, say a large wood-and-chicken-wire cone draped in black plastic, looking vaguely like a volcano; or the unselfconscious act of a child who digs a hole on the beach only to stand by and watch as it is engulfed by the incoming tide. What matters is to make a minuscule, human mark on a landscape and to claim a place within the world's vastness.

"We have ten minutes and counting until touchdown. All is go at Mission Control."

"Okay. I'm really looking forward to getting out of here." I respond with more honesty than I intended, unable to remain within the fiction of the space flight with responses like "roger that." I'm not panicking, but my emotions are extremely raw. I find the thought of my recently widowed mother particularly moving, still mourning in her quiet, stoic way, standing outside, vulnerable, here to enthusiastically support me. Art was not the career path my parents had imagined for me. I remember my father, who died several months previously, and wonder what he would think of all of this. And Diane, who has been having her own struggles and successes at graduate school while devoting time and energy to supporting me and this project. Have I reciprocated? Probably not. All of this and much more fills me with gratitude and sadness. As melodramatic as this sounds, I really am all tangled up in my feelings.

As I prepare for my exit, I take off the coveralls I've been wearing for the past seven days and start getting into the gold velvet Inner Space suit that Diane has carefully designed and made. It is spectacular: bell-bottom trousers with bold zippers that run up the sides, a jersey with similar zippers running up the length of the sleeves and two smaller zippers on the chest, flanking the zipper on the front that terminates at the top of loose folds forming the collar. Lots of zippers. More like an outfit for a glam rocker than an astronaut, but fitting for my inner space voyage. There is a strong odor surrounding me, a confluence of smells from my chemical toilet, residue from freeze-dried meals partially consumed, and a pungent stench arising from my unwashed body. Fortunately, having lived in their midst for a week, I am largely oblivious to them.

"Nine minutes and counting."

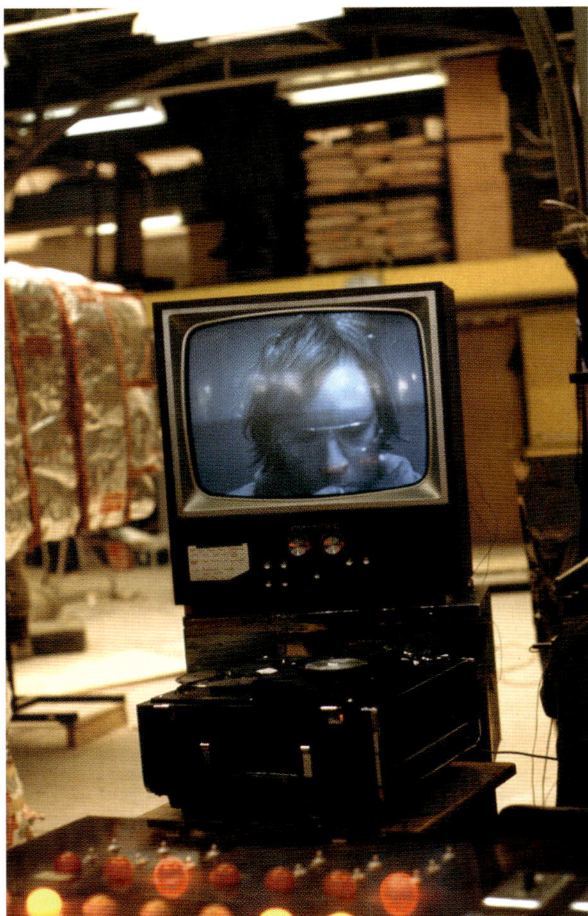

CCTV view at three days
Photographer unknown

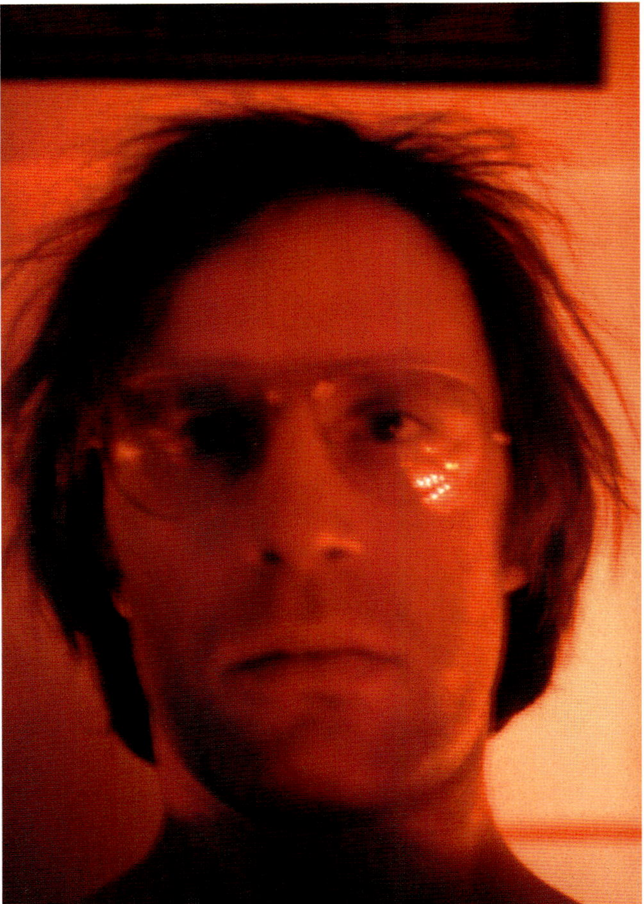

Self-portrait at three days
Photograph by Doug Hall

The idea for the project had been percolating since the previous spring semester, but it had remained out of reach. Obsessed as I was with NASA's Apollo program, I was stumped as to how to integrate this into a work that incorporated my emerging interests in duration, spectacle, and technology—how to make something experiential that claimed my body and psyche. My scattered thoughts had gained a little more clarity the preceding summer, away from the pressures of art school. I had started to visualize a stationary environment where my body remained in place while my mind traveled, stimulated by media rather than drugs. Not a deprivation environment but a high-frequency stimulation environment. But it was during my visit to the Manned Spacecraft Center in Houston that the idea of inhabiting the sculpture started to come into focus.

"Eight minutes to touchdown, Doug. A big crowd is gathering to greet you. All is looking good here."

"Thanks, Control. I'm preparing the module for the touchdown. All is go here. I'm going to need a little quiet while I gather myself for the reentry." I'm

still shaky but my voice is clearer than before. I'm feeling more composed, but I'm nauseous.

I've been subsisting on freeze-dried foods to which I can only add cold water. Norman Carlberg, director of Rinehart, insisted on two safety restrictions: there were to be no cooking or other electrical devices that could cause fires, and there must be an axe inside that I can use to break out in an emergency since the door is locked from the outside.

"Roger that. I will only be delivering the countdown at one-minute intervals between now and the time we open the hatch. No need for you to respond unless you feel like it."

In August, Diane and I flew to Dallas, borrowed her parents' Cadillac, and headed south to Houston. A close friend of my father's knew Wally Schirra, part of the first group of Apollo astronauts, and Schirra had arranged for us to have a VIP tour of the Manned Spacecraft Center, even agreeing to meet us at some point during the tour. We arrived in Houston Wednesday evening and checked into a Holiday Inn that Diane's father had generously booked for us. Since our tour was scheduled for Friday, we decided to spend some of Thursday cooling off in the motel pool.

"Seven minutes and counting. All systems go for reentry."

Once there, it became obvious that our art school bubble had not prepared us to seamlessly integrate into this conservative enclave of madras-clad, mainly blonde mothers and children who lolled about or played in the pool. Embarrassed by our difference, we settled into a couple of lounge chairs in a shady corner of the grounds away from the others. In our attempts to accommodate our surroundings, Diane, wearing a blue string bikini, not as brazen as contemporary bathing attire but revealing by the standards of the day, and I, in my black speedo, a tattoo on my right shoulder and my hair long, covered ourselves as best we could with our robes and towels, hoping that this nod to modesty would quell outside interest in us.

"Six minutes to reentry."

The situation escalated as the afternoon heat became too much and I, now bereft of my protective covers, quietly slid into the deep end of the pool while Diane, flesh exposed, moved toward the steps at the shallow end, near where most of the mothers and children were assembled. There, after gathering her long blonde hair into a loose bun, she stepped into the water and swam toward me. By the reaction of the parents, you would think flesh-eating piranhas had invaded the pool. Noticing the effect we were having and further embarrassed by the reactions, although equally amused, we quietly swam about, attempting to emulate a normalcy we hoped would ingratiate us into the surrounding community. To no avail. Concerned mothers, towels in hand, trying not to be too obvious, moved to the edges where they beckoned their children out of the water and into their protective embraces. This early lesson in difference would be reiterated numerous times over the next several years

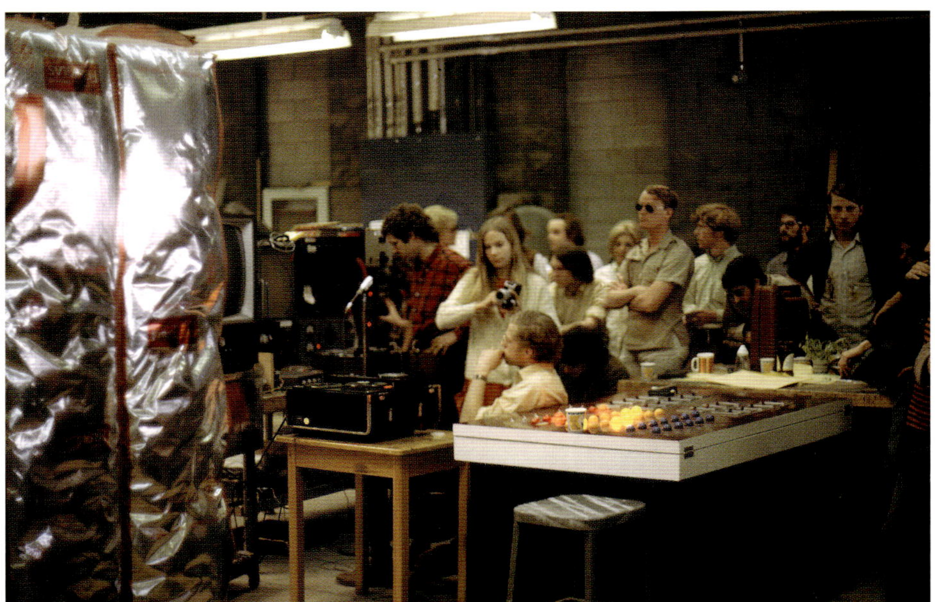

Ground Control Center shortly before touchdown on day seven
Photographer unknown

as we embraced ways of living and thinking that put us at odds with more traditional Americans, whom we arrogantly referred to as "straight" in contrast to "hip," the self-congratulatory epithet we assigned ourselves.

"Five minutes to touchdown. Spring is in the air, birds chirping, lilacs blooming." Sam has a strong Romantic vein coursing through him that can be a bit much at times.

"Sounds delicious," is all I can come up with. Unexpected emotions are sweeping over me again. Something fundamental is changing. It's as if I'm outside of my body watching myself, almost like I'm another person. Over the speakers, I hear the murmuring of what sounds like a lot of people and then silence as Sam cuts off the microphone. I think I can hear my heart pounding. The overhead lights flash on. By flipping a series of switches, I silently signal Control to turn the lights back off. The small room goes dark except for illumination from the red and blue instrument lights. Tears are coming to my eyes. How strange that something that is fake, a shoddy imitation, has become so real to me. And everyone is playing along, swept into the same fantasy, which has somehow mutated into something real. But that is the point, the exact thing I have been searching for: artifice made real, corporeal, experiential, vital. Why, then, this embarrassing display of emotion?

"Four minutes and counting. All systems are go."

To be continued . . .

Opposite: Module interior shortly before touchdown
Photograph by Doug Hall

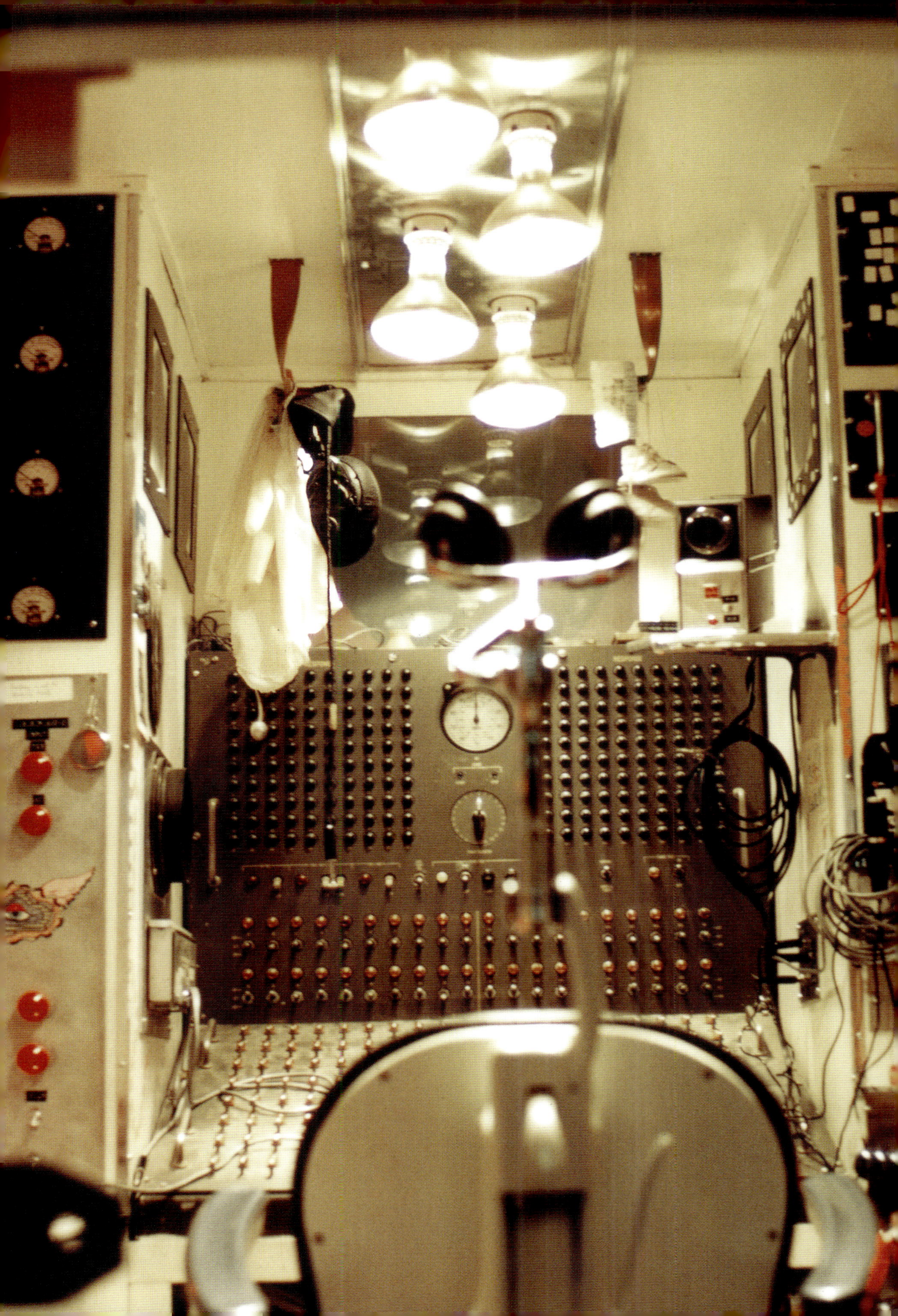

Berkeley in the Fifties

My first memories are attached to our home on Hillcrest Road, a street that wound up the hill from Claremont Avenue in Berkeley. Standing on a corner lot that overlooked the neighborhood, the two-story structure, built in the early 1920s, was covered with little peaks of white stucco, reminding me of whipped cream. The same treatment covered the four-foot-high retaining wall that stabilized the grass-covered ground that sloped down toward the street. One approached the house from the sidewalk on cement steps and a paved path leading to wooden stairs and a porch covered by the second-story overhang.

A large Washington palm stretched its late-afternoon shadow across the path and onto the porch where, in the spring and summer, Monarch butterflies would alight. I spent hours trying, with little success, to catch them by sneaking up from behind, moving very slowly with cupped hands, preventing my shadow from falling across them while I attempted my capture. In my memory the house on the hill appears white and gleaming, with the grass so green, particularly in the afternoon light that casts a warm glow over everything. Because the house and yard were unobstructed by other structures, it did in fact receive full light in the summer, which benefited the front garden my father could be found tending with a devotion approaching the spiritual.

As a child I felt protected, secure, and loved, or at worst, lovingly tolerated, by my sister Lyn, three years older; Marie, or Ree as we called her, my younger sister by two years; my mother, Carolyn Erskine Hall; and my father, Chaffee Earl Hall, Jr. By all indications my parents, who met as students at UC Berkeley, had a strong marriage that had survived the difficulties of separation during the Second World War. My father was associate dean of students at the university, and my mother was a stay-at-home mom who managed the daily lives of her three children. In my eyes, she was beautiful, carrying herself with grace and dignity. She was playful and affectionate toward us as she was toward my dad, and patiently drove us to our various activities from swimming lessons in Walnut Creek to my scout meetings in Oakland. There was a lot of hugging and a lot of cuddling from my mom.

My father expressed affection differently. Although he was not a cuddler, I felt his love in his patient attention to us, his gentleness, and his willingness to listen to and offer advice about our worries and concerns. When he was younger, he had entertained ambitions of being a writer, a dream he abandoned after returning from the war and committing to supporting a family. (My sister, the poet Lyn Hejinian, has a copy of a letter he wrote to Gertrude Stein when he was eighteen in which he thanked her for inspiring him to be more unconventional with his own writing style.) While he stopped writing novels and short stories, he pursued another passion, oil painting and collage, which he did most weekends in the small study off my parents' bedroom. Not the usual hobbyist's landscapes, his were small, bold abstractions that referenced the

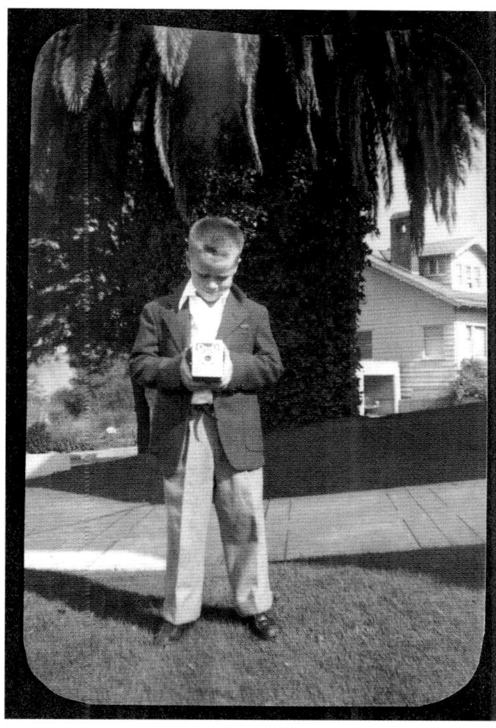

On the front lawn of our Berkeley house, 1952

natural and built worlds. The smell of oil paint, a sweet odor that to this day I find soothing, wafted through the house most weekends, usually dissipating through the week until reinvigorated the following Saturday morning.

My parents were both liberal Democrats, something I knew from an early age, when discussions at dinner might have included outrage that the African American singer Nat King Cole had been banned from buying a house in a Los Angeles neighborhood demographically like our own, or my parents' firm conviction that the so-called voice of conscience, Adlai Stevenson—an eloquent orator with an aristocratic air, who was discredited as an "egghead" by the more populist Republicans and too many Democrats—was a far better presidential candidate than war hero Dwight Eisenhower. I found out that "our" opinions weren't shared by everyone when I wore a "Stevenson for President" lapel pin to school during the 1952 campaign and was roundly ridiculed by my classmates, the majority of whom were the progeny of stolid Republicans. Both my parents were secularists, and my father probably an atheist. My mother had been brought up by a Christian Science mother and she retained elements of that religion throughout her life, although these didn't include what she considered absurdities like praying away injuries or sickness when a trip to a doctor would be the rational thing to do.

My parents resisted television and didn't relent until the spring of 1954, when they purchased our first black-and-white console so they could watch

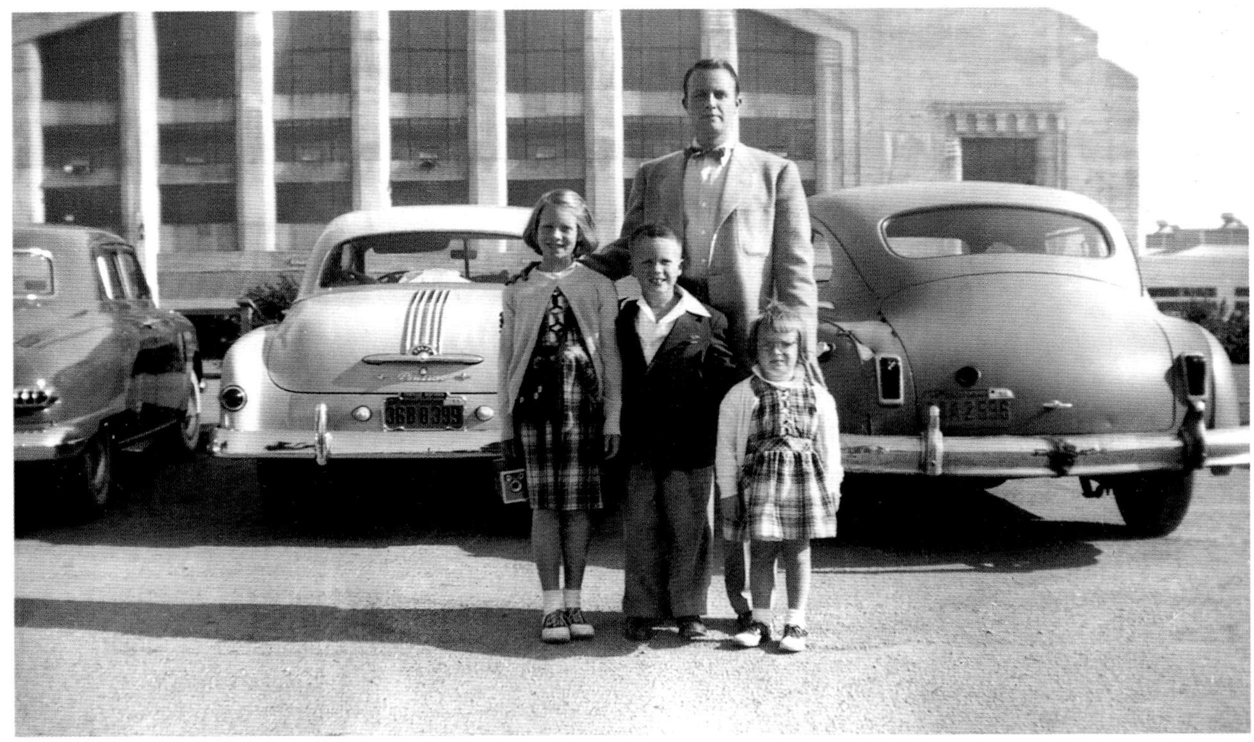

My father with my sisters and me outside the Cow Place, San Francisco, circa 1950

the Army-McCarthy hearings. Adamantly opposed to the politics and Red-baiting of Joseph McCarthy, they watched intently and encouraged us to join them from time to time. That's how we came to be huddled in front of the TV when army counsel Joseph Welch, responding to McCarthy's outrageous accusations against Welch's young colleague Fred Fisher, uttered with suppressed fury his famous line, "Have you no sense of decency, sir?" Those words brought my parents to their feet in celebratory whoops and, I suspect, relief that the autocrat had been exposed, presumably defeated.

Mother and Father expected, and for the most part received, our obedience, although of the three children I was the one who strayed. If the misbehavior was grave enough, I might receive the flat side of a hairbrush on my bare bottom, or if the infraction was foul language, my mouth washed out with soap. But these punishments, always inflicted by my mother, were infrequent. Mostly, my misbehavior was handled with words, not force. Other parental commandments were respect for and compassion toward all and, from my father particularly, honesty—all of which I could adhere to, more or less, without much difficulty.

Quiet Days in Felton

Every year, my sisters and I could look forward to time spent at our grandparents' summer place in Felton, California, a village in the Santa Cruz Mountains. Their land, comprising around seventy acres, including a vineyard, was situated close to the cooling summer fog that crept in at night and lingered into midmorning, but not so far inland that it left us sweltering in the afternoon heat.

Before I was born, my grandfather, a passionate wine connoisseur, in addition to being a corporate attorney, planted sixty acres with cabernet and Riesling grapes and built a small winery to process and age the juice into wine. Hallcrest Vineyards was one of the first boutique wineries in California.

The cultivation of the vineyard was handled by a querulous Portuguese, Manuel Silva, with assistance from his son, Fenton, and later, when their relationship became strained and Fenton departed, from Bill Bradley, a former prison guard. Both Fenton and Bill were extremely warm and accommodating of us children, whereas Manuel was all business and appeared to find our presence irritating and a hindrance to his work. He was also very hard of hearing, which to us children might have been misinterpreted as sternness. He always wore khaki work pants and shirt (as did my grandfather when he was there); he walked with a languid, smooth gait. His hands were rough, his fingers gnarled from his time as a catcher in the California Leagues in the late 1930s, or so he claimed. He smelled of sweat and the sweet odor of earth. It was clear from the way my grandfather interacted with him that he held Manuel in the highest regard while looking askance at his son, who preferred entertaining us kids to hard work.

Arriving at my grandparents' place never disappointed. The late-afternoon sky would still be light and the air warm before the evening breeze cooled everything down. The locust trees that shaded the two barns farther along the driveway filled the air with a familiar musky scent that mixed with that of peaches and apricots rotting in the small orchard adjacent to the swimming pool and behind "Aunt Marie's house." This one-room cottage was where my father's sister and her husband, Penry Griffiths, used to stay before they built their own home in the early 1960s at the top of the vineyard on the far western edge of the property. Their little house was flanked by a similar one, "the bunkhouse," on the other side of the outdoor sitting area we called "the circle." That was where one or both of my sisters and I usually slept.

It's curious the images, sounds, and smells that come wandering back as I recall a place so important to a childhood that existed before I understood how complicated the world could be. I can remember the kitchen screen door banging as food is brought out for lunch or dinner, with us gathered around the redwood table; at lunch the fear of yellow jackets buzzing around our tuna fish sandwiches or onto the cold cuts and cheese carefully arranged for the adults on a Wedgewood platter; the dappled light, filtering through trees that

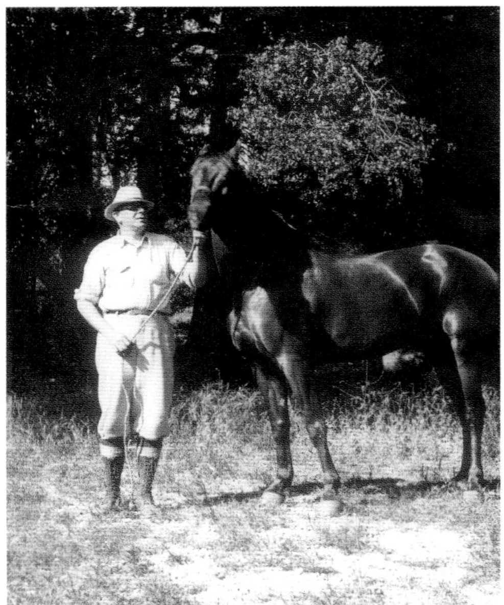
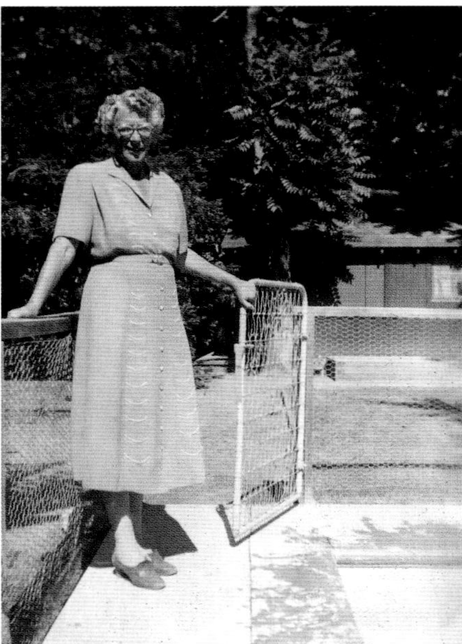

My paternal grandparents at their summer place in Felton, California

cast slow, undulating shadows across us and the surroundings; walks in the vineyard where the dust puffs up into small eruptions with each step and the alive smells of the warm earth; watching Manuel shoe the giant Shire work-horses at the forge or bringing them up from the pasture so he can hitch them to the sled with those massive collars, clicking and humming to them the entire time in some sort of horse language; climbing into the jeep with Fenton, or following him around as he does his chores; washing wine bottles at the large sink, which I can only reach by standing on a crate, on the ground floor of the winery where the wine ages pungently in oak barrels; feeling the coolness in that large, open room, and then stepping out of the cellar's darkness into the bright sunlight and to the sound of cicadas in the trees that run down the short hill to the gate leading to the pasture below; standing in the grove of fruit trees adjacent to the swimming pool, stalking bobbing birds, BB gun in hand; aiming my rifle carefully, steadily, and in cold blood, pulling the trigger, the thump of the tiny brass ball as it pierces the bird, its fall to the ground, my momentary sense of power followed by a much deeper feeling of remorse and sadness; the sensation of the cool water engulfing my body as I dive into the pool; the endless hours of playing Marco Polo with my sisters and the occasional adult who joins in; the voice of my mother pleading with me to get out of the water as the skin of my fingertips shrivels and my lips turn blue from the cold; feeling the hot sun on my body as I lie on a mat along the pavement that surrounds the pool; away from the property, taking walks alone or sometimes with Lyn along Fall Creek, which we reach after a fifteen-minute walk from my grandparents' place; Fall Creek, where we sometimes picnic in a clearing

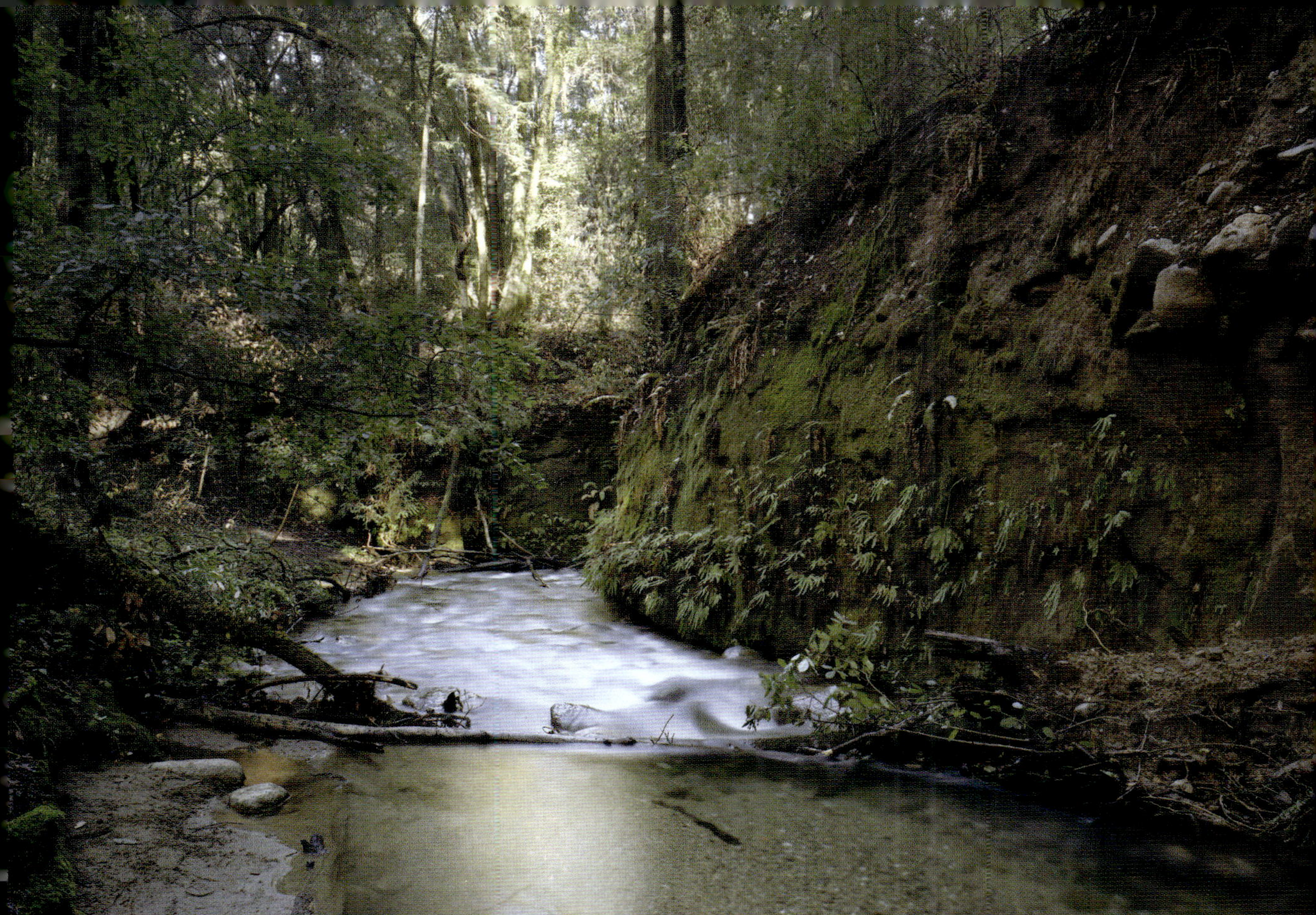

Fall Creek in early summer
Photograph by Doug Hall

surrounded by large fir and bay laurel trees that provide shade from the brilliant light; foliage and ferns growing along the creek's edge; Fall Creek, where I often go fishing and seldom catch anything beyond a few frustrating tangles; the patches of warmth and coolness as we come in and out of the sunlight on the trail next to the creek; the sound of the water as it flows, becomes partially damned to form large pools, and then breaks out into fast-moving sections that burble across the rocks, sounding a bit like children laughing; the murmur of insects and the call of birds, large and small; an occasional deer rustling through the brush or a snake moving across the path; my attempts to reach the "ghost town" that is supposed to exist just beyond the trail's end, but which I never seem to reach; back at my grandparents' the sounds and smells of dinner being prepared by Ida, their live-in cook, with the repetitive squeak and slap of the screen door opening and closing as dishes are brought out and the table set; the scent of meat cooking on the outdoor grill or, on special occasions, perhaps when guests are joining the adults, in the large concrete dutch oven, looking somewhat like a miniature nuclear cooling tower with a spit inside, that always seems to humiliate my exacting grandfather with unexpected results; the feeling of fatigue as dinner continues and the adults chatter;

the brief surge of energy as we toast marshmallows in the stone fireplace, mine often bursting into flame as I usually lack the patience for the slow-cook that produces the lightly browned skin that, once slightly cooled, I tenderly peel off with my lips from the white sugar blob still on the stick, repeating the process until there is nothing left; the signal from my mother that it is time for bed, which could have me in a tent by the pool with Lyn and Ree, a rare occurrence and one I don't like very much because I am afraid of bad guys, or in the room across from Gram and Pap's with one of my sisters, or in the bunkhouse with both of them; I prefer the bunkhouse even though there are spiders and other mysterious bugs that I insist be searched out with a flashlight and destroyed before I agree to climb into bed; falling asleep with the soft voices of the adults in the circle wafting through the screened windows, the logs in the fireplace popping; or maybe, if it is an unusually warm night and I am still partially awake, the sound of my parents, splashing and laughing while skinny dipping in the pool; and then sleep—long, peaceful sleep.

Summer Heat, Winter Cold

In late summer 1955, shortly after I turned eleven, we moved from California to Massachusetts, where I remained through college. Arriving in early summer so that my father could begin his new job at the Harvard Business School, my parents rented a gloomy house on a wooded hillside at the edge of the small Boston suburb of Lincoln. The surrounding thicket felt threatening to me as I imagined it occupied by angry bears. During that summer there was a nationwide polio scare, which meant communal swimming pools or even lakes, where we might find relief from the intense heat and humidity, were off limits.

Friendless, terrified of a bear attack that seemed imminent as soon as the sun went down, finding no relief from the damp heat that persisted even at night, and surrounded by woods filled with mosquitoes, large, unfamiliar moths, and beetles that after sundown slapped against the windows and outdoor lights on the back porch, I was experiencing a miserable summer, as were my siblings and probably my mother as well. Later, when I was acclimated, I would grow to love the New England summer weather, its richness and soft Nordic light, air moist with towering cumuli that often coalesced into electrical storms in the late afternoon or evening. Thunderclaps followed by torrential rain offered some cooling relief from the steamy day, and the complex cascade of smells released by the rain met the evening songs of frogs and crickets. But as a recent California transplant, this first summer's torpor added to my general longing for the familiarity we had left behind.

By late summer we settled into the house my parents purchased on Old Sudbury Road in Wayland that would be our family home for the next decade. I was enrolled in the sixth grade of the local public school. For a California boy,

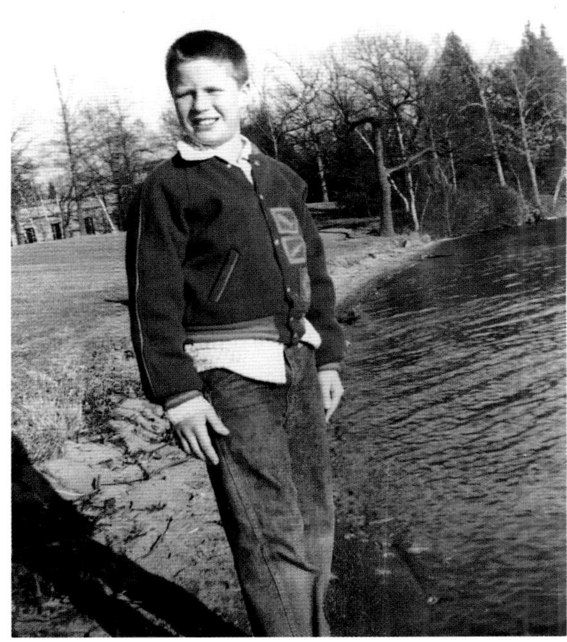

Shortly after our move to the East Coast, 1955

there was now the novelty of autumn and the frigidity of winter with its beautiful, pristine snowfalls that, along the streets and sidewalks, would eventually metamorphose into filthy, debris-strewn sludge. I began to understand how to take advantage of what winter offered. When the snow was clean, newly fallen, and containing the right amount of moisture, it could be gathered then crafted into fortifications for snowball fights or, if alone, chilly enclosures for fantasy. At night when it snowed, I would look out my second-floor bedroom window and notice how the flakes veiled and softened the streetlights, which glowed in the darkness like beacons on a stormy sea. In the morning not only would everything be submerged in white and, if the sun had broken through, this whiteness sparkle with blue specks of light refracting off ice crystals, but the acoustical world was also changed, muted and subdued. On these days everything slowed down, cars moved carefully along the streets, the muffled sound of shovels scraped against pavement as neighbors, me included, cleared driveways (one of the downsides of a heavy snowfall), government offices and many businesses were closed and, best of all, so were the schools.

I had a difficult time adjusting to my new school situation and, on the advice of my sixth-grade teacher, my parents sent me to Belmont Hill School, a private day school, where they reasoned I would experience a more challenging curriculum. As it turned out, it was a good choice for me. I was athletic,

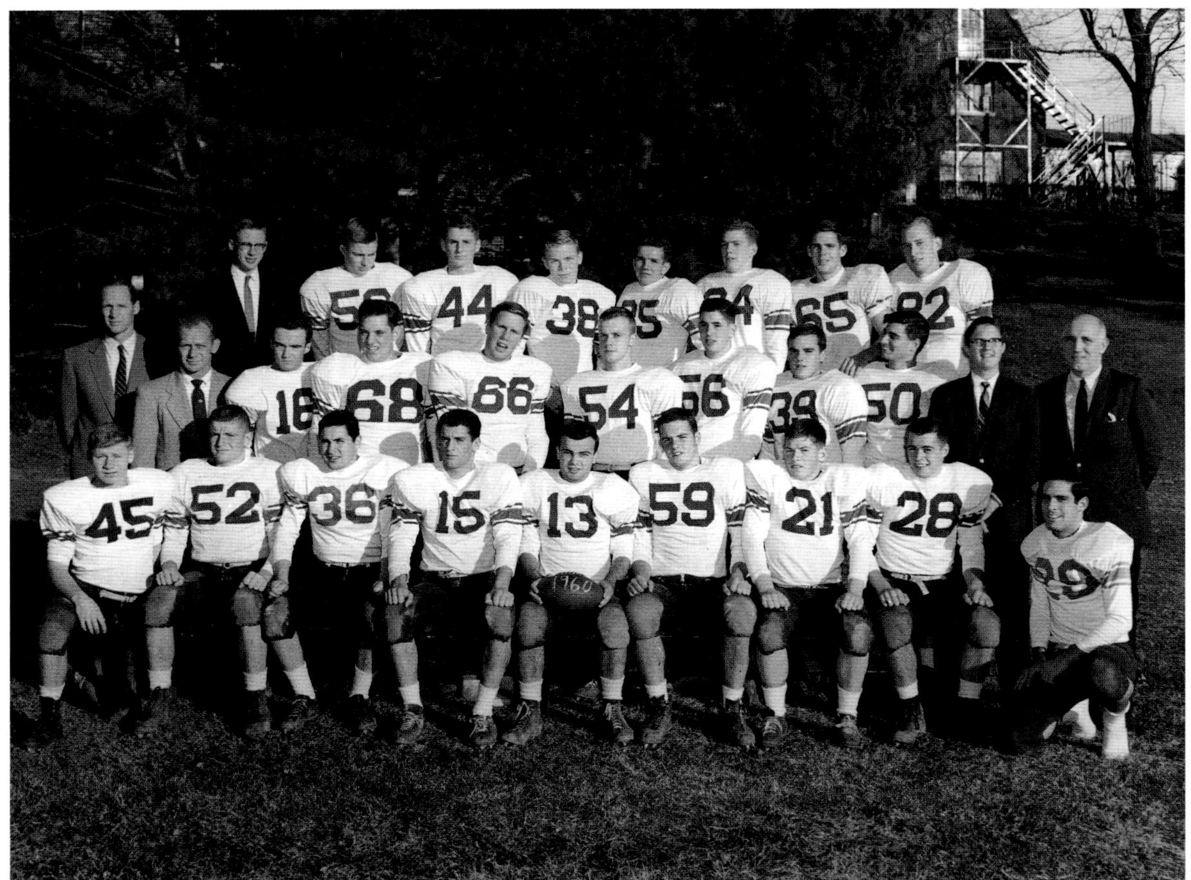

Varsity football team, 1961 (Pete is number 59 in the front row and I am number 66 in the second row)

excelling at football, which made me popular with the jocks, and smart and inquisitive enough to be accepted by the nerdier students.

My closest friend in high school was Pete Rowan. He was a year ahead of me and lived in Wayland not far from my house. We shared numerous interests—beyond football, which we both played, and girls, which we both craved—that could be summed up as a willingness (make that a need) to break the bonds of our suburban and prep-school restraints in search of adventure. Any kind of adventure, from cerebral to hedonistic to just plain physically risky, called to us.

By the time I was a junior, I had developed some intellectual interests that paralleled many of Pete's and which, unformed as they may have been, became more important and central in my life. We tirelessly consumed and discussed Ginsberg, Kerouac, Henry Miller, and Beckett while we smoked cigarettes that we stole (Parliaments from Pete's mom, Kents from my dad). Between stifled coughs we perfected nonchalant smoke rings or the more sophisticated affectation of exhaling smoke through the nose. After Pete got his driver's license, he could borrow his mother's blue Ford station wagon and we would take it to Cambridge to hear music at Club 47 or buy beer at the liquor store on the corner of Massachusetts Avenue and Brattle Street. Often, we ran into a Cambridge cop who turned the other way as the exchange was made or just stared into space, benignly. The Cambridge police were notoriously corrupt.

Club 47, the coffee house at 47 Mount Auburn Street just beyond Harvard Square, was our mecca. We would drink coffee, smoke, and listen to some of the best blues artists of the day. Lightnin' Hopkins, Muddy Waters, Mose Allison, John Lee Hooker, and B. B. King sang about things we would never experience, but were starting to be aware of—intolerance, racism, poverty, physical labor, violence, and desperate love. Their stories, direct and phrased in simple chords and poetic structures, took us far from suburban New England into the lives of people who toiled in fields and factories within a system that, the songs told us, were organized against them. I can still hear and see Lightnin' Hopkins singing "Baby, Please Don't Go" in a plaintive voice, both rough and smooth, thick with a Texas accent, the lyrics interspersed with impressive chord progressions and single-string picking.

Just as interesting and maybe easier to relate to, for a couple of restless White boys from the suburbs, was the exploding folk scene that was centered at Club 47. On Sunday afternoons, the club presented artists like Joan Baez, often accompanied by her sister, Mimi Fariña, who sang songs written by the Carters, Woody Guthrie, and others. Additional performers that I remember include Dave Van Ronk, Eric Von Schmidt, the Charles River Valley Boys, Tom Rush, and Pete Seeger. My friend Pete listened and watched more intently and knowledgeably than I. He fronted a high school band that played covers of artists like Buddy Holly and the Everly Brothers, as well as his own songs. In fact, Pete combed his hair Phil Everly–style, long on the side and formed into a dangled wave in the front. (Certain Belmont Hill teachers insisted that the dangle be brushed to the side into a look more appropriate for a young gentleman.) But Pete was a musician, who even then played the guitar elegantly and had a clear, beautiful voice that ranged from high baritone to tenor. I heard it often as we stood next to each other in Glee Club. After graduation, he attended college for just one semester before hightailing it to Nashville where he played with Bill Monroe and eventually formed his own bands; he continues to have a significant career as a country and bluegrass artist. I graduated the following year. Accepted at both Harvard and Stanford, I chose Harvard. And I lost contact with Pete.

I ran into him about twenty years later when he was performing with his band at a club in San Francisco. We briefly reminisced and, at my insistence, compared the tattoos we had gotten on our right shoulders one night in 1961 when, after guzzling several beers, we ventured to Jack Redcloud's tattoo parlor, just off Scollay Square, which in the late fifties, early sixties was a down-and-out section of Boston. At night drunks, prostitutes, and junkies staggered and circled about, some looking harmlessly disoriented, others more threatening. Redcloud's studio was up a flight of well-worn stairs and through a door with a dirty window with "Tattoos" boldly stenciled on it. In advance of our arrival, Pete and I had decided to get the same three-leaf clover to acknowledge our shared Irish heritage. When we entered the studio, Jack was busy finishing the outlines of a large eagle on a man's chest, with wings that stretched from shoulder to shoulder and talons that reached nearly to his navel. The wiry man was missing one front tooth, wore sailors' bell-bottom jeans, and appeared a little drunk. Judging from the grimaces as the electrical needle sparked and as Jack wiped blood from his chest with a rag, he wasn't having a lot of fun. Jack repeatedly sipped from a pint of Jack Daniels as he finished the outline of the eagle. From our angle standing above him, it was easy to see the face of Christ with a crown of thorns tattooed into the bald spot on the top of Jack's head. His own torso was concealed beneath a white t-shirt but if it was at all like his emaciated arms, it was decorated with a palimpsest of richly inked imagery.

After the poor guy left, his chest covered with an absorbent dressing beneath his shirt, it was our turn. We could tell by the way Jack moved about his studio and slurred his words that he was less than sober. I was having some qualms but thought it was no time to back out. He told us he had a quick errand to do and left briefly, returning with another pint of Jack Daniels, which he was sipping as he entered. He appeared unsteady on his feet as he plopped down onto his stool. I explained what I wanted and where. He made a quick sketch on my arm, grabbed his needle, dipped it into the black ink, and went to work. The flesh stung as the needle etched its path. Jack sipped from his bottle as he worked. Craning to get a peek, I was sad to see that it was less clover and, with points at the ends of the leaves, more poison ivy. When he finished the outline, filling it in with green ink, no more than half an hour had passed. The pint bottle was almost empty; Jack had consumed a lot of Jack and seemed to be having trouble staying upright on his stool.

Crudely bandaged, I got up from the chair and Pete sat down. Jack wiped Pete's upper right arm with alcohol as he had done with mine. But by now his movements were awkward and hesitant, as if he was imitating himself in slow motion. Pete started to get up to leave, which seemed like a great idea to me, but Jack, in his slurred but forceful voice and with more than a gentle tug, sat him back down in the chair. Then, rather than reach for the marker to make a sketch, he grabbed the electric needle. No longer in slow motion but now in jerky stop-motion, he stabbed it into the ink and into Pete's arm, at which point he lurched forward and collapsed onto Pete, pushing them both onto the floor. During the fall, Jack's outstretched left hand must have grabbed Pete's right shoulder while his right hand held the still-active tattoo needle. The needle trailed along Pete's upper arm from his shoulder to about two inches from his elbow. In its wake, it left a crooked four-inch black line. On the way home, after recovering from the shock and now completely sober, Pete laughingly referred to his new ornamentation as an "action tattoo," which I thought very cool in a Beat sort of way.

Learning to Think

If I were to write a one-sentence summary of my experience at Harvard, it would be, "The boy who entered college in 1962 was significantly changed by the time he graduated in 1966." Some would applaud those changes, others, perhaps including my parents and probably several of the students I associated with my first year, would have been less enthusiastic. As a freshman, I felt like a very ordinary kid with a growing sense that interesting things were possible, without any clear idea of what these "interesting things" might be. Nor was I thoroughly convinced that I could attain them. There was a yearning in me and perhaps a glimmer of realization that the preordained directions for a boy like me were not what I desired nor would even be good at. I'm not sure that, at the time, I had anything more than a slight understanding of how privileged I was to be able to think in terms of what I "wanted to do" as opposed to what I "had to do," which obviously was the only choice available to a lot of other kids my age.

Privilege in my case wasn't based on wealth, but more on the confidence that comes from a supportive and loving family. My politically and socially liberal parents believed in Enlightenment principles rather than any kind of religious dogmas. As college graduates in a long line of college graduates, they understood the importance of education and the role rational thought plays in our understanding of complex issues. They both read widely, fiction and non-fiction. They showed a deep appreciation for the arts and for artists, who were

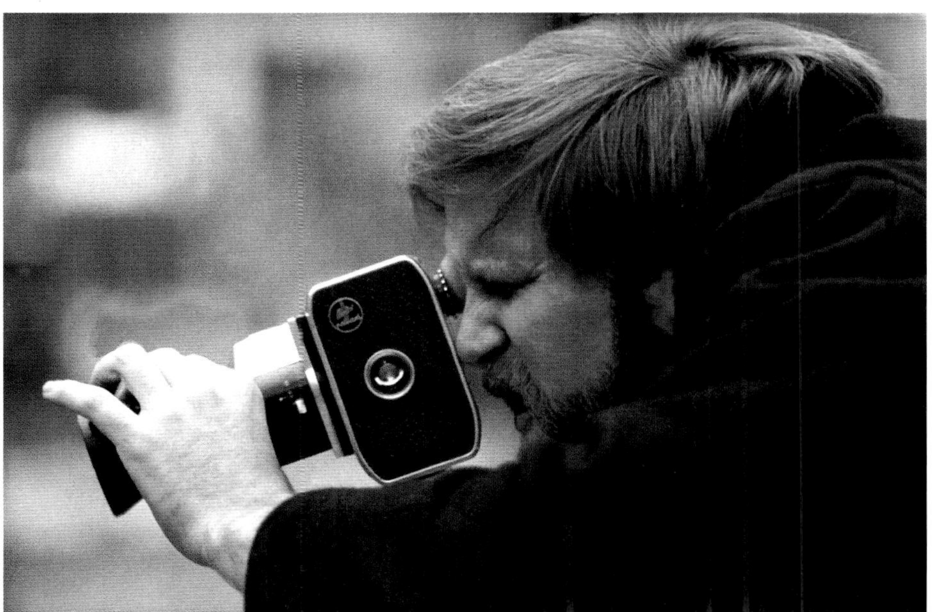

Shooting an assignment for Robert Gardner's film course, Harvard, 1965
Photographer unknown

among their friends; as kids we appreciated their special fondness for people who exhibited idiosyncratic mannerisms. If we would be categorized as a Waspish family, it was not in the restrictive sense that some old New England families are Waspish. We were, after all, transplanted Californians.

At Harvard some, though not all, descendants of families who had attended the college practically since its inception marched about Cambridge as if their elevated social station entitled them to privileges unavailable to the rest of us. An arrogant cynicism, perhaps learned from years at elite boarding schools, manifested itself in dismissive ridicule of ideas and intuitions that I was growing to value. I found them intimidating, but also sophisticated and mysterious in ways that I was not. By my sophomore year, when I had gained more confidence, I found a lot of these uber-preppies more amusing than threatening and would brush against the fringes of their scene: when not at the exclusive Porcellian Club, these blue bloods tended to gather at the Casablanca, the bar beneath the Brattle Theater, where they mingled with their doppelgängers from New York.

Despite some anxiety that I would flunk out before I even got started, I managed to bungle my way through freshman year with reasonable grades, and decided to major in anthropology; as a sophomore, I joined forces with others from my freshman dorm in Kirkland House, the college within the college, where we would spend the next three years. Important among them was Jody Procter. Jody and I established a firm friendship that was based on personal chemistry and a growing recognition of what we perceived as vast social and political injustices. Jody would become my brother-in-law for a few years, marrying my younger sister, Ree, and collaborator in the art collective T. R. Uthco several years later when we all converged in California.

Of course, Jody and I were not alone among our generation in questioning American attitudes toward class, race, gender, and war, or in blaming our parents' generation—fairly or not—for being complicit in these injustices. I gravitated toward anthropology because I hoped it might provide some insight into the complex social and cultural dynamics of our species. However, it didn't take me long to become disenchanted with the core of a curriculum that, to my quickly radicalizing soul, seemed racist and colonialist in its approaches to other cultures. As an antidote, I looked more to the Social Relations Department.[1] There I could take courses like sociologist David Reisman's, in which we explored his ideas about the inner and outer directedness of the American personality and how outer directedness contributed to acquiescent conformity. His was a portrait of the upper middle class: sequestered in suburbia, White and affluent, and where the residents sought neighbors' approval and feared being outcast from their communities. He was talking about the world

1. The Department of Social Relations was an interdisciplinary collaboration between anthropology, sociology, and psychology. Established in 1947, the department disbanded in the early seventies with the major disciplines then functioning independently of one another.

I came from and provided me with early insights into the source of my growing alienation.

Of the academic departments at Harvard, Social Relations was the most radical and experimental along the lines I was looking for. This impression was enhanced when, in spring of my freshman year, an article in the *Harvard Crimson* by its editor, Andrew Weil, exposed experiments with LSD, psilocybin, and other psychedelic drugs that were being conducted by Timothy Leary and Richard Alpert with students in the department. Although they were both terminated in spring 1963, the proliferation of psychedelics into the Harvard community wasn't: the drugs seeped out into the college community and beyond, some via participants in and followers of these early experiments and some from other sources. Their availability had an impact on a small population of the university that included me and several of my friends.

Despite my misgivings, I was able to navigate the Anthropology Department and find courses that interested me. Additionally, granted some flexibility by the administration, I was allowed to build a significant part of my studies around tutors with whom I could work on a one-to-one basis or as a member of a small group of students, many of whom shared my aversion to the core curriculum. Mostly non-tenured assistant professors, the tutors were younger, more adventurous, and less staid than the senior faculty. One of them, whose name I can no longer remember, introduced me to the structuralism of Claude Lévi-Strauss. This, in turn, steered me toward a more theoretical and literary approach to anthropology and a set of ideas that would grow throughout my adult life and, transformed by later thinkers, influence my thinking as an artist and a teacher. While I benefited from his patient instruction on structuralism, he was grateful that I agreed to get him marijuana, which we never smoked together, aware as we were of the potential punishment, particularly for him, had we been exposed. But, more importantly, through his mentorship an unformed idea began percolating in which I could imagine how the investigative tools of anthropology might be turned toward my own culture, which I saw as no less "primitive" than the societies we were studying.

At the newly opened Carpenter Center for the Visual Arts, housed in a building by Le Corbusier, I took ethnographic filmmaker Robert Gardner's class—twice, because I didn't do very well the first try. Crucially, it was at the Carpenter Center, home of the Architecture Department, that I found undergraduate design courses, the only classes that had anything to do with art practice. I thrived in the Bauhaus (form follows function) classes taught by former students of Josef Albers from Yale. More precisely, I responded to the formal rules imposed by the restricted materials we were given, and to the procedures that we went through to arrive at possible solutions. A typical assignment might be organized around a material, mesh screen for example. As we investigated the screen, it became obvious that it encouraged certain bends and folds while discouraging others. Rather than fight its proclivities,

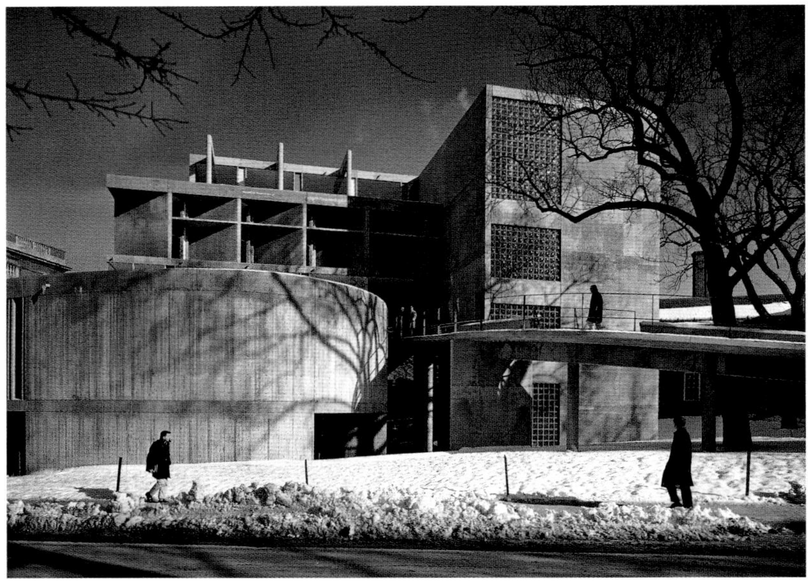

The Carpenter Center for the Visual Arts, Harvard University, circa 1964
Courtesy Harvard University Archive, UAV 605.295.4 Box 1

the sensible approach that we were encouraged to follow was to accept the material's inclinations and work creatively within them: a logic was worked out through a direct relationship with physical materials. I liked that every problem offered numerous valid resolutions, the values of which were based not only on the outcome but also on the process of getting there.

In this Bauhaus approach, making was a way of thinking and, in this setting, as legitimate as the more reflective kind of research that academia was based on. I was beginning to understand—no more than a first inkling—that one could make meaning through the manipulation of materials, and that the outcome of this operation contained the potential to continue this game of constructing and deconstructing meaning by inviting the interpretations of others. Later, I would theorize that the interpretative operation of art was political in that, freed of didacticism, the viewer was offered the free space to formulate their own assessments. I was thinking of politics as the arena in which we strive against controlling institutions or authorities to achieve the freedom necessary to evaluate the meaning of those things and ideas that come before us.

Although Harvard had no art practice curriculum (the university didn't believe that making art was a legitimate academic subject), it did have a Department of Fine Art. There I took several art history classes, starting with the basic Eurocentric survey class and moving through more period-specific courses dealing with the Northern Renaissance, Italian Renaissance, Baroque, up to the twentieth century.

Then, in 1965, Michael Fried, a graduate fellow in fine art, curated an exhibition at Harvard's Fogg Art Museum titled *Three American Painters:*

Kenneth Noland, Jules Olitski, and Frank Stella. His show was the first exhibition of contemporary art at the Fogg, which as an extension of the conservative Department of Fine Art, held that only pedigreed objects from the ancient to the just very old warranted scholarly attention. Fried's exhibition presaged many of the ideas he would commit to writing in his seminal 1967 essay "Art and Objecthood," which, in later years when I was teaching, I would describe to students as the last, dying gasp of Greenbergian Modernism. That Fried, as a junior fellow in the department, was able to mount such a controversial exhibition within that staid institution said something about the status this young art historian had achieved at credential-obsessed Harvard. *Three American Painters*, pro and con, was discussed endlessly and passionately by those of us who were interested in contemporary art as we milled about the Fogg and the Carpenter Center.

As much as I would like to pretend otherwise, I was no more than a mediocre student in college if judged in terms of my grades, which were generally Bs and Cs with the very occasional A. Truth is, I was distracted by all the people, ideas, and events I encountered beyond the formal boundaries of classes. One of the most significant of those people was Martin Peretz, a junior fellow in the Government Department and a resident tutor in Kirkland House. Marty, recently divorced, took most of his evening meals in the dining hall with the undergraduates and several of the house tutors. He was to my eyes erudite, extreme, and eloquent in his fast-paced New York way. He was charismatic, generous toward the many he chose to befriend and verbally belligerent toward those whose opinions he found reactionary or poorly reasoned, of which there were also many. The opposite of the staid academic, flamboyant and iconoclastic, Marty was an intellectual showboat who leaned heavily leftward, which put him in an unfavorable light with some of the more traditional academics, particularly those in the Government Department where the company line was determined by senior members like Henry Kissinger, whose own flamboyance was of a more acceptable type. It was through Marty that I was introduced to political theorists like Theodor Adorno, Herbert Marcuse (Marty's mentor at Brandeis), Leo Lowenthal, and others who helped ground my intuitively leftist politics.

As a college student filled with questions and doubts, my response was to fling myself out there with the belief that the best path for me was to find the least predictable ways of navigating the sea of information that roiled around me—although, to be clear, my reasoning then was more intuitive and reactive than carefully considered. In my search for a means to investigate the feelings and ideas that were percolating within, I gravitated toward the Loeb Drama Center, epicenter of the college theater scene. Perhaps it was a desire to be seen and heard that motivated me, or maybe it was just that I was drawn to these eccentric and expressive people with whom I felt some sort of kinship.

I acted in friends' movies and had minor roles in plays at the Loeb and other venues. The most memorable of these was when I had to suddenly replace the student who had been cast as First Servant to Gloucester (played brilliantly by sophomore John Lithgow) in *King Lear.* In my brief but pivotal scene, the servant turns against Cornwall, who has already stabbed out one of Gloucester's eyes, egged on by Regan, one of Lear's two unsavory daughters. I recall two lines from my epic performance: The first, as I faced the vicious Cornwall, "If you did wear a beard upon your chin, I would shake it on this quarrel." With that, a duel breaks out during which I wound Cornwall, who is belittled by Regan for being unable to outduel a mere peasant (me). She takes a knife from another servant and stabs the poor First Servant in the back, whereupon I cry, "Oh, I am slain! My lord, you have one eye left to see some mischief on him. Oh!" and I die. The problem was, having had almost no time to rehearse, I was extremely nervous and died awkwardly and over-theatrically, sprawling down and across a set of stairs and with a wavering and extended "Oh." This produced a very unwelcome laugh (a pretty loud one at that) during one of the gravest and most tragic moments in the play. Lithgow was nailing the tragedy of Gloucester before I did my bit. I learned that dying convincingly on stage was a lot harder than I imagined; by working with the director, I was able to tone it all down a bit so that by the last week of the run I could die with the best of them.

I had small parts in several other productions, including two Brecht plays: *The Threepenny Opera* with Susan (Stockard) Channing as Jenny and directed by Harvard legend Tim Mayer, and *Trumpets and Drums*. Tim was a fascinating figure around Cambridge. Disheveled in a suit jacket, hair uncombed, stooped from a deformity of his spine, he was elegant in a bohemian sort of way. He was, most of all, immensely talented as a writer and stage director. After college, he would go on to write and direct in Boston and Washington, D.C., often in collaboration with Peter Sellars, who is well known today as an innovative director of plays and operas.

Harvard was, and still is, a fortress of privilege. Students, and perhaps faculty as well, are swaddled in layers of self-approbation partially generated by the mystique of the place. I recognized this privilege. Was grateful for it. Yet, along with this gratitude was a growing awareness that we toiled under an unfair system that favored the well-connected over those less fortunate. This emerging realization was nurtured by my contact with scholars like Noam Chomsky who, through his teach-ins at MIT, provided us with a very different analysis of the Vietnam War than we were getting from our government or the mainstream press. Through my familiarity with the writings of Adorno, Marcuse, Lowenthal, Marx, Simone Weil, and others, I fully accepted the importance of questioning the institutions that held power over us. This awareness was further confirmed by the people I hung out with and, most profoundly, by the political and social unrest that seemed omnipresent. For a time, I was an eager

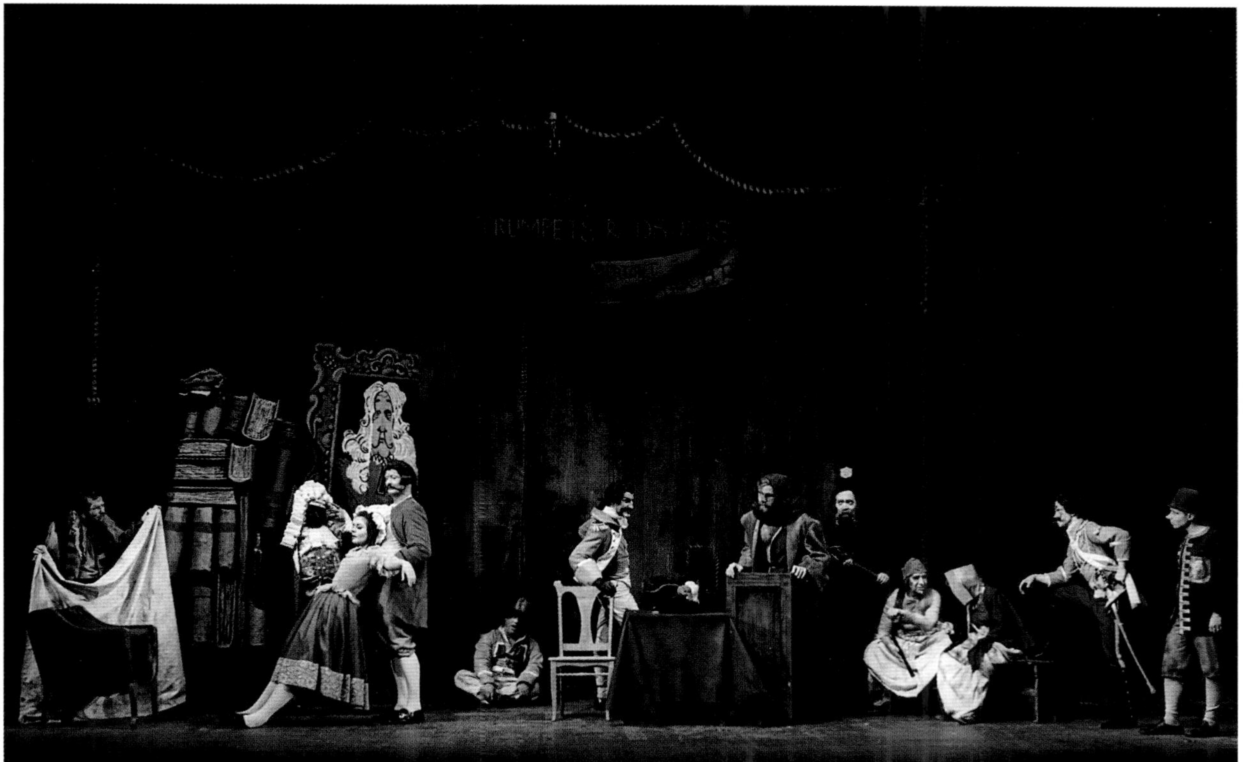

Being interrogated in Brecht's *Trumpets and Drums* at the Loeb Drama Center, 1965
Photograph: Loeb Drama Center, Harvard University

participant in Students for a Democratic Society (SDS), the major antiwar organization on college campuses. As a member, I delivered several fiery speeches, delighting in the attention. But, after a few months and lots of meetings, I became disenchanted and left when I witnessed the power struggles among the organization's leadership that, in my mind, exposed a hypocrisy in which their aspirations for power and organizational authority were more important than protesting the war in Vietnam.

War, Racism, Drugs

Many of my generation were shocked out of our 1950s slumber by the confluence of three events. One was the war in Vietnam, which to us was an unwinnable contest, racist and colonialist at its core, and based on outmoded theories about Communism as a monolithic force that would topple one country after the last, like a row of dominoes, with the final piece falling across the United States. To me and my peers, this narrative seemed absurd and defenseless.

The second major generational shock, more a social/cultural/political series of events, was the civil rights struggle and the realization—how could I have been so unaware?—that this country was corrupted by the terrible legacy of slavery and its everlasting companion, racism. The Deep South got the most attention, with its KKK, its advocates for segregation in governors, senators, and congressmen in outright defiance of federal laws, and its murders of African Americans. But it was not just the South that bore this burden. Boston, too, had its own segregationists, politicians like Rep. Louise Day Hicks who, first as a prominent and vocal member of the school board, proudly opposed desegregation of the public schools and attempted to halt court-ordered busing in the city.

And the third shock, perhaps as profound but in different ways than the other two, was the introduction of psychedelic drugs into American colleges and universities. If war and civil rights shook our political and social beings, psychedelics finished the job by completely reorienting our psychic beings. For me, the most shattering aspect was how my sense of self, as a unique entity living at a moment in time, came crashing in on itself. What made the experiences even more explosive was that these trips were done under casual circumstances without a guide to keep me from freaking out (an accurate expression of the sensation, by the way). Nor did I have the language to categorize the experience of time becoming incoherent—past, present, and future indistinguishably blurred—and space being perceived as something physical, pulsating, everywhere and nowhere at the same time. These drugs revealed another, palpable reality that lurked beneath existential reality as if a layer were stripped from the world as I ordinarily perceived it. Understanding the profundity of these experiences, I took them on infrequently since they often inserted as much anxious delirium (more with LSD than with psilocybin or peyote) as they provided delirious insight, or what Walter Benjamin, an author I would discover much later and who would have a huge influence on me, referred to in his essay "Surrealism" as "profane illumination."

By fall semester of my senior year, it dawned on me that I needed to figure out what I was going to do after graduation. The solemn specter of the military draft hung over all of us, which made the idea of continuing one's education attractive, since enrollment in a graduate degree program could qualify one for a student deferment. But it wasn't guaranteed, which made it even more imperative that, even if accepted into a graduate program, I be as unattractive as possible to my local draft board, which was in Concord, Massachusetts. My understanding, right or wrong, was that each draft district had a responsibility to provide a certain number of able bodies for military service. Being a small suburban community, I assumed the number from the Concord Board would be significantly fewer than from a district in Boston or Cambridge. I hoped it was an advantage, but I didn't know for sure if that was the case. Periodically, I would receive notifications from the board, all signed by the same woman, Gladys McDougal. One of them provided detailed information about how we were required to alert the board if we left town for any length of time, the implication being that they wanted to communicate with us immediately if we were called up. At least until graduation, I was protected by my student deferment. Nevertheless, my strategy was to enhance my posture as an unstable person by taking this instruction beyond what was required and providing Gladys with constant updates as to my whereabouts and how best to reach me. I wrote these on paper napkins, on brown paper ripped from shopping bags, on toilet paper, and on scraps I found in the street. I wrote with pens of all colors—sometimes with sketches in the margins—with pencils sharp and dull, with lipstick, and with crayons. I wrote her often; even, for example, if I was going away for the weekend, realizing that by the time she received my note, the weekend would likely have come and gone.

> Dear Gladys McDougal,
> I wanted to let you know that I will be visiting my friend Mike and staying at his parents' place in Truro this weekend. We might go swimming in the ocean if it is warm enough. It's supposed to be warm for the next several days, but I will bring a sweater just in case. If I get drafted you can contact me there.
> Sincerely,
> Douglas Hall

It was in this frantic, confusing atmosphere that I had to consider my options. I had vague thoughts about pursuing an academic career. But I was honest enough with myself to admit that I wouldn't do well under its rigid structures, nor was I scholarly in any traditional way. I looked for something more flexible, dynamic, and unconventional; something that wouldn't require me to spend all my time in a library. Of all the things I tried as a student, I felt most comfortable at the Carpenter Center where thinking was structured through the act of making things, the manipulation of materials and images. In my limited view of how art could function, I thought it was an approach that might accommodate my interests and aspirations. I was looking for a language of images through which I could begin to speak in my own voice. Late in the fall semester of my senior year, I applied to the UCLA Film School and the Rinehart School of Sculpture of the Maryland Institute College of Art and was accepted at both. Rinehart offered me a full scholarship and a generous materials allowance if I would agree to a three-year program rather than the usual two to compensate for my lack of undergraduate studio classes. I chose Rinehart. With my acceptance, I was reasonably assured of a military deferment, which allowed me to cease my compulsive letter-writing campaign to Ms. McDougal. After graduation and a short break, I headed off to Baltimore and Rinehart.

II

Thinking, Looking, Making

Love and Art in Rural Maine

It was a muggy July day in 1966 when I arrived at the Rinehart School of Sculpture in Baltimore, manifesting more than a little Ivy League rigidity. A well-trimmed red beard and a very serious demeanor masked my burning desire to succeed in this new environment. I worked through the summer in the large open studio that was located at one end of the converted nineteenth-century Mount Royal train station, replicating exercises I had done in William Reimann's 3-D design classes at Harvard. There were only a couple of grad students around that summer, and they were surprisingly kind and helpful considering how undeveloped I was as an artist.

Coming from Harvard, art school was a revelation, an awakening, really. For better or worse, I arrived with a bit of an attitude—not about making, where I had much to learn, nor about thinking visually through the formal logic of materials. But though I had yet to prove it to myself, let alone anyone else, I was convinced that I could develop a visual language that addressed relevant, contemporary conditions rather than one that was purely aesthetic, limiting itself to formal issues. Somehow, I already knew that this language had to operate expansively and provocatively rather than complacently or predictably. I look back at this as my emerging intuition that the vocabulary of art could be wide ranging, not limited to static objects, or maybe not even to objects at all, and that, most crucially, it could be, must be, interrogative and experiential.

My acceptance into the MFA program on a provisional basis had been orchestrated by Bud Leake, president of the Maryland Institute College of Art, the governing institution that oversaw the graduate programs in sculpture at Rinehart and in painting at the Hoffberger School. The idea, which was put forth by Leake with, as I would later learn, gentle resistance from Rinehart Director Norman Carlberg—like Leake, a Yale grad—was that I would be on a three-year course to reach my MFA. The first year was to be a trial year during which I would take intermediate drawing classes, figure modeling in clay, and metal casting, as well as work on my own ideas. Recognizing that talking and thinking art required a next crucial step into materiality, I was determined to learn how to make stuff. When the fall semester began, I was moved from the studio in the converted train station to a small space on the top floor of a row house above a ceramics studio that I shared with two other provisional students, both of whom would drop out after their first year.

Toward the end of the semester, Leake and Carlberg decided, I imagine after consulting with my drawing teacher and figure modeling instructor, that I would benefit from moving back into a space in the Rinehart studio, which I did shortly after returning from Christmas recess. Because the regular studios were full, they placed me in a windowless former storage room next to the bathroom in the hallway leading to Carlberg's private studio. Not yet a full-fledged Rinehart Fellow, I was closer than I had been and now able to benefit from

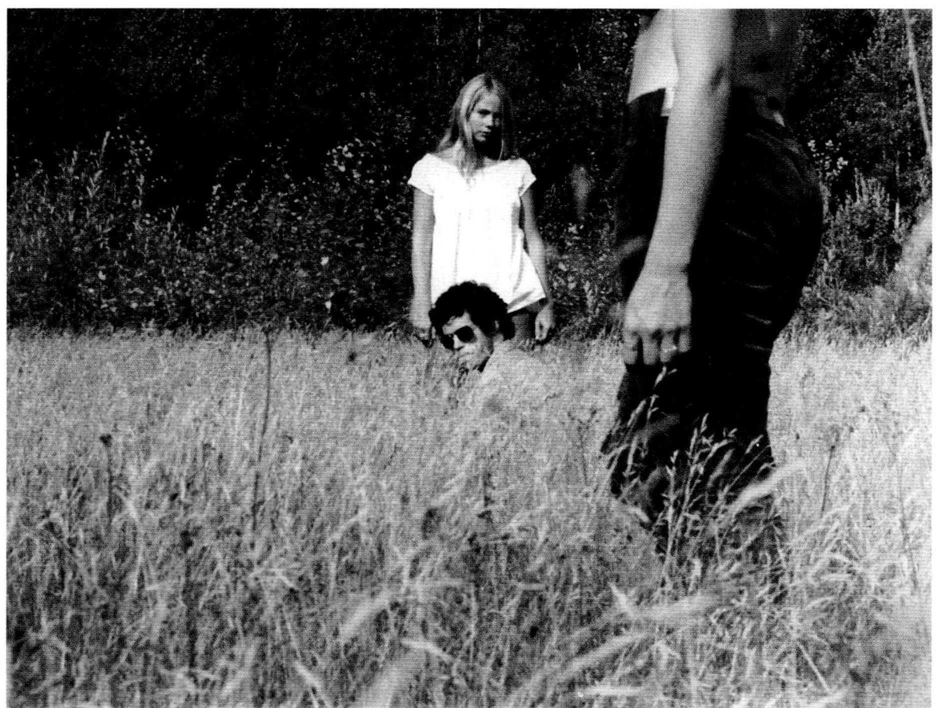

Fellow students at the Skowhegan School of Painting and Sculpture (Lea Douglas, right; Richard Olsen, seated; and Diane Andrews in the background), summer 1967
Photograph by Doug Hall

proximity to the graduate sculpture population of fifteen students, all of whom had completed rigorous undergraduate art programs: I watched, listened, and mimicked what I saw and heard as I struggled to figure things out. Apparently by the end of the first year, I had made enough objects that looked like sculpture and performed well enough in my classes to convince the faculty review committee that I should be fully accepted into the program. Even so, in my mind, I was far from where I wanted, or needed, to be. At the same time, I could imagine getting there and was further encouraged when I learned that the faculty had nominated me to attend the prestigious summer residency in Skowhegan, Maine. I was accepted with a full scholarship, including room and board.

So it was that, on a drizzly June afternoon in 1967, I pulled into the Skowhegan School of Painting and Sculpture in a rusty old Chevy station wagon that consumed vast amounts of oil, causing a constant smudge of dark smoke to spew from its exhaust. The rust on the undercarriage was so bad that from the passenger's side, you could look down and watch the asphalt race by; the roar of the tires on the pavement made it nearly impossible to carry on a normal conversation. The radio didn't work.

If indeed life is a balance between good and bad luck, then the opportunity to attend Skowhegan tipped way, way over onto the lucky side of the ledger, if for no other reason than it is where I met Diane Andrews.

After signing in at the office and dropping my things off in the room I would share with two others, I headed over to the sculpture facilities to check things out. Back then, the sculpture area consisted of a small building with various tools, including a table saw, hand tools, and welding equipment—the usual assortment for a small sculpture facility. Approachable through an open wall was a fenced-off outdoor area from which there came the intolerable racket of grinder against steel, sledgehammer against rock, and chainsaw against wood that I had been hearing long before I arrived at their source. It was the sound of earnest sculptors at work, all male, at least one shirtless and sweaty. I recognized that they were pursuing an aesthetic that I had little interest in, what I arrogantly referred to as "the Sweaty Armpit School of Art," the predictable outcome of which would be large, generally abstract works in steel or wood, requiring at least two people to move. Although, in all honesty, I had little clue what my aesthetic should be, I knew with great certainty what I did not want it to be. With my head hanging, feeling sorry for myself, wondering why in the world I had come there, and planning my escape—to where, I didn't know—I ventured along a path away from the sculpture area and its incessant clanging and grinding.

On one side of the path lay a series of sheds that were similar to horse stables, with the fronts open, their side walls going about three quarters of the way to the sloped ceilings providing some privacy on either side. These were occupied by painters. Brimming with self-pity, I glanced into them as I walked along. Near the end, far away from the sculpture area, I spied this beautiful girl with long, blonde hair streaming across her shoulders and down her back as she bent over the canvas she was stretching onto a frame lying on the ground. She wore light brown corduroy pants and a blue and white striped t-shirt. I stopped and stared. She turned and looked at me. Hers was the second-to-last of the painter's sheds. I noted that the one beyond was empty. It was then that I knew my summer destiny was to be a painter.

I quickly retraced my steps, rushing past the sculpture area to the main office. I burst in to explain that there had been an administrative mistake. I was a painter, not a sculptor, and I happened to notice that there was a space available at the far end of the painters' sheds and I would be happy to work there for the summer. After a little hemming and hawing on the administrative side they agreed to the plan, and I moved next door to Diane.

Over the next several weeks, Diane instructed me in how to stretch and prepare a canvas, and encouraged me to paint in acrylics (less difficult to control than her medium oil, she advised). I, for my part, when not applying color to the circles, geometric squares, and lines I'd meticulously drawn on stretched canvas, carefully marked off with compass and straight-edge (for which I would receive an award at the end of the summer that galled Diane then and still does over fifty years later), could be found pursuing her with passionate, and only occasionally frustrated, energy. I discovered that not only was she quietly and mysteriously sexy, but also profoundly talented and smart in ways that I was not. She drew and painted unselfconsciously with the skill of one who might have emerged from the womb with pencil and brush in hand. Whereas I tended to intellectualize, Diane, as I would discover over the course of the summer, was far more intuitive, less encumbered by a need to rationalize or conceptualize her painterly decisions. We were married six months later and, clueless at the time, destined for a deep love, many moments of profound joy, and a few of deep sorrow.

As central as Diane was to my time at Skowhegan, there were important interruptions to my incessant, if awkward, courting. By now, I had been through a year of graduate school, where I had become familiar with the esoteric language of critiques (in any case, Harvard had trained me in the fine art of talking with authority even if I was unsure of what I was saying), but I was far from a confident craftsman. I was awed by many of the students who represented the best from programs throughout the country. The most brash and confident were the few from New York, who saw themselves as the most aesthetically advanced, or perhaps that's how they seemed to me. While I was posing as a hard-edge, abstract painter to be close to Diane, others were earnestly painting, drawing, and sculpting in ways that were clearly accomplished, but to my eye, also traditional with a few exceptions.

One of those exceptions was Douglas Leichter, a born and bred New Yorker, who, from all appearances, seemed to be doing very little at Skowhegan. Doug was social but aloof, as if he knew something the rest of us didn't. He moved around with confidence, but he didn't spend much time in the painting sheds. Rather, along with another student, Richard Saba, he drifted about espousing aesthetic theories that were of interest to me, addressing the potential of a work of art being something other than a static object that rested on a base or hung on the wall in a gallery. It was an argument that I was becoming attuned to while groping for a way to actualize it. Doug and Richard were mysterious about what they were working on, only letting some of us know that it was site-specific (did we have such language at the time?) and was in a clearing in the woods some distance from the painting sheds.

During the summer, we had several critiques that were held in a former barn centrally located on the school grounds. Students would bring their work to the front where it would be available for discussion under the guidance of one of the resident faculty or visiting artists. When Doug's and Richard's turn came, they led us out of the barn.

It had been a rainy summer in Maine and the day was overcast, muggy, and buggy as we followed them from the barn into the woods and finally to the clearing, which, as we approached through the trees, seemed undisturbed. But as we drew near, we came upon a deep hole that they had spent a good part of the summer working on and which they were claiming as their art. My recollection is that they presented us with a void in which all the sides were equal, as if a cube had been removed from the ground. I was impressed. A hole in the ground as art! I had little context in which to think about this. None of us staring down into this void could have, because similar gestures into the landscape by artists like Robert Smithson, Michael Heizer, Nancy Holt, and others wouldn't reach our attention until a year or two later. Their simple gesture went off like an explosion in my brain. For me, it was another confirmation that the contours of sculpture were not as carefully defined as art history might lead us to believe but could be almost limitless.

I'm not sure that either Richard or Doug fully understood the implications of what they had done, since, as far as I can determine, neither followed up with similar projects, but instead carved out respectable careers as abstract painters. It would be some time before I could figure out how to take advantage of the insights I gained from these kinds of projects, but I stored them away along with a lot of other information I was gathering that summer, much of which came from artists who visited Skowhegan. For me, the most influential were John Cage and Merce Cunningham, who arrived as a couple, and Ad Reinhardt.

My recollections of Cage are more vivid than those of Cunningham, I suppose because I was familiar with some of Cage's work, and although I understood Cunningham's role as an occasional collaborator, I was ignorant about contemporary dance. What I found remarkable about Cage during his visit was the quiet calmness that surrounded him: the poetic, and yet pragmatic way in which he addressed his production as an artist, how he worked across media, and of course, the gentleness that he displayed toward all of us adoring and questioning students.

I vividly remember his quest for mushrooms that took us through the surrounding woods while he quietly commented on the things he noticed: the quality of the afternoon light as it broke through recent storm clouds, a spiderweb stretched between branches of a tree, a patch of wildflowers. He did this not at all in a teacherly way but as casual interjections, almost as if he were talking to himself, Merce, or one of us. Of course, the point wasn't really the mushrooms. It was the walk and being present and aware of the moments as they unfolded, and of the many things that were revealed in the process. And finally, after tramping through the forest with an entourage of about twenty art students, accepting the fact that on that day we would find no mushrooms.

I connected most deeply with Reinhardt. I was familiar with his black paintings and some of the discourse, from him and his critics, that surrounded this work. On learning that he would conduct a group critique, I worked up the courage to present my work. While it's fair to describe myself as something of a summer fraud—although I didn't see myself that way at the time—posing as a painter to escape the macho world of the sculpture area and to have proximity to Diane, it is also true that I took myself seriously and was trying to make the best paintings I could within the limited means I'd provided myself.

One of the great lessons I'd learned from the classes I took at Harvard's Carpenter Center was the necessity of establishing limiting rules within which to operate. By the time I arrived at Skowhegan, I was sophisticated enough to understand that producing art involved countless decisions and that, for me at least, this process had to have some sort of logic or order; otherwise anything seemed possible, with the result that nothing could be achieved. This is one of the reasons I was attracted to Cage, who used systems he derived from chance operations, like throwing the I Ching, to free himself from subjective and purely aesthetic operations.

What interested me so about Reinhardt was that although he also had rules, his were so strict that they resulted in works that, if one followed his logic, undermined their very reason for being: painterliness, the essence of painting. I loved this idea, outrageous, provocative, and logical in its endgame strategy. I am pretty sure that I couldn't have articulated it this way at the time, but I did recognize that Reinhardt—and later I would see this worked out by other artists in other ways—was getting at something that interested and motivated me: this notion that art was based on ideas and that these could be expressed "non-retinally," to borrow a term from Marcel Duchamp. In other words, art need not be merely visual (decorative, colorful, beautiful) but could be, again to quote Duchamp, "in the service of the mind."[1] Perhaps an art historian would shudder at this thought, but I will venture it anyway: while Duchamp took the everyday object and, by shifting its context, elevated it to high art, Reinhardt took the high art of painting and slammed it into a cul-de-sac from which there was no escape. In doing so, he wrote painting's philosophical endgame through painting itself. By my reasoning, Duchamp was undermining any conceit of purity that art may claim while Reinhardt was eradicating all elements—design, color, line, gesture, texture, light—that might prevent painting from achieving the purity for which he believed it was destined. I found all of this intoxicating.

I had anticipated that Rinehart's critique of our work would be as extreme as his art, but I was surprised to find him supportive and sympathetic, even playful, rather than harsh or antagonistic. What I found fascinating was the clarity of his remarks, as if he were presenting truths that would be obvious to anyone. He made it seem as if aesthetics was not subjective at all but a matter of applying certain precepts to the object in question and determining where there was or was not consistency. On this basis, he could point to a section of a painting and say things like, "This, here: it needs to be blue." Or "That red line that runs from here to there interferes with the rectangle nestled in the corner. Best to remove it." His approach was more about what not to do than what to do. I didn't fully understand this at the time, but much later, when I began conducting my own critiques of student work, I espoused a similar theory.

As a young artist, I noticed that I was inclined to try to put everything I thought about everything into what I made. I think when we are young, we

1. Marcel Duchamp, quoted in H. H. Arnason and Marla F. Prather, *History of Modern Art: Painting, Sculpture, Architecture, Photography* (Fourth Edition) (New York: Harry N. Abrams, Inc., 1998), 274.

have an urgency to say it all, maybe because of an unconscious fear that there will not be another opportunity—there is no future, there is only now. Or maybe we fear we don't have anything to say, and think we can conceal that by throwing everything but the kitchen sink into the object, an inclination that, over time, I learned to circumvent. Years later, as a college art teacher, I encouraged students to do likewise.

For me, the most striking impression of Reinhardt was that accompanying his pretense of logical objectivity, there was humor that verged on the mischievous. He was the master of a game, the rules of which he was teaching us, and the more fully we understood them, the greater was our pleasure in playing. There was nothing solemn about Reinhardt. In his iconoclastic comments about art, he was entertaining a sophisticated joke—one with profound aesthetic and philosophical implications.

I spent a lot of time with Reinhardt during his visit. Before parting, he invited me and Diane (as we had become nearly inseparable) to visit him in New York. And to prove that this was more than one of those empty invitations that we have all made with the hope that the invitee will never arrive, he gave me his address and a phone number where I could reach him. Of course, I was flattered, excited, and emboldened by the invitation. This all happened in July 1967. On August 30th, he died after suffering a massive heart attack while working in his studio.

Cautiously Confident

I returned to Baltimore for my second year with a confidence I hadn't known before. The initial awkwardness I felt in the transition from the oppressive academic atmosphere of Harvard to the freer strangeness of art school had been replaced by a growing sense that maybe I belonged there. It could also be that I was in love with Diane and, as surprising as it seemed to all who thought they knew me, we had plans to marry in December. As I've noted earlier, I had also made a couple of particularly close friendships by the end of my first year with John Hillding, a sculptor who was a year ahead of me at Rinehart, and Mike Zelenka, a graduate painter. John had grown up in Seattle and arrived at Rinehart after getting his BA degree from the Kansas City Art Institute. Whereas most of the students exhibited a formal monochromatic aesthetic that mimicked or built on the prevailing tendencies being exhibited in New York, John brought a wild, West Coast–influenced panache to his works. He made quirky tabletop-size fantasy landscapes with references to architecture, the terrain of the moon—or perhaps Mars—out of highly worked and polished fiberglass and related materials. What was most amazing to my untutored eye was how he treated the surfaces, which were painted using colorful automotive lacquers that masterfully enhanced the combination of amorphous, undulating, and

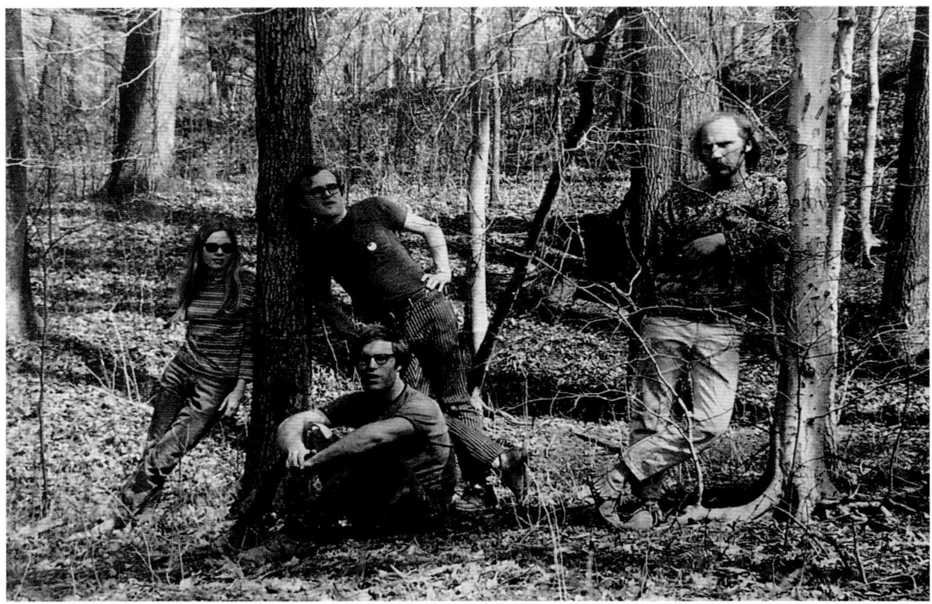

The Baltimore Gang: Diane, John, me (seated on the ground), and Mike

hard-edge shapes, giving the works a California hot rod reference that was anathema to the formal dictates of modernist sculpture. "Truth to materials" was the aesthetic of day, and polychrome surfaces were said to sully the "honesty" of the materials that lay beneath. The trend was also toward minimalist abstraction, whereas John's work had strong narrative content, even if the "story" was purely imagist rather than literary. I admired his stance and respected the calm, assured way in which he pursued it. He was serious about his art, and clearly very talented. He also had an appetite for adventure and fun.

As serious as I was, Mike seemed much more casual and carefree. Grace Hartigan, who oversaw the Hoffberger School of Painting where Mike was a student, was an artist who had little patience for pretenders. Here was Mike making hard-edge paintings (at a very leisurely pace) on boxes that he would arrange on the floor so that the chevrons and stripes carried the eye from one to the next. They weren't bad, but they didn't challenge or develop over the course of his tenure at school. And yet, Hartigan and the rest of the cohort not only tolerated Mike but clearly liked and respected him. I suppose everyone recognized what I did: that he was the art and his love of life and openness to others the medium. He was the perfect antidote to my tendency for overseriousness that could easily escalate into self-castigation and depression.

In the spring of my first year, John, Mike, and I rented a place on Mill Race Road, a dirt street with small, connected row houses of stone, perhaps gathered from the river running nearby. We later learned these houses had been built as quarters for the slaves who worked in the mill that spanned the river on the other side of the road. After their liberation, the buildings housed freemen and then Southern Whites who worked in the same mill. By the time we arrived, the mill had been long abandoned, and the living quarters were inhabited by poor Whites from Appalachia. Living there was like being cast back in time. I mean, way back in time to the Middle Ages. Although our apartment had a wooden floor, the others had dirt. Not only were the inhabitants desperately poor, they were also entirely uneducated, and since we were the only ones who could read, we were frequently asked to read letters and various government documents that our neighbors might receive. We would do our best to help them respond, including writing their letters in our longhand or, when appropriate, on a typewriter. We became the Mill Race Scribes along a small swath of Baltimore that felt more like the rural setting for the movie *Deliverance* than it did the periphery of a major American city.

Living a couple of doors down from us was a mother and daughter, Nona and Daisy, one of whose son—I think Daisy's—was in jail, awaiting trial on a murder charge. Helping them negotiate the complexity of the American legal system was beyond us, but we at least tried to help them have more direct communication with the court-appointed lawyer, which also meant our phone was occasionally usurped. The son was eventually found guilty, one of several from this little backwater who had run-ins with the law, mostly for theft (cars were a big item) and other nonlethal crimes.

Diane, who was admitted to the Hoffberger School, joined me after we were married in December 1967. I moved out of Mill Race Road, somewhat reluctantly as I recall, and into an apartment with Diane on W. Lafayette Avenue, right around the corner from the main building of the Maryland Institute. What had been a close friendship of three became an even closer friendship of four that expanded and contracted around other friendships as we navigated our individual and collective paths through our uncertain lives. By this time, my experience at art school had confirmed my earlier intuition that making could be a legitimate way for one to investigate and think, and I was open to all the influences around me. Norman Carlberg, as director of the Rinehart, was encouraging in a gentle, reserved sort of way. I really don't remember him "teaching" in any direct manner other than an occasional, almost informal, comment he might make in passing. He spent most of his time in his private studio, a large space off the central graduate studio where we worked. Norman and his Chilean wife, Juanita, who was as vivacious and outspoken as Norman was calm and quiet, were easy to like.

I was more directly influenced by fellow students like John, and by several of the full and part-time faculty who drifted through Rinehart, some of whom became friends. The most significant of these was the filmmaker Paul Sharits, who, not much older than I, arrived for his first teaching position at the Maryland Institute shortly after graduating with an MFA in design from Indiana University. As an undergraduate at the University of Denver, he had been a protégé of Stan Brakhage, with whom he maintained a close relationship. Sharits was charming, handsome in a dangerous sort of way, with clear brown eyes that seemed to flash when he was excited. He was charismatic, almost magnetic, particularly to women who were attracted to a kind of sexual energy that could quickly escalate from attentive flirtatiousness to obsessive animalism if alcohol or drugs were involved. He had a rapacious appetite for ideas as well as sensation. He loved to talk abstractly, particularly about film, which he did in a slow, measured way, even when intoxicated, as if pulling the words out of a brain overflowing with thoughts. He loved provocative ideas, which he pursued often with a bemused expression on his face, as if he were stifling a laugh as he pondered the absurdity or beauty of the thoughts drifting back and forth. I used to refer to this kind of conversation as "mind ball," and Paul played it better than anyone I have ever known. The skill requires a high degree of eloquence, a willingness to imagine everything from the sublime to the outrageous, and, importantly, an ability to pause and listen to the respondent so the ball can be received and batted around a bit before being returned. Paul, in short, was a great conversationalist. I loved talking to him. He was also mad.

To me, as a student, it was a seductive kind of madness, one that fit into the myth of the brilliant artist as a martyr to aesthetic cravings that were clear to him, often misunderstood by others. The history of western art is filled with examples of the impassioned, heroic artist who sacrifices everything, even sanity, in the service of his craft: Caravaggio, Van Gogh, Nijinsky, Artaud, the list is long and largely male. It is the artist as warrior and conqueror. (Yves Klein referred to himself as "the Conquistador of the Void," an epithet that accompanied a notorious photograph of him suspended in air, leaping from the side of a building, arms outstretched as if he were flying, miraculously held aloft and oblivious to the street that lay twenty feet below his outstretched body.) Paul inhabited the crazed artist convincingly with a combination of charm and poignancy, but also with terrible flashes of cruelty that could emerge suddenly, and if drunk at a bar, which was not unusual, end in violence.

Many of us flirted with madness. I allowed, even encouraged, a craziness within me that I enhanced with the occasional use of psychedelic drugs and other intoxicants to achieve levels of ecstasy, or at least illusions of transcendence, believing, I suppose, that it was a source of my creative energy. Sharits, on the other hand, embraced it. Not as an act, but as a true expression of neurological dysfunction coupled with personal experience. His mother had died by suicide and his younger brother, Gregg, who walked with a limp sustained when he hurled himself off the roof of his apartment building, successfully completed his self-destruction a few years later when he was suicided-by-cop.

In 1976, Paul was stabbed in the back during an argument on the street with a woman he was involved with. In 1982, apparently mistaken for someone else, he was shot at close range in the stomach outside a bar in Buffalo, suffering a wound that nearly killed him. Depressed, unable to fully recover from his injury, having lost his job at the University of Buffalo because of abusive behavior, he died at his home on July 8, 1993.

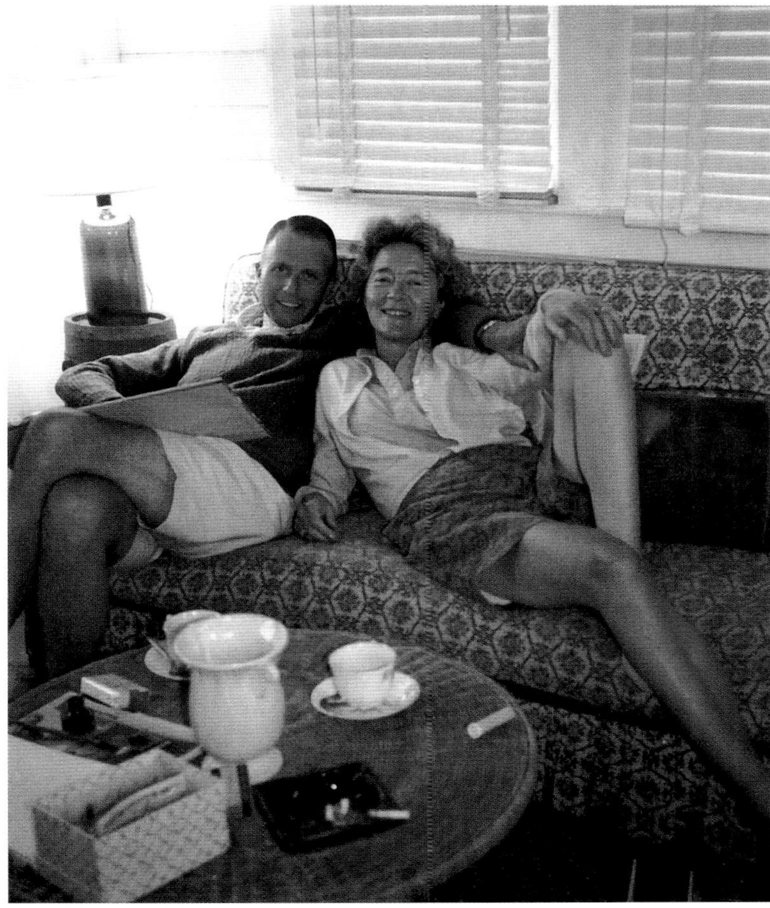

My parents during happier times, Martha's Vineyard, 1959

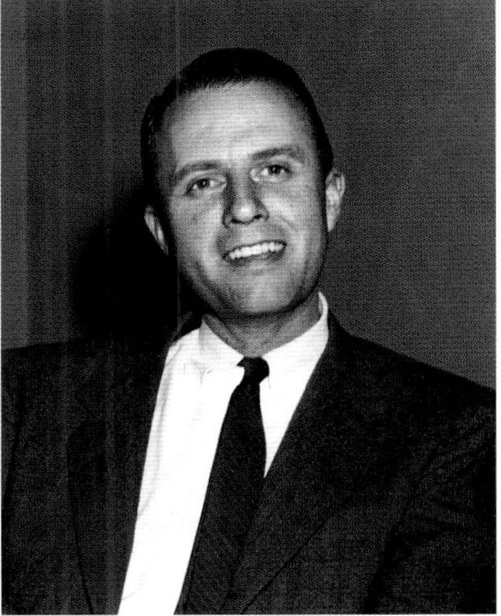

My father, circa 1962

A Death in the Family

In March 1968, shortly after Diane and I were married in Dallas, my father, who earlier had been diagnosed with incurable cancer, died at the age of fifty-one. I was devastated. Even though he had been desperately sick for several months, I was unprepared for his inevitable death.

My father was a gentle man with a wonderful sense of humor that was never boisterous or mean-spirited. As he had in my youth, he still loved visual art and, alongside his job as director of the MBA program at the Harvard Business School, pursued his passion for painting and collage and had several shows at small galleries in Cambridge and Boston.

I was completing my second year of graduate school when my mother called to tell me that, nine months after his melanoma diagnosis, he was nearing the end and I should come home. Diane and I flew to Boston to join my exhausted mother and dying father in their apartment on Beacon Street, originally chosen to please my father before he became ill. Aside from the light-filled rooms of the apartments, the major selling point for my dad was the building's rotating exhibitions of works by contemporary artists like Larry Rivers.

Thinking today about my father's illness and death, I am reminded of a passage by the Russian writer Victor Shklovsky. In his epistolary novel *Zoo, or Letters Not About Love*, unable to directly describe his love for Elsa Triolet, the woman he had left behind when he fled Russia, Shklovsky writes from his temporary self-exile, "Berlin is hard to describe." Berlin in this instance being a substitute for "love." One might say the same about the complex feelings associated with the death of someone we love: "Death is hard to describe."

At the time, melanoma was one of the most malignant and difficult cancers to treat. It first appeared as a discolored mole on my father's back and quickly spread throughout his body. Surely, he understood where his illness was headed, but he refused to acknowledge it; we, his children, were firmly instructed by my mother to make no references to the inevitable. He handled his illness quietly and privately, and from outward appearances, as if it were a temporary intrusion into his life—one that could be eliminated by simply ignoring it. I suppose that from his perspective, to name the disease was to recognize its power over him: a terrible malevolence entering his world that threatened to consume him while destroying the well-being of the family he loved and yearned to protect.

Although my father was obviously frail, we determined after consulting with his oncologist that his death wasn't imminent, so Diane and I returned to Baltimore. The call from my mother came a few weeks later. After our arrival, we followed her into the bedroom where my father lay in a hospital bed next to the twin bed where my mother continued to rest whenever she was able. I was shocked by what I saw: although covered by blankets, his frame looked small and fragile, complexion sallow, cheeks sunken, dark circles around his eyes, and his breathing was labored and slow. And yet he was clean shaven and well groomed, a chore my mother lovingly continued in recognition of his fastidiousness, which she insisted on maintaining even throughout his death march. Standing before him, it didn't take a medical professional to know that death was very near and that something had to be done to relieve the situation. At the very least, to provide rest for my mother. After some anguished discussion amidst frequent tears, we came to a terrible decision: we would quicken the process by significantly increasing the morphine that my mother was injecting into him. With me at her side, consoling as best I could, she pushed the needle into his emaciated thigh. The deed done, we waited through the night, seldom speaking, as his breathing became more and more labored and shallow. The night seemed to go on forever.

As I stared at him, I couldn't alleviate my own guilt and remorse over the pain I imagined I had caused him over the last few years. I had entered college as a typical suburban kid and, despite some significant infractions of rules and even laws along the way that had troubled my parents, I'd managed to get into Harvard as well as Stanford, which made both parents happy, even proud. It's what happened to me at Harvard and after that I think troubled them, although neither ever aggressively questioned me about the more radical path I had chosen. Sitting next to him as he lay dying, in a state that precluded any possibility for reparations or apologies, I grieved for any unresolved misunderstandings, any disappointments in me that he might harbor, in addition to the labyrinth of confusing emotions one faces as a parent, too young for death, draws those final breaths.

At some point in the early morning hours, my mother, fully clothed on top of her bed, stirred from a brief, troubled nap, and I, nodding off and on in a chair near my father's head, watched, frozen in anguished anticipation, as the seconds stretched between each breath, waiting, terrified for that final one. We waited. And we waited. And as the sun came up, the gloom of the night having dissipated, his breathing became more regular and he even regained semiconsciousness long enough to reach out a hand in recognition of my presence, calling "Lou," his nickname for me, before falling back into unawareness. Our attempts to kill him or, as we rationalized it, our attempts to ease him into death had failed, and neither of us had the capacity to try again. After a morning of discussion including consultation with his doctor, we decided to have him transported to the hospital, understanding that exhaustion and despair had finally overcome my mother's wish to allow him a death at home.

The last time I saw my father was in a private room at Mass General Hospital. He was sitting up in bed, softly speaking—almost cheerful—but making no sense. My mother was with him. Maybe one or both sisters. Despite a living will, and the explicit instructions of the family, the medical resident, believing that his patient should experience death consciously, had revived him. Barring intervention, we understood that death would overtake him in a couple of days, and we asked the doctors once again to allow this natural and inevitable process to unfold. They agreed.

With evening coming, the three of us returned to the apartment on Beacon Street. And waited. We waited through the night. And through the next day while my mother visited him, alone at her request, for what would be the last time. During our stay, Diane and I had been sleeping on a foam pad on the living room floor. We disconnected the phone in my mom's bedroom, leaving the one in the living room, so that if the call came from the hospital during the night, I could take it and relay the information to her. At three in the morning, the phone rang, a dreadful, brash, piercing sound knowing the devastating news that it signaled. "Hello," . . . neither the name nor the nurse's preamble registered as I anticipated the terrible words. "Mr. Hall passed away this morning at 2:30." Tears followed, but for my mother, I sensed that, lurking beneath a profound sadness that would last for years, there was relief. Many months of agony and powerlessness had ended.

. . . And I Stepped Out

I am approaching the final minutes of my week-long isolation within the Inner Space Simulation Module, *my MFA project at Rinehart. My mind is swirling with all kinds of rapid-fire thoughts and emotions. Interspersed are continuing recollections of the trip Diane and I made to Houston's Manned Spacecraft Center, one of the inspirations for the project.*

In 1968, the Manned Spacecraft Center, located near Clear Lake in Houston, consisted of numerous undistinguished buildings in the brutalist style situated within a sprawling campus. The array didn't look corporate as much as bureaucratic, matter-of-fact: a utilitarian place for visionaries and technicians who find their inspiration in mathematical models and in the challenge of solving confounding physical and technological problems. And like the surroundings, the mostly male practitioners we saw climbing in and out of their cars in the expansive parking lots or walking hurriedly along the paved pathways between buildings were unremarkable in appearance: lots of crew cuts, khaki pants, with some in suits with their jackets slung over one shoulder, revealing short-sleeved white shirts. Whether any were sporting those plastic pocket protectors, where pens and pencils are neatly arranged, I can't be sure, but if there was ever a mecca for the pocket protector population this had to be it. This was no-frills Nerdsville for sure, a complex community of brilliant individuals and their support staffs, sharing a single, shared obsession: getting men to the moon. I was thrilled beyond words.

"Three minutes and counting." At last, I'm getting out of here. I'm exhausted and emotional. I recall the past year, the support from some friends and advisers and the disdain from others, particularly other Rinehart Fellows, who are deeply wed to a more traditional practice. Carlberg, gentle by nature and very much a formalist, has been quietly supportive or at least not discouraging, occasionally asking challenging questions, but never aggressively, and always interested in and respectful of my responses. He is the opposite of the undergraduate sculpture teacher, who, in my eyes, epitomizes the swaggering, anti-intellectual cowboy sculptor, with no tolerance for ideas that abrade against his own. I quickly learned to ignore his digs, which angered him, a response that in my passive-aggression, I quietly enjoyed.

"OK," I respond. "What's it like out there?" I'm anxious, but calmer than I was a few minutes earlier. The overhead lights come on again, filling the small space with an uncomfortable brightness.

"A lot of people gathering, looking forward to welcoming you back." I look at the closed-circuit television camera above me and deliver a slow-motion wave to the people watching outside like I've seen some of the weightless astronauts do. Even without Sam's mic on, cheers permeate the soundproofing materials that surround the box I'm in. A new excitement courses through me.

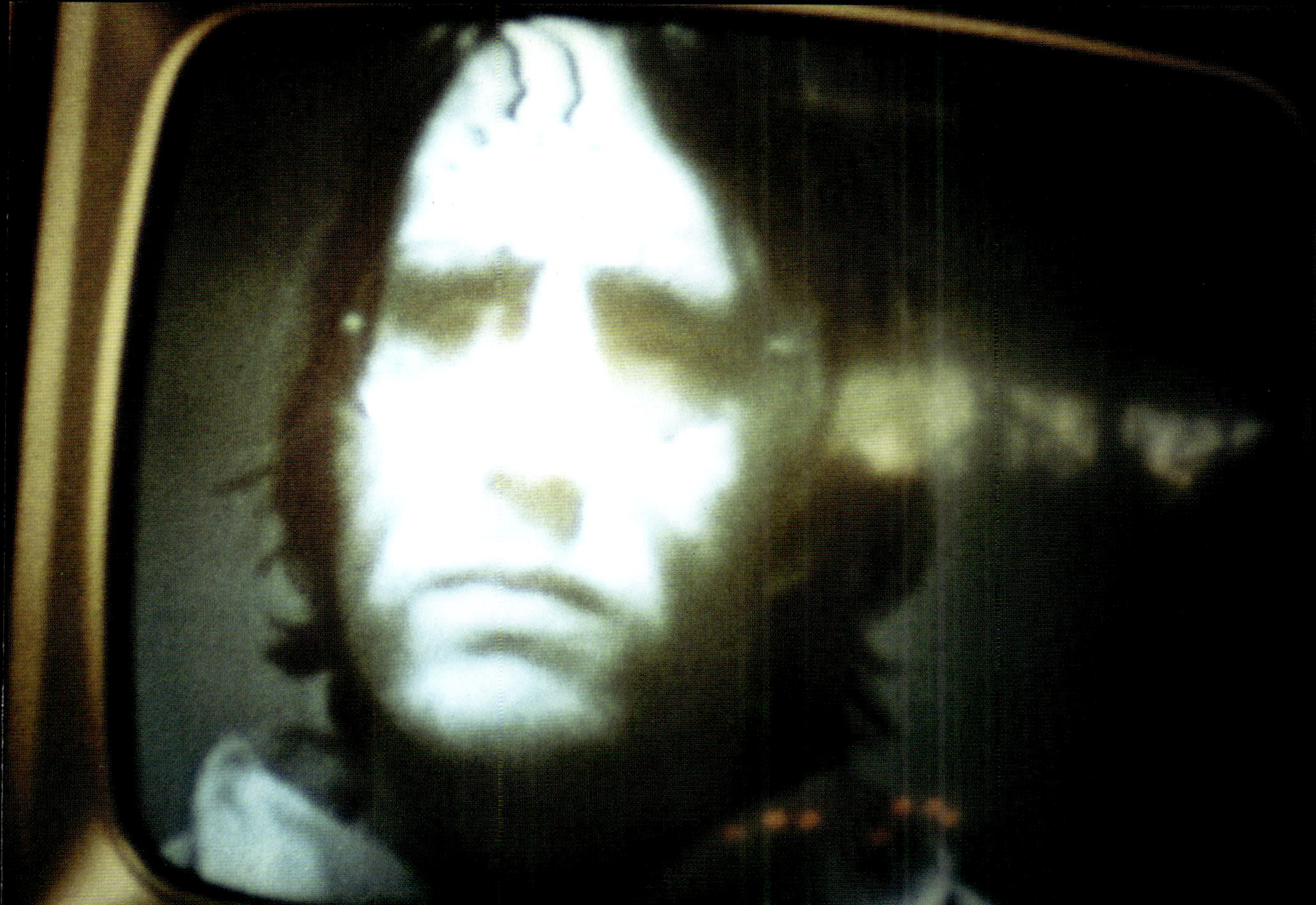

My face as seen on Mission Control's CCTV moments before touchdown
Photographer unknown

My memory of our visit to the Spacecraft Center, beyond general impressions, is surprisingly sparse considering how excited I was to be there. There were, however, unforgettable moments. One was standing in the Apollo Mission Control Center, which when we saw it was occupied by only a couple of technicians hovering around one of the workstations. Workstations were arranged in parallel rows that faced a convex surface of projection screens that, during launches, provided data and camera views. Each station consisted of a cream-colored instrument console and a similarly colored desk; on each desk was a black telephone, and on most, an amber ashtray. Built into the consoles were CRT monitors, numerous dials, levers, buttons, and the like all housed in institution green metal enclosures—the green you see in hospital corridors, or that I remember from my primary school classrooms. Being familiar with the surroundings as the set for a TV show that featured earlier Gemini launches, it was thrilling to be in the actual room; to feel the excitement and anxiety, even in the emptiness, that I was convinced still lingered there.

"Two minutes and counting."

I have no mirror, but I don't need one to know that after seven days, I am looking disheveled . . . which is putting it mildly. My unwashed hair is matted. But I've slipped into my gold velvet Inner Space suit, throwing my brown mechanic's coveralls on top of the foam sleeping pad under the main control

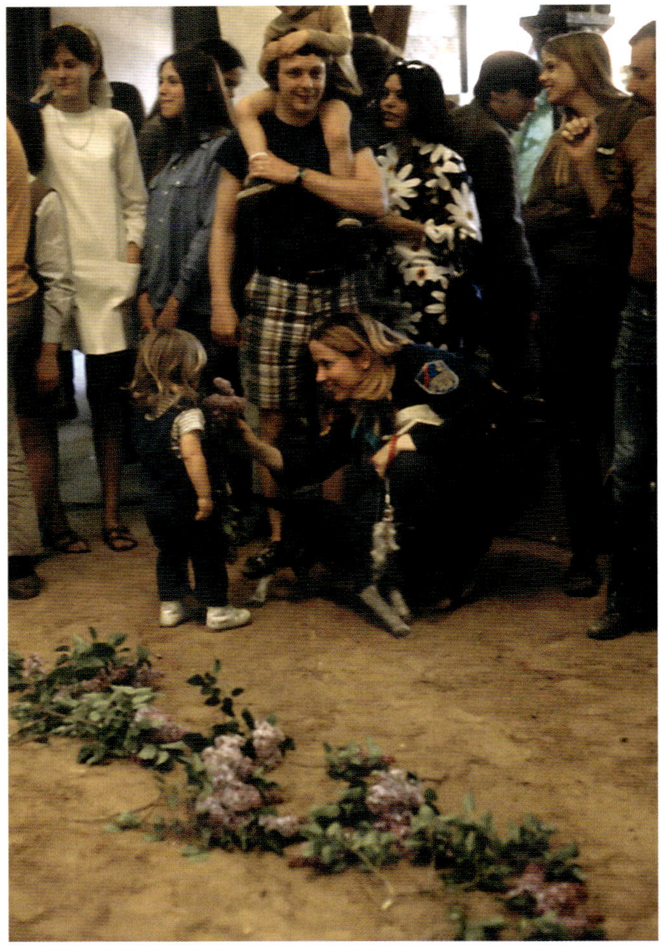

A small crowd assembles shortly before touchdown
Photographer unknown

console. I've checked all the waste containers, making sure they were properly sealed and in the airtight receptacle. I'm ready—at least I think I am.

Our Space Center guide stepped aside to make a quick telephone call. When he returned, he told us Captain Schirra was ready to meet us. We went along an outdoor path to a nearby building and onto an elevator that took us up a couple of floors. The doors opened onto a short corridor with an incredibly shiny floor flanked by doors on either side that led to rooms, a few of which were visible through sealed glass windows. Moving past the windows, I was too excited to notice what was behind them after just being told we would be meeting Schirra where he was trying on the new space suit, referred to by our guide as the A7L EMU.[2] (I loved all this abbreviated NASA-speak where

2. Extravehicular Mobility Unit was a new design, referred to as the A7L, that included a pressure suit and a portable life-support unit used in the space walks. It became the standard suit for the Apollo 7 through 15 flights.

complex systems could be reduced to a few letters. I was particularly delighted when these combinations, like E-M-U, ignited associations that had nothing to do with their technical designation—in this case that strange Australian bird that looks something like an ostrich.)

And then we were standing in a room and looking at Walter Schirra, famed pilot and astronaut of the Gemini missions. He, along with Donn Eisele and Walter Cunningham, would crew the October 1968 Apollo 7 Mission, the first of the manned Apollo missions that would eventually culminate in the lunar landings. These three had been the backup crew to Apollo 1, which in 1967 was to have been the first manned flight—a rehearsal in low orbit—but which famously never happened. A cabin fire had erupted during a preflight launch test, killing the three-man crew of Gus Grissom, Ed White, and Roger Chaffee.

In the brightly lit room, Schirra was standing on a slightly raised platform surrounded by technicians who were inspecting his bulky space suit with particular attention to the valves where the tubes from the life-support backpack connected. One of the technicians was holding his helmet, which he then placed on a shelf next to two identical helmets and above a couple of space suits stored neatly alongside matching backpacks and other gear.

I have zero memory of what conversation might have transpired between me and Schirra, which is fortunate because I'm sure if I said anything at all it would be humiliating to recall it now. I was thoroughly awed by the entire situation: the place and the person. The space program that had been ignited in our imaginations in 1962 when John F. Kennedy proclaimed, "We choose to go to the moon," was suddenly before me in the flesh of Wally Schirra, an actual spaceman.

"One minute and counting. We have someone in place to open the hatch. There's a crowd out here."

So, this is it, I'm thinking. My emotions are raw, stirred by a sense of accomplishment and by a, perhaps vain, belief that within this absurd action of make-believe there are buried truths that could point a way for me to become the artist of my imagination.

What has been surprising about the past seven days is how people, mostly students, including a few I didn't know, have interacted with me as if I were their confessor or psychiatrist. And the flow was in both directions, with them fulfilling a similar role for me. It seemed that the interface, in which they could see me on the video monitor and relate back to me through electronics, created a kind of distance and thus semi-anonymity. Perhaps because I could only hear and not see them—and to them I was a blurry, distant image—it was easier for us to speak intimately. I noticed this confessor dynamic around the third day. People would reveal anxieties, thoughts, and concerns of the most personal kind, and I would respond in kind, completely unselfconsciously, which is unusual for me. Although my perception of time was inaccurate, my sense was that these conversations occurred mainly in the evenings or later at night.

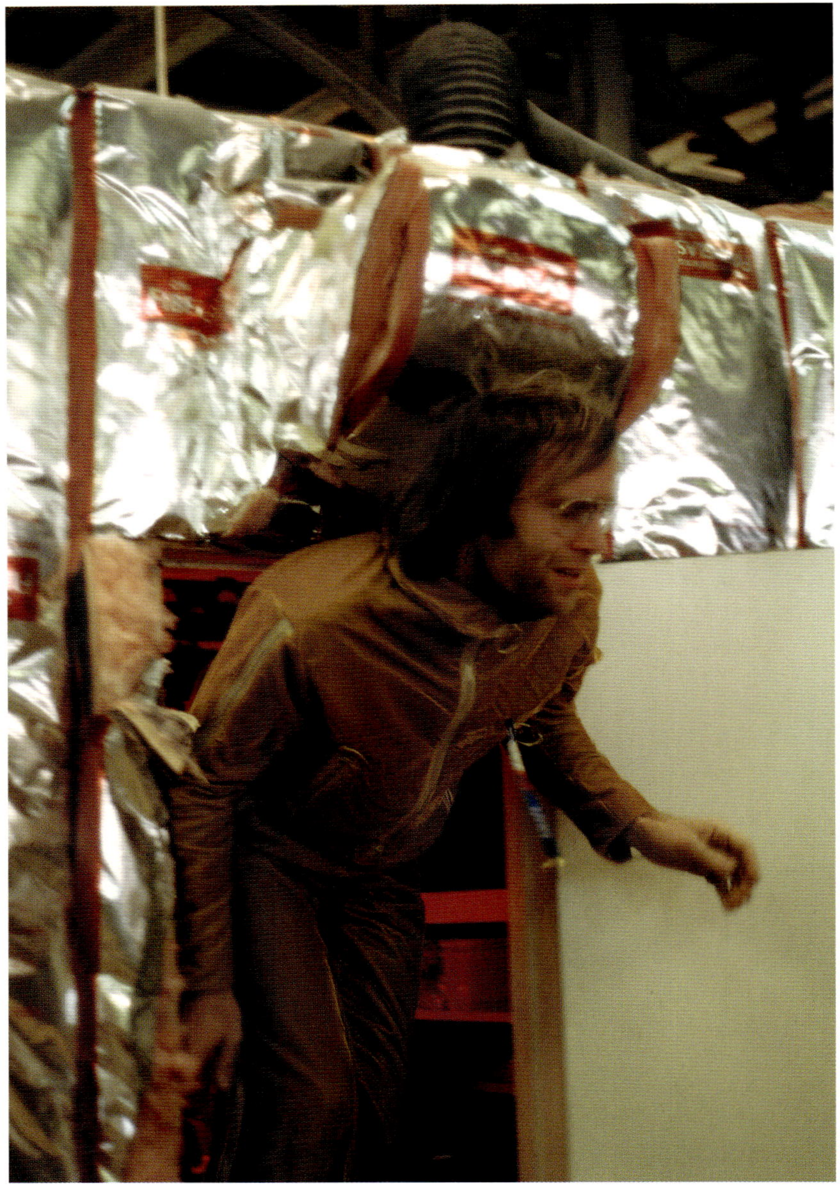

Exiting ISSM after seven days
Photographer unknown

I can only speculate, but I suspect the dynamic was partly related to the public display on the video monitor of my own vulnerability, a degree of pathos that grew over time as the experience wore on me.

"Ten, nine, eight . . ." The countdown has begun. Why the tears?

"Seven, six, five . . ." I can hear and see the turning of the locking shaft that will open the door.

"Four, three, two . . . The door opens, and I step out. Tears are streaming down my face. I try to hold them back but can't. I feel elated and embarrassed.

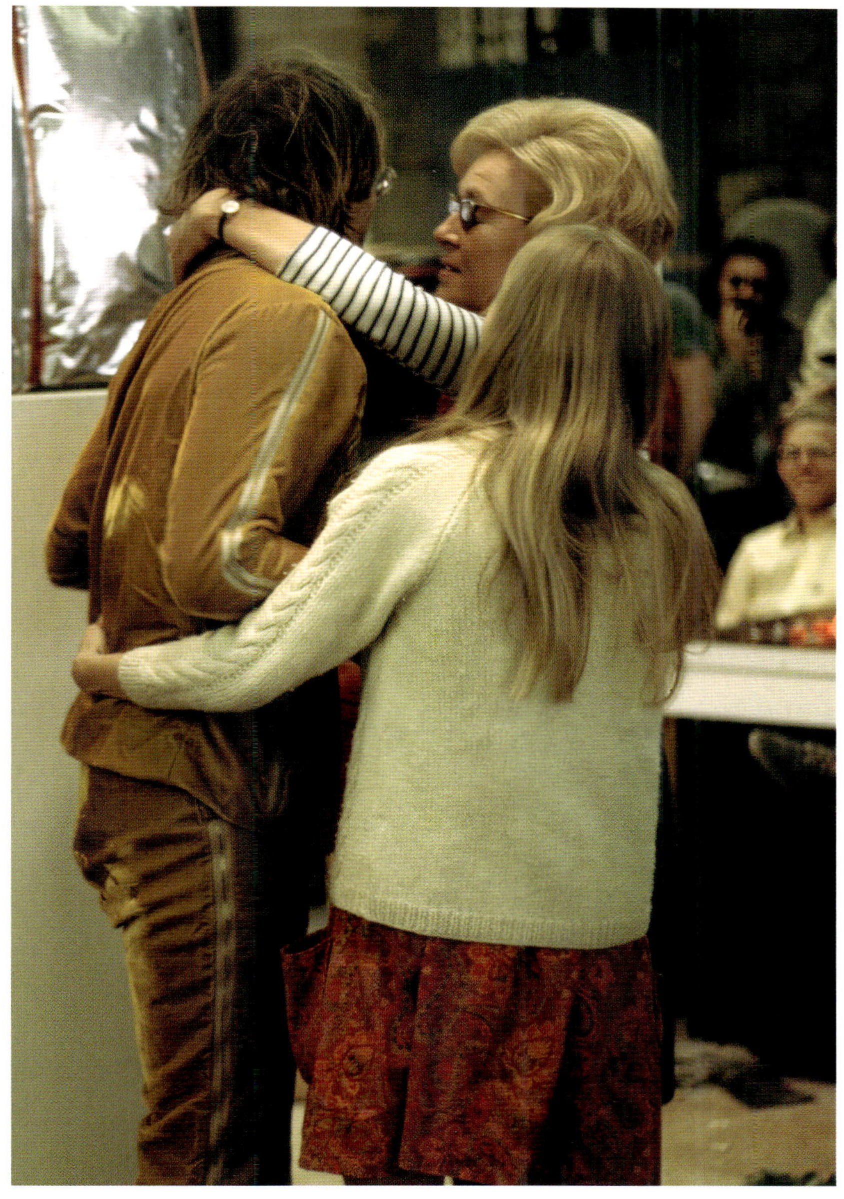

Greeted by Diane and my mother
Photographer unknown

Diane, looking beautiful and a little concerned, embraces me. My mother stands back. She holds her Hasselblad, looks down into the screen, and takes a photo.

Diane stays next to me as friends come up, some embracing me, others staring, perhaps not knowing what to say. I am quite a sight. Although the tears have ceased, I look worn. There must be a hundred people crowded into the room. The floor is covered with dirt and lilac sprigs people have cut from the flowering bushes outside and strewn about, welcoming me back to Mother Earth. It's all very moving. Not only the generosity of friends and strangers, but the realization that something has happened—something that is important to me. Something confirming my own intuition about what art could be for me. During a pause in the congratulations, my mother approaches and embraces me with a knowing and, I feel, deeply compassionate hug, which I interpret as her acknowledgment of me as an adult, perhaps as an artist. But it is also a poignant reminder of my father's absence, and that is overwhelming. As I have earlier reflected, the choices that brought me to this point were not always easy for my parents to understand. Not because they disdained the arts—quite the opposite—but because they feared for the kind of uncertain life I would be claiming for myself. My mother's embrace affirms her support and, in the absence of my father, his as well.

In truth, as melodramatic as this sounds, I felt this to be a defining moment in my quest to become an artist—an artist on terms that I could believe in. Stepping out of the *Inner Space Simulation Module* onto the dirt and lilac sprigs was my metaphoric rebirth, made even more meaningful by my mother's presence.

That was my perception. Unfortunately, it wasn't one shared by all the members of the Graduate Review Committee. Even before "liftoff" I had been hearing rumors that the faculty might not grant me a degree. The most resistance was coming from the aforementioned undergraduate sculpture professor, who was the proponent of a masculine, materials-based art, preferably oriented around the foundry that was located at the far end of the Rinehart studios. Luckily for me, the panel, which met a couple of weeks after the conclusion of my performance, included Robert Morris. Morris was a highly respected artist and an articulate defender of tendencies that were becoming mainstream in contemporary art, such as temporality, duration as a material, and expanded spatiality—that is, the ability of an object or performance to refer to spaces that exist beyond itself.

During the interrogation that followed my presentation, it was clear that Morris was enthusiastically supportive. Although he had missed the performance, the now abandoned *Inner Space Simulation Module* was available and, in advance of my review, we had stood in front of it and discussed the piece. Moreover, we talked more generally—actually, I listened more than I spoke—about shared interests in an expanded notion of what sculpture could be and why this was inevitable and even necessary. During the question-and-answer part of the review, as it became clear that Morris was on my side, those less enthusiastic voices fell silent, or at least became less obviously hostile. In the end, I passed the review and was awarded my MFA degree. A few weeks later, Diane and I packed up our white VW bus and headed for California.

Opposite: The abandoned ISSM following touchdown
Photographer unknown

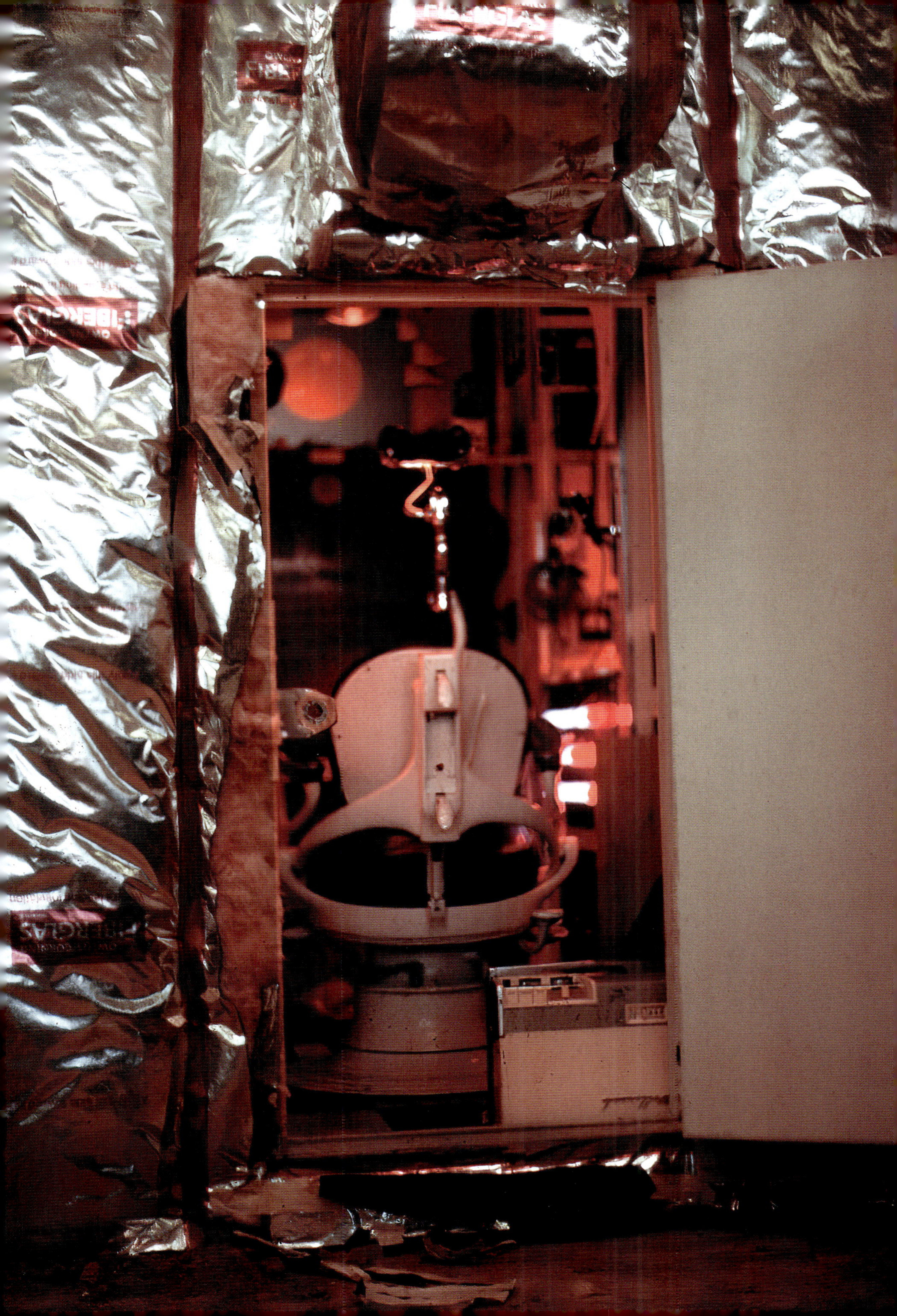

III

Some Madness in the Air

At the Western Edge

Diane and I arrived in San Francisco in the fall of 1969, after crossing the country from Baltimore, our VW bus fighting westerly winds a good part of the time, which reduced our speed considerably on some of the desert highways. In the bed I had built into the van, at a spot overlooking the Snake River Canyon, we conceived our son, much to our surprise, who was born in March of the next year. Gannon—not a family name, but an amalgam of names we both liked—would become a central focus of our lives: adored, often pampered, and after he matured into manhood, my closest friend.

After repeated discussions in anticipation of leaving Baltimore, we determined that there could be a cultural and existential advantage to living on the western edge of North America, in a city that had avant-garde traditions dating to the Beat era and before, embodied in City Lights Bookstore, Lawrence Ferlinghetti's monument to adventurous publishing, and of course, the hippie surge. The San Francisco music scene was pulsating with the incomparable Janis Joplin, Grace Slick, Country Joe and the Fish, It's a Beautiful Day, and Tracy Nelson with Mother Earth; and there were venues like Bill Graham's Fillmore West where, on occasion, we joined thousands of others in a community

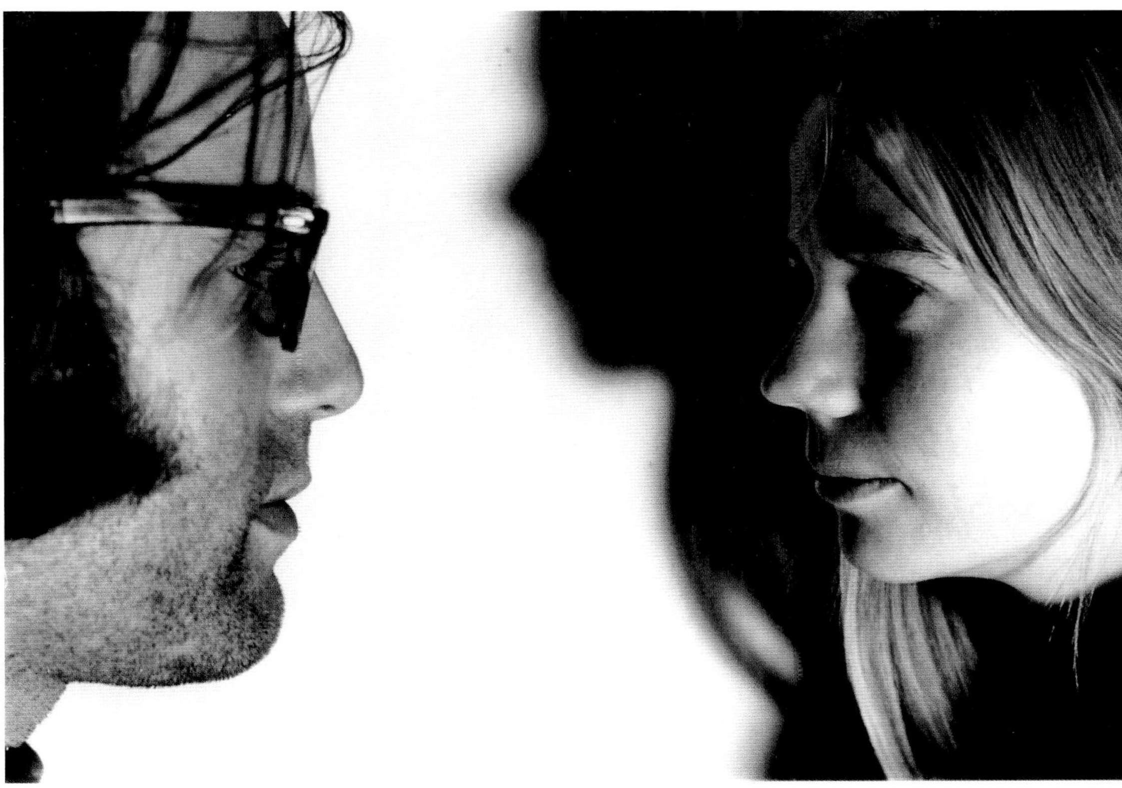

Diane and me shortly after arriving in California, 1969

of peers, mostly stoned, listening and gyrating to these artists and others. The pre-AIDS gay scene was flourishing with all its energy, both social and political, some of it ecstatically outrageous. In the early eighties, as AIDS became part of our vocabulary, this shifted into survival politics and passionate advocacy for help in fighting an epidemic that was claiming some of the most creative young men of our generation, as well as just ordinary people living their lives.

San Francisco and Berkeley were also the cities of my early childhood to which I returned repeatedly over the years after my family moved to the East Coast in 1955. A year after my father's death in 1968, my mother rented an apartment on Russian Hill to be close to my sisters, both of whom were living in San Francisco. (She remained in the city only until 1971 when she moved back to Cambridge and married Kenneth Andrews, a divorced colleague of my father's.) Lyn was married to John Hejinian, who was doing his residency in neurology at UCSF and was like a brother to me, having been part of our family since he and Lyn began dating as high school seniors. As the seventies progressed, Lyn divorced John, married Larry Ochs, an accomplished composer and musician, and over time, established herself as an important writer and professor at the University of California, Berkeley. My younger sister, Ree, was married to my college roommate and artistic collaborator, Jody Procter, another marriage that didn't survive the seventies. Eventually she left the Bay Area with her daughter, Sophie, and moved to Boulder, Colorado, where she studied with Buddhist teacher Chögyam Trungpa and became director of the visiting artist program at the Naropa Institute. Later, after numerous adventures, she returned to the East Coast, met and married Firoze Katrak, a native of India, and, having achieved emotional stability, pursued her love of collage and painting. To me, the Bay Area was both a familiar and an exciting frontier, overflowing with the potential for something different.

When Diane and I arrived, we knew little about the local art scene beyond the reputation of painters associated with the Bay Area Figurative movement including David Park, Richard Diebenkorn, and Wayne Thiebaud—none of whom interested me, although Diane, as a painter, felt differently. Over the course of the next several months, I became aware of several artists, labeled Funk, whom I found far more compelling: Jess, Wally Hedrick, Jay DeFeo, and Wallace Berman. Associated with this group was Bruce Conner, who worked voraciously across media and was the author of extraordinary films, and someone I would come to greatly admire.

Around the time we arrived there was also an emerging Conceptual art scene that included figures like Howard Fried, Paul Kos, David Ireland, Tom Marioni, and Terry Fox, all around my age. This group wasn't so much a movement as it was an association of artists, many of whom coalesced around Marioni's Museum of Conceptual Art (MOCA) and the San Francisco Art Institute where Fried taught sculpture. In the late 1970s, he would form the Performance/Video Department to work with students wanting to pursue sculptural practices that involved time, movement, and video. Predictably receiving far less attention than the men were women artists—Bonnie Sherk, Linda Montano, Lynn Hershman Leeson, Suzanne Lacy, and Sharon Grace—who were developing provocative projects based in media, performance, and other modes of working that would fall into the Conceptual art category. All of these artists were ignored by the more traditional art venues, but they showed, argued, and interacted at alternative and artist-run spaces that were proliferating around the Bay Area and other metropolitan areas. And it was with them that I eventually felt most at home. I would join the Performance/Video Department in 1979, along with Kos, Grace, and Tony Labat, a former student of Fried's.

Up until the mid-1990s, when the early disruptions of the tech boom began, San Francisco was an inexpensive place to live. Our rent, first in the outer Mission district and later in Noe Valley, never exceeded $200 a month. In 1974, with a small (but to us, large) inheritance I received from an unmarried great aunt, we were able to buy a house near our apartment; to say that it was a fixer-upper doesn't adequately describe the state it was in. Over the ensuing decades, we took out loans to cover renovations that provided Diane with a studio in the former basement with glass doors that led out to her beloved garden, and me a space that took up most of the top floor.

I had several part- and full-time jobs before I started teaching in the early eighties and selling some of my work. These included, in chronological order: phlebotomist at San Francisco General Hospital (a trade learned in a few hours by first practicing on an orange before graduating to human arms and then to the hospital wards where, because of our predawn arrival times, the patients referred to us as vampires); preparator at the San Francisco Museum of Modern Art; art packer and mover; and carpenter. Diane, as a mother, had less time, although she found part-time work as a freelance commercial photographer before she joined a gallery in the mid-1980s, and started selling her paintings and works on paper.

The seventies were a tumultuous time in the Bay Area, as they were throughout the country and beyond. The Vietnam War cast a pall over everything, and debates and confrontations were ongoing. Jim Crow remained alive and well in many Southern states and, one could argue, in Northern states as well. Also on the national level there was the Watergate burglary and its ever-unfolding scandals, and the resulting House impeachment inquiries that led to Richard Nixon's resignation in August 1974. More locally was the emergence of a new kind of African American self-awareness best typified by the Black Panther Party, which had a powerful presence, particularly in the East Bay, until the movement fractured into feuding bands. And of course, there was the vibrant hippie scene, centered in Haight-Ashbury, with its music, long hair, free love (is love ever really free?), and "dropping out," my generation's stinging catch phrase. Within a decade, the hippie phenomenon would become calcified on Haight Street where it remains today, as if frozen in time.

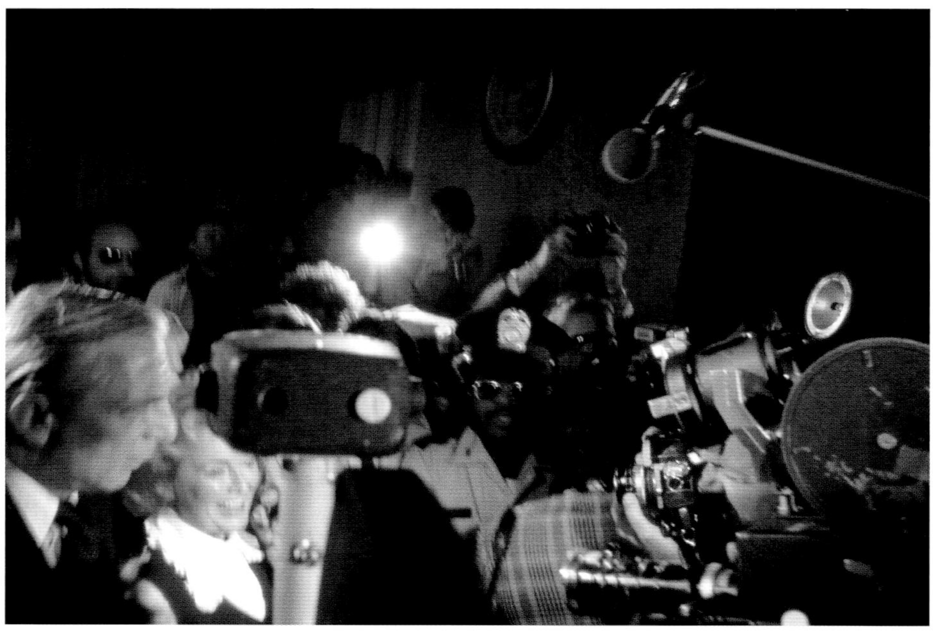

Catherine Hearst surrounded by press as she enters the federal courthouse following Patty Hearst's arrest, September 18, 1975
Photograph by T. R. Uthco from *Media Frenzy Surrounding the Arrest of Patty Hearst*

Imbedded within all of this, and particular to San Francisco and the Bay Area, were a series of events that grabbed the attention of locals and, in some cases, reverberated far beyond because they were threatening, socially disturbing, sad, or simply fascinating and strange. Taken in chronological order (and others might come up with a different list) they were the Native American occupation of Alcatraz Island in San Francisco Bay, starting in November 1969 and ending in June 1971 (socially disturbing, sad); the Zebra murders, 1973–74 (threatening, socially disturbing, strange); the Patty Hearst kidnapping, 1974 (fascinating and strange); the Reverend Jim Jones's Peoples Temple, culminating in a mass suicide at Jonestown, Guyana, 1978 (fascinating, strange, very sad); and the assassinations of San Francisco Mayor George Moscone and gay activist Supervisor Harvey Milk by Supervisor Dan White, 1978 (socially disturbing, very, very sad, and pretty strange). These events surged through the atmosphere and, when combined with other national and international events, inundated me with a disorienting combination of excitement and destabilizing confusion—thrilling and terrifying, like being caught in riptides or undertows over which I lacked all control.

In such times, art can sometimes be the only response, and the times were ripe for an art collective like T. R. Uthco. I, along with my T. R. Uthco cohorts, Diane and Jody Procter, became obsessed with the unfolding drama of the Patty Hearst saga, starting with the kidnapping of the publishing family scion by the Symbionese Liberation Army (SLA), followed by her participation with them in the Hibernia Bank heist, her disappearance, and her final capture by the FBI. We collected all the front pages of the *San Francisco Chronicle* where the story was featured day after day, week after week, and stole several of her wanted posters that were displayed in post offices throughout the state and beyond. We entertained fantasies, never realized, of making Diane over into a facsimile of Patty for a series of photos.

When Patty was captured and arraigned at the Federal Courthouse in San Francisco, we joined the crowd of media and gawking citizens in the foyer where we took photographs documenting the insane melee of reporters, police, lawyers, private guards, and the curious who had managed to sneak past security into the building. Eventually, Catherine and Randolph Hearst, still married but separated, entered the building within minutes of each other. The crowd surged around them. Catherine, the mother, jostled and attacked by reporters seeking statements and pictures, maintained a strange half-smile on her face, only her eyes indicating the grief and exhaustion she was suffering. Randolph, on the other hand, showed no emotion at all. He appeared stone-faced, dazed, his eyes seemingly unfocused as he and his wife, partially protected from the onrush by their private security and public relations personnel, were hustled through the large interior courtyard into a doorway on the other side and, finally, down a corridor where they disappeared on their way to see their daughter for the first time since her kidnapping.

The Hearst kidnapping, Patty's rejection of her family's privilege, her devolution into a bank robber, her willingness to ally herself with this obscure collection of insurgents promising "death to the fascist insect," and her rejection of her born name in favor of Tania, her nom de guerre, was for many of us the perfect narrative for our time. It was like a surreal soap opera that reached us episodically via headlines in the local newspapers and sensational snippets on the evening news. Maybe we could see a bit of ourselves in her rejection of straight society and apparent embrace of something that was radically different from everything she knew. At the same time, again for many of us, the entire sequence of events was hilarious. If *Saturday Night Live* had existed in 1974, one could imagine Gilda Radner playing Patty Hearst, socialite turned revolutionary. Even though real people died, starting with the murder of Oakland Schools Superintendent Marcus Foster with cyanide-laced bullets (sad, random), and ending with the death of the infamous Cinque (Donald DeFreeze) and others in a shootout in Los Angeles, the whole thing was—at least to my jaded sensibility—more absurdist theater than it was tragic drama. One would have a hard time imagining a narrative where the characters were as vivid, the plot as twisted, the outcome as dramatic and, at the same time, as outright wacky as was the sequence of events that exploded out of the Hearst kidnapping. For T. R. Uthco, as for me, it whetted our appetites for more.

It's somewhat of a cliché to say the sixties, perhaps starting with JFK's assassination in November 1963 and extending through the seventies, were an

WANTED BY THE FBI

NATIONAL FIREARMS ACT

William Taylor Harris
Date photographs taken unknown
FBI No.: 308,668 L5
Aliases: Mike Andrews, Richard Frank Dennis, William Kinder, Jonathan Maris, Jonathan Mark Salamone, Teko
Age: 30, born January 22, 1945, Fort Sill, Oklahoma (not supported by birth records)

Height:	5'7"	**Eyes:**	Hazel
Weight:	145 pounds	**Complexion:**	Medium
Build:	Medium	**Race:**	White
Hair:	Brown, short	**Nationality:**	American

Occupation: Postal clerk
Remarks: Reportedly wears Fu Manchu type mustache, may wear glasses, upper right center tooth may be chipped, reportedly jogs, swims and rides bicycle for exercise, was last seen wearing army type boots and dark jacket
Social Security Numbers Used: 315-46-2467; 553-27-8400; 359-48-5467
Fingerprint Classification: 20 L 1 At 12 / S 1 Ut

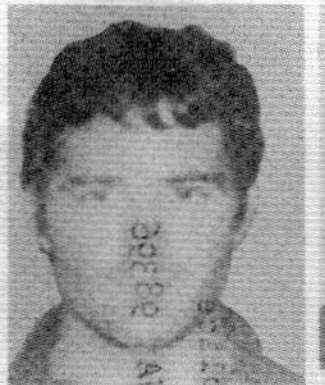
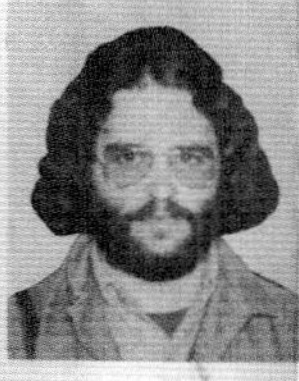
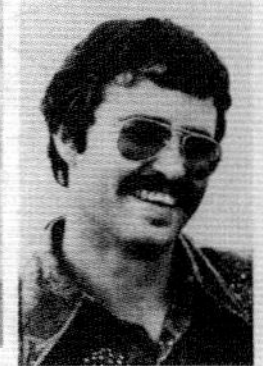
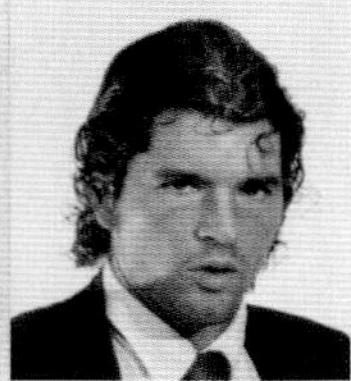

Emily Montague Harris
Date photographs taken unknown
FBI No.: 325,804 L2
Aliases: Mrs. William Taylor Harris, Mary Hensley, Joanne James, Anna Lindenberg, Cynthia Sue Mankins, Dorothy Ann Petri, Emily Montague Schwartz, Mary Schwartz, Yolanda
Age: 28, born February 11, 1947, Baltimore, Maryland (not supported by birth records)

Height:	5'3"	**Eyes:**	Blue
Weight:	115 pounds	**Complexion:**	Fair
Build:	Small	**Race:**	White
Hair:	Blonde	**Nationality:**	American

Occupations: Secretary, teacher
Remarks: Hair may be worn one inch below ear level, may wear glasses or contact lenses; reportedly has partial upper plate, pierced ears, is a natural food fadist, exercises by jogging, swimming and bicycle riding, usually wears slacks or street length dresses, was last seen wearing jeans and waist length shiny black leather coat; may wear wigs
Social Security Numbers Used: 327-42-2356; 429-42-8003

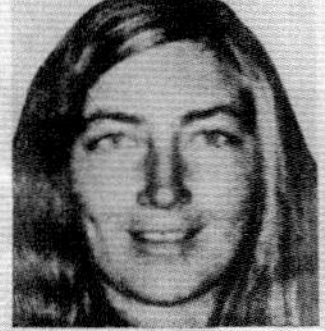
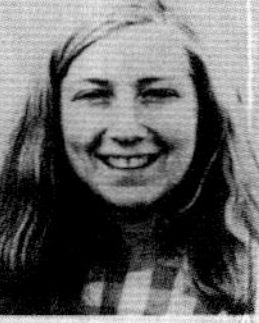
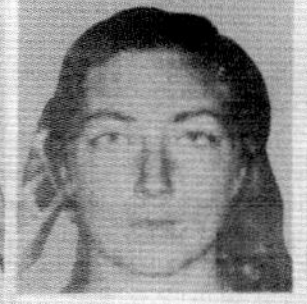
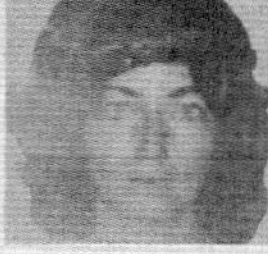

NATIONAL FIREARMS ACT; BANK ROBBERY

Patricia Campbell Hearst
FBI No.: 325,805 L10
Aliases: Tania, Susan
Age: 21, born February 20, 1954, San Francisco, California

Height:	5'3"	**Eyes:**	Brown
Weight:	110 pounds	**Complexion:**	Fair
Build:	Small	**Race:**	White
Hair:	Light brown, may be dyed blonde and cut short	**Nationality:**	American

Scars and Marks: Mole on lower right corner of mouth, scar near right ankle
Remarks: Hair naturally light brown, straight and worn about three inches below shoulders in length, however, may wear wigs, including Afro style, dark brown of medium length; was last seen wearing black sweater, plaid slacks, brown hiking boots and carrying a knife in her belt

Feb., 1972
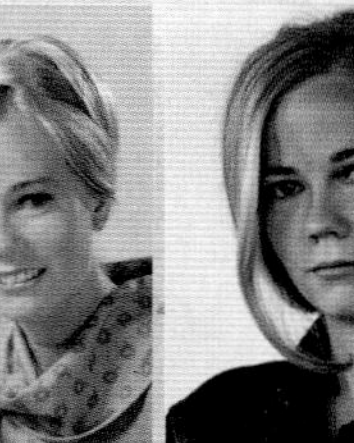
Dec., 1973
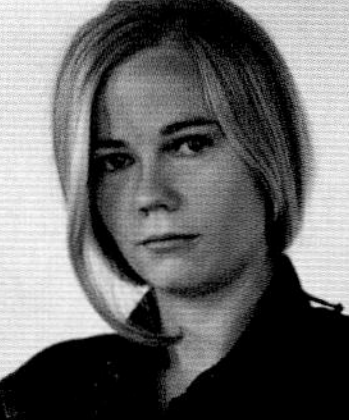
April, 1974
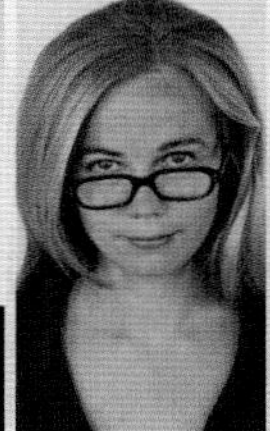
(artist conception) Summer 1974
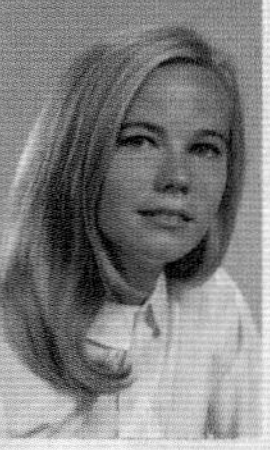

THE ABOVE INDIVIDUALS ARE SELF-PROCLAIMED MEMBERS OF THE SYMBIONESE LIBERATION ARMY AND REPORTEDLY HAVE BEEN IN POSSESSION OF NUMEROUS FIREARMS INCLUDING AUTOMATIC WEAPONS. WILLIAM HARRIS AND PATRICIA HEARST ALLEGEDLY HAVE USED GUNS TO AVOID ARREST ALL THREE SHOULD BE CONSIDERED ARMED AND VERY DANGEROUS.

Federal warrants were issued on May 20, 1974, at Los Angeles, California, charging the Harrises and Hearst with violation of the National Firearms Act. Hearst was also indicted by a Federal Grand Jury on June 6, 1974, at San Francisco, California, for bank robbery and use of a weapon during a felony.

IF YOU HAVE ANY INFORMATION CONCERNING THESE PERSONS, PLEASE NOTIFY ME OR CONTACT YOUR LOCAL FBI OFFICE, THE TELEPHONE NUMBER OF WHICH APPEARS ON THE FIRST PAGE OF MOST LOCAL DIRECTORIES.

C M Kelley
DIRECTOR
FEDERAL BUREAU OF INVESTIGATION
UNITED STATES DEPARTMENT OF JUSTICE
WASHINGTON, D. C 20535
TELEPHONE: 202 324-3000

Entered NCIC
Wanted Flyer 475 AA
(Rev. April 10, 1975)

Altered Harris and Hearst wanted poster, T. R. Uthco, 1974

uncommonly chaotic time in the United States. For starters, this is a vain presumption when we consider what my parents' generation had to contend with. But whether accurate or not, this was certainly the view of many of us who came of age during those years and found ourselves attracted to disparate unconventional communities—hippie, artist, spiritual, druggie, groupie, dropout—crudely referred to as counterculture. We all inhabit the time in which we live and, unless historians, tend to have a superficial understanding of the past. And because most of us are limited by our subjectivity, we see our time as the most this or that, forgetting that civilization has been fraught from its very beginnings. By drawing attention to the occupation of Alcatraz, the Zebra murders, the Patty Hearst kidnapping and its aftermath, and the Jonestown massacre, I make no claims other than that from my position, they along with other national and international events gave me the feeling that the world was unhinged, a condition that both frightened me and stimulated my imagination—which was much more stimulated than afraid. This only reinforced my conviction that art, as I understood it, was a system of thinking and making that could help me navigate through the madness of my time.

Altamont, the Un-Woodstock

If you were White, middle-class, young, and educated as many of the so-called hippies were, your experiences were not that different from my own. We rode the optimism of the age when postwar America was feeling its oats and saw itself as the center of the universe, the land of opportunity. When we left home and then college, our perspectives broadened and our idealism came up against the very things that our suburban idylls had hidden from us: poverty, racism, inequality, and the terrible disappointment of those who had no choice but to be overcome by them. For some of us, even as we rejected our privileged upbringing, our families were our safety nets, at least psychologically if not financially, as we mustered the courage to challenge these injustices. Many of my generation became politically active for the first time. Some of the bravest and most dedicated ventured into the Deep South to fight Jim Crow and sacrificed their lives in the process. Some swarmed to San Francisco, to communes in Colorado or Vermont. Many wanted to entirely drop out of conventional society while others joined religious or social cults—another kind of dropping out—and there were a few, like members of the Weather Underground, who wanted to arm themselves and fight back, violently.

I never thought of myself as a hippie as embodied in the image of the blissed-out reveler in a crowd of stoned kids in Golden Gate Park, swaying to the Grateful Dead or Jefferson Airplane. Rather, I associated with the generations of artists, my own and those that had preceded me, who looked to their times in search of a language that was appropriate to describe the world they found themselves in. And I was inspired by my recognition of kinship with others who shared my politics while being from different backgrounds than my own. Although I would never have equated—nor would ever equate—my disenchantment with that of Brown, Black, or poor White Americans, who had to tolerate a level of oppression that I can barely imagine, I did, when finally confronted by the hypocrisies embedded in "American exceptionalism," succumb to profound disappointment and disillusionment. This was caused not by oppression but by the friction between *my* ideals—the morals and ethics I'd grown up with, which had become more entrenched with age and experience—and the governmental duplicity I saw around me.

Political and social disillusionment, like the loss of religious faith, is perhaps a gradual process, a sort of chipping away until the concealing facade crumbles to expose difficult truths. The hippie scene and its less frivolous mutations and subgroups self-validated through expressions of what we might call our better angels: brotherly love, compassion, egalitarianism, peace—all the platitudes that many of us believed the previous generation had lost sight of or that had been ignored and belittled by its governmental representatives. We were the "make love not war" generation, who came together at certain moments to declare our solidarity—most memorably in August 1969 at Woodstock, a gathering of the tribe for a celebration of the Aquarian Age, on a dairy farm in Bethel, New York. It was billed as "Three Days of Peace and Music," and over its course many of the great artists and bands of the era famously performed before a mostly well-behaved crowd of 450,000 celebrants. It was here that Jimi Hendrix, the final act of the festival, first played his riveting, psychedelic, ecstatic version of the "Star-Spangled Banner" to a rain-soaked crowd that had diminished to 200,000.

The Altamont Free Concert on December 6, 1969, was supposed to be the West Coast version of Woodstock, a love-fest. Instead it took a large chunk out of whatever illusions of peace and love the idealists of my generation might have harbored. Participating in Altamont was like stumbling into the darkness, not just for me but for most of those who attended. Looking back, I see it as the end of a shared utopian dream held by the youth of middle-class America and beyond, one that dared to imagine a more egalitarian society in which American postwar prosperity would be shared across classes, rather than horded by the powerful, and institutional racism overcome. Instead, we found "Sympathy for the Devil" and the beginning of the Nixonian Age.

Resorting to the language of the time, "Altamont was a fucking bummer, man, from beginning to end."

It started for me early on the morning of December 6th, when Jody, my cousin Steve Hall, who lived in San Francisco after having returned from a two-year stint in the Peace Corps, and I climbed into my VW bus and headed east across the Bay Bridge toward the Altamont Speedway near Tracy, about sixty miles away. It was one of those smoggy days that I describe as "the acid

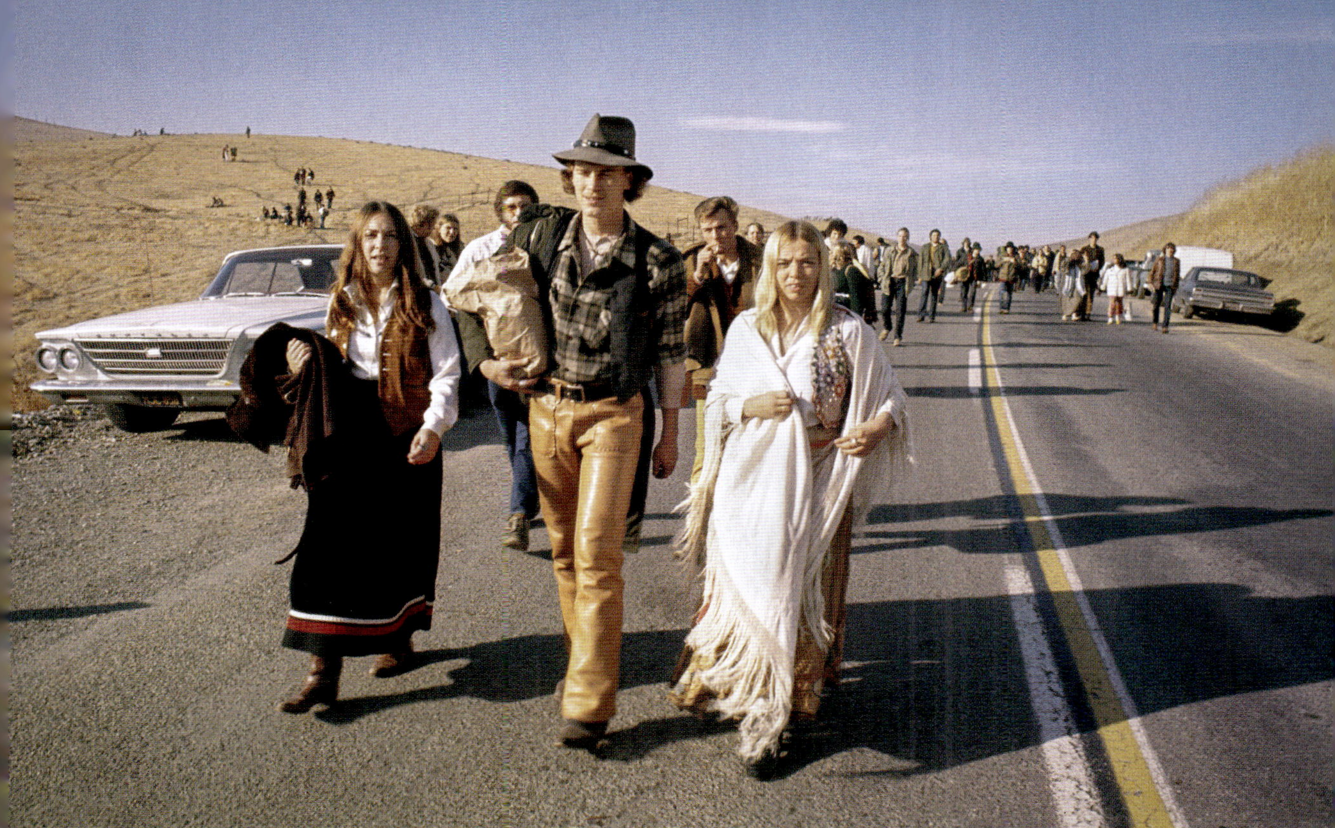

The long march to the Altamont concert site
Photo credit: © Bill Owens, 1969

days," when the light, filtered through pollution, is murky orange and the haze feels aggressive and corrosive to the eyes and throat. Tracy and Livermore, two towns on the edge of the Central Valley, were, even then, home to the immense industrial farms that extend between Sacramento to just north of Los Angeles where the fertile land becomes irrigated desert.

A few miles beyond Pleasanton, the concert traffic became dense and slowed, many of the cars pulling onto the shoulder along a stretch that went far into the distance. As we added our car to the collection, we watched the bearded and the beaded, including many with children, carrying coolers, picnic baskets, and backpacks as they crossed the six-lane highway to join a throng of similarly clad young people marching in long lines through the tall, dry grass toward what we assumed was the most direct route to the concert venue.

We followed, passing beneath the soaring high-tension towers whose wires hummed above our heads. Rather than celebratory, the procession through the parched alien landscape seemed oddly morose, almost funereal. We trudged and we trudged in this joyless, nearly silent parade. Occasionally individuals, sometimes pairs, passed us from the opposite direction I recall one wild-eyed person called out prophetically, "The devil is waiting out there."

"A bad trip," I thought and tried to dismiss the encounter, but it added to a sensation of dread that reminded me of those scenes in war movies where the fresh troops moving toward the battle pass the wounded and broken coming back, and look at them with a mixture of horror, fear, and respect.

After we had been walking about forty minutes a guy came up to us and handed Jody a couple of joints. (Why Jody was always the one approached in these kinds of situations rather than me, I'll never know.) "This is great shit, man. Enjoy the show," he said and moved on as we stood there contemplating the two items in Jody's outstretched hand.

Laughing, but also a little cautious, since one rule of responsible drug use is to know what you are ingesting or smoking before taking the plunge, Jody asked, "Well, what do you think? Should we or shouldn't we?"

We looked at one another, briefly, before I blurted out, "We should. It's our constitutional duty as Americans." But the whole time I was thinking, "Get stoned in this godforsaken place surrounded by all these hippie strangers? Could be disastrous." And so, the waking nightmare began.

We lit both and passed them around while sitting on the ground on a little rise above the lines of people trudging quietly toward some destination. We could see the line in both directions, and we commented on it looking more like a forced death march than a parade to a musical celebration. A darkness was descending upon our psyches as we warily rose to join our brothers and sisters in their mournful trek.

I don't know for sure what these joints were laced with, perhaps PCP and other stuff, but whatever it was, it was not pleasant. The effects came on strong and hard. Of the three of us, Jody had smoked the most, with me second, and Steve not much at all. But we trudged on, me clench-jawed, paranoid, quiet, wondering how I was going to get through this ordeal, and Jody, the loquacious one, babbling in stream of consciousness, in a private, dystopian hallucination. Steve, only moderately dysfunctional, tried to guide us to a place where we could sit and be safe.

About an hour and a half after we had started the great march and thirty minutes after we lit the joints, we reached a highway on the other side of which we could see the back of the stage and in front of that, a gentle slope filling with people. Jody had stopped chattering by the time we reached the edge of the stage, and I assumed he was in a similar state of agitation and escalating paranoia to mine. As we tried to move past the stage toward the seating area beyond, a group of Hells Angels gathered, two of whom appeared to be facing off for a fight, slinging insults while a circle of spectators, mainly fellow Angels, began to grow around them. Into the middle of this scene— which even I, in my semi-delirious state, and certainly Steve, carefully circumvented— strode an oblivious Jody. I don't know how he got out of the way of the two combatants, who came at each other like charging bulls. It must have been Steve who looked back in time to grab Jody by the arm and pull him to the edge of the tightening circle where the two of them fell together in a heap. Standing on the outside, I could only glimpse my compatriots through arms

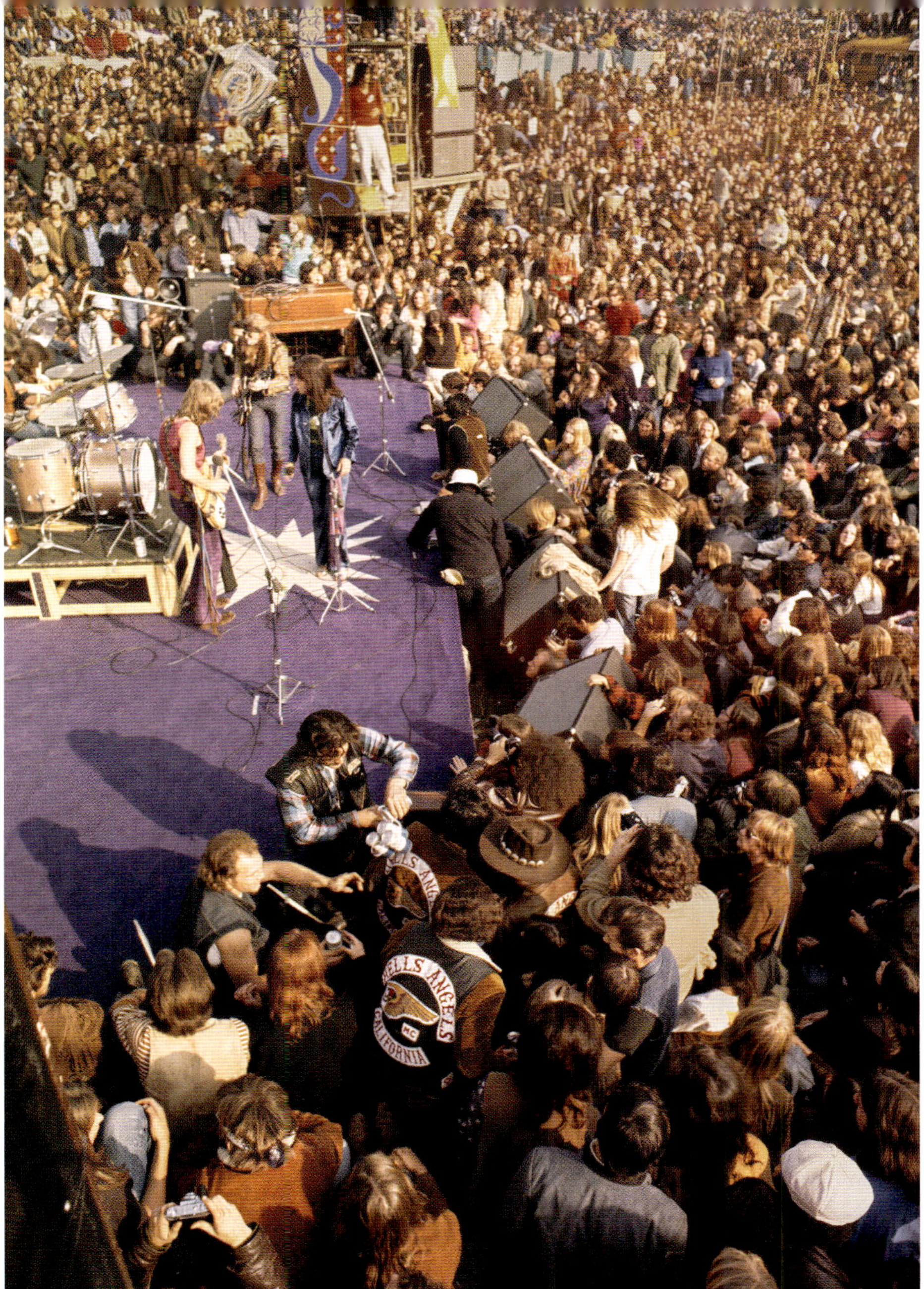

Hells Angels distributing beers at the front of the concert stage
Photo credit: © Bill Owens, 1969

and legs as they gingerly pushed their way out, in the end receiving nothing more than nasty stares and a couple of slight shoves from the crowd.

Eventually we reached a spot around a hundred feet up the hill in front of the stage where we settled and hoped to come down from the adrenaline-filled high we were on. I have very little recollection of the actual concert. I do recall periodic violent stirrings that took place around the front of the stage throughout the afternoon and a few fist fights, one of which broke out near us. Beer bottles were thrown. It was as if everyone there was on the same drug, one that made you feel aggressive, bold, speedy, paranoid, and, worst of all, invincible.

This was an ugly and potentially dangerous state of mind to have while in a crowd on the verge of becoming a mob. As afternoon turned into evening, more fights broke out. During the Jefferson Airplane set, one of the performers, it might have been Marty Balin, jumped off the front of the stage to intercede in some sort of dispute. He never returned, and we later learned he had been hit in the head by a Hells Angel and knocked unconscious. Clearly, all the peace and love stuff hadn't migrated west from that farm in Woodstock.

In the early evening, we heard the whomp-whomp-whomp of helicopter blades as the Rolling Stones descended from heaven to join us in our little hell. Assembling on the stage, it didn't take them long to realize that all was not well. Even before the first note, Jagger, addressing those near the stage, pleaded for calm as the assembled Angels intimidated and harassed those nearby. Things were getting dicey around us, so we got up and moved farther up the hill where the crowd was not as dense. I was feeling less fried now, as was Jody, but Steve remained protective, dutifully taking charge of our movements like a mother hen. In the middle of "Sympathy for the Devil"—appropriately enough—the Stones stopped and once again begged the audience for calm. From our vantage point, it was hard to tell if the Hells Angels were attempting to restore order or incite violence. They had been agitated when we passed them in the late morning, and one could guess what kind of shape they were in now. The Stones played a couple of more songs before some guy jumped onto the stage, followed by others who pulled him back down. The interloper was easy to spot in a bright green jumpsuit.

I don't remember if the Stones got through another song before the crowd in front of the stage began to surge, clearly reacting to some incident. They played on a bit . . . and then stopped, and we could hear Jagger calling out for a doctor. Somehow, the music picked up again and their set ended without further incident. It wasn't until later that we learned that the green-clad stage jumper had been stabbed and killed by one of the Hells Angels, a fitting end to a miserable day.

Recalling our wilderness trek of hours earlier, my cousin Steve came up with the obvious and brilliant observation that the highway we crossed before entering the speedway was the same I-580 where we parked the car. Therefore, rather than taking the cross-country route in the dark, it made sense to walk along the shoulder even if it would take longer. Fifteen minutes later we were at the car.

Jody shrieked, "What the fuck! Are you kidding me? We were this close, and we walked all that distance?"

Still a bit wired from the drug, but much less agitated and deeply relieved to have survived the ordeal with our minds and bodies relatively unscathed, we couldn't help but laugh about the absurdity of it all. The torturous march that really did feel like a walk through Hades was somehow the perfect metaphor for the day that unfolded, and maybe for the twilight of a cultural moment.

Great Moments

In 1974, the collective T. R. Uthco—Diane, Jody, and I—put together a series of nine sketches in a stage show we titled *Great Moments*. Influenced by early vaudeville—we referred to our act as Avant-vaudeville—it premiered at Mills College's Center for Contemporary Music, which was under the direction of the composer Robert Ashley. We received generally positive responses from an audience made up of friends and others with a taste for avant-garde performance, and this encouraged us to look for additional places to perform.

In order to attract potential venues beyond the Bay Area, we assembled a publicity package that included a brochure of staged stills from the performance with a brief description; a résumé, some of which was true, that made us appear far more accomplished than we were; and as a clincher, a "*Newsweek*" review, written by Jody in recognizable artspeak and with a photo from the performance, all formatted to look like a crude photocopy from the magazine. Our rationale for this deception was simple: we needed the work, and we couldn't get work without validation. As supposedly creative individuals, we would fabricate that validation.

We mailed this package to colleges and a few museums where we had connections and by the fall had confirmed stops in New York, Baltimore, Washington, Richmond, Pittsburgh, Detroit, and Chicago. The following year we would do a second tour that included John Hillding, my grad school roommate, who would start his own branch of T. R. Uthco in Seattle.

John's involvement started in the early 1970s, when Jody and I, along with several of Hillding's friends, came together for the Bumbershoot Festival, Seattle's annual weeklong summer extravaganza of art and entertainment held at the Seattle Center, the recreation area that includes the Space Needle. Over three summer festivals we erected large, inflated sculptures in and around the center's International Fountain.

However, on our first foray east to perform *Great Moments*, it was just Jody and me. Bidding farewell to Diane, who would remain at home with our three-year-old son, we packed our props—media in the form of slides, audio tape, and film; tape recorder for four-channel audio playback; a 16mm projector and two slide projectors; and costumes—into my van and set off with our rolling art show for the Midwest and East Coast.

In an unpublished book about our T. R. Uthco days, Jody provides his recollection of one of the more memorable—fair to say catastrophic—performances of *Great Moments.* Jody's narrative is in italics while my comments, interspersed with his, are unitalicized.

The guests, around one hundred fifty I estimate, are filing in from the adjacent dining room, where we had joined them earlier for dinner. Peeking through the stage curtain inside the arched proscenium, I watch them take their seats in the modern auditorium. Our elevated stage is exactly the right scale for our work. The house lights dim. The murmuring subsides.

We are at the Art Institute of Chicago where T. R. Uthco has been invited to do a presentation for Friends of Contemporary Art, a group of wealthy patrons who assemble monthly to hear lectures by established contemporary artists like Jasper Johns, Willem de Kooning, and others of that ilk. Being anything but established, it's a fluke that we are there, and we wouldn't be were it not for the influence of John Neff, a curator at the Detroit Institute of the Arts where we had performed earlier. He had recommended us to Mrs. M., director of the Friends, when she had a sudden vacancy that needed to be filled. Trusting Neff, while knowing nothing about us, she booked us.

From backstage, Doug starts the tape recorder and the taped sound of applause from a massive unseen audience fills the room. The curtain pulls back to reveal a chair, a podium, and two small floodlights. Doug comes out, sits down, and the "Graduation Speech," the first of our nine-episode performance, booms out over the speakers with Doug's Gertrude Steinian monologue about the meaning of meaning. At its conclusion, he stands up, turns around to face the audience and emits a scream, augmented by its deafening pre-recorded version. It only lasts about a minute, but it is long enough to stimulate a noticeable murmur of disapproval arising from the audience. Already, just with our opening act, we seem to be tapping into a rich vein of acute hostility. "Isn't this great!" Doug whispers to me as we pass backstage in the dark. For us, hostility from the right demographic is tantamount to a resounding affirmation.

For the next piece we carry out a wooden box, which doubles as a container for our gear when we are on the road, and place it at center stage. The box is about two and a half feet wide, four and a half feet high, and painted on one side with a strange, unidentifiable white shape against a black background. Doug walks out into the middle of the audience where a slide projector is set up a few rows back. I start the tape recorder again and over the loudspeakers comes the voice of classic crooner Jim Nabors (aka Gomer Pyle) singing "Full Moon and Empty Arms": "Full moon and empty arms, a night like this, the moon is full, but where are you?"

While Nabors sings, Doug starts the slide projector, revealing the initial slide of the backside of a full-figured woman that fits perfectly into the outlined white space on the back of the box. Bent over, the audience sees her backside in a full-length floral skirt. Slowly, slide by slide, with Nabors' schmaltzy song in the background, she lifts her skirt. Ankles, calves, knees, thighs, and finally her big, white ass staring out at the audience. At this point I return to the stage and place a large plastic costume ass onto two invisible hooks, so that the fake ass is superimposed on the photographic ass. The song builds toward its full-throated, booming finale, and as Nabors hits the last big note, Doug unleashes a live arrow from his position behind the slide projector (he had the

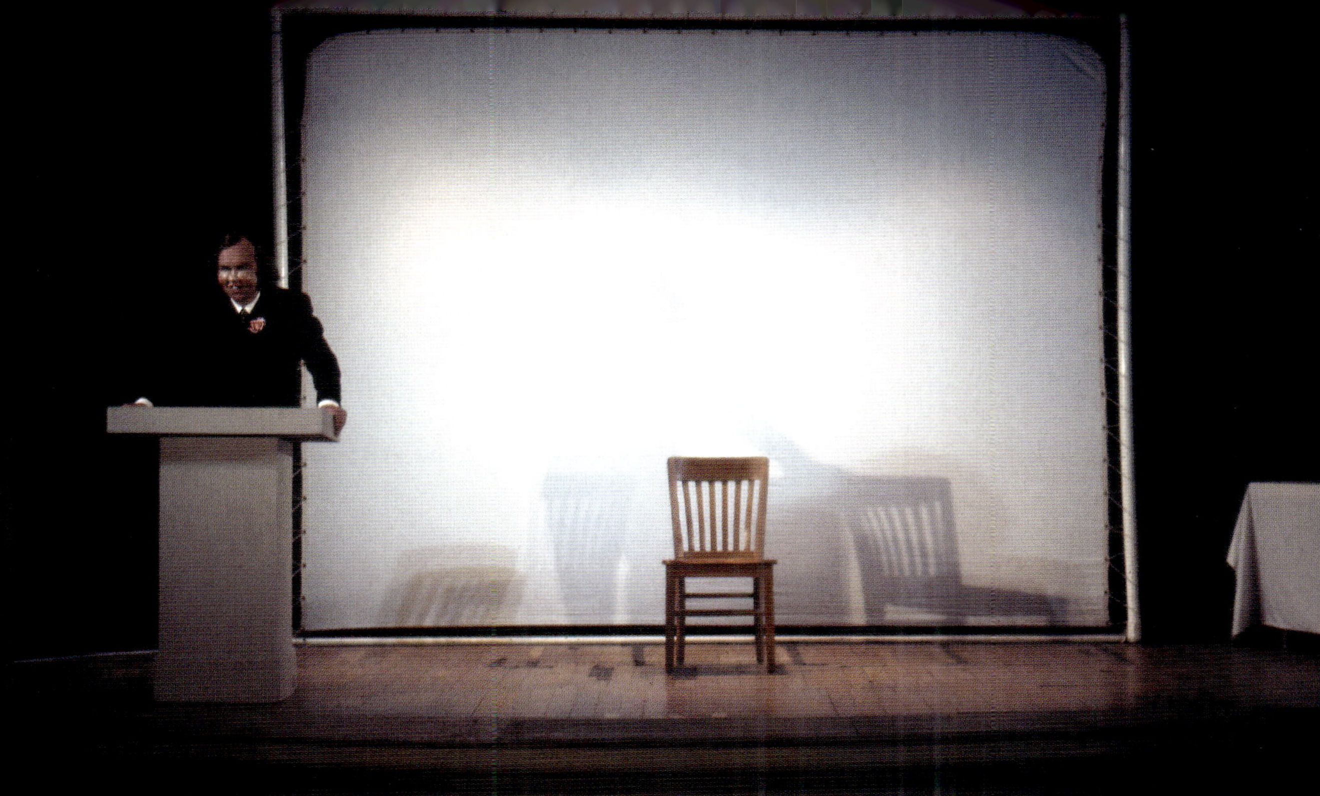

John Hillding performing "The Graduation Address" during our second East Coast tour of *Great Moments*, T. R. Uthco, 1975
Photographer unknown

bow and arrow stashed under the slide table), the arrow hitting and sinking into the white plastic ass, a few inches to the left of the crack. "Fwouuuuuuuu . . . piling . . . twack." I cut the lights immediately to darkness, as, with a pencil-thin pocket flashlight, Doug makes his way back to the sanctuary behind the curtains and we prepare to set up for #3. "What's the atmosphere like out there?" I asked. "Wooahhh boy. I'd say the natives are getting a leetle bit touchy. Particularly the male natives."

It's easy to understand why the natives were "getting a leetle bit touchy." This was a long way from the refined discussions the Friends were used to, more puerile infantilism than inspiring aesthetics. I don't think our primary intent was to offend, since our imagined audience was our contemporaries who would be more amused than outraged. They would certainly get the jokes and art-world references. But there is no question we found a perverse, but noble, satisfaction in undermining what we perceived as the bourgeois expectations of this audience by playing off the raunchy irreverence of vaudeville, while quoting, and perhaps ridiculing, some of the tropes of contemporary art and popular culture. We understood and undeniably delighted in the realization that some with vested interests in high capitalistic culture, which in our minds included high art aesthetics, might find our antics offensive.

A worse possibility, one that haunted me, was that they simply saw us as an annoying nuisance, like a teenage child who displays uncouth manners at the dinner table.

We can hear the coughing, the squirming, the low hostile whispers through the backstage darkness, as we prepare for piece #3—"Shooting." I come onto an empty stage dressed in an all-white outfit with a white plastic mask covering my face. I hold a pistol in my hand that looks something like a snub-nosed .38. It's a stage pistol we picked up at a theatrical supply house. I stand silently, in a small pool of light, looking back towards the curtain. If you listen carefully, you can just hear the almost sub-audible tape hiss as blank tape rolls through the heads on the tape recorder. One of the things we had learned, just in our short time of performing, was that nothing makes an audience more uncomfortable than extended silence on the stage.

After a proper, prolonged interval, Doug finally emerges from behind the curtain. Also dressed in white, he is carrying something that resembles a large shield-like device that he holds in two hands as he walks across the stage. Mounted to its front is a full-length dime-store mirror. Doug positions himself on the opposite side of the stage, in another small pool of light, hunkering down slightly and holding the mirror as if he were bracing for some force or impact. Once he is settled, a loud, authoritative pre-recorded voice starts a slow countdown. "10 . . . 9 . . . 8 . . . 7 . . . 6 . . . 5 . . . 4 . . . 3 . . . 2 . . . 1" During the count, I slowly raise my gun and take aim at the mirror, which is some thirty feet away. When the voice reaches "0" I fire a single shot and the mirror explodes in a burst of glass, made possible by Doug's surreptitious release of a spring-loaded device, invisible to the audience, that shatters the mirror from behind. A cacophony of electronic music, made by piling and looping the sound of glass breaking repeatedly, follows us as we walk slowly off the darkened stage, and continues for a few minutes with neither action nor illumination on stage.

The unmistakable buzz of dissatisfaction from the audience continues to grow as we reconnoiter backstage for the next act.

One of the themes we were pursuing in *Great Moments* was deception. It wasn't that we intended to fool anyone. In fact, the opposite was true. We wanted the tricks to be transparent, so the mechanisms of deception were revealed. That was the joke. For us it was a joke that had wider implications beyond the crude illusion of a mirror supposedly shattered by a bullet. These had to do with what we called the "authority or tyranny of images," the opprobrium we attached to media channels like network television and the advertising that supported them. Later, we would get at these ideas much more directly in pieces like *The Artist-President* and *The Eternal Frame.* But for the time being we wanted our Avant-vaudeville to contain, embedded within its intentional meaninglessness, some implications beyond absurdity.

The following act, "Standing Men," was based on a series of slides Jody found in a dumpster behind one of the photo labs whose detritus he would go

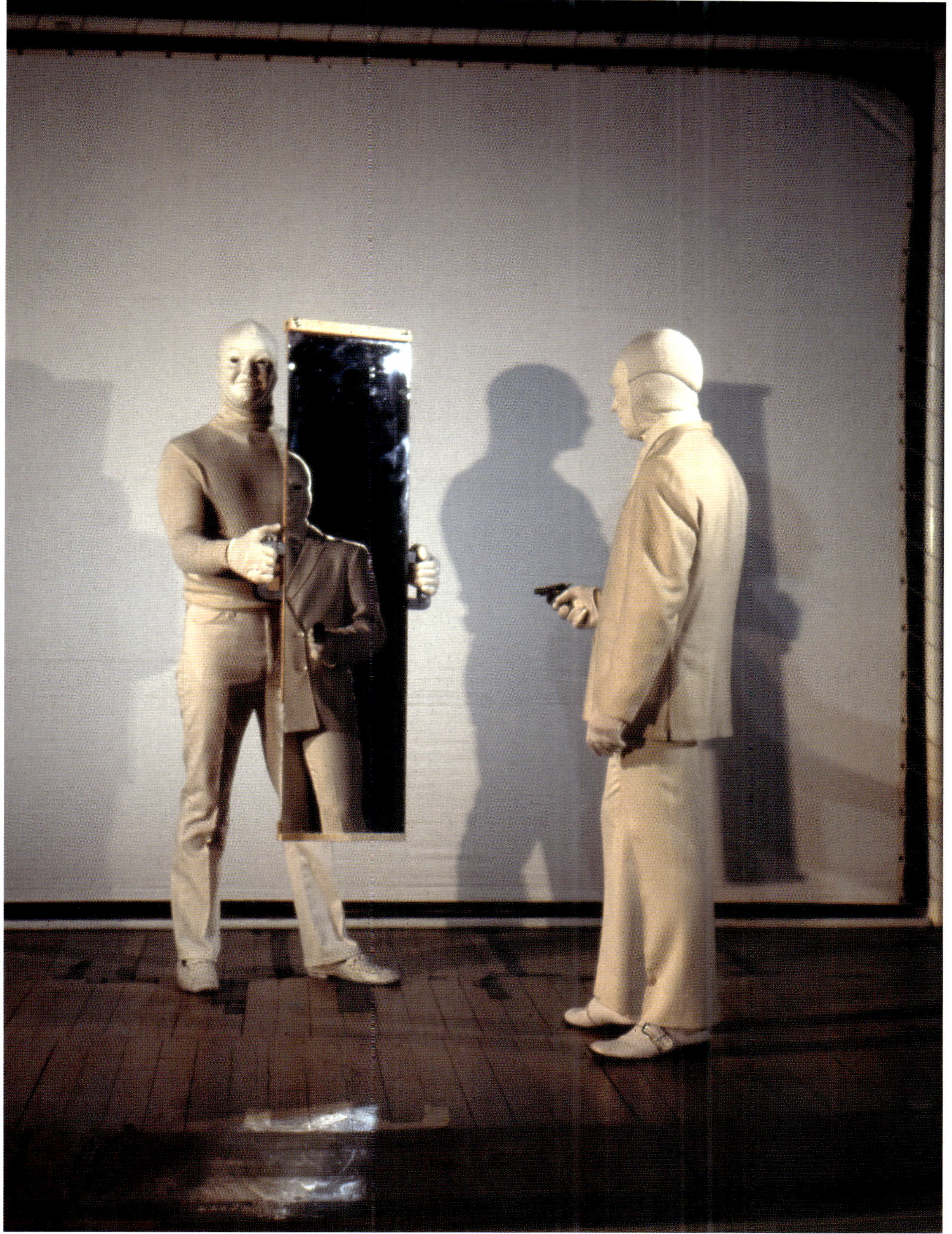

"Shooting," *Great Moments*

through periodically in search of interesting images. On this one occasion, he found what we considered a gold mine, a sequence of slides that depicted two men, each photographed individually, wearing suits and ties, hair neatly combed, and standing in positions with outstretched arms as if they were shaking hands. "Very Uthco," Jody proclaimed as he returned to our studio (at that time my dining room) with his haul.

In the performance, we projected the slides, side by side, onto the portable projection screen that was part of our set. Interspersed were clear slides that created an illuminated rectangle into which we would periodically step from opposite sides of the screen, assuming the poses of the figures we replaced. This dance went on for a while. Toward the end, we left the stage and the projections alternated between portraits of the mystery men and our own portraits with our heads in the same positions, mimicking them. This provided time for Jody to go backstage where he changed into a white shirt before returning to center stage to face the audience while holding a white tie in his right hand. When he was in position, I turned off the slides and started a 16mm projector that showed a film of him wearing an elaborately embroidered blue cowboy shirt and tying a wide multicolored tie that was projected onto him. Aided by a mirror in front of the projector, invisible to the audience, he was able to time his similar actions to coincide with his projected self, which was superimposed onto him, providing a curious offset between the action in real and mediated time.

Several acts followed, often punctuated by the now very audible groans of the audience. One man even decried in a near shout, "I could be at home watching television," which was received with sympathetic laughter from others in the house, more than one catcall, and light applause. Clearly, we were bombing. Undeterred, although noticeably rattled, we knew the show must go on.

One of my favorite moments in *Great Moments* was "Framers Framing," another piece in which we interacted with projected slides. It began with slides of a picture frame, followed by a dissolve to a slide of the first frame framed, then with Jody, the framer, framing the framed frame. These actions and projections were accompanied by an authoritative voice proclaiming what was going on. In our imaginations, the process was like a reverse zoom in cinema where the camera starts close-in (for us, it's the single picture frame, noted as "frame") and pulls back to reveal the full context of the scene (in our case, "framed framer framing framed framer framing framer framing framed frame").

After "Underneath the Arches: A Tribute to Gilbert and George," "A Trick My Grandmother Taught Me," and a couple of other acts, we ended, as we always did, with a pie in the face, which we alternated delivering to each other. This would be accompanied by a prerecorded drumroll and then loud applause,

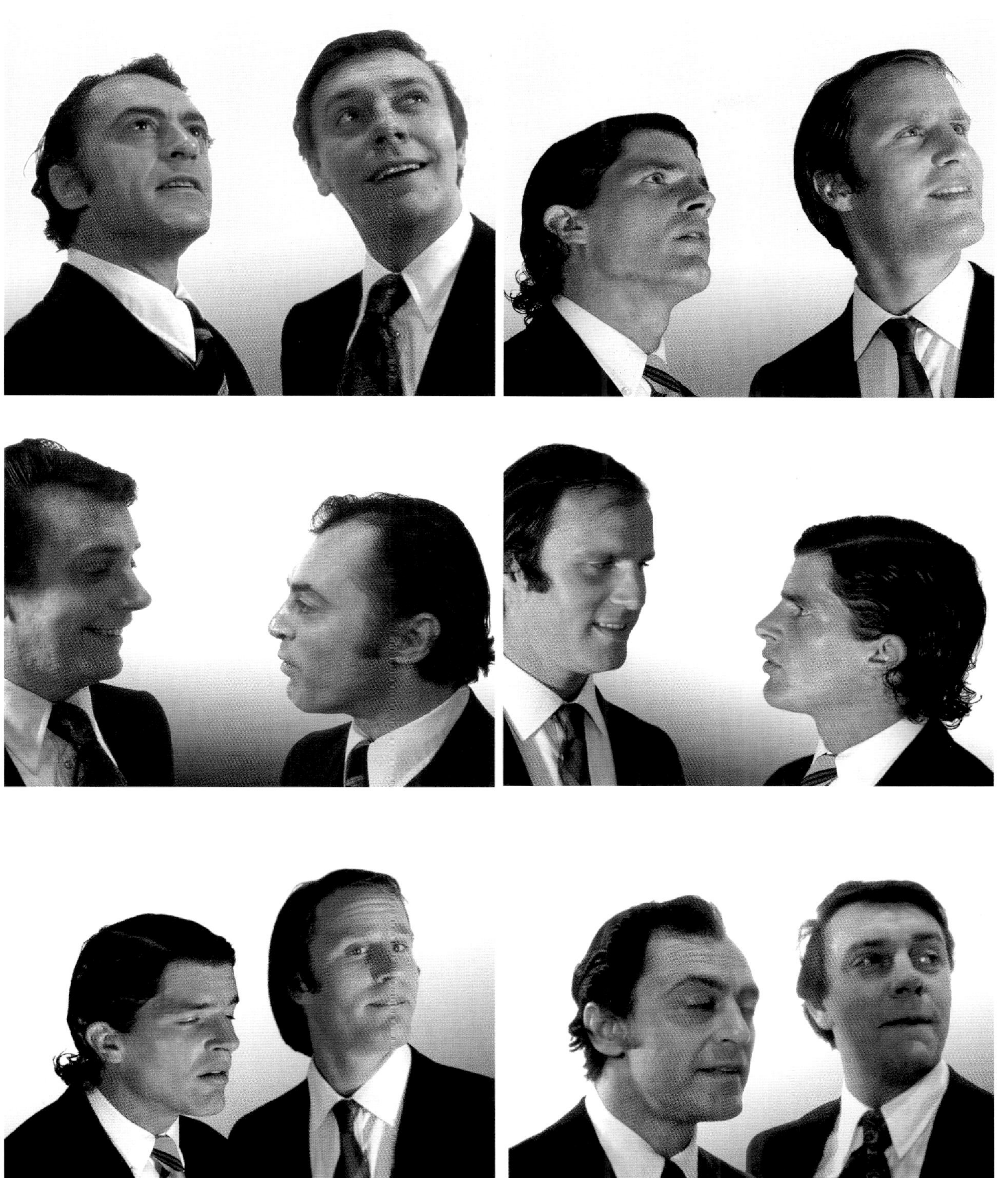

“Standing Men,” black-and-white reproductions of original color slide projections, *Great Moments*

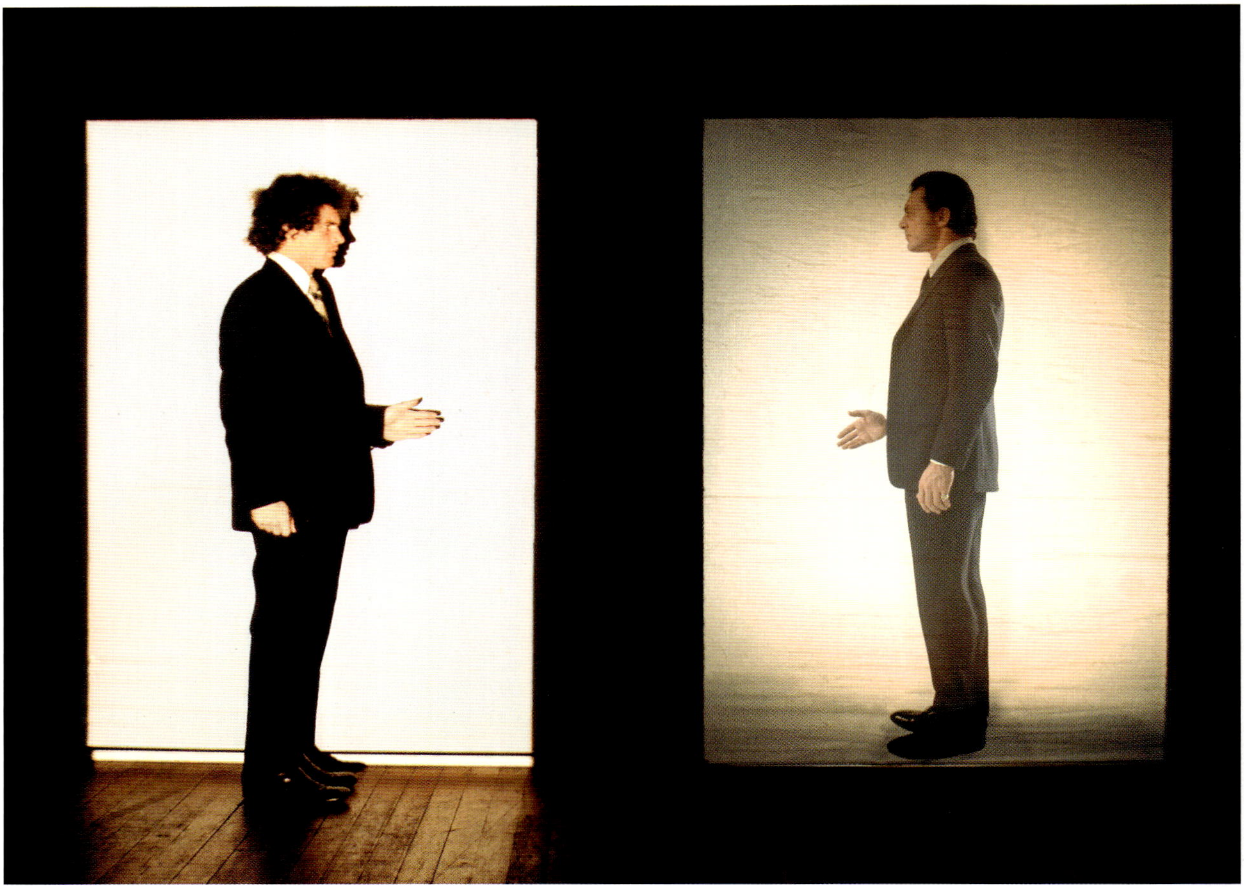

Performance still from "Standing Men" showing projected slides and live action, *Great Moments*

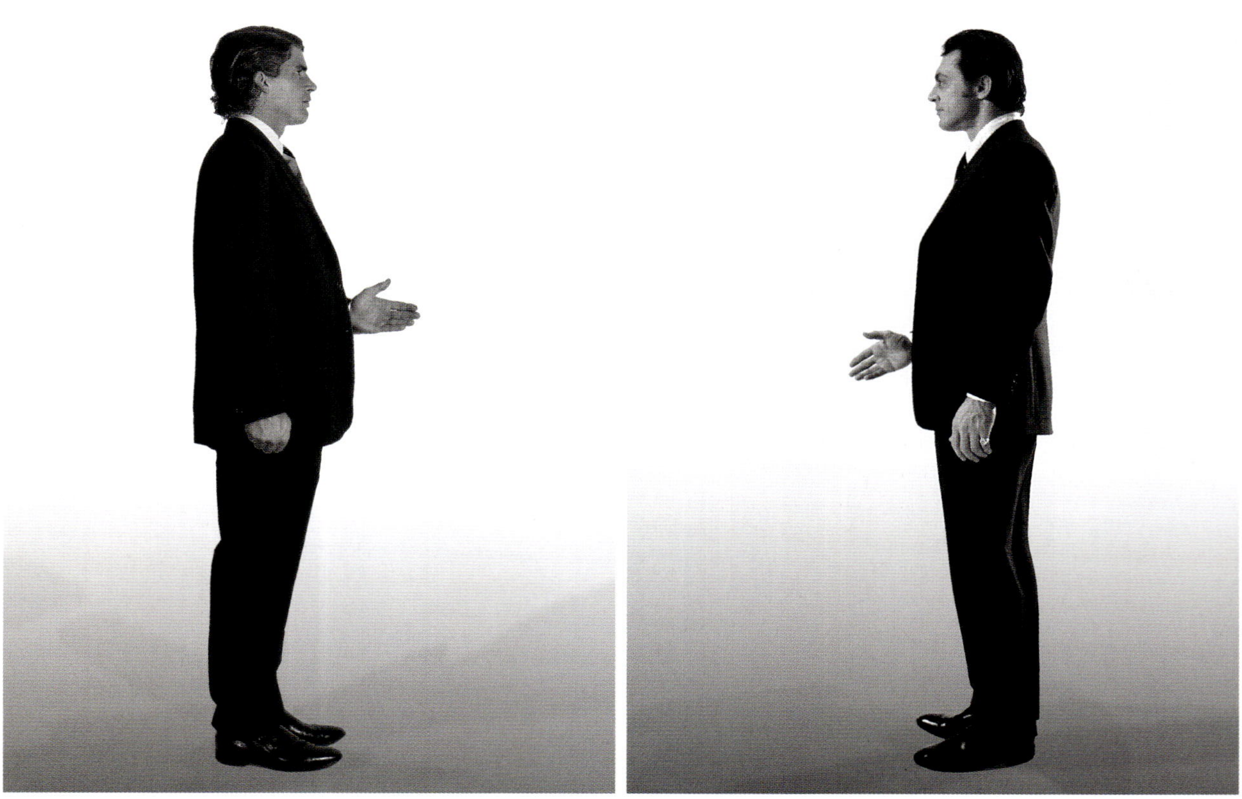

"Standing Men," black-and-white reproductions of original color slide projections, *Great Moments*

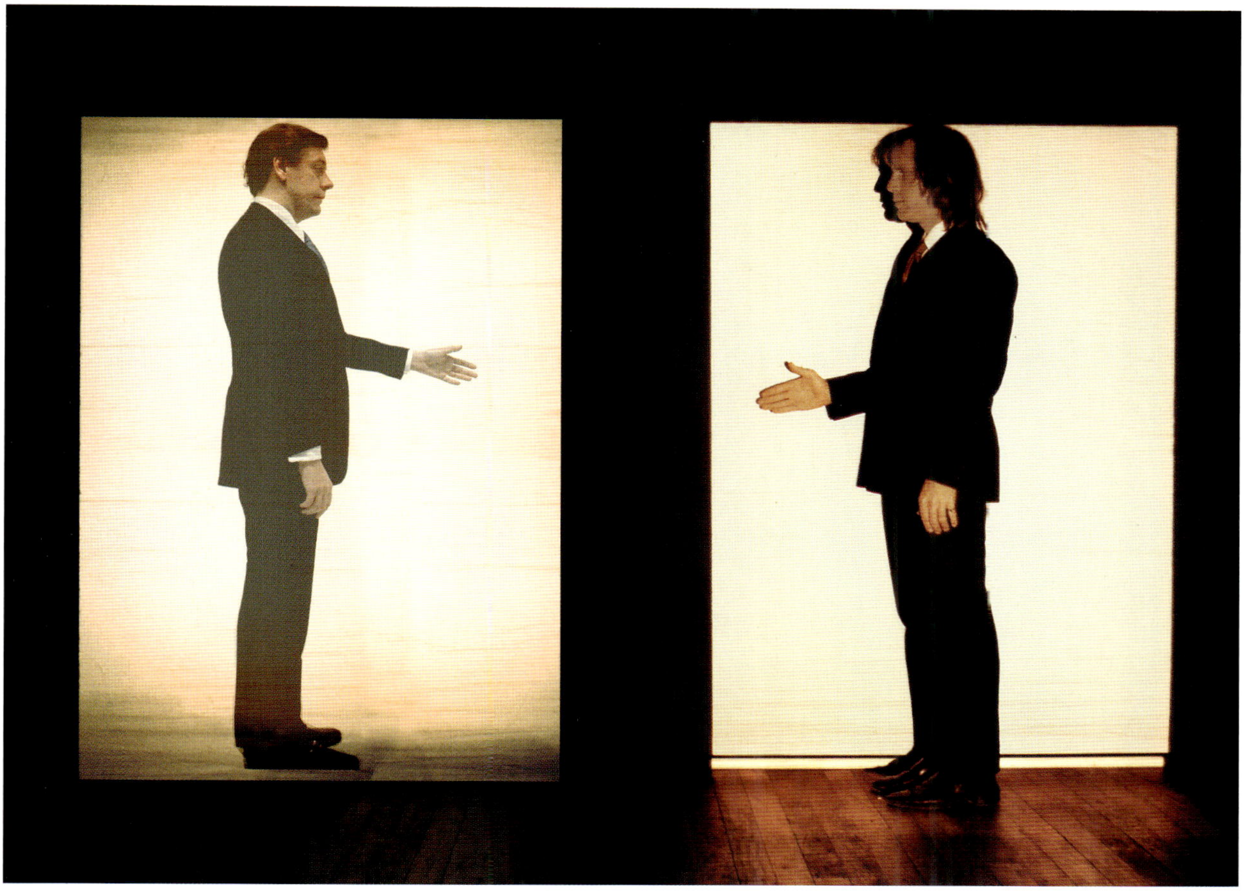

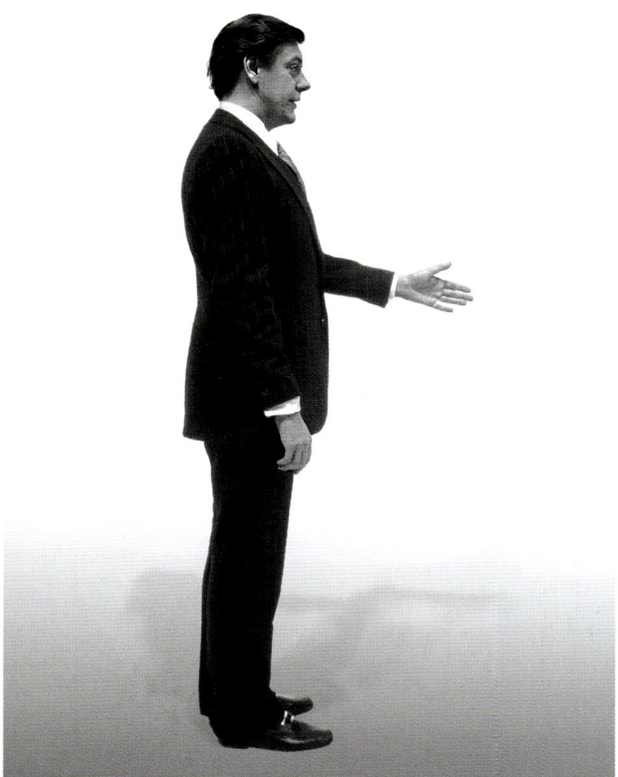

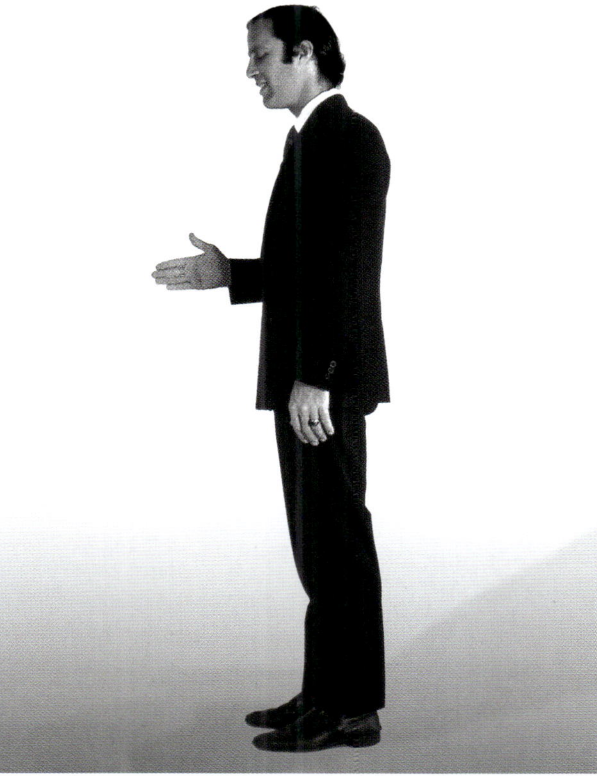

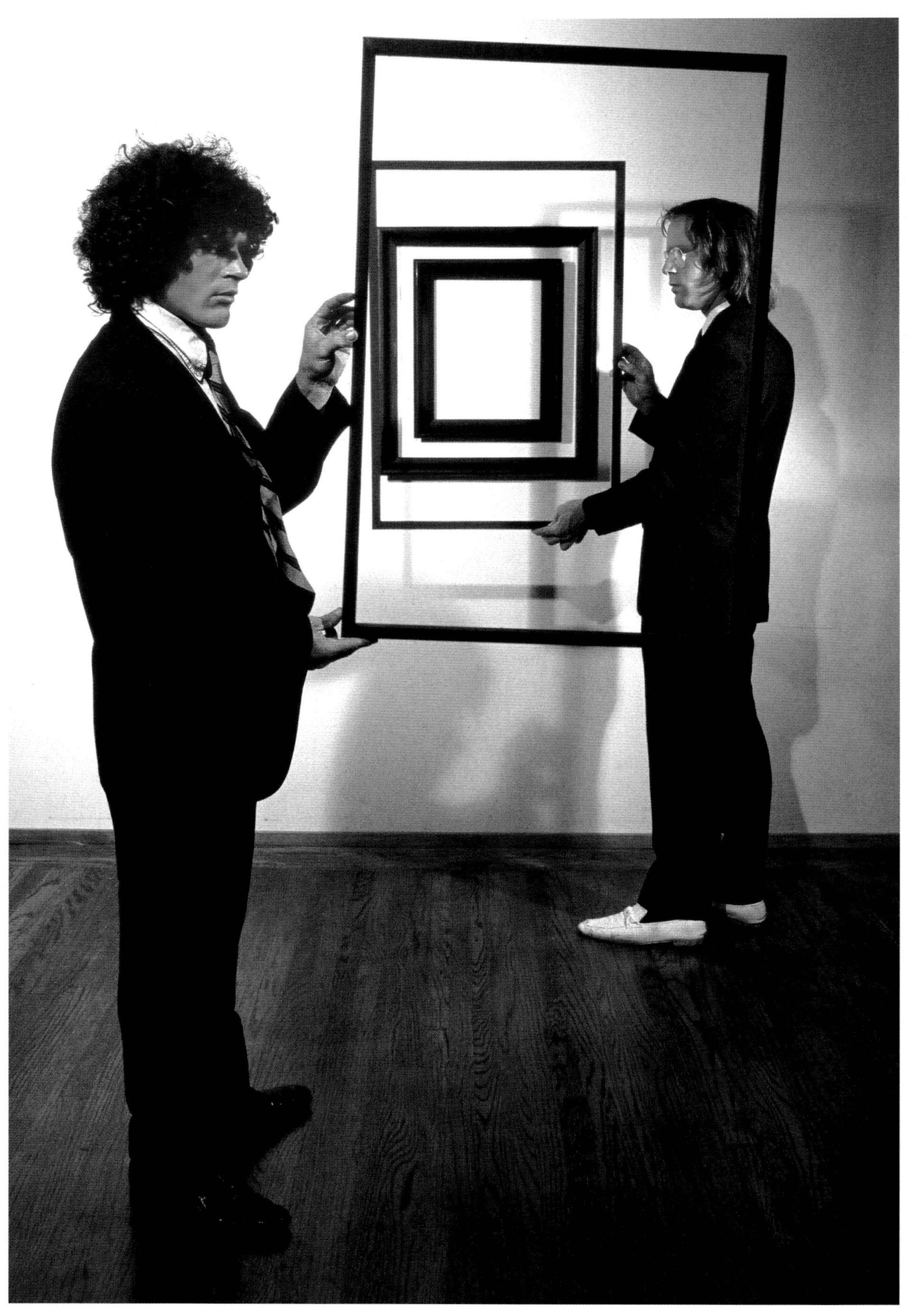

“Framer’s Friend Framing Framer Framing Framed Frame,” black-and-white reproduction of original color slide projection, *Great Moments*

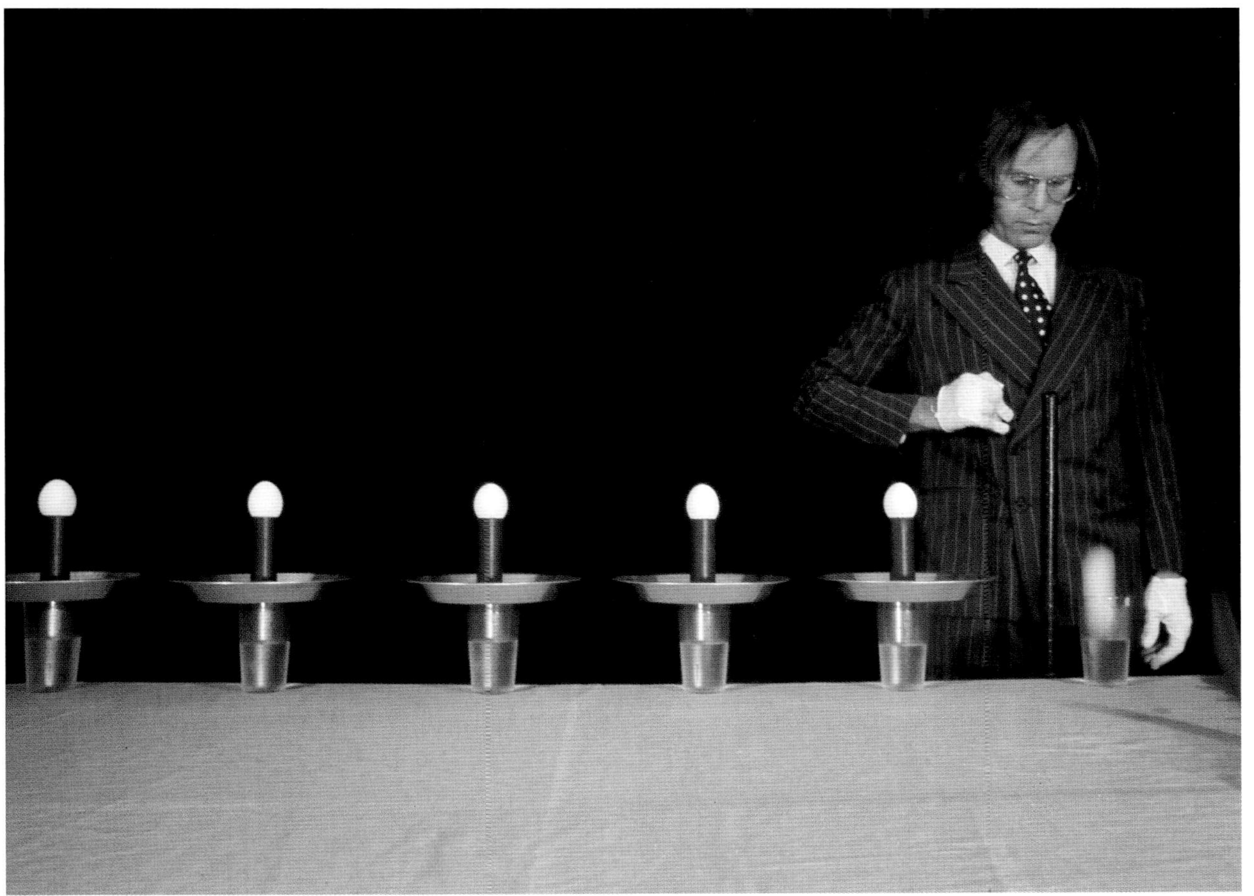

"A Trick My Grandmother Taught Me," *Great Moments*

which on this chilly night in Chicago was just about the only applause we received. Jody's description:

Great Moments *is over. When we kill the tape recorder, we hear a smattering of boos from the audience as they get out of their seats and head towards the exits. No one comes back to congratulate us. No one comes back to ask us how we ever thought up all these zany ideas. There is to be no post-performance celebration no one is offering to take us out to some swank lake-shore bar for a few tall cool ones. Even Mrs. M., our host, who finally appears around half an hour after I had cleaned the shaving cream off my face, seems to do so only out of some sense of hideous obligation. Her face is wan and pale and her eyes flit away from us, nervously. Her hair seems a bit disheveled, as if she has been grabbing at patches of it with her clenched fists. She hands Doug an envelope with our check and mumbles something like "Well, that certainly was . . . ah . . . unusual," and then turns and rushes away down a brightly lit corridor lined with early American landscapes and is gone.*

The night guard stayed around until we had repacked and loaded all our equipment into the van, and by midnight we are back out on the road, heading east toward Detroit and then to Pittsburgh where we have a gig at the University Theater in three days. There are a couple of six-packs of Coors on the

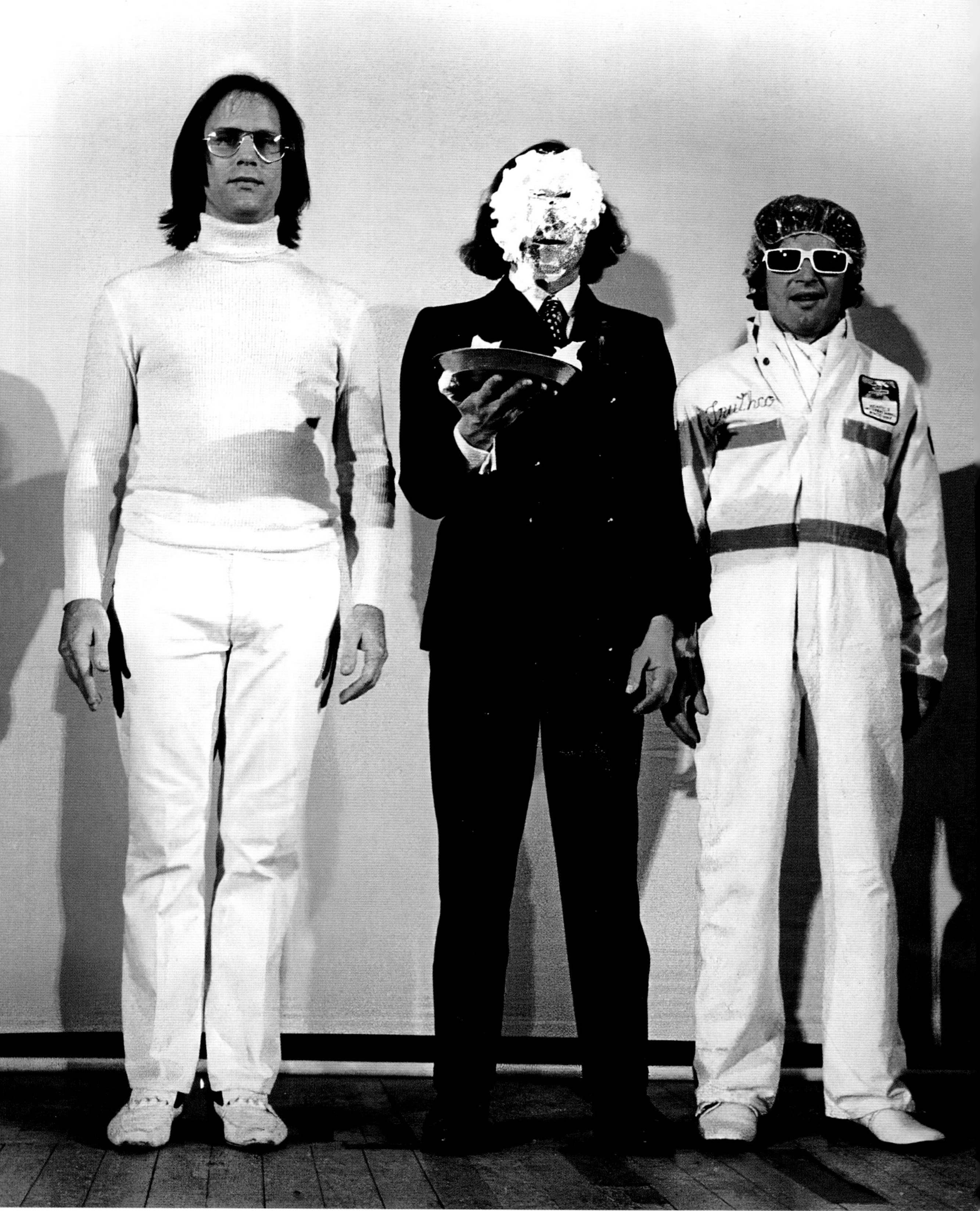

Concluding act, *Great Moments,* (l to r) Doug Hall, John Hillding, Jody Procter

floor. I roll a joint as Doug drives. The radio is playing country music out of a megawatt all-night station in southern Indiana, the highway is out in front of us, the big bright lights of Chicago receding in our rearview mirror.

One detail that Jody forgot to mention is that a few minutes after Mrs. M. "rushed away," I opened the envelope she had handed me to make sure that our check was enclosed. I immediately saw that there was a check, but it was made out to a plumbing company, not to me, and the amount was considerably more than we were supposed to receive. This forced me into the humiliating position of rushing out of the building with the hope that I could catch her before she drove away. Luckily, she and her husband were just pulling out in their black Mercedes. Mrs. M., in the passenger's seat, saw me frantically flailing my arms as I raced toward her. She rolled down the window and I, shivering in my shirtsleeves, explained the problem to her. She laughed nervously, apologized, took the $560 check from me, and handed me the correct one made out for $200.

Into the Strange

Starting in the early 1970s, numerous artist-run and small independent spaces cropped up in many of the major cities in the United States and Europe that were eager to share the artist's risk by offering places for aesthetic experimentation. La Mamelle Art Center in San Francisco was one of those—a place that welcomed T. R. Uthco and supported several of our performances. The best known of these was *Thirty-two Feet Per Second Per Second* (1976), in which Jody and I performed one of our "dual monologues" while sitting in chairs bolted to the facade of La Mamelle's building, three stories above the pavement. Dressed all in white, with even our faces and hair white with stage makeup, we were part of the building's architecture, living sculptures high above the ground, neatly centered just beneath the peak of the roof. Our plan was to remain there from nine to five, the duration of a normal working day, but we only made it to three o'clock as the sun shifted and we found ourselves in cold shadow, shivering in the frigid wind of a San Francisco summer afternoon.

Over the years, Jody and I had developed a character in our imaginations. He had no name and was always referred to as He. In performances, we pursued a technique of simultaneous speaking we termed "double monologues." These were governed by simple rules, similar, we thought, to those that might be used by improvising musicians. The first was to listen to each other, allowing enough space so that we weren't always speaking at the same time. Second, once a mood began to develop, which was invariably bleak but sprinkled with what we considered humor—if Kafka, Beckett, and Buster Keaton had melded into one another—we would try to maintain that mood in both voices, even as the details of our narratives differed. Part of our strategy was to put our bodies

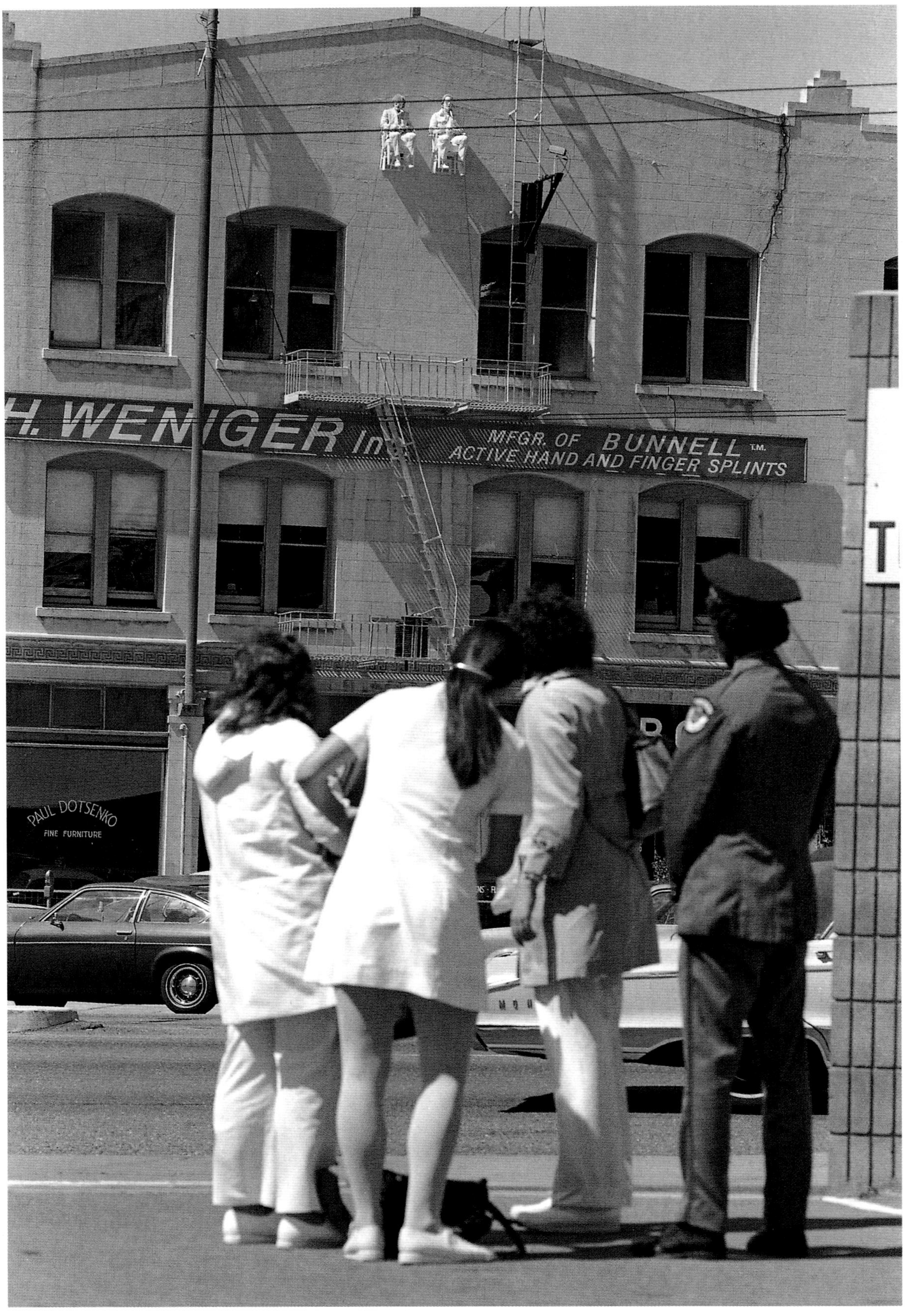

Thirty-two Feet Per Second Per Second, T. R. Uthco, 1976, street view
Photograph by T. R. Uthco (Diane Andrews Hall)
Opposite: *Thirty-two Feet Per Second Per Second,* roof view
Photograph by T. R. Uthco (Diane Andrews Hall)

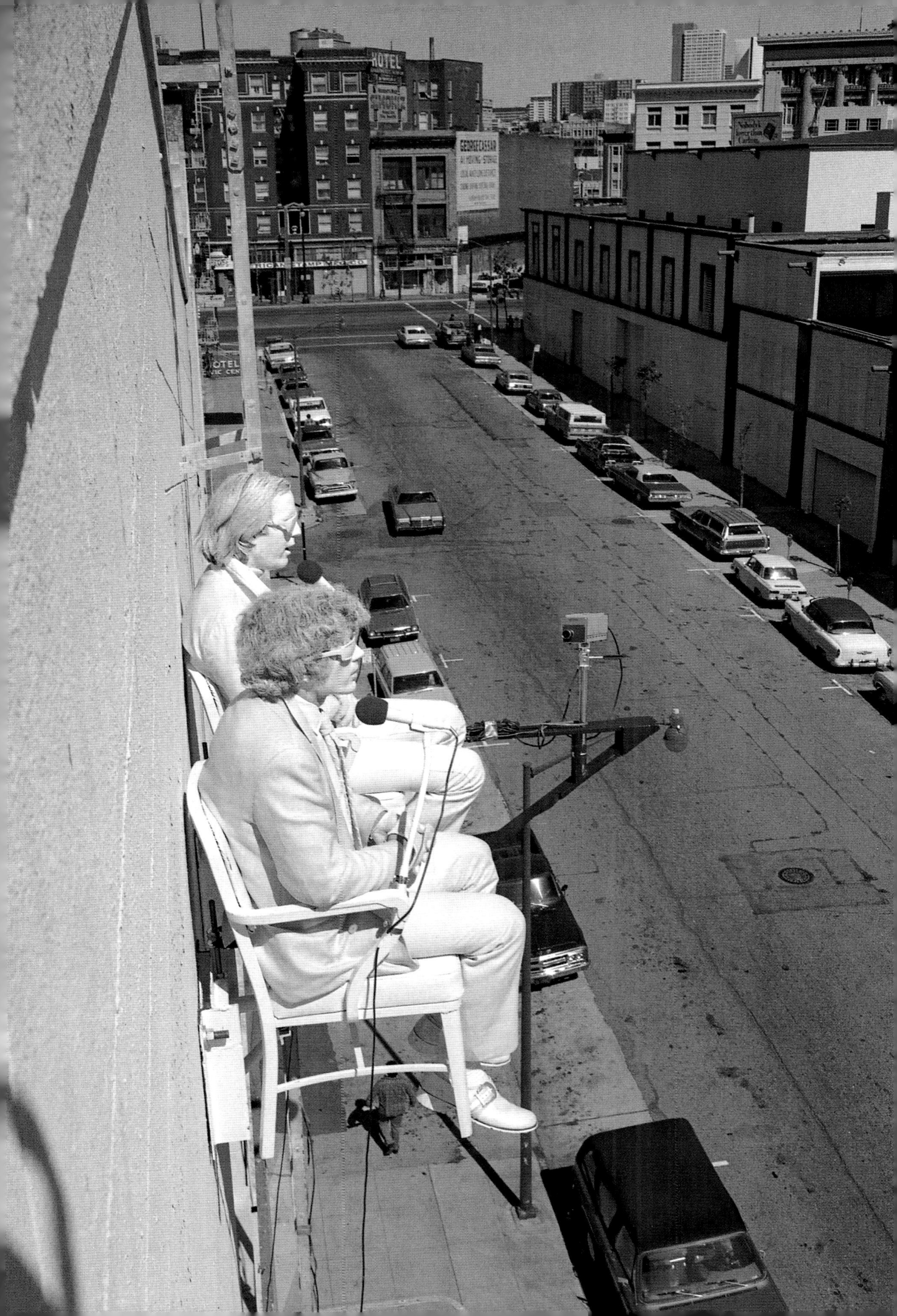
HOTEL
GEORGECASSAR

and psyches into trying situations that could mirror the tribulations of our characters. We also thought that the stress stimulated our imaginations by taking us from the Ordinary and transporting us into the Strange.

First Speaker (Doug)

He liked bright lights in his apartment. Darkness frightened him.

Second Speaker (Jody)

He wondered where he was. He had been dreaming, dreaming of other times, dreaming of his dreams.

First Speaker (Doug)

Night was falling. "Darkness frightens me," he said. The one-room apartment was strewn with lamps.

Second Speaker (Jody)

He dreamed a dream he thought he had had several nights before. Or perhaps he wasn't dreaming at all. It was hard to tell where dreaming began, and non-dreaming ended.

First Speaker (Doug)

Strewn throughout the apartment were lamps of all kinds and shapes. Some had decorative porcelain bases, others were plainer. There were floor lamps, formal table lamps with ripped and stained shades, desk lamps with dented metal shades. Electrical cords crisscrossed the floor and were draped over the foot of the bed and across and under the one table that was pushed against the wall, under the window.

"I do not like the darkness," he said.

He walked slowly around the room, pausing at each lamp as he turned it on. Finally, when all of the lamps were on and the room filled with intense light, he walked to the switch by the door, flipped it on, and moaned in anguish when he saw that the bare bulb in the ceiling fixture did not illuminate. "This is not good," he said. "This is not good at all."

He took the ladder from the nook by the refrigerator, placed it beneath the ceiling light, holding in his hand a new bulb he had taken from the bulb drawer to the left of the stove, he carefully climbed the ladder.

"There will be light," he announced as if to a room full of people, while unscrewing the dead bulb.

After climbing down from the ladder, he crossed the small room to the switch next to the door, flipped it on, and as the light came on proclaimed in a commanding voice, "And the Lord said, let there be light. And there was light."

"I think I am having a crisis," he said out loud. He was worried that he couldn't continue. "How can I continue when I don't know where I have been and don't know where I am going?" he asked himself in silent thought.

He heard laughter. Suddenly he was aware that he was standing on a sidewalk and that he was dressed in blue pajamas that were decorated with repeating images of a cowboy on a bucking horse, separated by single cactuses. There was a small crowd around him, mainly of children. The children were laughing. He could feel their eyes on him. There was a lone man in the crowd. He wore a disheveled suit and was pointing. "Why is that man pointing at me?" he wondered to himself.

He blinked his eyes and realized that he was standing at a window, looking out at a group of children playing basketball in the court below. On the sidewalk there was a man and a woman looking up at him. With panic in his voice, he shouted, "Who are those people and why are they staring at me?" He moved abruptly away from the window and half fell into the overstuffed chair that was nearby.

He continued, mumbling now, "Light brings comfort. Light brings life. Light frightens away the dark forces." He raised his arms and stretched them out at shoulder height while slowly turning as if celebrating the entire room that was now blindingly bright.

"Who are those people and how can I be in two places at the same time: on the street and in this room?" The light of late afternoon was fading, and his room was filling with darkness.

With *Thirty-two Feet Per Second Per Second*—the title referencing the mathematical calculation for the speed at which a body falls from a height—we had an additional interest: the distinction between intimate, private space and public space. We anticipated the perception of us as seen from a distance (from the street, sidewalk, or the windows of surrounding buildings) in contrast to what people might experience if they ventured up the stairs to the gallery where our live voices and video images were transmitted through closed-circuit television and audio feeds.

At a distance we were these strange, inexplicable intruders into everyday life, framed by a fragment of urban architecture high above the turmoil below. Those pedestrians who looked up or followed the gazes of others stopped and stared. People gathered at the windows of the Bank of America building across the street; one could only imagine what they were thinking or saying to one another. We could see none of this since most of the time our eyes were obscured by glasses whose lenses had been covered in opaque white paint.

I'm not sure it's accurate to describe the experience from inside the gallery as "intimate," since we were still unapproachable, situated on the exterior side of a gallery wall; but there is no question that seeing us on the two monitors and hearing us through the speakers allowed a proximity, one filtered through media, that contrasted with the view from the street. Thinking about it now, I realize how similar this dynamic was to the one I set up years earlier in my *Inner Space Simulation Module*. In *Thirty-two Feet,* however, visitors could walk across the gallery to one of the open windows below us where, if they looked up, they would get a third, unfiltered perspective. This interest in the effects of shifting perspectives on our abilities to understand, to become knowledgeable,

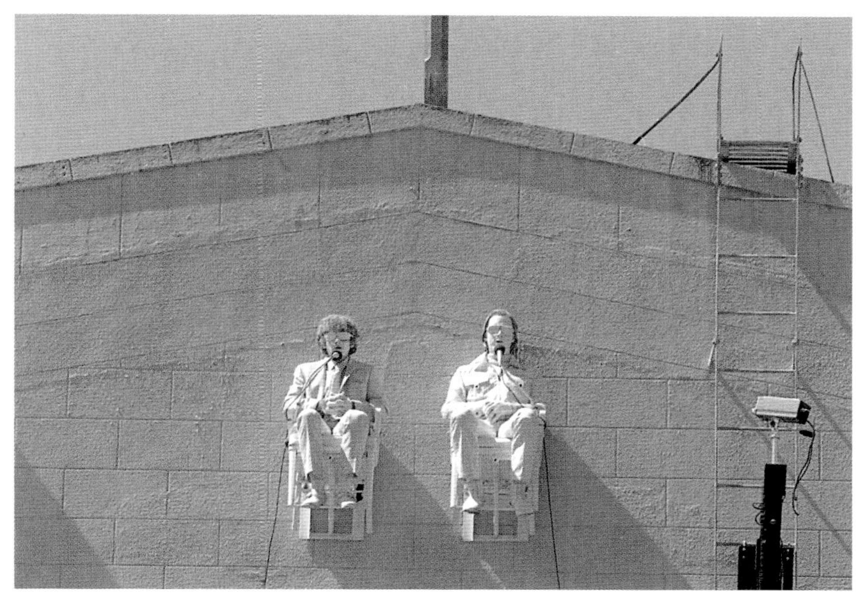

Thirty-two Feet Per Second Per Second, view from building across the street
Photograph by T. R. Uthco (Diane Andrews Hall)

Below: *Thirty-two Feet Per Second Per Second*, gallery view
Photograph by T. R. Uthco (Diane Andrews Hall)

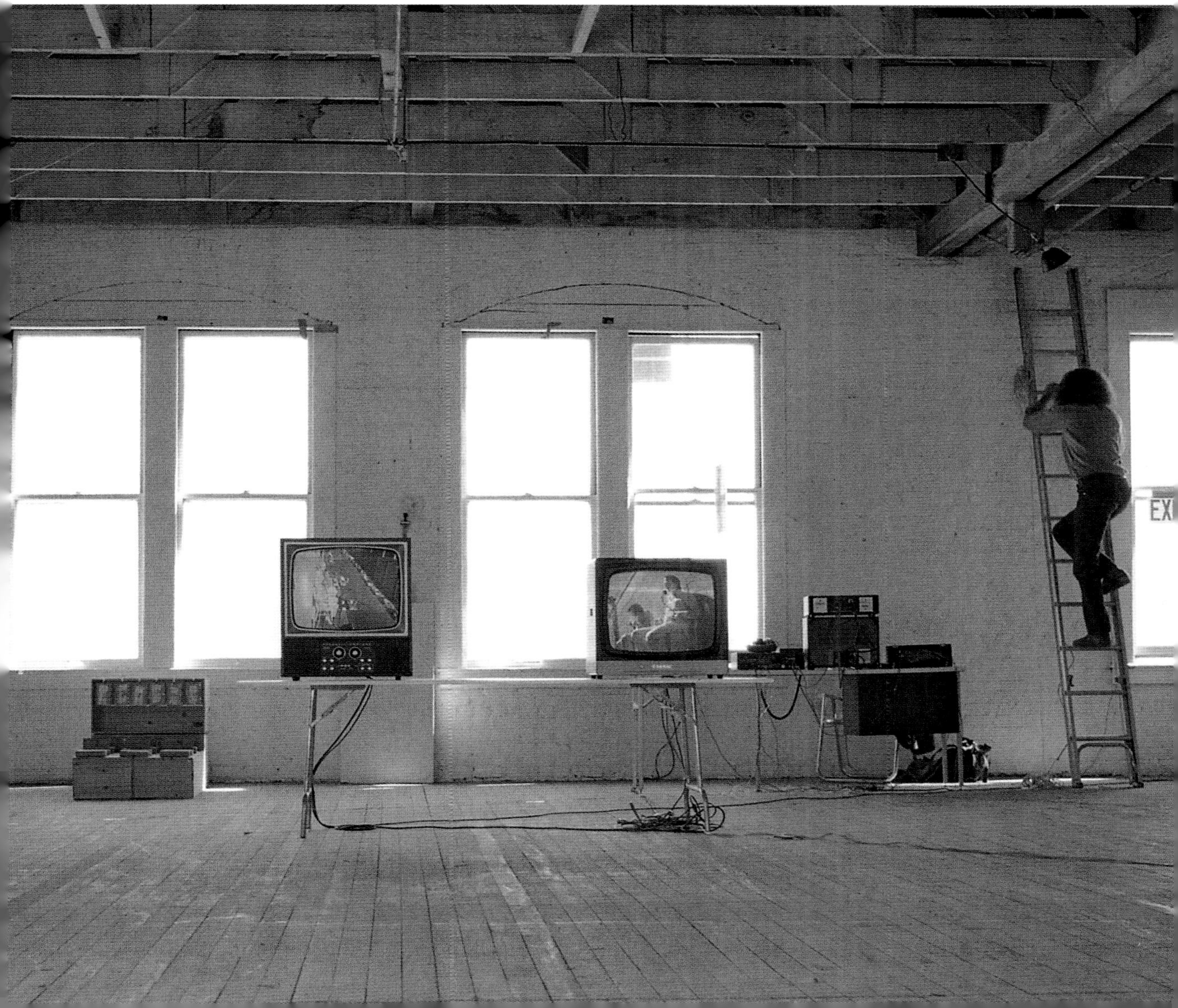

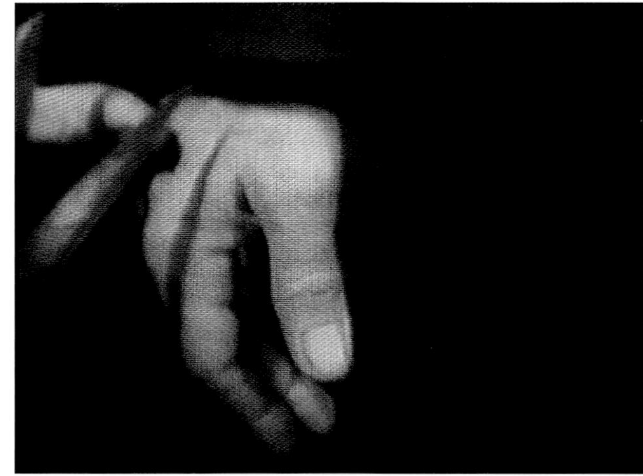

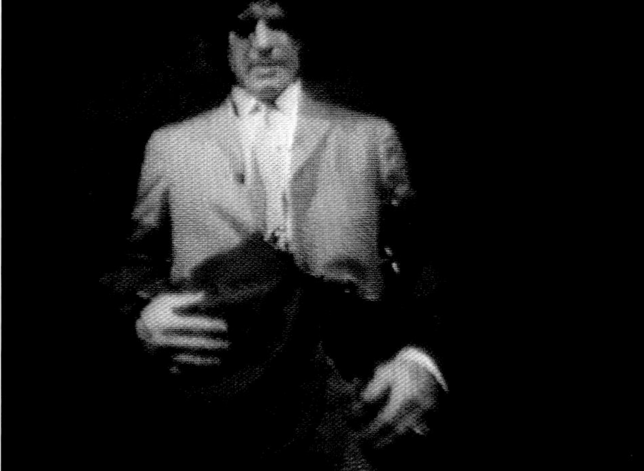

"Really, I've never done anything like this before," he said, T. R. Uthco, 1977, central images showing live performance, flanked by images from the accompanying videos
Photographs by T. R. Uthco (Diane Andrews Hall)

although not fully examined or clearly articulated by us at the time, grew in importance in subsequent years, particularly for me as I ventured off on my own.

We explored such thoughts about proximity and distance a little more explicitly in a speaking piece we performed sometime later. In this performance, *Really, I've never done anything like this before, he said* (1977), we were in a small gallery with a door that could be closed off from the larger main gallery. We secured the door so that it was slightly ajar. In the main gallery, we set up two monitors that showed two related pre-edited, black-and-white videos of us doing strange things to each other—cutting off each other's suits, reattaching my disembodied suit fragments to Jody's and vice versa, and wrapping each other's heads in string. In between the two monitors was a third one that displayed a live feed without audio from the small gallery where we were performing. In the live action our heads were bound together with string, a little like conjoined twins. We wore canvas harnesses with loop handles that we could grip to lean into each other, stressful body positions to

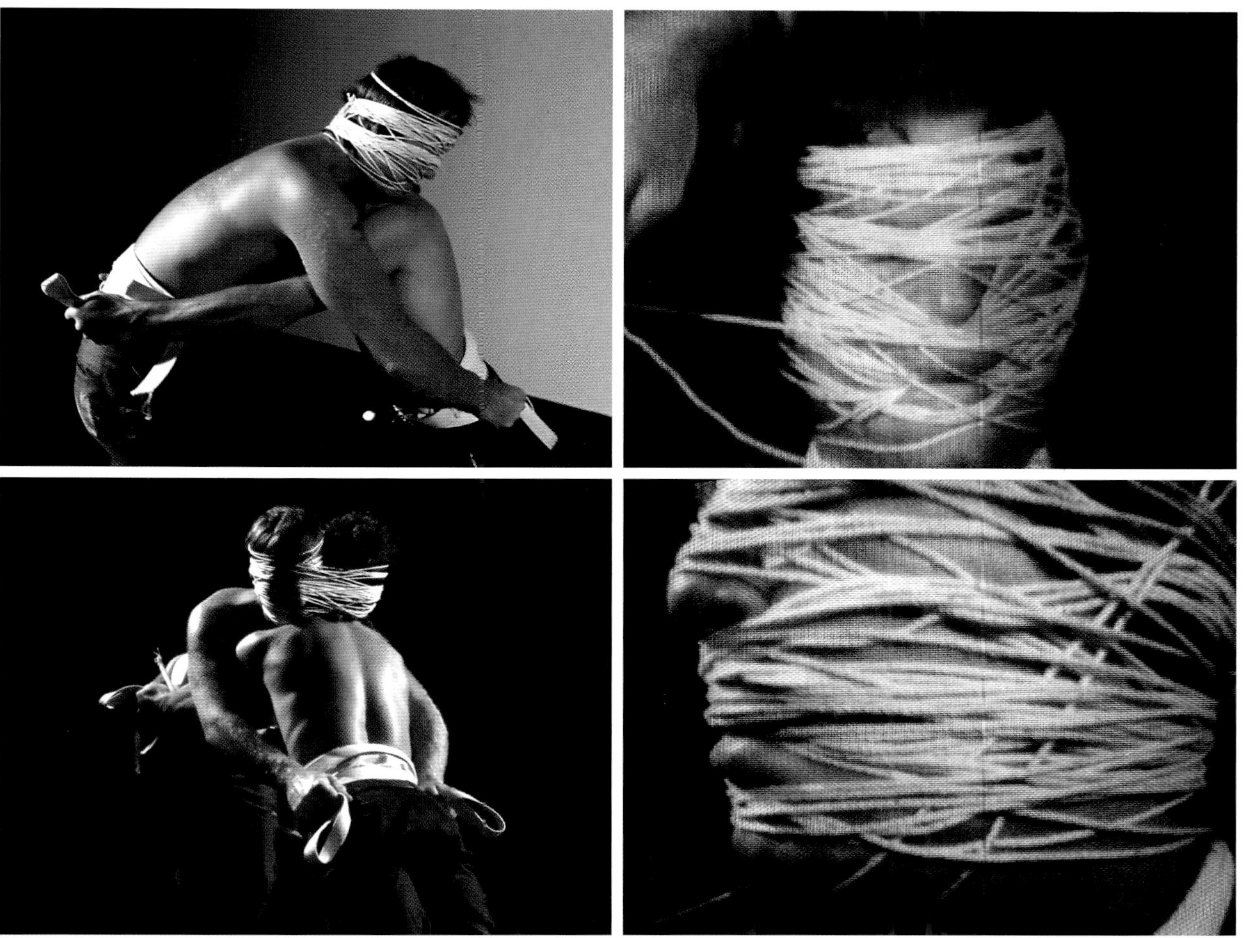

maintain for an hour. This binding together created a third person—the He of our narratives. The dominating view was from the three monitors, but one could lean an eye into the small crack in the door to see fragments of us and the vivid shadows cast along the walls by light from a dozen flashlights that circled us in brackets on the floor. If you listened carefully, you could make out what we were saying. We called this the Peeping Tom View.

> Let us imagine that moved by jealousy, curiosity, or vice I have just glued my ear to the door and looked through a keyhole. . . . [B]ehind that door a spectacle is presented as "to be seen," a conversation as "to be heard." The door, the keyhole are at once both instruments and obstacles.[1]

1. Jean-Paul Sartre, *Being and Nothingness*, trans. Hazel E. Barnes (UK: Routledge Classics, 2006), 282–83.

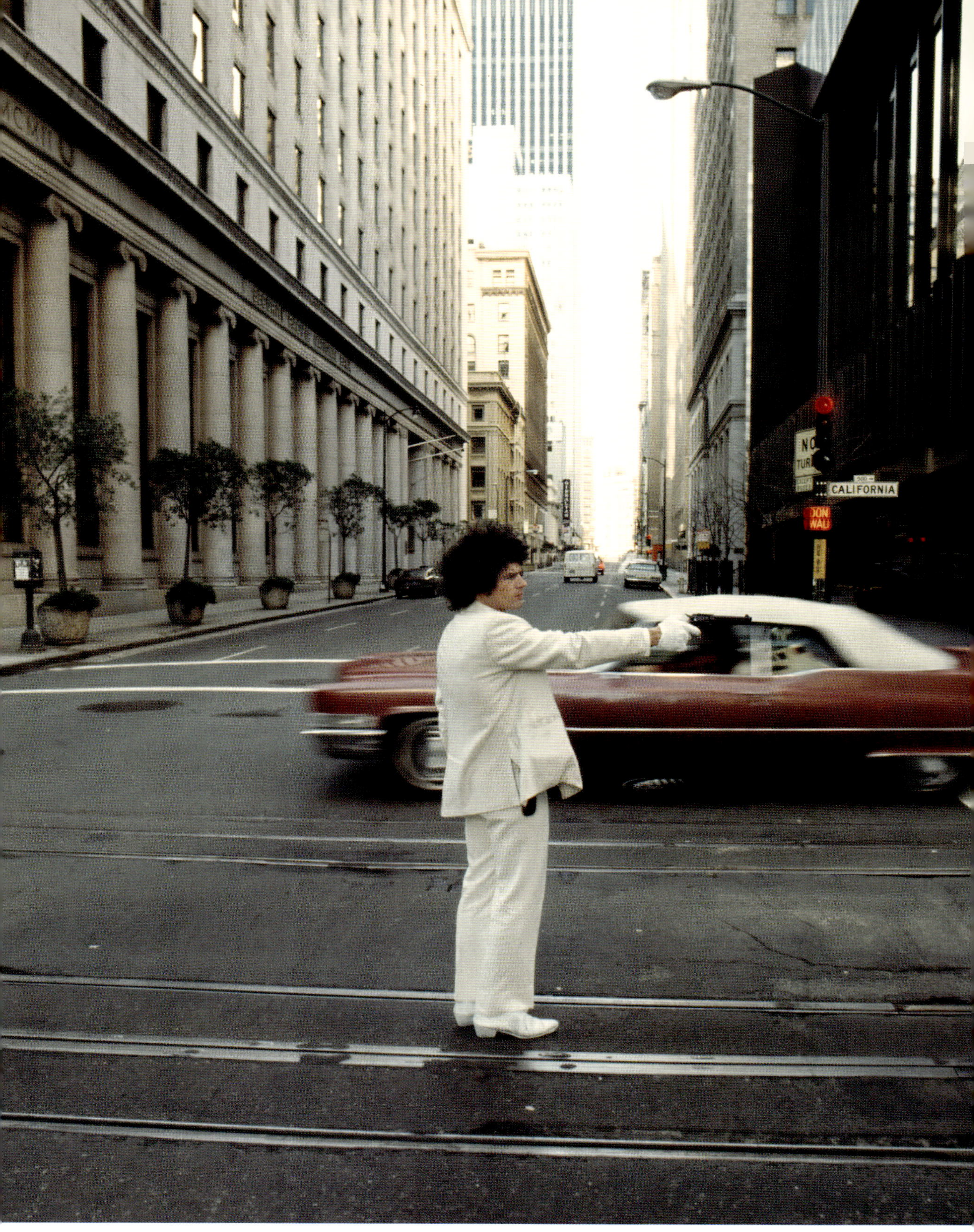

Shooting in the Financial District, T. R. Uthco, 1972
Photograph by T. R. Uthco (Doug Hall)

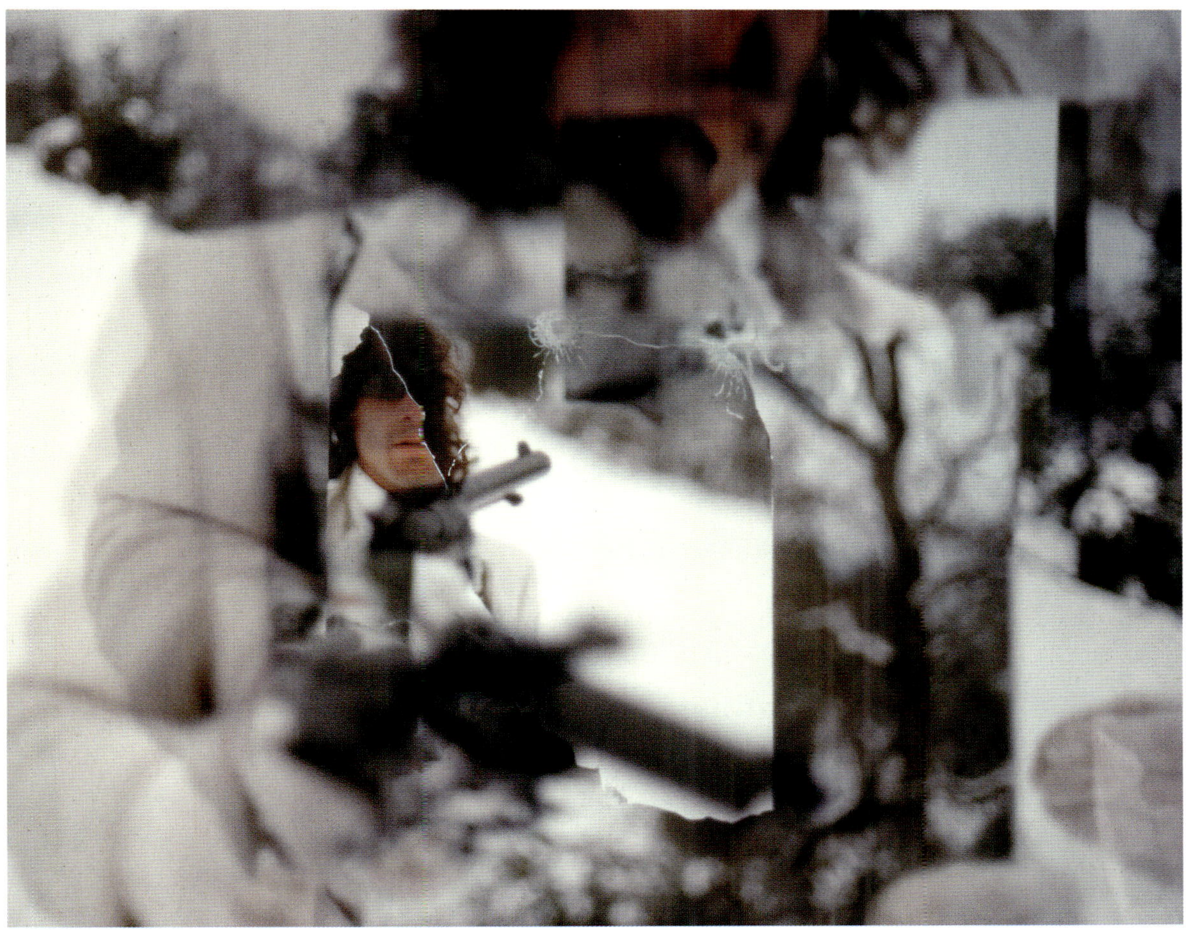

Fracturing, T. R. Uthco, 1972
Photograph by T. R. Uthco (Doug Hall)

In the early to mid-1970s, T. R. Uthco performed numerous "street actions" in which we introduced images into urban settings that disrupted expectations by adding intrusive elements that couldn't easily be accounted for. Most were lighthearted, intended to provide a gentle shock, a disturbance of the everyday through humor or surprise. Some, like *Shooting in the Financial District*, in which Jody, standing in the middle of the street, raises a pistol as if about to fire it, were more sinister. This image had morphed from *Fracturing* (1972), an earlier private performance for the camera that was also the inspiration for "Shooting" in *Great Moments. Fracturing* took place in a snow-covered field on land we held communally in Mendocino. Jody, wearing a white suit and a mirror that covered his torso, fired a pistol at another, full-length mirror a few yards away, resulting in the fracturing of his reflection and its eventual disappearance as the mirror shattered into pieces. It suggested, we soon realized, the dissolution of his personhood—a frightening proposition given Jody's fragile psyche at the time. Despite this momentary nod to urban violence, we recognized and appreciated that the streets of American cities in the 1970s, including San Francisco where poverty and social unrest fomented, were violent enough without us blithely commenting on it. Our street instincts steered us toward less confrontational imagery, although we remained committed to responsible provocation through operations that unsettled social complacency.

In *Walking Mission Street* (1975), we paraded along the major thoroughfare that starts at the southern edge of Daly City and extends to the Embarcadero along San Francisco's northeastern waterfront. With periodic stops so Diane could take photographs, we continued our promenade for a couple of miles, piercing San Francisco's periphery through working-class neighborhoods of used car lots, trailer parks, burger and fried chicken joints, liquor stores, nail salons, and barber shops until exhaustion and boredom overcame all of us. Whenever possible, we walked side by side in unison without speaking or responding to occasional comments from bystanders. As it happens, venturing through predominately African American and Hispanic neighborhoods, clad in all white, we were greeted more by startled amusement than by anger at our display of whiteness. Our intention, naive in retrospect, was to introduce strangeness, not racial commentary, into these settings. One of the better comments hurled at us came from a group of Black teens, one of whom called out, "Hey, White boys!" followed by a chorus of similar greetings from others in the group who, while laughing, suggested muffled hostility as well as derisiveness. The racial implications, which should have been obvious to us, were unavoidable.

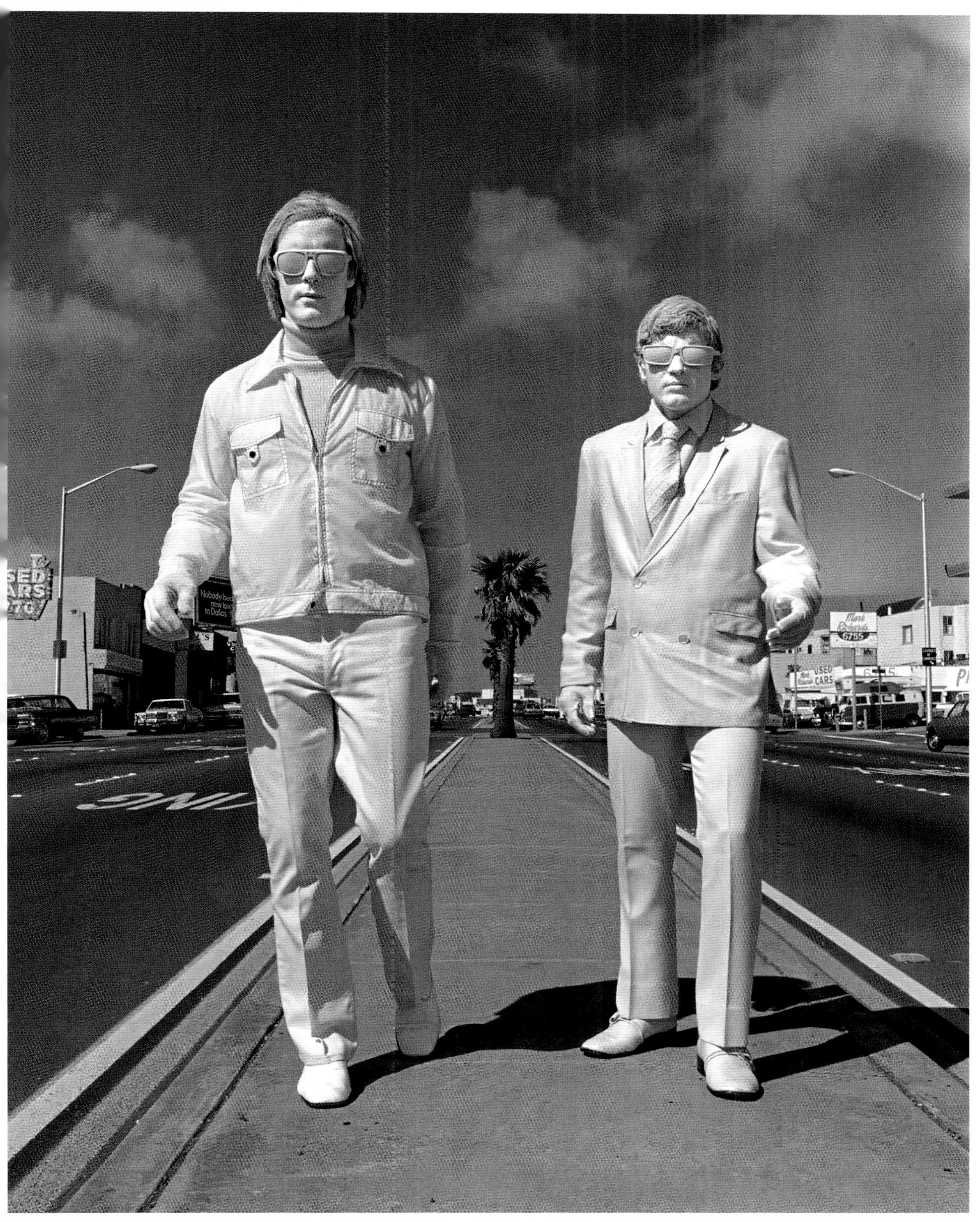

Walking Mission Street, T. R. Uthco, 1975
Photograph by Diane Andrews Hall

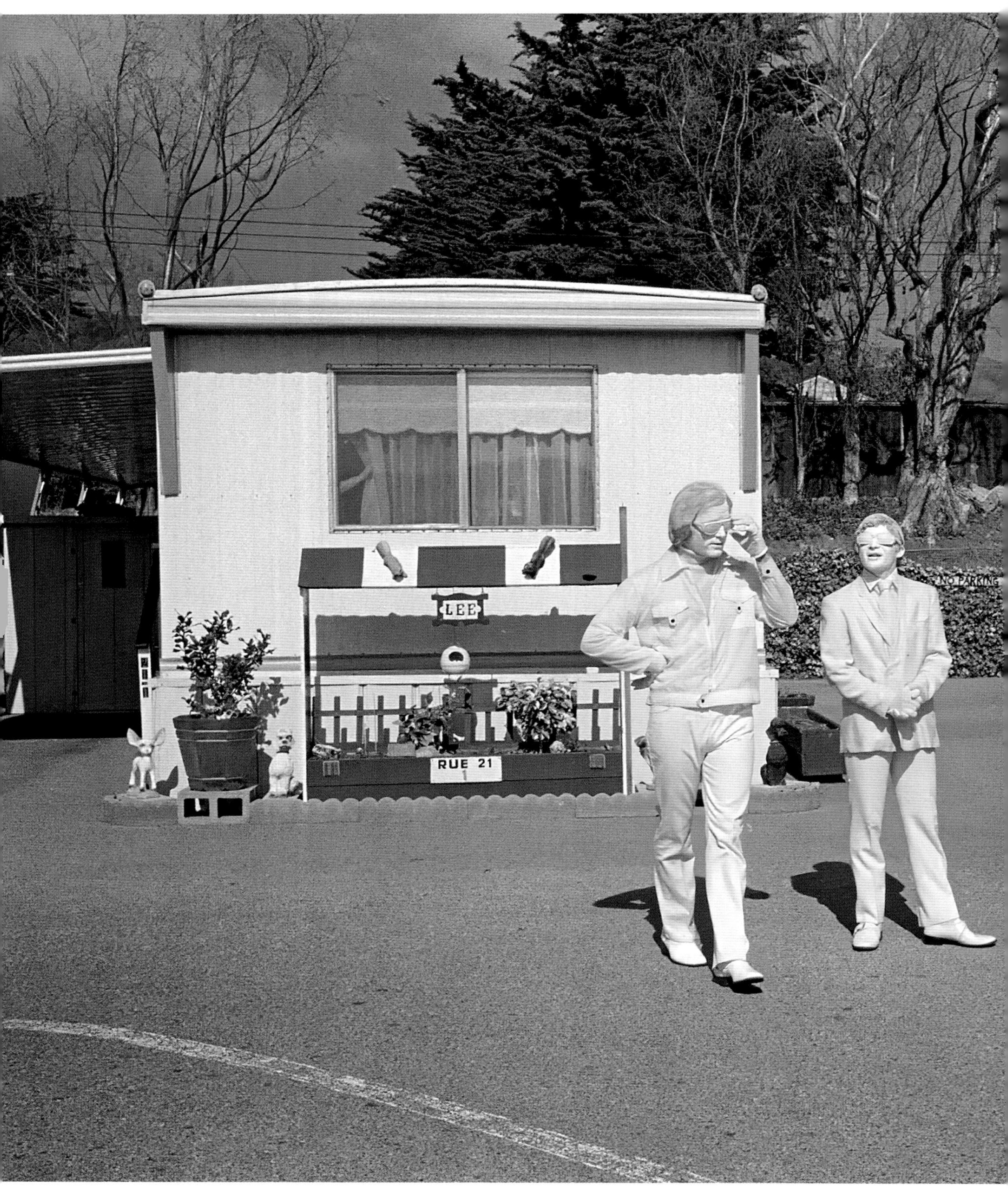

"Rue 21, Bon Air Mobile Home Park, Daly City" (from *Walking Mission Street*)
Photograph by Diane Andrews Hall

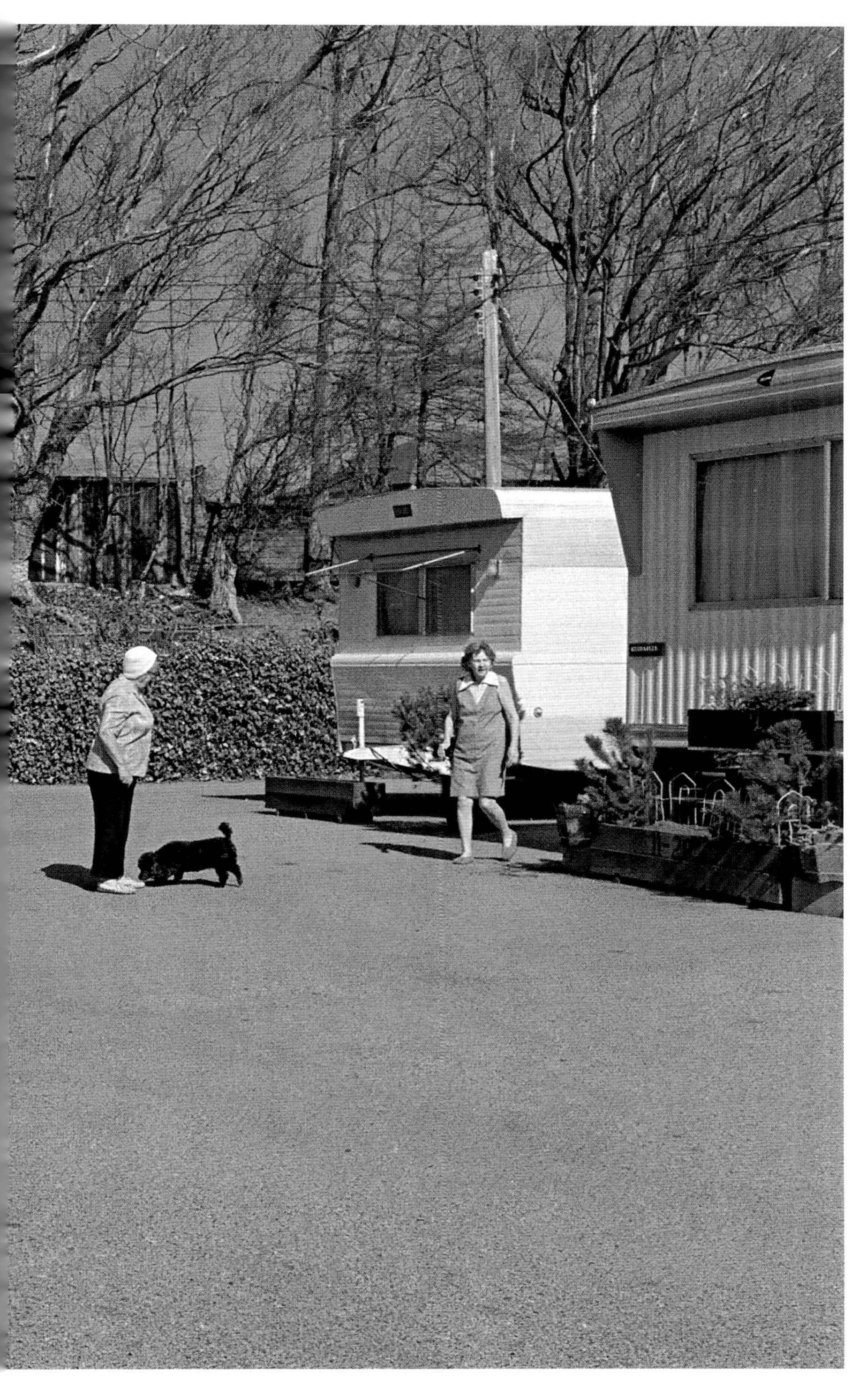

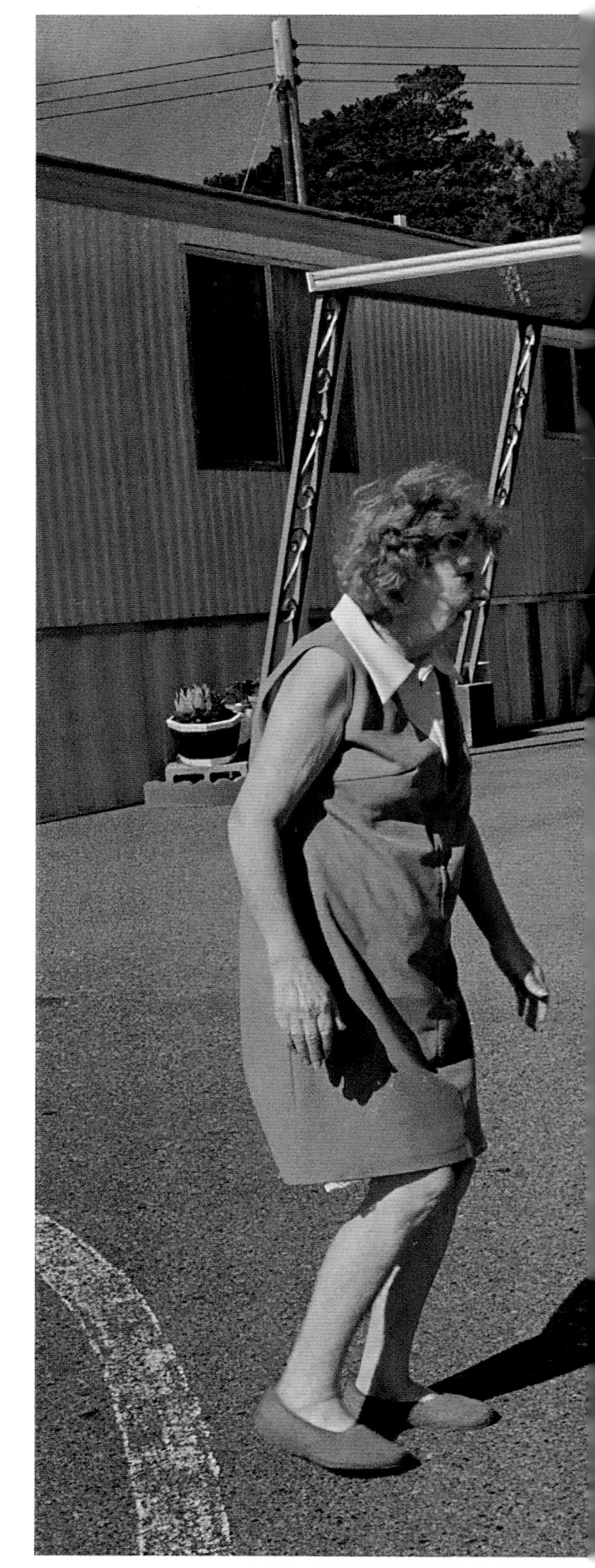

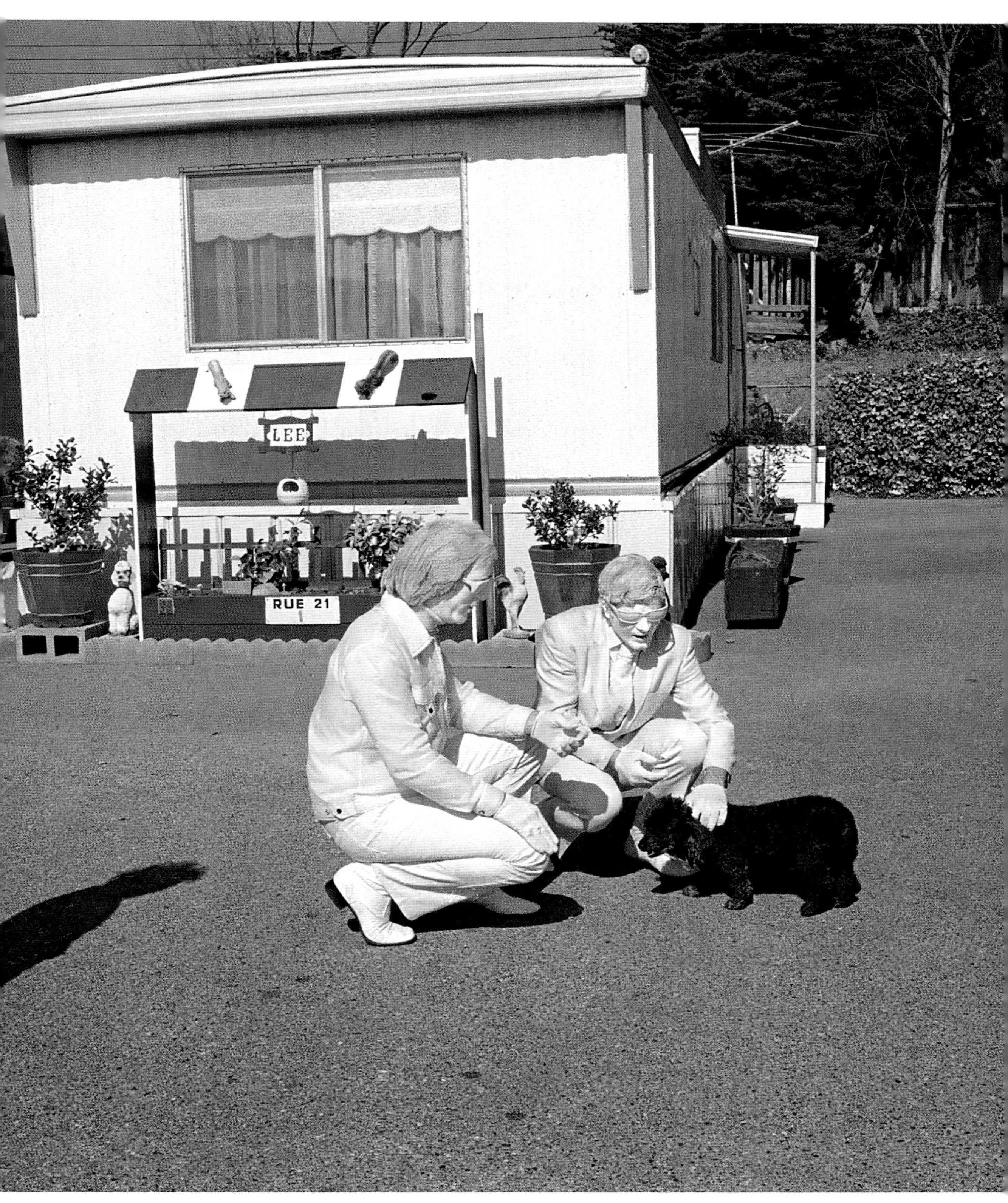

"Concerned Dog Owner on Rue 21, Bon Air Mobile Home Park" (from *Walking Mission Street*)
Photograph by Diane Andrews Hall

From Weird to Weirder

Delirious is the word that comes to mind when I think about the seventies; delirium fueled by my unrequited ambition, confusion, utopian ideals, arrogance, doubt, and optimism. I experienced all these states in staccato-like intervals, or sometimes even simultaneously. And they were enhanced by occasional drug use and more than frequent consumption of alcohol.

It's early December 1972. Jody and I are driving up Cedar Street in Berkeley to visit Philip E., his wife Carol, and others who live communally in a house in the hills above the UC campus. I met Phil and Carol at a small party a few weeks earlier where we ended up in sporadic conversation, periodically interrupted by other guests and the usual distractions that happen when groups of intense people get together. We talked about art, politics, social change, psychiatry (his specialty), and when the evening broke up vowed to meet again. I was captivated and curious.

"That's it. Buena Vista. Turn right. Are the numbers going in the right direction?" This is way pre-GPS. A short pause. I'm concentrating on navigating the tight turns. "There it is. I think. Yes, that's the house." It's big, with large glass panes that we will soon discover provide a panoramic view of the city and the bay below, extending to the Golden Gate Bridge in the far distance. After parking, we climb steep steps toward the house; to our right, ivy climbs part way up the trunk of a palm tree that casts a shadow across the modern facade. Slightly out of breath, we reach a flat area just below the front entrance and the few remaining steps to the front door. I ring the bell. We wait. Nothing. We continue to wait. Still nothing.

"Should I ring again?"

Before Jody can respond we hear stirrings, and Phil opens the door.

"Hello, Doug. Come on in."

Carol, a few feet behind, steps forward and extends a hand. "Hi," she offers, a little hesitantly it seems to me. Phil and Carol have a reserved formality about them that is a contrast, one that I appreciate, to the exuberant informality of the hippie scene with its ostentatious embrace of egalitarianism and its insistence that we all "have a nice day."

When we met a few weeks earlier, Phil had started to explain how he arrived in California a year earlier to become chief resident in psychiatry at a state mental hospital in Santa Clara, south of San Francisco. In his telling, the hire had been controversial because of his radical approach to the treatment of schizophrenia, which was based on the ideas of the Scottish psychiatrist R. D. Laing, with whom he had studied and later worked. Laing's teachings, which Philip E. was pursuing through his own research, proposed that schizophrenia, rather than an illness, was an alternative perception of reality that, although not the norm, perceived truths about the world that should be affirmed rather than dismissed as madness. The proper treatment was not electroshock therapy or pharmaceuticals, but a form of psychoanalysis that was intended to help patients accept and learn from their condition. Philip took this further than I think Laing advocated by spending time with his patients while under the influence of LSD "in order to have a better sense of their world view."

This is pretty much where our conversation had ended at the party a couple of weeks earlier. My curiosity tweaked, I wanted to know more, which is why we were standing at his doorstep on a smoggy Saturday afternoon in early December. We followed Phil and Carol into the foyer and then into the adjoining living room. And this is where things started to get really weird.

In the living room are two men. One is standing and is introduced to us as Jalal. I will later learn that he is the Pakistani leader of a notorious London-based civil rights group advocating for South Asian immigrants. He had fled England to avoid possible indictment for his activism, which had in some cases led to violence, and also in response to threats on his life from far-right nationalists. He says nothing when we are introduced, only delivers a slight nod. His attention is directed to the man sitting on the couch. Carol and Phil, too, after we are quickly introduced, appear to lose interest in us.

All eyes are on the tiny man in white garments I associate with a Hindu ascetic. Harish is sitting on the couch, legs crossed, eyes closed, apparently meditating or, for all I know, napping. The room has a solemnity, a heaviness that feels as leaden and suffocating as the air outside. Harish's eyes momentarily flash open. He gestures toward a couple of empty chairs opposite him, indicating where we should sit. I'm feeling very uncomfortable as Jalal lights a joint, hands it to Phil, who passes it on to the rest of us. I take a tiny hit, knowing that this is exactly the kind of situation where, if stoned, I can completely lose my bearings and fall into deep, persistent paranoia. Jody is even more of a wimp than I and yet takes a deep toke. This could end badly.

Being the last in the chain, I get up to hand the joint to Harish, seemingly still in the lap of Morpheus, but Phil steps forward and gently guides me back to my chair.

"Harish is on LSD. He takes it a few times a week as a way to take his meditations deeper," Phil says in a hushed voice as I return to my chair. Nobody speaks as the joint gets passed around again. Jody takes a big hit before passing it to me. It's a roach by now. I take a toke, hand it to Jalal, who grasps it between the tongs of an alligator clip and takes a couple of hits before disposing of it in an ashtray that contains a pile of similarly spent joints. The dope is strong. I'm very stoned. All is very quiet. Harish's emaciated chest and stomach rise and fall with each breath. We are all looking at him as if in anticipation of . . . what?

"What do you know?" Harish, eyes suddenly wide open, directs his question at Jody. He laughs, a sustained guffaw. His entire body briefly quakes with laughter. The rest of us try to join in with a chuckle, as if we might get the joke.

I look over at Jody. He isn't laughing at all. He's ashen. Abruptly, Harish stops laughing.

Staring directly at Jody while pulling a wrap around his bare shoulder, "What do you know? Do you think you know something?" he challenges him in his heavy Indian accent.

"The eternal space poom," Jody replies after an uncomfortably long pause and with a mild smirk on his face. A total non sequitur that only I could appreciate, since we use it and similar phrases to express confounding stoned reality. Jody has the tendency, when confronted by a difficult social situation, to default into a kind of wiseass posture as a defensive maneuver. It's his suit of armor, meaning it's a nearly impenetrable shield that discourages anyone from trying to get at whatever may lie within. Sufficient to repel most verbal or psychological onslaughts, it works best on strangers but can be almost as effective with those who know him and the ploy well.

Now, this is when things went from weird to weirdest. I will do my best to describe what I saw and heard as accurately as possible, and I will understand if the reader ends up doubting the veracity of my tale.

Harish's eyes seem to lock on Jody, whose smirk has been replaced by a bewildered, extremely vulnerable, almost vacant expression. In a quiet voice, void of any aggression, speaking quietly but firmly, Harish says, "You know nothing. You can know nothing. You stand by the river, but you do not jump in. You stand by the river and watch the water flow past. You watch and you talk but cannot know."

I look at Harish, though not too closely for fear that he might single me out, and then at Jody. But Jody no longer looks like himself. His face is drawn, his complexion waxen; he looks like he is shrinking. All of that is frightening enough, but what is worse is that there appears to be some sort of mass, a roundish something, suspended above his head. I am thinking I am mighty stoned, and I must be hallucinating, but judging by the expressions of others in the room, all focused on poor Jody, they are seeing the same thing. It looks like Jody is trying to speak. I'm afraid he might be choking but I'm unable to move, caught in a force field that has me plastered to the chair. My very strong sense is that the thing suspended above Jody's head is his consciousness and Harish, in an ostentatious display of power, has extracted it so he can look at it and play with it the way a cat might play with a mouse before issuing a death bite.

I don't know how long this went on, with Jody paralyzed and Harish offering his terse, enigmatic insights, extracting them from Jody's hovering consciousness like a skilled surgeon removing a difficult tumor, all punctuated by Harish's occasional bursts of hysterical laughter. What was probably no more than five minutes felt like an eternity.

Harish persists, "You wear your fear the way a young girl wears a new dress, but your shoes are dirty. There can be no party for you." A short spurt of raucous laughter. No one else is laughing. No one is even smiling. Nor do the other three in the room look particularly surprised or alarmed, as if they have seen this before. The object above Jody's head glows, now more like a vapor than a hard object. It's bluish at the center and becomes whiter toward the edges. Jody's eyes are wide open with the almost comical expression of a cartoon character who has seen a ghost. It goes on like this a while longer.

"What are you afraid of? Put on your dancing shoes and dance alone." A long pause. No one else speaks. Jody's mouth is slightly ajar, eyes wide in fright or astonishment.

"You can't be afraid to go where you have to go." Harish tucks his garment around his waist. His eyes remain intently on Jody. Another pause, longer than the last.

"But you are hiding, and you are lost." He coughs. His eyes dart across the room and then back to Jody. A quick spurting laugh.

"I could show you the way, but you need to find it on your own. Put on your dancing shoes." A burst of unsmiling, mirthless laughter.

More follows in a similar vein. Harish makes uncanny statements about Jody: his aspirations as a writer and artist, the tensions in his relationship with his wife (my sister), his privileged background, which he attacks amid displays of derisive laughter. How does he know all of this? It's as if he's reading Jody's mind, going deep where his insecurities reside like little foraging demons. Meanwhile, I'm totally freaked out, appalled by the cruelty of it all and plotting how to get the fuck out of there even as I'm immobilized by paranoia and the apparent force that's anchoring me to the spot. And then as suddenly as it began, it's over. The entity above Jody's head dissipates, like a patch of fog seen in time lapse evaporating into the air; Jody, still pale, stirs in the chair. Although my paranoia is redlining, I feel as if an invisible weight has been lifted from me while those around me come back into focus. Harish draws his legs tighter beneath him in a meditative posture, which he had never entirely left, and with a relaxed, contented expression on his thin lips, closes his eyes, looking very much the way he appeared when we entered the room.

After sitting numbly for a few minutes, surrounded by a cumbersome silence, Jody and I exchanged time-to-leave eye contact, gathered what was left of our psyches, and, following awkward farewells, fled from the house to our car. As we headed west toward our homes, we struggled to make sense of what had just happened. The only statement that made any sense under the circumstances was Jody's comment, "Something is definitely amiss in the eternal space poom."

IV

Teaching to Learn

These Are the Rules

By 1978 my activities, both individually and as a member of T. R. Uthco, had attracted enough attention that I was invited to be a visiting artist for the spring semester in the Sculpture Department at Virginia Commonwealth University in Richmond. The invitation was in response to a couple of short visiting-artist stints I had done there at the behest of faculty member (and Fluxus artist) David E. Thompson (aka Davi Det Hompson). The first of these was when Jody and I were touring in 1974 with our performance *Great Moments*, and the second was a 1977 gig that involved a public lecture on my/our work followed by short critiques with individual students. I wasn't an unknown to many of the students this time around: all upper-level undergraduates, they had elected to work with me based on the information that had been provided by the department or through their own research. Several had seen my talk the previous year.

To say I was nervous about this first major teaching job would be an understatement. It was softened, but also further complicated, by our decision to have Diane and eight-year-old Gannon make the trip east with me, which we did in our Dodge van. This was long before seat belts or booster seats for children, so Gannon bounced around in the back of the van as we plodded along through the late-December ice and snow. Resilient as he was, he approached the trip with a minimum of complaining. However, he had some difficult, tear-inducing moments adjusting to a new school where some of the children saw him as an outsider and thus a convenient target for bullying.

The situation wasn't any easier for Diane, who abandoned the familiarity of her home and work routine to support me. She did it with as much love as she could muster, but not without moments of resentment and frustration that grew to the point that her leaving us for a couple of weeks to stay with a friend in New York was, we agreed, the best way to preserve our marriage.

It would be fair to say that my approach to this first teaching job was more instinctual than carefully worked out. Still, I came to the situation with a few precepts, if I can call them that. Some were based on my own experiences in college and fine arts graduate school, where I first encountered the rarefied language that was used in critiques.

My first precept, then as now, is not to emulate the undisciplined use of language that had been employed so uncritically in those seminars. As an art student, I had been appalled when an instructor would say things like, "I want to see more of you in the work," or "This just doesn't work," or "What are you expressing?" or "I reject the beauty in your work," or "Where is your anger?" Where, indeed. I considered art to be an exchange of ideas, a two-way conversation—the sensibility of the artist availing itself through the object or action and that of viewers through their interpretation of that object. Art is thinking made manifest through material: artists' thinking flows into the things they make, from which viewers construct meaning. This meaning, however, is not static and in turn invites further thinking. In my view it is impossible to rise above the most superficial and subjective discussion if empty terms are thrown around without being scrutinized. The first precept, then, is that the terms we use to discuss and describe our work need to be looked at critically—as critically as the work itself. Language matters.

Art education in the sixties and later was very much dominated by a White male world view, and I was as much a product of this thinking as anyone else. But even at the time I recognized it as a problem because, along with marginalizing women, it failed to account for art that was going on in communities outside the supposed mainstream of contemporary art. This of course was defined by a select number of galleries and museums in New York along with a few in Europe, and supported by the major art magazines like *Art Forum*. If I had learned anything from my undergraduate study of anthropology, it was that there are structural differences between cultures and that although some universals link them, those differences matter and need to be honored. It isn't such a great leap to apply this to a diverse group of young artists: we are not all the same, and we see the world from vastly different points of view. In other words, how we engage with works of art is contextual. In order to have a meaningful conversation in a seminar, one in which the students are coming at their ideas from different perspectives and employing different materials and strategies, we need to address the fact of difference. My second precept is to recognize the significance of context when looking at and discussing works of art and to respect the differences among us.

It is a common default to reduce the experiences of art to short phrases such as "I like that" or "I don't like that." My third, deceptively simple precept is to disallow an expression of one's likes or dislikes when discussing a work because, I argue, they are nothing other than subjective terms that, being personal and private, discourage serious thought and investigation.

My final insistence, more procedure than precept, is that the presenting artist show the work without prior explanation, unless the explanation is itself part of the work, so that the group can discuss what it is seeing or hearing without being prejudiced by the artist's statement of purpose. The idea is that the student becomes like a fly on the wall while a group of informed contemporaries carry on an in-depth conversation about the work before them. The assumption is that this will provide the student with a reasonably unfettered, honest view of how others interpret the work. Of course, at the conclusion, the student is invited to add whatever they like.

In all of this, I am recognizing something basic and important about visual art—its most important attribute in my estimation—which is that art is always in a state of becoming as opposed to having arrived. This isn't to say it is, from the artist's perspective, unfinished. What it does say is that the experience, its reception, doesn't close meaning down but opens it up to a kind of completion that can only take place when the viewer steps in. It is this condition of becoming that I think is the great gift art offers us (and it may be true to all forms: dance, music, film, performance): by not over-defining itself, by maintaining itself in a state of becoming, it gives us the privilege to be with the work, to establish our own relationship to it, and to arrive at our own provisional interpretation. One of the great pleasures we receive from experiencing art, sometimes in the quiet of a museum, gallery, or concert hall, is the invitation to freely follow our own thoughts that have been ignited through a specific kind of looking or listening.

The art that interests me is essentially mute, that is, it stands before us without providing explanation as to its reason why. It pulls us in, interests us or moves us, perhaps even threatens us. At the same time, it stands aloof, unconscious of our existence, contained within itself. Much later in my teaching career while leading a seminar based on the writings of Jacques Rancière, I came across Friedrich Schiller's "Fifteenth Letter" from *On the Aesthetic Education of Man in a Series of Letters* (1795), which is an important reference for Rancière's ideas about the politics of aesthetics. In it, Schiller expresses this ability of art—one that I could only crudely conceptualize with the students at VCU—to embrace us (I imagine it like a kind of seduction), while simultaneously holding us at a distance by not resolving its own mystery. Schiller writes,

> It is neither charm, nor is it dignity, that speaks to us from the superb countenance of a Juno Ludovici;[1] it is neither of them, because it is both at once. While the womanly god demands our veneration, the godlike woman kindles our love; but while we allow ourselves to melt in the celestial loveliness, the celestial self-sufficiency holds us back in awe. The whole form reposes and dwells within itself, a complete closed creation, and—as though it were beyond space—without yielding, without resistance; there is no force to contend with force, no unprotected part where temporality might break in. Irresistibly seized and attracted by one quality, and held at a distance by the other, we find ourselves at the same time in the condition of utter rest and extreme movement, and the result is that wonderful emotion for which reason has no conception and language no name.[2]

1. From Wikipedia: "The Juno Ludovisi (also called Hera Ludovisi) is a colossal Roman marble head of the 1st century CE from an acrolithic statue of an idealized and youthful Antonia Minor as the goddess Juno. Added to the Ludovisi collection formed by Cardinal Ludovico Ludovisi, it is now in the Palazzo Altemps, Museo Nazionale Romano, Rome."
2. Friedrich Schiller, "Fifteenth Letter," *On the Aesthetic Education of Man*, trans. Reginald Snell (Mineola, NY: Dover Publications, 2004), 81.

These moments of being embraced and held at a distance by a work of art, of comprehension and persisting mystery, allow us an acknowledgment of our own freedom to think, to be simultaneously hidden away in our own thoughts while recognizing ourselves in the world, because what applies in the quiet of a museum also applies when we leave and find ourselves on the street. For one willing or able to engage with art in this way, the world can open in all its complexity and diversity. I'm tempted to call this condition, which is aesthetic, psychological, and cultural, the "poetics of doubt," because rather than finalizing judgments, it recognizes, even celebrates, uncertainty. And this uncertainty, rather than something to fear, creates the space—what I call a free zone—in which a viewer comes to terms with meaning as it evolves out of the experience of standing before a particular object or experience.

The negotiation of meaning, uninhibited by external forces that demand a certain interpretation, is, I propose, the real politics of art. Political because, as viewers, we are expressing our freedom to think on our own terms without external hindrances other than the normal baggage that we carry into any unfamiliar situation. I think it is important, even curious, that the ruminations taking place when our eyes intersect the objects before us happen in conjunction with language. And this brings me full circle to my first precept: The language we use when we think and talk about art is important. At least it is in a critique seminar where students and the seminar leader are striving to make sense of what is before them by applying words to a sensory experience. This conversion of the visual into language is influenced by all our previous experiences that are beyond the object itself—books we've read, conversations had or overheard, walks in the city or the country, sad moments, ecstatic moments—all of these and so many more are carried with us and are tapped into when we look at art. And in most cases, this intersection of our bodies and minds with art produces many more questions than it resolves. Art allows a process of coming-to-terms-with. It turns "that which is" into "what is that?"

As luck would have it, my first teaching experience in Virginia included a group of extraordinarily talented, directed students. They were unexpectedly generous and open, offering their work, insights, and references to writings, artists, and ideas some of which were new to me and outside of the iconic mainstream of contemporary art. With them, I was able to approach teaching as something of a collaborative art project, one that could adapt to what was happening in front of us based on the work shown and the issues that arose as a result. Perhaps the biggest lesson I learned from my VCU experience, one that I kept in clear focus over the next two and a half decades, is that students not only learn but they also teach; that teaching and learning are vectors operating in parallel directions simultaneously. As the teacher, the designated adult in the room, the challenge is to create and maintain an atmosphere in which that can happen. Of course, I wasn't always successful in doing this.

The School on a Hill

The San Francisco Art Institute[3] was founded in 1871 and is situated in a campus consisting of a Brutalist building by Paffard Keatinge-Clay adjoining an earlier Italianate building with a campanile that rises above its Russian Hill location. The school has an illustrious history. Artists who taught there during summer classes or for longer periods include Dorothea Lange, Imogen Cunningham, and Minor White who joined the first fine art photography department that Ansel Adams started in 1945. In the 1940s, the painting faculty included Clyfford Still, David Park, Elmer Bischoff, and Richard Diebenkorn, and in the summer of 1945, visitors Ad Reinhardt and Mark Rothko. In a large, light-filled room off the school's inner courtyard is Diego Rivera's 1931 fresco *The Making of a Fresco Showing the Building of a City*, which many scholars and historians consider his finest work in the United States (except, perhaps, for his fresco at the Detroit Institute of the Arts).

Knowing of this history and of the school's continuing repute, it was with humility and some trepidation that I began my teaching career in the Performance/Video Department, the new department that artist and teacher Howard Fried established to provide a curriculum for the exploration of time-based work in video, performance, and installation.

As an educational institution, the Art Institute was unique and unlike anything I'd encountered before. Rather than a "college," it felt more like a place where artist/teachers met with artist/students and where the distinction between the two was blurred and often entirely obliterated. At least this was my initial experience when I joined the small faculty in 1979. Fried, as department chair, had the authority to hire whomever he liked and to construct a curriculum free from much oversight. Faculty throughout the school taught on year-to-year contracts. There was no tenure, and a starting teacher would be paid the same as someone who had been around for a while, which wasn't much. That was about it for protocol.

The theory was that as working artists we would be drawing some income through our work outside of teaching, which some did. San Francisco in those years was an inexpensive place to live, as I've noted, so one could cobble together a modest living by combining teaching with other part-time jobs, and again, some did. Because our department had a growing reputation for accepting practices that to the more traditional minded would seem outlandish or simply "not art at all," it attracted visitors who shared our values. Some would be in residence for a few days, others for one or more semesters. The list includes Kathy Acker, Brian Routh (The Kipper Kids), Vito Acconci, Marina

3. The San Francisco Art Institute, which had faced financial difficulties in the past, finally succumbed in spring 2022 when it graduated its final cohort of BFA and MFA students. In March 2023, it declared bankruptcy and is, at the time of this writing, in the hands of the court. It is unclear what will happen to the building on Russian Hill or Diego Rivera's renowned fresco.

Abramovic, curators Richard Simmons and David Ross, Lynn Hershman Leeson, Tony Oursler, Tom Marioni, David Ireland, and Linda Montano, among many others. Faculty, visitors, and students represented myriad perspectives, aesthetics, and ways of working. The idea wasn't to create a movement of like artists. On the contrary, it was to recognize and encourage a wide range of tactics for engaging with the world of ideas, social practices, and aesthetics. And it was to create a context in which these practices and ideas could come up against one another—sometimes in conflict—in a forum in which this mess could be sorted out while understanding that this "sorting out" was provisional and available for reexamination on another day with perhaps different conclusions or different participants.

It's not as if we were all best friends. In fact, our faculty, although holding certain principles in common, differed in how we approached our own work and teaching. Relationships could become strained over ideas or just personal conflicts. But for the most part, we got along or at least remained civil and respectful of one another. Importantly, our department had the enthusiastic support of the college president, Stephen Goldstein, which allowed us to prosper in the early years even when there was some skepticism from the more conservative faculty.

Most of the students, undergraduate and graduate, were in their twenties and older, long out of high school. They were perhaps more sophisticated and certainly more jaded and streetwise than the students at VCU, and with few exceptions, up to speed on all the most trendy and hip art fashions of the day. Like the VCU students, most weren't versed in canonical art historical texts from the likes of Heinrich Wölfflin or Erwin Panofsky. They consumed popular culture, had a workable, although limited, knowledge of contemporary art criticism from writers like Hal Foster, and would likely have read essays by Clement Greenberg but not Michael Fried. With few exceptions, their background or interest in critical theory was lacking. Although I was better informed about its various strains than most of the students, my engagement with thinkers like Theodor Adorno, Walter Benjamin, the French structuralists and post-structuralists, Michel Foucault, Martin Heidegger, Jürgen Habermas, and others was eclectic, undisciplined, and amateurish. This never changed, even later, as I passionately dove into these and other difficult texts to satisfy my own curiosity, contextualize ideas that were forming in my mind, or share with students as potential sources that could help ground theirs.

Over the years, I've pursued more deeply and seriously a range of literature, including theory and fiction, that is relevant to my interests and that I felt could inform discussions around students' work. Coming from an earlier academic tradition that demeaned knowledge that wasn't supported by impeccable research, preferably legitimized through a PhD, I was at first shy to bring some of the more challenging materials into a studio setting; art school tradition celebrates practice while denigrating theory and the thinking that

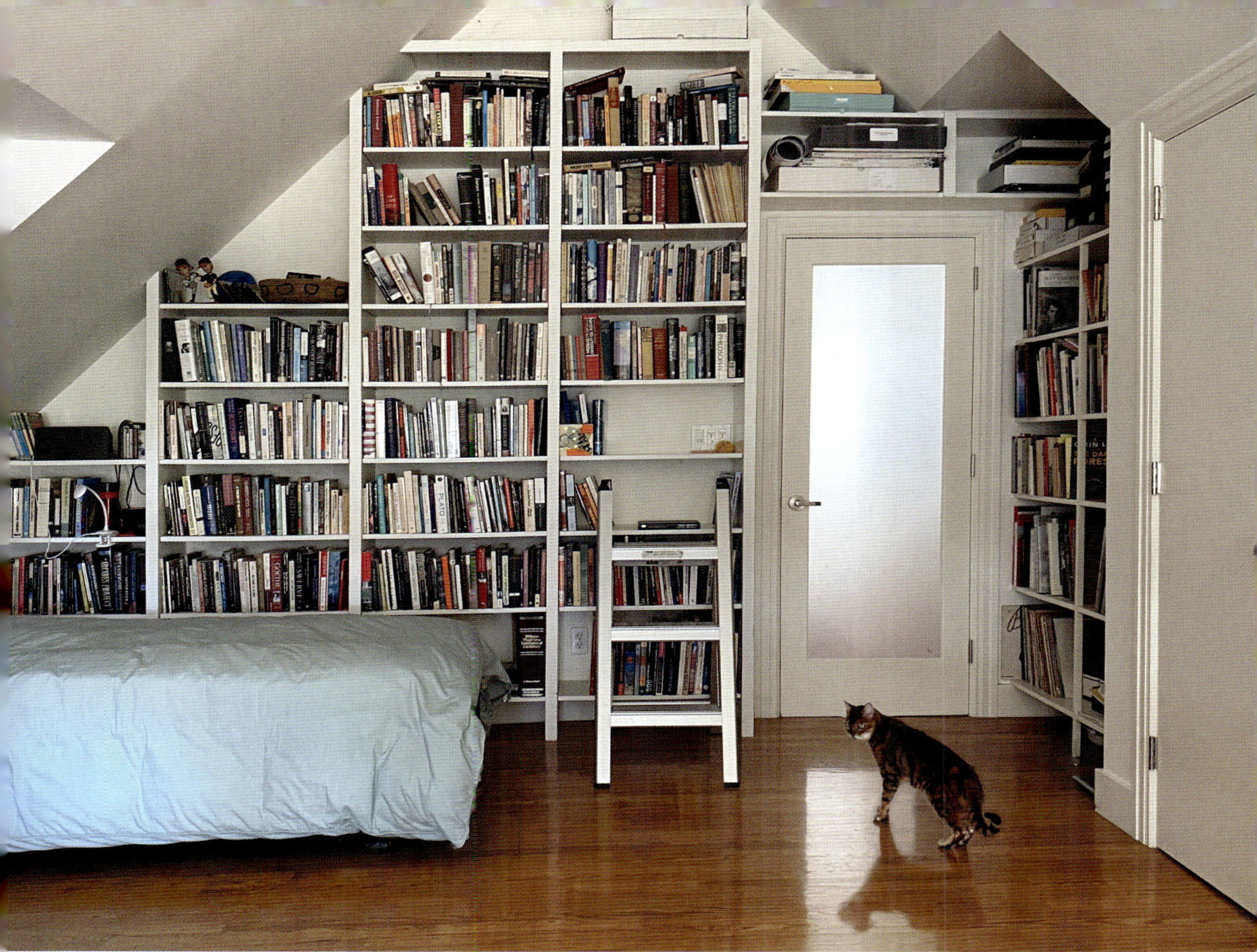

My studio with our cat, Dante, looking for a comfortable place to recline

generates making. In my mind, as exemplified by my practice, the interplay between thinking and making is natural and necessary. My arguments in favor of considering theoretical and literary texts as part of a studio class were based on the idea that being better informed never hurt anyone and that we didn't have to be experts to wrestle with difficult texts. In fact, for the artist, the mistakes that might evolve out of the amateur's misreading could have as much benefit as an academically correct reading. This isn't to make a case that anything goes, and any interpretation is correct. Rather, it is to contend that an argument can be reasoned, rationally and provocatively, without adhering to strict academic protocol—we were not creating scholars with PhDs in philosophy, cultural theory, or rhetoric. The process I wanted to encourage in students was to use the ideas and observations of others to gain more insight into what they were doing. It was on this basis that I encouraged them to read texts that had inspired me and to bring in those that inspired them. To help the process, I put together an ever-expanding annotated reading list, which became notorious around the school, appreciated by some, ridiculed by others. None of the reading was required and the list was eclectic, offering a wide range of ideas, at least a couple of which I hoped would be relevant to

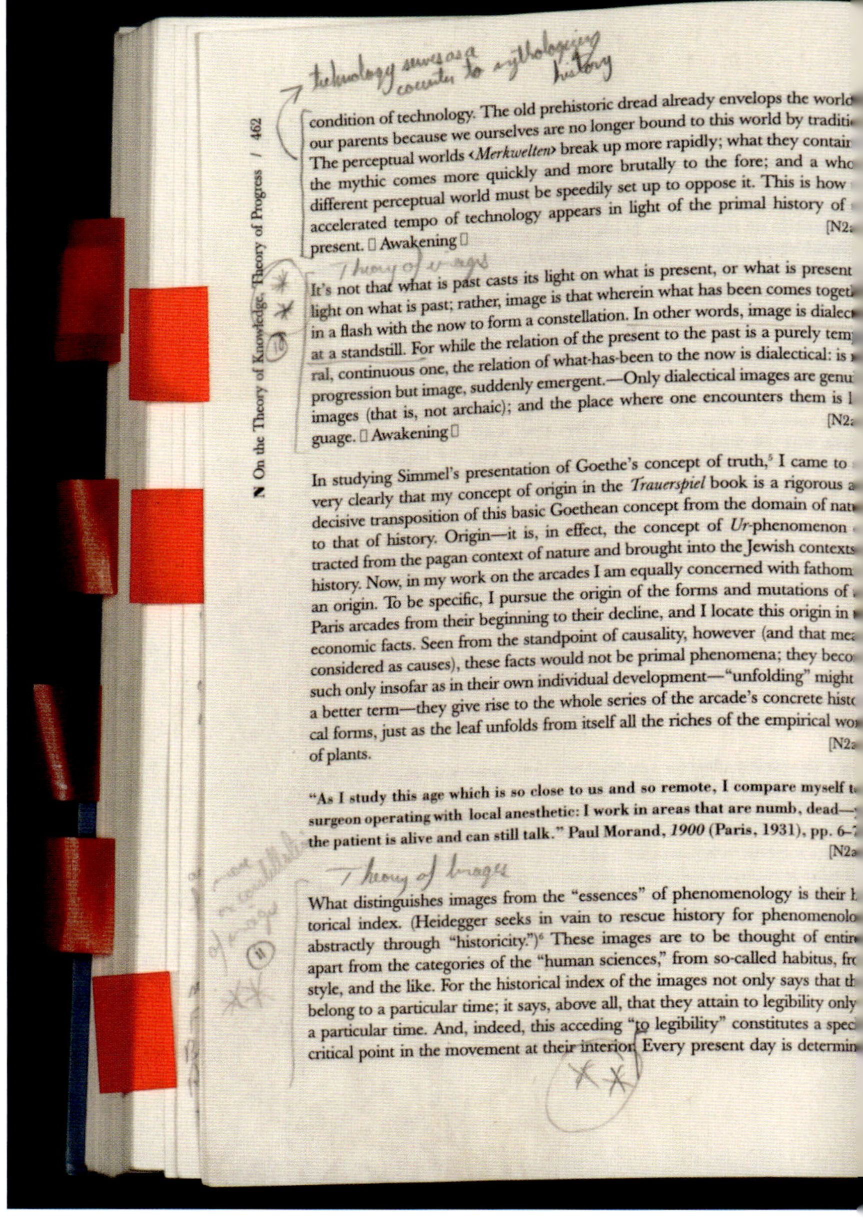

N On the Theory of Knowledge, Theory of Progress / 462

condition of technology. The old prehistoric dread already envelops the world
our parents because we ourselves are no longer bound to this world by traditi
The perceptual worlds ‹*Merkwelten*› break up more rapidly; what they contair
the mythic comes more quickly and more brutally to the fore; and a who
different perceptual world must be speedily set up to oppose it. This is how
accelerated tempo of technology appears in light of the primal history of
present. ▯ Awakening ▯ [N2

It's not that what is past casts its light on what is present, or what is present
light on what is past; rather, image is that wherein what has been comes toget
in a flash with the now to form a constellation. In other words, image is dialec
at a standstill. For while the relation of the present to the past is a purely tem
ral, continuous one, the relation of what-has-been to the now is dialectical: is
progression but image, suddenly emergent.—Only dialectical images are genu
images (that is, not archaic); and the place where one encounters them is l
guage. ▯ Awakening ▯ [N2

In studying Simmel's presentation of Goethe's concept of truth,[5] I came to
very clearly that my concept of origin in the *Trauerspiel* book is a rigorous a
decisive transposition of this basic Goethean concept from the domain of nat
to that of history. Origin—it is, in effect, the concept of *Ur*-phenomenon
tracted from the pagan context of nature and brought into the Jewish contexts
history. Now, in my work on the arcades I am equally concerned with fathom
an origin. To be specific, I pursue the origin of the forms and mutations of
Paris arcades from their beginning to their decline, and I locate this origin in
economic facts. Seen from the standpoint of causality, however (and that mea
considered as causes), these facts would not be primal phenomena; they beco
such only insofar as in their own individual development—"unfolding" might
a better term—they give rise to the whole series of the arcade's concrete hist
cal forms, just as the leaf unfolds from itself all the riches of the empirical wo
of plants. [N2

"As I study this age which is so close to us and so remote, I compare myself t
surgeon operating with local anesthetic: I work in areas that are numb, dead—
the patient is alive and can still talk." Paul Morand, *1900* (Paris, 1931), pp. 6– [N2a

What distinguishes images from the "essences" of phenomenology is their h
torical index. (Heidegger seeks in vain to rescue history for phenomenolo
abstractly through "historicity.")[6] These images are to be thought of entir
apart from the categories of the "human sciences," from so-called habitus, fr
style, and the like. For the historical index of the images not only says that th
belong to a particular time; it says, above all, that they attain to legibility only
a particular time. And, indeed, this acceding "to legibility" constitutes a spec
critical point in the movement at their interior. Every present day is determin

My heavily notated copy of Walter Benjamin's *Arcades Project*, "Convolut N, On the Theory of Knowledge, Theory of Progress"

the wide mix of students. A random sampling includes writings by Giorgio Agamben, Louis Aragon, Hannah Arendt, Homi Bhabha, Franz Kafka, Rosalind Krauss, Edward Said, W. G. Sebald, and Susan Sontag.

The readings I assigned in studio classes were usually short essays selected in response to specific works being shown or as a reaction to a discussion that was going on that could be amplified through the reading. I recognized that some artists are averse to theory. Some are dyslexic and for them, reading, particularly difficult texts, is agony. For me, however, coming upon a particular writer could be like finding a friend in a crowded party filled with

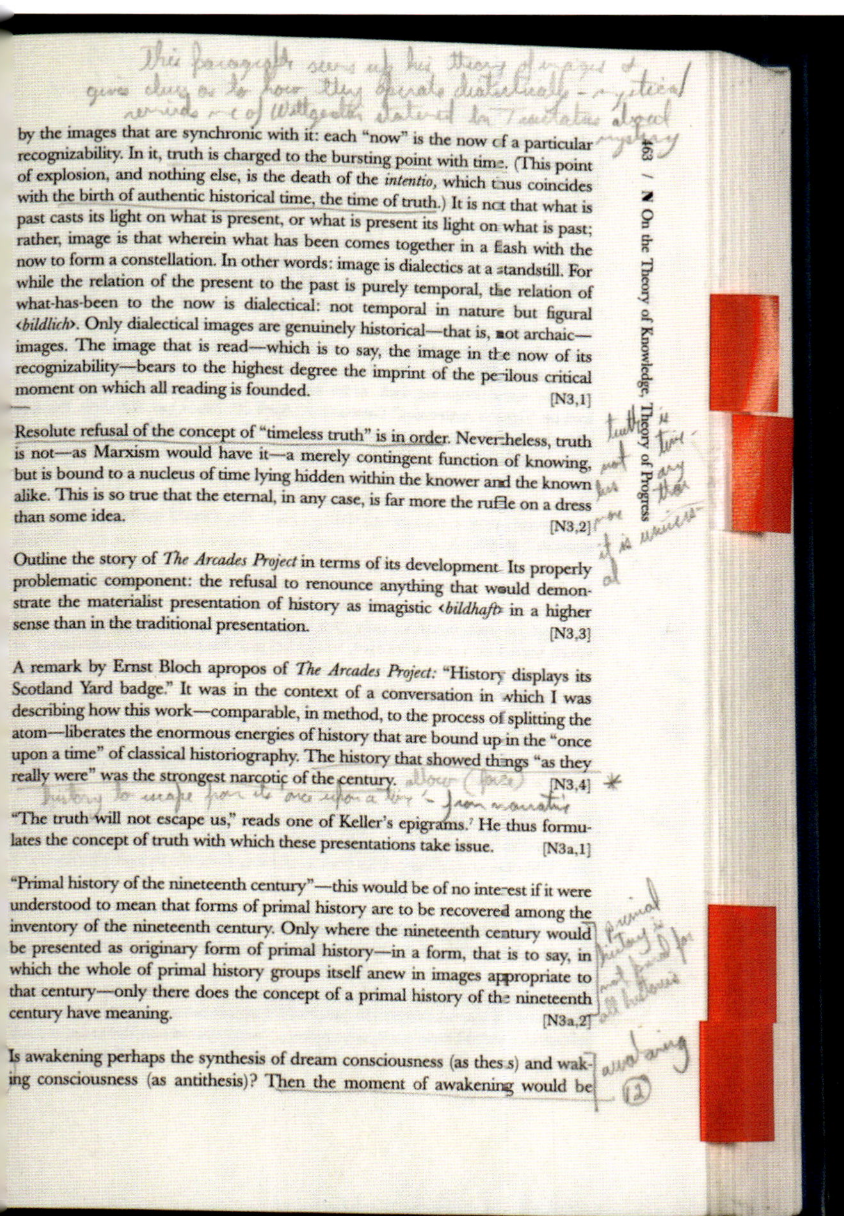

by the images that are synchronic with it: each "now" is the now of a particular recognizability. In it, truth is charged to the bursting point with time. (This point of explosion, and nothing else, is the death of the *intentio,* which thus coincides with the birth of authentic historical time, the time of truth.) It is not that what is past casts its light on what is present, or what is present its light on what is past; rather, image is that wherein what has been comes together in a flash with the now to form a constellation. In other words: image is dialectics at a standstill. For while the relation of the present to the past is purely temporal, the relation of what-has-been to the now is dialectical: not temporal in nature but figural ‹*bildlich*›. Only dialectical images are genuinely historical—that is, not archaic—images. The image that is read—which is to say, the image in the now of its recognizability—bears to the highest degree the imprint of the perilous critical moment on which all reading is founded. [N3,1]

Resolute refusal of the concept of "timeless truth" is in order. Nevertheless, truth is not—as Marxism would have it—a merely contingent function of knowing, but is bound to a nucleus of time lying hidden within the knower and the known alike. This is so true that the eternal, in any case, is far more the ruffle on a dress than some idea. [N3,2]

Outline the story of *The Arcades Project* in terms of its development. Its properly problematic component: the refusal to renounce anything that would demonstrate the materialist presentation of history as imagistic ‹*bildhaft*› in a higher sense than in the traditional presentation. [N3,3]

A remark by Ernst Bloch apropos of *The Arcades Project:* "History displays its Scotland Yard badge." It was in the context of a conversation in which I was describing how this work—comparable, in method, to the process of splitting the atom—liberates the enormous energies of history that are bound up in the "once upon a time" of classical historiography. The history that showed things "as they really were" was the strongest narcotic of the century. [N3,4]

"The truth will not escape us," reads one of Keller's epigrams.[7] He thus formulates the concept of truth with which these presentations take issue. [N3a,1]

"Primal history of the nineteenth century"—this would be of no interest if it were understood to mean that forms of primal history are to be recovered among the inventory of the nineteenth century. Only where the nineteenth century would be presented as originary form of primal history—in a form, that is to say, in which the whole of primal history groups itself anew in images appropriate to that century—only there does the concept of a primal history of the nineteenth century have meaning. [N3a,2]

Is awakening perhaps the synthesis of dream consciousness (as thesis) and waking consciousness (as antithesis)? Then the moment of awakening would be

463 / N On the Theory of Knowledge, Theory of Progress

strangers. Somehow a writer's words—which writer depended on my preoccupations at the time—could bring a degree of clarity, or, in some instances, increased confusion, which for an artist can be as instructive as certainty: both knowing and not-knowing are part of an operation which, for the artist, finds its resolution in the making of things.

As important as I claimed theory to be, I also entertained a healthy suspicion of it, particularly during the final few years of my teaching career. This isn't to say I rejected theory, but I saw what could happen when it was embraced with such fervor that it imposed a rigid academic chokehold on a student, becoming in the process another inhibiting orthodoxy. This is ironic when you consider that theory's gift—the thing that makes it useful for an artist—is that, rather than providing dogmatic rules to stabilize meaning, it introduces uncertainty by recognizing that interpretation is subjective and influenced by a wide set of variables that inform the maker and the viewer. Deconstruction is a way of accounting for those variables, to help us understand how difference emerges among us. But this process can get out of hand when it overpowers an artist's ability to physically make something. There is a time to think in order to construct the platform from which making can happen and a time to actually make something. I am reminded of Ludwig Wittgenstein's warning in his second-to-last entry in *The Tractatus*, where he writes, "My propositions serve as elucidations in the following way: anyone who understands me eventually recognizes them as nonsensical, when he has used them—as steps—to climb up beyond them. (He must, so to speak, throw away the ladder after he has climbed up to it.) He must transcend these propositions, and then he will see the world aright."[4] At a certain point the artist must transcend theories, silence the inner voices that may be derived from those that support our speculative propositions, so that we can hear and see the work itself, and only then will we "see the world aright." For the artist, making is thinking. That can only happen when one is present with the experience as it is taking place.

What I enjoyed about critique seminars, particularly with graduate students, was the give and take that happened among the participants when trying to come to terms with someone's work. To my mind, among the most interesting discussions—also the most contentious and problematic—were the debates around the questions of quality. Is the work being presented good or bad? Is it even legitimate to ask such a question? And if one is willing to offer judgments, what are the criteria upon which they are based? The problem, a most curious one, is that if you accept the idea that "art is a creative act that changes something"[5] then you recognize that the boundaries separating disciplines are extremely porous. Artists are constantly crossing back and forth between mediums—sculpture, video, performance—with the result that, lacking fixed models for establishing hierarchies, any standards for connoisseurship dissolve with a shrug of the shoulders and perhaps a tentative (and critically useless), "I like that."

This conundrum was much less fraught in the late modernist period when there were critical proclamations by Clement Greenberg and others that established rigid aesthetic rules that claimed domination over others with enough self-assured authority and panache to be convincing to most arbiters of high art. Today, to the relief of many, art has been liberated from this kind of

---

4. Ludwig Wittgenstein, *Tractatus Logico-Philosophicus*, 6.54, trans. D. F. Pears, and B. F. McGuinness (London and New York: Routledge Humanities Press International, 1988), 74.
5. This is the answer my eleven-year-old grandson, Atticus, provided when I asked if he could define art.

orthodoxy, so that the process of rendering judgments must take place within an environment that recognizes heterogeneity and the positive role that difference can and must play in our perceptions. This only further problematizes the question around quality: is what I am looking at good or bad and how would I know which?

Earlier I referred to the influential essay "Art and Objecthood" that art writer and scholar Michael Fried wrote in 1967. In the essay, he celebrates the modernist principles that, he argues, rule painting and sculpture to defend them against the infiltration of minimalist or "literalist" sculpture that, by his telling, introduces a kind of theatricality into the mix. According to this line of thinking, the "objectness" of these minimalist sculptures engages the viewer as an active, bodily participant—an actor if you will. This undermines the pure engagement between a person and the relational or formal properties of a work of art that, to be distinguished from any other ordinary, worldly experience, must take place within a moment of quiet reflection. Fried writes, "At this point I want to make a claim that I cannot hope to prove or substantiate but that I believe nevertheless to be true: theater and theatricality are at war today, not simply with modernist painting (or modernist painting and sculpture), but with art as such—and to the extent that the different arts can be described as modernist, with modern sensibility as such."[6] He then claims that this assertion can be broken into three propositions. I will just quote the heading of each (these are numbered and italicized, either entirely or in part, in his original text): The first reads, "The success, even the survival, of the arts has come increasingly to depend on their ability to defeat theater." Here, he is proposing that any distraction that diverts attention from the formal qualities of a work defeats what is essential in our experiencing of art. His second proposition reads, "Art degenerates as it approaches the condition of theater," which relates to the first proposition and prepares us for the third, which reads, "The concepts of quality and value—and to the extent that these are central to art, the concept of art itself—are meaningful, or wholly meaningful, only within the individual arts. What lies between the arts is theater."[7] I have always admired this essay even as I recognized that Fried's formalism, although perhaps comforting in how it sets manageable limits to aesthetic pleasure and in so doing establishes guidelines for a determination of quality, does so by segregating art from any real-world experience (the exact theatricality that he laments) and dooms it to another kind of death—death by irrelevance.

Since the world is a mess, we shouldn't be surprised that the art of our world can also be messy. The problem of good or bad then is not a problem at all, or at least if a problem it has been poorly phrased. Thinking in these terms

6. Michael Fried, *Art and Objecthood: Essays and Reviews* (Chicago: University of Chicago Press, 1998), 163.
7. Ibid., 163–64.

is about as helpful as liking or not liking, which are perfectly acceptable responses—we all exercise them—but are useless if we experience art as thinking made manifest and want to get at this thinking. I want to stress this notion of experiencing: a state of being in which body and mind intercept an object that comes before us. If the object is of interest to us, which is to say arrests our attention for any number of reasons (it is odd, it is beautiful, it is hideous, it is glorious, it is depraved), a process of interpretation takes place that arises out of deep looking. Robert D. Richardson in his biography of William James discusses James's "radical empiricism." This philosophical position relies on experience rather than absolutes, and proposes that experiences are constructed out of many colliding parts, much, I think, in the way that Walter Benjamin writes about fragments of knowledge as constellations.[8] What we call knowledge is a sorting out of these fragments and as such is contextual (what do they refer to? where do they come from?), dynamic (they are mediated by their time and ours), and most of all provisional (what is true now may be less true or not true at all later). Richardson writes, "Empiricism, [James] insists, is the opposite of rationalism. Rationalism tends to emphasize universals and to make wholes prior to parts. Empiricism on the contrary lays the explanatory stress upon the part, the element, the individual, and treats the whole as a collection, and the universal as an abstraction. To be radical, an empiricism must neither admit into its construction any element that is not directly experienced nor exclude from them any element that is directly experienced."[9] This idea that experience comes to us in parts that we add up into *some thing*, that this resulting thing is not universal—in other words, is contextual and may well be seen differently by different individuals looking from different prior experiences and points of view—is relevant when critiquing art.

So, where does this leave us, say, in a critique seminar of students working differently and embracing different ideas, methodologies, materials, sexual orientations, races, economic backgrounds, and the like? At its worst, it can doom us to a perpetual state of indecisive relativism in which one point of view is as valid as another, a deadly recipe for a process that is attempting to experience and be critical of the proliferation of things. At its best, it reminds us that proclamations about such things as quality are compromised by all

---

8. Admittedly I am distorting Benjamin's thoughts about how images organize into constellations, since he's thinking about how the past collides with the present, and the images he refers to are words not pictures. But I believe his concept is relevant to how we experience and come to terms with works of art. They tend to smolder or burst forward in much the same way as Benjamin's past and present flash into legibility. He writes, "It's not that what is past casts its light on what is present, or what is present its light on what is past; rather, image is that wherein what has been comes together in a flash and with the now to form a constellation. In other words, image is dialectics at a standstill." Walter Benjamin, *The Arcades Project*, "Convolute N, On the Theory of Knowledge, Theory of Progress," trans. Howard Eiland and Kevin McLaughlin (Cambridge, MA: Belknap Press of Harvard University, 1999), 462.

9. Robert D. Richardson, *William James: In the Maelstrom of American Modernism* (Boston: Houghton Mifflin Harcourt, 2006), 449.

kinds of cultural assumptions and that a serious critique of art requires that we address these assumptions directly and honestly. There are no universals here. There are no fixed truths. There are paths toward understanding, fluid, not static, like temporary lanes cut through the surf by a swimmer.

We are encouraged to confront works of art on their own terms. Perhaps we start by asking, "What have they set out to do?" Regardless of their vastly different aesthetics, motivating influences, and differing agendas we can, with few exceptions, identify a series of facts about what we are looking at. From these and our own subjective responses to them, we can venture informed insights as to where the work is taking us—what I call "the work of the work." There may not be agreement about this, which in itself is interesting. We may find ourselves critiquing our own assumptions. We look at the details. At how things add up, or don't. We may determine that the work is trying to do too much; using a literary metaphor, we might argue that it has too many dangling modifiers that muddy the experience, neutralizing rather than enhancing our experience or understanding. And there may be strong disagreements about this. That our disagreements cannot be resolved is not a problem. Art is conversational. It is not about certainty. The artist, through the work, takes us on a tour of thoughts and ideas. There can be no question that some works do this better than others. But it isn't a question of good or bad or right or wrong. It is a matter of what processes best convey the intention of the artist, and of recognizing that there are as many intentions as there are people with them. We stand before works with our own baggage—White heterosexual male, African American, transgender woman, Latinx. One of us was raised in the suburbs of New England, another in the Bronx, or in the barrio of El Paso. What we can know of one another will have limitations based on our separate experiences, but I would make the claim that if we are blessed with the normal amount of empathy and we have had enough experience in the world, both personal and perhaps through education, we should be able to at least imagine the life of another, and walk gently in their shoes. And there are a lot of human experiences that we all share regardless of where we were born or our race. This isn't to discount difference, which is real and is central to the work of some artists, but if the work is good (here I go doing the good and bad thing) it shouldn't eliminate others from sharing in some aspect of the experience.

I recall many years ago when the artist Nayland Blake was living and working in San Francisco, and they declared that they made their work for a queer audience. And there could be no question of that in their imagery, which in this body of work consisted of tools and apparatuses one would equate with sadomasochism, and yet, as a straight male, I was captivated by the work. Why was that? The provocative nature of the devices was both alluring and disarming because one could imagine one's own body under assault. I felt, or at least could imagine, my own vulnerability to pain and sensation. I would also accept that I missed a lot that would have been obvious, perhaps even funny, to those more familiar with the world the works referred to. Aside from the imagery, there was also something—dare I say it— formally satisfying in the way the surfaces and materials interacted with one another. As sculpture, the objects were interesting and captivating. You didn't have to be queer or into S&M to appreciate them.

Critique, particularly group critique, can be a fraught experience. The presenting artist is before colleagues and a seminar leader who collectively open the artist's work to intense scrutiny. For the more vulnerable, it can be like having your emotions mercilessly probed. I believe that critique should be direct and honest, but it also needs to be delivered with a degree of humility and a great deal of respect for the process, both of making art and of turning the art into language. All of this requires trust. Critique should not be a brutal confrontation for anyone participating but a means to a discussion. If this process is carried out with integrity, including mutual respect for all voices, then everyone benefits. Indeed, the lessons of empathy and rigorous investigation stand together, not as opposites but as complements, and are relevant far beyond their rarefied applications to art school pedagogy.

On Language as Such

A work of art cannot claim itself as such randomly—the idea that it is art simply because I say it is. Part of the context in which art exists is cultural, established by precedence, by the rules of the game, so to speak. These rules are constantly being expanded and shifted, and part of what we experience as we look at and think about and discuss art is how and why this is taking place. Another way to think about this is to consider the making of art as an operation that occurs within historical, philosophical, and cultural norms into which the artist intercedes. Poetic language, for example, is a figuration (a manipulation of linguistic rules governing grammar, phonology, and semantics) of normative language that, when subverted by the poet, allows new meanings to be revealed that are buried beneath the ubiquity of everyday language.

Group critique was a crucial part of my studio classes where we attempted to find language to describe and explain our reactions to the work students presented. In the early 1980s, I had a surprising indication of the response that language, even a single word, could trigger when I was teaching an advanced undergraduate class in the Performance/Video Department at the San Francisco Art Institute. We were in the middle of a discussion and one of the students was expressing her thoughts about a triptych of synchronized videos by another student in which each monitor showed a segment of his nude body: head, shoulders, and upper chest; abdomen and genitals; legs and feet. At the start, the three sections were aligned with the full figure facing the viewer, his torso and head propped up by his elbow, arm, and hand. Eventually the segments fell out of alignment as the figure moved, creating the uncanny impression that the body was in fragments.

The conversation was all very congenial and straightforward, the comments preceptive and generous. At some point, one of the students (I'll call her Isabel) jumped up and ran out of the room in an apparent state of anguish. I was stunned. We all were. What had happened? Was something said that was so offensive as to warrant such a response? It wasn't even Isabel's work that was being discussed. No doubt she was an unusual student. She often appeared on edge and could quickly change from being present and engaged to acting distant and perhaps bored. Her work, usually performances with erotic overtones or similarly themed videos, could be brilliant, unique, and well considered and at other times appear thrown together. But even the thrown together moments contained at least a spark of intelligence and passion. In conversation she was always lucid and came at things from unusual, unpredictable angles that we all learned from. She was a respected and important member of the group, which made her sudden rush for the exit that much more mysterious and disconcerting. I needed to get to the bottom of it. Moreover, I had been teaching long enough to know that a respected student who suddenly expresses discontent with a class can sabotage the entire enterprise, so that whatever atmosphere of rigor and trust we have managed to foster deteriorates into something negative and destructive.

We took a break, and I went to find Isabel. I didn't have to go far. She was sitting on a wall right outside the studio. The other students had the good sense to drift away so that we could talk privately. She had been crying and was clearly still upset. "Are you okay?" I awkwardly asked since it was clear she was not. Her response was fascinating. First, she apologized profusely for her behavior and then went into an explanation of what had happened. She told me that she suffered from schizophrenia and perhaps other mental health conditions, which, for the most part, her medications kept reasonably under control. But certain words when spoken by others triggered unpredictable reactions in her that were diagnosed by her psychiatrist as severe momentary panic attacks. The thing I found so interesting was that, according to her, these reactions had nothing to do with the content of the words, with what they meant, but only with how they sounded to her. "The weird thing," she explained, "is there seems to be no pattern about which words will cause the reaction. A word that caused a panic attack on one occasion might not do the same on another."

Whatever instinct I had to comfort her, which of course I did initially, had now been replaced by curiosity. Perhaps she was relieved to see how interested I was, or the attack had simply run its course. In either case, her anguish or embarrassment dissipated and as it did, some of the students drifted over as we continued to discuss the idea that certain words could be toxic. She did note that often it was polysyllabic words that affected her and sometimes they contained the sound we make with words that have the *ch* sound (like cherubic, I thought to myself without daring to say it out loud). But she went on to say this was not always the case. Furthermore, the reaction was so spontaneous and fast she often didn't know what word had caused it. One of the students asked if other sounds, music for example, ever had the same affect. She said no. It was just words.

As she was obviously over the crisis and as interested in the discussion as the rest of us, we drifted back into the studio, where the conversation continued. "How do you know," I asked, "that it isn't the content of the word and only the sound?" She admitted that it wasn't out of the question that the content of the words registered in some unconscious way. We talked about the idea of taboo in which certain words were seen as magical or potentially dangerous and could only be spoken by designated people, usually from the priestly cast, and only under particular circumstances. Within groups that recognized such taboos, it was believed that breaking them could result in bad luck for the individual or, worse, famine or plague for the entire clan or larger tribe. This led us into a short discussion about William Burroughs and his famous quote: "Language is a virus from outer space."

I recognized we were veering off the immediate subject since, as I recalled, perhaps inaccurately, Burroughs's idea was that language was like a virus in that it can spread information wide and far but also can lead, through those who control it, to social and political domination. After about a half an hour of further speculation, we decided it was time to get back to the critiques we were doing while agreeing to avoid any polysyllabic words with the *ch* sound, a condition that made Isabel laugh, which, in turn, dissipated whatever tension remained in the room.

When I got home that evening, still vibrating from what I had now come to think of as the magical potential of language, I recalled Benjamin's "On Language as Such, and on the Language of Man" (1916). In this essay, he claims that all things have language; the language of man is given sonic representation, whereas the language of things is mute. We can only know those things we resemble. Things (objects) recognize their thingness in each other, and language (an ability to name) is our way of establishing similarity between ourselves and things. But the language of modern man has stepped outside of itself and has lost its ability to merge with the energy of objects. Instead, we are left with a language of judgment and analysis. Although lost, the explosive potential of language, its capacity for immediate participation, has not disappeared. It can be found, for example, in the languages of preindustrial people where the magical, unmediated connection between language and thing has not been corrupted. The capacity for recognizing the similarities between language and thing is magical—language, therefore, is a survival of ancient magic in which name and thing were of the same order. The "primitive" mind perceives living forces in things that the civilized mind considers dead. For us, a name is only a label and, as such, conceals what is essential rather than conveying the interrelatedness of people, things, and the powers of each. Thinking about Isabel's panic attack in this context, I wondered if what she experienced during these occasional disruptions was a sudden awareness of the mystical force of language—a jolt that in its uncanniness disabled her but also allowed her momentary insight that remained unavailable to the rest of us. That evening I finished my thoughts about language by listening to Laurie Anderson's "Language Is a Virus from Outer Space":

> Paradise is exactly like
> Where you are right now
> Only much much better
> (It's a shipwreck)
> (It's a job)
> You know?
> I don't believe there's such a thing as TV
> I mean – they just keep showing
> The same pictures over and over
> And when they talk they just make sounds
> That more or less synch up
> With their lips
> That's what I think
> Language
> It's a virus
> Language
> It's a virus
> Language
> It's a virus[10]

10. Laurie Anderson, "Language Is a Virus from Outer Space," Warner Bros. Records, 1986.

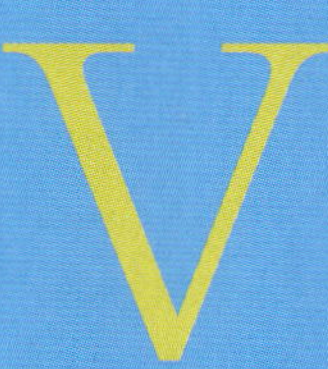

What It Is Is Figuring Out What It Is

The Eternal Frame

Jody, Diane, and I met members of Ant Farm, a collective of renegade architects and media artists, in 1969, shortly after we arrived in San Francisco. The introduction was through Hudson Marquez, a member of the group whom Diane knew from Tulane where they had both been undergraduate art majors. The other Ant Farmers were Doug Michels, a graduate of the Yale School of Architecture; Chip Lord, also a Tulane alumnus; and Curtis Schreier, who received his BA degree from the Rhode Island School of Design. It was a fortuitous meeting that led to deep friendships, particularly with Michels, who tragically died in 2003 from a fall while whale watching in Australia, and Lord, who has remained over the years a close friend, collaborator, and confidant.

It was in late 1975, on the second floor of our newly purchased house on Twenty-third Street, now our studio, where Jody and I, with Diane popping in and out, plotted with Chip and Doug our outlandish idea to reenact the Kennedy assassination in Dallas. By this time, Hudson had left Ant Farm to work with the pioneering video collective TVTV. Curtis, still an important member of Ant Farm, had little interest in our subversive assassination fantasies, although he helped modify the Lincoln convertible that would eventually carry the Artist-Presidential party through Dealey Plaza.

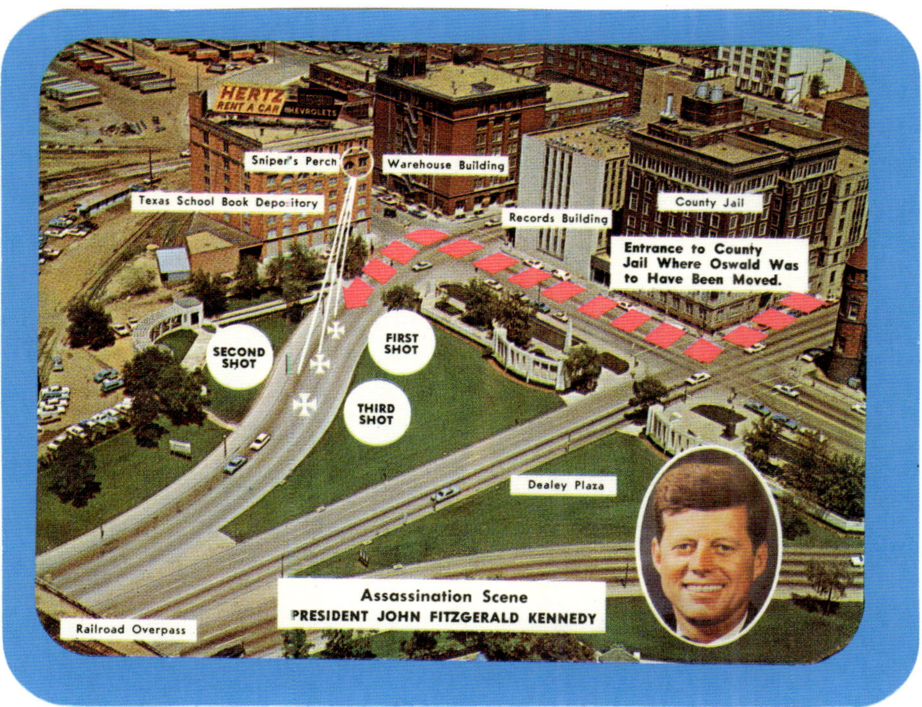

Commemorative postcard, sold at the Kennedy Museum, located on the ground floor of the Texas School Book Depository, Dealey Plaza, Dallas

Jody's and my shared investment in politics dated back to our college days—some of our more substantial political insights grew out of our exposure to leftist academics with whom we brushed shoulders while at Harvard. Jody was a serious modern history major who wrote a magna cum laude undergraduate thesis on some arcane historical event, and he was always fun to engage with in political discussions that often mixed absurdist musings with well-grounded insight. My academic interests tended to be more anthropological and cultural. As an artist I was fascinated by how power could be expressed through gesture, language, intonation, and staging. I saw politics as a form of theater and was not alone in thinking that no politician managed the elements of the role better than John F. Kennedy.[1]

Inaugurated in 1961, the young, debonair Kennedy along with his elegant wife shimmered and glowed from within the nation's TV sets. The media fell in love with them and encouraged us to do the same. JFK became the gallant prince and Jackie his princess. Later, shortly after Kennedy's assassination, which added martyrdom to the growing heroism myth, the former first lady in a *Life* Magazine interview with the historian-journalist Theodore H. White made a comparison between her husband's short presidency and Camelot, the fabled chivalrous kingdom of King Arthur and Lancelot. She claimed Kennedy was taken by the lyrics of King Arthur's final song from the 1960 Broadway production *Camelot,* "Don't let it be forgot, that once there was a spot, for one brief shining moment that was known as Camelot." That image only grew and ballooned over time and, despite more honest contemporary counternarratives, persists in some circles to this day.

We love our heroes and love them even more if martyred. Time stands still for those who die young. They linger before us, uncontaminated by future bad fortune, questionable morals, ethical missteps, or the ravages of age. If martyred in glory as was JFK, a person can become an icon, a symbol, or a cipher that absorbs all the emotions or fantasies we care to bring to it.

A country that was obsessed with the Kennedys became transfixed by JFK's assassination, empathetic to Jackie's grief, horrified by the televised shooting of suspected assassin Lee Harvey Oswald by nightclub owner Jack Ruby—and deeply moved by the spectacle of the fallen president's funeral. The world watched in unison, momentarily linked in shared grief, as the military pallbearers stepped out of Saint Matthew's Cathedral carrying the slain president's flag-draped coffin, followed by Jacqueline Kennedy, veiled in mourning, a restless child grasping each hand. It was here, at the bottom of the cathedral steps, where the former first lady leaned down and whispered in her toddler son John's ear, and he responded to her urging by saluting his

1. Although by today's standards, the media landscape in the early 1960s was primitive, with only three major networks, each with its own evening news anchor. At NBC it was Huntley and Brinkley; CBS had Walter Cronkite; ABC had several different anchors in an attempt to move up from their dismal third-place standing in the Nielsen ratings.

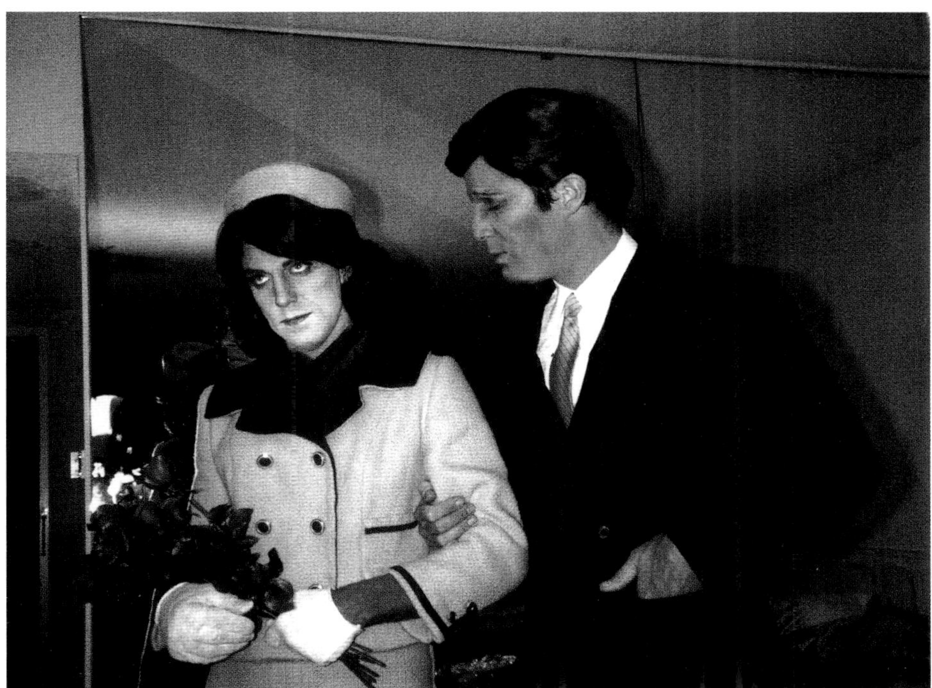

Artist-Jackie (Doug Michels) and the Artist-President (Doug Hall) on their way to Dealey Plaza, *The Eternal Frame*, 1975
Photograph by Diane Andrews Hall

father's coffin. America and the world sighed and dabbed tissues at its collective eyes. The pathos mounted as the horse-drawn caisson made its way along Connecticut Avenue to Arlington National Cemetery. Behind it strode a riderless horse, black boots reversed in the stirrups, restrained by a Marine handler. Family members and heads of state from around the world followed. After them, soldiers from all the services marched in perfect unison, and military bands played mournful, patriotic songs; flags waved, and tearful, silent citizens lined the funeral route. It was all heartbreaking. And it was strangely beautiful.

Over the course of his presidency, culminating in his assassination, I and others began to see Kennedy as the first media or televisual president, an idea of a president as youthful, charismatic, worldly wise, and modern (even if the Prince of Camelot). It was a representation constructed around a willing participant through careful marketing and a deep understanding of how an image can gather weight and veracity when artfully and strategically injected into the media streams of popular culture. Of course, there had been others. FDR comes to mind, but television galvanized us in ways that radio and newsreels never could. Kennedy lived and essentially even died on TV.

Although I couldn't articulate this contemporaneously, I began to understand that images of this sort can become so dense and, in some cases, so magnificent that they transcend the ordinary and ascend into the iconic. When this occurs, meaning migrates. The images surrounding an event (in this case, the assassination of a president) separate from the event itself and assume unrelated significances. Analogically, it is like a snowball rolling down a hill. As it rolls, it picks up much of the debris that lies in its path—sticks, pebbles, maybe a mitten or two, a lost charm bracelet—so that in the end it contains more than the original snowball. It is a repository of everything that stuck to it. So it is with certain images. As representations of events circulate through our media landscape, playing over and over in some sort of structuralist film loop, they become magnets for the myriad ideas and feelings we bring to them. These they then release back to us, packaged by media companies for our consumption with logos, inspiring graphics, and theme songs. We easily fall under the spell of these troubling episodes.

Meaning is not stagnant. The facts about what has happened are plain and simple in many cases. Then, if the event is significant enough, it circulates, rolls along collecting emotions, feelings, stories that lie in its path. Meaning is distorted, and is always distorting. It migrates from the truth of an occurrence to the fictions and beliefs that stick to its mediated representations. They in turn ricochet through the culture until they take up restless residence in our shared consciousness. In the case of Kennedy, and particularly his assassination, the snowball is penetrated by everything from conspiracy theories and mythic hyperbole to feelings of deep patriotism and even love, but most significantly with loss of innocence. Terrible events—assassinations, dictatorships, wars, political corruption—were seen from the American shores as happening "over there," never here. Suddenly, this American conceit was annihilated. Little did any of us know at the time that Kennedy's violent death was a harbinger of things to come. Walter Benjamin wrote, "History decays into images, not into stories."[2] I would modify this observation somewhat by suggesting that history decays into images that become ciphers through which all kinds of stories circulate, proliferate, and mutate.

And so, one winter evening in 1975, Ant Farm and T. R. Uthco, joined in a commitment to subvert media culture, met in our attic studio to muse and conspire around the event, the terrible image—a sacred icon—that haunted the American psyche: the assassination of JFK.

Jody and I had a significant head start when it came to playing with—in later times, we might call it deconstructing—the Kennedy image going all the way back to our college days, although our approach then was more along the lines of a prank than anything serious. During my junior year, I was invited to join the Signet Society, Harvard's only literary club, which was populated by the more artsy undergraduates, including students like Doug Kenney of the *Harvard Lampoon* (and later *National Lampoon*) and Tim Mayer, the Harvard theater producer, director, and playwright I had briefly worked with. It was Mayer, at the time president of the Signet, who invited me to join. As part of

2. Benjamin, *The Arcades Project,* "Convolute N11,4," 476.

the initiation, one was required to do some sort of oral presentation following lunch at the club on Dunster Street; this was expected to be clever, filled with obscure literary and cultural references as well as amusing anecdotes that would titillate the minds of the aspiring, in some cases actual, literati gathered around the dining tables. The prospect of addressing this group of cynical sophisticates gave me the dry-mouth terrors.

When with friends, as a rule, after a few drinks I could be coaxed into doing my JFK impersonation that was inspired by the immensely popular LP *The First Family* by the comedian Vaughn Meader, in which he spoofed Kennedy in an overstated version of the famous accent. But for the Signet I needed something more. After serious thought and with only increasing anxiety, I approached Jody with the idea that he would be my "speechwriter" and help me write a speech about making a speech at the Signet. We decided it would only be interesting if we drew some of the content from the club's history, details of the room where the speech would be delivered, and references to some of the better-known former club members such as Robert Frost, T. S. Eliot, and Norman Mailer. With a strategy in mind, we managed to gain entry to the club in advance of my presentation and took note of pictures on the walls, architectural flourishes, furnishings, and the like. We fashioned a speech that probed the pretensions of the event while I, using my best Kennedy accent, dressed in my charcoal gray suit, assumed "presidential" poses and gestures associated with the deceased president. I thought my speech about making a speech while mimicking the theatrics of the political speech was outrageously funny (in retrospect, maybe more outrageous than funny, since in 1965 Kennedy's death was still recent history). I recall there were a few chuckles throughout (no catcalls or Bronx cheers), but I must admit the response was more tepid than I had hoped for. Little did we know, at the time, where all of this was leading.

When we all moved to California, formed T. R. Uthco, and in the early to mid-seventies put our show on the road, we needed performances to fall back on when we were unable to mount the elaborate stage show *Great Moments*. We settled on a couple. My favorite was a series of odd, generally unfathomable gestures that Jody and I would enact together, always dressed in our suits, under the title *Eight Gestures*. The performance consisted of holding a series of poses for a short period as tableaux vivants. Each would be introduced by one of us coming out onto the stage and announcing it. "Gesture Number One," one of us would say before leaving the performance area to return a moment later with the other. All very restrained as we quietly arranged ourselves, perhaps changed position, maybe one of us would go up to the other and slightly alter the position of a hand or arm before assuming our own pose. The only sounds would be our footfalls, perhaps the creaking floorboards, and sometimes a rustle or an anxious murmuring from the audience. Once in position, we would hold it there for a few minutes before one would decide to break, followed by the other, and would exit the stage before returning for the

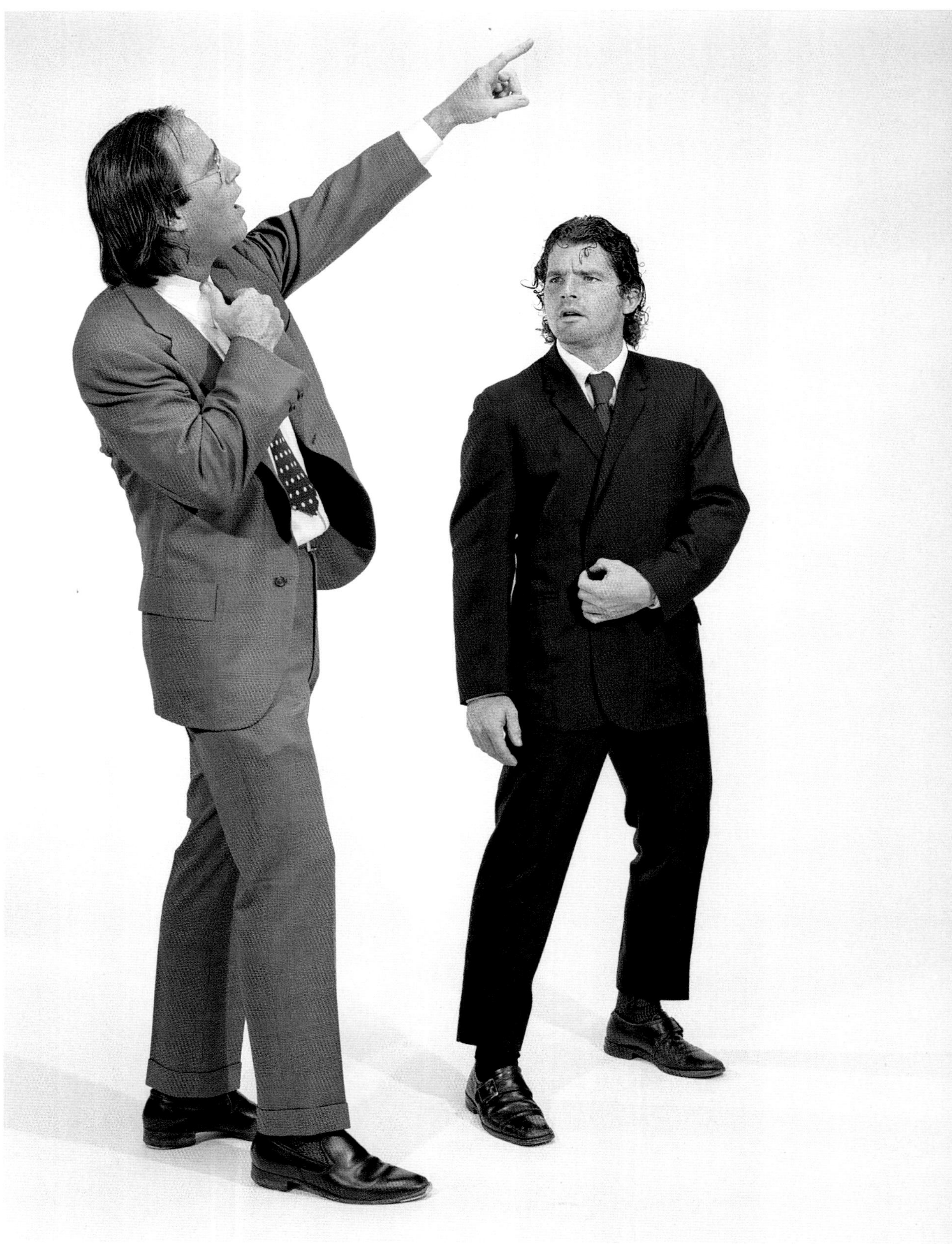

"Gesture III" from *Eight Gestures,* T. R. Uthco, 1972
Photograph by T. R. Uthco (Diane Andrews Hall)

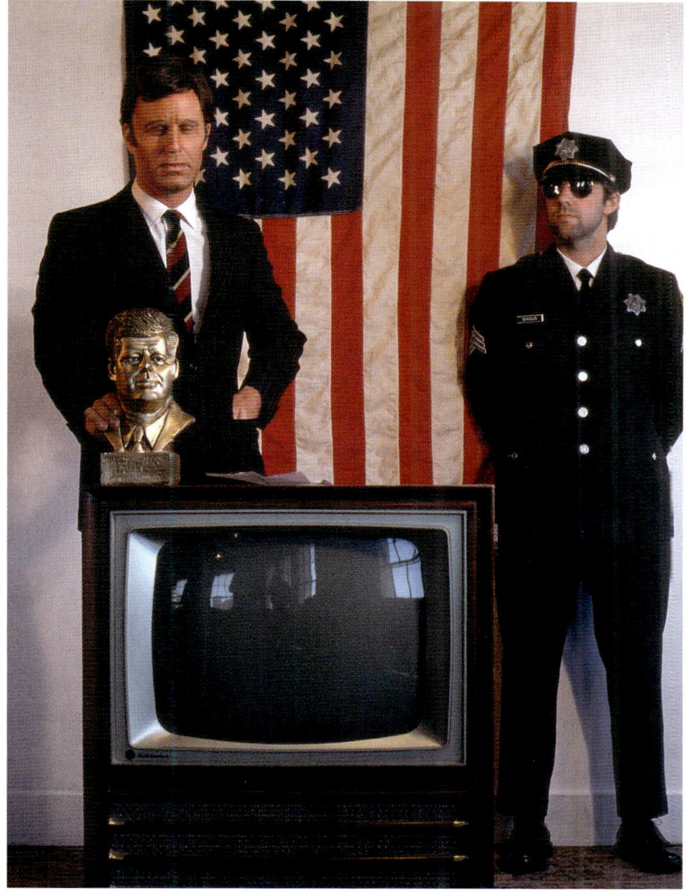

The Artist-President with Officer Dingus (Doug Michels)
Photograph by Chip Lord

next pose. Our appearances were usually sponsored by college art departments with small audiences consisting of students, some required to attend, a few just curious, and if we were lucky and there had been adequate publicity, interested people from the local arts community.

Our other performance consisted of a speech I would make as the Artist-President with Jody acting as Secret Service. We even had an Artist-President seal that we could stick on the front of a lectern to give us that added touch of credibility. Like our earlier Signet foray, these performances were heavily gestured, spoken with my Kennedy accent, and included verbal play and references to the act of delivering a political speech, including comments about the audience and sometimes my own actions ("I am placing my left hand into my suit jacket pocket, indicating self-assurance, confidence, and a generally relaxed demeanor"). We might combine the two, *Speech* and *Gestures*, by ending *Gestures* with the Artist-President's speech. It depended on the amount of time we were expected to fill.

I don't recall who, on the winter evening in 1975, came up with the outlandish idea of reenacting the assassination of JFK at the site of the actual,

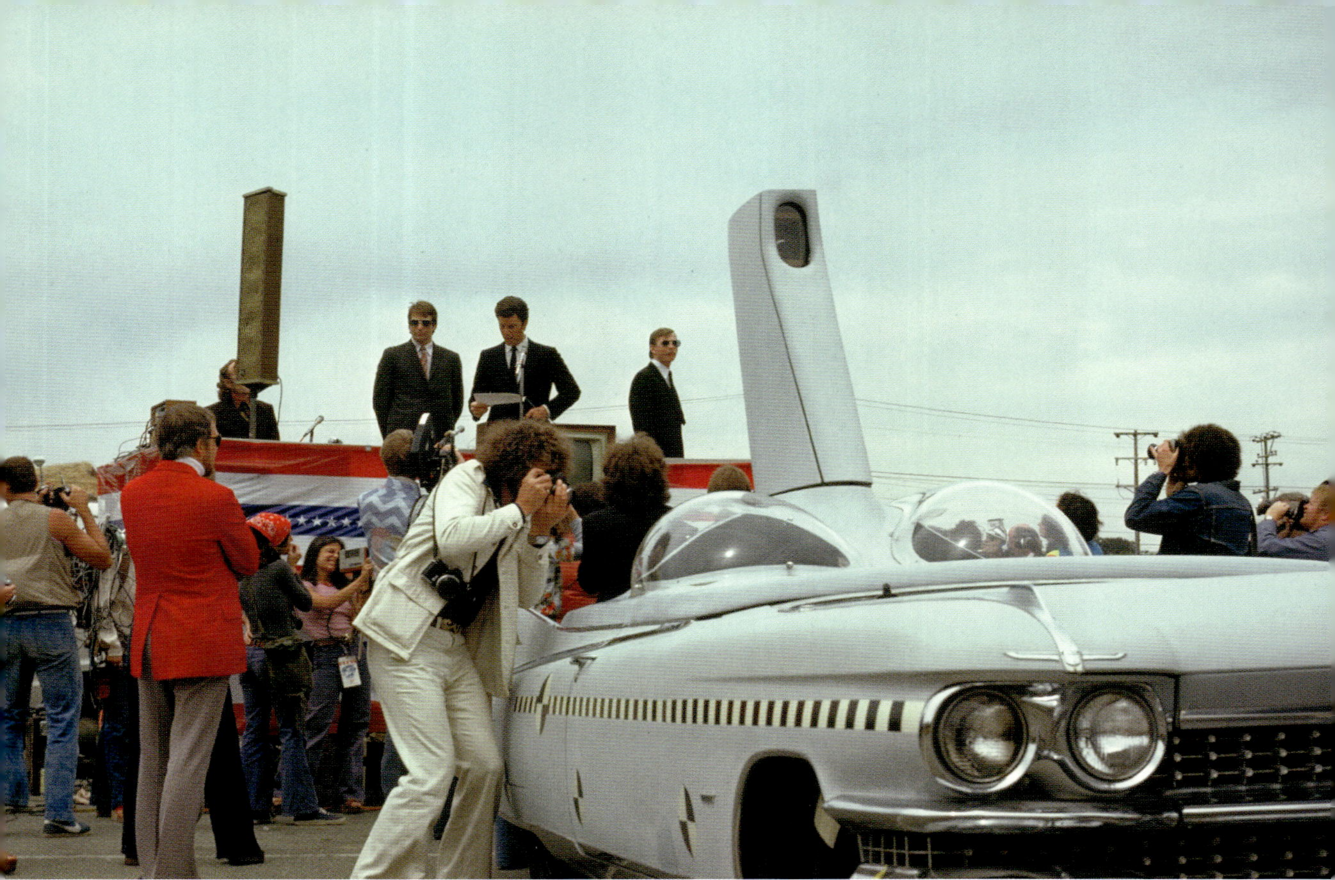

The Artist-President delivering the keynote address at Ant Farm's *Media Burn*, Cow Palace, Daly City, July 4, 1975
Photograph by Chip Lord

traumatizing event. I do remember that while recognizing the perversity of our intention, there was an overriding investigative impulse to interrogate an image—one that seemed almost untouchable, as well as impenetrable—and we knew the only way to achieve that was to fully embrace it. We needed to throw our bodies and psyches into the image and do it on the same stage in Dallas, Texas, where the actual event occurred, and the image originated.

While we were organizing our assassination reenactment, Ant Farm was preparing *Media Burn*, their spectacular critique of the media, featuring, as the central metaphor, a customized Cadillac (the Phantom Dream Car) crashing through a wall of burning televisions. Their event, scheduled for July 4, 1975, was to take place a month before our anticipated August performance in Dallas, and seemed a perfect stage for the Artist-President to deliver a major address. This would both provide a context for *Media Burn* and also be a dress rehearsal for my future role as a JFK surrogate, destined for assassination in Dealey Plaza.[3]

Originally, Jody as my Ted Sorenson (speechwriter and adviser to President Kennedy) was commissioned to write the *Media Burn* address, but Chip and Doug decided, correctly in hindsight, that Jody's writing was too

3. For a detailed and compelling account of *Media Burn*, see Steve Seid's *Media Burn: Ant Farm and the Making of an Image* (Los Angeles / San Francisco: Inventory Press / RITE Editions, 2020).

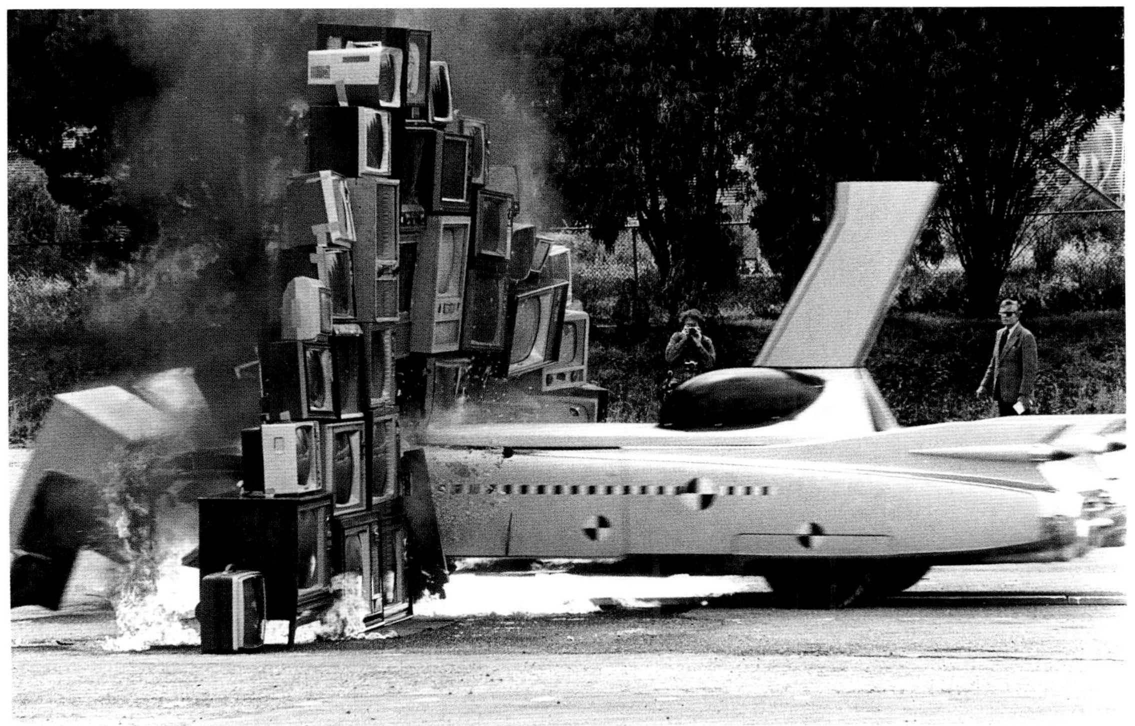

Ant Farm's Phantom Dream Car crashing through a pyramid of flaming televisions at *Media Burn*
Photograph by Diane Andrews Hall

satirical and demanded a rewrite. They turned to a speech by senator and defeated presidential candidate George McGovern printed in the March 13, 1975, *Rolling Stone* titled, "The State of the Union." It formed the basis of the Artist-President's *Media Burn* speech, with our alterations to make it more appropriate for their event. Jody and I tweaked it further to better capture the Kennedy-esque cadence.

To secure funding for our Dallas adventure, we had put together a proposal that included a brief rationale and a budget. Doug Michels contacted Doug Kenney at the *National Lampoon*, whom I knew superficially from Harvard. Michels was an excellent pitchman and managed to convince Kenney that we could produce a series of still images that would make sense for his magazine. Much later, we learned that his acceptance and willingness to fund our project as a multipage spread in the magazine led to a heated debate that pitched Kenney and a few of his allies against most of the staff, who found the proposal offensive and stupid.

Stanley Marsh III, a wealthy Texan, on whose land Ant Farm's *Cadillac Ranch* was installed, agreed to help finance the project with a stipulation: Marsh would play the role of Governor John Connally, who along with his wife, Nellie—played by Natasha Hubsman, Michels's girlfriend—accompanied the Kennedys in the car when the fatal shots were fired.

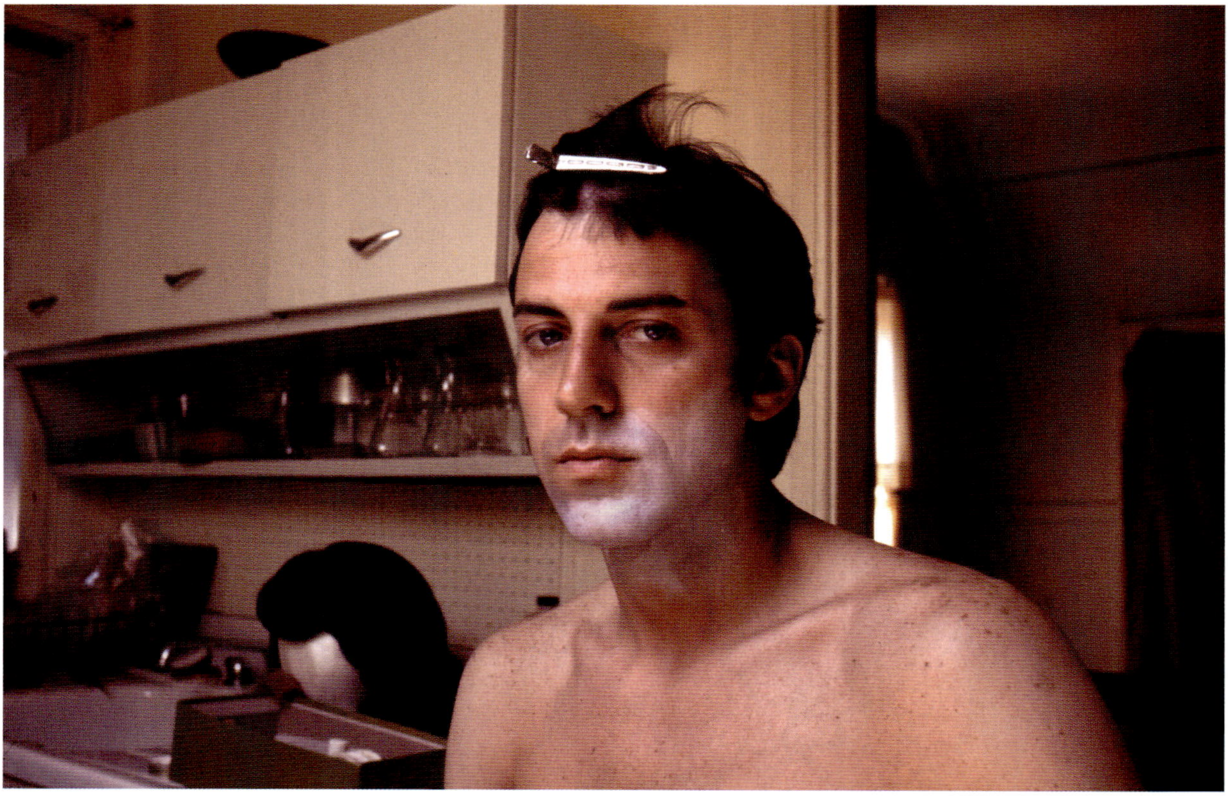

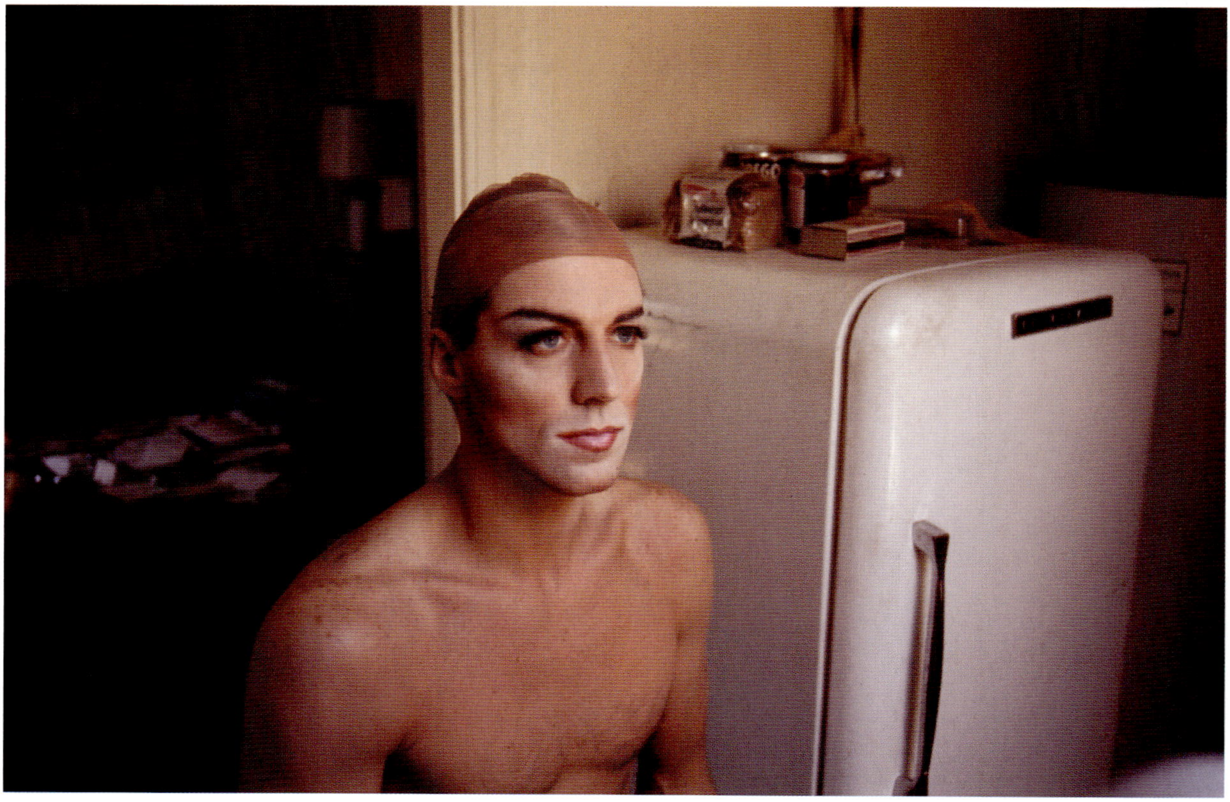

Doug Michels becoming Jackie
Photographs by Chip Lord

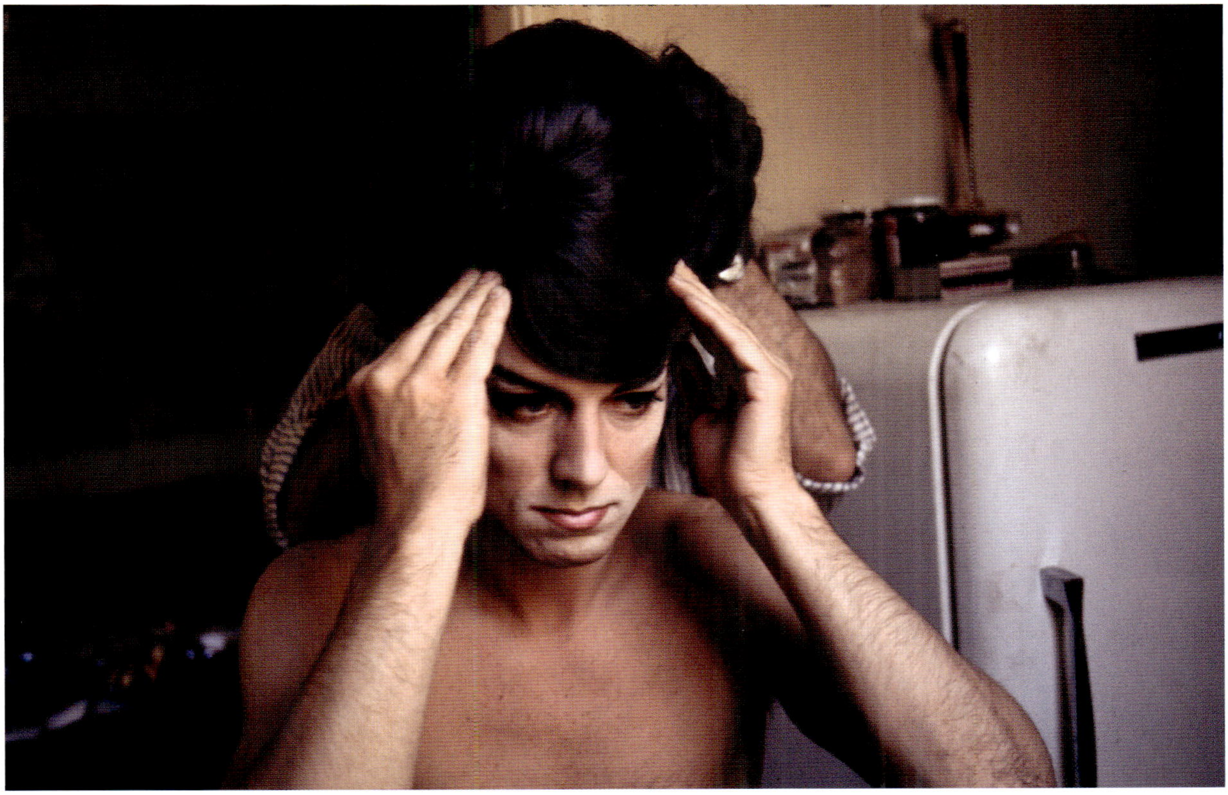

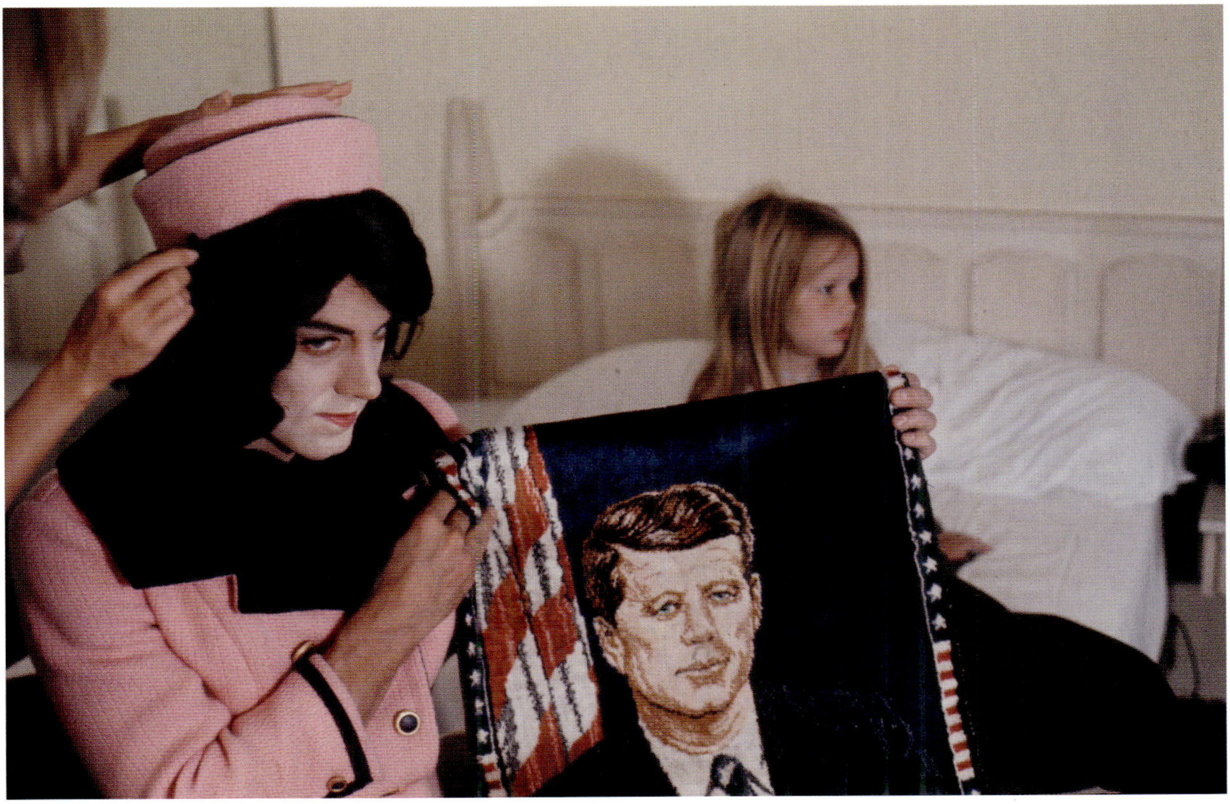

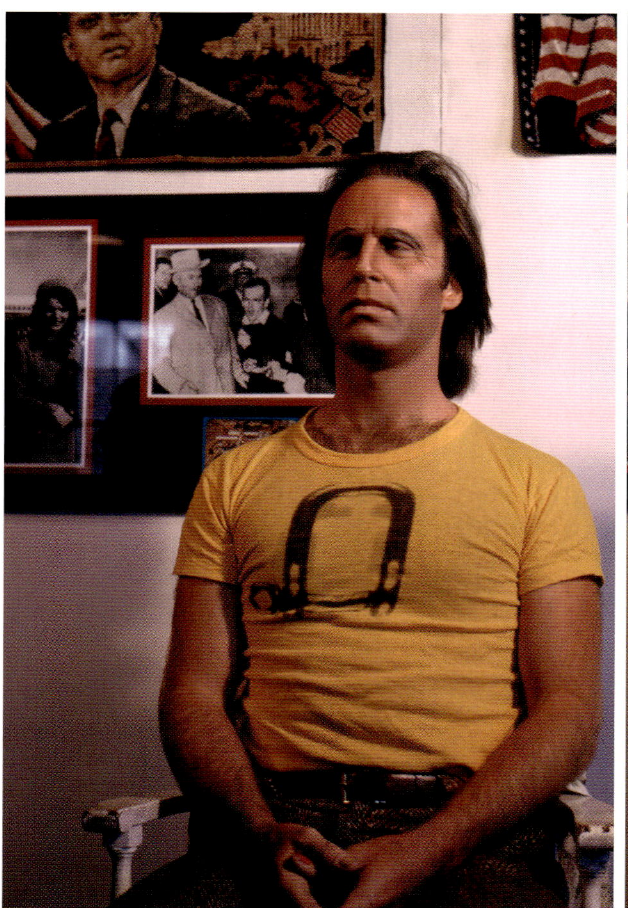
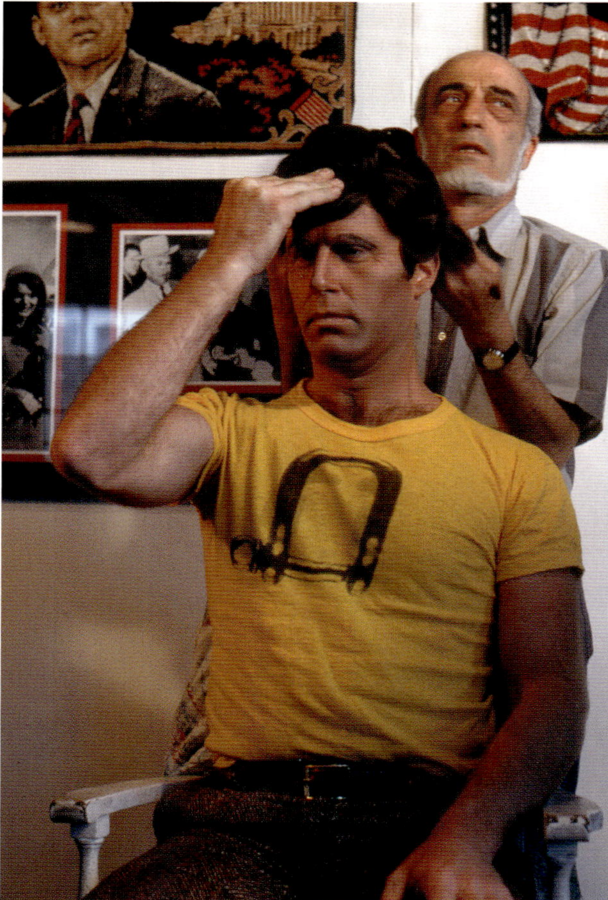

Makeup artist Leslie Sherman creating the Artist-President
Photographs by Chip Lord

The first assassination imagery that any of us saw were selected stills from Abraham Zapruder's home movie that appeared in the November 29, 1963, issue of *Life* Magazine. Zapruder gave *Life* permission to publish stills from the movie except for frame 333, which shows the gunshot that exploded the president's head. That frame was withheld from public view until it was shown within the film on Geraldo Rivera's show *Good Night America* in March 1975. Around the same time, bootlegged versions of the movie began to appear, and we managed to get our hands on one. It, and to a lesser extent a second film shot from the other side of the plaza by Orville Nix, became the source materials for our "authentic reenactment" of the assassination.

The release of the film spawned all kinds of conspiracy theories, none of which interested us. As Alexandra Zapruder, granddaughter of Abraham Zapruder, explains in her book *Twenty-Six Seconds: A Personal History of the Zapruder Film* (2016), "They [T. R. Uthco and Ant Farm] sought to use artistic collaboration to tackle that fixed, iconic imagery—the Zapruder film itself—

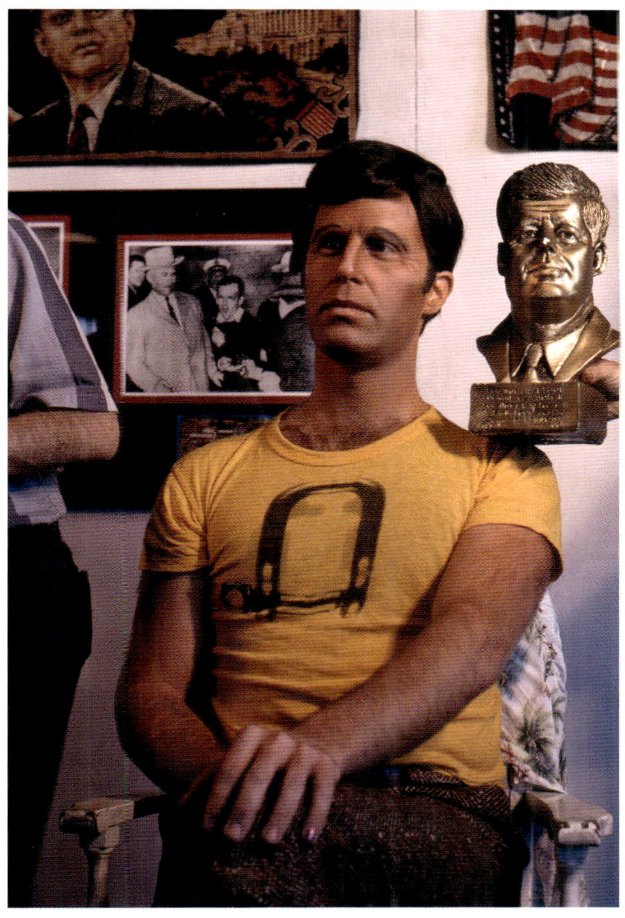

that so dominated the public imagination. But as avant-garde artists critiquing accepted norms, they could not operate within traditional structures. They had to do something inappropriate, radical, even taboo. In correspondence with me, Doug Hall explained it this way: 'Our need was to break down that wall, to cause fissures to appear in its facade with the belief that these cracks would widen and other hidden truths would reveal themselves. I won't presume that we succeeded, but I will stand by our intent.'"[4]

More discussions. Lots of planning. If I was going to be the Artist-President then a member of Ant Farm would have to be the Artist–First Lady and the obvious choice was Doug Michels. And so, the two Dougs came to be Jack and Jackie. Chip took the role of the film director, who acts as if he is directing the performances in Dealey Plaza; and Jody became Clint Hill, the

4. Alexandra Zapruder, *Twenty-Six Seconds: A Personal History of the Zapruder Film* (New York: Twelve, 2016), 260.

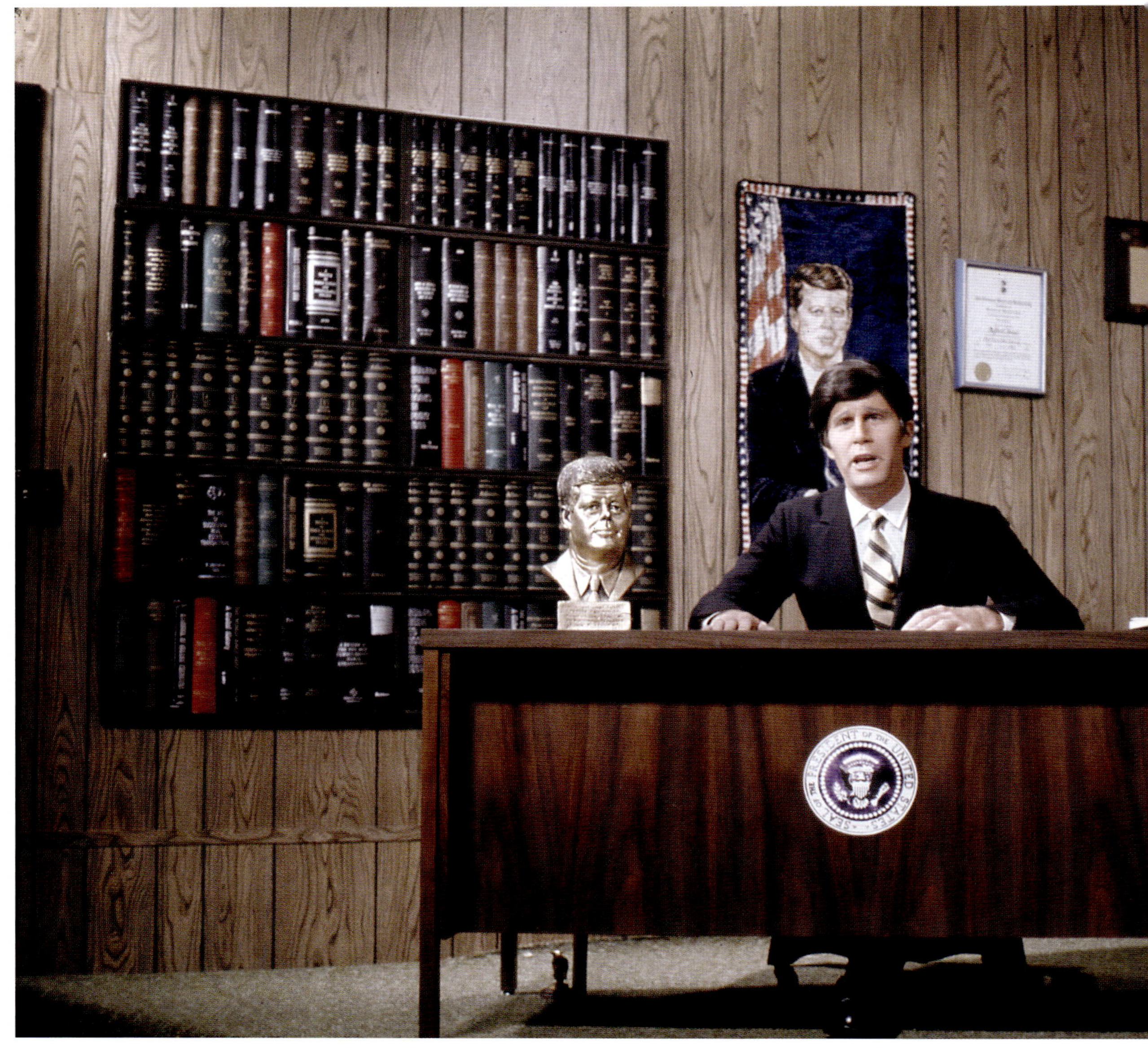

Secret Service agent who jumped onto the back of the presidential limousine after the shots were fired and as it sped off to Parkland Hospital. Diane, always shy before the camera even though she supported herself through college by modeling for magazines, was to be the primary still photographer.

We hired a friend, Sandra Woodall, costume designer for many film and theatrical productions, including for the San Francisco Opera, to design and fabricate Jackie's pink Chanel suit with blue piping and matching pillbox hat. Also from the opera, we hired makeup artist Leslie Sherman to create the face and hair of my JFK and Doug's Jackie, and to pass those skills along to Diane so she could apply the makeup when we were in Dallas.

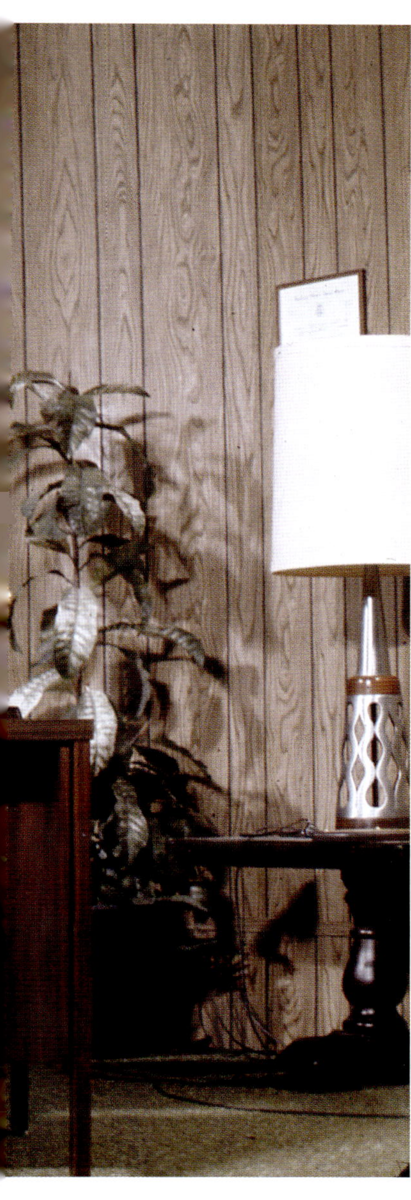

The Artist-President at the KVII Television studio, Amarillo, Texas
Photograph by Chip Lord

From a junkyard we rescued a Lincoln Continental convertible that could stand in for the presidential limousine (which we crassly referred to as the assassination mobile). It ran, but just barely. The side of the car that would be away from the Grassy Knoll and Zapruder's camera was heavily dented, and because it wasn't running on all its cylinders, the car spewed dark exhaust. Curtis Schreier from Ant Farm fashioned a roll bar that replicated the one on the actual limousine and at a hardware store bought a couple of cabinet handles that he attached to the trunk, mimicking those the Secret Service would hold on to in an emergency.

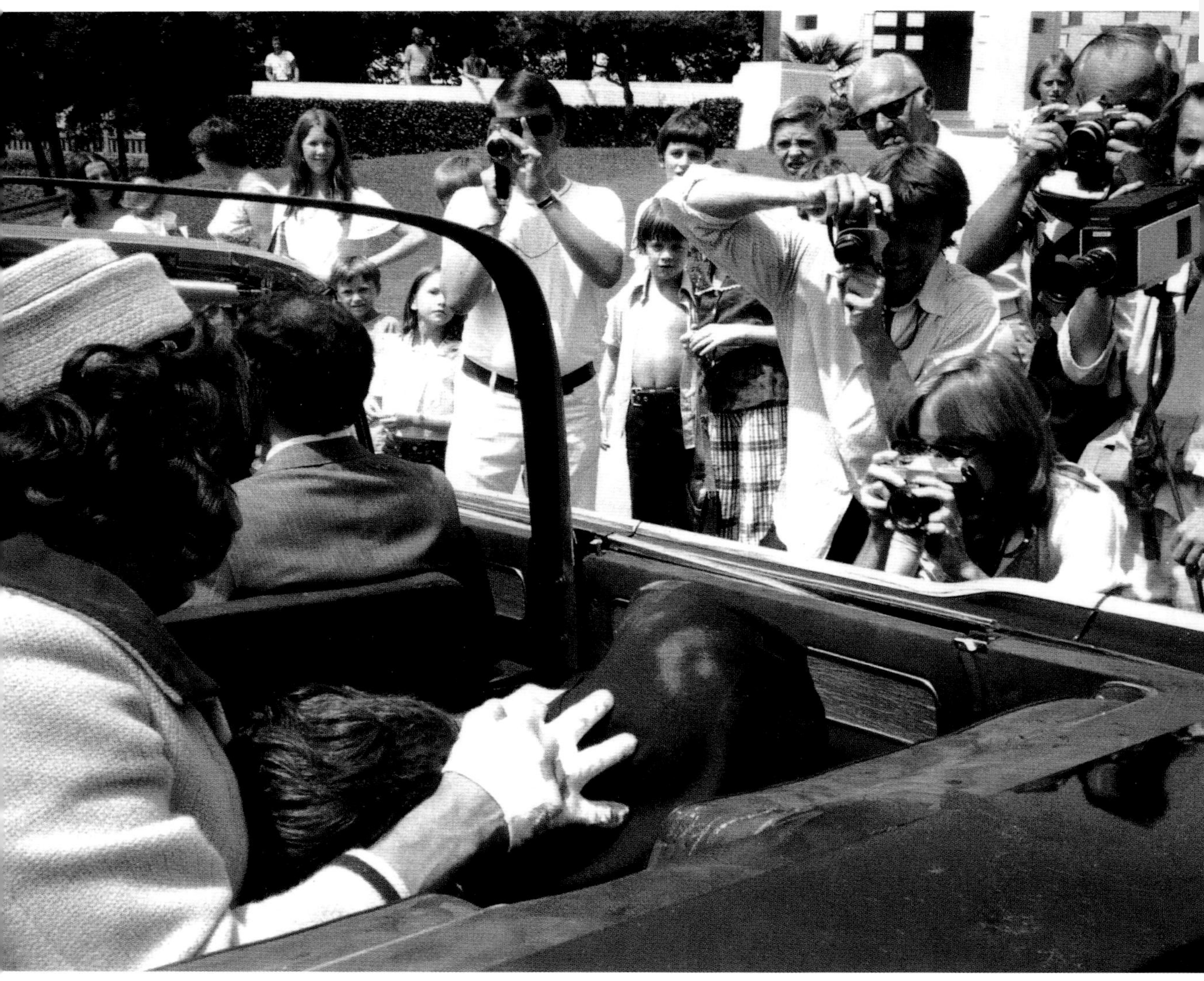

Posing for tourists and our camera crew below the Grassy Knoll, Dealey Plaza
Photograph by Chip Lord

We needed a skilled camera crew to shoot video and film in Dallas. We asked Jim Newman, a friend and the former owner and director of the Dilexi Gallery, the first avant-garde gallery in San Francisco, to cover the Orville Nix angle with 8mm, which Nix had used to film from the other side of the Grassy Knoll to where Zapruder filmed with his 16mm camera. Pepper Mauser, a friend of Ant Farm's and part of a Texas collective called South Coast, shot the counterfeit Zapruder movie. Most important, we needed a small crew who could move around easily with a Sony Portapak and get the kind of details we would need for the anticipated video documenting the event. Ant Farm had a close relationship with the pioneering guerilla video group Videofreex and talked two of their members, Skip Blumberg and Bart Friedman, into joining us in Dallas. They turned out to be the perfect choice. With Skip doing most of the video and Bart the audio, they managed to move in and out of events, capturing small details while getting the crucial shots. Skip was also a talented interviewer, an ability he demonstrated while engaging spectators in Dealey Plaza who witnessed our crude reenactment. One of the most revealing moments in the video shows the closeup of a woman's face: "Oh look, he's reenacting it," she declares to her friends. "Oh, no," she gasps. Obviously moved, she strains her neck to get a better view while wiping tears from her cheek. "I feel like it's the real thing. It looks so real," she says as she turns to her friends, who commiserate and recall what they were doing on the fateful November afternoon. Another woman is heard wondering about what she is witnessing and assumes it must be staged "for tourists and the like." She wasn't alone among the visitors that day who thought our reenactment was an entertainment put on by the city of Dallas.

We converged on Dealey Plaza on an already hot August morning, prepared to get one or maybe two passes through the plaza before the local police shut us down. The camera crews were positioned at the two crucial film positions, those of Zapruder and Nix, as we made our first pass.

The silent shots are fired. Kennedy is pushed forward and then violently back as the second shot hits. Jackie twists and stretches toward the back of the limousine where the Secret Service agent is climbing onto the back of the car. A wounded Governor Connally slumps as Nellie slouches down in her seat. The limousine picks up speed and heads beneath the overpass on its way to Parkland Hospital. But in our case, instead of going to the hospital, we make a U-turn so we can quickly return to our starting point before making another pass through Dealey Plaza. After our sixth or seventh time, we knew we had a lot of the crucial images we were after, which allowed Skip and Bart to concentrate on the people who were gathering to watch the spectacle.

Those of us in the car were getting a little bored with the repetition and decided that Jackie and Jack would go into the Kennedy Museum, which was housed on the ground floor of the notorious Texas School Book Depository. I was surprisingly good at coming up with things to say in these improvised situations but on this occasion, I was tongue tied. A lot of people were milling about and several had gathered around a counter where a short, dark-haired man in a shirt and tie appeared to be selling memorabilia. As we entered, we heard a woman say, "Oh my god, it's Kennedy and Jackie."

Not knowing what to say I just opened my mouth and hoped for the best. "I want to thank you all for coming to the Kennedy Museum. And I also want you all to know as you watch the history of my life . . ."

Suddenly, the Artist-President, as captured in the video, is interrupted by the man behind one of the glass display counters. His timing is perfect, since I had drawn a complete blank about what to say next. "Sir," he gestures toward me with his hand as if to sweep me away.

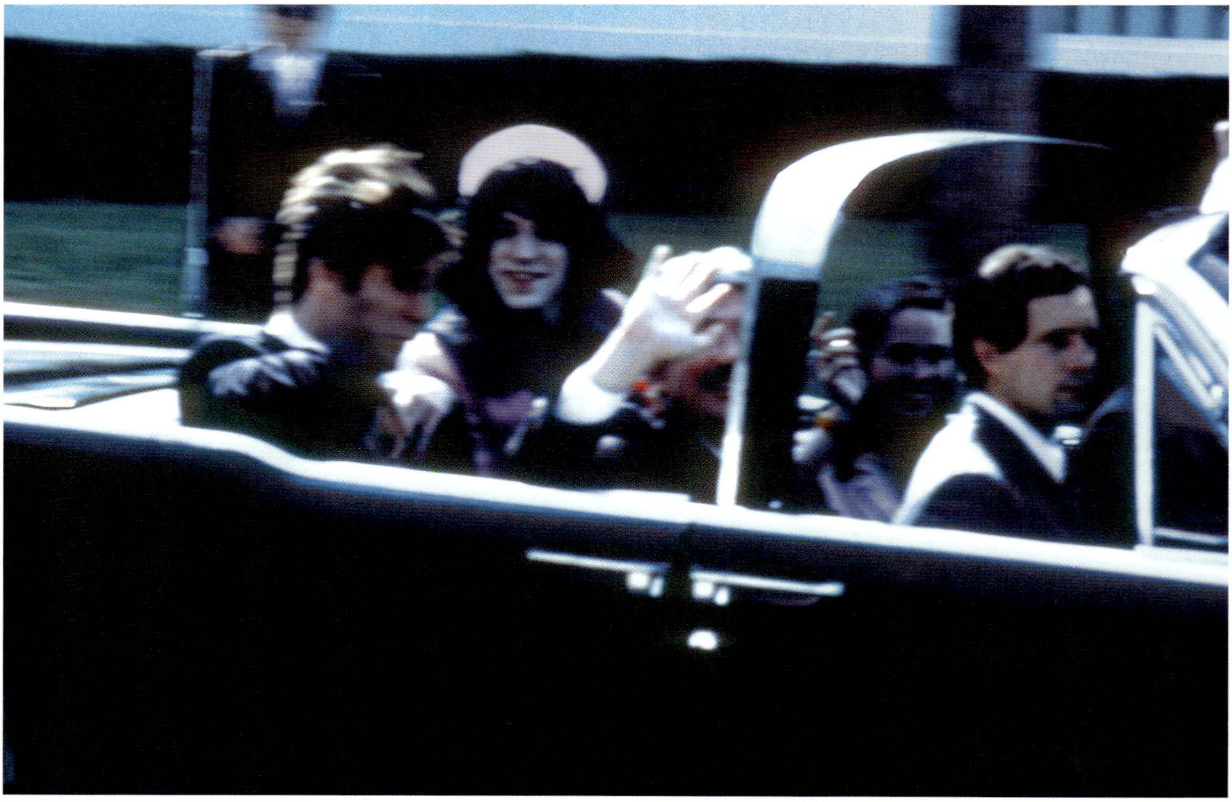

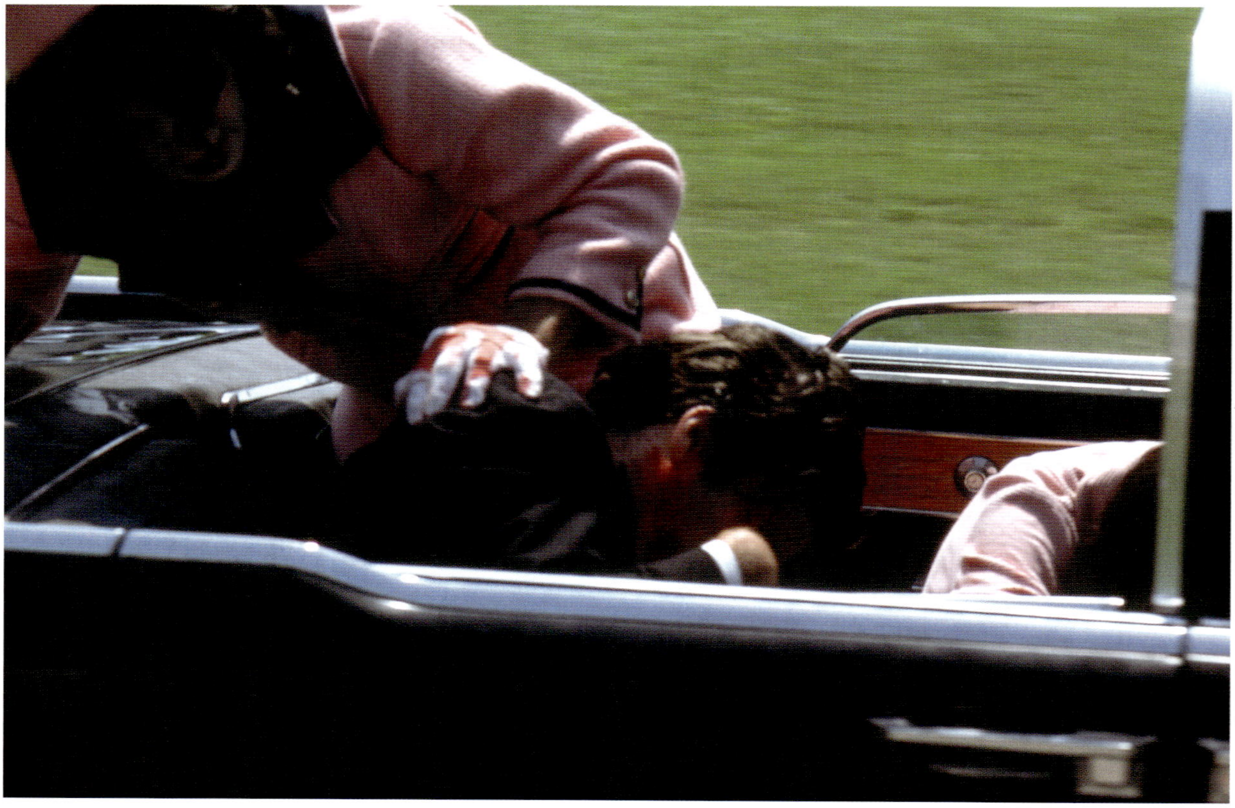

Assassination sequence, Dealey Plaza
Photographs by Diane Andrews Hall

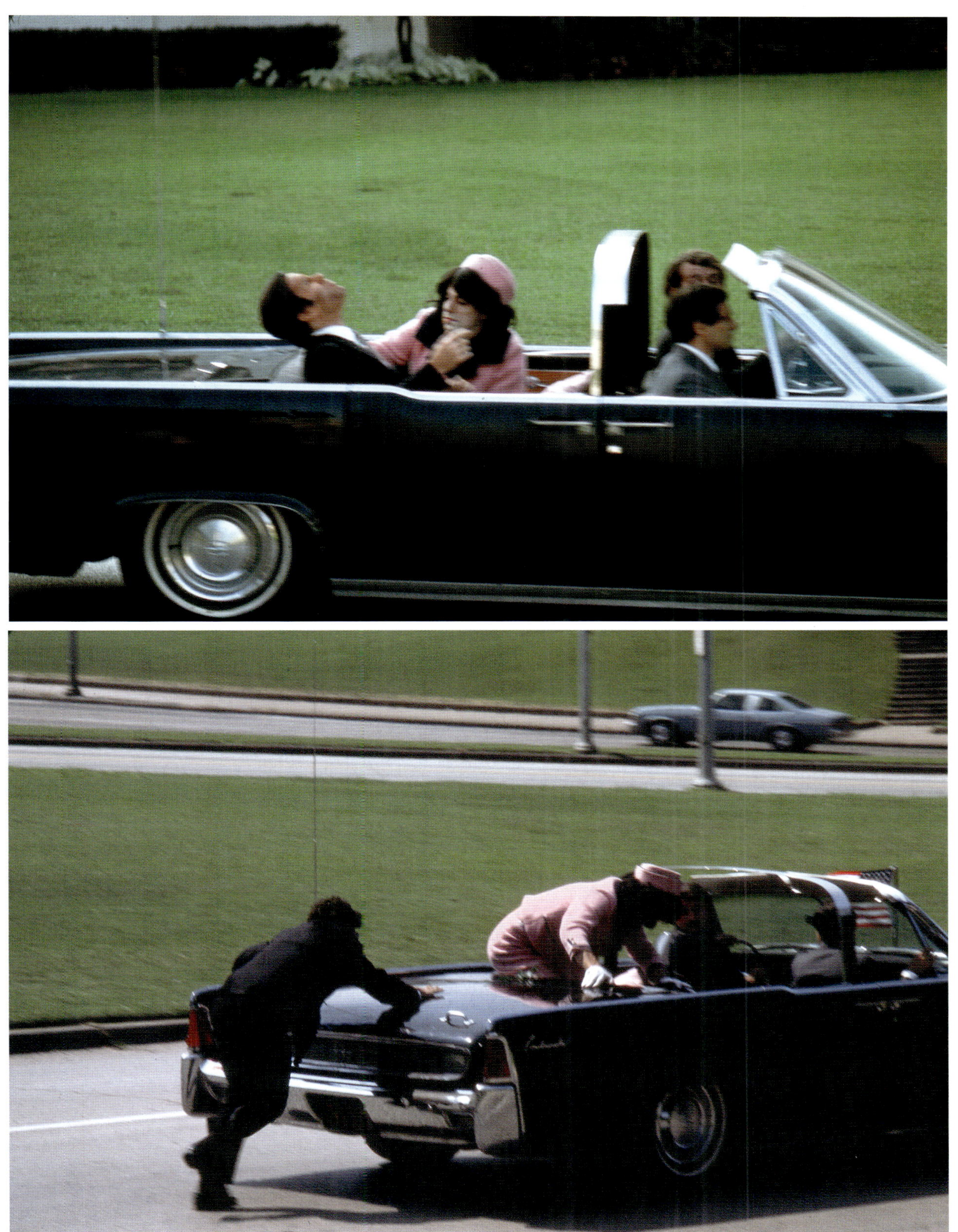

"Yes?"

"Uhh, please," he says with an exasperated, twangy Texas accent, "not now. I'll talk to you later about this."

"Fine, thank you very much, sir. It's a good, worthwhile thing you are doing here."

"Please step outside." The man is clearly irritated.

And the Artist-President, banished from his museum responds, "Yes, sir." And then addressing those around him, he says, "It doesn't seem that the uhh . . ." The sentence remains incomplete as the entourage leaves the museum.

It was around noon when we climbed back into the assassination mobile and headed out to do some more passes through Dealey Plaza. After about three more times through, a couple of police cars arrived. We figured that at the very least they would shut us down. But after one of Stanley Marsh's on-site lawyers, who was doubling as the chauffeur of the presidential limousine, gave them a brief explanation, the cops offered to control the traffic so we could get video without interference from other cars passing through. With the aid of the Dallas police, we made several more passes through Dealey Plaza—seventeen in all—before exhaustion set in and we called it a day.

As irreverent as all of this was, there was a rationale to our collective madness. That people, gathered at Dealey Plaza, could accept our crude simulations as a stand-in for that tragic moment in American history was fascinating. No one recoiled. No one rebelled at our tastelessness. No jeers. No outrage, even with a man in drag as Jackie. (One woman in the video declares, "Oh my god it looks just like her doesn't it!") The people who came to Dealey Plaza that day—where they went to remember, to offer tribute—embraced the spectacle and allowed themselves to be drawn in; to be moved and uplifted by what they saw. It took so little, really, to jump-start their emotions, which has to say something about how we navigate through the images we encounter every day and draw meaning from them.

One interpretation might be that the true nature of catastrophe becomes diluted through its mediation, a transformation that allows one to engage with the horror rather than be overcome or incapacitated by it. Turning horror into narrative creates an acceptable, approachable surrogate of the original: the distancing and aestheticizing mechanism allows the truly horrible to linger more gently in our minds so that our sentiments can grab hold and find avenues for expression and momentary release. This reduces our sense of powerlessness before those tragic public events that invade our lives and are beyond our control. Because true horror is, in its raw, visceral reality, indeed unfathomable. I think this is what Jacques Rancière means when he writes, "The real must be fictionalized in order to be thought."[5]

5. Jacques Rancière, *The Politics of Aesthetics: The Distribution of the Sensible*, trans. Gabriel Rockhill (London, New York: Continuum, 2004), 38.

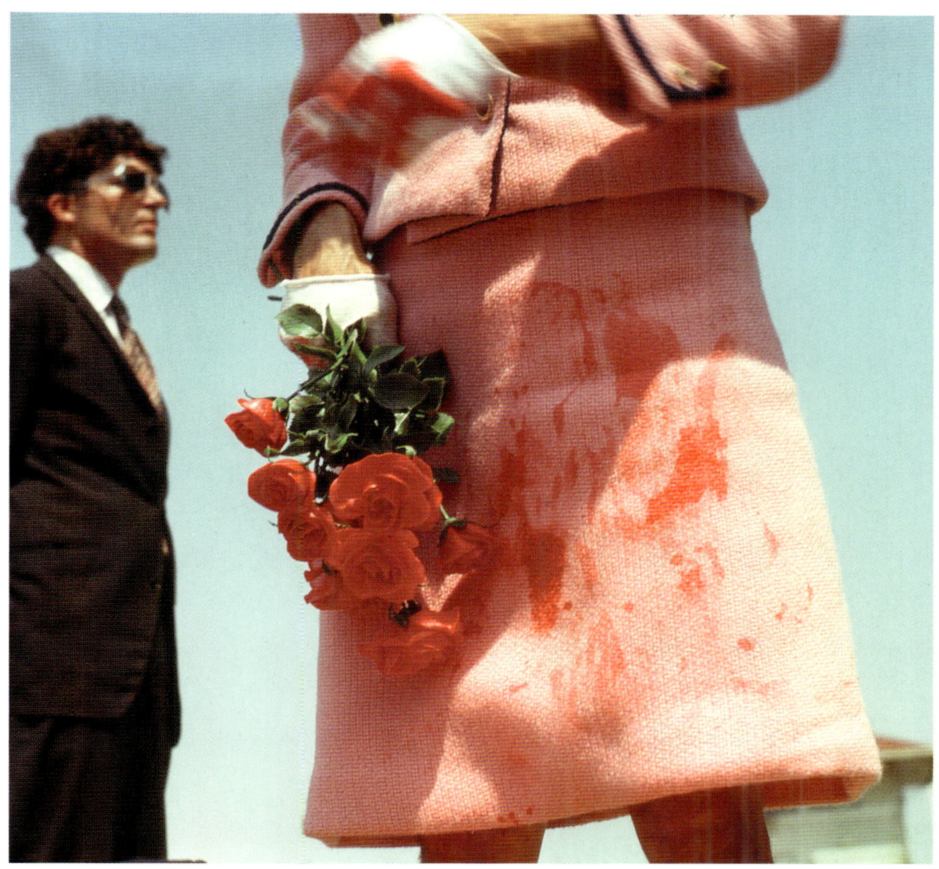

Doug Michels (Artist-Jackie) with Jody Procter (Agent Clint Hill) following our reenactment, Dealey Plaza
Photographer unknown

As Marita Sturken and others have pointed out, the television coverage of the aftermath of the Kennedy assassination, which played out over several uninterrupted days, provided a public space for our shared mourning. She writes, "Zapruder's documentary footage is not the only means through which Kennedy's death became a media event. The networks covered the events surrounding Kennedy's death and his funeral over many days with uninterrupted television coverage, making of the events a public spectacle and creating an opportunity for mass-mediated participation in the ritual of mourning."[6] What I find interesting is that this "public spectacle," as identified by Sturken, had all the same ingredients—narrative flow, emotional hooks, and most importantly, catharsis—as classic tragic theater, literature, or cinema.

6. Marita Sturken and Lisa Cartwright, *Practices of Looking: An Introduction to Visual Culture* (New York: Oxford University Press, 2001), 181.

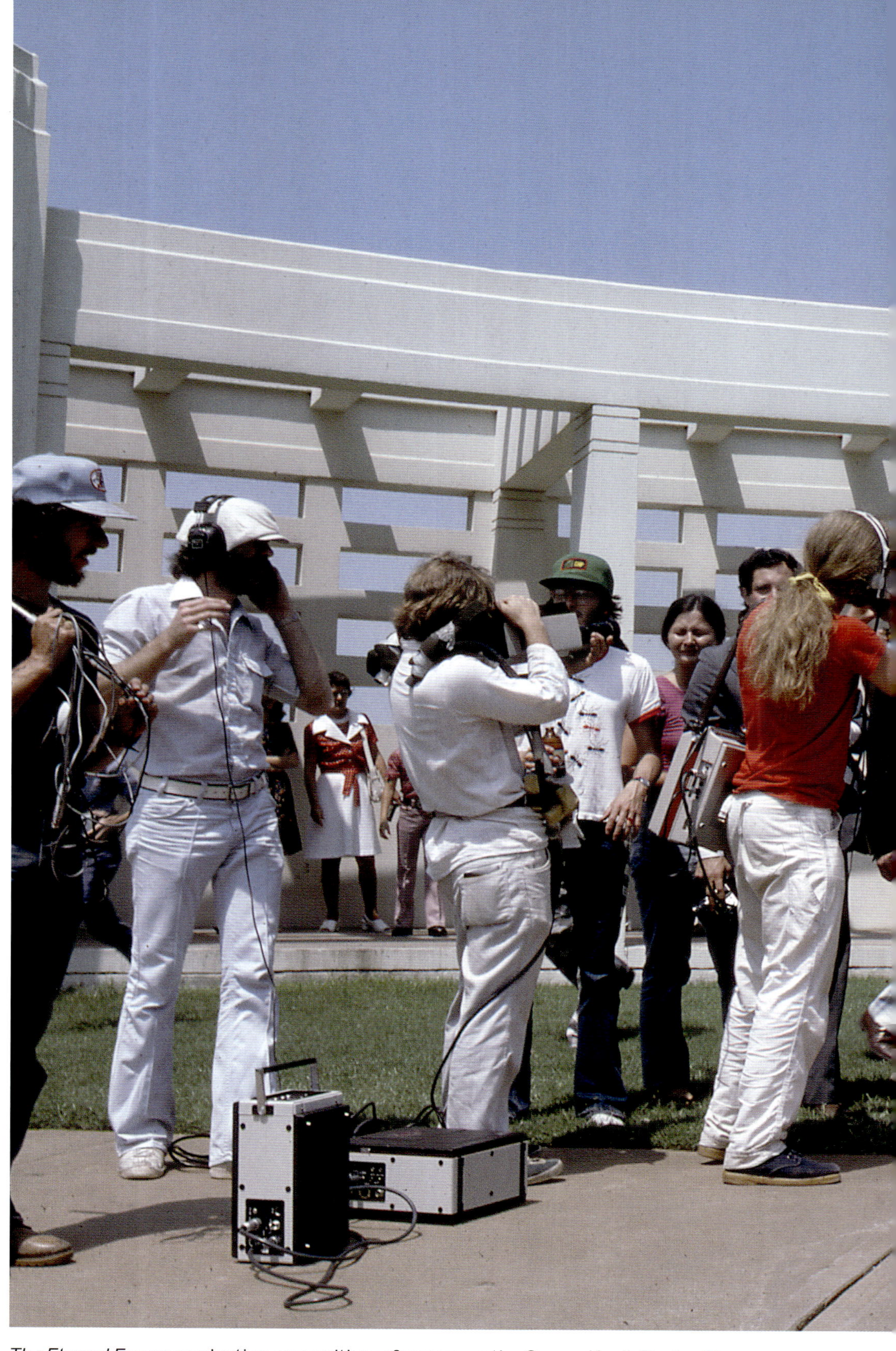

The Eternal Frame production crew with performers on the Grassy Knoll, Dealey Plaza
Photograph by Diane Andrews Hall

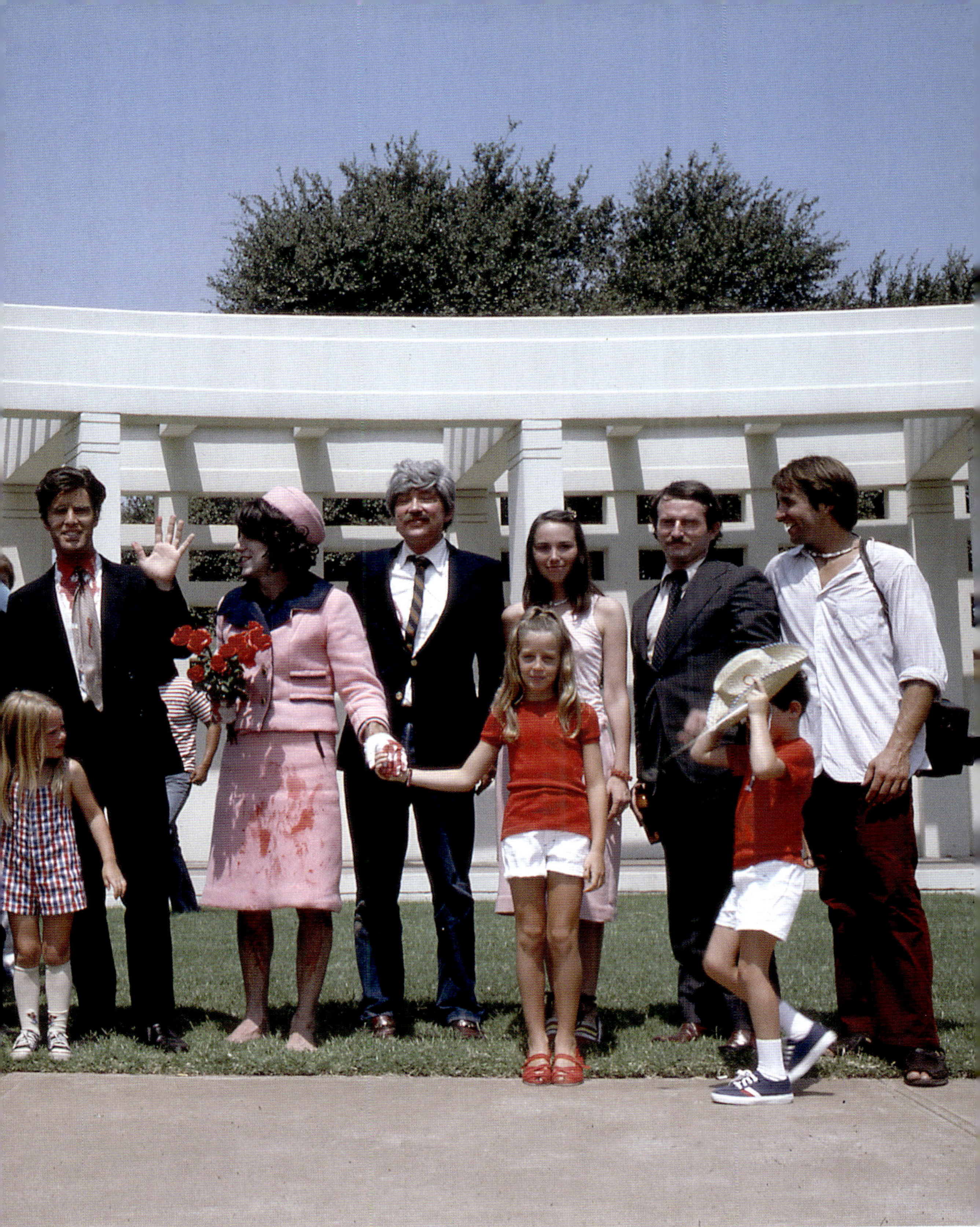

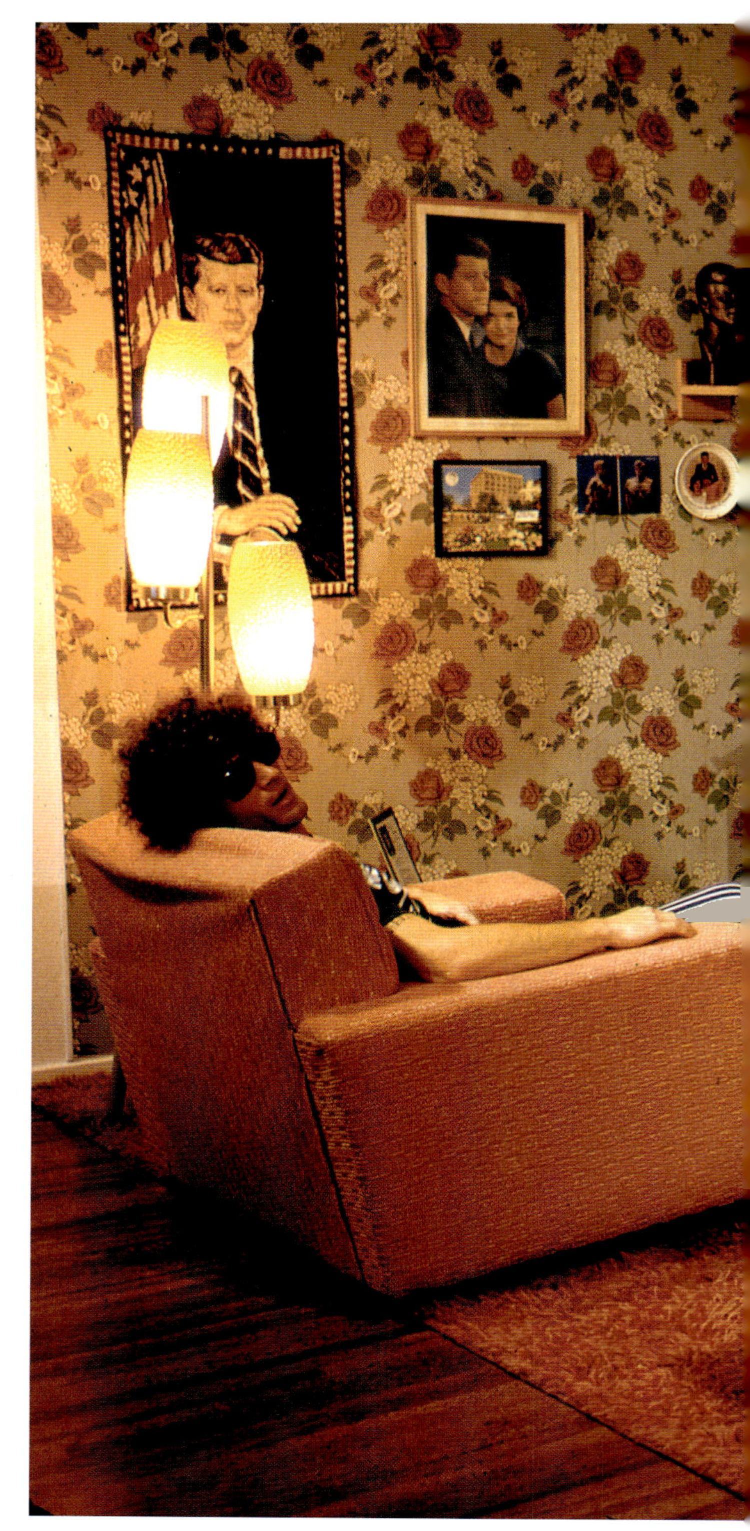

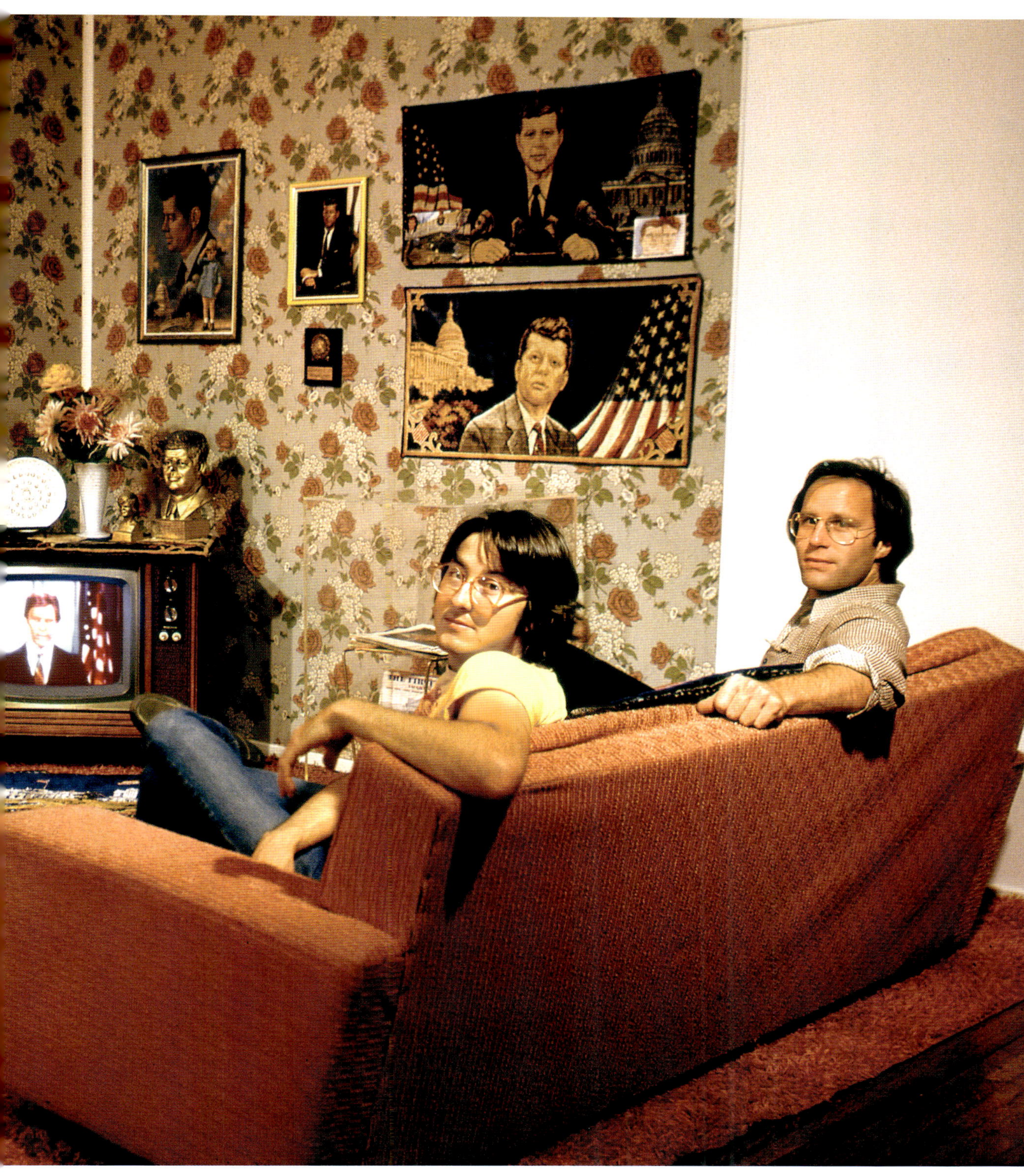

The Eternal Frame, installation view, Long Beach Museum of Art, California, 1976
(left to right: Jody Procter, Chip Lord, Doug Hall)
Photograph by David Ross

Interventions

On September 2, 1975, Lynette "Squeaky" Fromme, standing at arm's length from President Gerald Ford, who was in Sacramento on his way to visit Governor Jerry Brown, raised a pistol, pointed it at Ford's head, and pulled the trigger. Nothing happened. Fromme, already notorious as a member of the Charles Manson cult, had failed to chamber a round.

Ford was scheduled to visit San Francisco twenty days later for a meeting of the World Affairs Council at the St. Francis Hotel. Having survived a near miss in the capital, the media announced, the San Francisco Police along with the FBI, Secret Service, Highway Patrol, and officers from the Oakland Police Department would provide the highest level of security ever arranged at the municipal level for a visiting dignitary, foreign or domestic. On hearing this, and not particularly concerned where art stopped and everyday life began or even convinced that there could be a legitimate division between the two, Jody, Diane, and I decided to initiate a project in which we would explore the secure perimeter that was described by local papers as impenetrable. Was it an art project? Did it matter?

Of the three of us, Jody and I were the most interested in spectacle, the modes through which capitalist institutions demonstrate, sometimes subliminally or obliquely, their dominance over the less powerful. We executed numerous forays into this vaguely defined arena of the politiical sublime. Some of these were successful in that something tangible and exhibitable came out of them, but more were unsuccessful, if measured along those lines. However, for us, being present as witnesses—with cameras whenever possible—was sufficient justification for our efforts.

Our intention, on this warm September morning, was to see if we could infiltrate the security surrounding Ford's San Francisco visit. Earlier that year, we had created a pseudo-company that we called Avant Guard Security, an obvious art-world pun that initially expressed itself as words printed in white block letters on black t-shirts. At some point, we decided that we needed an official-looking uniform with badge and cap that could approximate a police officer, or at least a security guard. We rummaged through the various thrift stores around the city and finally located a discarded security officer's uniform with matching cap that was too small for me, but fit Jody perfectly. The outfit was in excellent condition, and we were set, but with no place to go. The uniform fit Chip and Doug Michels, as well, and we took several photos with the two Ant Farmers posing, cop-like. I think it was Chip who decided our uniformed officer needed a name and a name tag. He came up with Officer Dingus, and we all agreed that was perfect. Officer Dingus it was, but still with no place to go.

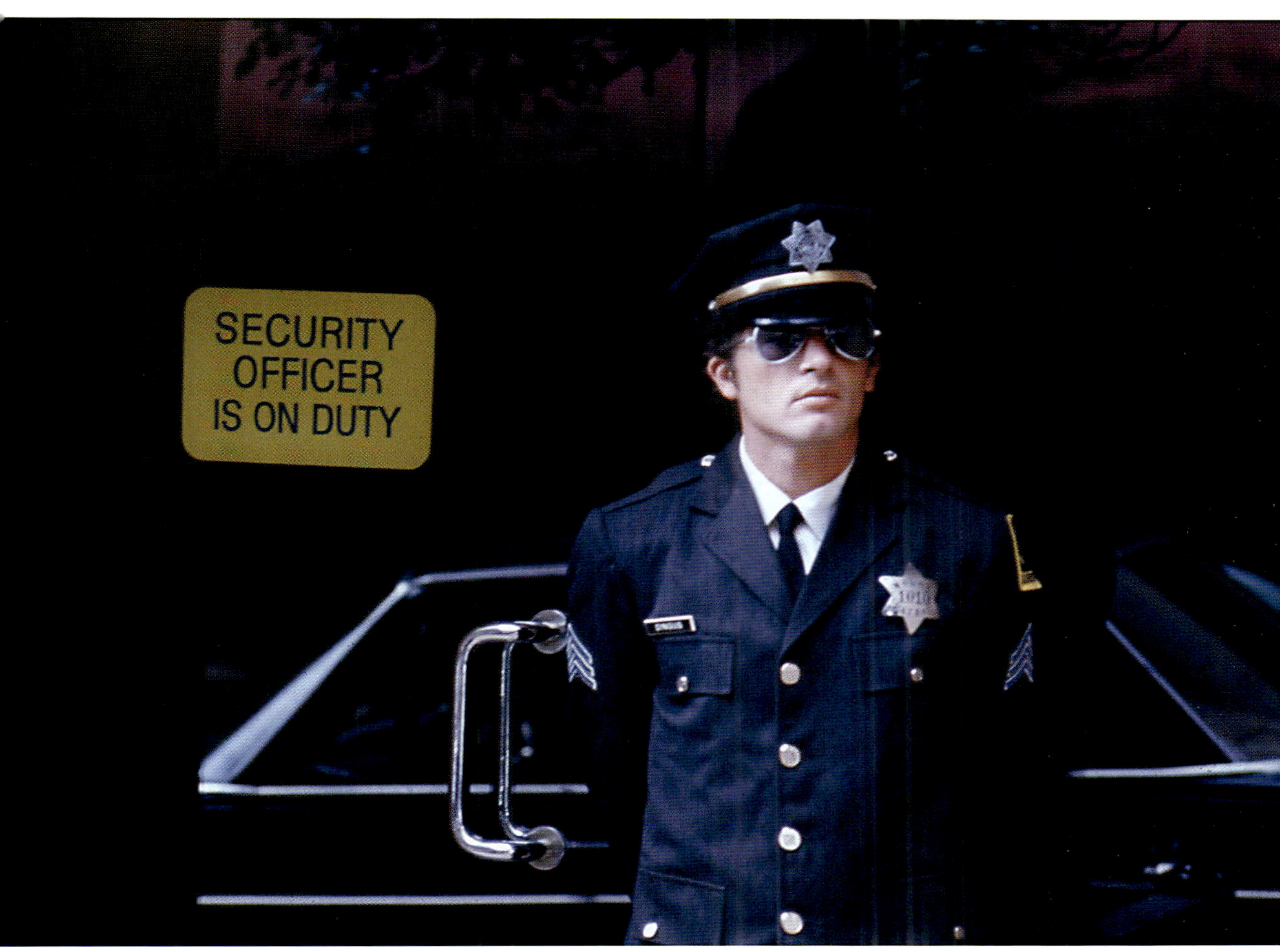

Jody Procter as Avant Guard Security officer Dingus
Photograph by Doug Hall

"Did you hear that Ford is coming to San Francisco on the twenty-second?" Diane asks us as we sit around the dinner table finishing our bottle of wine while Jody rolls a joint.

"Yeah! That's in just a couple of days. After Sacramento, they're arranging a huge security presence," I respond. Jody hands me the lit joint. I take a hit and offer it to Diane who declines with a wave of her hand. She gets up and peeks through the open door into the hallway where Gannon and Sophie, Jody's daughter and our niece, are taking turns riding his Big Wheels as fast as they can and screaming as the three-wheeled vehicle caroms off the hallway baseboards. Diane makes them stop and they disappear into another room where they become mysteriously quiet, as kids do.

She comes back into the dining room and, standing before us with a mischievous expression on her face, declares, "Sounds to me like a job for your Officer Dingus."

Momentary silence; our eyes pass from one to the other as we try to fathom what Diane is suggesting.

"You mean send Dingus to Ford's arrival?" I blurt out.

Before I can finish or Diane can respond, Jody pipes in, "I mean isn't that a little risky? There's supposed to be a lot of cops. And Secret Service all over the place. It's going to be crazy downtown."

We've lost interest in the joint that now sits on the edge of the ashtray. "Do you think we could infiltrate that police presence? Get close to Ford? Do you think it would be a crime trying?"

"It's impersonating an officer," Jody answers.

"But look at Dingus's uniform! I mean it doesn't say San Francisco Police. He won't be carrying a gun or anything," I say as it becomes clearer in my mind that we must do it.

"Right. I think we have a right to assemble, and we can do that dressed however we like," Diane adds.

"Sure, as long as we aren't impersonating a police officer or behaving in ways that could cause harm to anyone, particularly the president."

"And we won't be impersonating a police officer. We'll be impersonating a security guard. Come on. We have to do this," I say, pleadingly.

"Well. We are sort of. And it will be me doing the impersonating," Jody says but with a tone in his voice of rising excitement, clearly on the verge of buying in.

Our eyes are now on Jody. He's right. I can't fit into the uniform. He will be the one out there. Diane and I will be hidden behind cameras.

Not one to avoid the adventure of confronting authority, Jody adds, "I think Dingus will look enough like the real thing, so that people will respond to him the same way they do to the cops."

"Yeah, sort of like the assassination mobile and our fake Jack and Jackie. Just enough to trigger the right responses."

Diane chimes in, "The question isn't how people will react but what the police might do when they see you acting cop-like."

And Jody says, after reaching for the roach on the edge of the ashtray and lighting it, "Well, are we not Uthco? Only one way to find out." And so, it was decided. We would try to probe the security that was being assembled for Gerald Ford's visit.

When we arrive at Union Square, we are amazed at the number of police that line not only Powell Street, location of the St. Francis, but the crossing and surrounding streets. The sidewalks are framed by uniformed police, standing shoulder to shoulder, who contain the protestors—on one side, those petitioning for Palestine and on the other, those advocating for Israel—and keep them away from the areas near the hotel entrance and from blocking traffic. Sharpshooters and uniformed men with binoculars are poised on the roofs of buildings around the square. Motorcycle cops sit on or lean against their

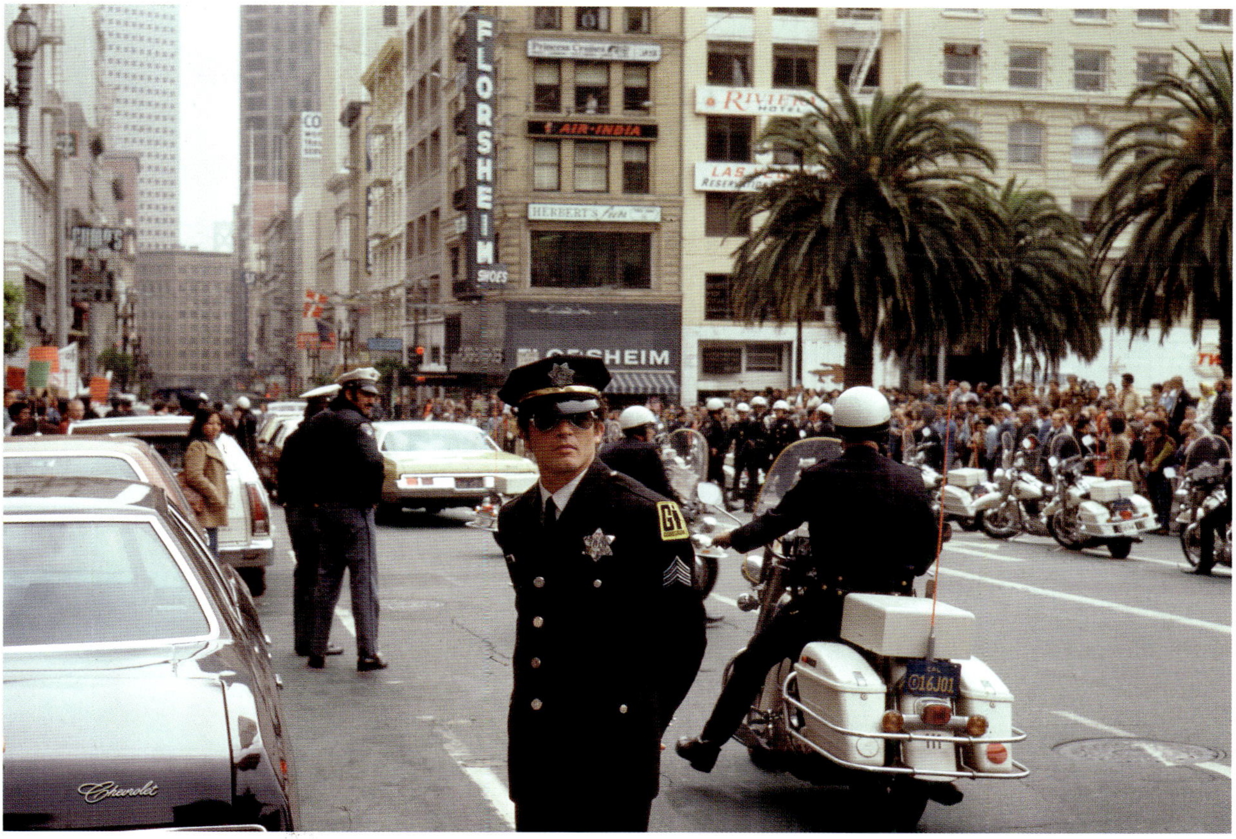

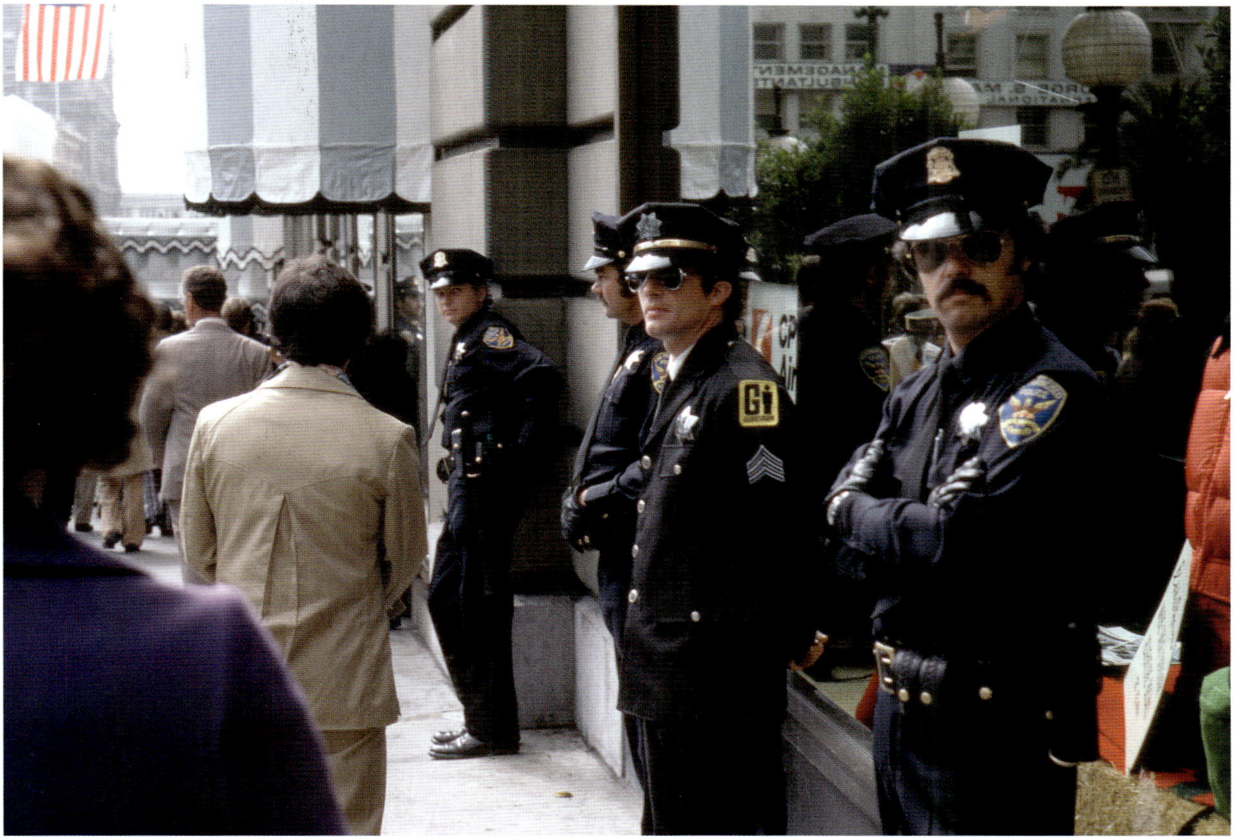

Officer Dingus providing presidential security
Photographs by T. R. Uthco (Diane Andrews Hall, Doug Hall)

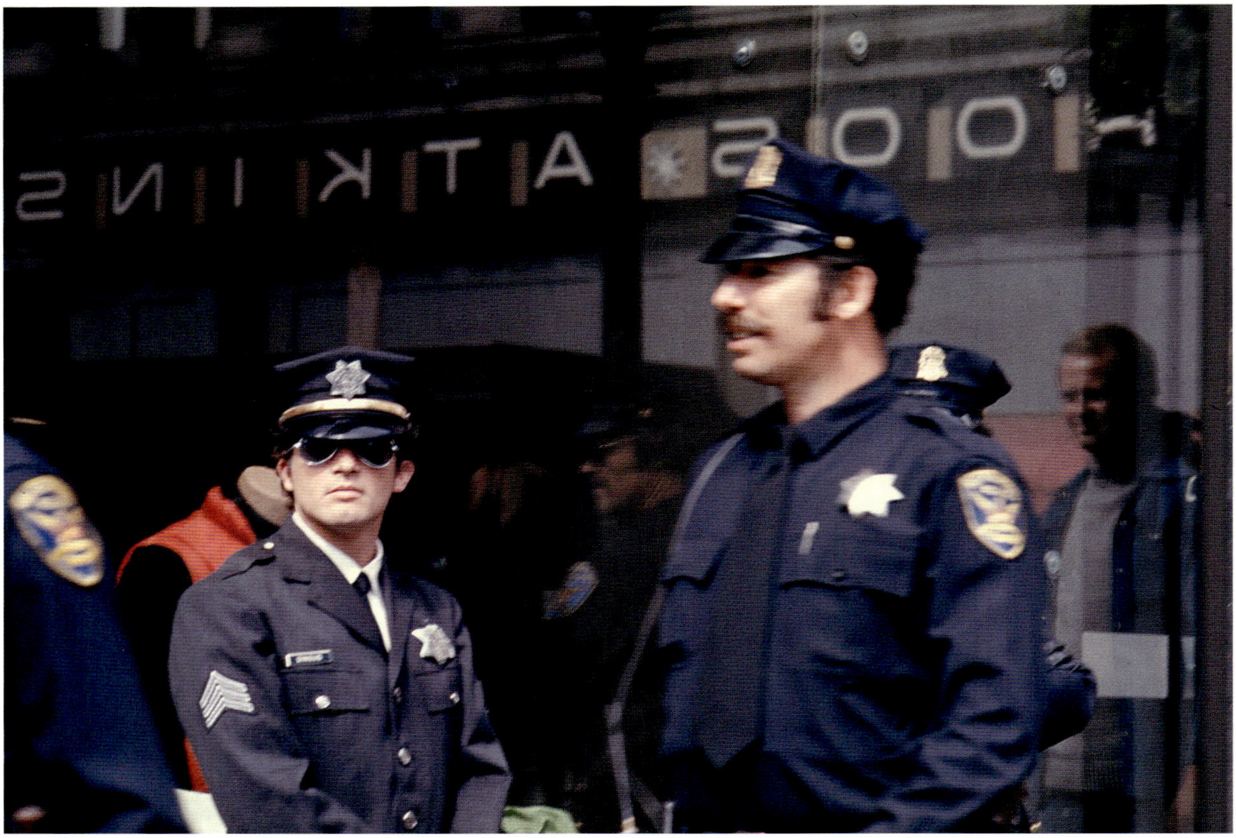

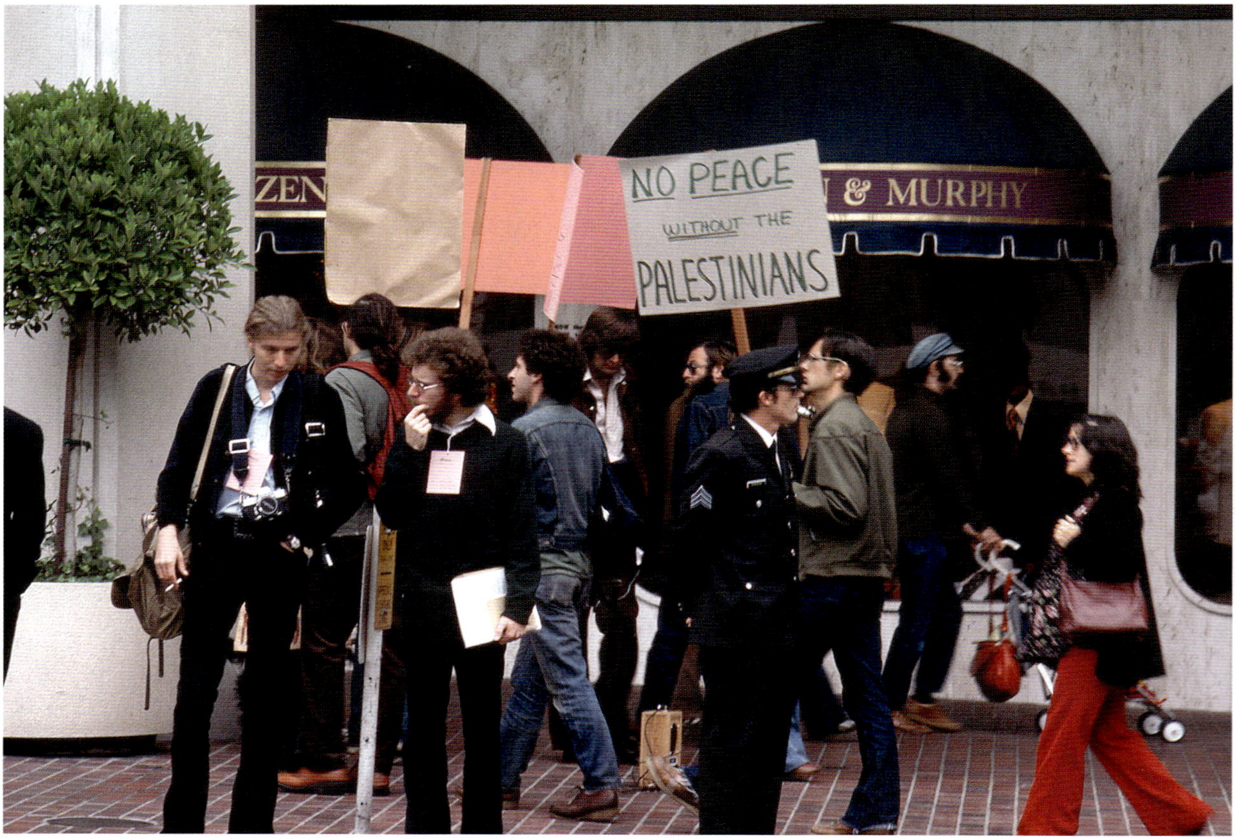

Officer Dingus providing presidential security
Photographs by T. R. Uthco (Diane Andrews Hall, Doug Hall)

bikes, arranged in long lines on the north and south sides of the park. It is a cop-o-rama for sure.

Several Secret Service agents, some holding clipboards, others talking into their wrists or to one another, some sporting sunglasses and all with a coiled wire extending to one of their ears, mingle in front of the hotel. It looks as impenetrable as advertised, but before we can chicken out, Jody has crossed the street where he begins, with cop-like bravado, to admonish members of the Palestinian contingent who had started interrupting traffic by stepping into the street.

"Please step back onto the sidewalk," he politely commands, "and don't block it. People need to get by." The protestors quickly obey, and the police officers who are nearby, although several look surprised, do nothing. Diane and I, after recovering from the momentary shock of Jody's actions, click away with our cameras, trying to stay far enough back so that we won't draw too much attention to our Officer Dingus.

It goes this way for the rest of the morning as we await Ford's arrival. Now, at the crosswalk, while Jody is stopping traffic for pedestrians, an older woman asks him when Ford is expected to arrive. He responds, looking at his watch, "He's presently scheduled for a noon arrival at the St. Francis." Gesturing to the woman, he commands, "Please keep moving," and then saunters along with her, releasing the cars that had been holding at his direction.

As his courage increases, Jody mingles with the cops as they stand in a line in the shadow of the buildings, waiting for trouble to erupt, or as they gather in small groups at the barricades erected to prevent traffic from entering the section of Powell Street where the president is scheduled to arrive. Throughout, Diane and I take photos, becoming bolder ourselves as it is apparent that the three of us have seamlessly merged with the surrounding security and the growing crowd awaiting the spectacle of a presidential arrival.

Our plan is to get Jody as close as we can to Ford as he arrives at the hotel, our hope to capture Officer Dingus in the frame with Ford and a couple of his Secret Service agents as he climbs out of the presidential limousine or as they enter the hotel. We gradually make our way to what we think is the best location, across the street from the hotel entrance, which is as close as anyone can get who isn't part of the presidential party.

We watch as the black advance cars with blinking blue and red lights stream into the underground parking lot. Finally, the presidential limousine arrives along with several other black SUVs, doors fly open, and out of one steps Ford, who waves as he moves away from the car and toward the hotel entrance. Jody, on the opposite side of the street along with the police, holds back the crowd that is gently pushing to get a better view. I manage to get a distant photo of Ford as he turns toward us and waves but am unable to position Jody in the same frame. Ford is surrounded by Secret Service who push him along through a door, where he disappears. Other agents linger at the

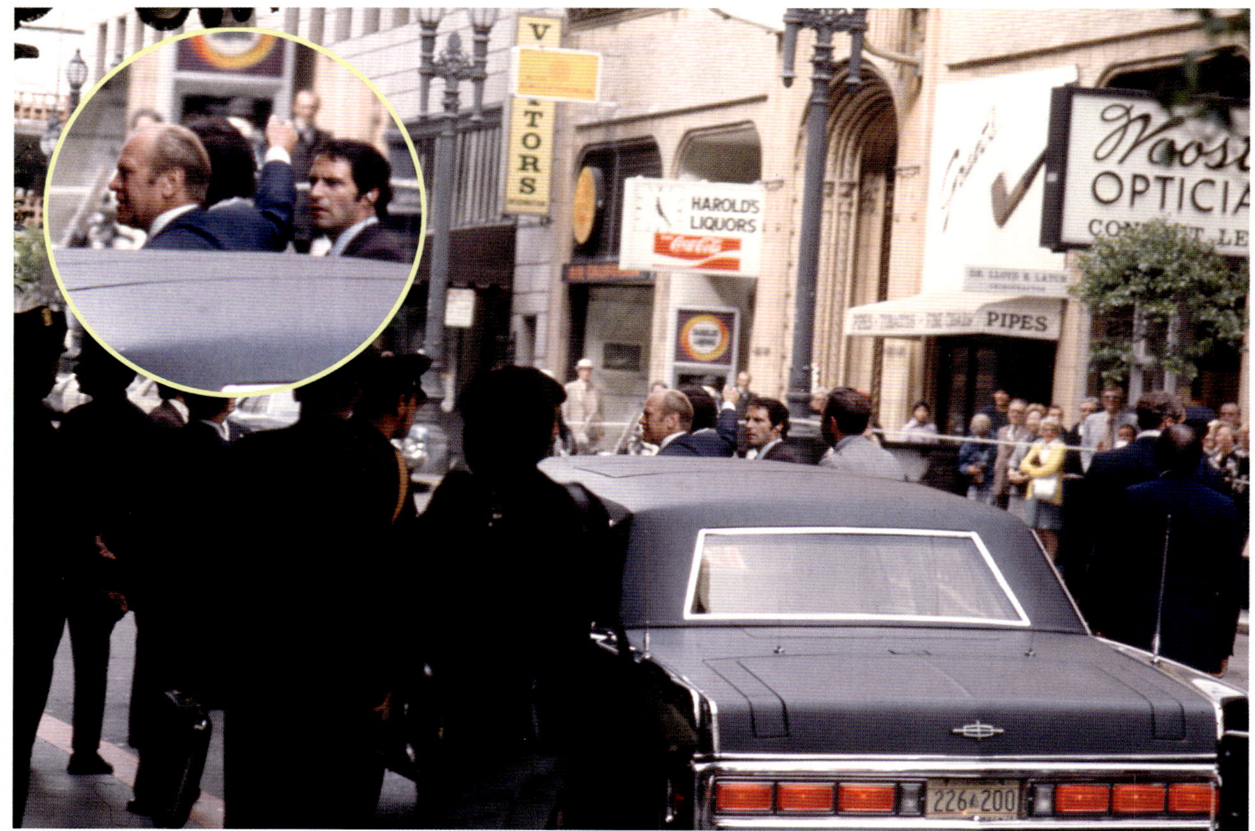

President Gerald Ford's arrival at the St. Francis Hotel, San Francisco
Photograph and collage by T. R. Uthco

landing, looking out through their aviator glasses like eyeless specters peering at the throngs of people, who begin to slowly disperse, us among them.

Later that afternoon, when Ford exited the hotel after his meeting and we were back at our studio, Sara Jane Moore, standing very near to where we had been that morning, raised a .38-caliber pistol she had purchased that morning and fired a single shot at Ford that narrowly missed him. She raised her hand to fire a second shot but was restrained by a citizen, making the second shot go astray, hitting a bystander who suffered a non-life-threatening injury.

There is a revealing moment in *The Eternal Frame*, our reenactment of the Kennedy assassination in Dallas, where Doug Michels, standing in the hotel lobby in front of the elevator soon after we arrived in Dallas and before the events in Dealey Plaza, looking perplexed and tense, is asked by the interviewer: "Is there some way you could describe this event? Would you call this art? Is it an art event? I mean what is it really?"

Doug responds, "That's what it is. What it is is figuring out what it is."

His statement summed up a lot of our thinking at the time. To us, Dingus's infiltration of the presidential arrival was art, but in fact, we didn't worry if it was for others. We didn't know or care if it was process or product. We threw ourselves out there, often motivated by a perverse curiosity, spurred on by one another, almost as in a dare, to engage the structures that pervaded our lives,

EXTRA

San Francisco Examiner

111th Year No. 88 ☆☆☆ SU 1-2424 MONDAY, SEPTEMBER 22, 1975 Daily 20c FINAL EDITION COMPLETE STOCKS

SHOT FIRED AT FORD

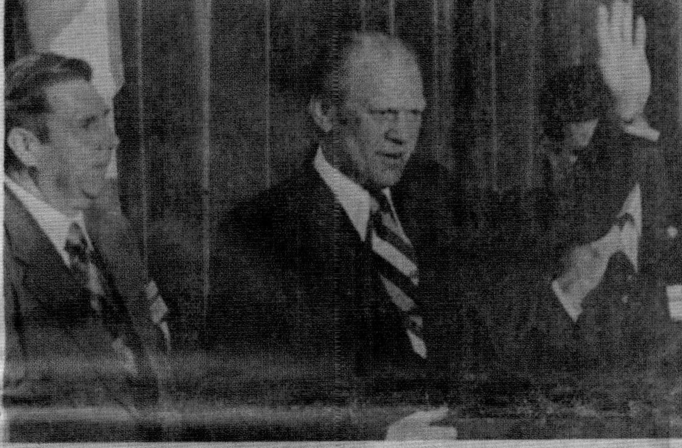

President Ford finishing speech at Hyatt Union-Square Hotel. With him is Charles Pillard, electrical union chief

Examiner Photo by Bob Bryant

A shot was fired at President Ford by a woman today as he lef the St. Francis Hotel.

The shot came from across the street.

The woman fired once as Ford left the hotel waving.

The President immediately ducked behind his limousine.

Witnesses said they saw a flash of metal from a handgun. The woman was immediately wrestled to the ground while others fell to the pavement to duck away.

The president was not hurt.

He was hustled into the car by Secret Service agents and the limousine sped away. Three agents appeared to be lying on top of the President to protect him.

Police cordoned off the area.

The suspected gunman was pushed into the St. Francis Hotel.

Officer Richard Benjamin said he was standing 10 feet away when the shot was fired.

"I took a quick look at the President," he said. "I heard a shot and turned around. A silver gun sort of hung out of the crowd.

"After the shot I heard a crack."

"I saw some smoke and then they were on him."

Patrolman Gary Bemos jumped her and wrestled her to the ground.

Bail hearing tomorrow

Patty expected to end silence

By Stephen Cook

Patricia Hearst, who has said almost nothing publicly since her arrest Thursday, is expected to end her silence tomorrow.

The 21-year-old kidnap victim turned "urban guerrilla" will probably speak for her release on bail, either directly from the witness stand or through an affidavit, during her bail hearing before U. S. District Judge Oliver J. Carter.

"It is possible she will testify on the limited question of what her intent would be if she ever gets bail," said E. J. Kleines, one of the lawyers preparing Miss Hearst's legal defense.

The legal danger is that any testimony would leave her open to cross-examination by U. S. Attorney James Browning, Kleines said.

Another option would be for Miss Hearst to speak through an affidavit, but Browning could challenge that paper declaration and demand to question Miss Hearst anyway, the lawyer said.

Miss Hearst is represented by a team of attorneys including James Martin MacInnis, Terence Hallinan, Kleines and John A. Knutson. The latter two are members of a law firm regularly representing the Hearst Corp.

Meanwhile, Miss Hearst was visited by an old school friend and six family members at the San Mateo County Jail in Redwood City yesterday.

They spoke by telephone separated by a glass wall, and talked only of "family matters," said her mother, Catherine Hearst.

Her cousin, William Randolph Hearst III, who was accompanied by his brother, Austin, and parents, Mr. and Mrs. William Randolph Hearst Jr., said Miss Hearst warned that the family conversations were probably being taped.

Her mother found her "better today. She seemed to have improved more. She's a little more in touch with reality."

Miss Hearst was not as nervous and no longer was smoking cigarettes as she had been during their first meeting in 19 months early Friday, Mrs. Hearst said.

"The first time we saw her she was not herself," she said. "She seemed to be spaced out up here (motioning to her head). Today she wasn't smoking and she was much better. She's getting better every day."

Mrs. Hearst said Patty asked about a black cat she used to have. The pet, called "Patty's cat" by the family, is still alive, the mother assured her.

Her cousin, Will, said she seemed bored, was uncertain if

—See Back Page, Col. 6

INSIDE

Weather: Foggy

Full report: Page 16

Rare press conference

Hirohito talks gently of his part in War II

By Carl Irving
Examiner Staff Writer

TOKYO — Emperor Hirohito knew about Japanese plans to attack Pearl Harbor, but doesn't want to talk about it because many who were involved still live.

In a rare press conference, the emperor said he is studying what to say to the American people about World War II, when he visits the United States next week.

But he made clear that he would not delve into his own role at that time, beyond the fact that he carried out what the pre-war constitution required of him.

In an interview earlier this month with Newsweek Magazine, Hirohito said he played a decisive role in ending the war, confirming many historians' accounts.

But the emperor declined today to comment on a book published recently that asserts he led militarist movements for nearly three decades before World War II. He said he had heard of the book, but had not read it, and therefore would not want to comment.

The 74-year-old monarch answered 17 questions during the 35-minute session with some 30 correspondents in a salon adjoining the Imperial Palace.

The emperor strode quickly into the room and began answering questions after a nod of the head.

—See Back Page, Col. 1

U.S. plans to speed arms talks

By John P. Wallach
Examiner Correspondent

NEW YORK — Secretary of State Kissinger disclosed a three-way American peace offensive today in a major speech to the U.N. General Assembly.

• In a conciliatory move toward Soviet positions, he said the United States is ready to promote an Israel-Syria agreement as the next step toward a general Mideast settlement.

• He proposed a four-power conference of the U.S., China, and North and South Korea to discuss preserving the 1953 armistice that ended the Korean war.

• And he announced plans to speed strategic arms negotiations with Russia so that a Ford-Brezhnev summit can be held in the U.S. before year end.

"Opportunities must be seized or they will disappear," he said, so the U.S. is ready to explore alternatives to a Geneva conference to get on with peace in the Mideast. Alternatives could include, he said, "perhaps a more informal multilateral meeting . . . to assess conditions and to discuss the future."

Israel has balked at including Palestinians in such a meeting and up to now has had some support from the United Sates for this. The Soviet Union, however, is understood to advocate Palestine Liberation Organization participation in such a conference.

Kissinger's remarks about the Mideast were seen as edging toward positions of the Soviets and Arabs who want the United States to press Israel to withdraw from its fronts with Syria and Jordan now that it has pulled back in Sinai.

"I want to emphasize that the

—See Back Page, Col. 3

Self-sufficient U.S. urged in talk here

By Sydney Kossen
Political Editor

President Ford disclosed a $100 billion plan here today to give the nation energy independence in 10 years.

He told a convention of the AFL-CIO Building and Construction Trades Council the project will be carried out by a government corporation.

Addressing a union whose ranks are plagued by alarmingly high unemployment, Ford said the proposed Energy Independence Authority can help create jobs.

"I want to see millions of new jobs in the next 10 years with healthy widening ripples throughout the economy," the President said.

Arriving from Monterey under heavy security, Ford addressed the 500 labor leaders at the Hyatt-Union Square Hotel.

After a slow drive past crowds lining Union Square, he stopped at the St. Francis Hotel to address 1,000 members of the World Affairs Council of Northern California on the sensitive subject of intelligence gathering.

As they did yesterday in Palo Alto, Secret Service agents with automatic weapons rode on the fenders of a car behind the President's limousine.

San Francisco police and Secret Service sharpshooters stood on rooftops, and a security helicopter flew overhead.

This was the President's second "non-political" trip to California in two weeks.

The President will return to San Francisco and Los Angeles in late October on a purely political mission — to take part in two Republican fund-raising dinners with former Gov. Ronald Reagan, his potential rival for the 1976 GOP presidential nomination.

Ford said in a weekend interview that he welcomed competition from Reagan. The President said he is confident that his Administration's policies "put us in a pretty good position."

At Stanford University yesterday, however, Ford failed to stir much enthusiasm in an outdoor audience of more than 12,000 during a speech on individual rights.

His appearance at the Stanford law school dedication marked the first time Ford was greeted on a campus by protestors reminiscent

—See Back Page, Co. 1

'Threatening note' brings one arrest

A man was arrested in Union Square today for allegedly threatening the life of President Ford.

Two others were picked up by police and Secret Service agents but were released after questioning.

Heavy security measures were in effect in the square as Ford arrived in The City, stopped briefly at the Hyatt Union Square Hotel, then drove the one block to the St. Francis Hotel for his noontime speech.

There were several demonstrations, but the crowds were not large.

Ford did not mingle with the people — as he had been doing when an attempt to assassinate him was made recently in Sacramento.

The only major incident was at the St. Francis, before he arrived there.

The man involved was identified as Ronald Carlo, 24, who said he is a fisherman from Mobile, Ala., and has been staying here at 1139 Market St.

William Greener, chief deputy White House press secretary, said the man approached the hotel cashier and "handed her a note threatening the President's life."

"The cashier read the note and went for help," Greener said. "When she returned the man and the note were gone."

Greener said Carlo spoke to the doorman on the way out, telling him in effect to "get out of here . . . . He showed him the handwritten note, and said 'Here's what's going to happen.' The d

—See Back Page

Front page, *San Francisco Examiner*, September 22, 1975

many of which were invisible or, if evident, were veiled and not easily ascertained. In the case of the Ford visit, it had to do with exploring the theatrics of presidential power and the security that was part of the show. These were themes we had enacted performatively as the Artist-President and in *The Eternal Frame*, and would later in videos of mine like *The Speech* and *This Is the Truth.* By placing ourselves in the center of the spectacle, we owned it for a short time. It was no longer something that existed mysteriously at the peripheries of our bodies, but was brought in close, embodied, unmasked to a certain extent, and put into human scale. No longer epic, unassailable, or sublime by being "over there," but more comprehensible and less frightening by being "right here."

It was in this spirit that Diane and I, cameras in hand, mingled with the crowd, made up of the curious and reporters armed with larger cameras, that had assembled at the Federal Courthouse on Golden Gate Avenue, where Patty Hearst was being held shortly after her arrest that same September of 1975. And why, a year earlier, Jody and I showed up at the New York trial of John Mitchell, Nixon's attorney general, and Maurice Stans, finance chairman for the Committee to Reelect the President (CREEP), who were charged with criminal conspiracy related to their roles in Nixon's reelection campaign. Interacting with this and similar spectacles was our way of penetrating obfuscating bureaucracies, allowing us to witness stories on our own terms rather than as interpreted by the media. In the case of the Stans trial, we thought of ourselves as observers and as bit players—extras without speaking parts—in the unfolding show. We weren't deluded into thinking that we could alter the narrative, but being there gave us a sense of participation and perhaps the illusion of some degree of control.

Similar thoughts were the impetus behind a trio of projects I proposed in the late 1970s. The idea was to infiltrate as "artist-in-residence" three bastions of American life: the office of the president of the United States (at the time Jimmy Carter); professional sports (specifically the San Francisco Giants baseball team); and finally, a small-market television news station. Of the three, only the television news project produced acceptable results.

The White House project came close to becoming a reality thanks to the help of Barry Jagoda, Carter's main media adviser and the friend of a friend, but became impossible when the White House, which had been very open, almost loose in its interaction with the press and public, pulled back following a scandal involving a cabinet member.

In 1977, I did get permission to be artist-in-residence with the San Francisco Giants. I spent time with them at their Arizona spring training camp where I became friendly with several of the players, particularly third baseman Darrell Evans, formerly of the Atlanta Braves.[7] After the team

7. Evans was on first base when Hank Aaron hit his historic 715th home run.

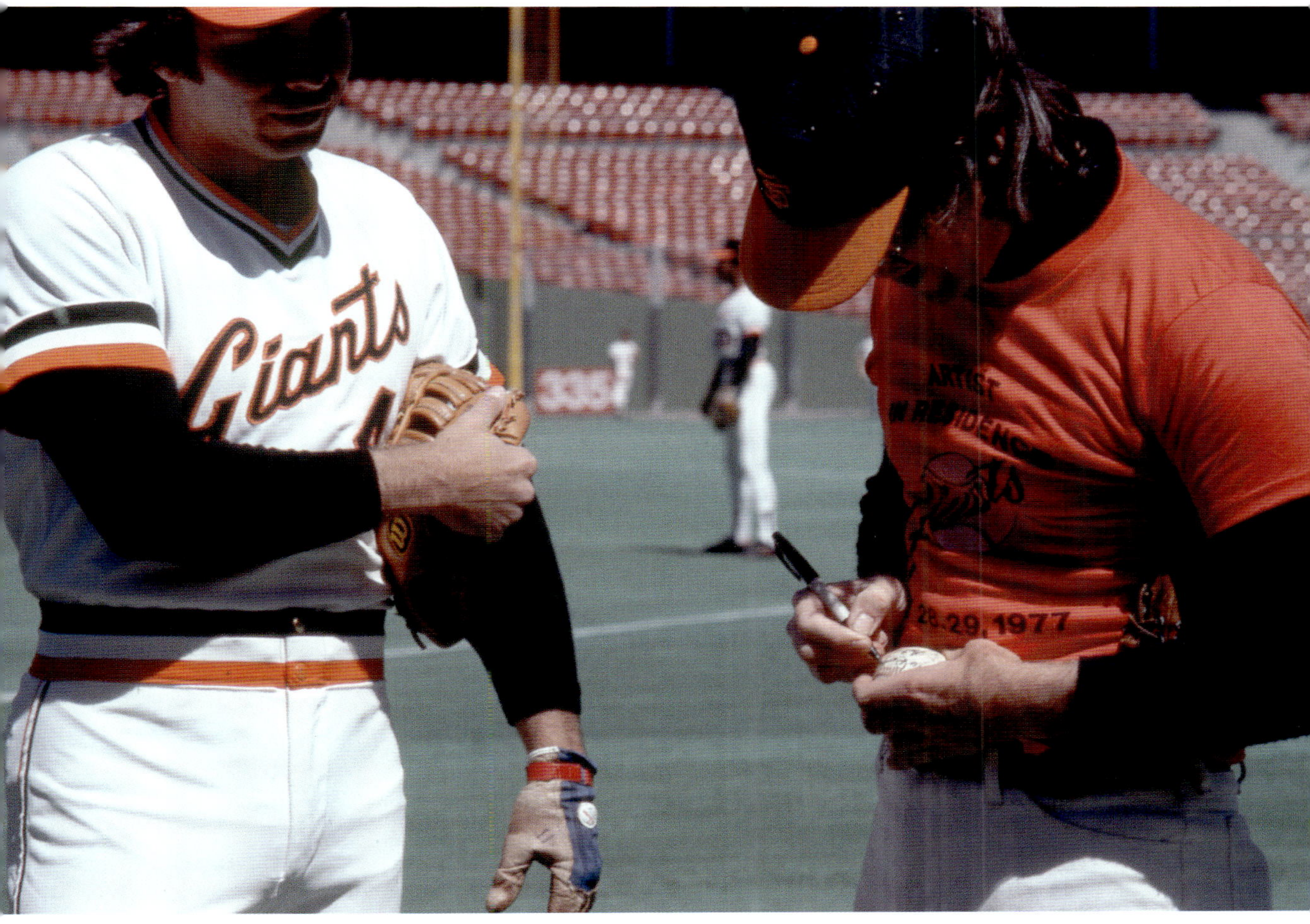

Autographing a baseball for Giants third baseman Darrell Evans from *Game of the Week,* 1977
Photograph by Diane Andrews Hall

returned to San Francisco, we produced a video, *Game of the Week*, which mainly consisted of my learning from the players such things as how to look cool when chewing tobacco, or the correct way to interact with fans when signing an autograph. In the end, the results were considerably less than what I had hoped for. Not a home run.

More successful was *The Amarillo News Tapes*, which I made in 1979, collaborating with Chip and Jody shortly after both Ant Farm and T. R. Uthco disbanded. As in the other projects, we were interested in examining a cultural institution, in this case, a small-market television station in Amarillo that was conveniently owned by Stanley Marsh III. Marsh, the flamboyant, controversial businessman and rancher I had met in 1975 when he assumed the role of Texas Governor John Connally for our assassination remake in Dallas, had a penchant for supporting unusual art projects. Among them were Robert Smithson's *Amarillo Ramp*, installed on Marsh's property close to where Smithson

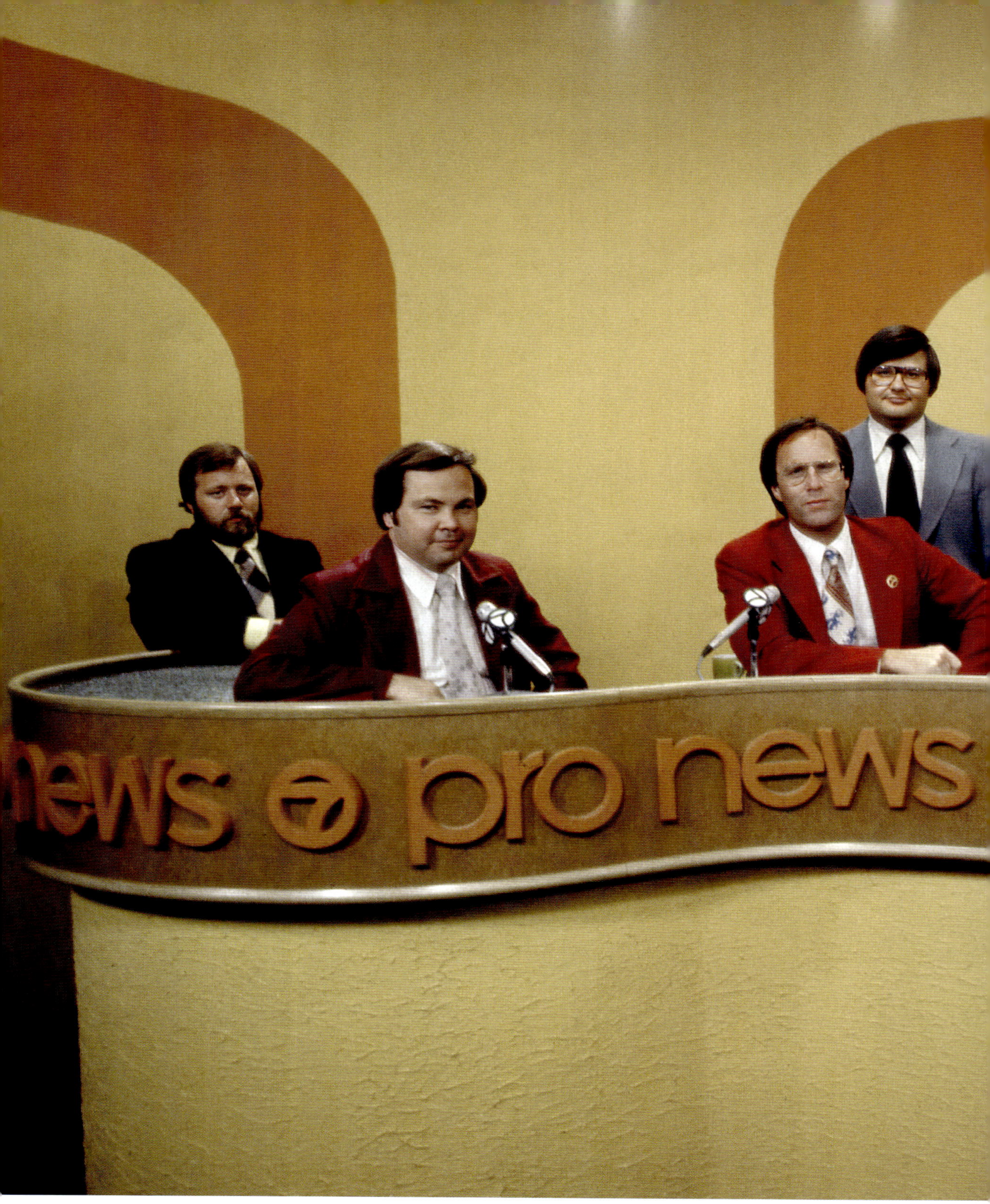

The Amarillo News Tapes, Artist News Team with Pro News Team (front row, from second from left: Doug Hall, News Anchor; Jody Procter, Sports Anchor; Chip Lord, Weatherman)
Photographer unknown

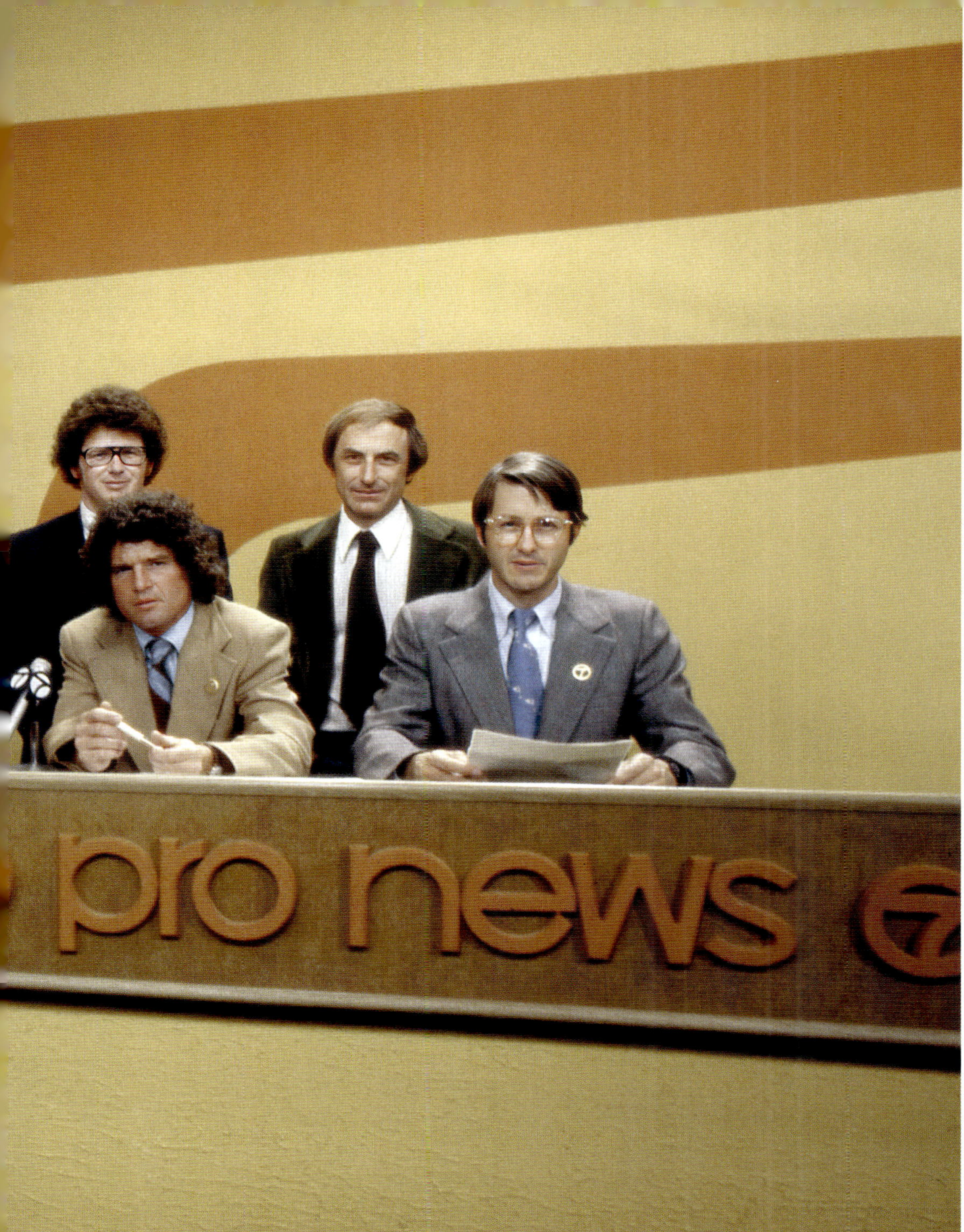
pro news

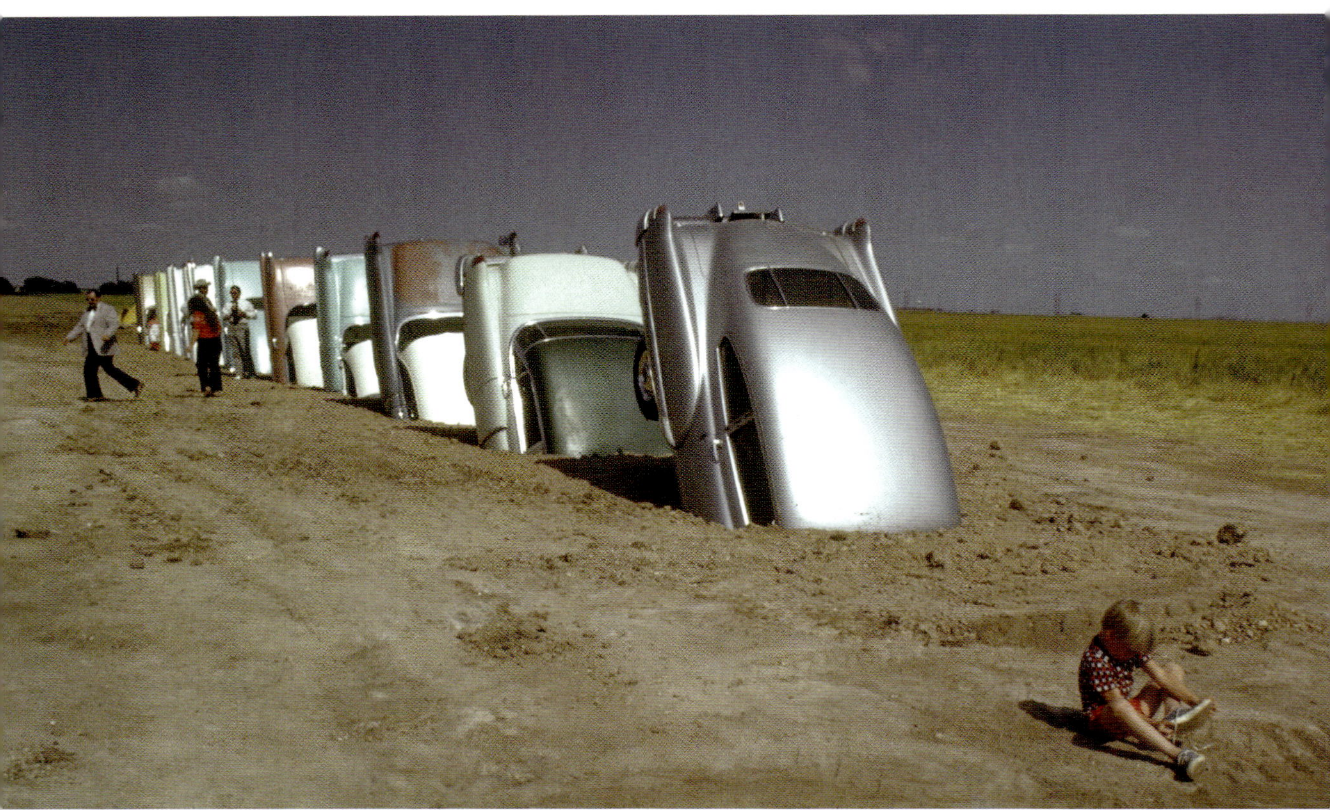

Ant Farm's *Cadillac Ranch* shortly after it was installed in 1974
Photograph by Chip Lord

died when the plane from which he was photographing the finished sculpture crashed. Ant Farm, learning of his aesthetic adventurism, reached out to Marsh in 1972 when the group proposed their roadside sculpture, *Cadillac Ranch,* which Stanley eventually funded and had installed on one of his many properties, a wheat field that was visible from the nearby highway. The now well-known public art installation, completed in 1974, consists of ten Cadillacs from 1949 to 1963, defining the rise and fall of the tail fin, that are buried nose first.

For our intervention into the television news department, Stanley gave us permission to do as we wished as long as we didn't interfere with the broadcasts or prevent the staff from doing their jobs. The video shows the three of us in our respective roles as anchor (me), weatherman (Chip), and sportscaster (Jody) interacting with the real Pro News Team on the set. In such episodes as "Opening Routine," "Liberal Fire," and "Two Stories," we drew attention to the oddities of language, gesture, and setting that constituted the ubiquitous theater of small-market television news. Although the episodes are humorous, our purpose was not parody for its own sake but to examine how local news is packaged and ritualized to create a program—a show—that is both familiar and a trusted authority.

In "Two Stories," the station's real news reader, in an authoritative and deadpan way, and with the perfect cadence and inflections we expect from our television anchors, reads a nonsensical script that we (Jody, I think) wrote for him. With his eyes moving between the script in his hands and the camera in front of him, he reads:

> The windshield was dirty, and the brakes had failed on at least three occasions. The rear bumper was dented and there were several rust spots around the door. But the tires were old and and some threads could be seen. Little tufts of foam rubber were peeking out of the upholstery where it had been ripped. There was brown tape attached to the ceiling and there were stains on the dashboard. The radio no longer worked, but on the television, there was a man laughing at a woman. The woman wore a white hat and talked in a foreign accent, possibly Czechoslovakian. She said she had been in the basement when the phone rang and that when she answered it there was no voice.[8]

In the midst of our detached, deconstructive examination of a news station—where the usual stories featured nearby fires, the price of sorghum, local politics, and prices at the daily cattle auction—a devastating tornado ripped through Wichita Falls, Texas, leveling sections of the city, killing forty-five people, and injuring many more. Suddenly the game had changed. A real news story.

In the early morning hours of April 11, we climb into the Pro News van with the two senior reporters and head southeast on Highway 287. Four hours later, in the predawn morning, we arrive in Wichita Falls and slowly make our way into the most stricken area of the city. It is a ghostly scene as the first light of morning casts an eerie glow across the destruction. Trees, entirely shorn of leaves, limbs fractured, are silhouetted against the sky; a massive combine, battered and bent, lies on its side, like a stricken beast resting in the median between the two lanes of the highway. As the sun comes up, we come upon a car surrounded by firemen with the Jaws of Life, prying open the crumpled door to free the bloodied, inert body inside.

And finally, the residential neighborhood—or what remains of a neighborhood: utterly flattened, debris everywhere. Dazed residents, some weeping, others staring blankly, move slowly, almost mechanically, like zombies or robots, bending from time to time to pick up a tattered photograph or some other salvaged keepsake. The air is still, punctuated by an occasional siren, the intermittent scream of chain saws, and the chatter of bystanders and

8. Doug Hall, Chip Lord, and Jody Procter, "Two Stories," excerpt, *The Amarillo News Tapes*, 1979–80, video, 28 min.

survivors. Emergency vehicles are everywhere. And, of course, members of the press, local and national, wander through the wreckage looking for people to interview. And we are right there with them, sticking our microphones into the same faces that all the other reporters have been hounding. What is striking is how predictable both the questions and answers are, a required ritual-of-testimony to accompany a disaster.

Our reporter asks, "Could you tell us what it was like here when the tornado hit? It must have been terrifying."

A man stands in front of what had been a kitchen but is now half a kitchen, its front wall gone, but with unbroken dishes still in the sink and an open cupboard where cups and plates are still neatly stacked. He responds in a heavy Texas drawl, "I was watchin' television when the whistles started blowin'. I knew we could be in for it. I ain't got no storm basement so I go into the bathroom and climb into the bathtub. It sounded like a freight train was comin' through. It sounded like a thousand freight trains. The whole house was shakin' and I could hear the wood rippin' and stuff. Darn, I thought I was done for."

But the prize interview—the one everyone is looking for—is that of a reasonably attractive person, preferably a woman under forty, who can deliver that heartfelt moment, perhaps with a few tears but not hysterical weeping, which can signal defeat. The treasured interview must include a positive note of triumph over adversity. We wait to speak to a youngish woman who is talking to another news crew. She is wearing a denim skirt, t-shirt, and a blue patterned scarf to control her long hair. Her tennis shoes are muddy; there are mud splatters on her skirt and shirt and a smudge on her cheek that looks like it might have been placed there by a makeup artist. Watching her talk to the reporter we can see she is relaxed and well spoken. Our Pro News guys are salivating.

When our turn comes, our reporter moves in and, after a few introductory remarks, asks, "How are you doing?" And with a deeply sympathetic inflection adds, "Looks like you lost pretty much everything."

Her eyes well, but no actual tears as she responds with a resigned look, somewhere between a grimace and a slight smile, "Yeah, it's all gone." Pause.

"How does it feel?"

She looks at our reporter for a moment then answers, "Terrible. We've lost everything." (I'm thinking, how do you think it feels?) "Even our dogs, Cherry and Sam, are gone. Maybe they ran off, but we can't find them."

"I'm so sorry for your loss. Hopefully the dogs will turn up."

"Well, we are alright. My daughter and me. We can rebuild. We will rebuild." (We have struck reporter gold.) "The Lord has a purpose for everyone, and we can't question that." Pause. She turns her head down and slightly to the left before raising it gain. "He never gives us a burden we can't handle." Another pause, a slight, resigned—but not self-pitying—smile and then, "There are people a lot worse off than we are."

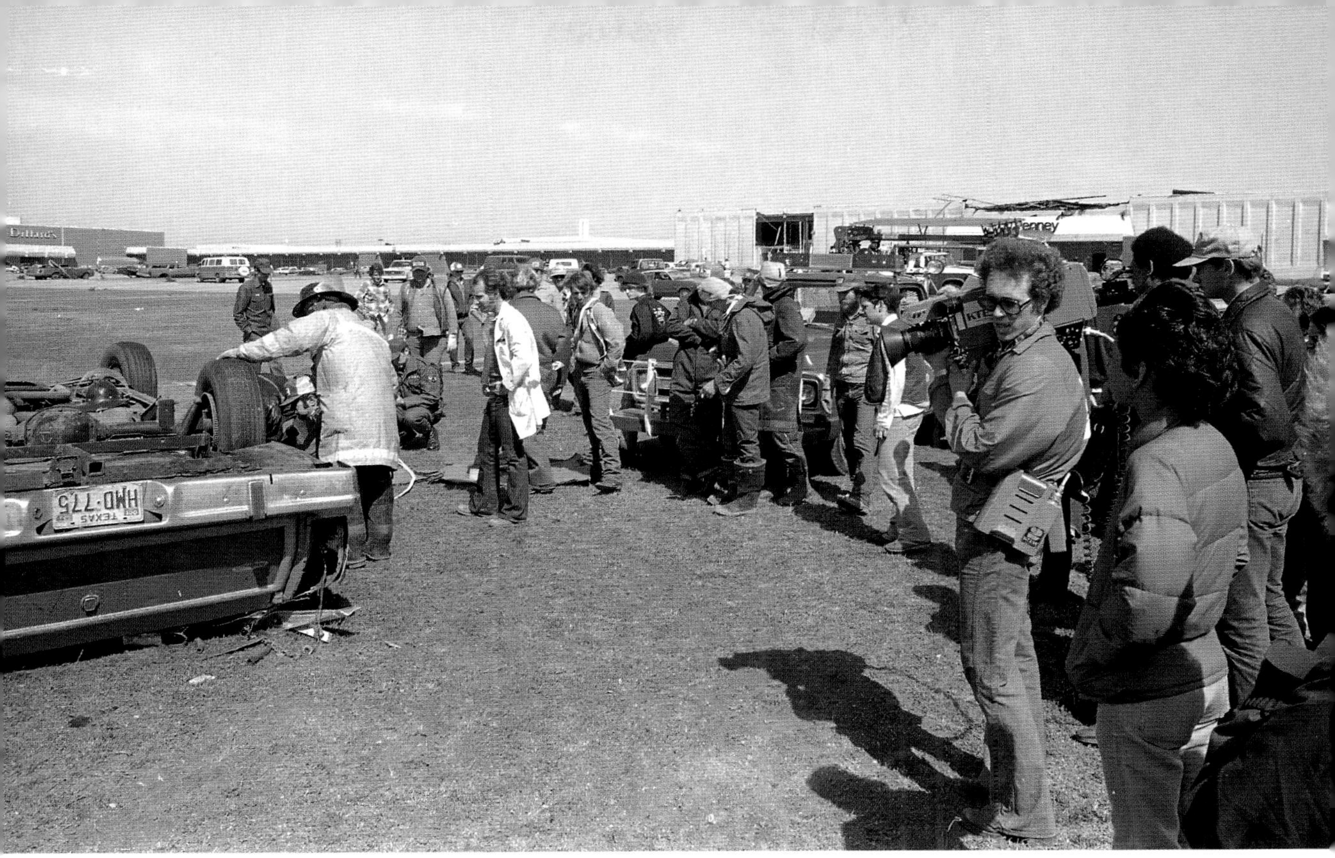

Firemen using the "jaws of life" to pry open a car door to extract the body within
Photograph by Hall/Lord/Procter

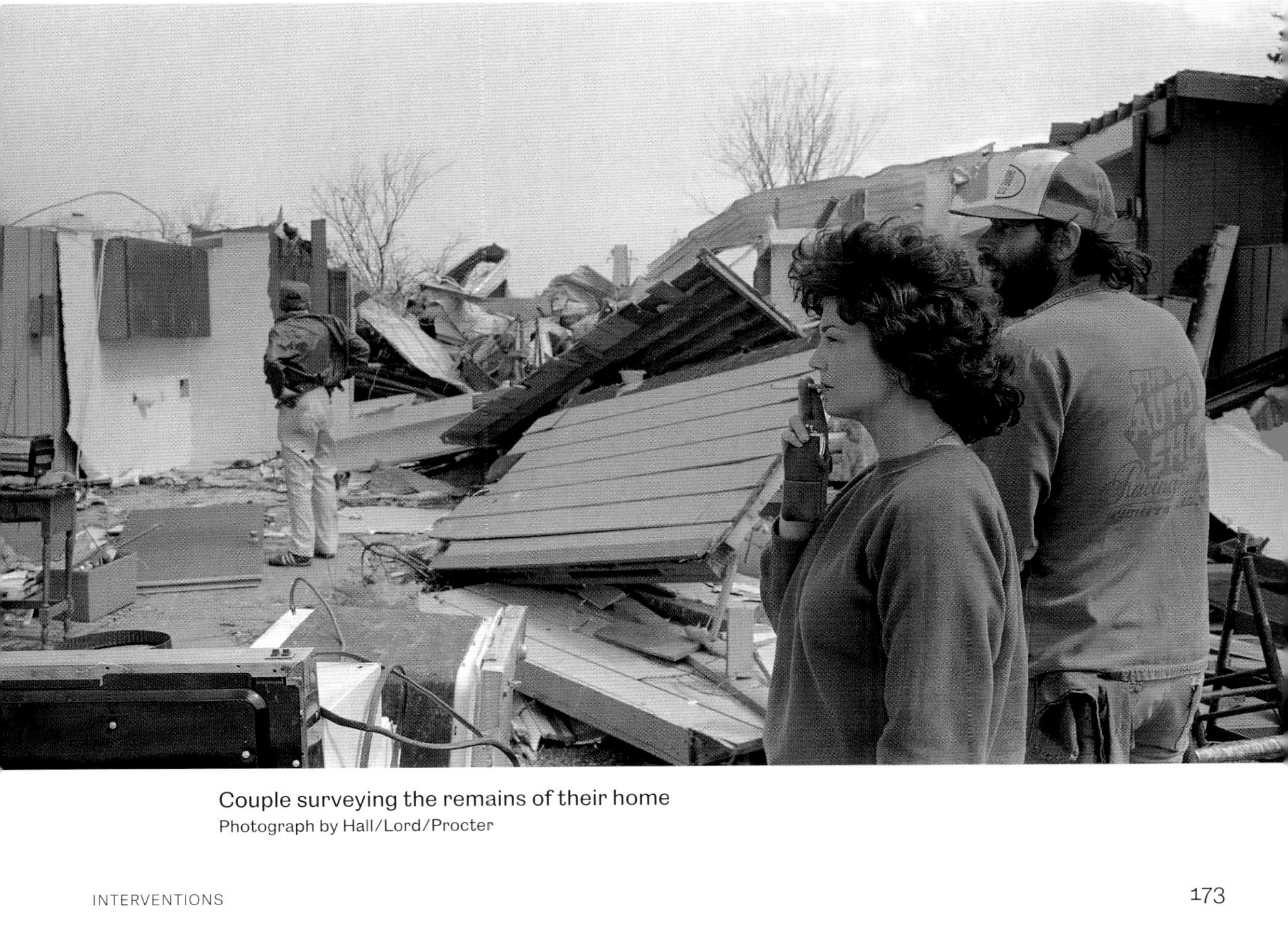

Couple surveying the remains of their home
Photograph by Hall/Lord/Procter

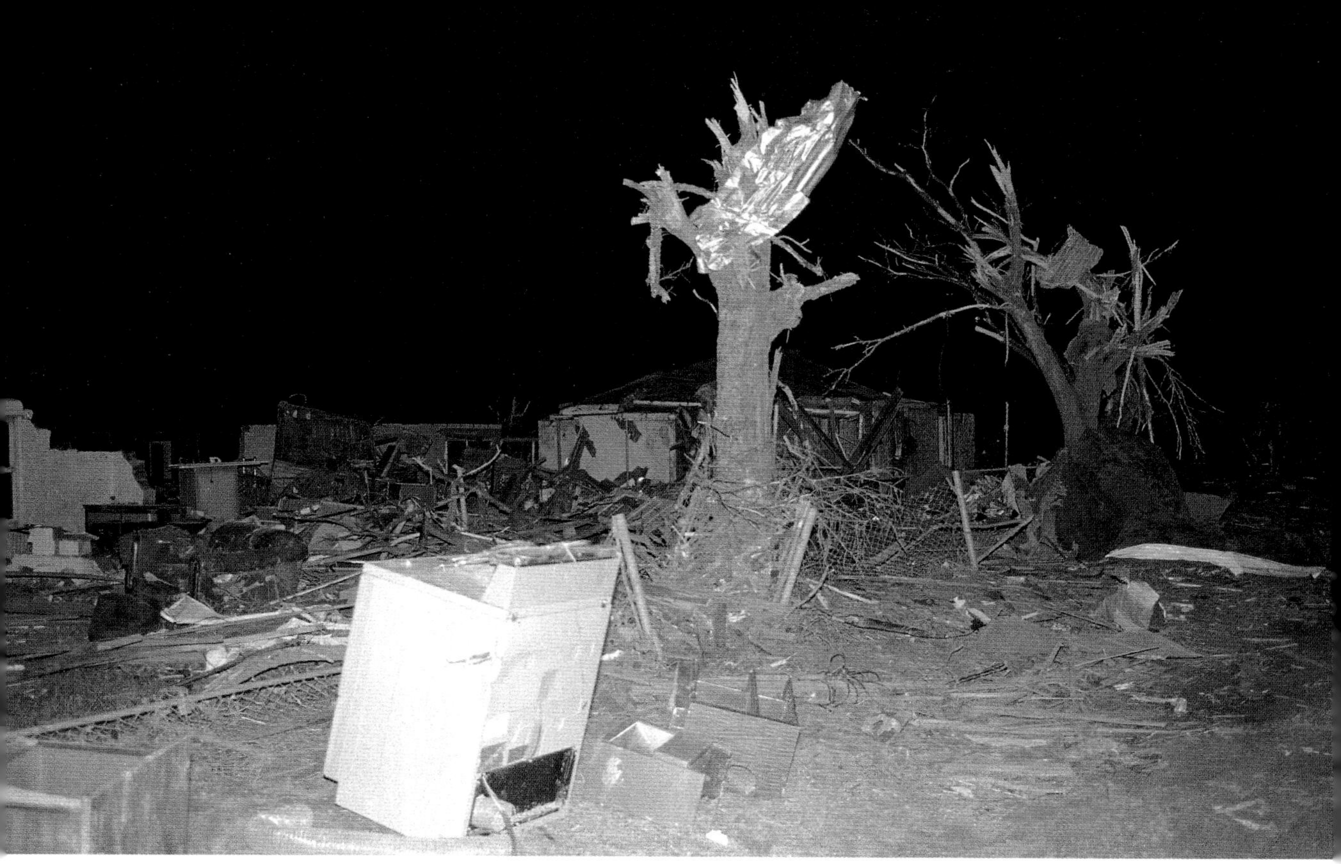

Tornado devastation illuminated by the headlights of the Pro News van
Photograph by Hall/Lord/Procter

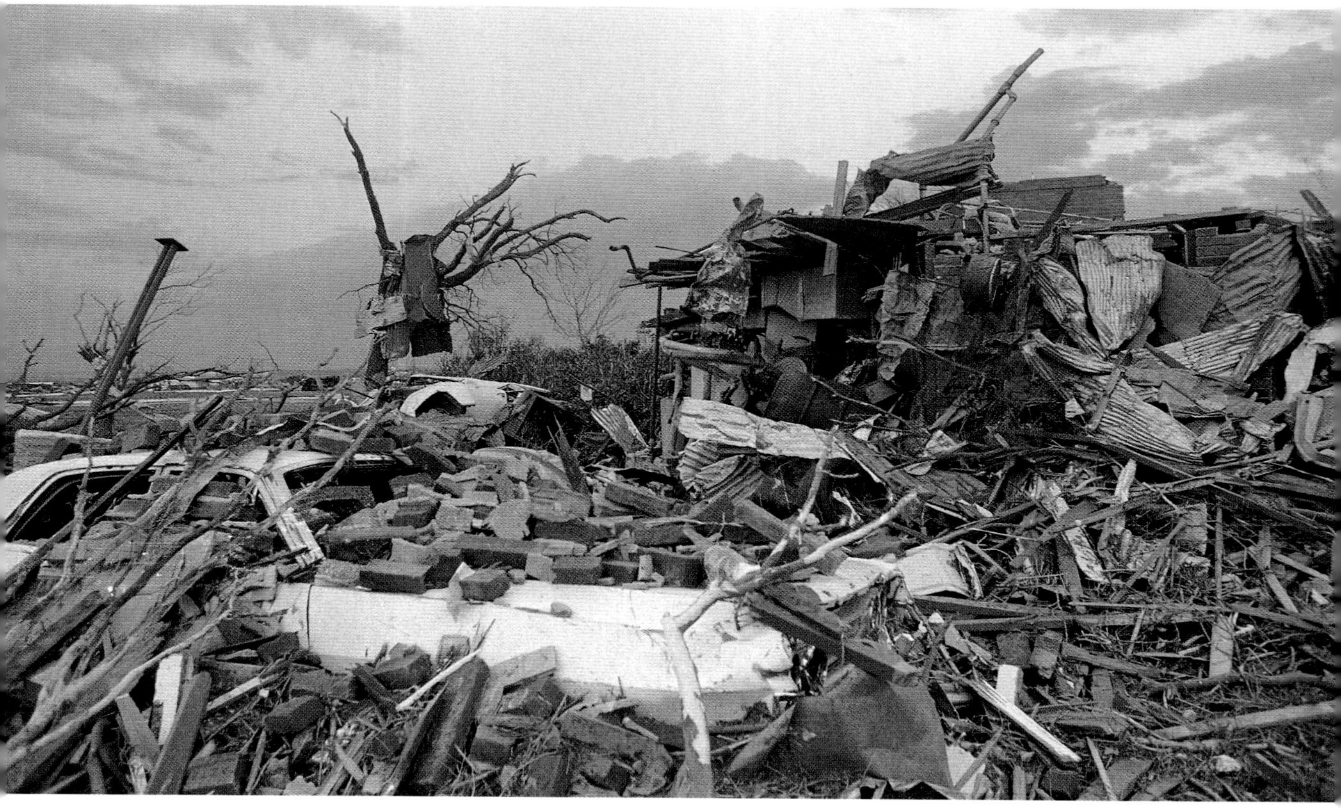

Tornado's destruction revealed in morning's early light
Photograph by Hall/Lord/Procter

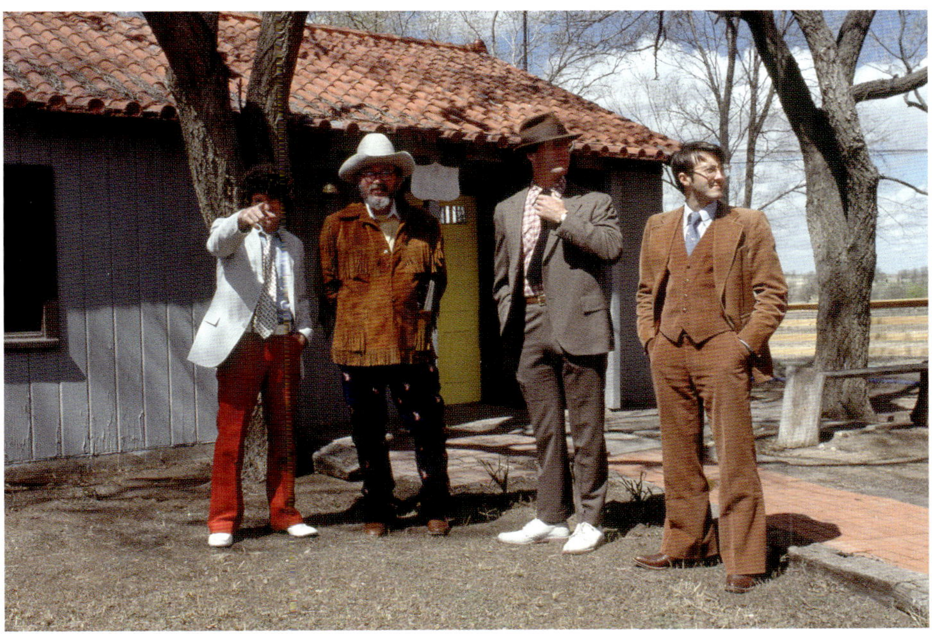

At Toad Hall, Stanley Marsh's ranch in Amarillo (l to r): Jody, Stanley, me, Chip

It goes on like this for a while as our reporter milks every drop he can from this agreeable respondent. After the interview concludes and the woman has been claimed by other reporters, we exchange the equivalent of high fives through our facial expressions. Once back in the van on our way to Dillard's department store, which has been ripped apart and promises to be another good site for interviews and devastation video, we congratulate ourselves for our brilliant reporting with whoops and "hot damns." We are now seen by ourselves and the two reporters as fully part of the Pro News team.

Later that night while I sit in the van heading back to Amarillo, my head bobbing as I fall in and out of sleep, I have some thoughts about what unfolded earlier. The elation we feel is partially explained by the pure excitement of finding ourselves in the middle of life and death drama. Perhaps doctors experience something like this performing triage at a disaster sight. But in our case, there is a significant difference. Whereas the doctors are trying to save lives, we in our roles as make-believe reporters, along with the real thing, are controllers of the narrative. We are the storytellers, tourists of the terrible. Arrogant about the importance of our mission, we revel in our subjectivity. In our minds, we are bold witnesses to destruction and even death, who bravely plod through the wreckage, cameras and microphones in hand, unharmed by the frightening events that preceded us, and so feeling a sense of power and control. Without judgment, I accept that, among other things, our sense of importance is a self-aggrandizing fantasy.

Some Ideas Are More Unusual than Others

Throughout the seventies, T. R. Uthco, and I individually, explored a more sedate, and I suppose more traditional, studio practice in photography. These works were based in performance, and until recently, none of them made it out of our archives to be exhibited. One reason for this was that no one, including dealers or curators, knew of their existence, but the reason for *that* is a little more complicated than laziness on our part.

Not recognized as "photographers," we lacked a context for showing photography. As a result, these works, never publicly exhibited, were largely forgotten and buried away in mislabeled boxes scattered in various locations. That is, until a few years ago when I started pawing through old cartons and flat files. Discovering these projects from our distant past was like coming across old acquaintances I'd lost contact with. I was reminded how important these photographs had been to our collective and to me personally in providing ways to develop or discard ideas that we were pursuing.

Most were done as studies for performances. They allowed Jody and me to see what we were doing and to gain a little critical distance so that, working with Diane, we could establish the kind of gestural language we were after. It was later, in the early 1980s, that I organized some of them into finished works. One set shot in 1972 became *8 Gestures*, a sequence of photographs in which, dressed in our customary suits, Jody and I strike ambiguous postures. As studies, the photographs provided a way for us to examine and ultimately choose gestures that, when done live, would comprise a series of performative non sequiturs. It was Diane who recognized that they might be interesting in themselves, insisted on printing them on quality fiber-based paper, and encouraged me to organize them into the sequences that exist today.

It must have been on the same day that we took the photos for *8 Gestures* that we did another series, later organized under the title *Unusual Ideas*. A sequence of fifteen photographs was arranged into five separate episodes of two to four photos. Accompanying each episode was an oblique narrative, typed on a small, lined page that could have been ripped from a 3 x 5–inch notepad.

Among the photo series that I did on my own with Diane behind the camera were those that fell under the general heading, "Imitations of Everyday Objects." One set, *The Way Things Look*, consists of ten 8 x 10–inch photos of me standing in front of a wall in contorted body positions. Under each photo is a title on a lined filing card that identifies the action in the photograph. For example, below an image of me blurred by rapid movement are the words, "An abstract expressionist painting." Titles for other photos read: "A soggy kitchen sponge," "A crack in the sidewalk," "A glass of curdled milk," and so on.

They understood that the
worst ideas are those
that can lead to other
ideas. These ideas can
be dangerous. Religion
is of this type. And
perhaps politics. Clearly
some ideas are better
left unthought.

Unusual Ideas, "Episode V," 1972. Text on notebook page with four gelatin silver prints, 10 × 8 in. ea. (25.4 × 20.3 cm)
Photographs by T. R. Uthco (Diane Andrews Hall)

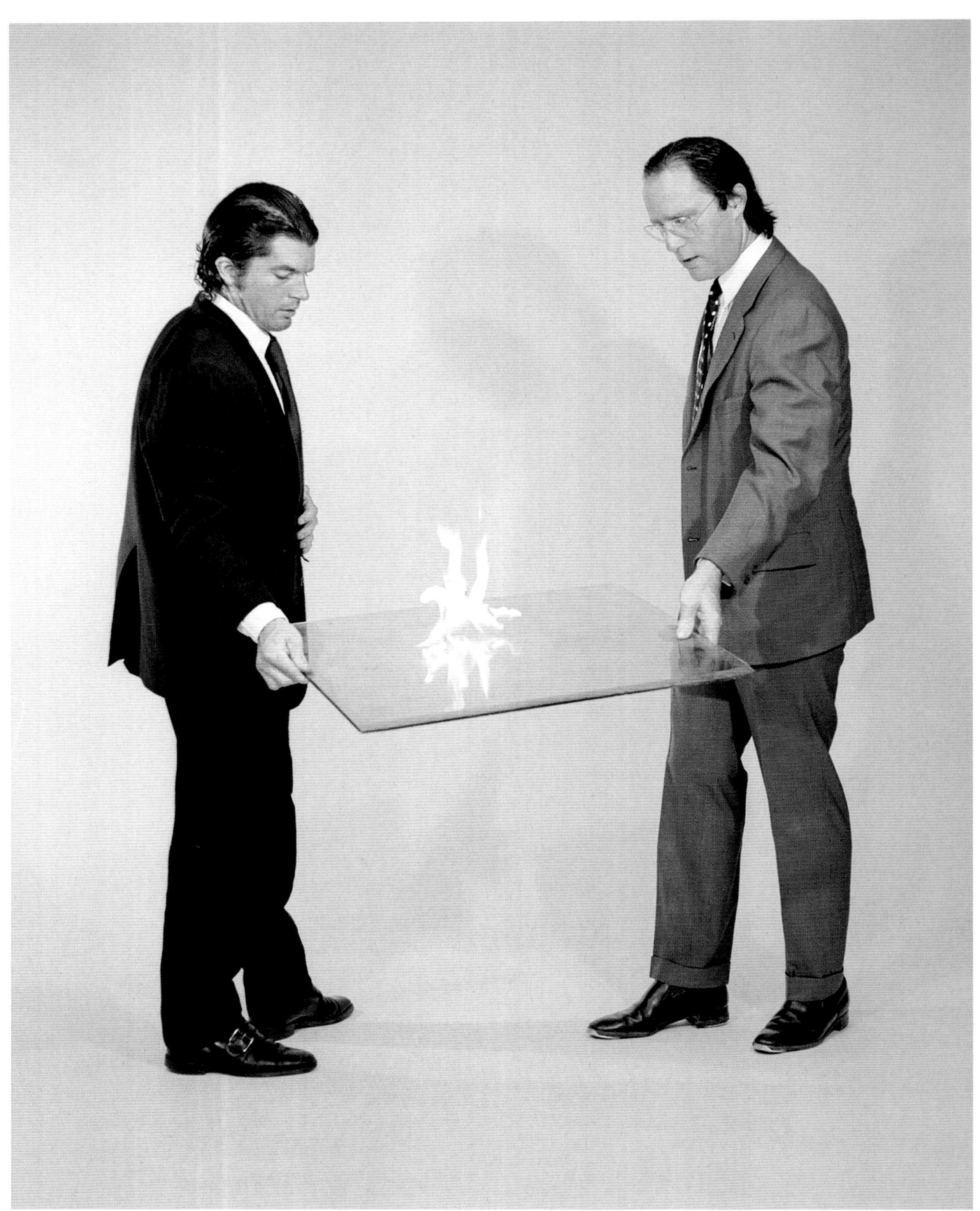

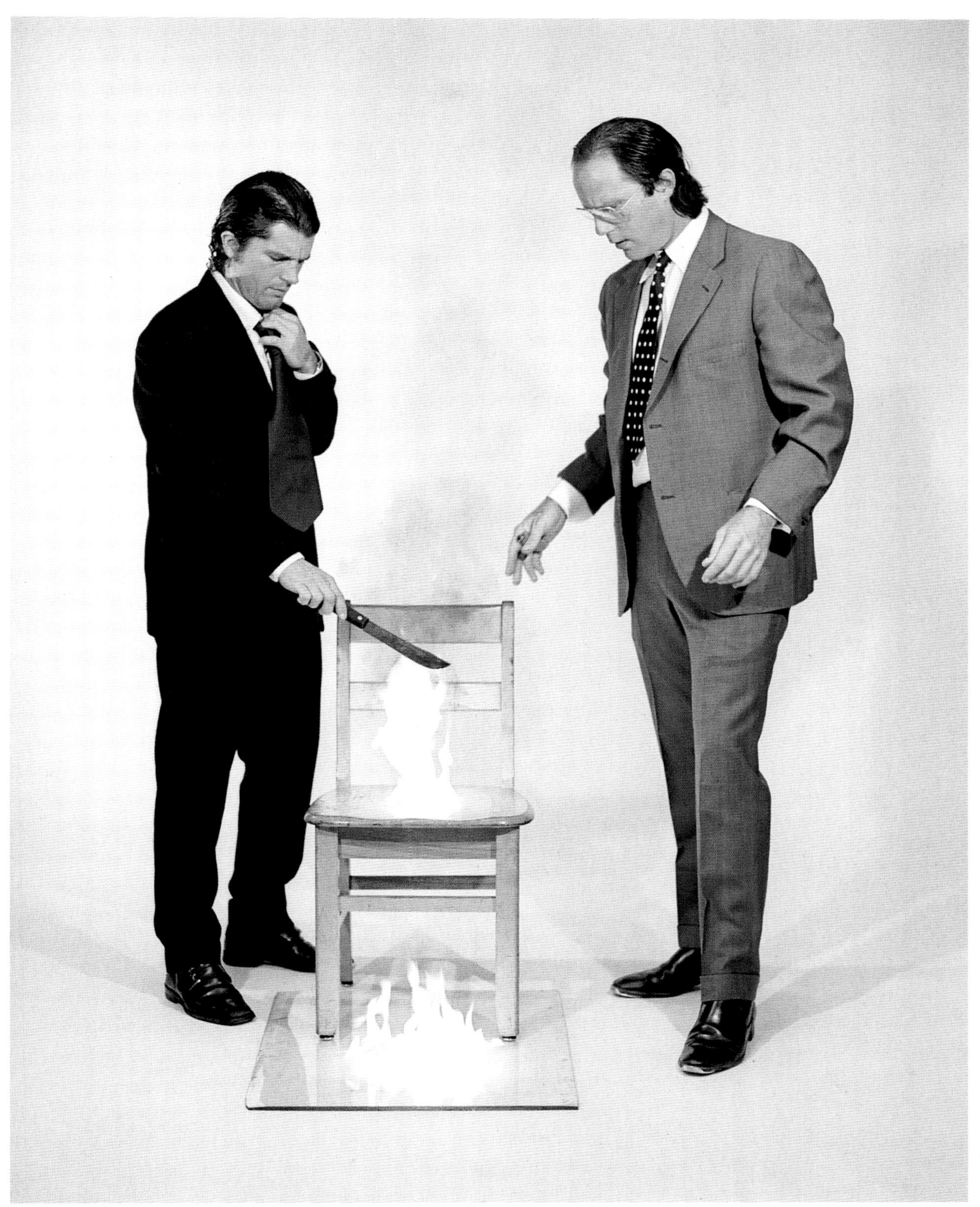

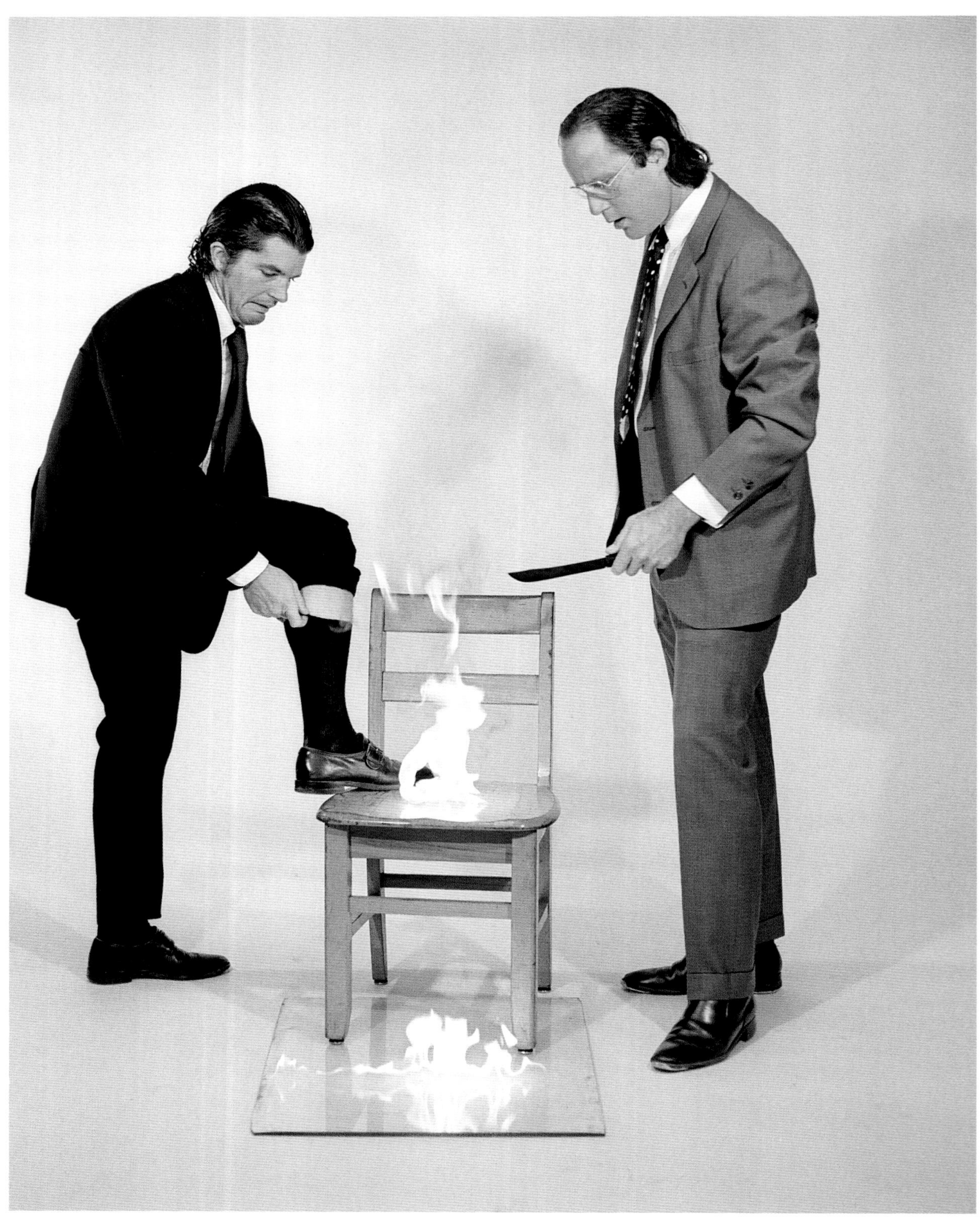

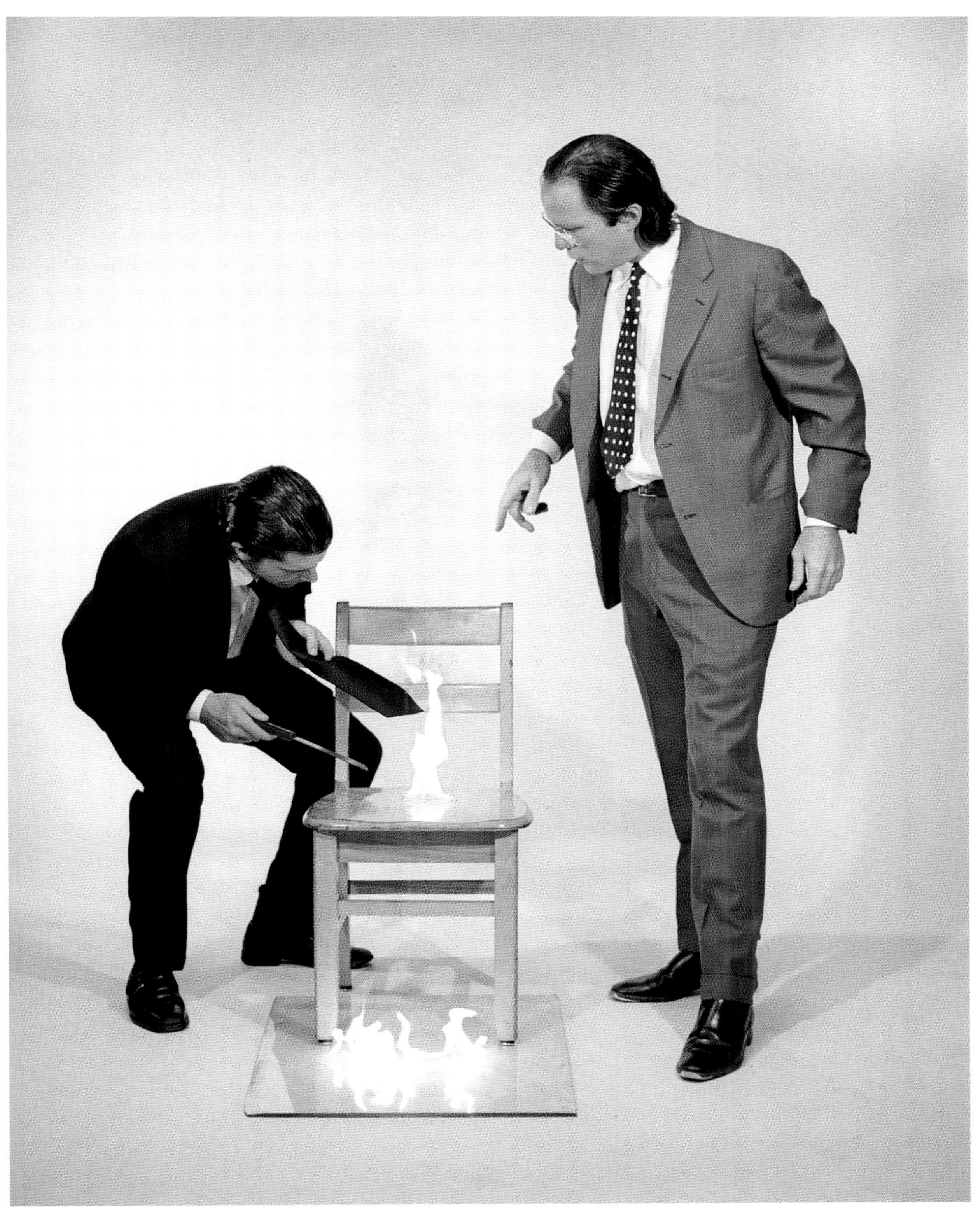

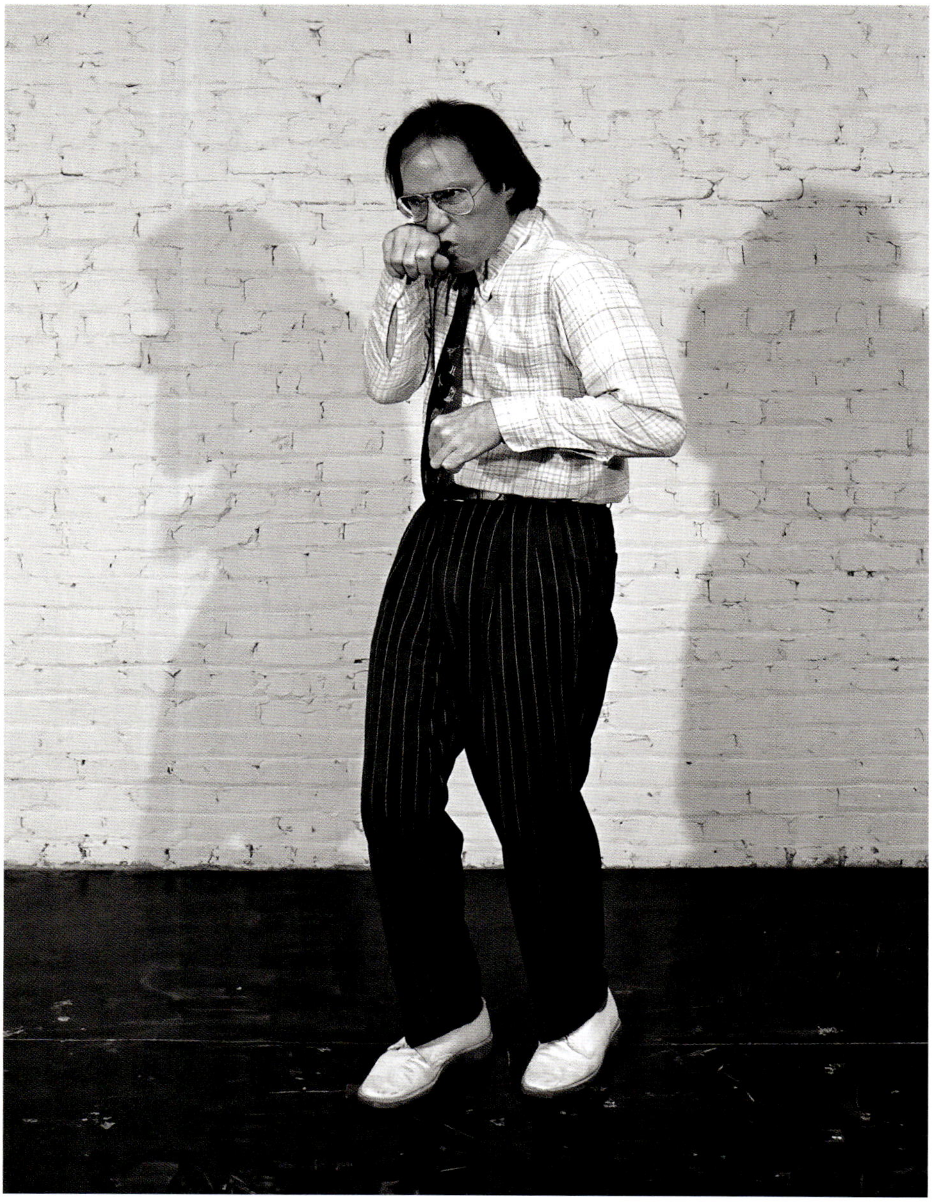

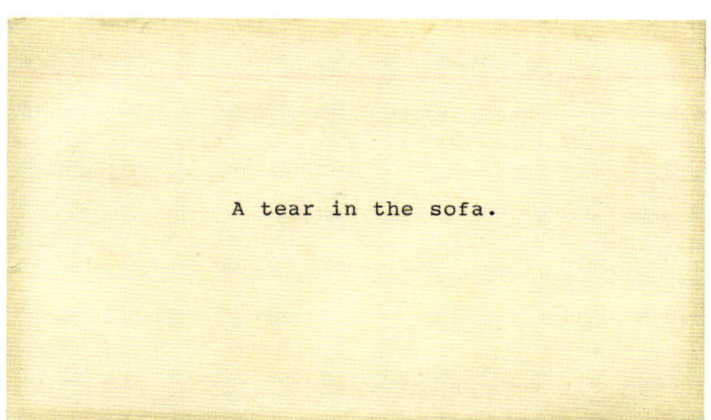

From *The Way Things Look*, 1974. Text on filing card with gelatin silver print, 10 × 8 in. (25.4 × 20.3 cm)

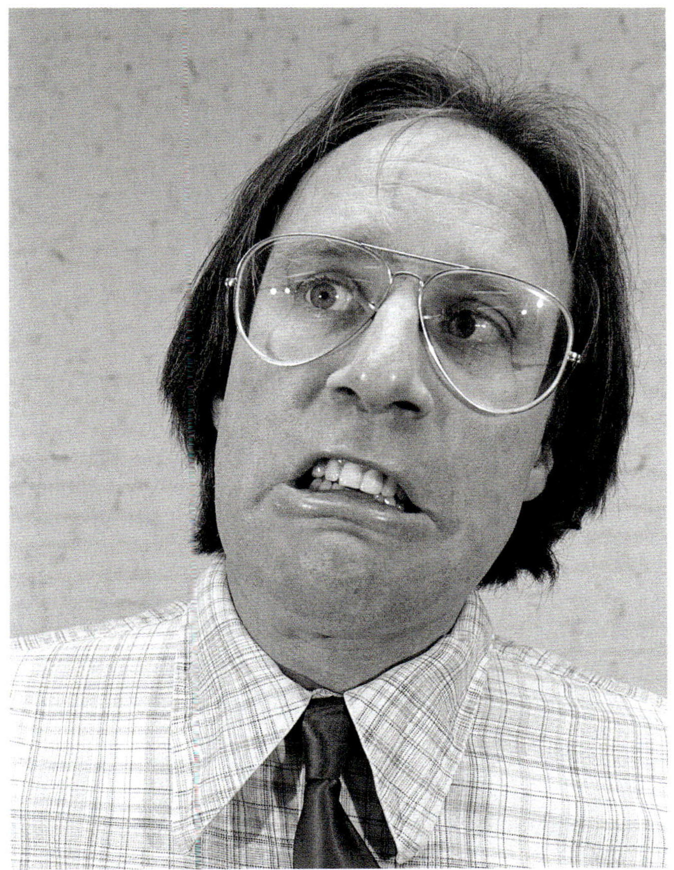

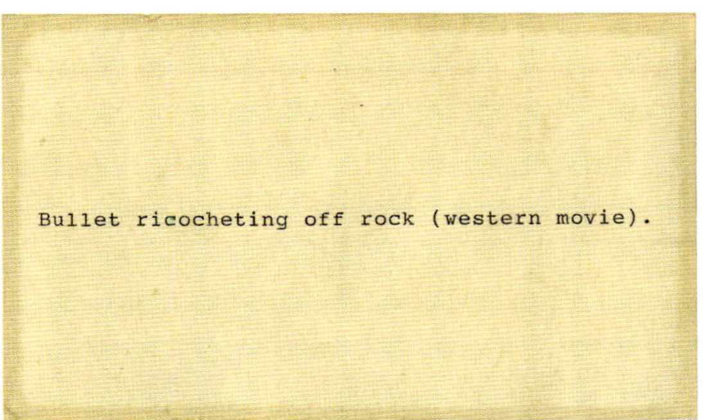

From *The Way Things Sound*, 1974. Text on filing card with gelatin silver print, 10 × 8 in. (25.4 × 20.3 cm)

I did a similar series based on sounds and appropriately titled *The Way Things Sound* with titles like "Machine gun fire (gangster movie)," "Toilet flushing," and "Squeaky right shoe." These and other modest photographic works were the ingredients for a game—to me a serious game—about language and image, sense and nonsense, and the limits of representation. They were visual notes that provided me with ways to think and make at a time when I had very limited resources.

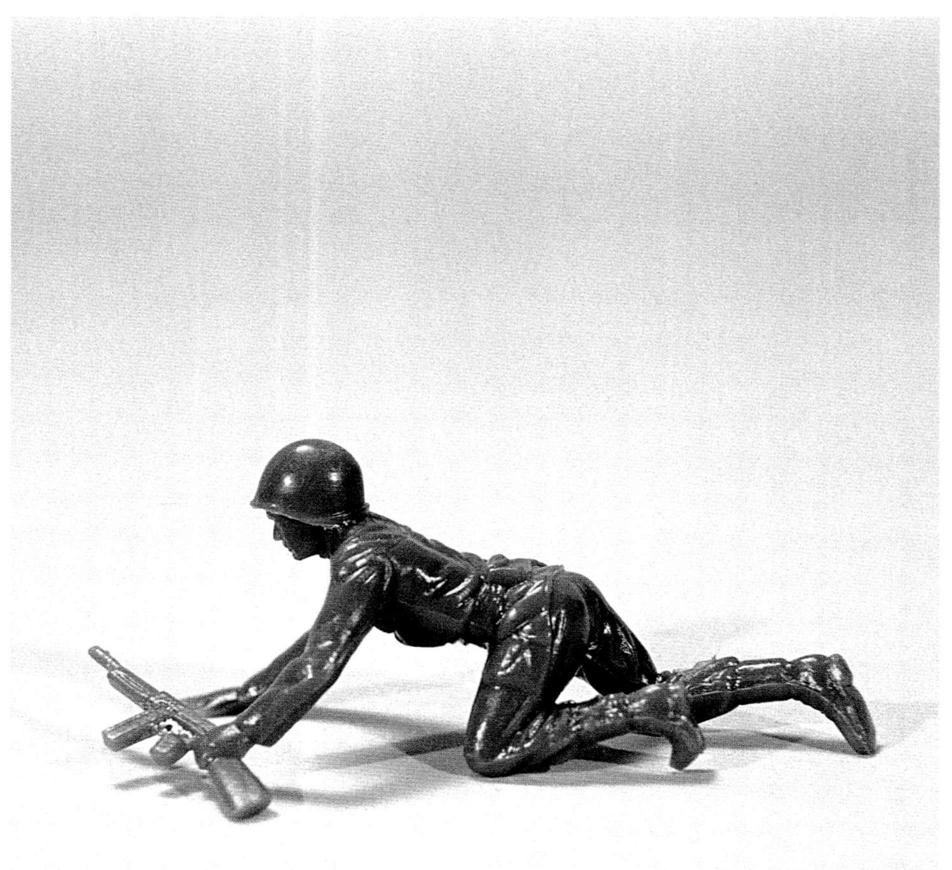

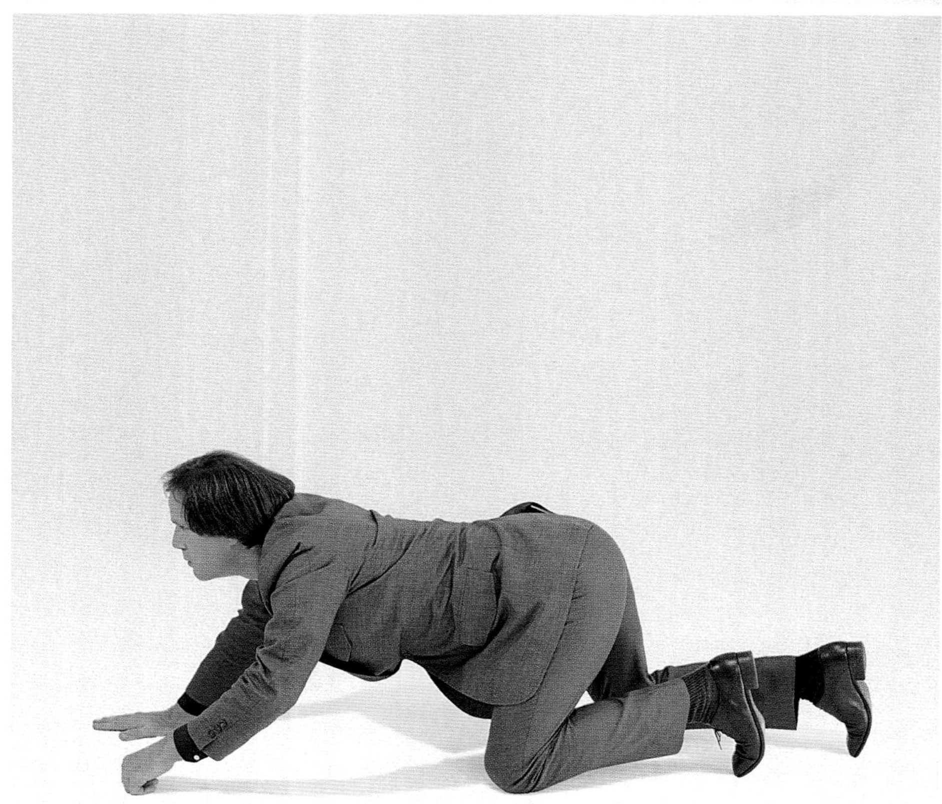

“Soldier Crawling with Rifle,” from *Imitations of Everyday Objects: Plastic Soldiers*, 1972. Diptych, gelatin silver prints, 5 × 5 in. (12.7 × 12.7 cm)

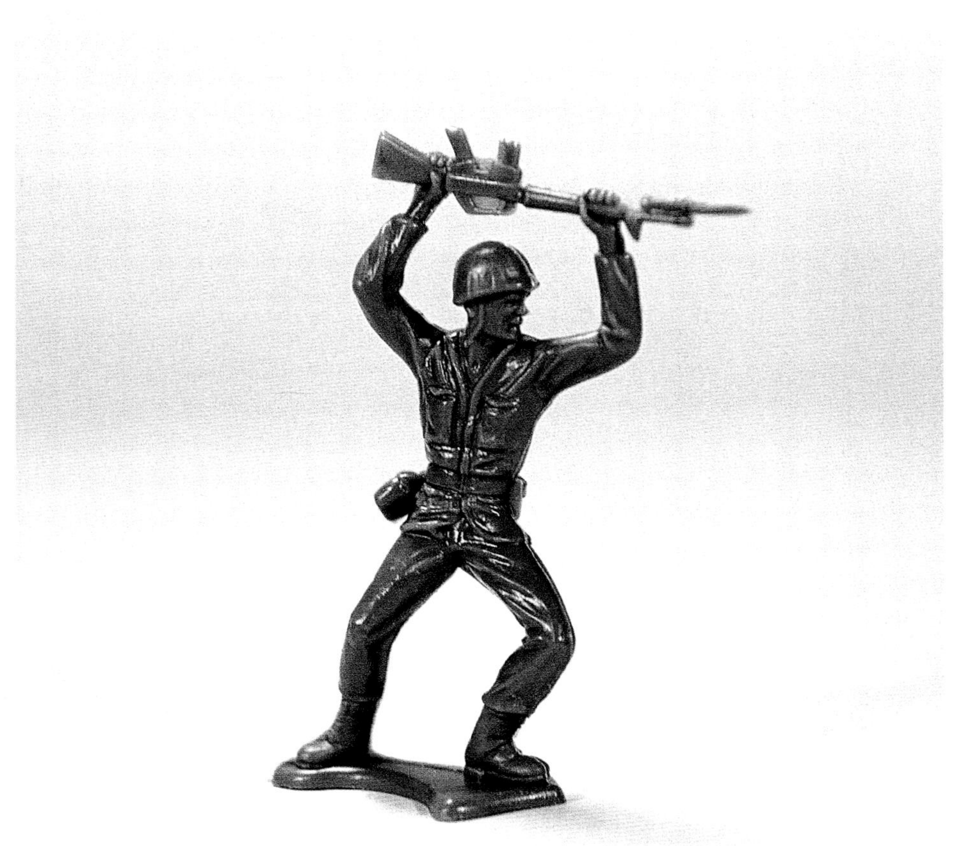

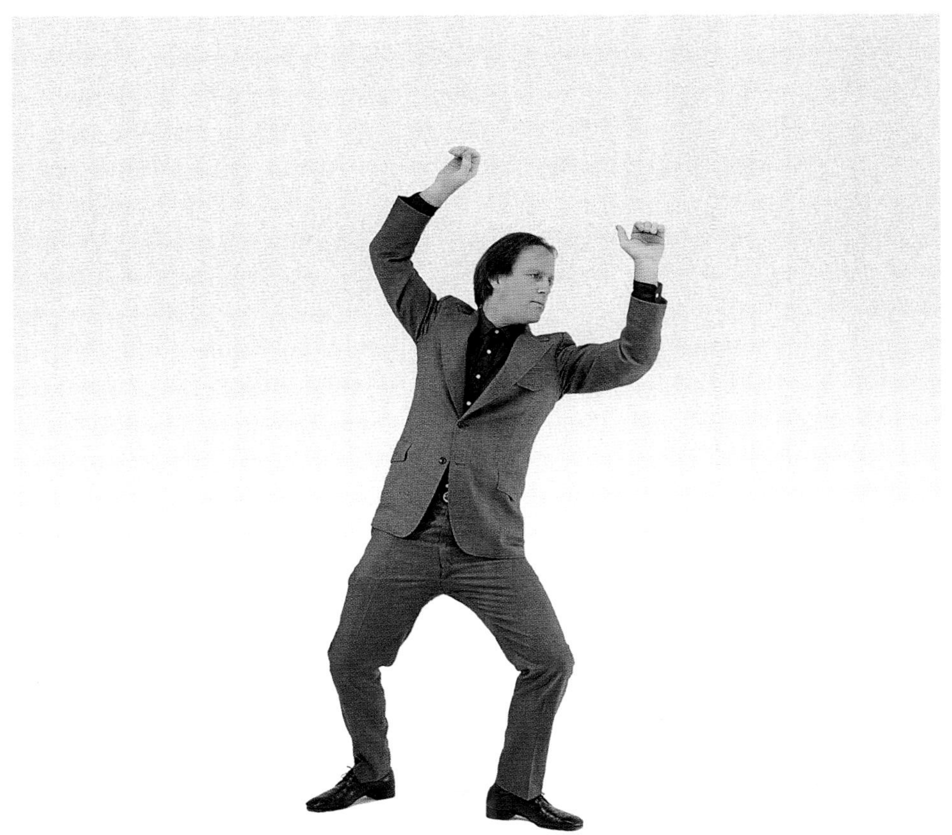

"Soldier Lunging with Bayonet and Rifle," from *Imitations of Everyday Objects: Plastic Soldiers*

Escape from Performance

Performance for me was a kind of controlled, choreographed madness—not exactly a sustainable practice. The problem with embracing an art form in which you act out temporary lunacy is that it can start creeping into your life in ways you can't control. Eventually, it starts to wreak havoc within and around you, as it threatened to do with me. That fact, coupled with the realization, obvious to the three of us, that the collective energies behind T. R. Uthco had run their course, made it evident by 1979 that it was time for a change. The end had ungraciously announced itself on August 7, 1978, when San Francisco's Pier 40, where we had our studio across from Ant Farm's, was destroyed by fire. We were a little slow to accept the finality of the event, clearly a sign from the gods, as we continued to express verbal commitments to our shared enterprise for several months after the fire. But we knew it was over.

This became very clear in winter 1979, when T. R. Uthco was invited to do a project as part of the 1980 San Francisco Art Institute Annual. Rather than work together, we decided to make individual contributions. Or rather, I decided, with support from Diane, that we would work independently; both of us were frustrated by the limitations the collective was putting on our diverging interests and sought a way out. Jody, more of a literary than visual artist, relied on T. R. Uthco as a vehicle for investigating our shared interests, and was less enthusiastic about going it alone. His resentment of our decision to disband contributed to his 1982 move to Southern California and eventually to Eugene, Oregon, where he returned to his first love, writing fiction, supporting this by working as a carpenter. Our parting ways led to a painful fourteen-year estrangement that lasted until his daughter's (my niece's) wedding in New York in 1996. After reuniting in his hotel room, where we tearfully embraced, it was as if the anger-filled, saddening years had never happened. And so it is, or can be, with the people we truly love. In 1998, Jody was diagnosed with small cell lung cancer, and six months later, at home with his wife Kit and teenage daughter Tara, he died. Jody was fifty-one, the same age as my father when he died. And again, I was heartbroken.

As a visual artist, Jody's aesthetic was shock, pure and simple. His contribution to the Art Institute Annual was to install, with commentary, a series of deeply disturbing photographs of the Jonestown massacre that he had pillaged from the dumpster behind the photo lab where most of the images for local press photographers were processed and printed. These were mounted below a series of *San Francisco Chronicle* front pages that documented the terrifying events taking place at Jim Jones's agrarian commune in Guyana. Jody's interests were firmly rooted in the political and social disruptions of our times, and at least in this instance, he displayed them with no distancing mechanisms whatsoever. Later, after moving to Los Angeles, he became friendly and collaborated with Paul Krassner, a notorious sixties iconoclast

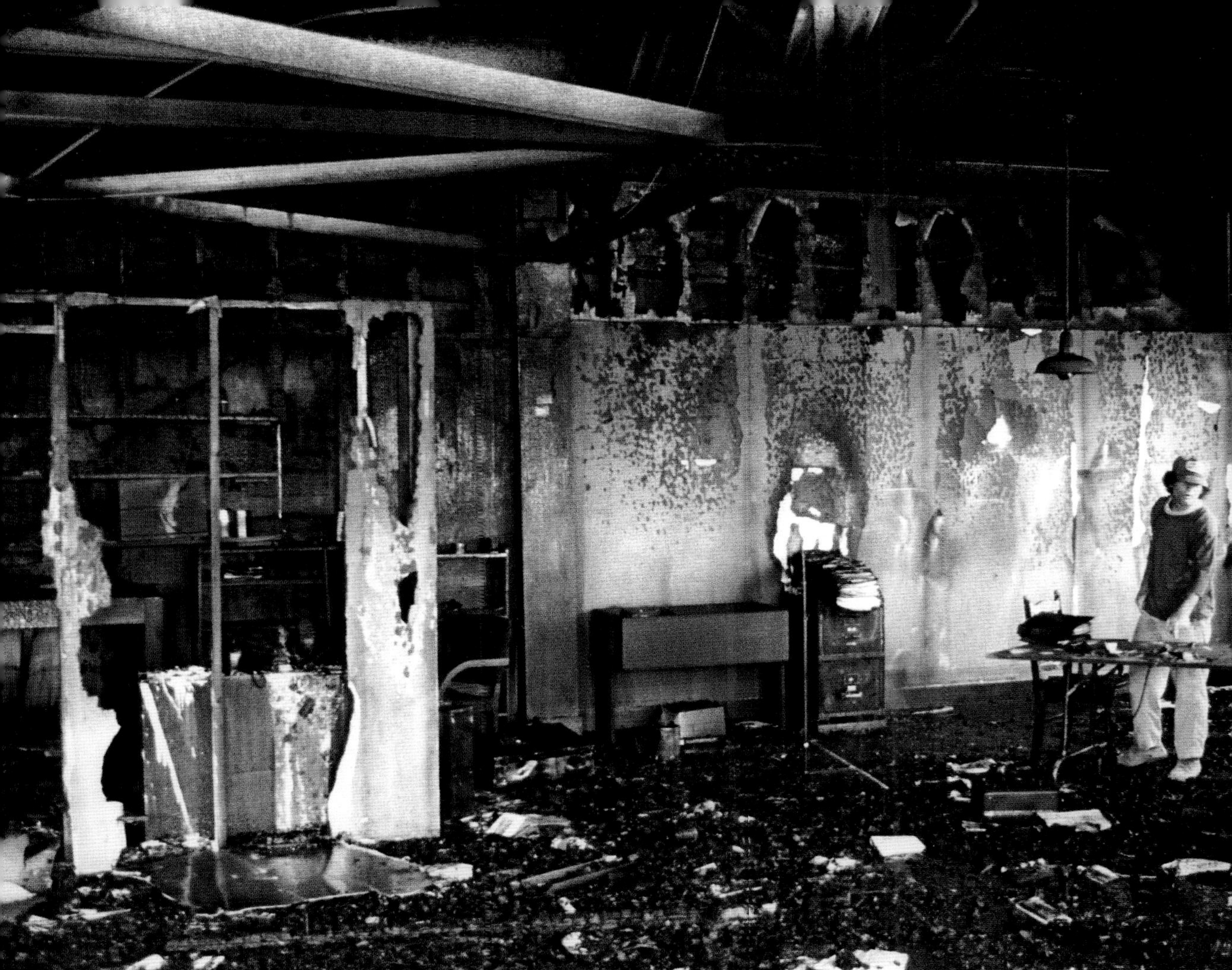

Jody sorting through the wreckage of our fire-damaged studio following the Pier 40 fire, August 7, 1978

and contributor to *The Realist*. In addition to working on his personal writing, Jody provided biting and funny stream-of-consciousness riffs on social and political events as part the video magazine *The 90's*, produced by Tom Weinberg, an early member of the radical documentary group TVTV.

Diane, on the other hand, looked out at the world and felt its fragile temporality, which she had started expressing through large pencil drawings that brought the fleetingness of things to a temporary standstill: passing clouds, a swimmer moving through the water, the movement of ocean waves, a beam of natural light in the corner of a room, and for the Annual, a triptych of a young woman brushing her long, luxuriant hair. Over the years, these and other subjects, like the momentary presence of birds alighting in our backyard, would evolve into the exquisite, painstakingly crafted paintings for which she is now known.

I remained deeply committed to ideas that had motivated me from the beginning, but was searching for a way out of performance, which, being all

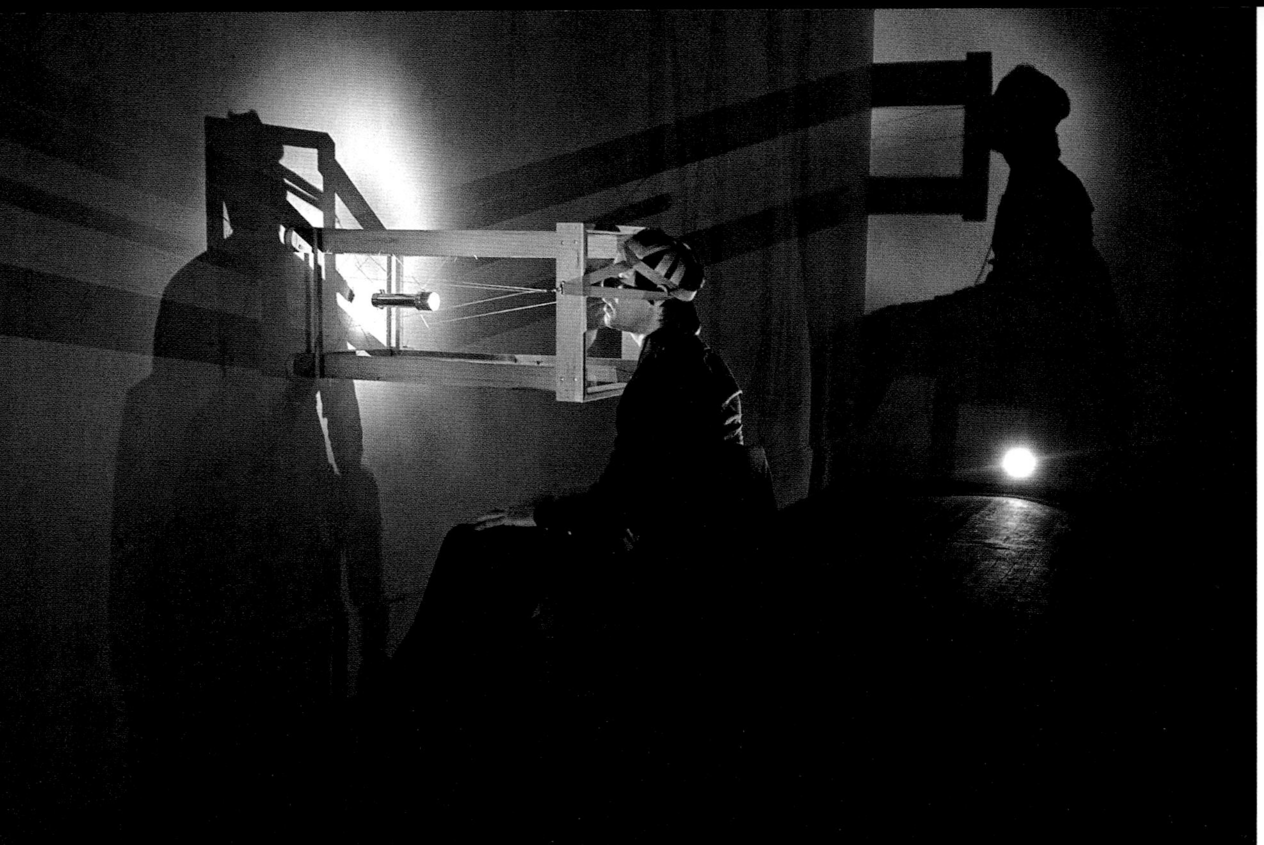

"Chapter III," from *Seven Chapters from the Life of . . . (A Soap Opera)*, 1980
Photograph by Diane Andrews Hall

about me as medium and means, was becoming a burdensome, solipsistic trap. I reasoned that if I could establish a connection between an action and the objects associated with that action, I could remove my body from the situation, leaving the remaining objects as a stand-in for my body and for what had occurred between me and them. The motivating idea was that having been imbued with the energy of their use, the configuration of objects had a reason for being—one that transcended formal aesthetics. On a philosophical level, this harked back to my attraction to Walter Benjamin and the language of things. On a practical level, my hope was that this way of operating, although firmly situated in performance, the very thing I was trying to escape, would provide me with a way out by shifting the emphasis from me to the installation of remaining objects.

Over seven nights in January at SITE, a beautiful loft space–studio that artist Alan Scarritt made available to others whose work he admired, I did a sequence of performances within different sculptural settings under the general title, *Seven Chapters from the Life of . . . (A Soap Opera).* Loosely based on the structure of a television soap opera, the work consisted of episodes performed on consecutive nights over the course of a week. Each performance lasted about an hour. Some involved live speaking of the sort Jody and I had finessed in our double monologues. Others were silent, while others were accompanied by prerecorded sound. Each tableau was illuminated by flashlights that were

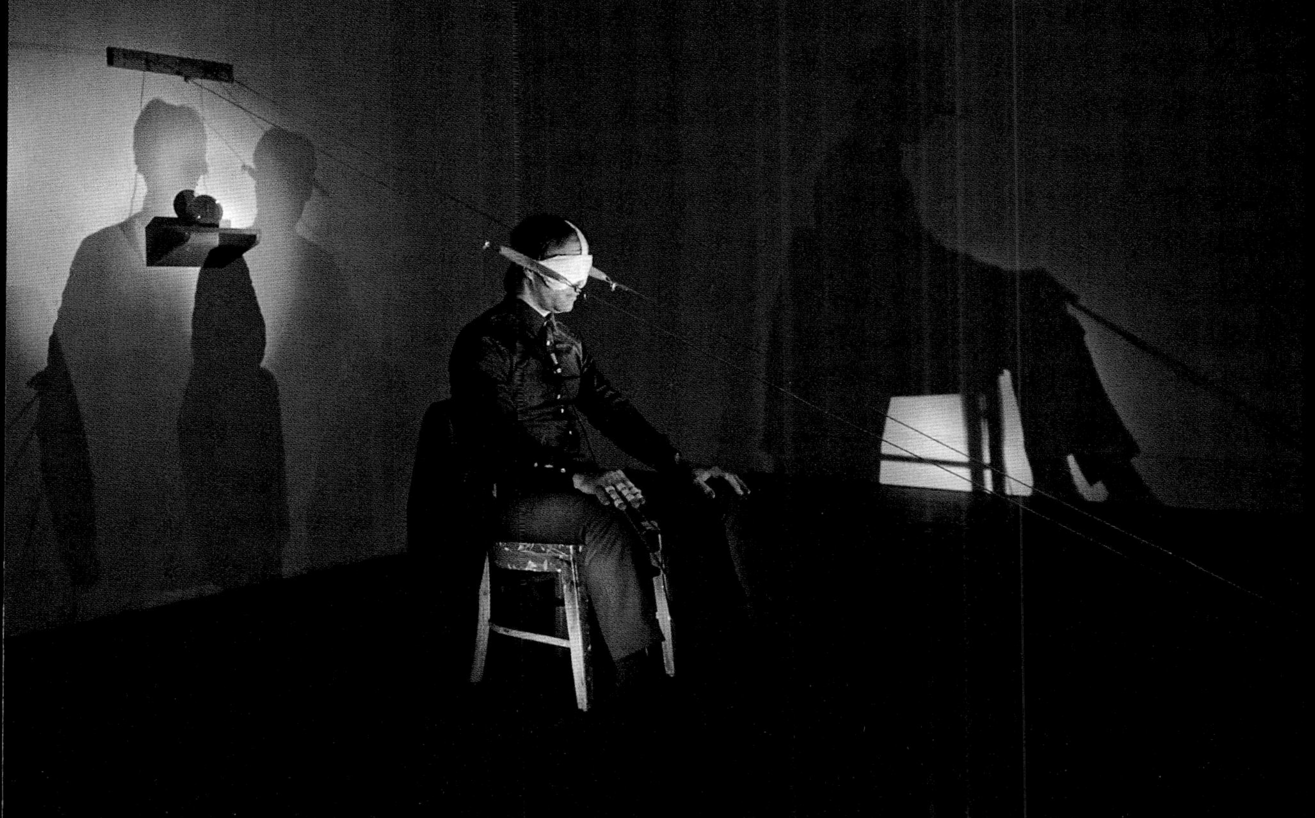

"Chapter IV," from *Seven Chapters from the Life of . . . (A Soap Opera)*
Photograph by Diane Andrews Hall

arranged on the floor and angled so that the light cast dramatic shadows across the gallery. For example, in "Chapter Five," dressed in my gray suit, I sat in a chair beneath a slowly dripping galvanized metal bucket suspended high above me on a board that extended from a wooden scaffolding. The drips of water fell into a wine glass that I held in one hand while the index finger of the other rubbed around the rim creating a tone that changed in pitch as the glass filled.

As the series of performances evolved, the flashlights from the earlier actions remained on, gradually dimming as their batteries wore down; the fading light illuminated the remaining set of objects and contraptions like disappearing memories. Before each performance, I tacked a handwritten title to the wall next to the door where people entered and exited. These accumulated so that by the final evening all seven titles were on the wall. They read:

"Chapter One: He was born very young and had everything to look forward to."

"Chapter Two: He was having more fun than people realized and when it rained, he dreamed of going to Miami and wearing green shoes with yellow laces."

"Chapter Three: Some days were uneventful and for long periods of time he found himself staring at the wall."

"Chapter Four: At one point he actually forgot just about everything he knew and had to start all over again."

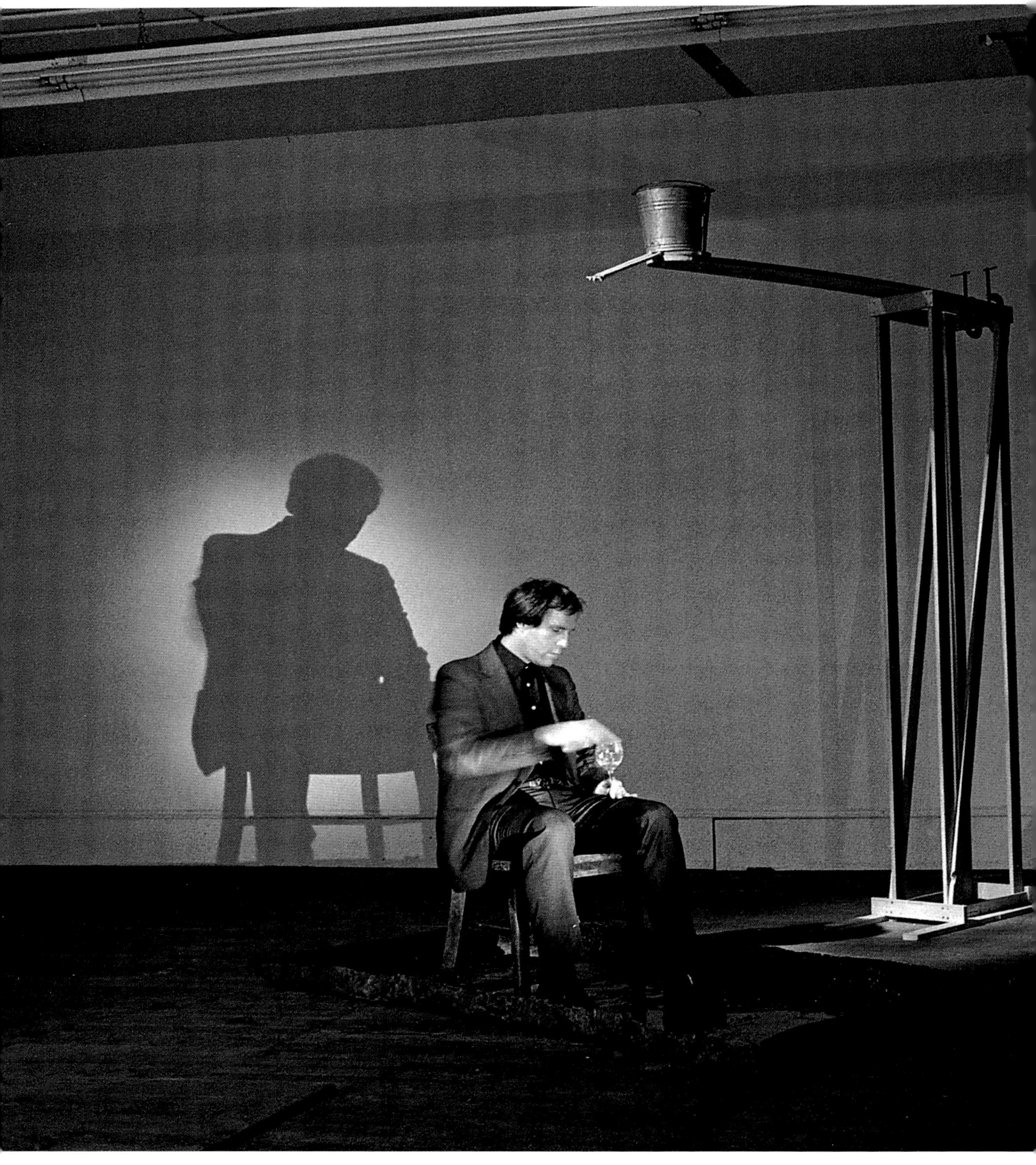

"Chapter V," from *Seven Chapters from the Life of . . . (A Soap Opera)*
Photograph by Diane Andrews Hall

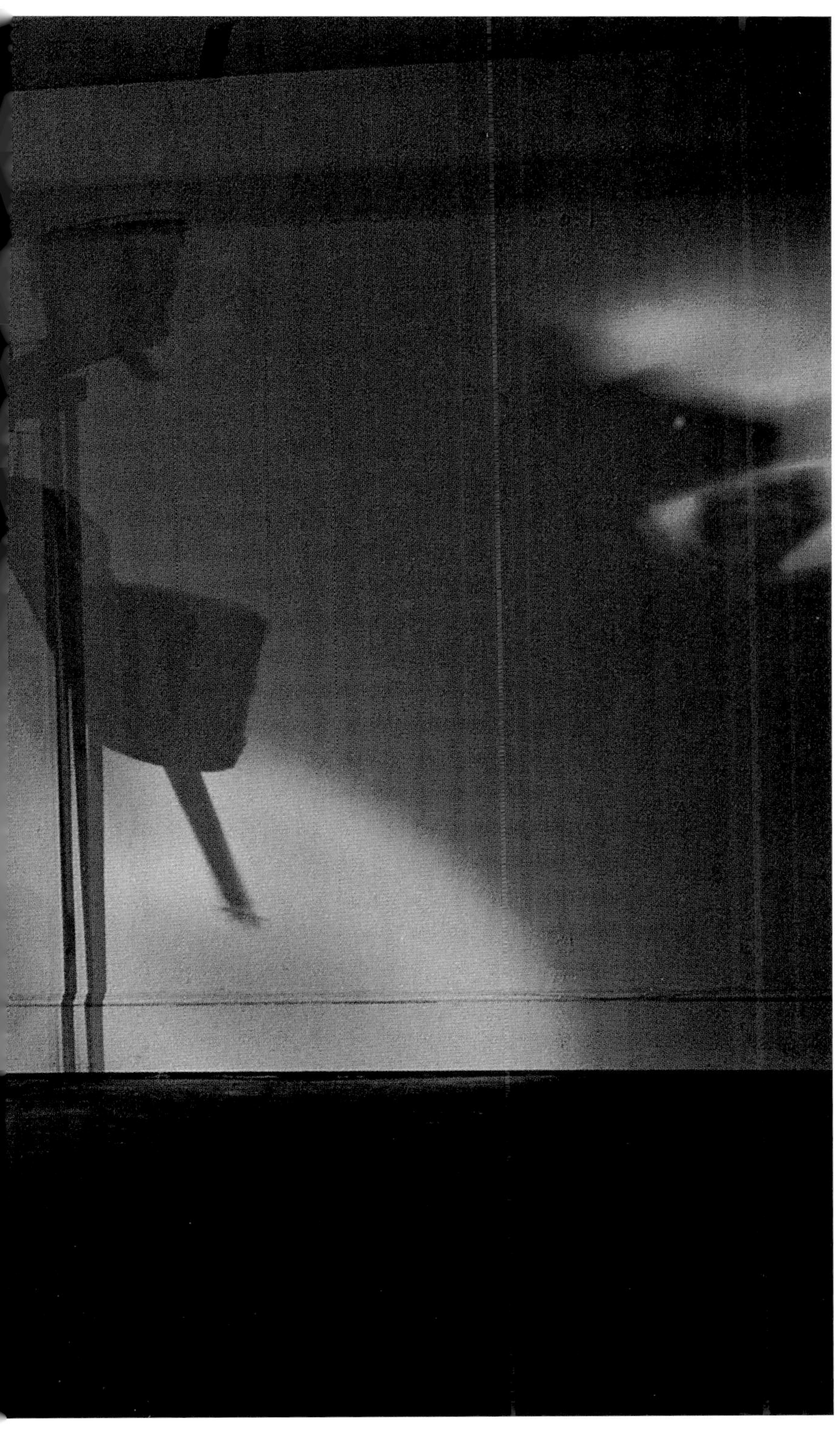

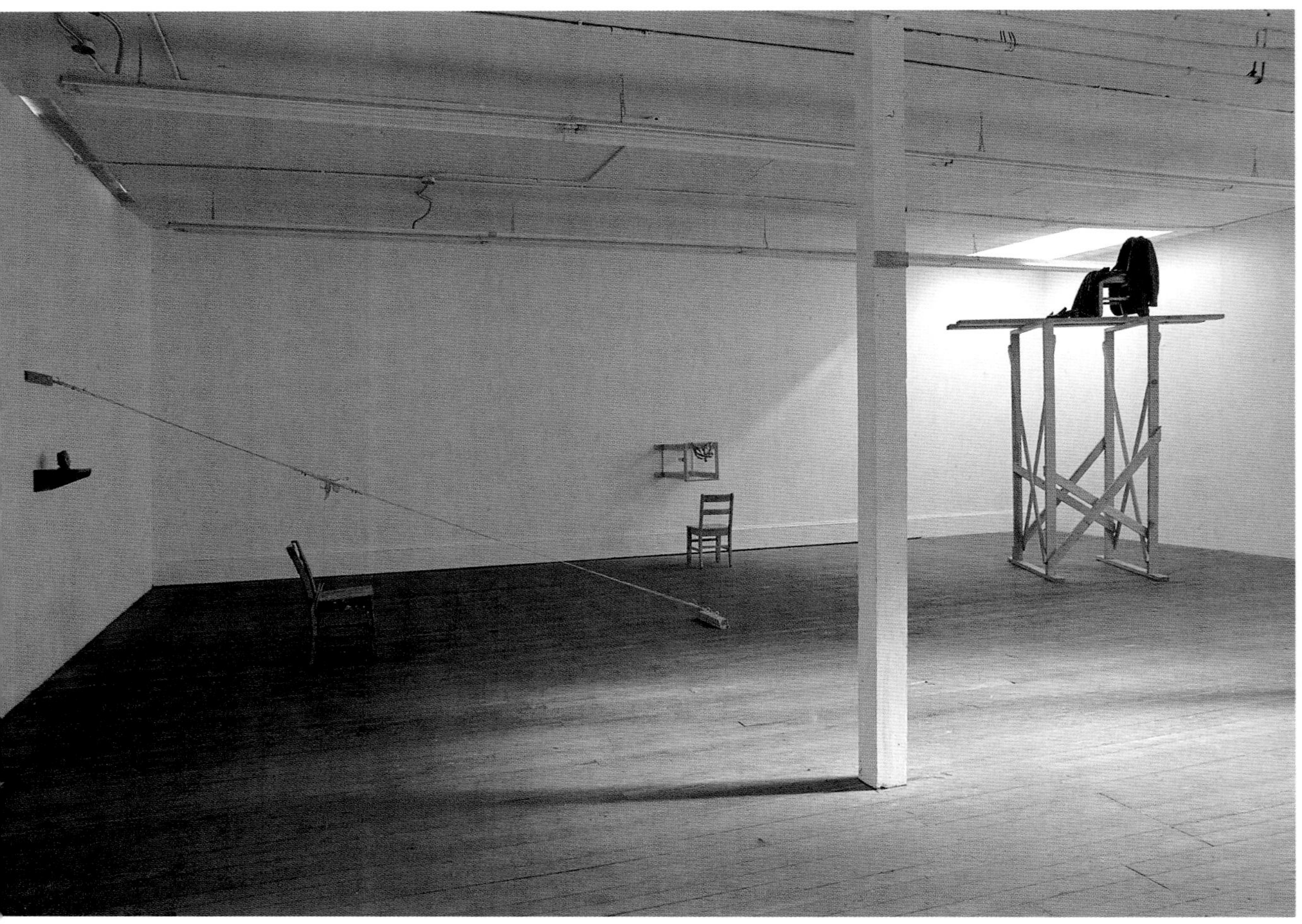

Seven Chapters from the Life of . . . (A Soap Opera), installation view
Photograph by Diane Andrews Hall

"Chapter Five: He was neither young nor old, but the roof leaked, and his shoulder ached when he laughed."
"Chapter Six: As he piled the dirt from the cellar onto the kitchen floor, he understood that some things could only be understood later."
"Chapter Seven: He never knew how he had gotten there or why, but he left through the back door."

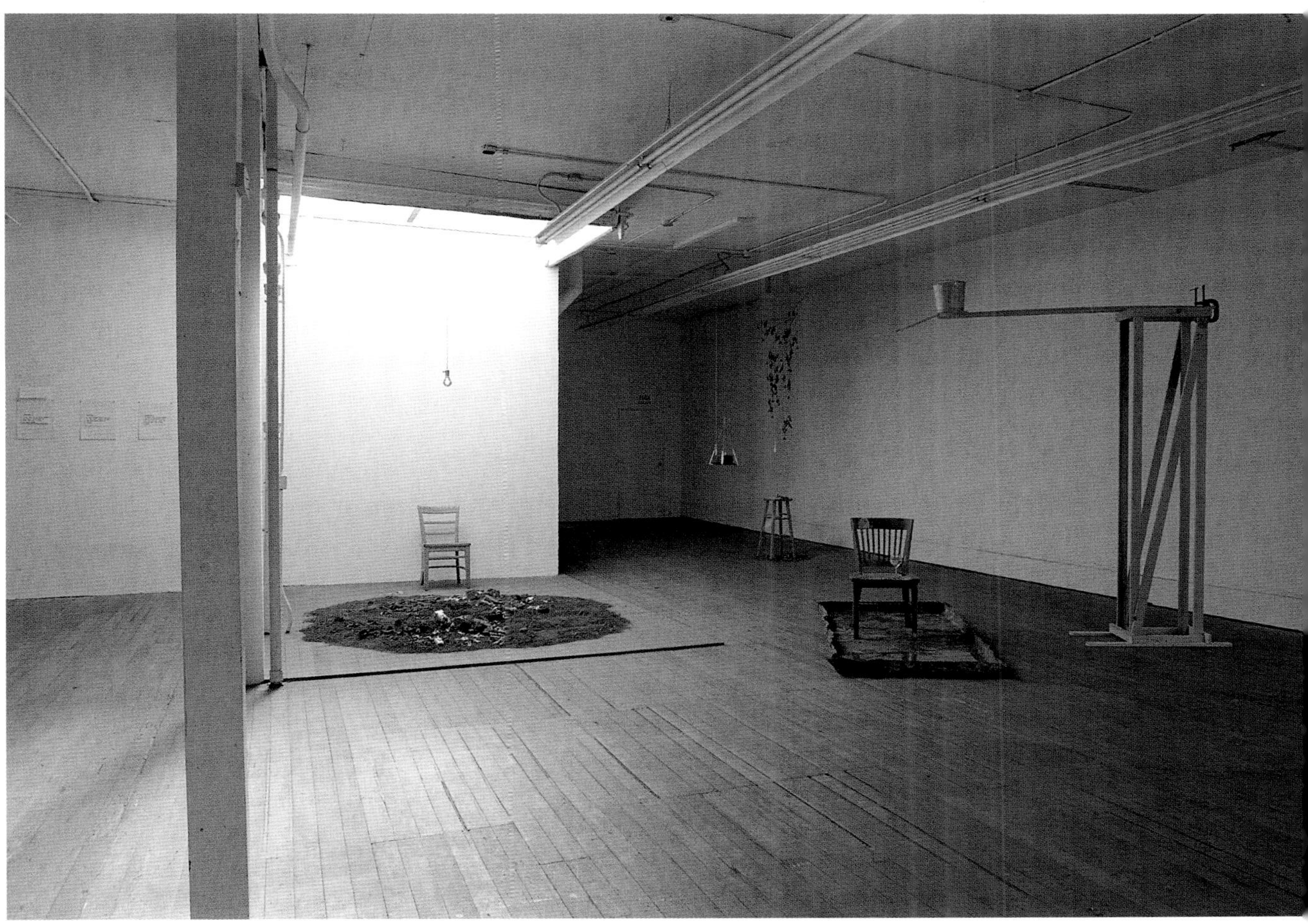

Seven Chapters from the Life of . . . (A Soap Opera), installation view
Photograph by Diane Andrews Hall

For three weeks following the performance of the final chapter, the props and devices used in the performances were on view as seven independent but related installations that referenced earlier actions, but which were now entirely mute. By this I mean the objects that I had energized—made real, at least in my imagination—circulated on their own without being overdetermined by my presence. I was freed by an organization of objects that existed in relation to my body and its actions but that could persist without me.

VI

The Spectacle of Image

Image, Language, Power

There is a position that I associate with Theodor Adorno and the Frankfurt School that sees modern humans as passive victims of an industry of images, slogans, and propaganda before which we are defenseless. Guy Debord, the French political theorist, referred to this condition as "spectacle," which he describes through a series of short, aphoristic statements in *The Society of the Spectacle*. He writes, "The spectacle manifests itself as an enormous positivity, out of reach and beyond dispute. All it says is: 'Everything that appears is good; whatever is good will appear.' The attitude that it demands in principle is the same passive acceptance that it has already secured by means of its incontrovertibility, and indeed by its monopolization of the realm of appearances."[1] In this picture of passivity, we are seen foundering in our ignorance, defenseless against the persuasiveness of advertising, television, mass media, and, if we are to bring it up to date, social media.

In 1984, inspired in part by the book of that name by George Orwell, I made a media installation, *Machinery for the Reeducation of a Delinquent Dictator*, that explored spectacle through the demagoguery of authoritarian images and further suggested that we are not so much passive as we are complicit in what I termed "the spectacle of the image." In the program notes for its exhibition at the Whitney Museum of American Art, I wrote that we are, for the most part, willing participants in this phantasmagoria of images and information, flirting or toying with them as they presume to dominate us the way a sky diver might toy with the forces of gravity. I described this as "the terror of mediation," a fearful exultation of an information environment that lords over us, terrorizing while seducing. I claimed that these forces have a relationship to the aesthetic category that Edmund Burke and others classified as the sublime. Burke writes, "Whatever is fitted in any sort to excite the ideas of pain, and danger, that is to say, whatever is in any sort terrible, or is conversant about terrible objects, or operates in a manner analogous to terror, is a source of the sublime; that is, it is productive of the strongest emotion which the mind is capable of feeling."[2]

Machinery for the Reeducation of a Delinquent Dictator attempted to explore how politics and capitalism deliver their products through the subversive power of Debordian "spectacle"—that is to say, how power exerts itself through images. Debord writes, "For one to whom the real world becomes real images, mere images are transformed into real beings—tangible figments which are the efficient motors of trancelike behavior." And later in the same paragraph: "The spectacle is, by definition, immune from human activity,

1. Guy Debord, *The Society of the Spectacle*, trans. Donald Nicholson-Smith (New York: Zone Books, 1994), 15.
2. Edmund Burke, *A Philosophical Enquiry into the Origin of Our Ideas of the Sublime and Beautiful*, ed. James T. Boulton (Notre Dame, N: University of Notre Dame Press, 1958), 39.

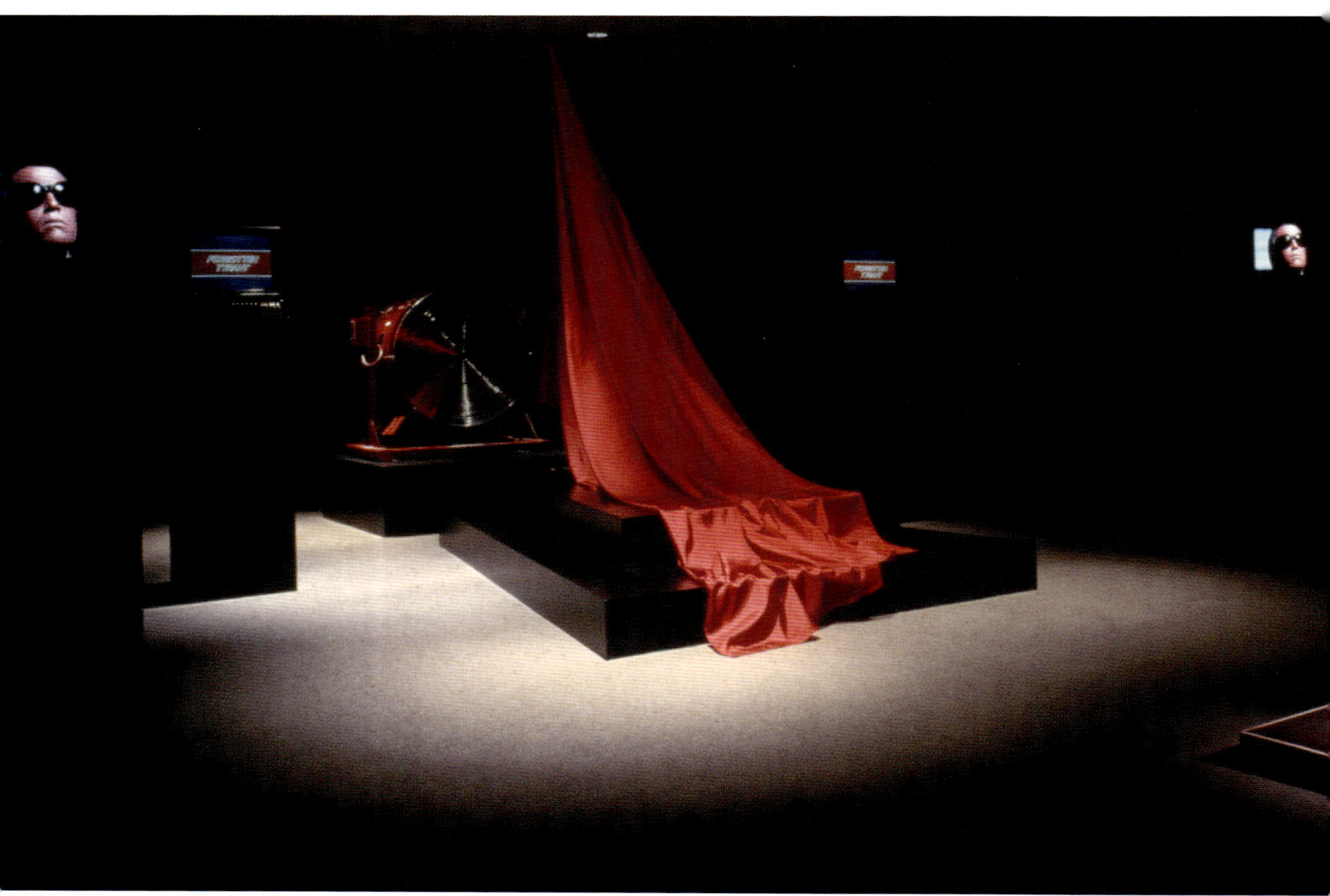

Doug Hall, *Machinery for the Reeducation of a Delinquent Dictator*, 1984.
Video installation
Photograph © Peter Aaron/OTTO

inaccessible to any projected review or correction. It is the opposite of dialogue. Wherever representation takes on an independent existence, the spectacle reestablishes itself."[3]

My reeducation machine referred to Debord's "efficient motor," but whereas Debord asserts that the motor induces "trancelike behavior" and is "immune from human activity," I was convinced that we fully and actively participate in the spectacle, sometimes playfully, even joyfully, and other times because we find it dangerously stimulating and exciting or we have no choice.

The installation, now in the Whitney collection, consists of four CRT monitors on matching black plinths flanking a black stepped platform that narrows as it recedes from the viewer. On the monitors are closeups of a man's face (mine), meticulously covered in red makeup. He is haranguing the viewer, although what he says is difficult to discern because his voice is slowed and

3. Debord, *Society of the Spectacle*, 17.

processed to the point that it is more roar than articulated speech. Listening intently, one can barely discern that he is saying the kinds of things a parent might say to an unruly child: "Don't be jealous of your neighbor. Be happy for his successes," or "Be polite at the dinner table. Don't speak with your mouth full of food," or "Listen when others speak. Don't dominate the conversation." Interspersed is slow-motion video of a blowing red flag.

Draping across the platform like an immense skirt is a large red flag, fastened to a rope stretching to the ceiling of the gallery. A smaller platform sits a few feet in front of the flag base. When a viewer steps onto this platform, the pressure triggers a switch that turns on an industrial fan situated behind the flag that makes it snap inches from the viewer's face. It is the viewer—neither passive nor trancelike—who initiates and participates in the spectacle of the flag. In the darkened gallery, spotlights illuminate the flag and the spectator who becomes part of the spectacle, thus completing the installation.

The sublime, initially attributed to an ancient treatise by Cassius Longinus, has come to refer in modern times to forces, often natural, whose greatness is beyond our human ability to calculate. It can also refer to frightening conditions that are unfathomable because they are unseen even as their presence is powerfully felt or sensed. My claim is that the sublime is not just a description of our relationship to natural phenomena or their representations but to all kinds of overbearing experiences such as those manufactured through media and political spectacle—aspects of the capitalist or political sublime that Debord simply refers to as spectacle. My further claim is that artists, rather than passive, actively engage these forces, both the seen and the unseen, through diverse strategies and aesthetic stances, including parody, irony, and appropriation. These procedures allow us to calculate the incalculable, to bring the overbearing down to a more human, and therefore vulnerable and manageable, scale. This is very different from Debord's passive victims who unwittingly participate in their subservience to the spectacle of images. Artists have a need to talk back, to assume some degree of agency, to better understand by holding close that which wants to remain at a distance.

These aren't new practices, although it might be fair to call them modern ones. Modern and contemporary art histories are filled with examples from Picasso's *Guernica* (1937) to Sarah Charlesworth's *Movie-Television-News-History, June 21, 1979* (1979), works that occupy distant poles from which each talks back. Both artists take actual events and, in a sense, reenact them through manipulations, although we get very different tones and meanings from them. Picasso's deeply moving painting is based on the horrific bombing of the small Basque town of Guernica by Nazi Germany and fascist Italy at Franco's behest in 1937. Charlesworth's prints chronicle a single day as represented by the front pages of twenty-seven international newspapers that reported on the on-camera killing of an ABC news correspondent who was covering the Nicaraguan Revolution. She removed the descriptive content from

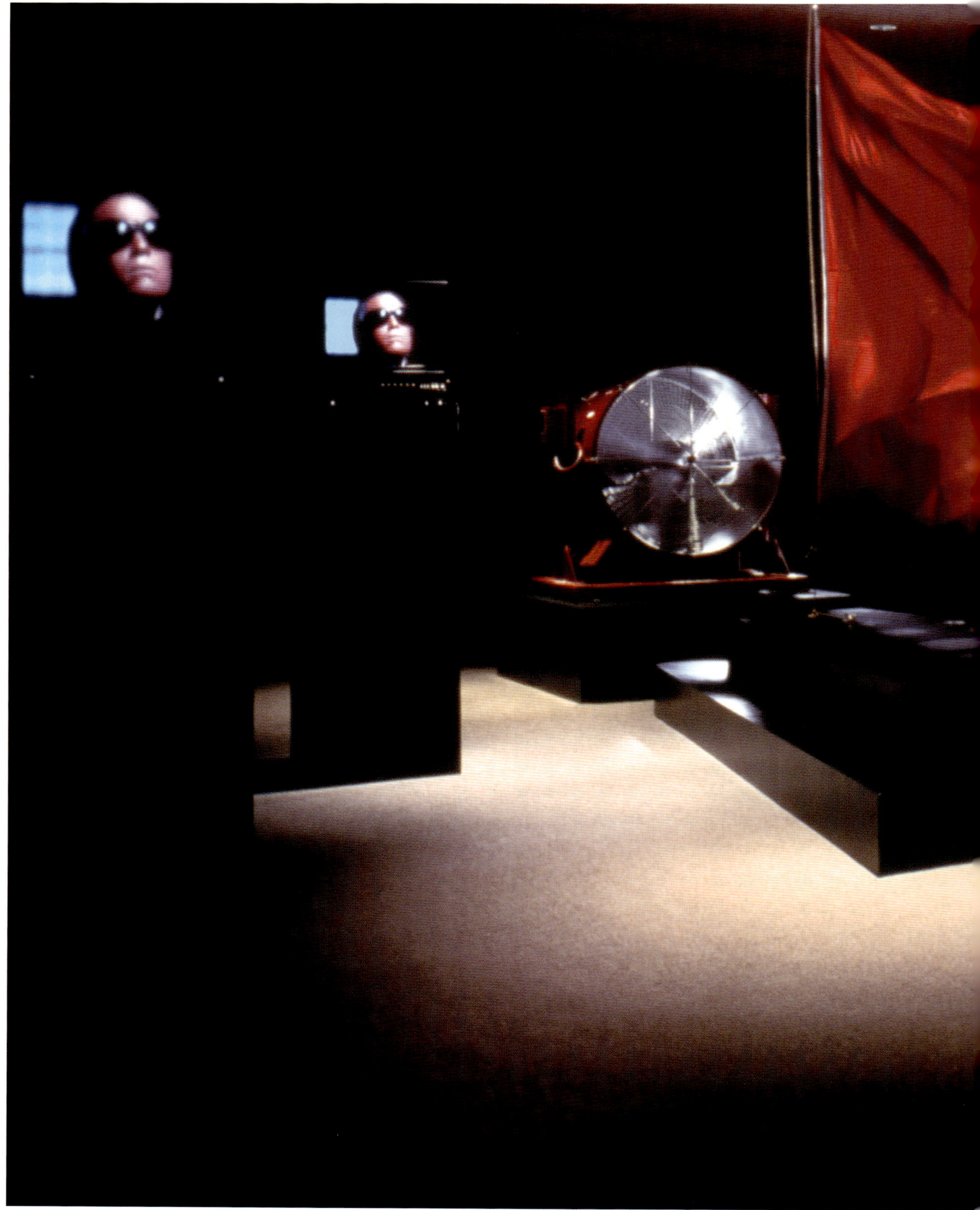

Doug Hall, *Machinery for the Reeducation of a Delinquent Dictator*, 1984. Video installation
Photograph © Peter Aaron/OTTO

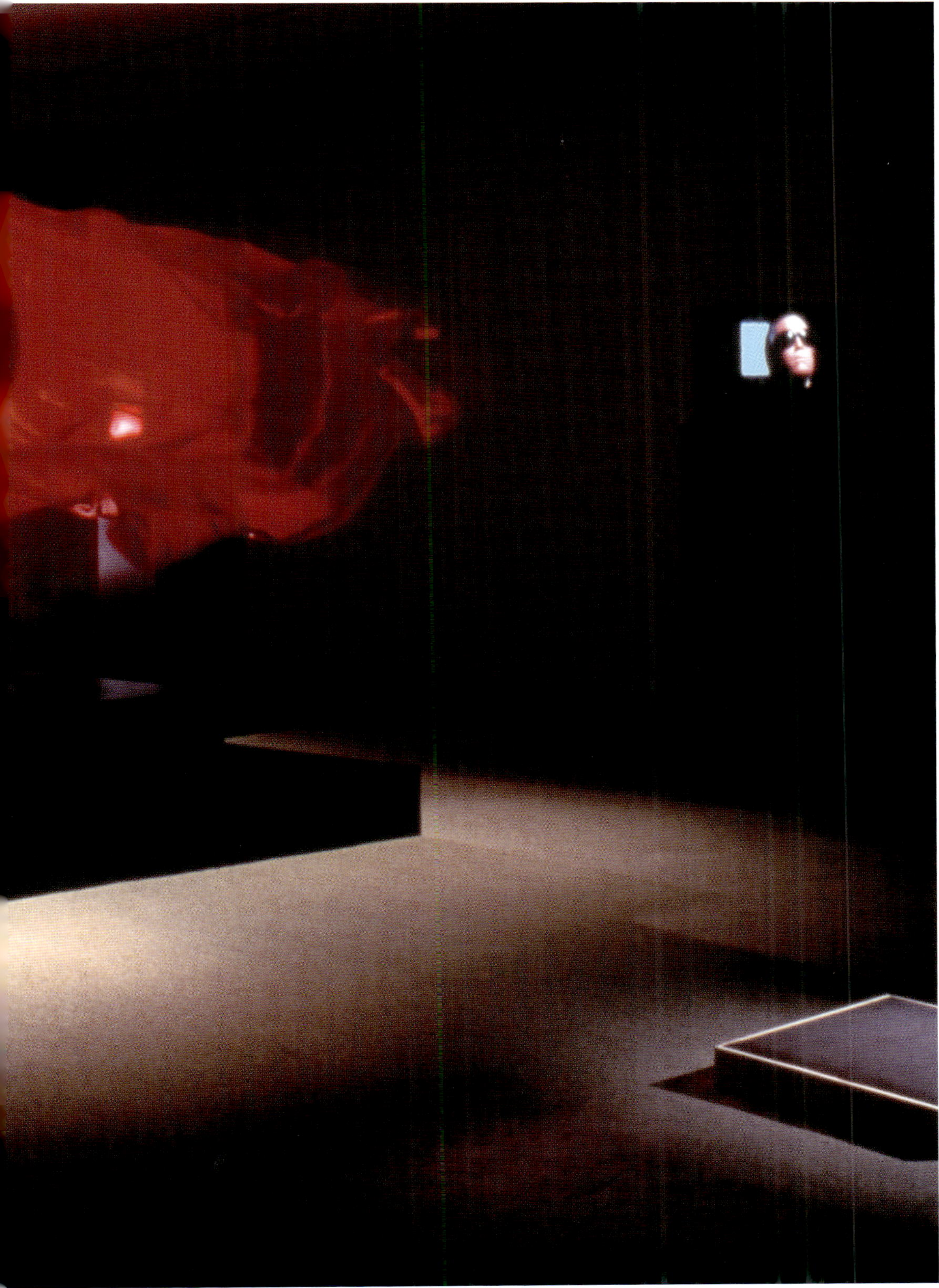

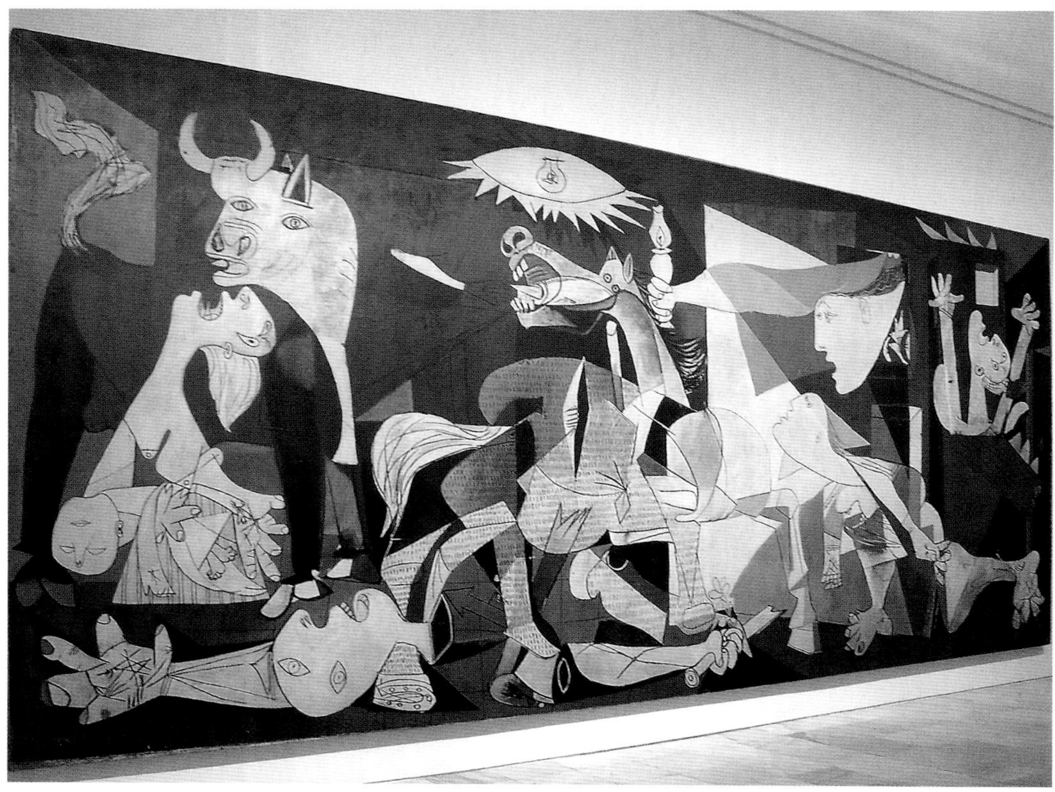

Pablo Picasso, *Guernica,* 1937. Oil on canvas, 137⅜ × 305½ in. (349.3 × 776.6 cm). Collection Reina Sofia, Madrid
Photograph by Peter Collins

the newspaper pages, leaving just the images, captions, and headings. By showing how these were arranged on the page, she revealed how differently each paper represented the event, an indication of the relative newsworthiness the editors ascribed to the murder.

While Picasso's approach is visceral and sentient and Charlesworth's is cerebral and analytic, both artists dip into the stream of violent public events and base their representations on newspaper accounts, which they manipulate to uncover what had been previously concealed. As we did in *The Eternal Frame*, they personalize the events by imposing themselves into them. Events that can be nothing but abstract and distant to those who haven't experienced them firsthand are made at once allegorical and accessible—are made human.[4]

4. See Martin Minchom, "The Truth about Guernica: Picasso and the Lying Press," in which he makes a strong case about the crucial role published materials like newspapers and political propaganda played in the making of *Guernica*. The Abraham Lincoln Brigade Archives (ALBA), March 9, 2012, https://albavolunteer.org/2012/03/the-truth-about-guernica-picasso-and-the-lying-press/.

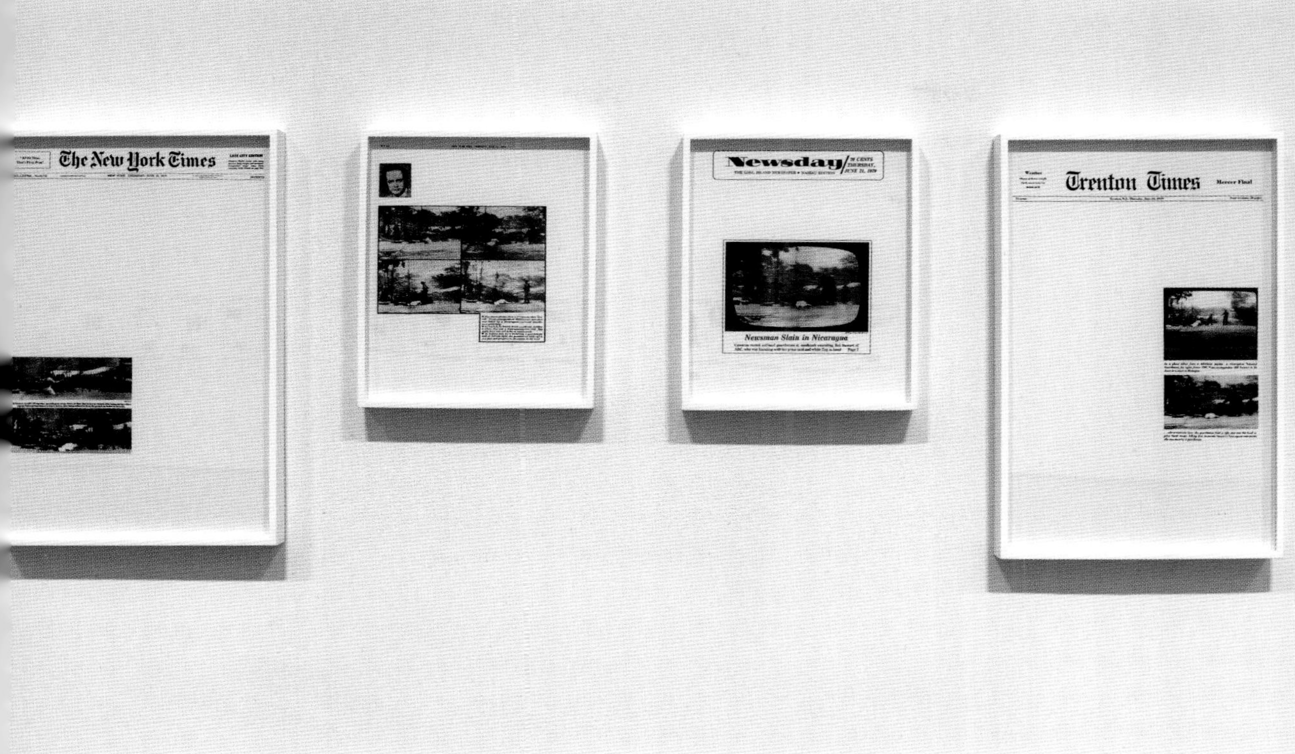

Sarah Charlesworth, *Movie-Television-News-History, June 21, 1979* (detail).
27 black & white prints, varying sizes, approximately 22 × 16 in. (55.9 × 40.6 cm)

Photograph by Steven Probert

People have the potential for immense creativity in innumerable ways. What separates artists from non-artists is that our creativity is focused in ways that produce visual evidence of its existence, an object (I want to call it a monument) that is the sum of all the thoughts and decisions that went into its making. Artists gather material from the world of things, transposing images, thoughts, and sounds into unexpected configurations from which new meanings and emotions arise. When we marvel at this culmination of the artist's efforts it's because we are taken by its craftsmanlike skill, its relevance to our own thoughts or sentiments, or perhaps because it carries our intellect and emotions to places we'd not ventured before. I can't speak for others, but for me this making-of-things creates markers that accumulate as points of reference to help locate me in space and time. Without them, I would be adrift, feeling dangerously unmoored. This is what I mean when I say art is a necessity, not an avocation.

The artist's job is to close the gap between here and there. One way we accomplish this is by constructing an image-based figuration or poetics in which images are set into dynamic constellations or collision courses with one another. It's the resulting abrasions that produce the flashes and ruptures that can lead both artist and viewer to insight. This insight, or deep recognition, circumvents the limitations of conventional language by replacing language's descriptive powers with the image's revealing immediacy. Much in the way a poetics based on words distorts language's usual meanings through figuration, a poetics of image applies figuration to the objectively familiar so we can access emotions and feelings beyond their representational grasp. This process gives meaning to events in our lives by identifying or naming them. Ironically, it's a nonverbal naming: a recognition that is both concrete—situated in the world of objects—and transitory. I think all relevant art derives its deepest meaning, its ability to move or stir us, in this way.

In my interpretation, a poetics based in nonverbal naming has the following characteristics: it is experiential rather than expository and, as a result, is taken in somatically and sensationally before it's dissected intellectually. It is nondidactic and, indeed, it might even be difficult to say what a work composed in this way is about. In other words, such a work might be made up of a single image or combinations of images that are self-referential and defy—even discourage as being inappropriate—linear analysis or judgment. Admittedly, this is an odd sort of naming. It's a naming that refuses to name but provides, instead, a fluid and sentient medium in which to comprehend, if momentarily, those aspects of our lives—those most important events or emotional states—that we can't easily speak about. Our words for human emotions, for example, attempt to represent our most complex feelings. But they are expressively dead, inadequate for the task. Representations of these emotions call for another "language" or medium of address, one that is analogical rather than specifically representational. It is a language that must compress the gap dividing the objective world from us so that rather than holding experience at a distance, it knows no boundaries. It becomes us so that we might become it—if even for just a moment. Mediated, the unnamable becomes immediate and, fleetingly, part of us.

Power, Authority, and the Sublime

I continued doing performances into the early 1980s, but few were done in front of a live audience. Most took place before a camera, videotaped as segments to be used in video installations—the emerging hybrid that combined video's temporality with sculptural or architectural settings. Video installation could be accommodated within contemporary art museums because most of the work behaved like a theatricalized form of sculpture rather than narrative film, with its demands on the viewer's attention from beginning to end. In these early media installations, the moving images were often short, looped sequences that could be experienced, along with the sound, in the moment, the way one might view a painting or a sculpture.

In 1986, I received grants through the New Works Program of the Massachusetts Council on the Arts and Humanities to produce two video-based projects. These became *Storm and Stress,* a sixty-minute video for the Contemporary Art Television Fund, a program of WGBH Television and the Institute of Contemporary Art, Boston; and *The Terrible Uncertainty of the Thing Described*, an expansive multichannel video installation that reconfigured imagery I had shot over the course of two years for *Storm and Stress* with my cameraman, Jules Backus.

Both works expanded my interest in the sublime by suggesting an equivalence between the tumultuous landscape as represented by extreme meteorological events like tornadoes and severe electrical storms, and industrial power as represented by forms of scientific and industrial technology in which machines are constructed to mimic aspects of the natural world to better understand it or are created to harness or redirect the forces of nature.

Of the two works, *The Terrible Uncertainty of the Thing Described*[5] was the most entangled in the questions I was obsessed with at the time: how power is manifested through spectacle and the role that the sublime, as a philosophical category of judgment, plays in our reception of these displays of power.

Near the midpoint of Edmund Burke's *A Philosophical Enquiry into the Origin of Our Ideas of the Sublime and Beautiful* (1757), he writes, "I know of nothing sublime which is not some modification of power."[6] My intent was to both create the sublime spectacle and reveal the mechanisms by which it operates.

The Terrible Uncertainty of the Thing Described is a sprawling media installation composed of three channels of synchronized video that are displayed on six monitors on steel stands that elevate them slightly above the heads of the viewers. One of the video channels is also projected onto the gallery wall. The video consists of heavily edited sequences of violent weather: tornadoes, electrical storms, forest fires, floods; and their equivalents in science and industry: an immense wind machine, power plants, dams, high-energy testing facilities (Los Alamos, New Mexico), radio telescope arrays (the Very Large Array, also in New Mexico), a tornado simulator, and the like. The flow of images is accompanied by a soundtrack that rivals their scale through percussive roars, moans, and hisses separated by moments of relative silence or natural sounds—the songs and twitters of birds, for example, as they feed in grasslands after an intense thunderstorm. Along with this cacophony of

5. The title of the work is taken from a statement that appears in Edmund Burke's *A Philosophical Enquiry into the Origin of Our Ideas of the Sublime and Beautiful.*
6. Burke, *A Philosophical Enquiry*, 64.

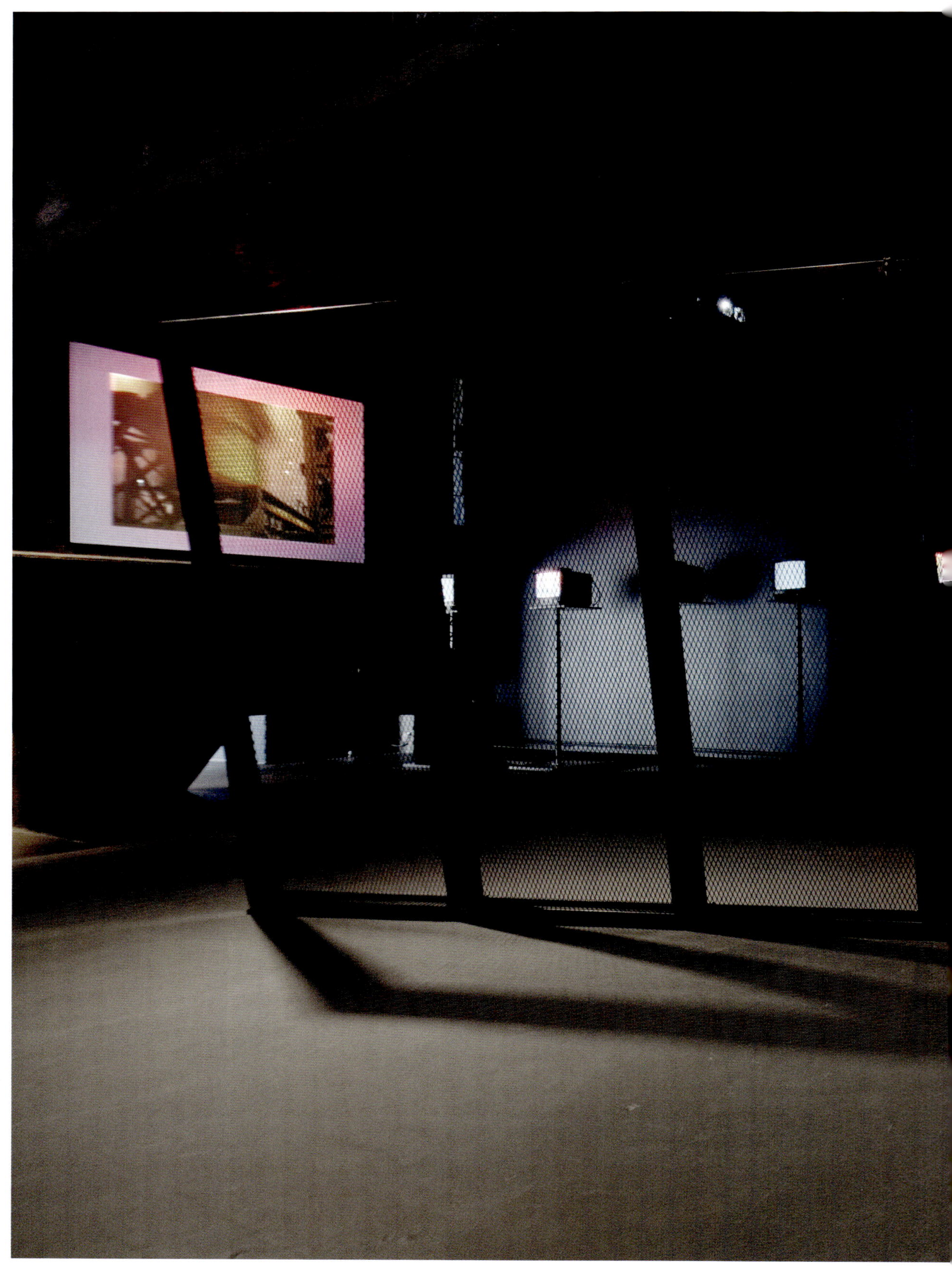

Doug Hall, *The Terrible Uncertainty of the Thing Described,* 1986. Video installation (installation view at the San Francisco Art Institute, 2015). Collection of SFMOMA, Purchase through a gift of the Modern Art Council and the San Francisco Art Dealers Association
Photograph by Gregory Goode

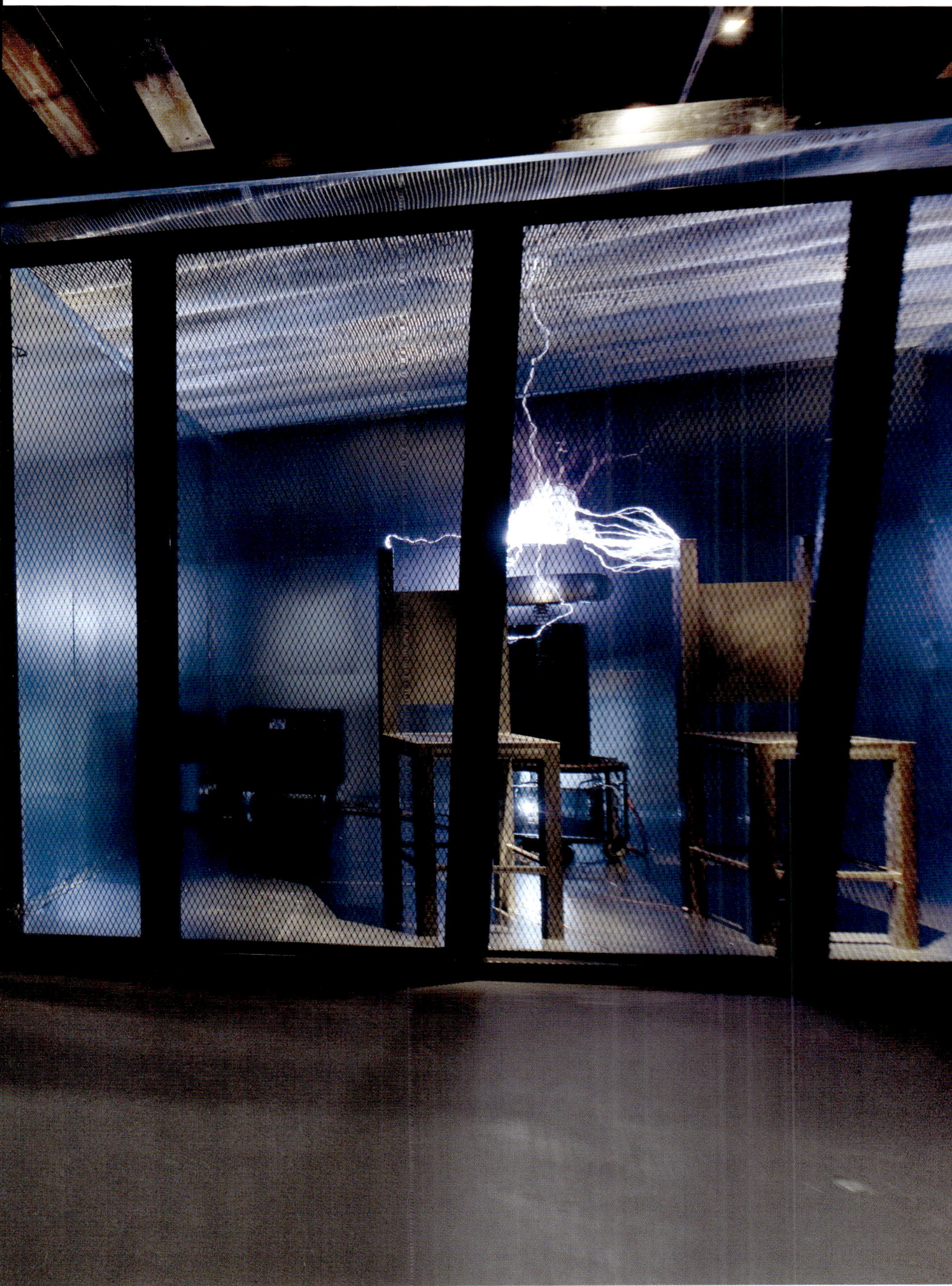

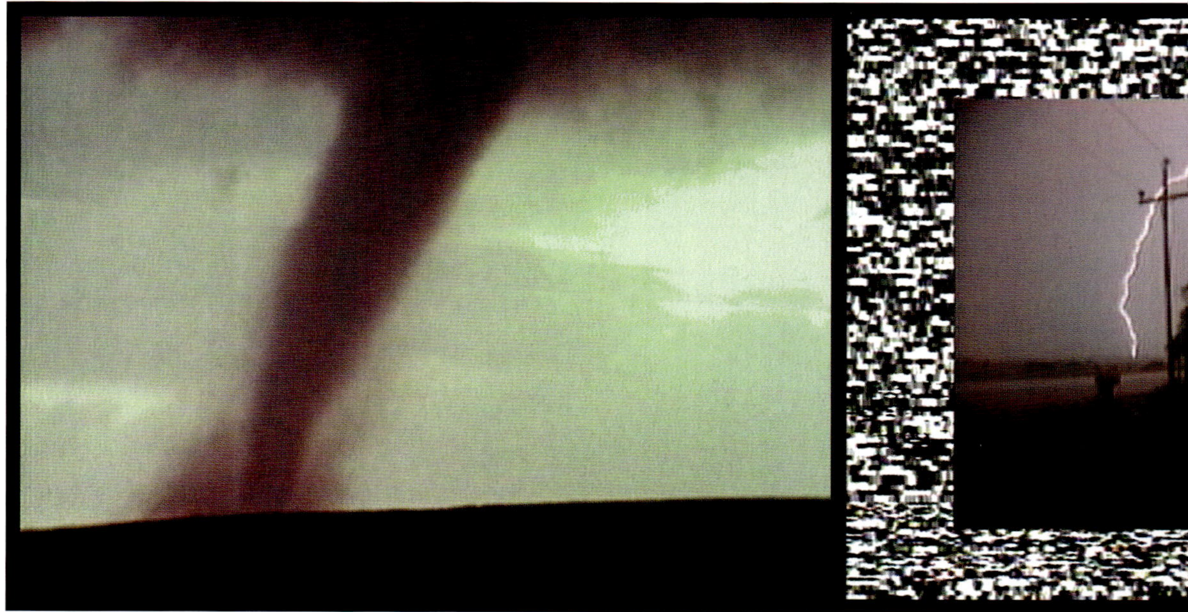

The Terrible Uncertainty of the Thing Described, showing the relationship between the three projections

image and sound is a ten-foot-high steel mesh fence that leans toward the viewer threateningly. Behind the fence are two oversize steel chairs and behind them, a Tesla coil that periodically emits a million-volt discharge of hissing, crackling electricity that dances along the chairs and the steel mesh on the ceiling above them.

With the explosive snarl of the Tesla coil, viewers are made suddenly and frighteningly aware that the industrial and natural power they thought safely corralled within video image and sound is in the gallery with them, no longer as mere representation but as disruptive fact. Tucked into this visceral experience, which presents power rawly and directly, I was proposing an analogy between the coil's explosive discharge and the controlled beaming of video images onto the glass faces of the cathode ray tubes (CRTs) and from the projector onto the wall of the gallery.

Both the coil and the televisions are emitting data. The data coming from the coil appears chaotic, incoherent, and an expression of pure energy, whereas the data coming from the televisions and projector is refined, providing recognizable moving images. The coil's oscillating transformer that emits bolts of electricity to the steel chairs in the installation—an obvious reference to the executioner's electric chair—is technically similar to the electron gun that shoots beams onto the phosphorescent surface of the cathode ray tube. What is vastly different, of course, is the contrasting data coming from each, and how we experience and draw meaning from them. By analogy, I was implying that there is something frightening about the never-ending flow of televi-

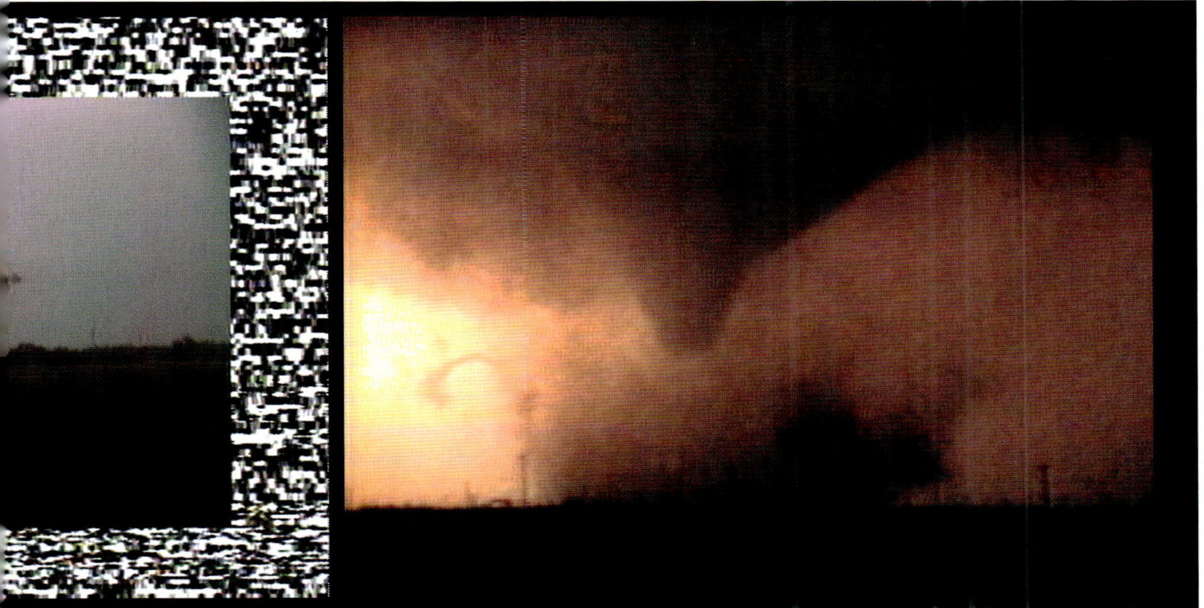

sual images. They have their own power, based not on voltage or amperage but on unrelenting cascades of data, at times subliminal and at others overpowering, almost physical. It is the terror of mediation.

It's worth noting that Nikola Tesla's ideas about the potential for his coil to transmit information in the form of electrical energy are compatible with my own more metaphorical assertions. In the early part of the twentieth century, he built the Wardenclyffe Tower and laboratory at Shoreham, Long Island. The base of the 187-foot wooden tower supported an immense steel ball at the top that was sixty-eight feet in diameter. His intention, which went unrealized after his funding was lifted and his theory proven incorrect, was to build enough of these giant Tesla coils across the planet to electrify the atmosphere, delivering free electricity throughout the world, wirelessly.

The obvious irony of using spectacle and raw power to critique spectacle and power is that one creates an experience that is all about spectacle and power. I was not unaware of this contradiction. As I write these words, and recall some of the controversy around this piece, I am reminded of a highly critical review that Roberta Smith wrote in reaction to *Art at the Armory: Occupied Territory*, a group exhibition in Chicago organized by the Museum of Contemporary Art that included *The Terrible Uncertainty*.

In her *New York Times* article that was spread across the front page of the Sunday arts section, she panned the entire show under the headline, "In Installation Art, a Bit of the Spoiled Brat." No one came out looking good, but few came out looking worse than I. While my contentious side delighted in

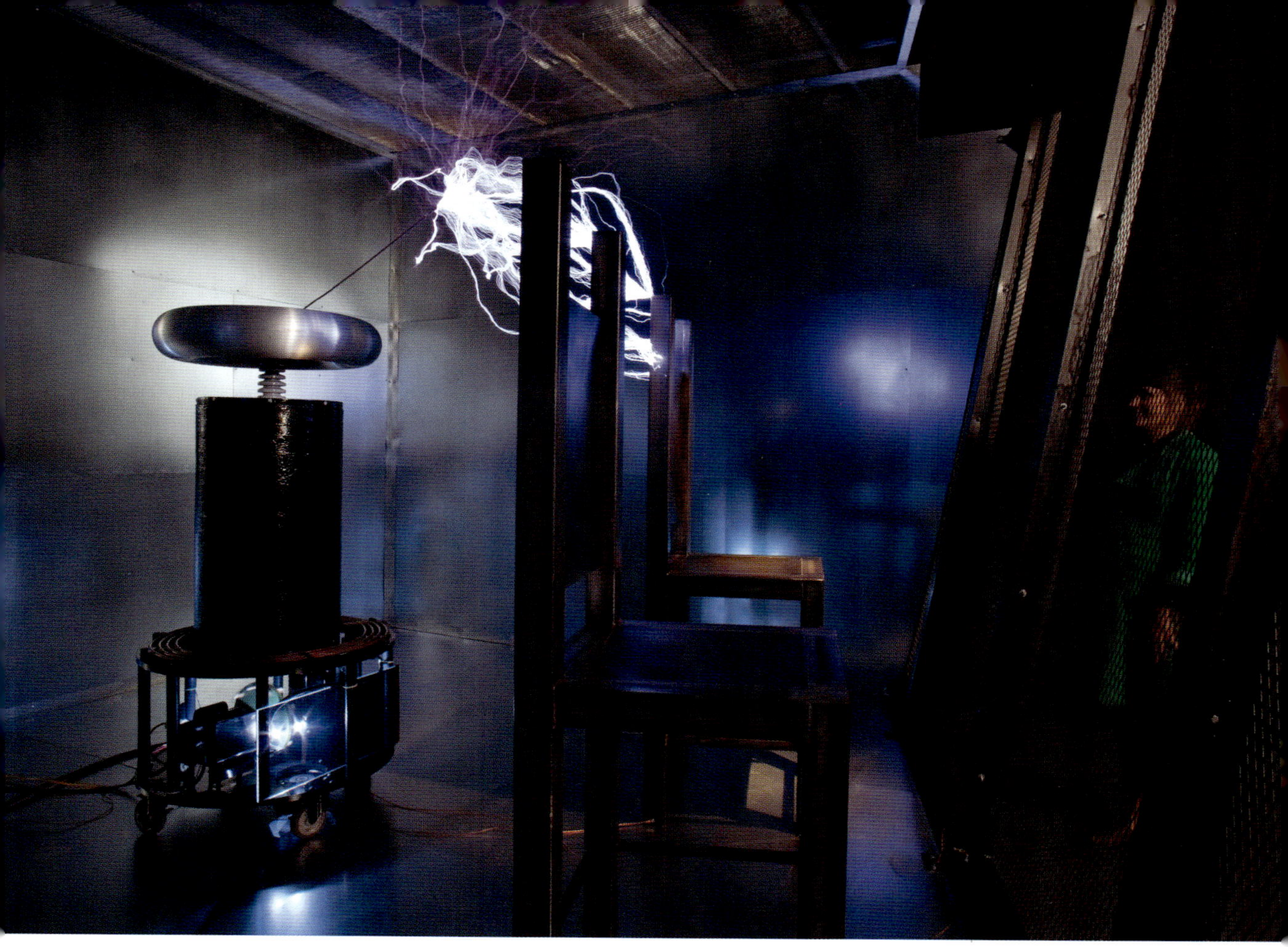

The Terrible Uncertainty of the Thing Described, showing detail of the Tesla coil discharging to steel chairs
Photograph by Gregory Goode, courtesy San Francisco Museum of Modern Art

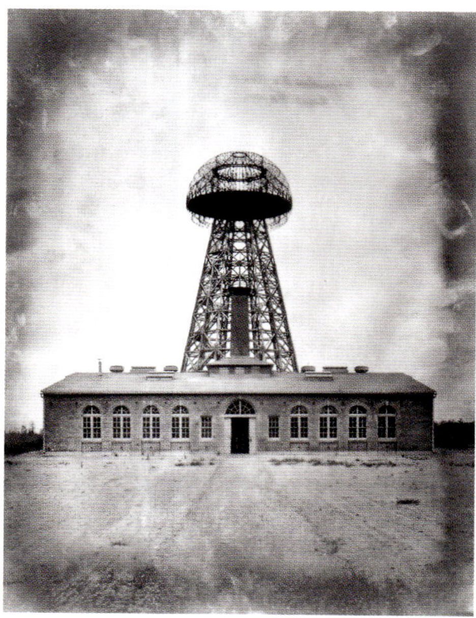

Nikola Tesla's Wardenclyffe Tower Laboratory, Shoreham, Long Island, 1903
Photograph courtesy of the Science Photo Library

rubbing the critic the wrong way (Fuck the critics! They can't make art!), my ego was injured, resulting in a bout of self-loathing. Over time, I came to understand that the opinion of the critic, when situated within a prestigious publication, is its own expression of power—insignificant to the world at large but formidable within the smaller ecosystem of the art world.

Smith wrote, "*The Terrible Uncertainty of the Thing Described* uses video to overbearing effect, projecting natural disasters on six big screens to the accompaniment of ear-splitting Dolby sound. But the real climax of the piece is actual lightning that, at 30-minute intervals . . . leaps dramatically between two steel chairs in a mesh cage. There must be a name for a spectacle, apart from amusement park rides and certain horror movies, that reduces the spectator to speechless fear—but it may not be art."[7]

Recalling Smith's critique, I can't pass up the opportunity to express my own judgments on her kind of corporate-sponsored criticism and about contemporary art criticism in general. I make what I think is an important distinction between the review and the longer critical essay. Smith offered a review, which is her personal assessment or judgment about the works in an exhibition, based on her experience of looking at and commenting on visual art. It is typical of a kind of art writing that is generally brief, singling out work that supports the author's thesis, expressed as their likes and dislikes, although the writer couches her assessments in the more sophisticated language of contemporary art-speak. If, for example, the writer believes that installation art is an aesthetic travesty because of its excessive theatricality or that it is overly immersive, disallowing critical or aesthetic distance in the modernist tradition—a position that Smith may or may not have held—then a negative review would be no surprise.

Because column space is limited (more so in the pre-digital age) for art writers in major urban publications, their weekly reviews tend to be superficial, uncompromising, and hard hitting, landing at the extremes of the like-dislike scale. This, after all, is what their readers want, as do advertisers and others with financial interests in the health of mainstream newspapers. These critics fulfill their roles as valued professional reviewers. Roberta Smith, as the primary art writer for New York's most trusted newspaper, had great credibility; her assessments influenced gallerists, collectors, and curators, affecting artists' careers both positively and negatively. The crux of the issue, at least from my perspective as an artist, is that the voice of a respected, institutionally validated reviewer, who reaches a broad art-interested audience, carries more weight—let's call it power—than the work of the artist, which, even if loud and bombastic, remains mute on the subject of its validity.

Works of art are vulnerable in this way, as is the artist who made the work. The art does the artist's speaking. We put the work out there because

7. Roberta Smith, "In Installation Art, a Bit of the Spoiled Brat," *New York Times*, January 3, 1993.

we believe it is significant enough to deserve a response, proposing that visual art is a discussion between artist and audience. As I expressed earlier, this dynamic is one of the major pleasures we have when looking at art: it makes us think and feel things we couldn't have thought or felt otherwise or would have experienced differently had we never seen the work in the first place. In my case, and for others in the show, Smith gave her assessment, which is perfectly fair and legitimate, given the expectations of her audience and the limitations of the form. I wasn't offended by her position as much as I was sorry that her opinion wasn't based on a more insightful analysis of why I did what I did in the way that I did it. In other words, she offered a judgment about product at the expense of process (the thinking and decisions that led to the product).

We all come to art with certain preconceptions of what it is and what it is supposed to be. This is particularly true for artists and those who write about art. In a sense, we are professional lookers. We have historical and philosophical contexts from which we view things, and we have, as well, our own personal idiosyncrasies. These form and frame our biases, which all of us have. The problem for me with most reviews is that they don't allow the space to reveal the author's biases, nor the rationale used to arrive at their opinions.

Professional looker or not, reactions to art occur within a cultural and historical context. For example, when I was emerging in the 1970s, the prevailing aesthetic was the one coming out of Modernism. It tended to support the work of White, generally male artists who worked in modes that seemed fully compatible with what scholars and writers perceived as Modernism's natural evolutionary cycle. But Modernism's linearity was restrictive, unable to account for a world culture that is heterogenous and complex. Those who didn't fit into the narrative were placed into marginalized categories: feminist art, naive art, African American art, and so on. This freed the main critical line from ideas or ways of seeing that could undermine the prevailing modernist narrative, with its historical roots firmly planted in Europe where it could be traced from Giotto to Picasso and beyond. Late-modernist aesthetics—the ideology of the postwar period through the early 1990s—with its reliance on the formal attributes of color, shape, and truth-to-materials, is precise about the criteria for judging and evaluating art, as the writings of Clement Greenberg and others made clear. In the case of the Smith review, when she ends by asking if the work is art (a perfectly legitimate and potentially interesting line of inquiry) the question falls before the reader as a condemnation with the implication that it is not. No reason is given for this evaluation other than it is the opinion of the writer, an opinion we are asked to accept without explanation. And many do, since she writes from a place of power: the pages of the *New York Times*.

As most of us have noted of late, the world is a lot messier than the clean line of Modernism can account for, and this is represented in contemporary art. Much has changed since the 1970s. Today, and for the first time certainly in my life, artists and styles of work that had been marginalized are front and center where they are being seen and intelligently discussed. The best art writers are struggling with this multicultural complexity to engage us in difficult conversations about aesthetics, White privilege, institutional racism and power, gender identification, and other sociopolitical issues that, until recently, had fallen outside the range of formal discussions in the arts. For the most part, these investigations are occurring not in the short review but in the longer form, the critical essay.

Such essays are where ideas and controversies initiated by works of art have best been explored and debated, and when written by talented authors, they embody literary, even poetic, style. The most compelling of these writers burrow into the work, less intent on judging and more engaged in mucking about, moving toward some sort of interpretation and leaving crumbs behind for the curious to ponder in the process. This approach, based in curiosity, is one that cannot be achieved in the short newspaper review; it requires the time and space of the essay.

One of the most accomplished at this was the poet and art writer Bill Berkson, who was a colleague at the San Francisco Art Institute and a dear friend. Bill wrote inspiringly about the artists he knew and whose work he admired such as New Yorkers Alex Katz, Philip Guston, Willem and Elaine de Kooning, and Jasper Johns, as well as many California artists, including me. He approached art through the connecting rhythms of the poet he was.

In a eulogy I delivered at the San Francisco Art Institute on the occasion of Bill's memorial in 2016, I made several comments, delivered as if I had written him a letter, that are relevant to the distinction I am making between the reviewer and the essayist, the former based on judgment, the latter on curiosity and imagination:

> Bill, I am trying to come up with some historical antecedents that could shed light on this talent you had of involving us in your pursuit of those questions, generated by doubt, that promised no static or final resolutions but instead involved a process of thinking-things-through. I keep circulating back to Michel de Montaigne, the originator of the essay as a literary form, as one likely progenitor. I'm hoping you won't be uncomfortable with this connection. I'm recalling how the French title for his collection of anecdotal and philosophical writings, *Essais*, is literally translated as trials or attempts. In your critical writings, poems, essays, teaching, one has the sense that you are on a journey of discovery, of understanding, of coming-to-terms-with, and that you've invited all of us to come along with you. And these journeys, or trials, or attempts are conducted with such grace, honest curiosity, and elegance that we can't help but join in, pulled along, lending our voices here and there, and thoroughly

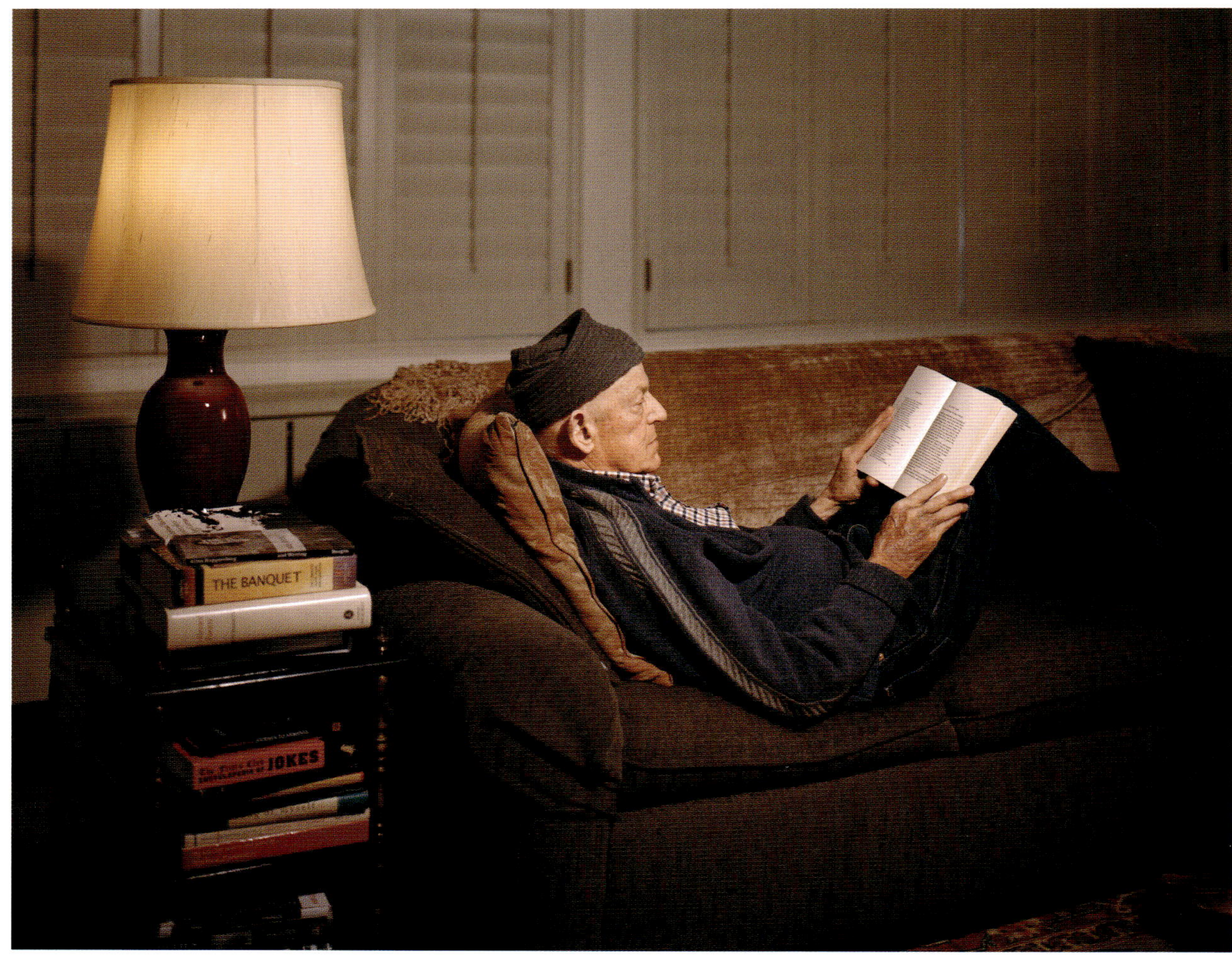

Doug Hall, *Bill Berkson Reading at Home*, 2014. Digital chromogenic print, 30 × 36½ in. (76.2 × 91.4 cm)

enjoying the ride wherever it may take us, appreciating the bumps, abrupt changes in direction, and occasional vertiginous drops that might occur along the way.

As I tried to say in my eulogy, Bill's writing was remarkable in how he approached the art he admired with the sentiments of the poet, the curiosity of a precocious child, and the rigor of the scholar. In the sense that an artist reveals in their work the decisions that led to the conclusion we see before us, Berkson's writing places us on the winding paths he takes to discover his own insights, which we receive not as pronouncements but as questions we are left to ponder. The writing expands the scope of the work itself and, like the art, it doesn't presume to close the door on multiple meanings but allows them to remain like stones placed along a path to help us navigate our way home. We are carried along not only by the essay's content but by its literary style, which is generous and beautifully composed. His writing takes us deep into works of art and back out again, noting what he sees and feels along the way—not ideological at all, as most writing is today, but transparent, experiential, placing us in close contact with the work and with the sentiments of one who can look deeply into art.

Delirious Space

By the early 1990s, digital technology was starting to push aside its analog precursors. Walking into an office, one no longer heard the clacking of IBM typewriters but instead sensed the much quieter tapping of keyboards connected to computers, interrupted by printers loudly spewing out their scrolls of perforated pages. If fax, an earlier technical breakthrough, offered fast and efficient transmission of documents across the globe, email—connected to the emerging Internet with crude dial-up modems, their unique audible signal clattering—seemed almost instantaneous in comparison.

The mechanical world, offspring of the industrial revolution, ponderously expands the human grasp through machines able to carry out the myriad industrial tasks that are beyond the physical capability of the human body. Many of the devices are heroic in scale and appearance and awe-inspiring in the force they generate. These prosthetics magnify our measly human strength thousands, perhaps millions, of times over. In that sense, they make us more productive. The earth can be more quickly drilled to remove its oil, forests obliterated to allow more acreage for farming or to make space for expanding cities; entire mountains are flattened, their mineral-rich soil carted away on trucks with tires twice the height of a man; factories belch while highways are built to carry their products across the country.

Like a human body, these machines require fuel to run and, like us, they create waste that must be eliminated. In their wake, we see expanses of land contaminated by their excretions and skies polluted by their deadly residue. Into the mid-twentieth century, industry's capacity for environmental destruction was on a scale as heroic as the devices that caused it. Although describing nineteenth-century London, Charles Dickens could as easily be describing Pittsburgh or any number of American cities in the 1950s or even early seventies when he writes, "Smoke lowering down from chimney-pots, making a soft black drizzle, with flakes of soot in it as big as full-grown snow-flakes—gone into mourning, one might imagine, for the death of the sun."[8]

While analog devices extend the physical strength of our bodies, digital technologies enhance the subliminal power of our brains. The former are aggressively visible as they clatter and clang, the latter mostly invisible and nearly silent, although in their own way even more powerful. The monstrosities of the industrial age, both the beautiful and the hideous, seem permanent, immoveable,

8. Charles Dickens, *Bleak House,* 1853 (London: Collector's Library, 2006), 9.

and monumental; those of the digital age transient, impermanent. Even much of the architecture of the postmodern period seems to lack substance, as if temporarily installed the way a theater director might erect a set for a play.[9]

Rather than appearing solid, anchored to the earth, postmodern buildings with their snap-on exteriors and flamboyant surfaces can seem unserious, gaudy, and superficial. At the same time, these structures are often playful, more welcoming than "serious" modernist buildings that can feel forebodingly humorless and stern in their refusal to accommodate the softening pleasures of decoration. It is in this anti-decorative spirit that the influential Austrian architect Adolf Loos wrote, in 1908, "A person of our times who gives way to the urge to daub the walls with erotic symbols is a criminal or degenerate. What is natural in a Papuan [Loos's example of the primitive urge to decorate] or the child is a sign of degeneracy in a modern adult. I made the following discovery, which I passed on to the world: *the evolution of culture is synonymous with the removal of decoration from objects of everyday use.*"[10] [italics in original]

Postmodernism's embrace of ironic playfulness, rejection of universalizing narratives, and preference for the virtual at the expense of the real form a deep contrast to the monuments of the International Style,[11] designed by early twentieth-century architects like Le Corbusier, Frank Lloyd Wright, Ludwig Mies van der Rohe, and others. Mies's Chicago and New York skyscrapers, with their soaring facades punctuated by expansive windows, provide transparent portals through which the production of the workers and executives within is framed, as if to celebrate the power, solidity, and ubiquity of American capital. I am not the first to make this claim, which I first came across in an essay by the writer/artist Victor Burgin where he writes, "The transparent wall, used by such socialist modernists as [Walter] Gropius to unite interior with exterior, was destined to become the very index of capitalist corporate exclusivity."[12] Much postmodern architecture favors flamboyant surfaces or one-way glass facades that mask the interiors or create mirrors that project the exterior back at us. They seem to suggest that surface is all there is. It is as far as we need go, as far as we are allowed to go. Superficiality is its own reward and endgame.

---

9. I find the term "postmodern" to be sloppily unspecific. I am using it to describe an approach to architecture that prevailed in the sixties, reached its heights in the seventies, and faded as a style by the mid-nineties. It was an architectural expression of a philosophical position that rejects the universalizing assumptions of the Enlightenment in favor of theories that see all interpretations as contingent on the perspective from which they are made. Claims to objective fact are dismissed as naive realism.

10. Adolf Loos, "Ornament and Crime," from *Ornament and Crime: Selected Essays*, ed. Adolf Opel (Riverside, CA: Ariadne Press, 1998), 167.

11. The International Style in architecture is "characterized by an emphasis on volume over mass, the use of lightweight, mass-produced, industrial materials, rejection of all ornament and colour, repetitive modular forms, and the use of flat surfaces, typically alternating with areas of glass," per the Getty Research Institute as cited in Wikipedia.

12. Victor Burgin, "The City in Pieces," in *In / Different Spaces: Place and Memory in Visual Culture* (Berkeley, CA: University of California Press, 1996), 147.

While the architecture of surfaces might have reintroduced fantasy into the sobriety of high modernist architecture, it did so by eliminating spatial depth and consequently introducing, or at least accentuating, the psychological disorientation and alienation caused by an unsettling sense of placelessness in which "everything conceals something else."

> With cities, it is as with dreams: everything imaginable can be dreamed, but even the most unexpected dream is a rebus that conceals a desire or, its reverse, a fear. Cities, like dreams, are made of desires and fears, even if the thread of their discourse is secret, their rules are absurd, their perspectives deceitful, and everything conceals something else.
>
> —Italo Calvino, *Invisible Cities*[13]

Nowhere has the art of architecture-as-surface been more flamboyantly addressed than in Tokyo and other East Asian cities. If the European city is the site of a rational space based on Renaissance perspective, then modern-day Tokyo exemplifies where this rational space is blown to smithereens. It is superseded by a surrational, or anti-perspectival, space whose sources are to be found in the televisual expanses of a post-Euclidean geometry, not in the equilibrium of the humanist grid. In rational space, one enters public spaces that unfold one after the other, always leading or directing, and constructed with one's body in mind. If one drifts through these spaces—in the tradition of the flaneur, for example—it's a controlled drift, corporally defined and taking place within prescribed boundaries, reassuring intersections, squares, and focal points. The public spaces of Tokyo, on the other hand, inspire an entirely different sensation.

I am standing in Shibuya, staring across a vast expanse of people, all moving in different directions, at a building whose facade has just transformed itself from glass and steel into an immense electronic display of constantly changing scenes—at one moment it's yellow wildflowers bobbing in a lush field and the next an animated dinosaur several stories high lumbering across the facade until it disappears into the opposite corner. There is no discernible logic to the sequencing of images. Nor is there any cohesion between these displays and the numerous similar ones taking place on and above buildings in whatever direction I might look, buildings that are crowned with huge advertising billboards, neon signs, company logos, and brand names—some in English, most in Japanese. The sounds of jingles or hysterical sales pitches—I assume they're advertising something—come at me from every direction. From

13. Italo Calvino, *Invisible Cities*, trans. William Weaver (San Diego, New York, London: Harcourt, Inc., 1974), 44.

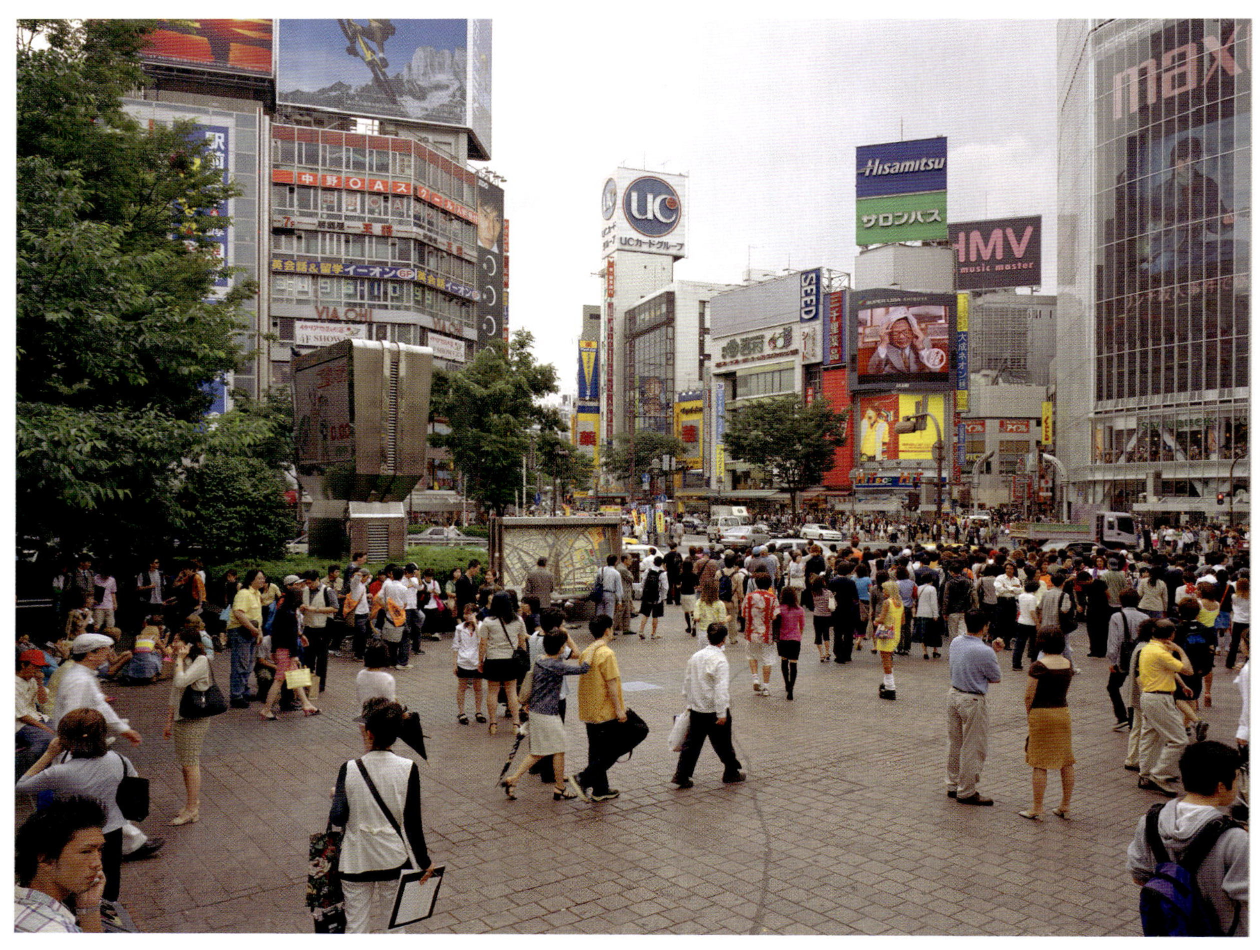

Doug Hall, *Shibuya, Tokyo*, 2001. Diptych, pigment prints, 50 × 126 in. overall (127 × 416.6 cm)

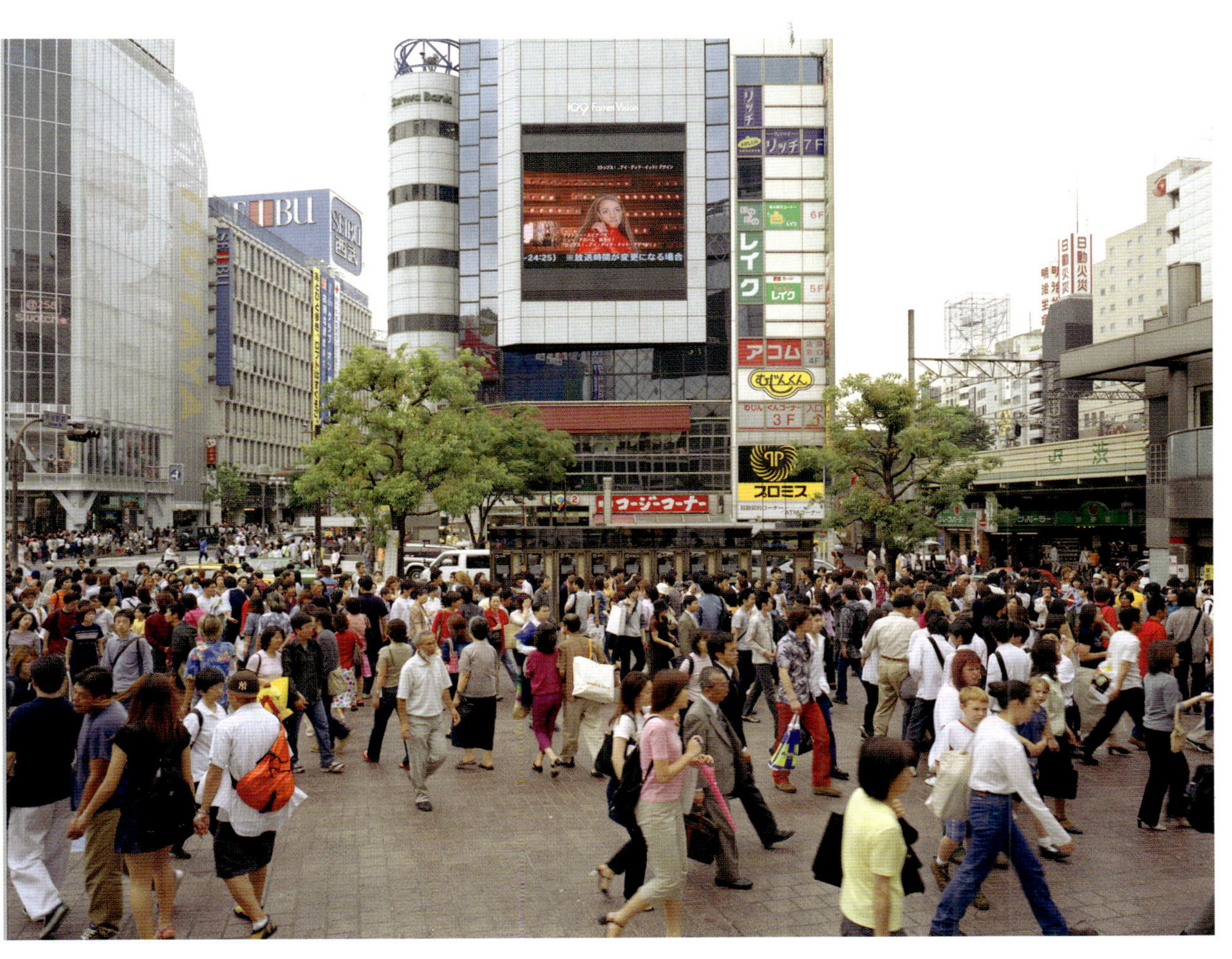
BU
SEIBU
TSUTAYA
リッチ
リッチ 7F
6F
レイク
5F
アコム
4F
むじんくん
3F
プロミス
コージーコーナー
日動火災

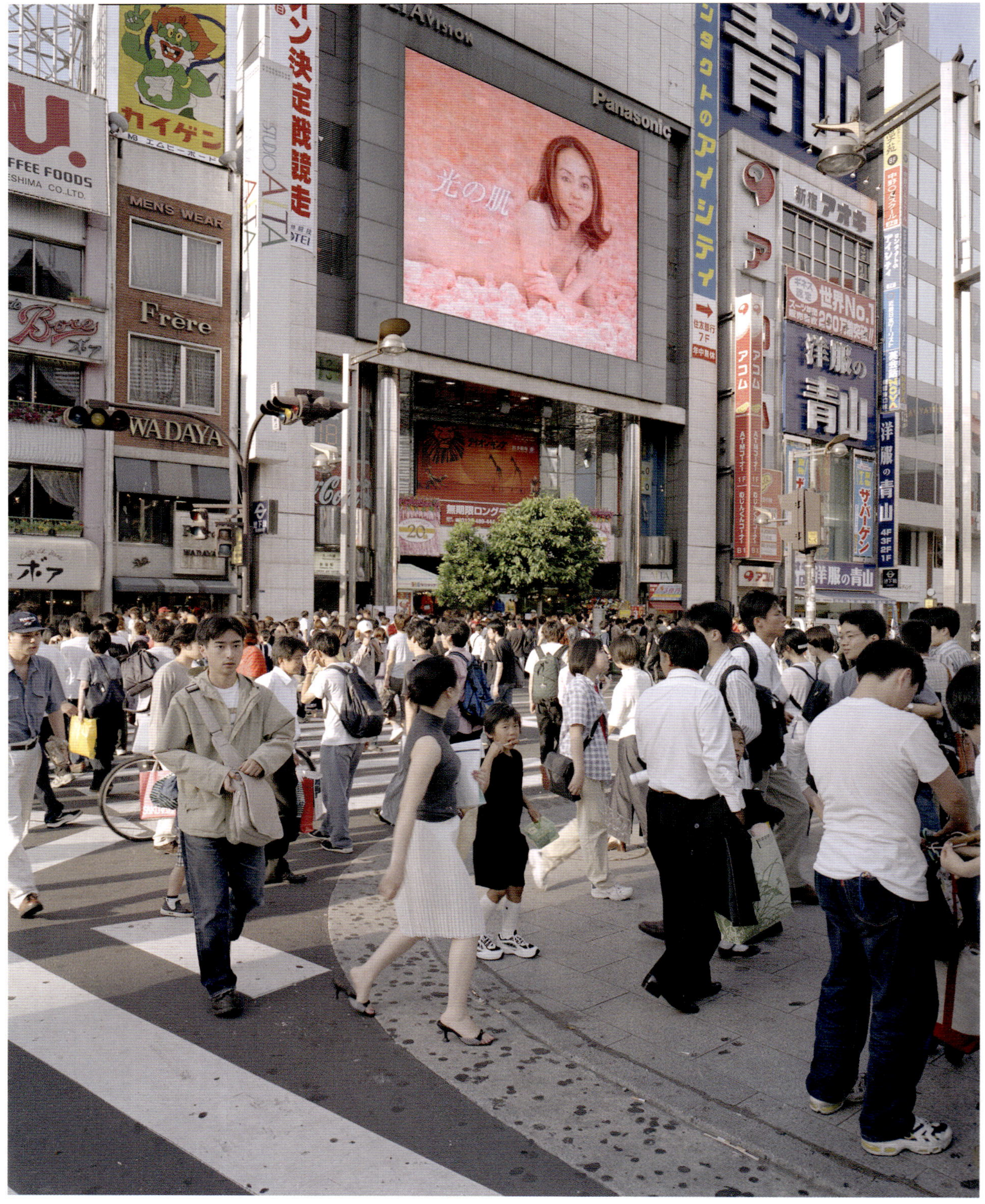

Doug Hall, *Shinjuku, Tokyo, Saturday Afternoon*, 2001. Digital chromogenic print, 62 × 50 in. (157.5 × 127 cm)

the edge of the open space where I am standing, I watch thousands of people, some milling about talking on cellphones hanging from their necks, others hurrying along, a few grasping shopping bags. There are people flirting and laughing and talking. Some stand in groups, others in pairs, and others alone. Every age is represented, and every style of dress from the most conservative to the most outlandish. I stare at a young woman who stands nearly motionless within the throng. I can't figure out what she's doing. I think she might be selling or pitching something but if she is, it's being done at a nearly subliminal level. Her long, bleached hair is swept back from her face and falls midway down her back. She wears black platform shoes that add six inches to her height and heavy white knee-socks that she's pulled down to mid-calf so they bunch around her legs and over the tops of her shoes. Her bright yellow sleeveless dress—cotton, I think—hangs loosely and extends to the top of her thighs. She carries on a clear strap from her shoulder a large transparent purse that's filled with all kinds of brightly colored objects. Looking out into this throng, I am aware that I have never felt more "other" in my life. Nor, I realize, have I ever felt more transported by the dream—the dream city—that's unfolding in my imagination.

Why is this? I think it has something to do with how contemporary Tokyo feels more like a media environment than a solid city made from steel, glass, and stone; as such, it introduces an inescapable otherness into my personal space. And this, while liberating, contributes to the destruction of whatever illusions I may have had of myself as the center point on a neatly organized perspectival grid. The order of the world decomposes into a palimpsest that relocates me at its periphery, not its center.

The televisual is without center and exists as multiple planes that are constantly shifting, intersecting, and folding in on one another; proximity and distance are indistinguishable. In this state, I can never occupy anything other than the edge. This centerless space is furthermore a place of diminished gravity, and it is its lack—this sense of boundlessness—that frees my imagination, allowing it to float and drift directionless and liberated rather than corralled by the phantasmagoria that surrounds it. Fredric Jameson might identify this psychic condition as momentary schizophrenia, in which there is a complete "breakdown in the signifying chain," with the result that the schizophrenic is reduced to "an experience of pure material signifiers, or in other words a series of pure and unrelated presents in time."[14] I would describe it more simply as euphoria, both terrible and exhilarating.

These and similar thoughts were behind several of my media installations in the late eighties and into the nineties, such as *People in Buildings* (1989) and *Terminal Landscape* (1995).

14. Fredric Jameson, *Postmodernism, or, the Cultural Logic of Late Capitalism* (Durham, NC: Duke University Press, 1991), 26.

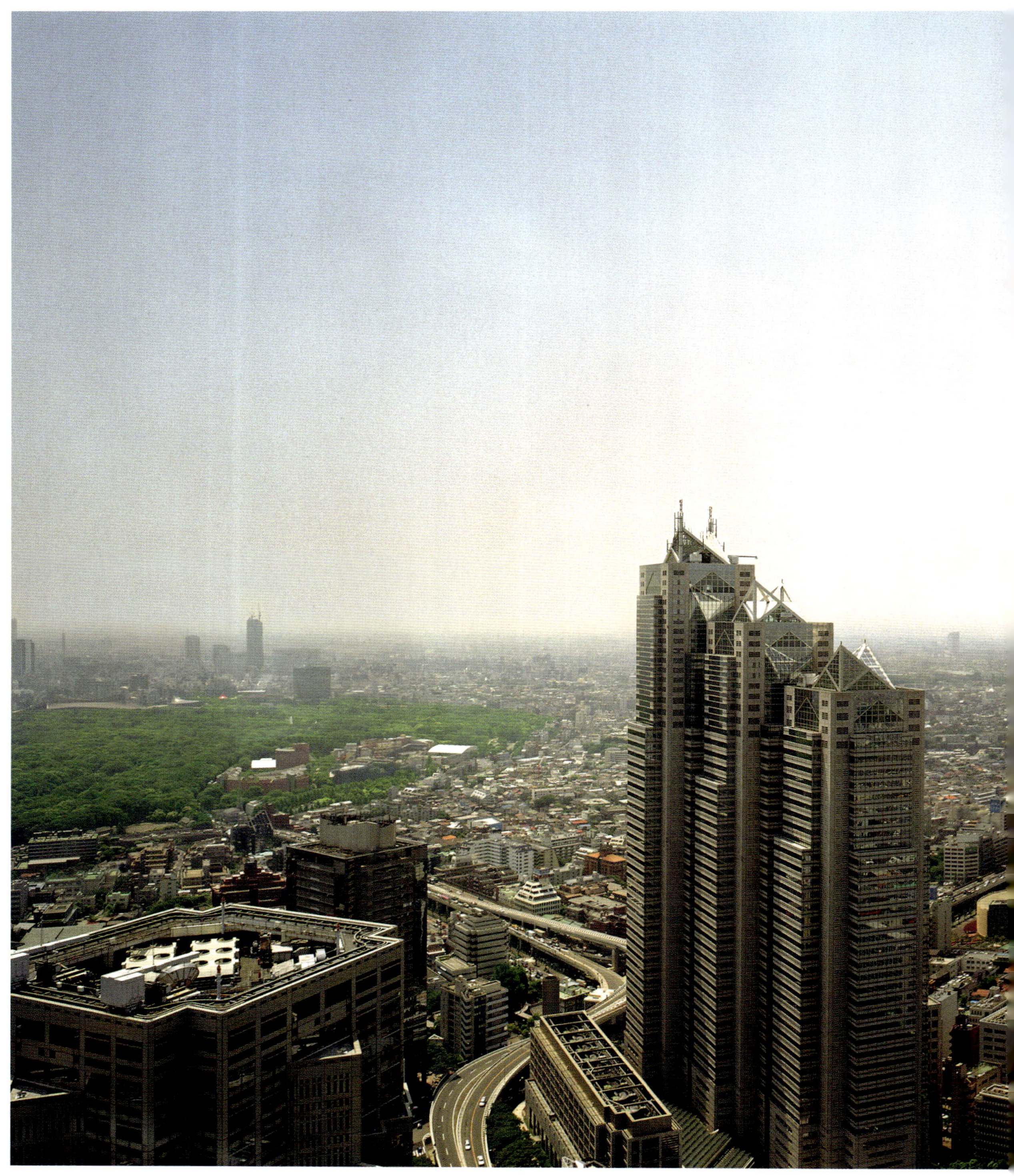

Doug Hall, *Tokyo, Looking Northwest*, 2001. Digital chromogenic print, 40 × 70⅞ in. (101.6 × 180 cm)

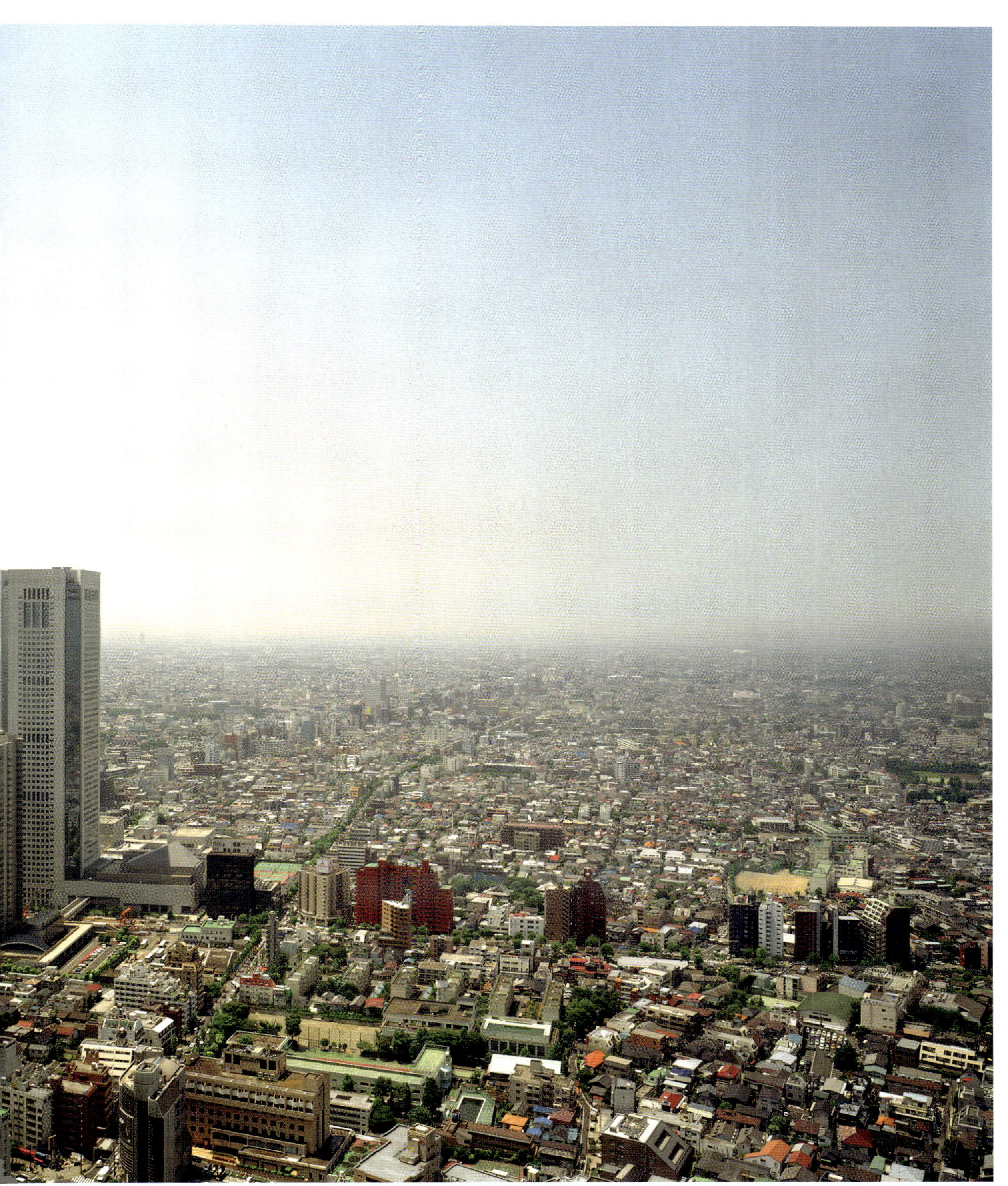

Allegories of Omniscience and Oblivion

I made *People in Buildings* in order to investigate my claim that postmodern architecture, in its obsession with surface, deceives us by presenting what I called a "dilemma of surfaces." I hoped the two-channel projected installation would make my theoretical claim visceral. That, in any case, was its original inspiration, although such an assertion makes me appear far more rational in my art-making than I actually was, or am.

The installation is organized around two walls onto which video is projected. The first presents a constantly changing surface of projected video. Through an opening in its center, a second projection can be seen. The first wall, partially influenced by Charles Moore's Piazza d'Italia in New Orleans (1978), is a decorative video facade created by combining video of random architectural details with elements from eclectic sources: television snow and interference, flowers in corporate parks, urban fountains, city signage, and clouds. The disparate images combine into patterns that circulate around the cased opening. One enters the opening into the shallow room beyond to encounter a rear-screen video projection of people interacting in the mostly banal spaces: working, searching, waiting, looking, in malls, offices, hospital waiting rooms, institutional corridors, art museums, DMVs, courtrooms, bookstores, and libraries—the places where we carry out the ordinary activities of

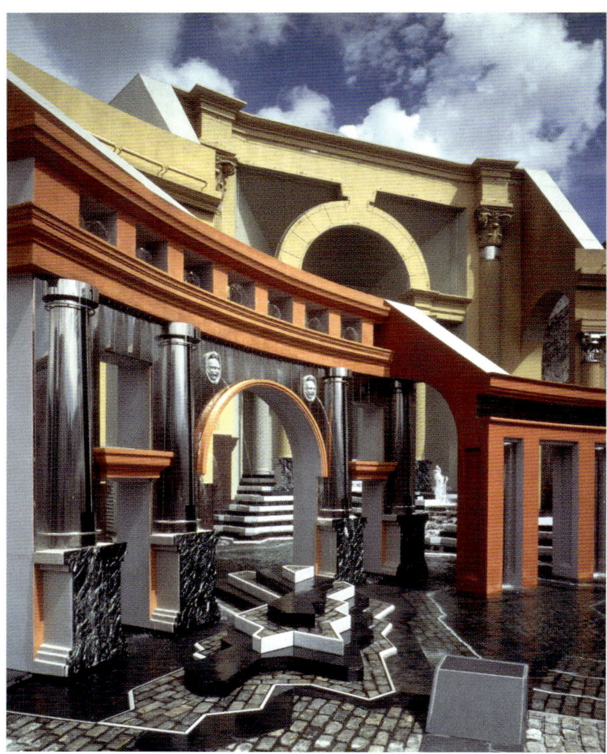

Charles Moore (with Perez Architects), *Piazza d'Italia,* New Orleans, 1978
Photograph © Norman McGrath

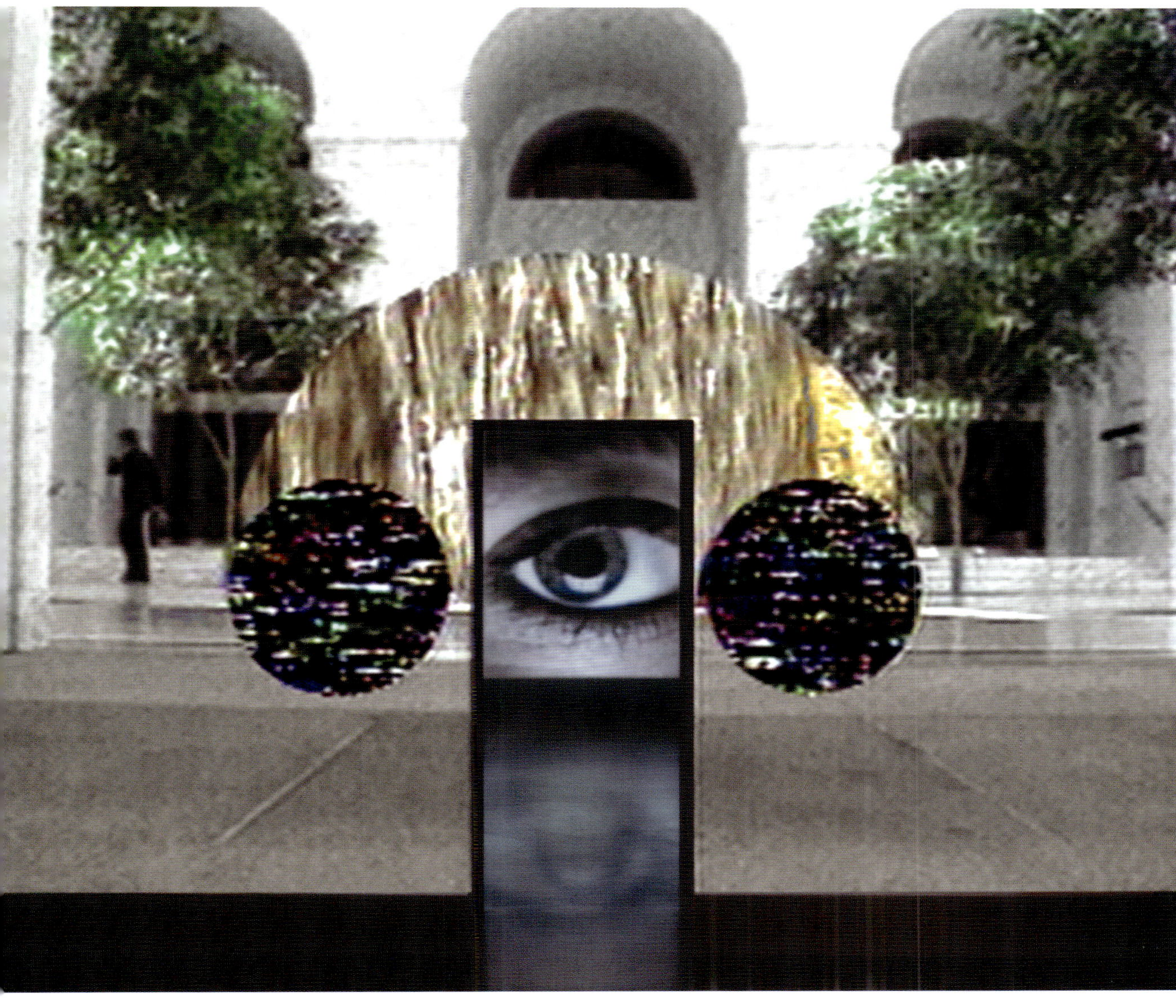

Doug Hall, *People in Buildings*, 1989. Two-channel video installation with sound (installation view)
Photograph by Ben Blackwell

our lives. Through the opening, the playfulness of the first surface gives way to the mundanity within.

It was while filming for this project, particularly when standing in long institutional corridors, stultifying in their bland ordinariness, that I had a minor epiphany: I needed to stop time, to arrest the spaces and free them from the narrativity that video imposed on them. Only then, as static images that allowed contemplation, could they express what I was coming to think of as their allegorical potential. I turned to large-format photography, with its ability to at once freeze the moment and provide images with remarkable detail at a scale that feels cinematic—something that in the 1980s was beyond the capability of analog video.

By "allegorical" I mean that the photograph, in its stark literalness, distances itself from the world-as-fact even as it explicitly refers to it. Combined with other images, on a gallery wall perhaps and at a scale that relates to our own bodies, the photograph can insinuate itself into our consciousness in ways that are unlike time-based media. One reason is that we are not propelled by video's built-in temporality. We can linger, meander, enter, and exit at our own speed, not yanked from our reflections by the onrush of a narrative, as is the case in video and film. Undisturbed, we can dream ourselves into the image.

Perhaps it is also that the image is beyond real—not real at all, and certainly not true—in that it provides a level of detail and focal depth that is beyond the capability of the naked eye. It is this frozen, unrealistic pictorial literal*ness* that frees the image from the literal, making it hyperreal. And being static, the photograph stands as a recollection that awaits our return, unlike moving images that have little patience for our dalliance. In the moment when we stand before the photograph, our imaginations adrift, it abandons its false and less important claim of accurately describing the world and assumes its more important (and interesting) job of helping us imagine ourselves in the world.

These are some of the thoughts that led me to venture into large-format photography. The first photographs in 1989 were taken looking down the institutional corridors where I had been spending so much time while filming *People in Buildings*. With meticulous care, I placed the camera in the center of the corridors so that the resulting photos reveal the cone-like perspective that radiates between the lens of the camera (the viewer's monocular eye) and the point in the distance where the lines converge. Herein lies the allegory—actually, dual, conflicting allegories—of omniscience and oblivion.

"*Perspectiva* is a Latin word which means 'seeing through,'" Albrecht Dürer wrote in the latter part of the fifteenth century.[15] Erwin Panofsky, art historian and iconographer, proposes in *Perspective as Symbolic Form* (1924) that linear perspective evolved not just because it solved a practical problem of how to translate three dimensions into two but because the solution it provided was consistent with the humanistic philosophies that were fast developing at the time, namely Humanism with its reliance on logic and reason—what might be paraphrased as Cartesian rationalism. Putting my own twist on this, I suggest that perspective represents two conflicting conditions simultaneously.

The first, dating back to the Renaissance, offers linear perspective as an abstraction of a world that is rational, static, homogeneous—one that can be

---

15. Quoted in Erwin Panofsky, *Perspective as Symbolic Form* (1927), trans. Christopher S. Wood (Princeton, NJ: Zone Books, 1997), 27.

plotted as a series of precise, geometrically derived points within a stable grid. Symbolically, the message is that physical space, and all it contains, reaches our eyes through a cone of vision that situates us as the knowing centers of all things—godlike. In this model, the world lays itself out for us as the masters of our fate, the omniscient ones.

The conflicting condition, one that better suits our time, reverses this cone of vision so that instead of vision emanating from our eyes outward to a stable and conforming world, we have a funnel with a drain hole at its farthest end through which, symbolically, our subjective worldview evacuates, casting stability and our sense of wellbeing into uncertainty. In *Being and Nothingness*, Jean-Paul Sartre claims that this sense of worldly disintegration occurs when one's subjectivity is intersected by an Other, by one-who-is-not-me.

> Thus, suddenly an object has appeared which has stolen the world from me. Everything is in place; everything still exists for me; but everything is traversed by an invisible flight and fixed in the direction of a new object. The appearance of the Other in the world corresponds therefore to a fixed sliding of the whole universe, to a decentralization of the world which undermines the centralization which I am simultaneously affecting. [W]e are not dealing here with a flight of the world toward nothingness or outside itself. *Rather it appears that the world has a kind of drain hole in the middle of its being and that it is perpetually flowing off through this hole.*[16] [my italics]

In my corridor photos, the distant point of converging perspective represents the allegorical portal through which a destabilized world flows.

16. Jean-Paul Sartre, *Being and Nothingness*, trans. Hazel E. Barnes (New York: Washington Square Press / Pocket Books, 1992), 343.

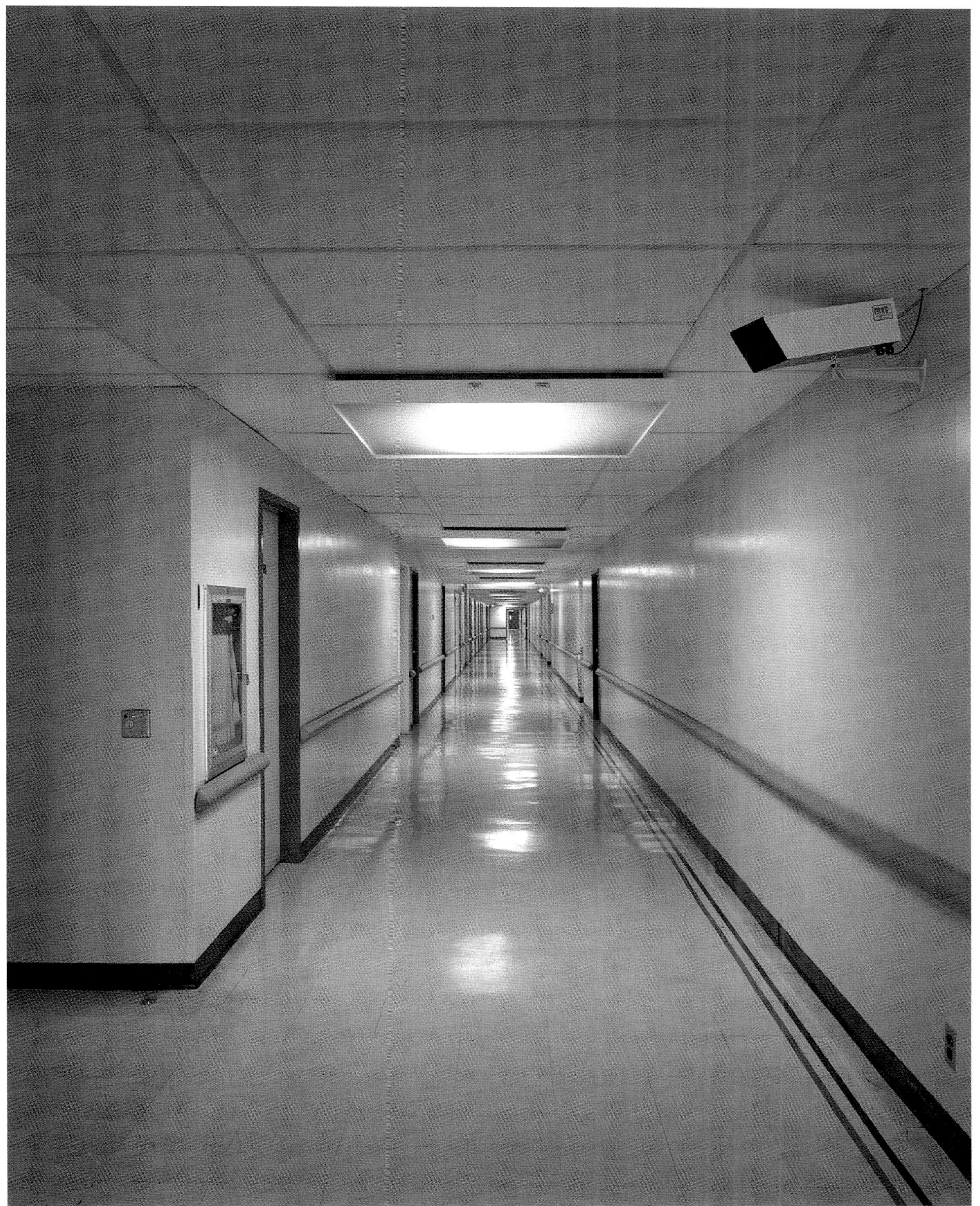

Doug Hall, *Nonplace 35*, 1989. Gelatin silver print, 62 × 48 in. (157.5 × 121.9 cm)

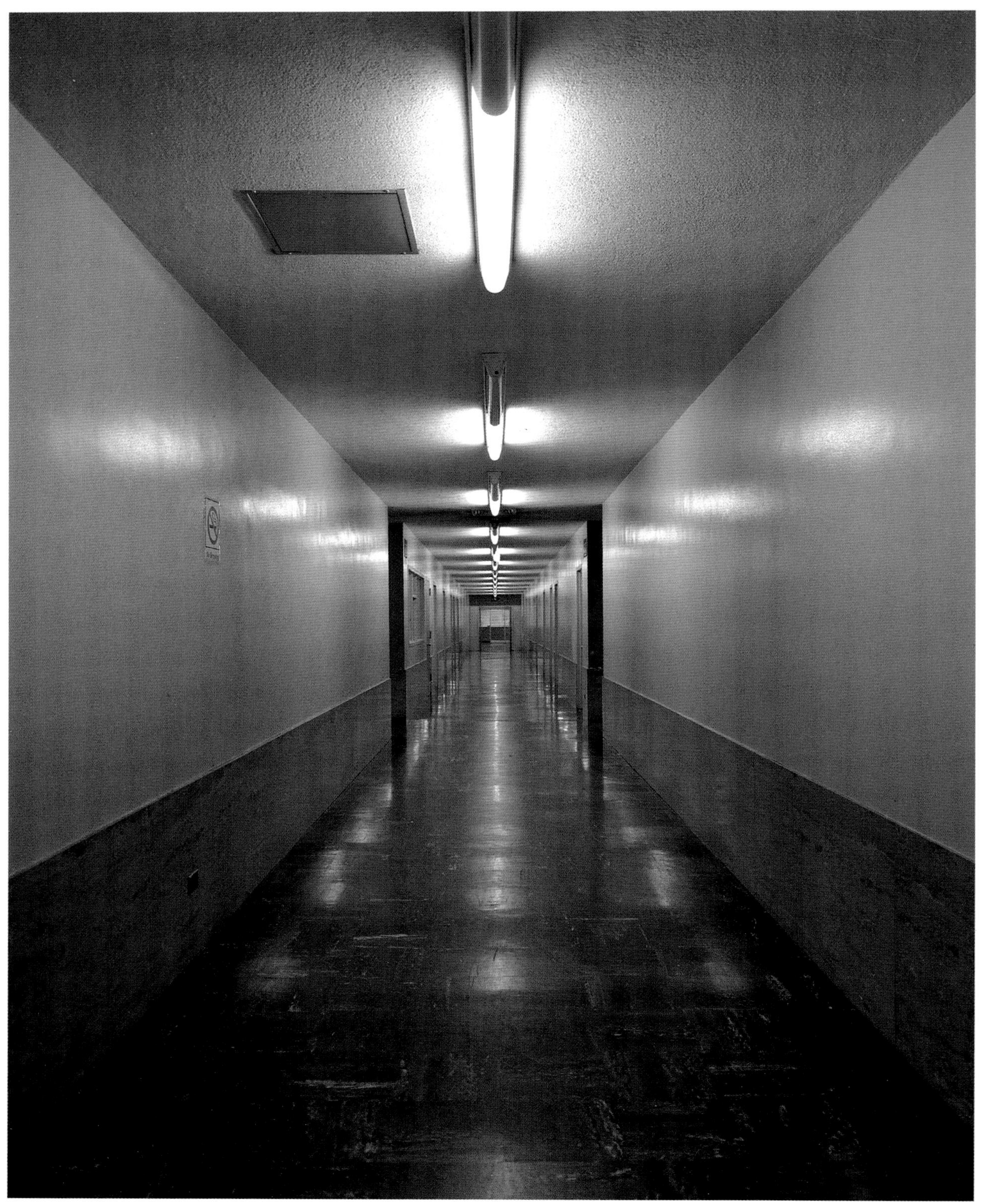

Doug Hall, *Nonplace 17*, 1989. Gelatin silver print, 62 × 48 in. (157.5 × 121.9 cm)

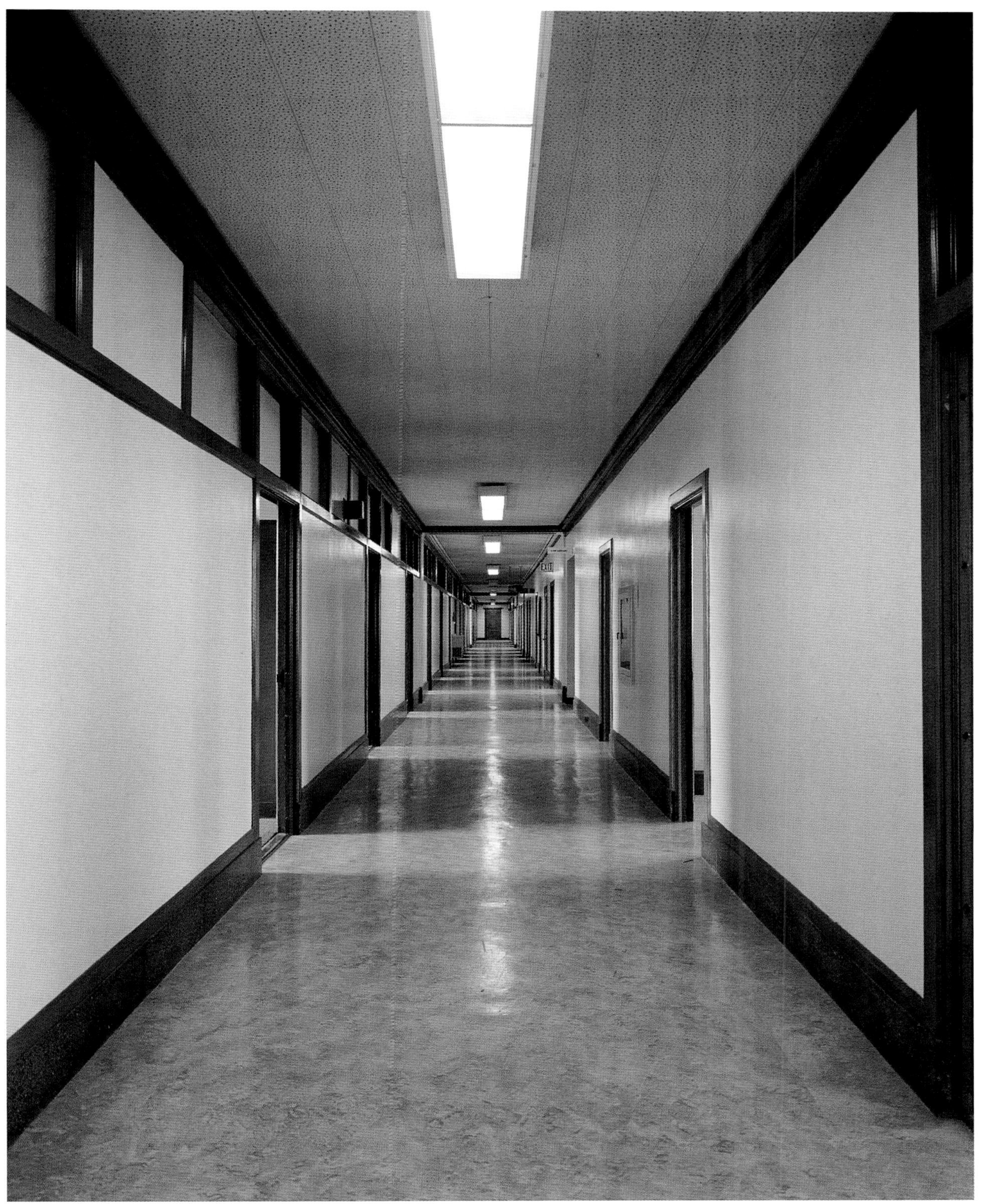

Doug Hall, *X Corridor*, 1989. Gelatin silver print, 62 × 48 in. (157.5 × 121.9 cm)

Mnemonic Space

In the 1990s I began thinking about how governmental architecture strives to articulate the underlying principles and power of the state. I was struck, for example, by how classical motifs—massive Ionic and Corinthian columns and majestic domed buildings—are the primary architectural forms employed by both authoritarian and democratic governments. Although advertising opposing political viewpoints, the architectural language of Nazi Germany with its classical forms and soaring eagles is not unlike that of democratic America, which adorns its federal buildings with similar iconography. In the case of fascist Germany, the buildings of Albert Speer and other architects of the Reich take stripped-down modernism, inflate its scale a hundredfold, and enhance it with classical references to express the dominance of the state over everything under its purview. This was the intention behind Speer's gargantuan Volkshalle. Inspired by Hitler's 1925 sketch based on his visit to Rome's Pantheon, the building was to be the centerpiece of Germania, the massive rebuilding of Berlin that was planned to symbolize the perseverance of the thousand-year Reich following the war.

In 2002, I was invited by an architectural preservation foundation in Moscow to photograph some of the buildings from the Soviet Union's constructivist/modernist phase. As symbols of the collective, communal aspirations of the first phase of the revolution, these structures provide a marked contrast to the Germans' contemporaneous architectural authoritarianism as well as to later Soviet periods. One example among the several I photographed is the Communal House of the Textile Institute, designed by Ivan Nikolaev and built in 1929–31 to accommodate 2,000 students. The building,

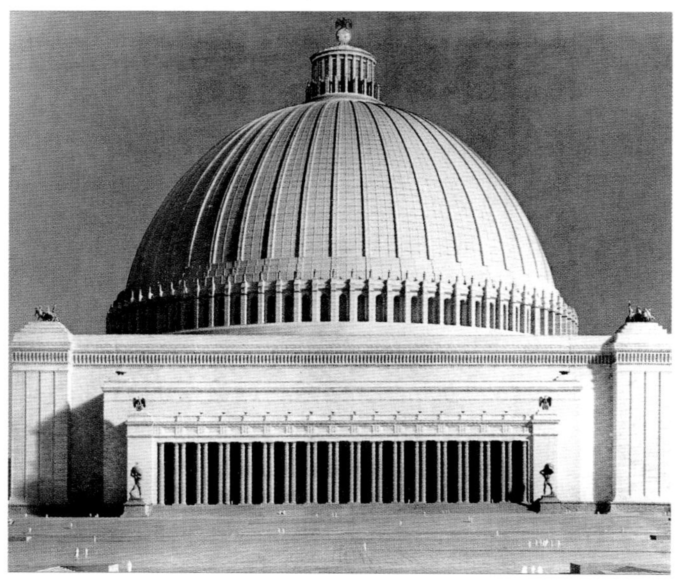

Albert Speer, model for the Volkshalle (based on an earlier drawing by Hitler to be built after the war in a reconstituted Berlin that would be renamed Germania), 1940
Credit: Photograph by Ullstein Bild via Getty Images

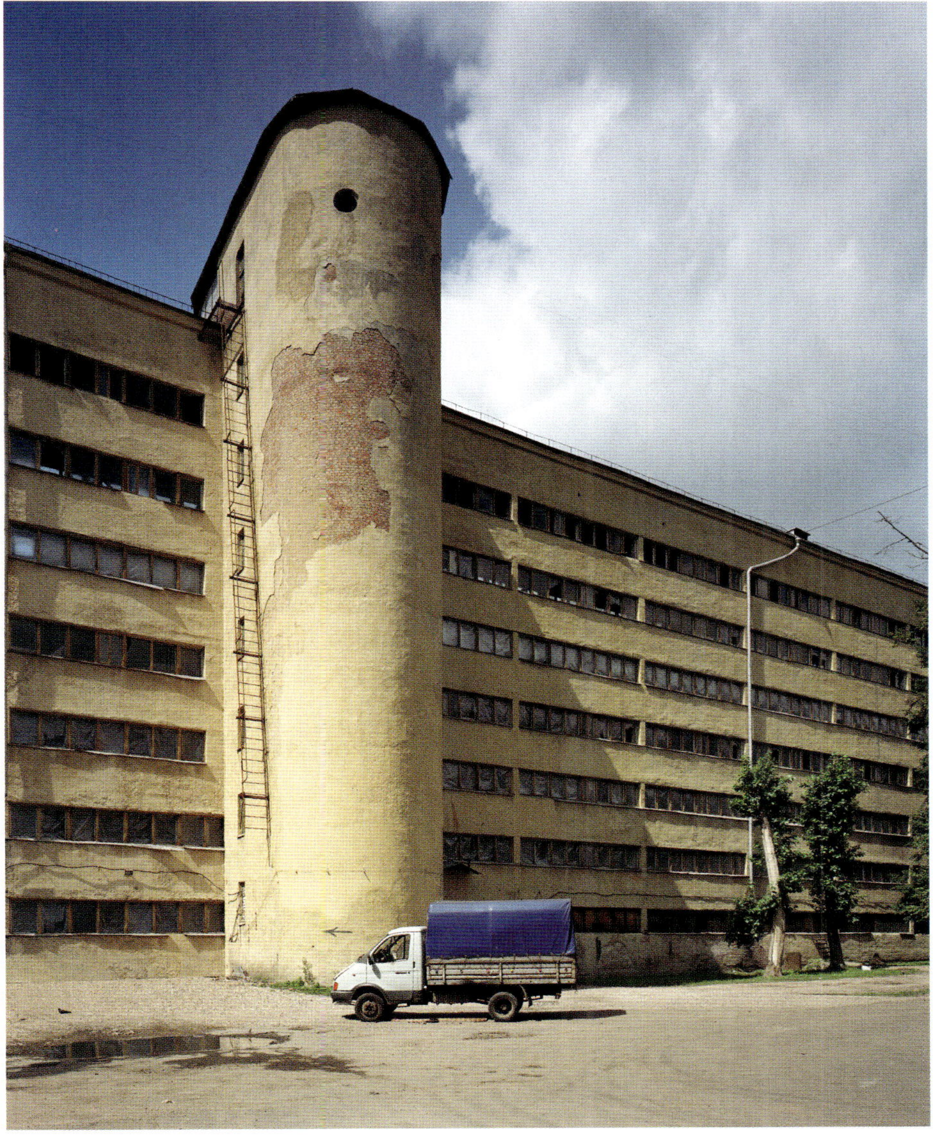

Doug Hall, *Communal House of the Textile Institute*, 2002. Pigment print, 40 × 32 in. (101.6 × 81.3 cm)

abandoned and in disrepair when I photographed it, consisted of small two-person sleeping cells located in the tower—individualism was discouraged—and, in the long horizontal block, expansive communal spaces for studying, reading, eating, and showering.

Once Stalin's rule was solidified, Moscow's modest constructivist architecture, no longer representative of the state's aspirations, was surpassed by utilitarian housing blocks for the people and large vertical buildings for the state. If these had some similarity to New York's monuments to capitalism, they lacked their proportioned gracefulness. Whereas New York's skyscrapers

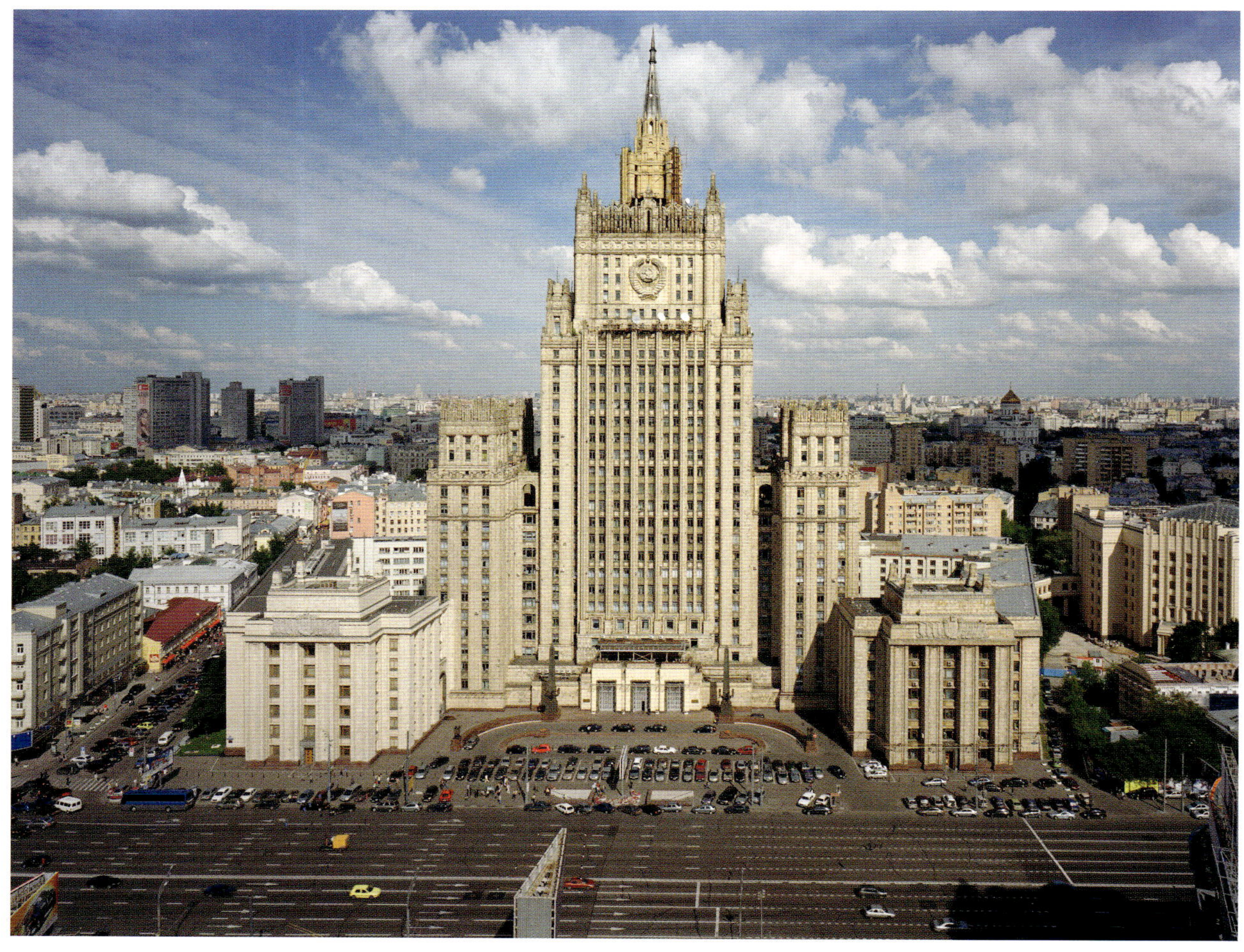

Doug Hall, *Ministry of Foreign Affairs, Moscow*, 2006. Pigment print, 32 × 40 in. (81.3 × 101.6 cm)

soar toward the heavens, Moscow's are squat, anchored to the earth—massive and weighty, like fortresses or maybe prisons. Their insistent symmetry suggests stability, regularity, and authority. That, in any case, was my impression of the Ministry of Foreign Affairs and the other similar buildings, all built between 1947 and 1953, that comprise the so-called Seven Sisters.

A decade earlier, in 1992, supported by a grant from the Guggenheim Foundation, I had traveled to the former East Berlin to photograph three abandoned government buildings that had been the center of power for the Communist regime of East Germany. The Palace of the Republic (Palast der Republik), built in the 1970s, was both a popular social center and, separated from the public by locked glass doors, the seat of the People's Congress (Volkskammer). The State Council Building (Staatsratsgebäude), situated on the south side of Marx-Engels-Platz, had been headquarters for the General Secretary of the Central Committee, Erich Honecker in the final days of the

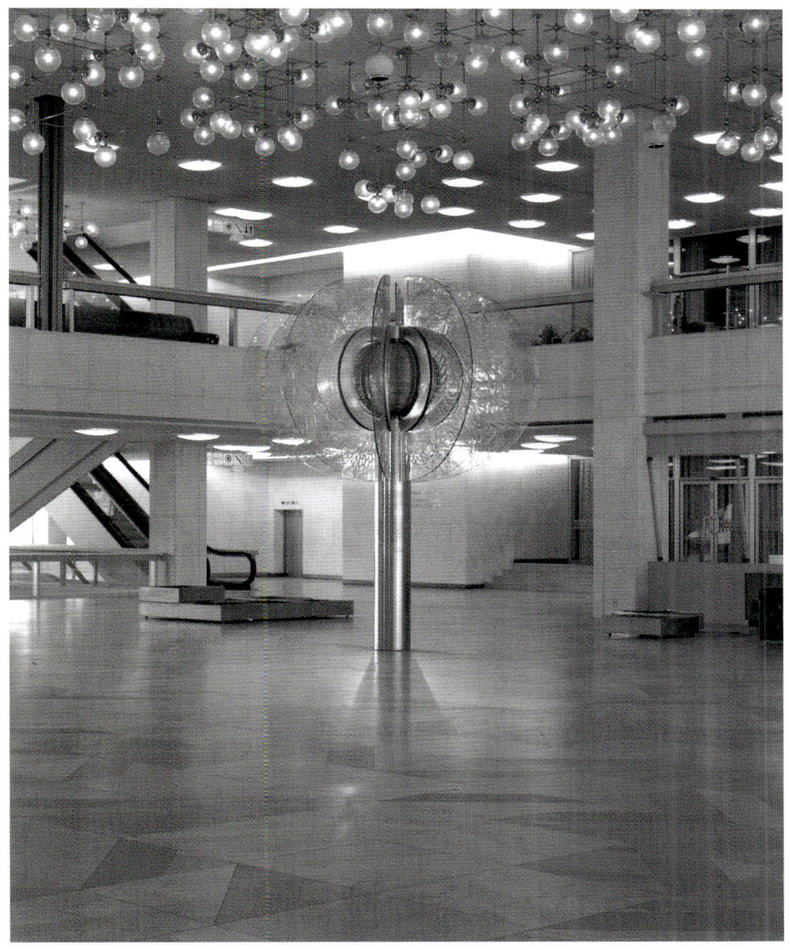

Doug Hall, *Central Court, People's Palace (Palast der Republik), Berlin*, 1992. Pigment print, 24 × 16 in. (61 × 40.6 cm)

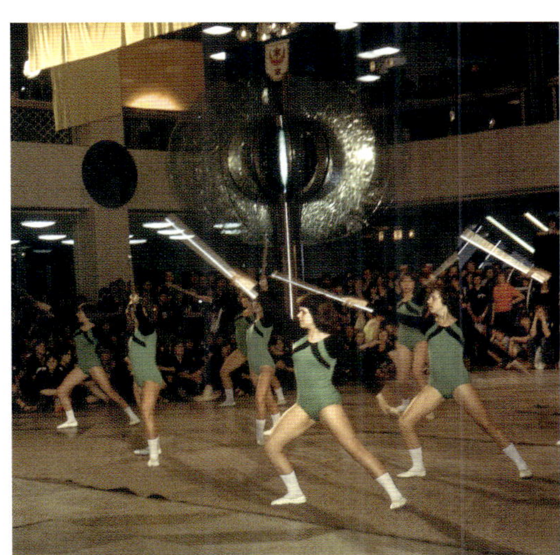

Synchronized Baton Demonstration, People's Palace, (East) Berlin, circa 1972. Archive of the German Democratic Republic

Communist regime. The third building, on the other side of the square, the Central Committee Building of the Communist Party, was built in 1934 by the fascist architect Heinrich Wolff as the Reichsbank, and after the war was transformed into headquarters for the Politburo.

While photographing inside the Palace of the Republic and the State Council Building, I was struck by their anonymity: how alike they were to each other and to similar places in the East and West, and how placeless they felt. There were areas within the Palace that could easily be mistaken for an airport lobby in Buenos Aires, a convention center in Omaha, Nebraska, or a state building in Geneva. Perhaps we should not be surprised by this sameness. We have all experienced how most bureaucratic and public interiors throughout the world blend into one another, becoming indistinguishable. These are non-places where our identities threaten to dissipate into the ordinariness of our surroundings.

And yet one expects, maybe even hopes, to find in governmental architecture, particularly in the buildings that house the highest levels of government, a physical equivalence to the grandiose rhetoric that nourishes and mythologizes its ideology. In the case of East Berlin, however, one enters interior spaces of resolute blandness, which are both psychologically and spiritually numbing. While some, like the State Council Building, try to create an illusion of grandeur, even cursory examination reveals the superficiality of the affect—surfaces of humble materials masquerading as palatial elegance. These are spaces that abhor surprise, and if surprise is a metaphor for hope and change, they speak to the values of continuity over innovation, of drudgery and conformity over epiphany. Unlike the Stalinist buildings of the Soviet Union, which monumentalized commonality and the will of the state, there is nothing celebratory about the East German buildings of the Communist period. They are as devoid of joy as they are of humor, parody, or critique. It is an architectural language in which neither past nor future is imaginable beyond the horizon of an endless and mundane present.

My experience of the Communist-era East German buildings was very different from what I encountered in 1996, when, as a Fellow of the American Academy in Rome, my interests turned to archives in Rome and Naples. In their richness of accumulated history, these proved to be the opposite in tone and feel from the deadening spaces depicted in the earlier non-place photographs or in the pictures of the government buildings of East Berlin. Most of the Italian archives and libraries were built during and after the Renaissance by churches and wealthy aristocrats to house their vast collections of books and documents. Some of the holdings were prosaic financial records of a diocese or an estate; others included exquisite illuminated manuscripts or rare texts copied by scribes from earlier Roman or Greek originals. Over the years, as many churches and aristocratic families were no longer able to maintain their collections, the Italian government took them over, housing them in state-owned archives.

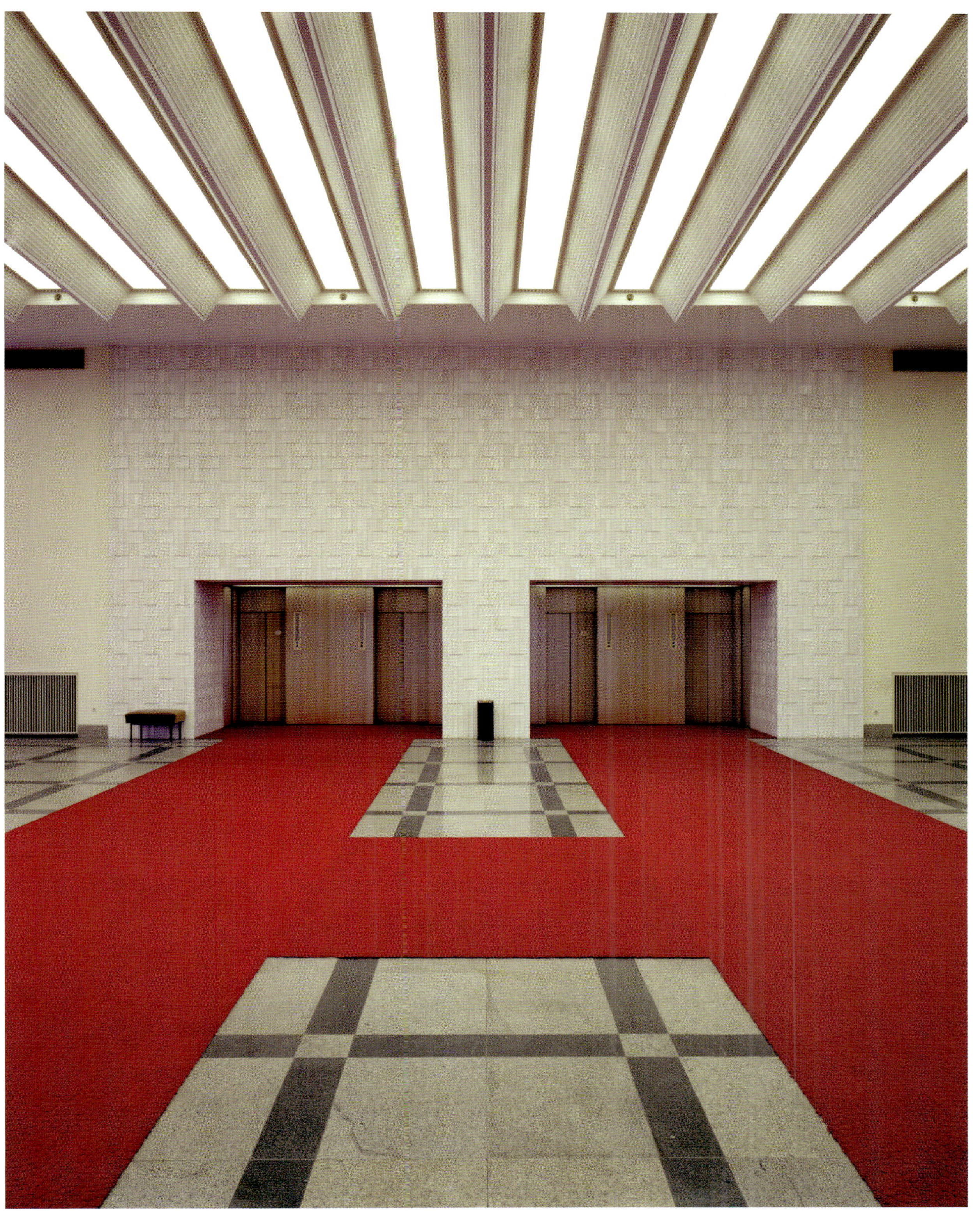

Doug Hall, *Main Entrance Hall, Council of State Building, (East) Berlin*, 1992. Pigment print, 48 × 60 in. (121.9 × 152.4 cm)

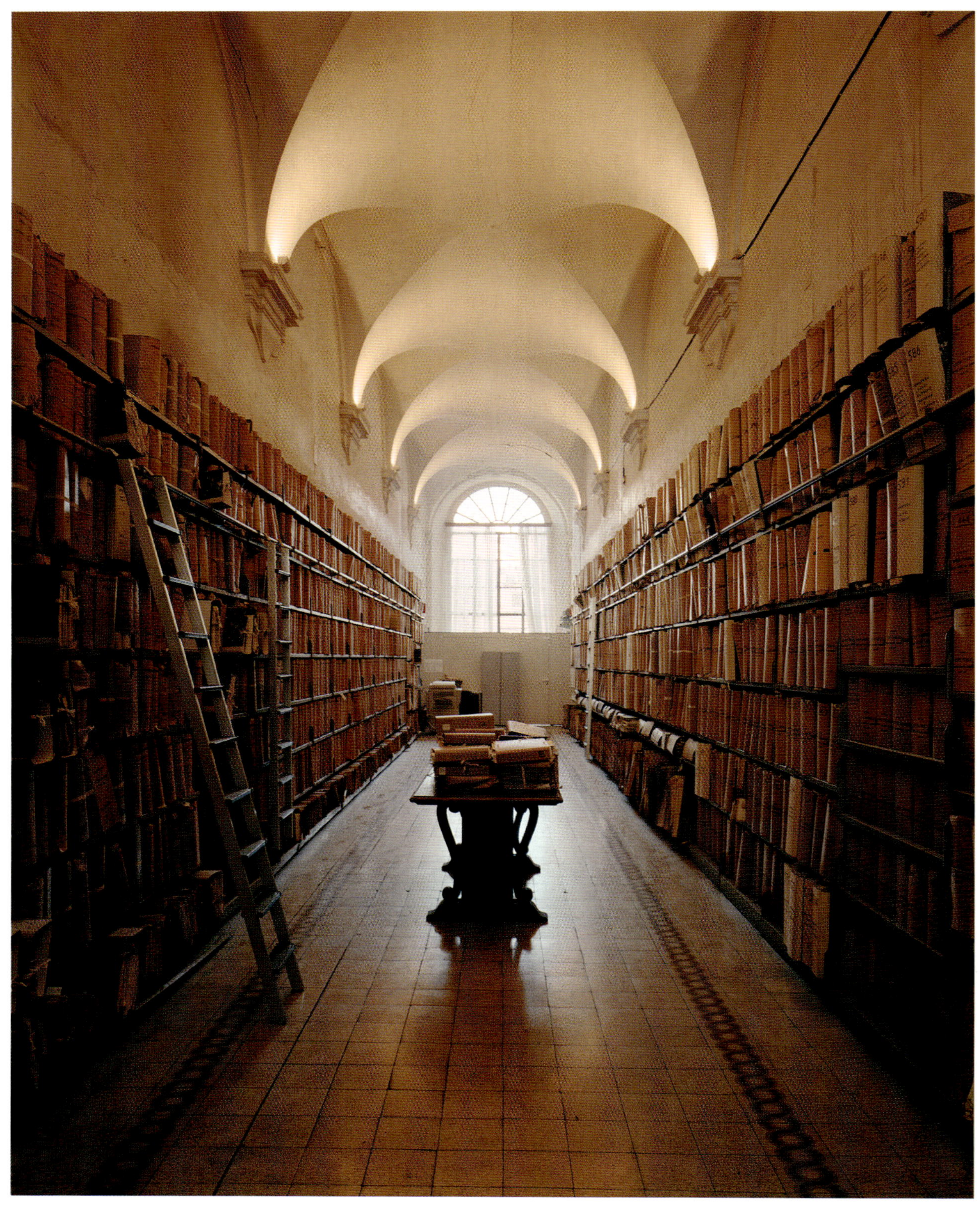

Doug Hall, *State Archive at Sant' Ivo alla Sapienza, Rome,* 1996. Pigment print, 61 × 48 in. (154 × 121.9 cm)

Of the several I visited during my year in Italy, the Historical Archive of the Bank of Naples, which houses several private holdings as well the financial records from the bank dating back to the sixteenth century, is among the most memorable. Moving through the rooms, one dedicated to records from the fifteenth and sixteenth centuries, others to different periods, is like surfing an ebb of backward-moving time. If history can be said to have an aura, then one experiences its full force within those musty rooms. It is as if the spaces breathe into me: their modesty, their stained walls; the subdued natural light; the sheaves of paper, books, and folders in yellowing covers stacked, seemingly abandoned, on their shelves; objects from the past tentatively and obliviously occupying our present, appearing more randomly placed than ordered. And the near silence: whatever sounds I hear are muted and faraway, as if occupying a different galaxy, a different time. The air is like that of my grandparents' attic, filled with smells of arid decay and remembrance. I feel subdued within these rooms, overcome with the sort of reverence one might experience when eulogizing or recalling a deceased friend or relative. I welcome these sensations even while realizing, perhaps precisely because I do realize, that these repositories of the past are disappearing anachronisms—relics of the humanist need to order—and are being replaced by the vast, dynamic digital archives available to nearly anyone in the world. The Internet's democratization of knowledge turns traditional, hierarchical archives like the ones depicted in my photos into an accessible plain of information. As liberating as this surely is, it does so while devouring epistemological palpability, the physical manifestation of the past, its aura as well as its vain urge for historical coherence.

Not surprisingly, the Vatican Library presents itself very differently: in its large central reading room, rows of tables are arranged beneath a highly decorated, vaulted ceiling and surrounded by portraits of former library prefects, popes, and other religious figures. When I was in Rome, Father Leonard Boyle, an Irish and Canadian scholar in medieval studies and paleography, was the prefect of the library. Before he took the position in 1984, it had very strict protocols controlling who was granted access and a dress code for those who were admitted (coats and ties for men; for women, knee-length skirts and conservative blouses). Father Boyle changed all of this, making the library and its holdings much more widely available. It was under his auspices that the Vatican Library began high-resolution digitization of its early illuminated manuscripts, and because of him that I was permitted to photograph the library's grand reading room.

We *experience* the archive spaces and the more formal reading room very differently, as well. In the library, it is as if knowledge is being staged, a measure of the papal state's power to control that knowledge. The main reading room exuberantly and ostentatiously expresses its power. In marked contrast is the modest archive, which abhors or at least is oblivious to ostentation.

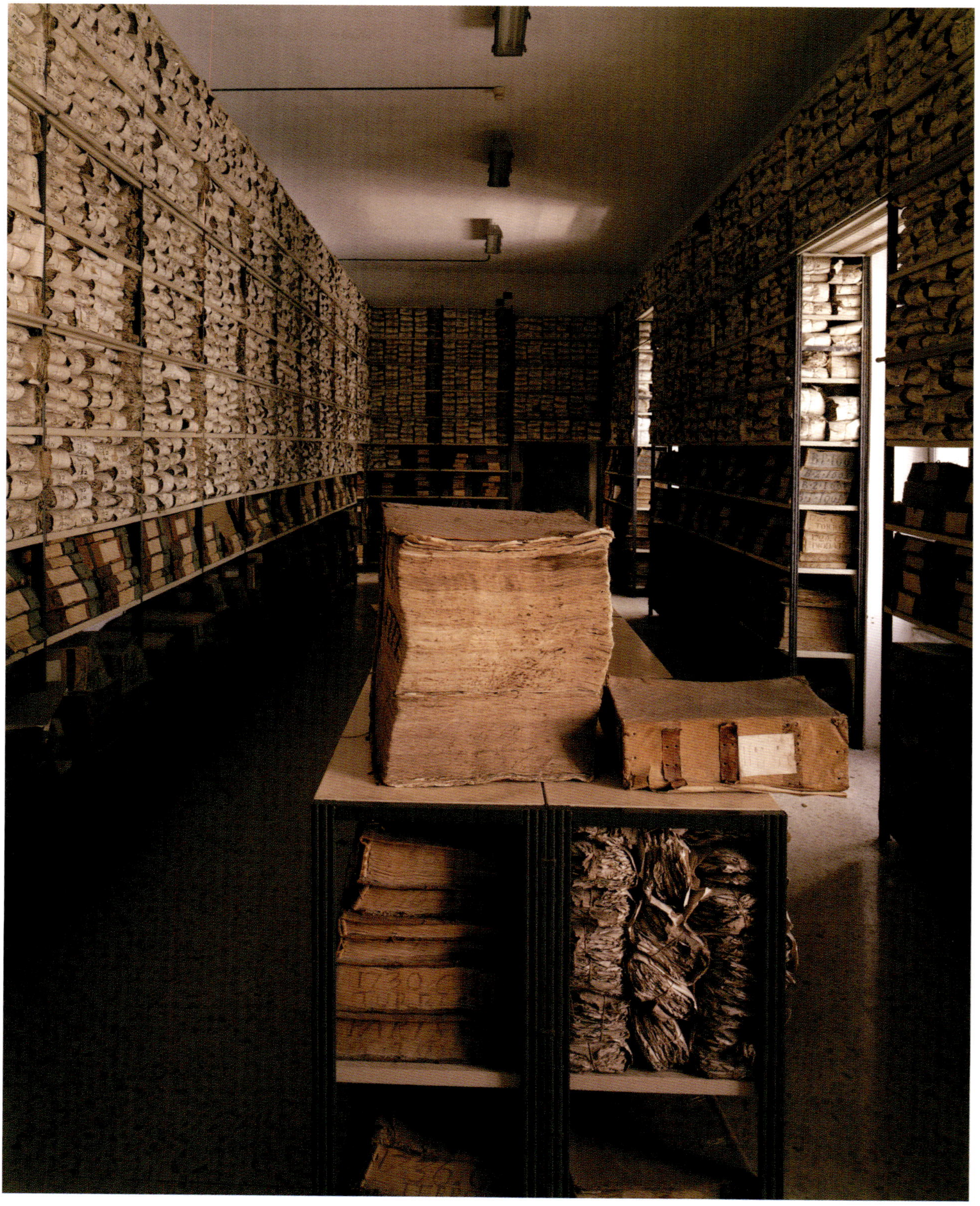

Doug Hall, *Archive of the Bank of Naples, 1780s Room*, 1996. Pigment print, 61 × 48 in. (154 × 121.9 cm)

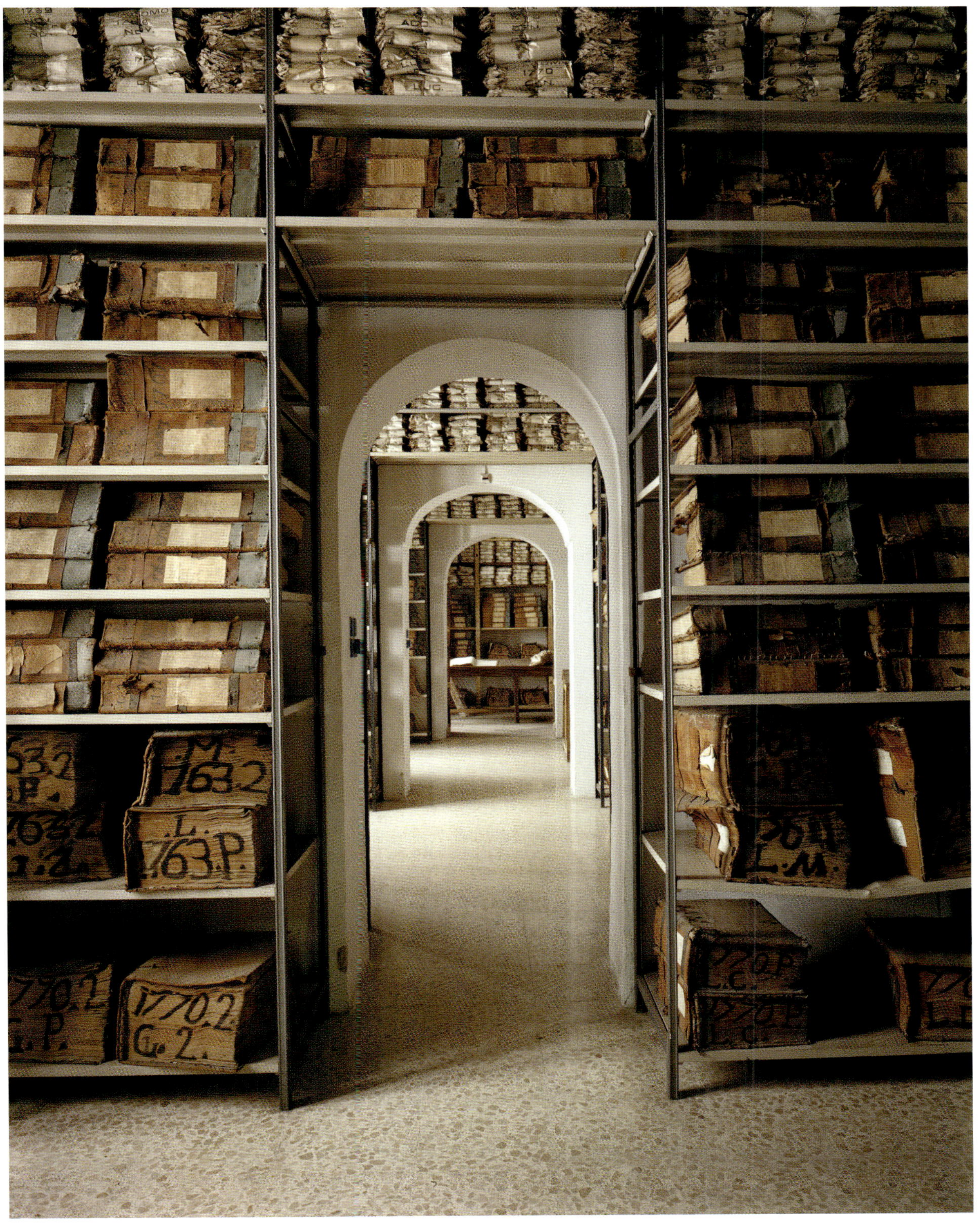

Doug Hall, *Central Passage, Archive of the Bank of Naples*, 1996. Pigment print, 61 × 48 in. (154 × 121.9 cm)

Those spaces, humble and unselfconscious, are more beautiful to me than the Vatican's elaborately decorated reading room. They contain the reserved dignity of functionality within the framework of historical time.

It's fascinating how time is preserved in Italy: the ancient is buried in layers that start beneath the ground, and as the new replaces the old, terminate in remarkable structures that themselves have survived the vicissitudes of the ages. In some cases, the remaining buildings and artifacts reveal social and political currents that surge into our own time. This is what initially interested me about the opera houses scattered throughout Italy, in large cities and small towns.

The first opera house to admit a paying public was Teatro San Cassiano, which opened in Venice in 1637. Before that, opera was performed in small halls as entertainment for royalty. By 1700, large public opera houses had been built in Venice, which had nine, and in other cities throughout Europe. They emerged as the wealthy, mercantile elite arose and demanded its place in social and political affairs while the landed aristocracy, with its hereditary connections to royalty, diminished in importance. The unique horseshoe plan of eighteenth- and nineteenth-century opera houses consisted of tiered boxes and balconies arranged around and above an open seating area and the stage beyond. The plan brought those seated in the boxes closer to the action on stage and provided better acoustics than possible in a rectangular room. More interesting from my perspective, the structure revealed the broader social hierarchies that were in place. The most prestigious seats were those along the curve of the horseshoe directly opposite the stage. The Royal Box, the most important location of all, was situated on the second tier in the center of the curve and directly opposite the stage. From there, the occupant could see everyone in the hall and be seen in turn, and of course have full view of the stage. It was, however, not the best location for hearing the opera. Nevertheless, one's stature within the social hierarchy was revealed according to where one was seated in relation to the Royal Box.

In Italian, the word for the stage, the location where the opera or play takes place, is *palcoscenico*. The word for the box containing seats in a theater is *palco*. Etymologically,

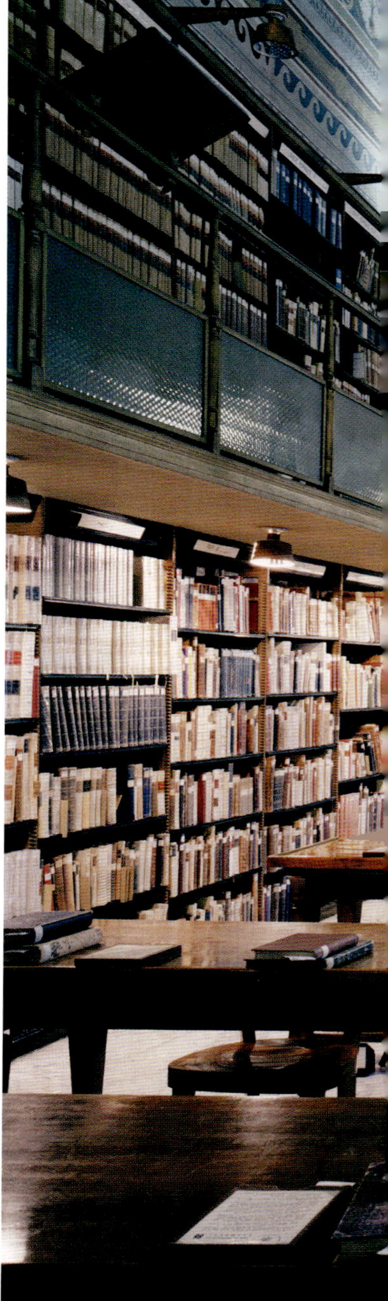

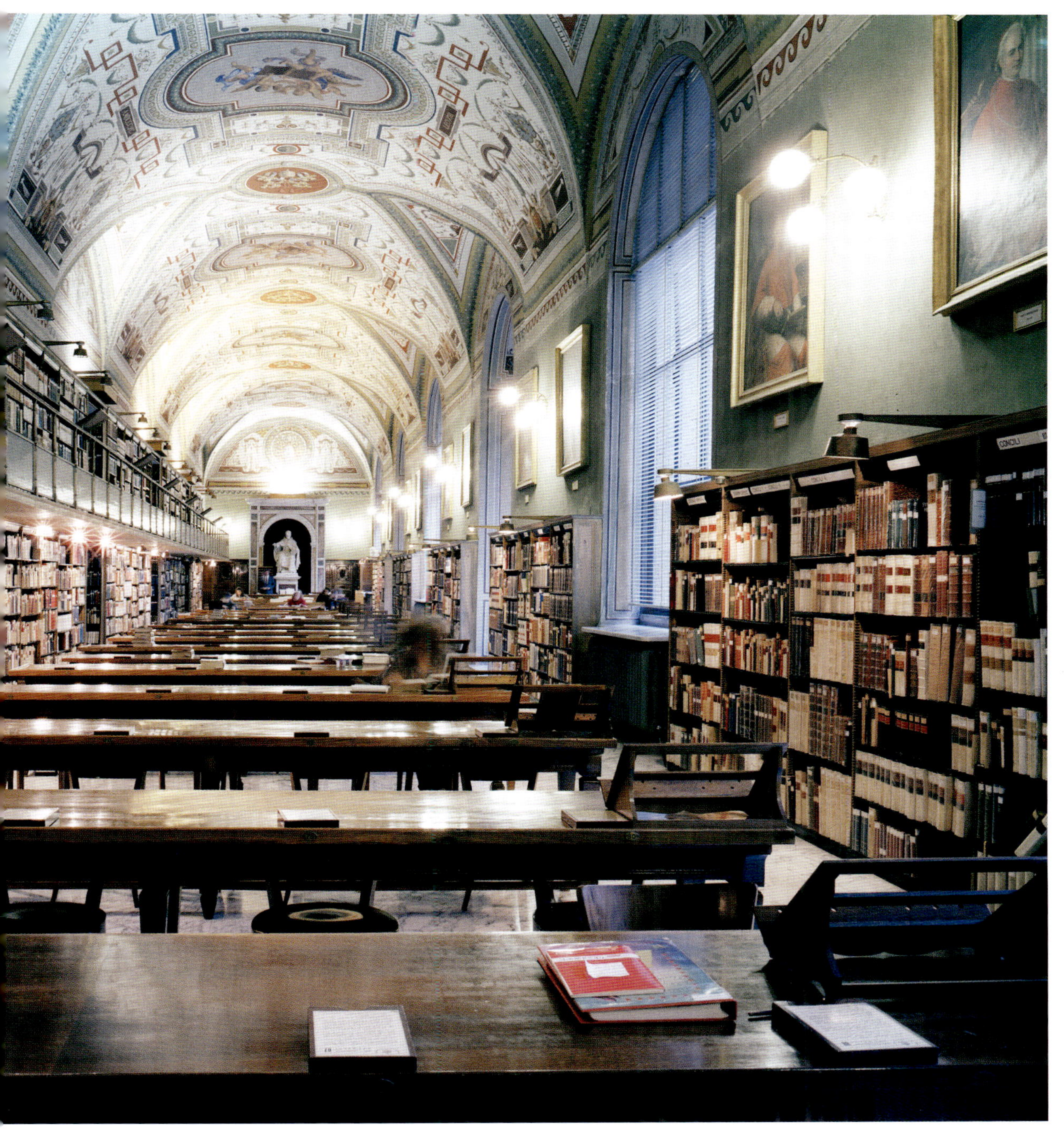

Doug Hall, *Main Reading Room, Vatican Library, Vatican City*, 1996. Pigment print, 24 × 30 in. (61 × 76.2 cm)

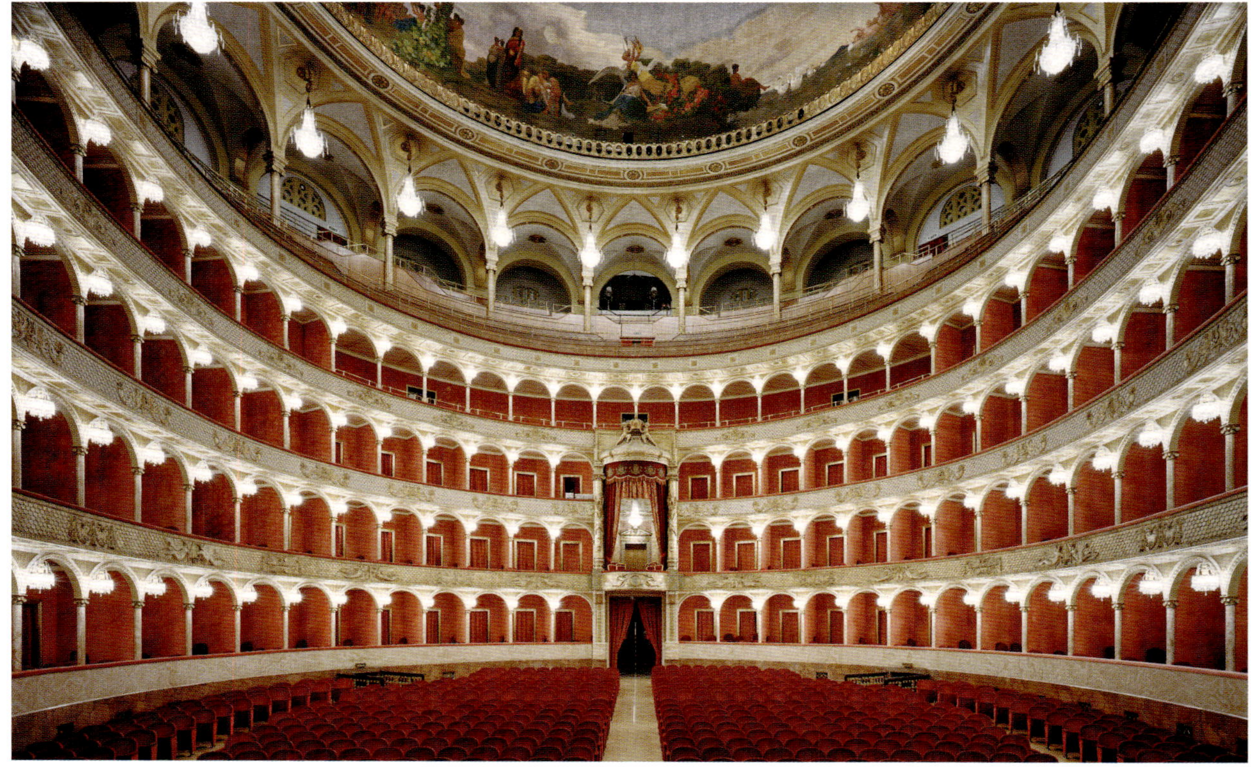

Doug Hall, *Teatro dell'Opera, Rome*, 2002. Pigment print, 48 × 75½ in. (121.9 × 191.8 cm)

both words imply the idea of a stage. In the former, it is the stage upon which the central action occurs; in the latter, it is the stage from which the social drama of class and status is acted out and observed. From the eighteenth through nineteenth centuries, *palci* framed the dramas in which members of the new bourgeois elite performed their roles of social status. Wealthy individuals entered their boxes much as a prima donna might enter the stage and like her, each would look out from a lavishly draped and cushioned interior of bright silks and velvet, framed by an ornate arch. Along the sweeping wall of the opera house were arranged tiers of small individual stages, each one displaying its unique drama of gesture and expression, tableaux that signified one's position within a dynamic social hierarchy. It was within these opera houses that two elites met: the ascending bourgeoisie and the descending aristocracy. The status of the former was based on the accumulation of wealth, drew its power from the marketplace, and was the future. The gentry based its privilege on heredity and was the past.

While this might explain how these buildings inscribed social hierarchies, it doesn't account for the uncanny experience I had when making the photographs. On more than one occasion, the ornate spaces seemed to be staring back at me. I felt as if caught in the gaze from a source I couldn't identify, and

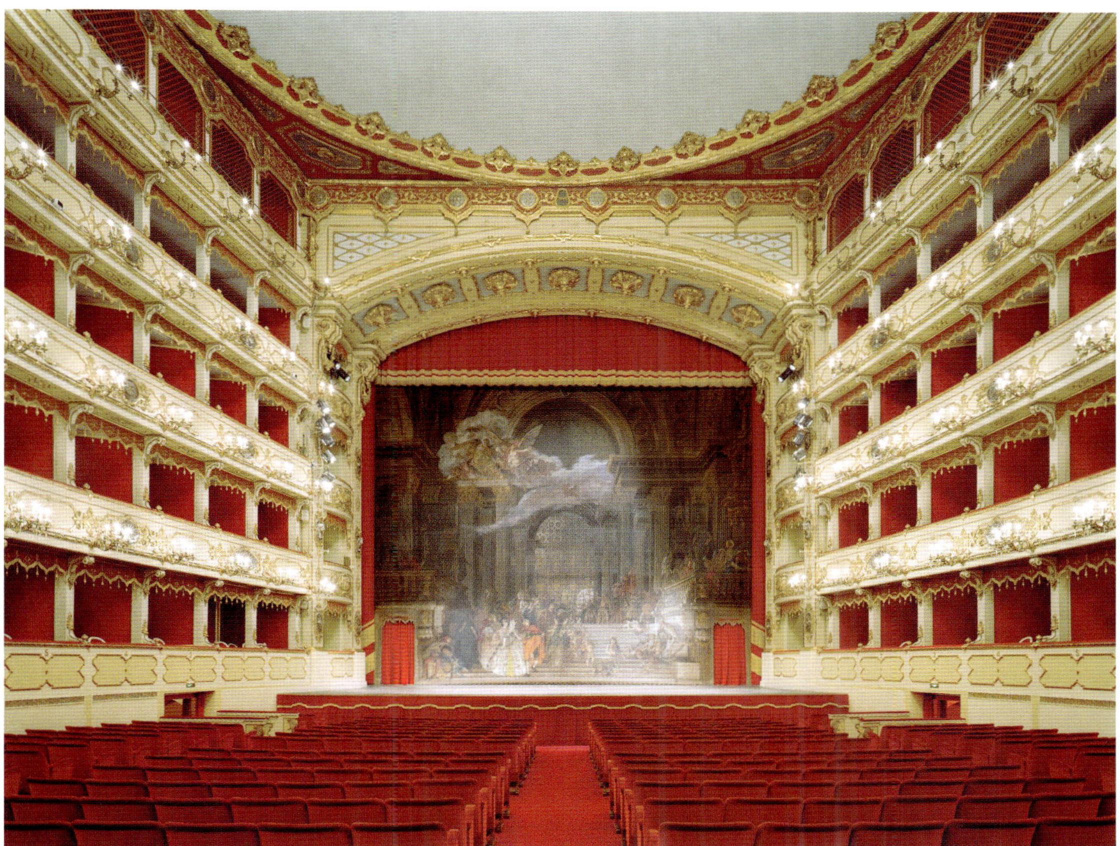

Doug Hall, *Teatro Comunale Ponchielli, Cremona*, 2002. Pigment print, 48 × 60 in. (121.9 × 152.4 cm)

that what I was photographing was not just a room, but the act of looking itself. On the surface, this is understandable: the center stage where I was standing (and where the viewer of the photographs is also positioned) is the optical and perspectival hub toward and from which all vision radiates. The result is that I, the photographer, and you, the viewer of the photograph, find ourselves at the center of the world at least as it is defined by this interior. With the empty seats and vacant tiers of boxes arrayed before us, we are aware of ourselves as both the ones seeing and the ones being seen. The sensation that I found unsettling, and had certainly not expected, was the impression of being caught in the act of looking. It reminds me of the embarrassment one might feel if caught while staring at someone, a stranger on the bus, perhaps, or at an adjoining table in a restaurant. My tentative explanation is that this being "caught-in-the-act" produces a self-consciousness that turns looking, a kind of objectless seeing, into watching—a looking that locates an object, almost possessing it, at the end of its gaze. My intuition tells me that there is something erotic, something primitive and biological, at the root of this sort of visual possession.

Time at a Standstill

In the nineties, the growing availability of digital technologies (Photoshop, drum scanners, and printers for large-scale photographs) allowed a degree of control over the image that had been impossible with analog photography. Depending on one's point of view, this was either a good or a bad thing. To those who believed that the photograph had a responsibility to represent a unique occurrence, captured as a moment in time—that its significance was tied to its veracity—the manipulative capability of digital photography was a travesty. Although I was fully committed to digital imaging, having more interest in fictions that appeared true rather than so-called truth itself, I understood and appreciated the criticism from these skeptics.

Even while recognizing the technical and physical complications that digital technologies imposed on the traditions of photography, I fully embraced the expanded possibilities they afforded me. With the aid of computer software, I constructed images by arranging figures extracted from numerous scanned negatives that I carefully placed in relationship to one another and to their surroundings within large seamless photographs. This practice was compatible with my assertion that, like architecture, landscapes are stage sets where we act out our relationship to place and to those with whom we share those places. In my heavily populated photographs, I position the figures within the scene the way a theater or film director might position actors and scenery on a stage. This approach not only allows me to control everything within the photographic frame (to get it to say what I want it to say) but it also defies one of the celebrated attributes of photography by compressing time into the illusion of a moment—one that is, in fact, composed of many moments, a palimpsest of sorts, spread out over several hours. I think of these scenic pictures as cinema at a standstill.

My embrace of large-format photography was born out of my interest in how our interactions with built spaces inform us, sometimes subconsciously or, as Walter Benjamin put it "in a state of distraction."[17] They impose on us unstated behavioral rules that give rise to thoughts, feelings, and bodily postures that are partially governed by the way buildings and public spaces are organized and purposed. The subjectivity of our experiences ranges beyond the built world to include more natural surroundings. I contend that when we view large-scale, deep-focus photographs, we allow our imaginations to enter the image, which, due to its scale and fidelity, welcomes our bodies as well as our minds. As we meander in and through the representation, loitering here and there, recollections and recognitions are triggered as if in a waking dream. The nature of these dreams is, of course, related to how the photograph expresses itself to us and the preconditions we bring to it. Regardless of the content, large-scale photography can transport us much in the way that nineteenth-century American landscape painting or European history painting provided viewers entry into their unique representational dreamworlds.

17. Walter Benjamin, *Illuminations*, ed. Hannah Arendt (New York: Schocken Books, 1969), 239.

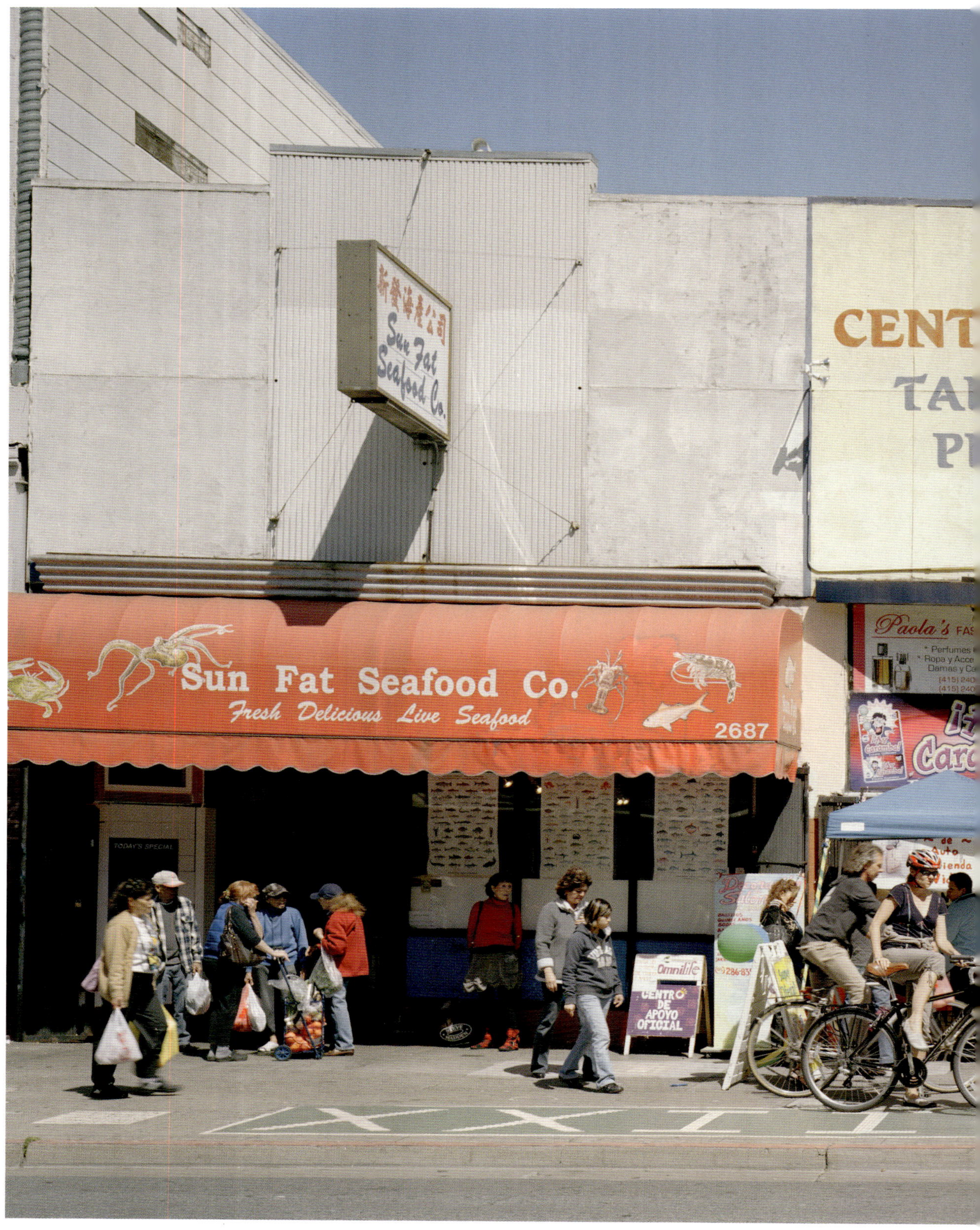

Doug Hall, *1689 Mission Street, San Francisco*, 2011. Pigment print, 37¾ × 62 in. (95.9 × 157.5 cm)

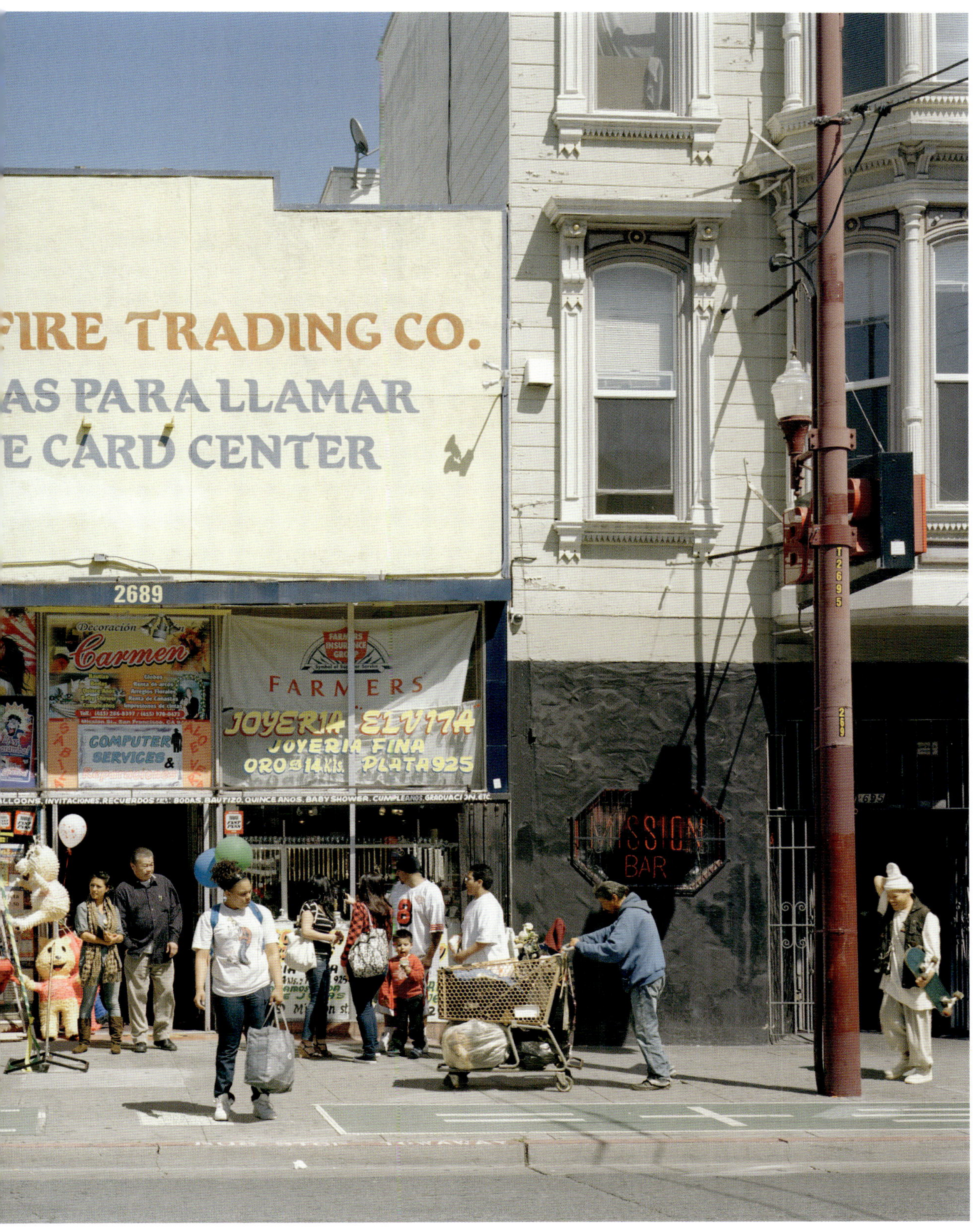

We are not immune to the different spaces we move through or inhabit. As they surround and embrace us, we unconsciously adopt different postures, mental and physical, that are appropriate to each situation. Absentmindedly, as we move about, we wear and replace these postures the way we might our clothes.

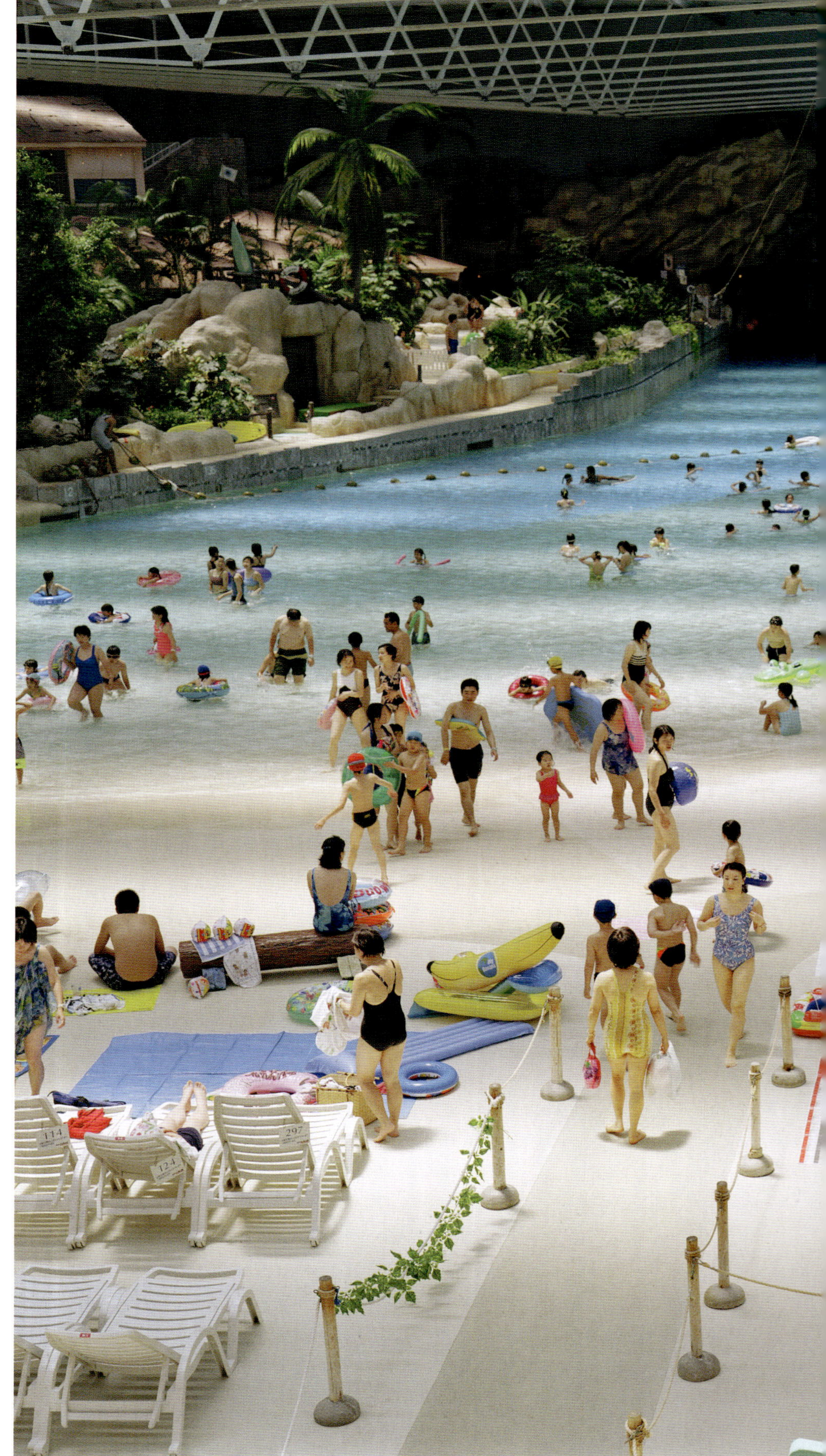

Doug Hall, *Wild Blue Yokohama*, 2000. Pigment print, 48 × 61 in. (121.9 × 154.9 cm)

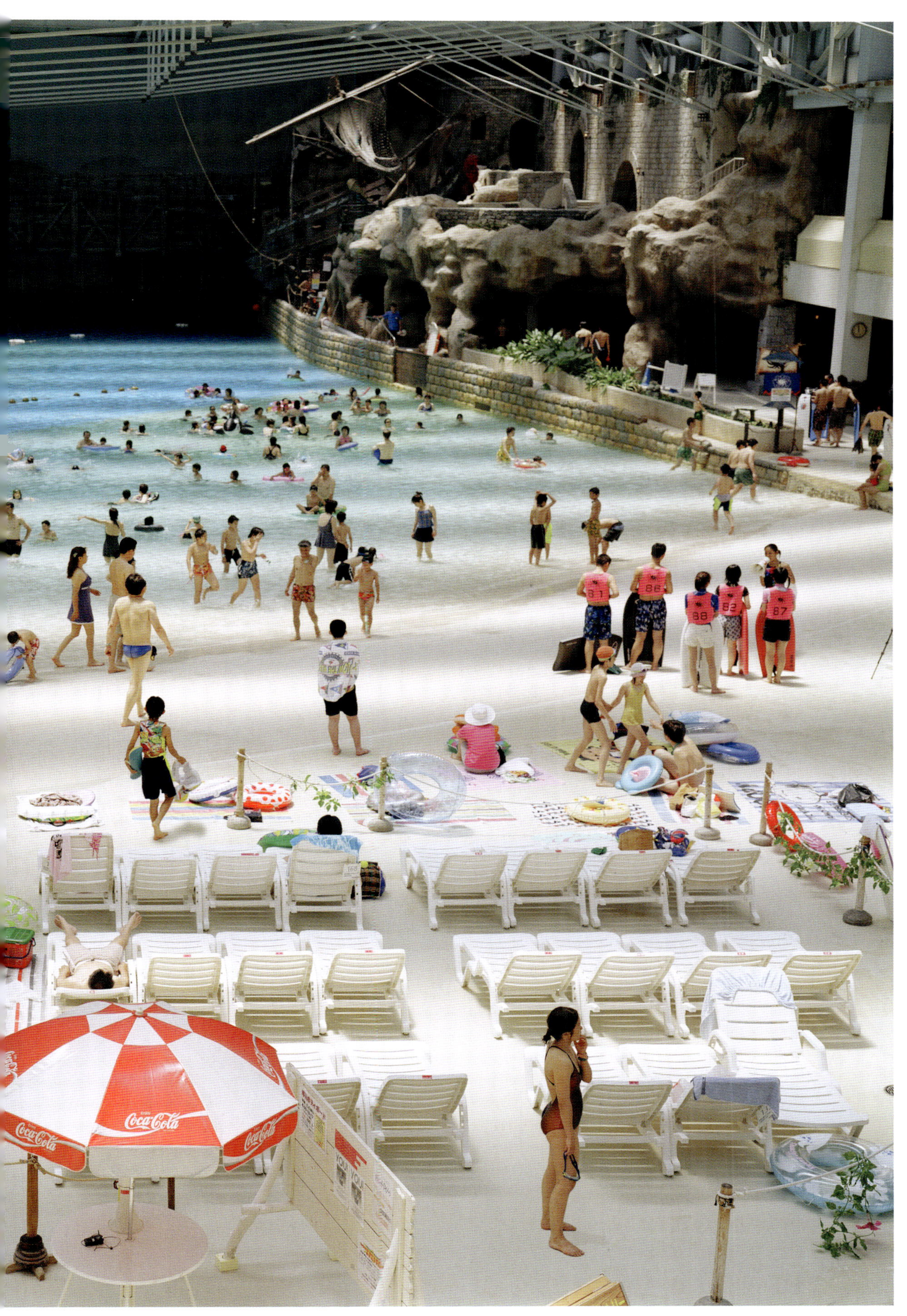
Coca-Cola
Coca-Cola
Coca-Cola

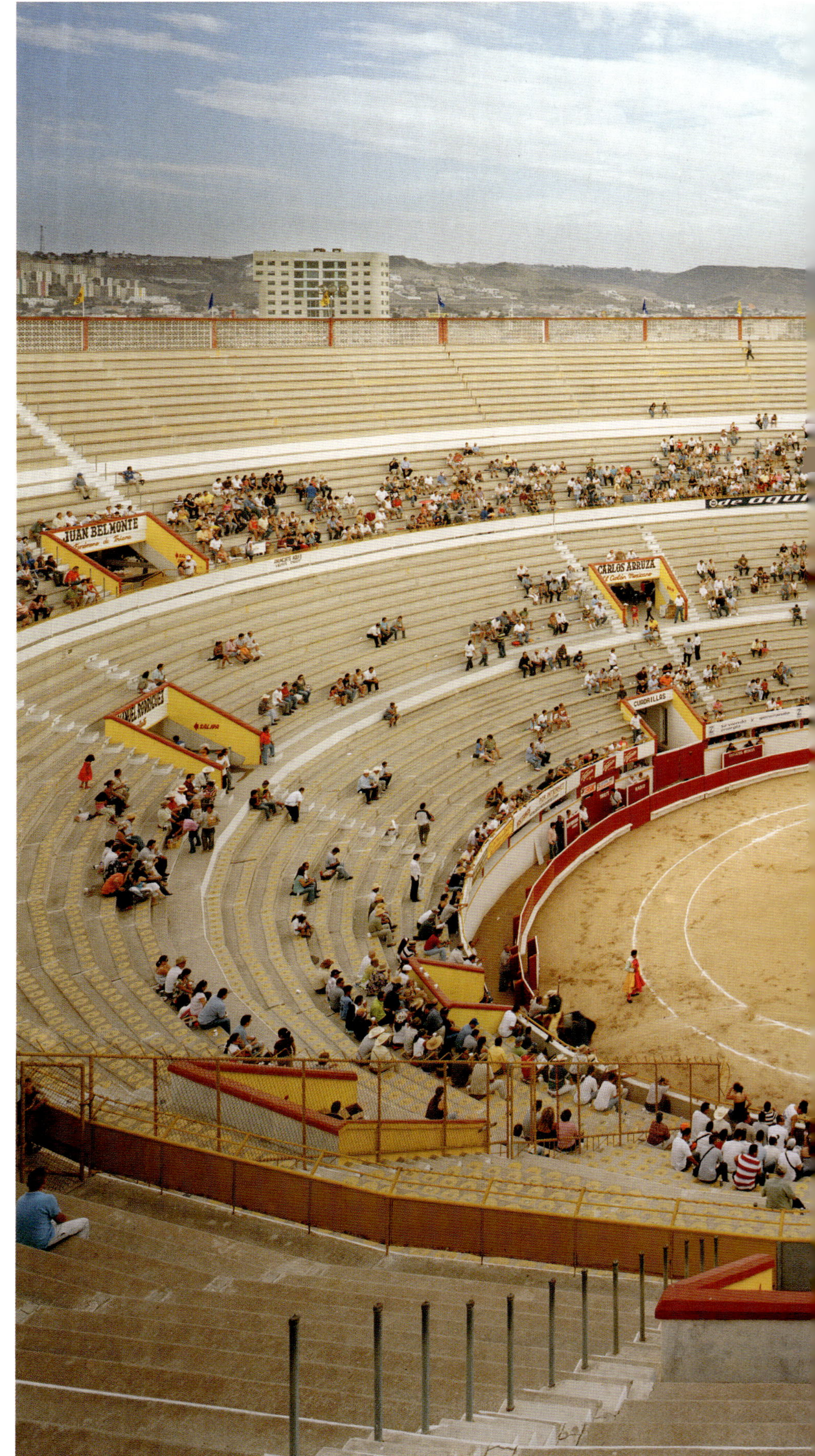

Doug Hall, *Plaza Monumental Tijuana,* 2007. Pigment print, 32 × 39 in. (81.3 × 99.1 cm)

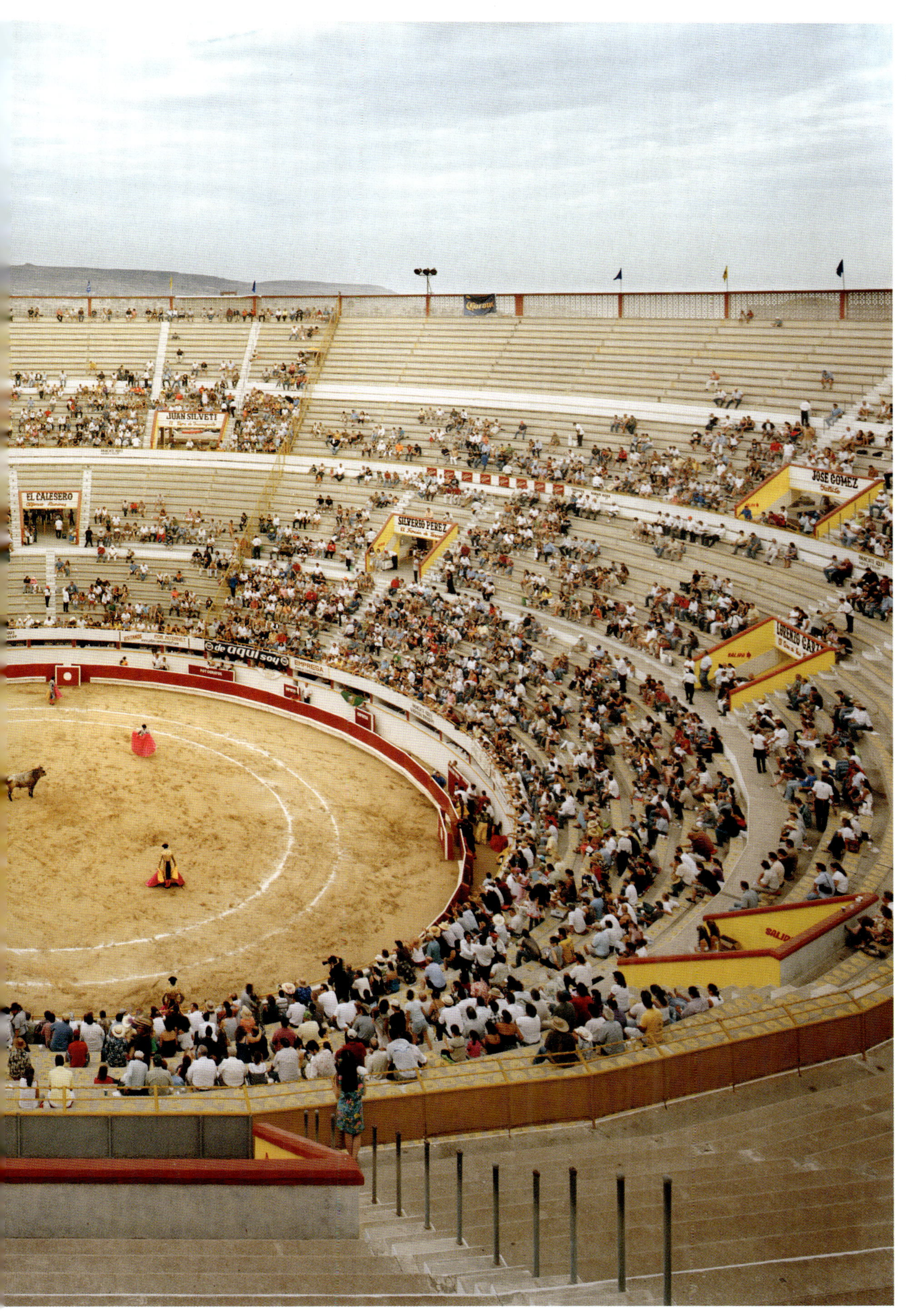
JUAN SILVETI
EL CALESERO
SILVERIO PEREZ
JOSE GOMEZ
de aqui soy
EMPRESA
SALIDA

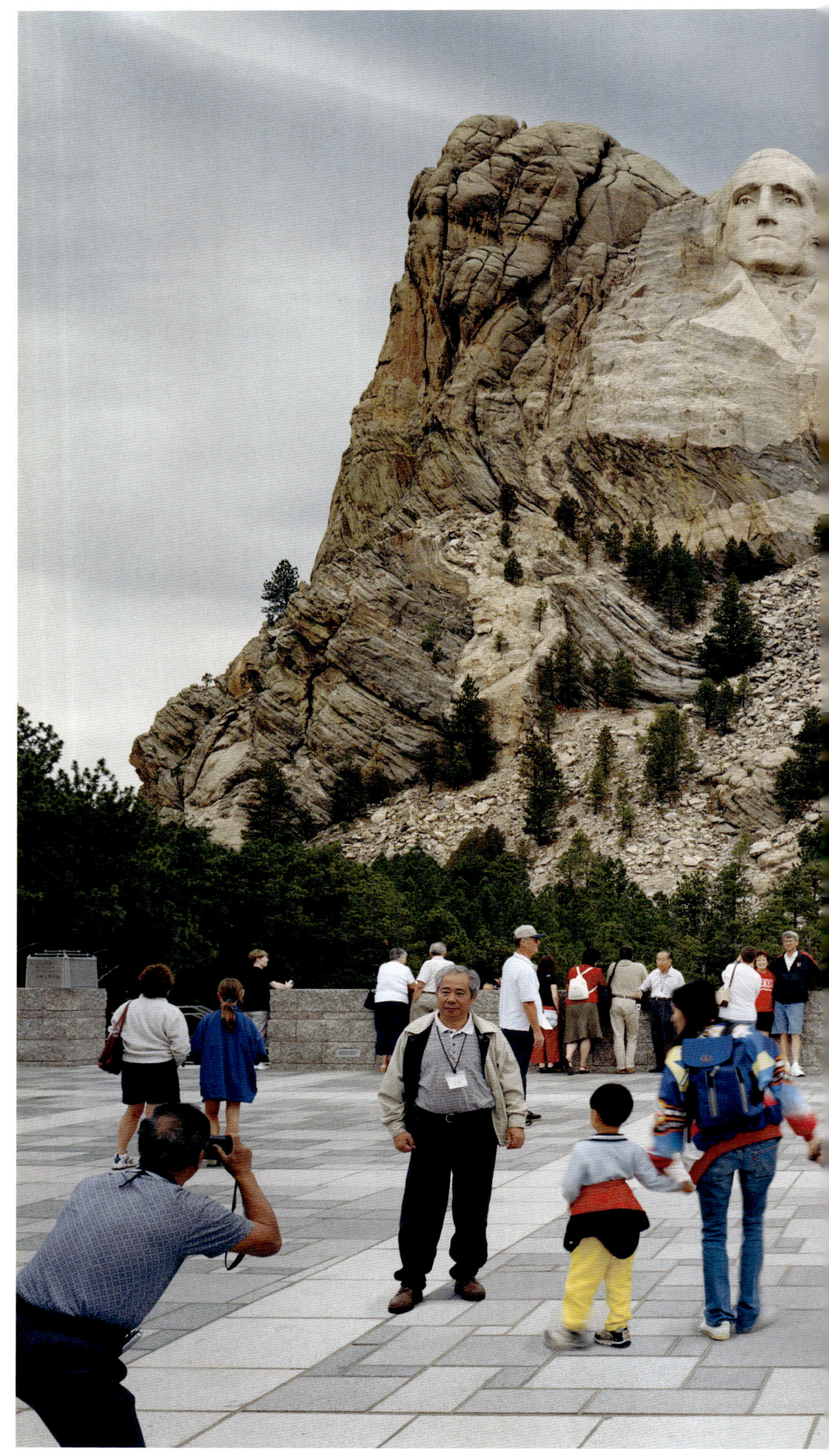

Doug Hall, *Mount Rushmore*, 2004. Pigment print, 48 × 63 in. (121.9 × 160 cm)

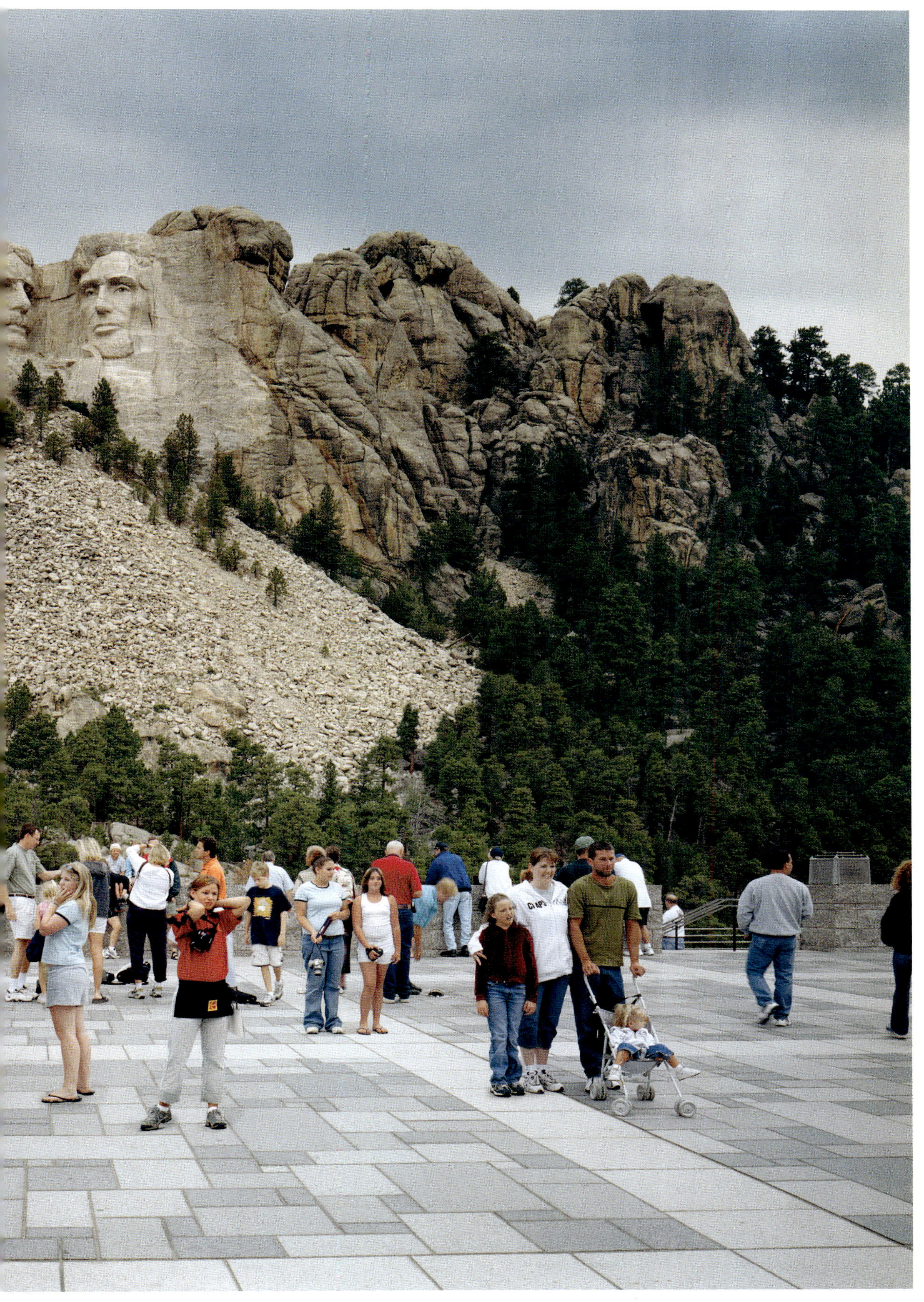

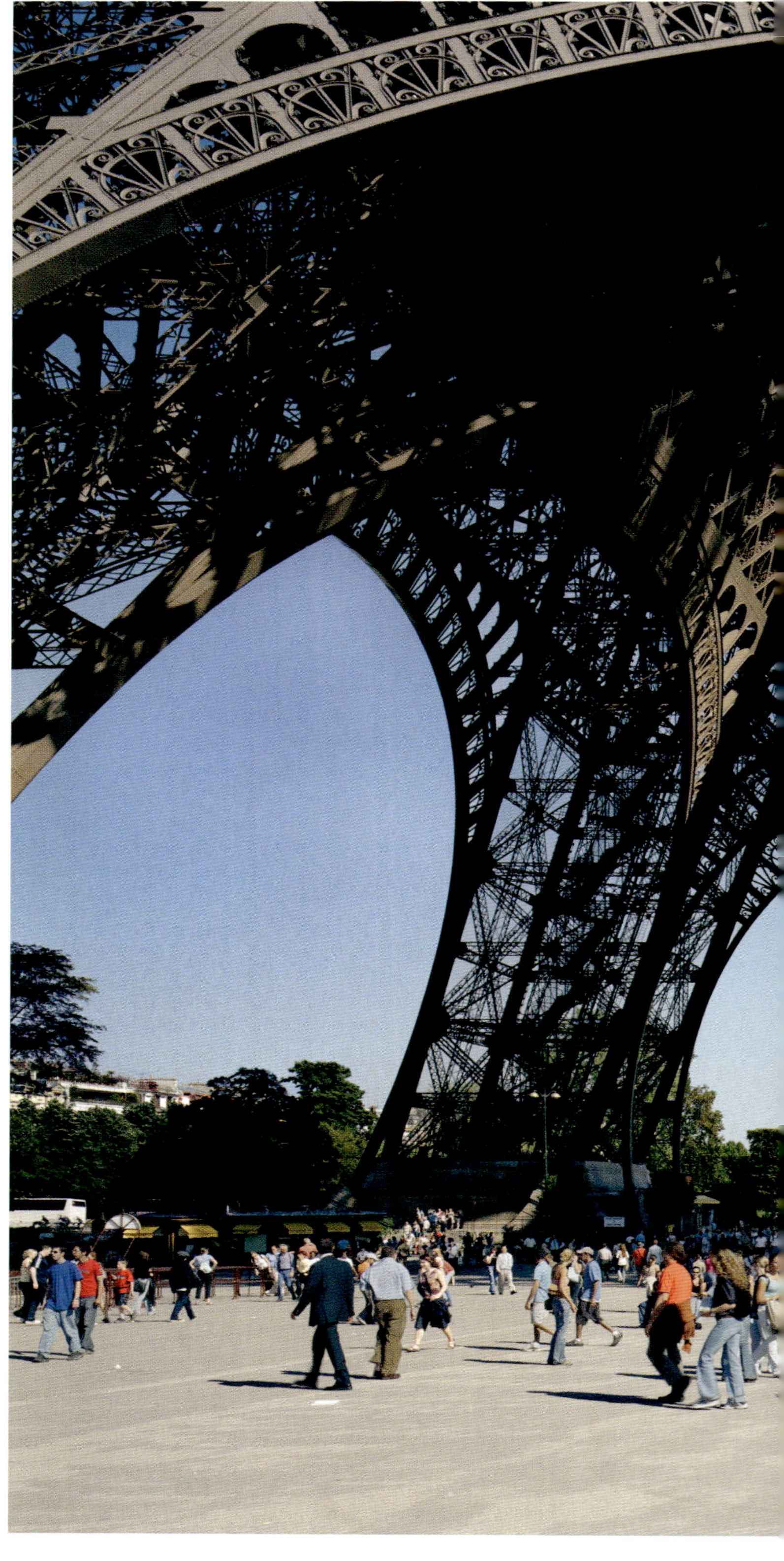

Doug Hall, *The Eiffel Tower,* 2004. Pigment print, 48 × 65 in. (121.9 × 165.1 cm)

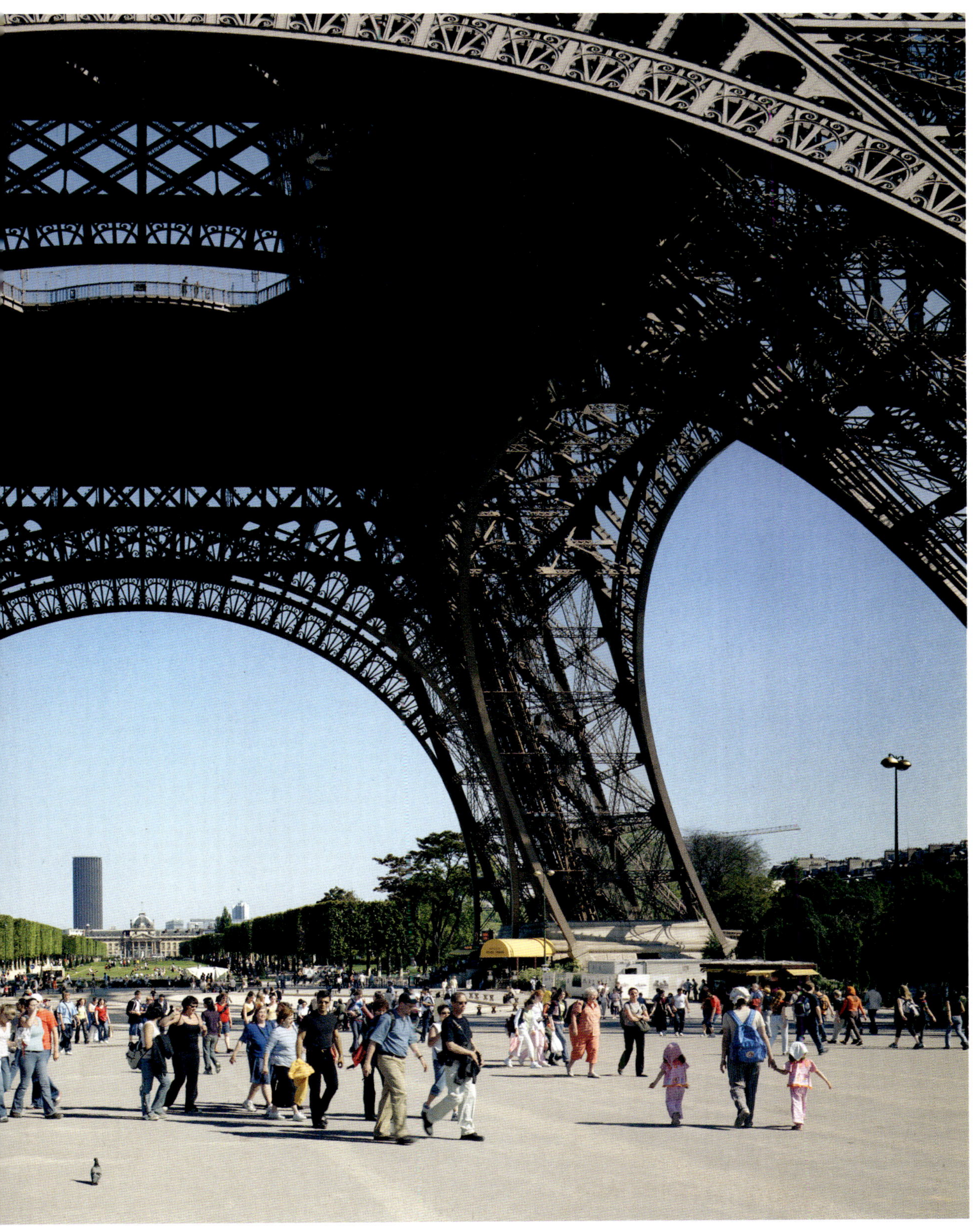

There are cities so vividly etched into my imagination that I don't feel the need to physically travel in order to visit them. Paris, Rome, and Moscow are places I frequented long before I actually saw them.

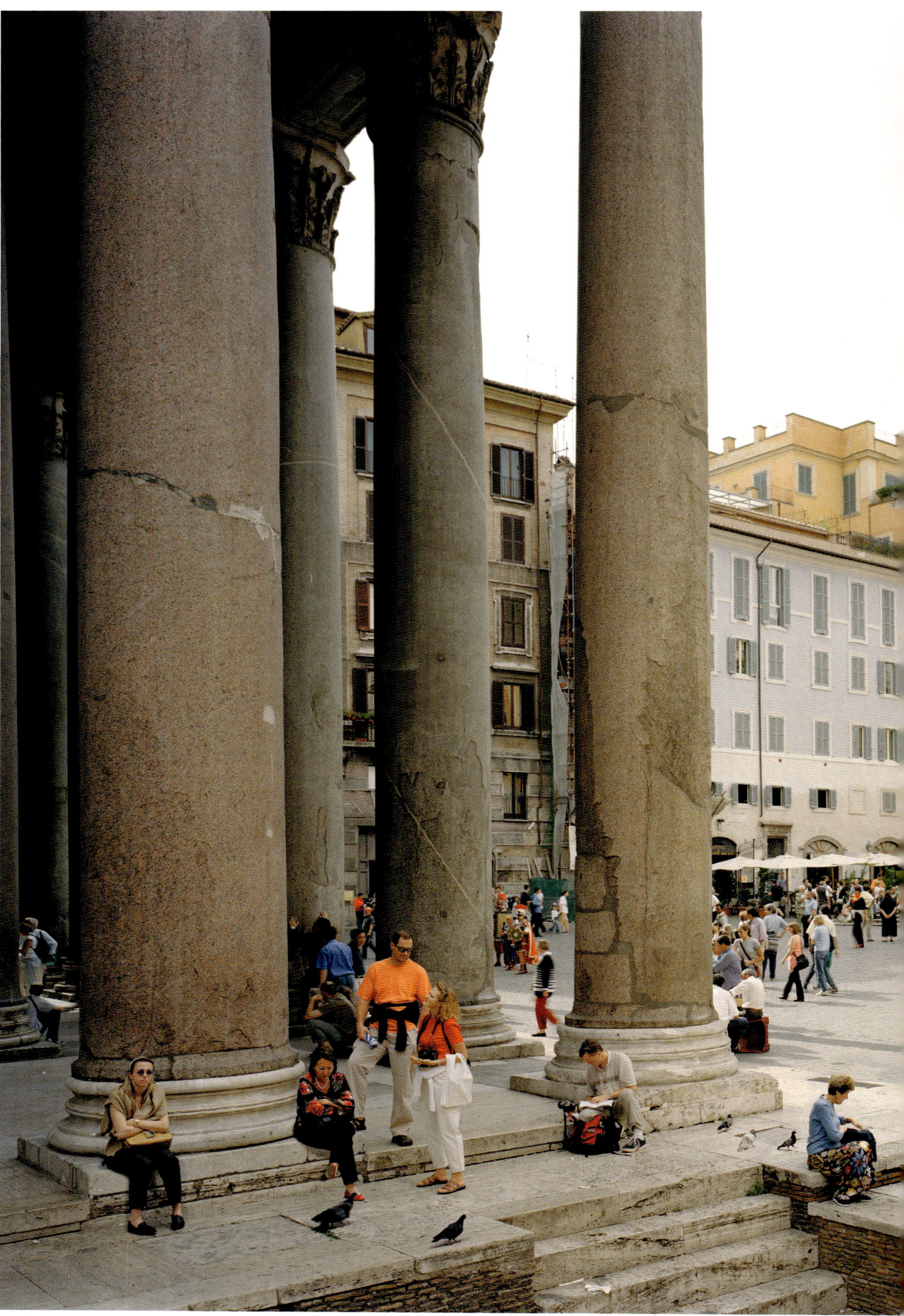

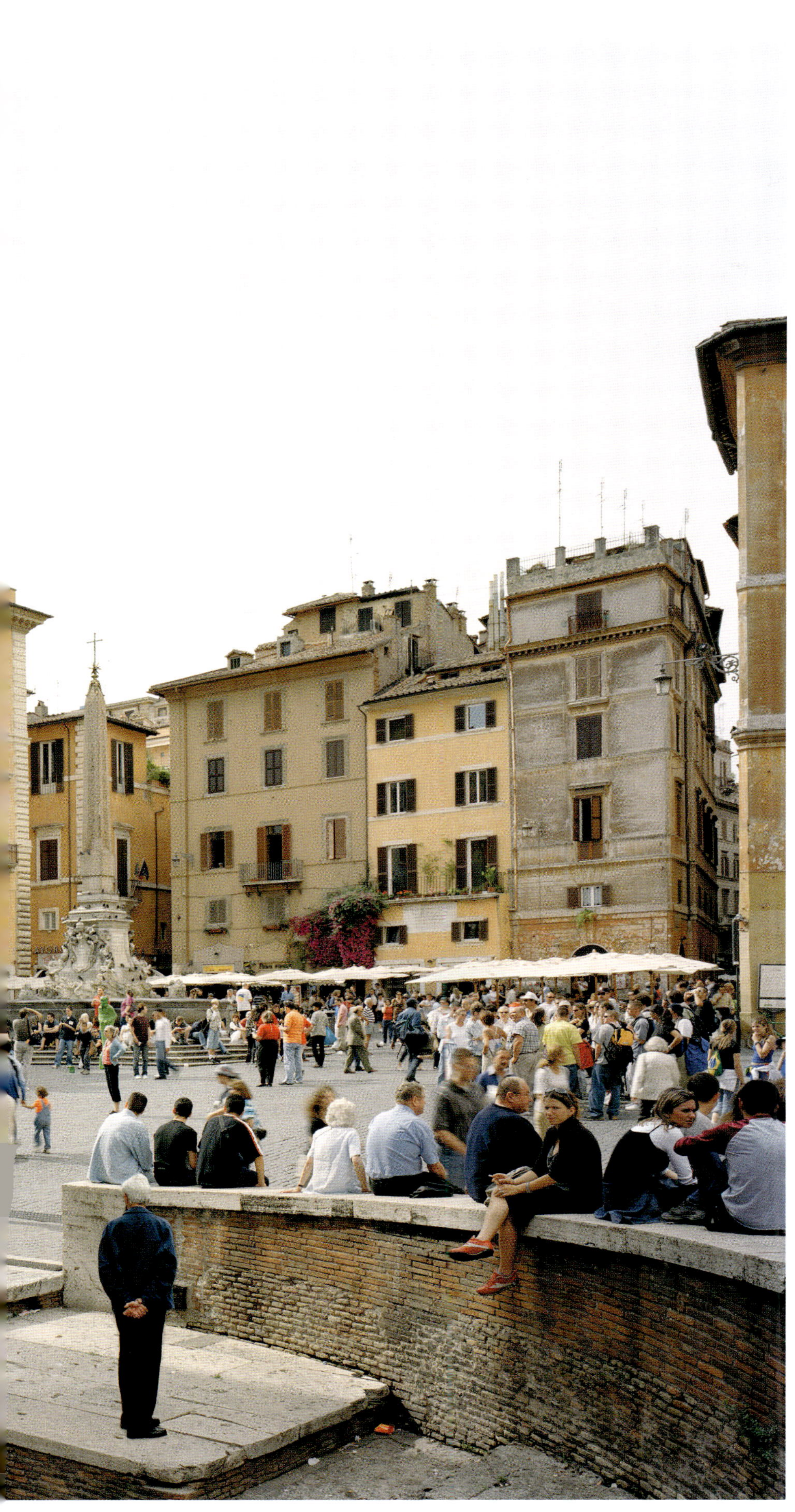

Doug Hall, *Piazza della Rotonda, Rome*, 2002. Pigment print, 48 × 61 in. (121.9 × 154.9 cm)

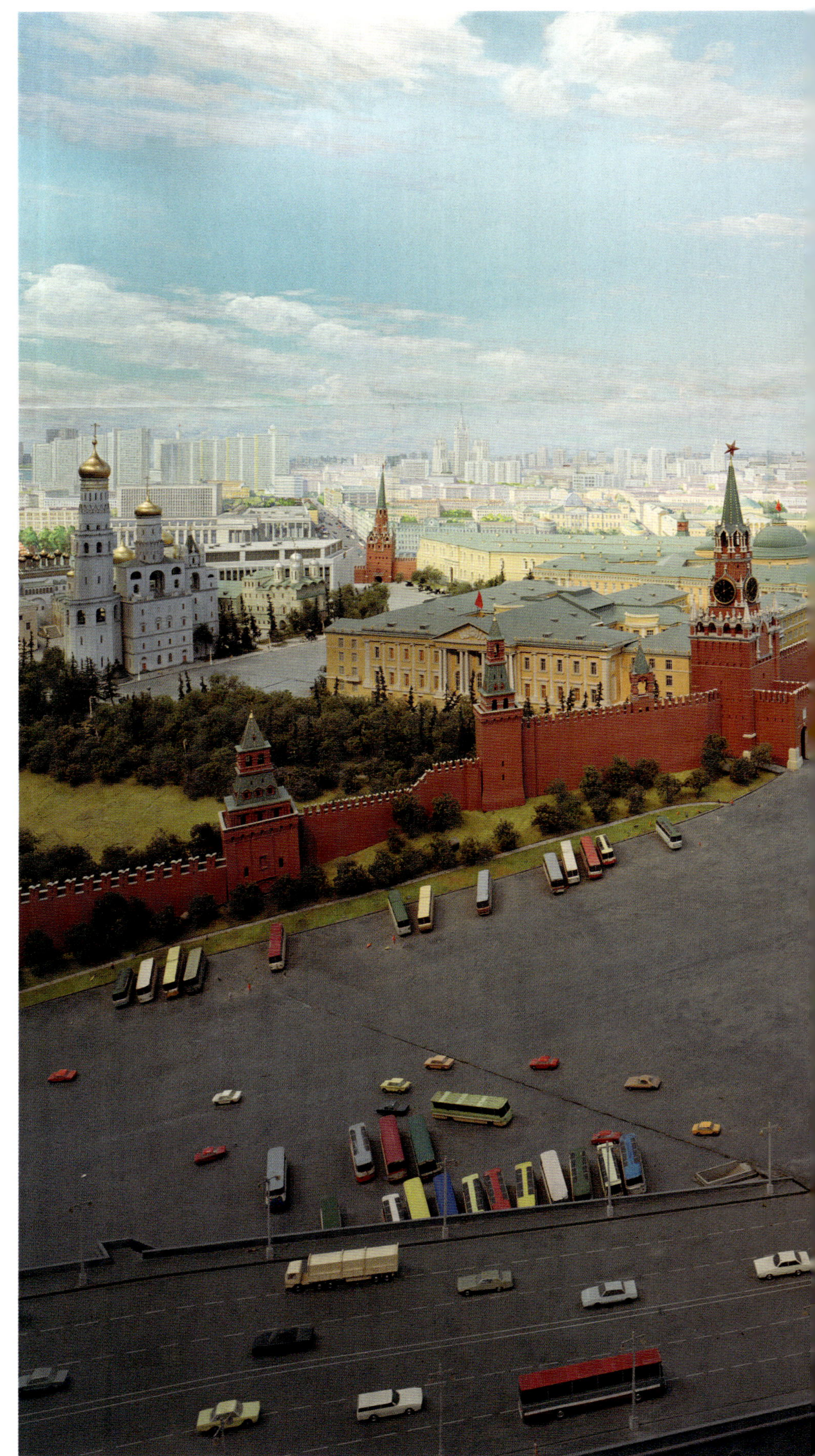

Doug Hall, *Moscow Diorama circa 1976*, 2006. Pigment print, 30 × 40 in. (76.2 × 101.6 cm)

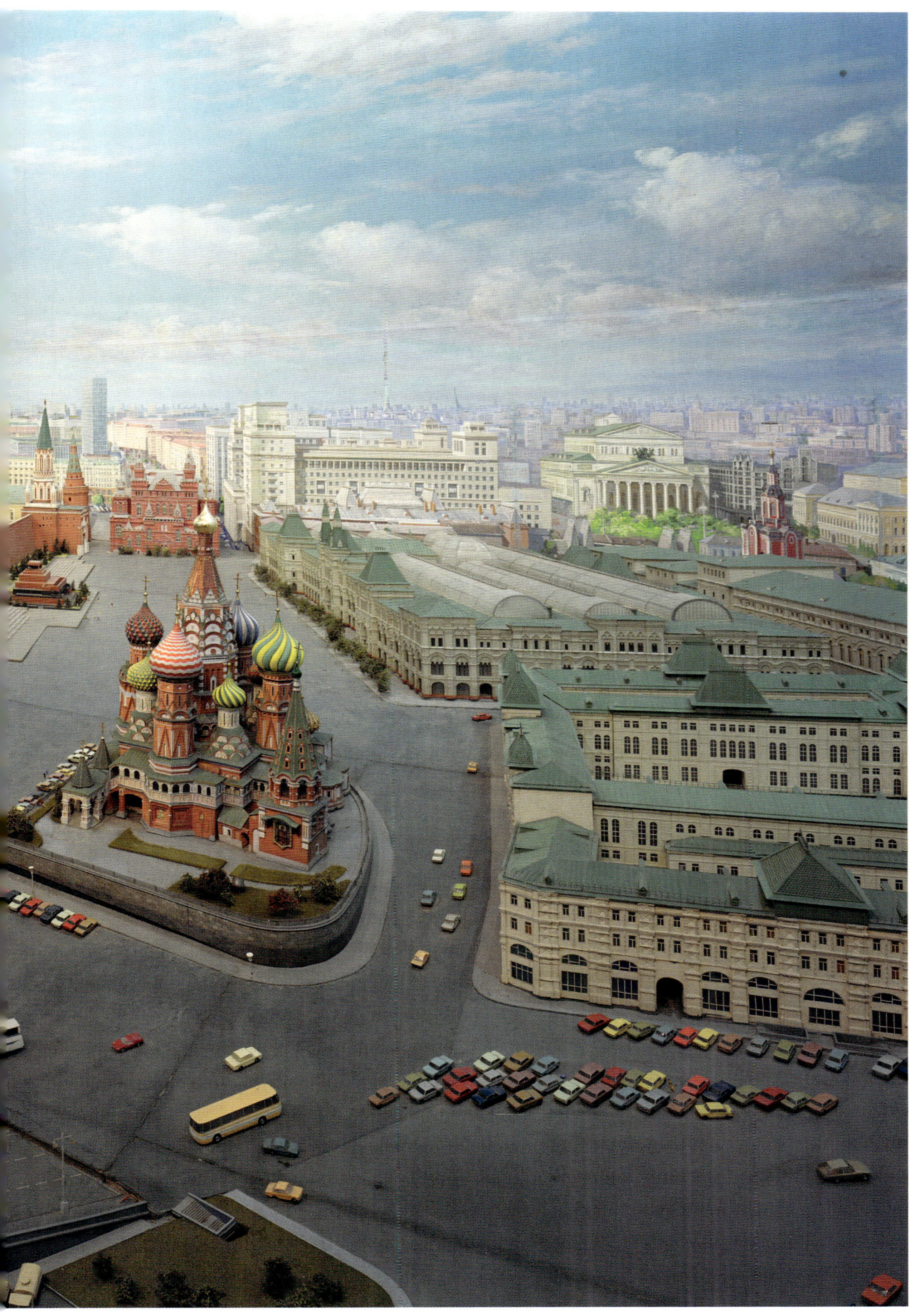

One of my favorite passages in Georges Perec's "Species of Spaces" is that in which he asks us to imagine "a space without a use." He writes, "[I]t wouldn't be a junk room, an extra bedroom, or a corridor, or a cubby-hole, or a corner. It would be a functionless space. It would serve for nothing, relate to nothing." My attempts to imagine Perec's useless space produce results like those I got from my youthful contemplation of infinity or timelessness: a momentary lightheadedness followed by a slight headache located somewhere behind the eyes.

A friend recently told me that she became anxious and afraid when she entered the boundless territories surrounding the western city where she lived. She said, "To me, even the most beautiful landscapes can seem desperate and voracious. I feel like I will be devoured by all that space surrounding me."

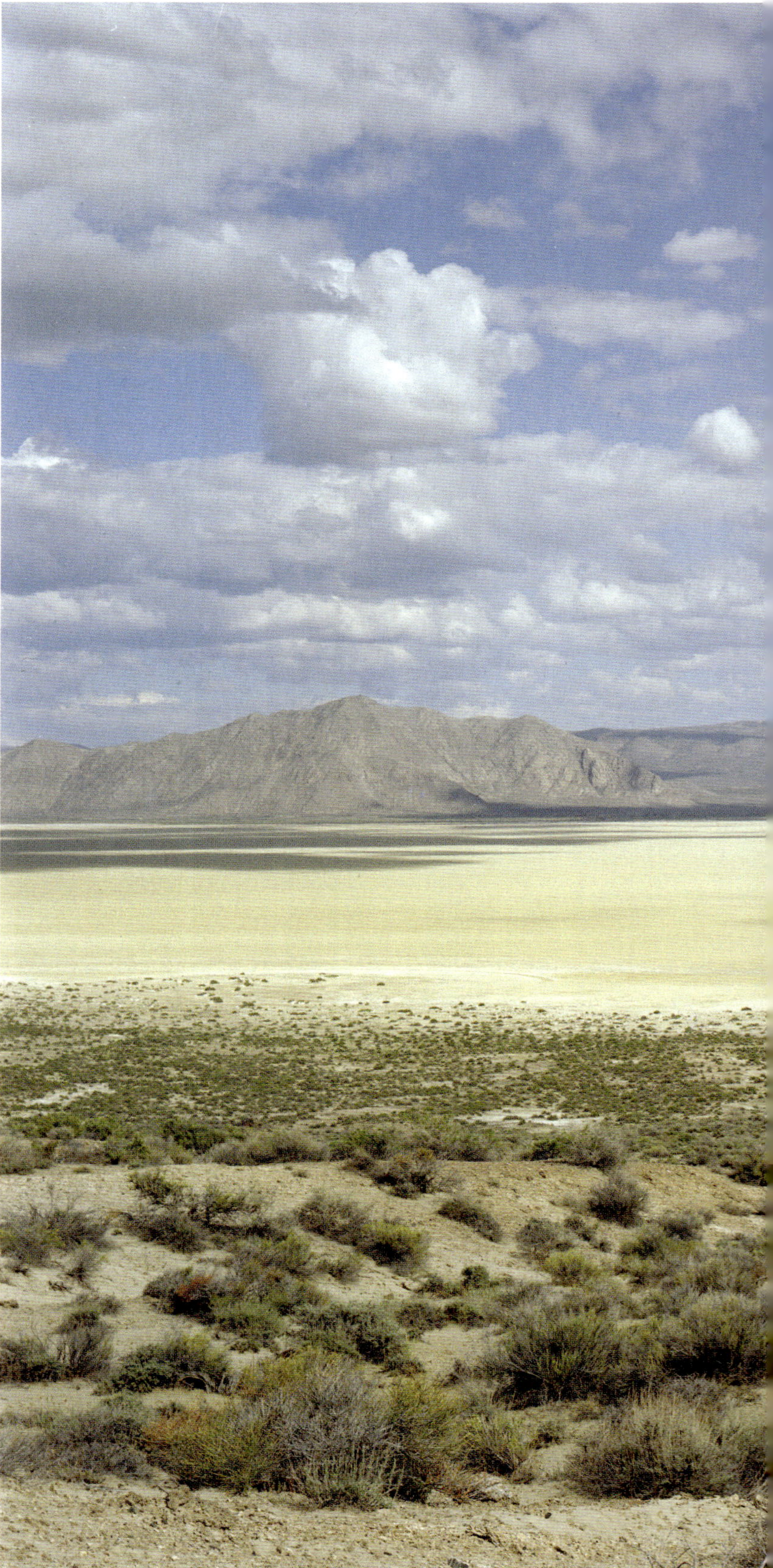

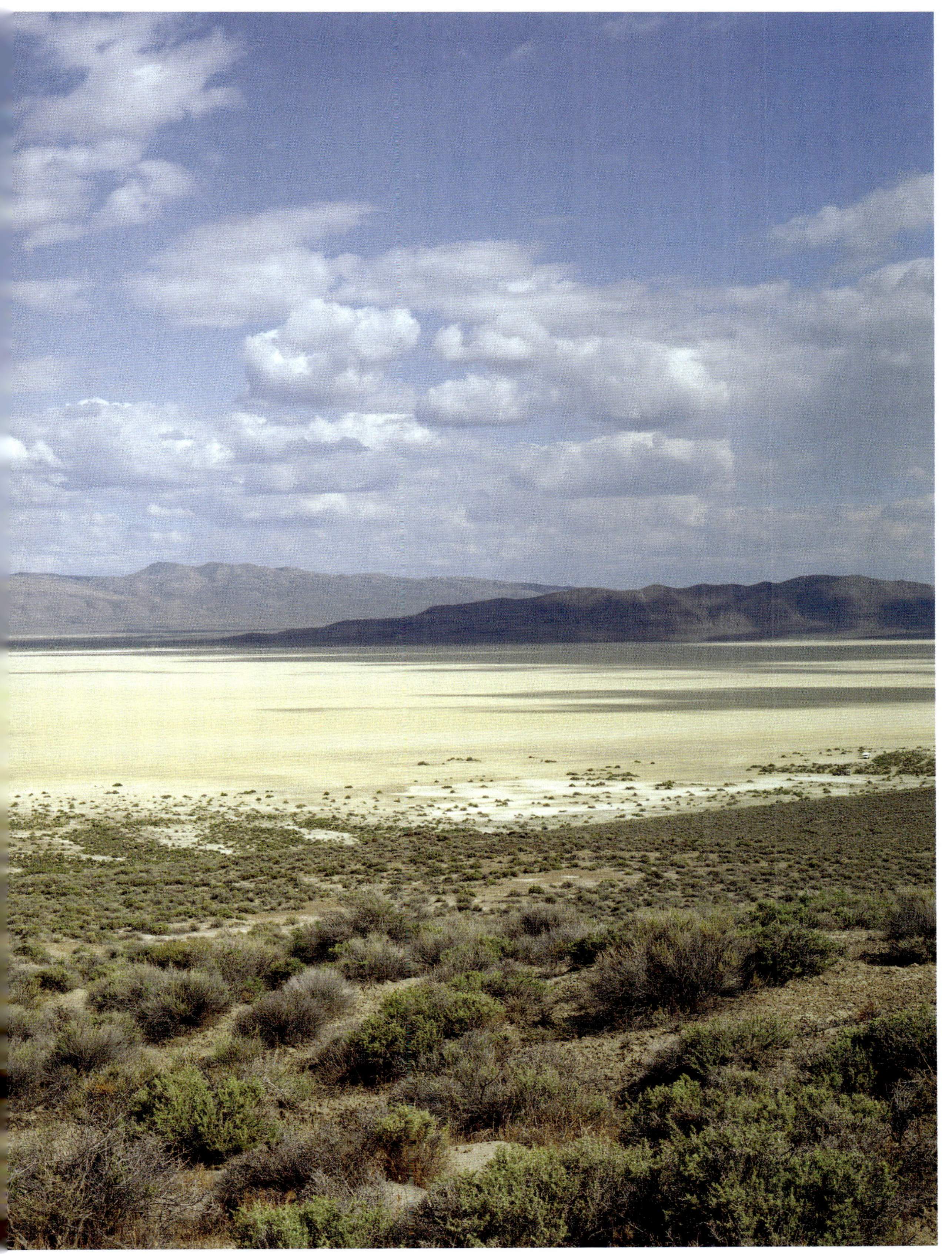

Doug Hall, *Terrain North of Gerlach, Nevada,* 2009. Pigment print, 48 × 63 in. (121.9 × 160 cm)

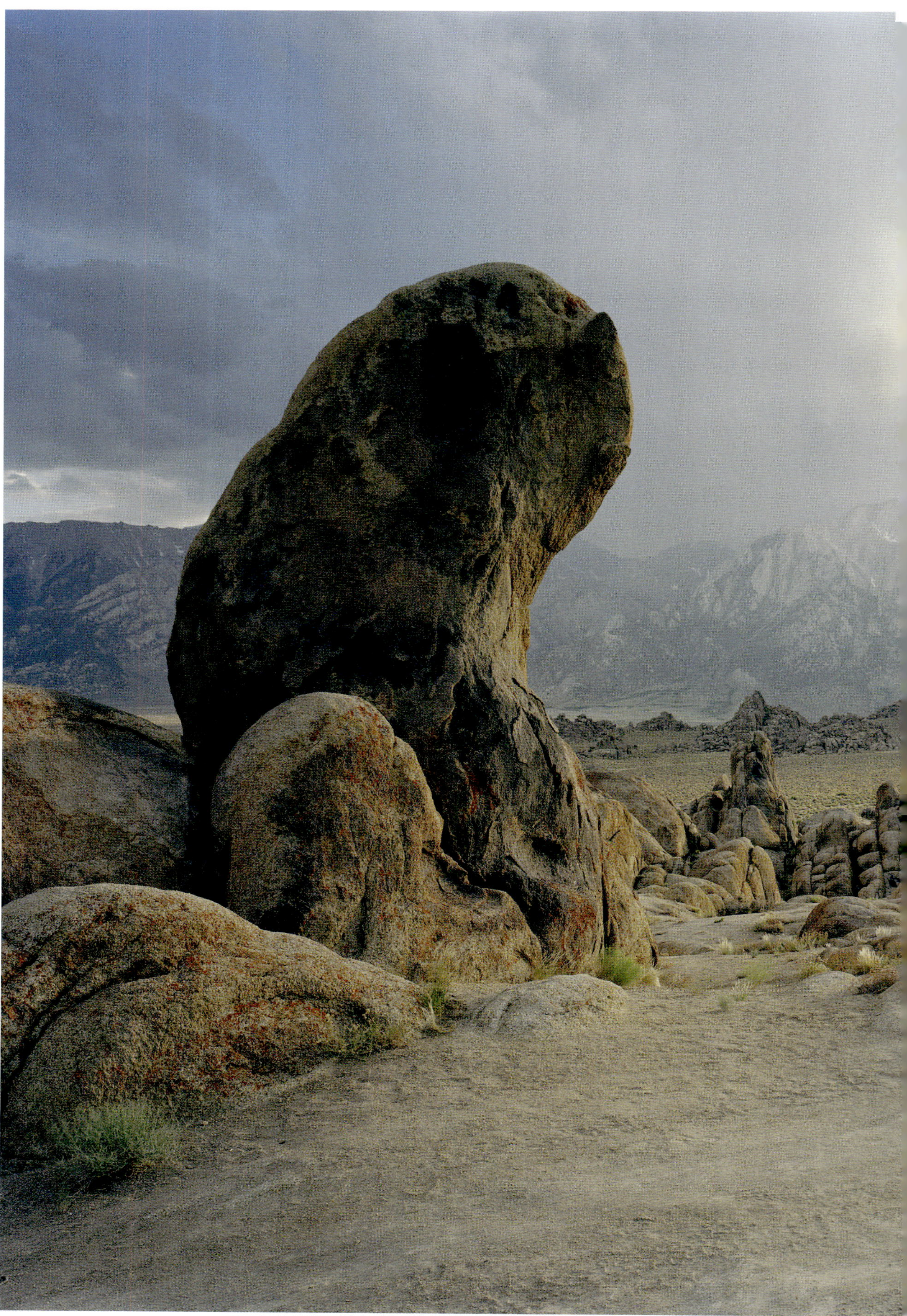

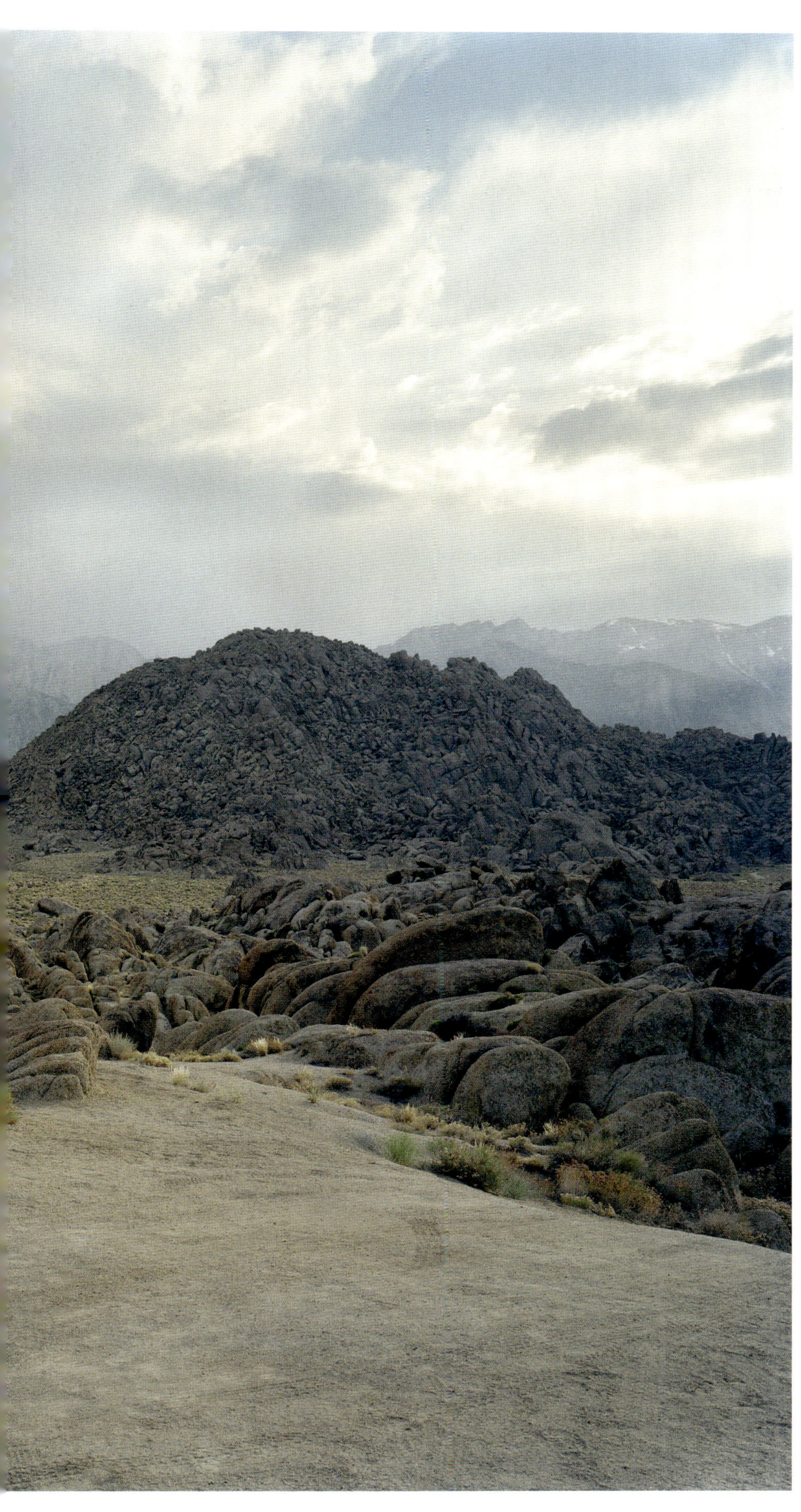

Doug Hall, *Gene Autry Rock, Alabama Hills, California,* 2002. Pigment print, 48 × 61 in. (121.9 × 154.9 cm)

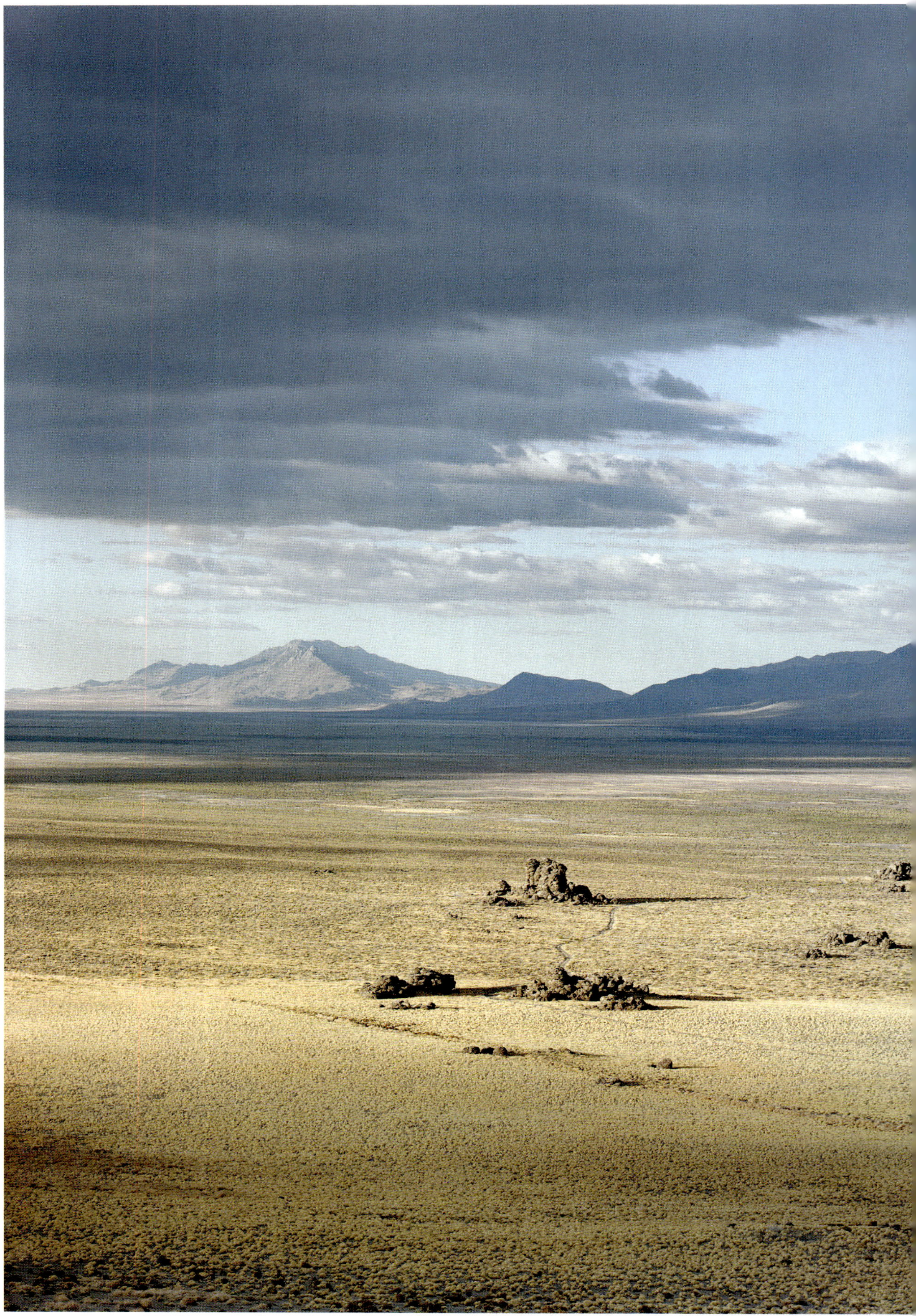

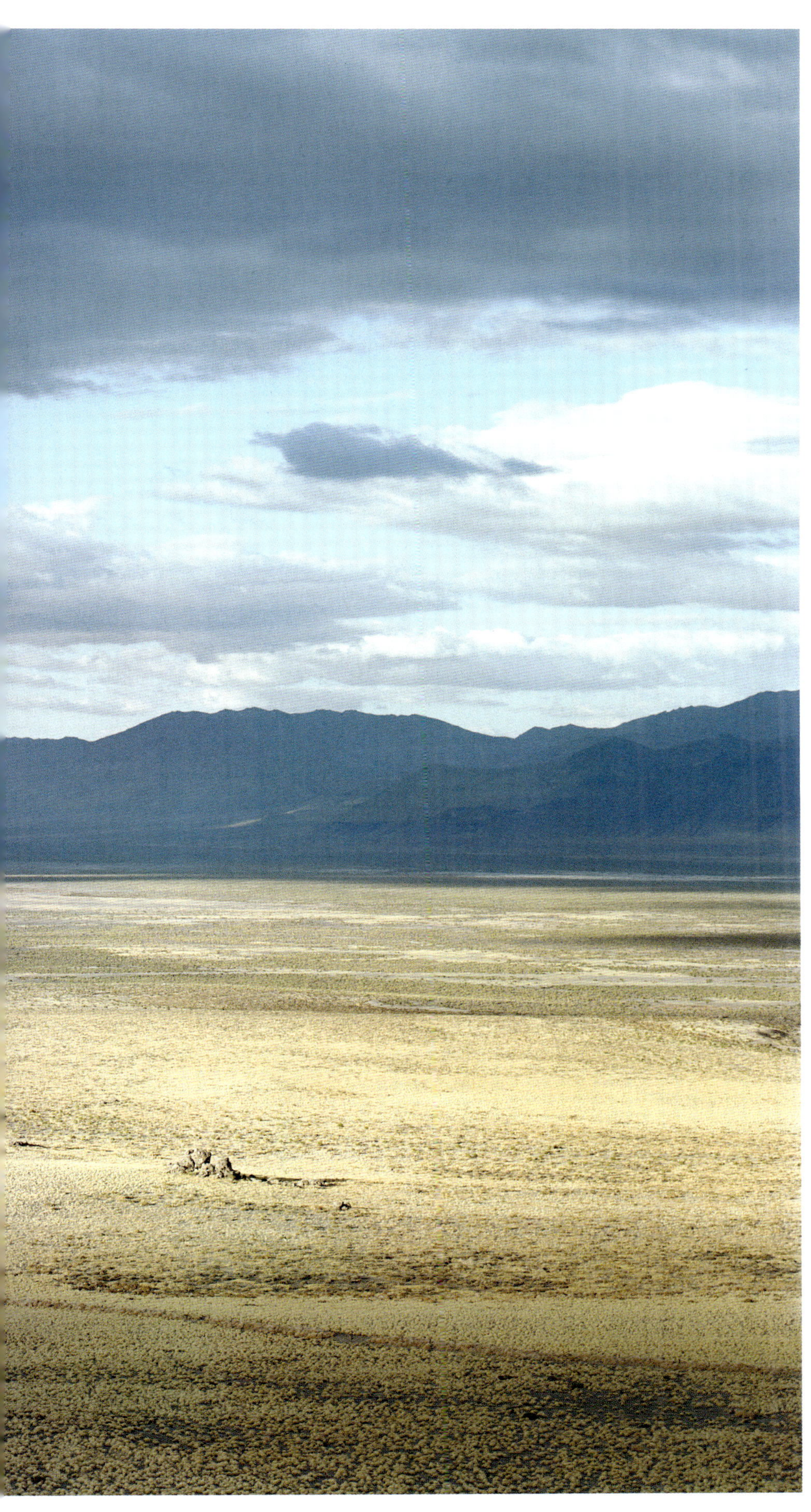

Doug Hall, *High Desert, Northern Nevada*, 2008. Pigment print, 48 × 60 in. (121.9 × 152.4 cm)

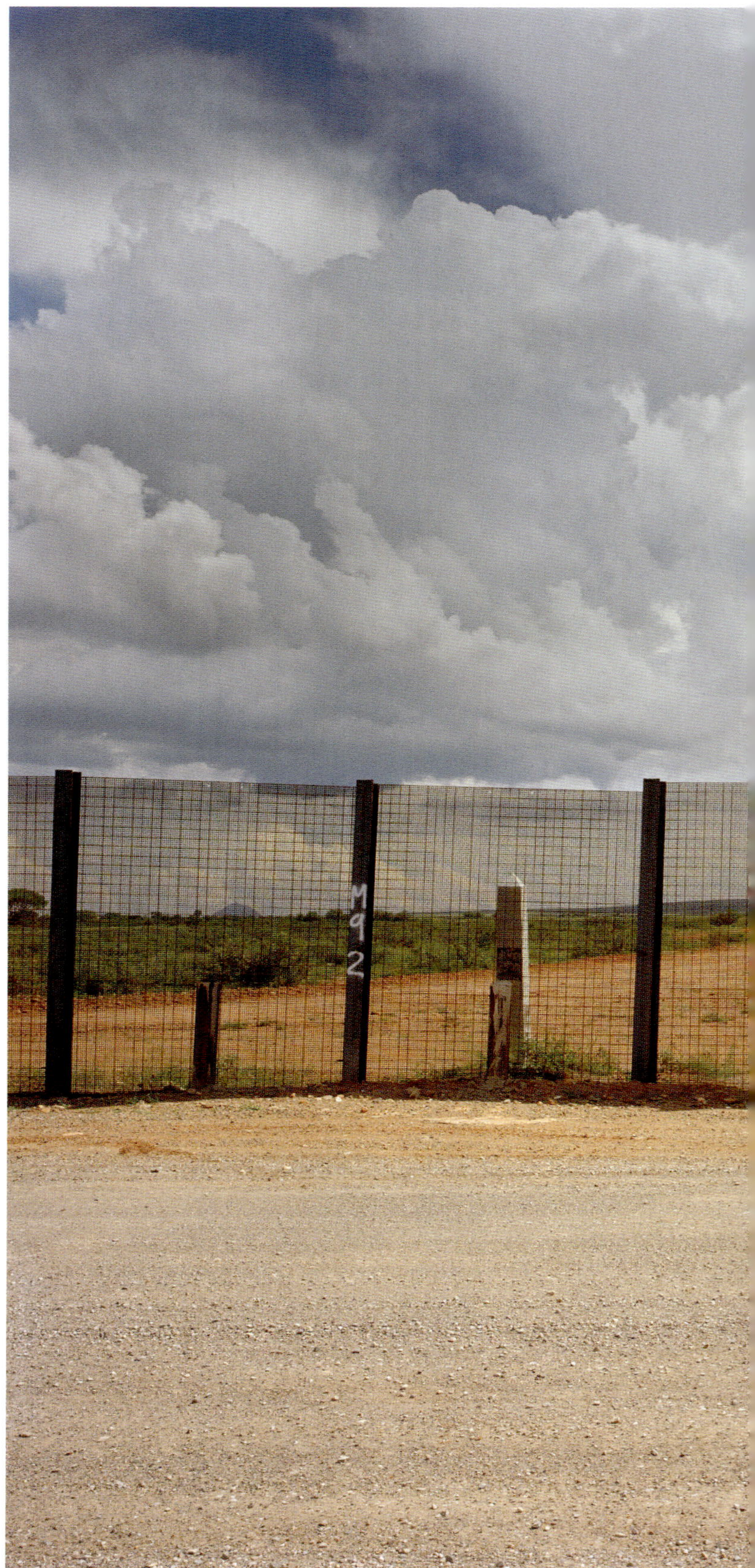

We are all aware of margins, borders, the edges of things. What we are less clear about is how relative and subjective these designations are. Sometimes boundaries are clearly defined, but more frequently, the region where one thing ends and another begins is blurred. In those areas where space is forcibly delineated, the edges can become brittle and hostile.

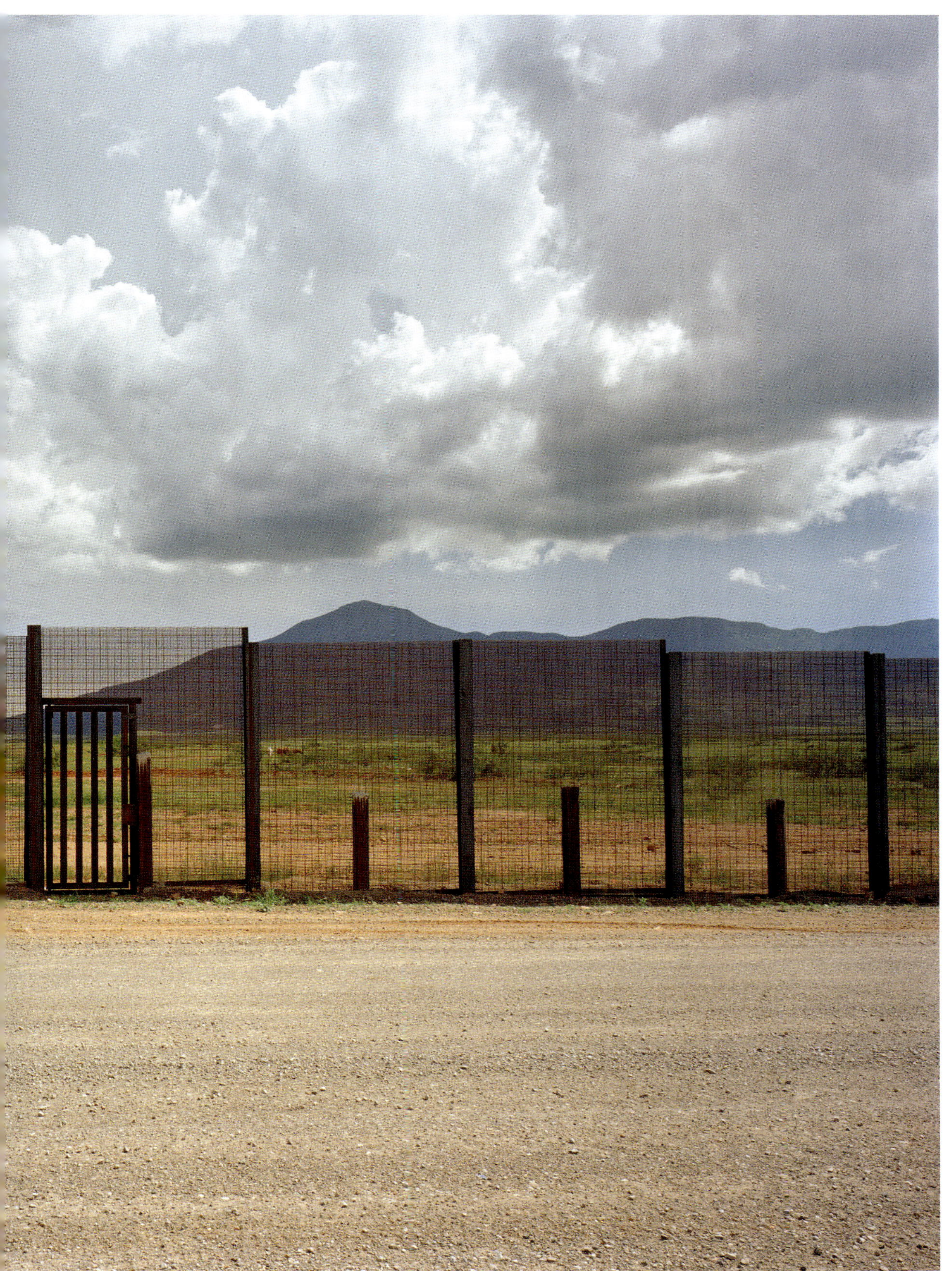

Doug Hall, *Border Fence, Naco, Arizona*, 2008. Pigment print, 48 × 60 in. (121.9 × 152.4 cm)

When I was a child, I liked to pretend that the world was a blank screen and what I was seeing was being projected onto it by rays coming from my eyes.

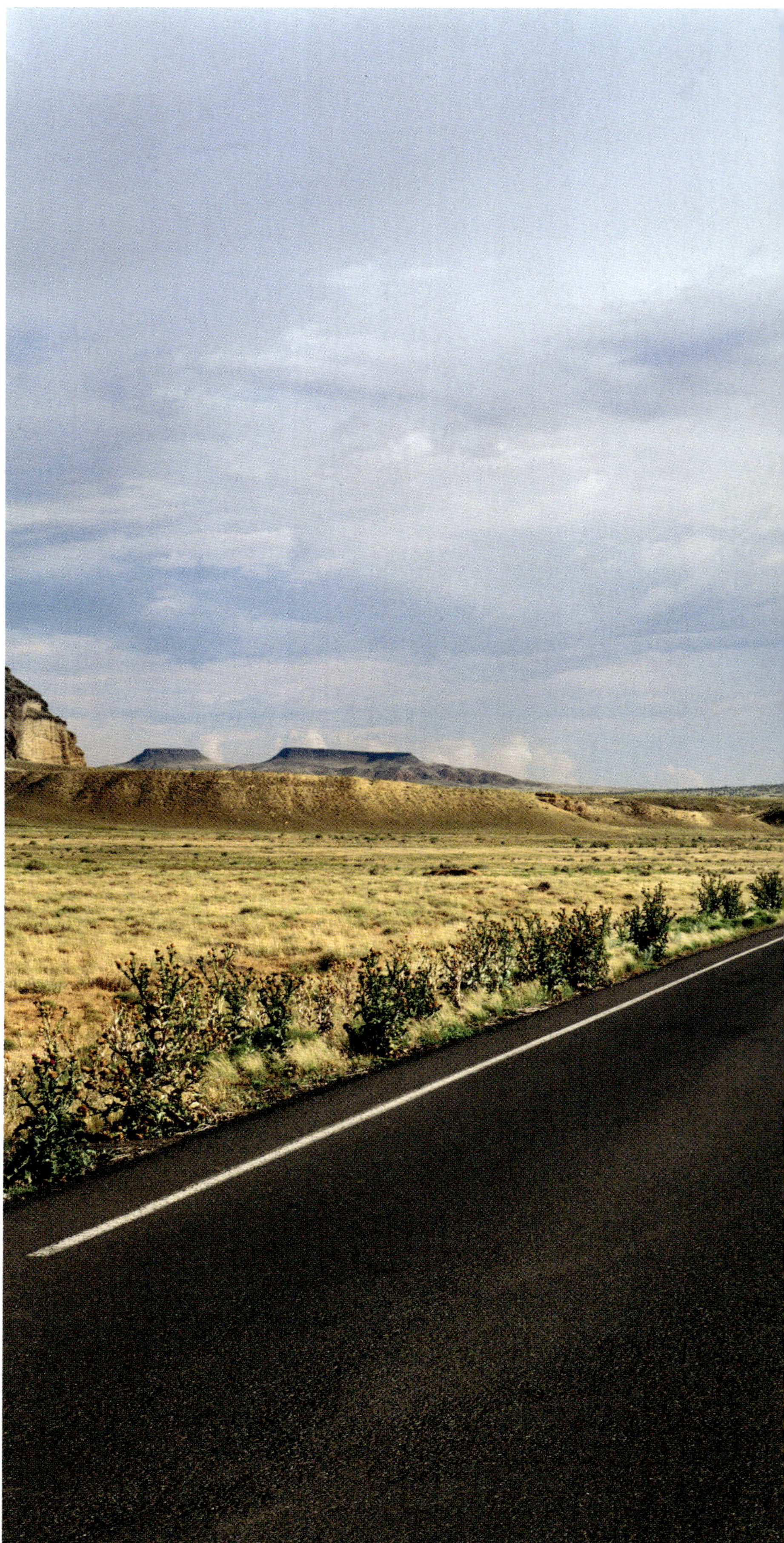

Doug Hall, *Highway 442, Arizona,* 1998. Pigment print, 48 × 62 in. (121.9 × 157.5 cm)

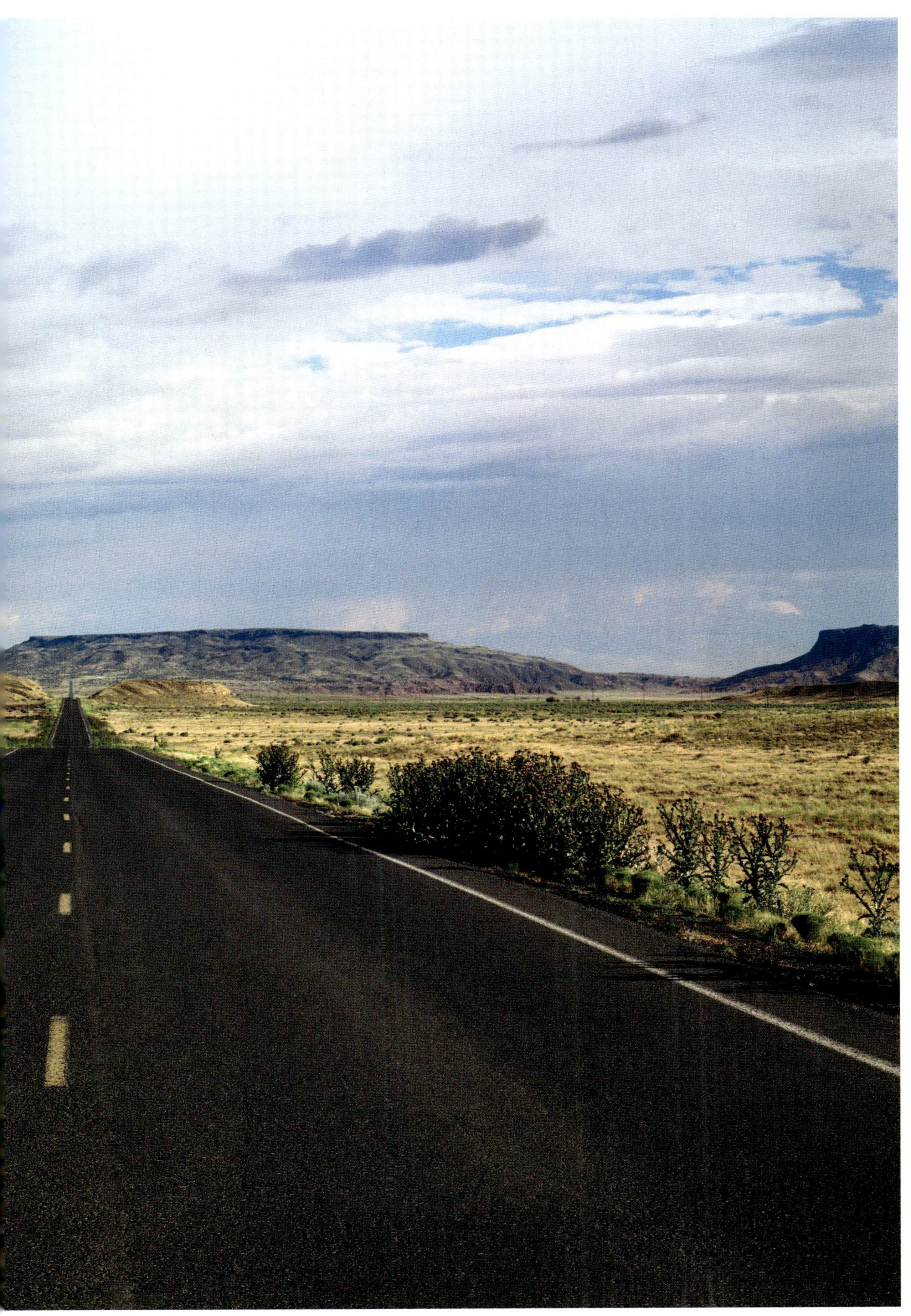

VII

All the Coming and Going

Do Elephants Mourn?

The rituals of birth and death are poignant affairs. Birth, of course, is a grand hello, a greeting accompanied by an understanding on the part of those on the welcoming committee of the myriad joys and sorrows this new life will experience. We are moved by the miracle that something so fully formed and yet so vulnerable and defenseless can slip out of another body into the light of day. As parents and, in my case at least, also as grandparents we are tempered by the associated responsibility and pain that loving can bring us.

Death is the big good-bye. There is no "see you tomorrow." The door slams shut, and that's the end of it. The sadness I felt when I was twenty-three and my father died persists to this day.

Or does the door slam shut? I have encountered my parents on a few occasions, as I have others who were present in my life and are now gone. They come to me sometimes as shape-shifters that drift through my dreamscape like a breeze through an open window. At other times, they seem solid, substantial—not dead at all—occupying a more familiar world. When happened upon in dreams, they often mingle with more surreal inhabitants of strange places, and the contact, usually brief, is fraught with a sense of imminent danger, often suggested by a warning from one of these murky apparitions. Whereupon, I awaken with a dread or at least an unease that haunts me well into the morning.

Although not as profoundly as in dreams, I have experienced momentary waking encounters with deceased loved ones. These are like flashes, a feeling of a person without recognizable substance that starts in the back of the neck, ripples through the body, and then is gone with the speed of a blinking eye, leaving little residue. Infrequently, they happen when I am alone, sitting quietly or taking a leisurely stroll in a natural setting. I like to think I've come upon the energy of the departed person that reaches out to me, touches me ever so slightly and then, unable to enter my world, retreats into that other dimension where it lives with all the greater energy of the cosmos.

But here, back on earth, death is devastatingly final.

"Doug, I have some very sad news." Diane has reached me on the phone in my hotel room in São Paulo where I am participating in the 2001 São Paulo Biennial. I can tell that she is quietly crying and she chokes out the unexpected news, "Your mother passed away last night in her sleep." My immediate response is shock, followed by a flood of tears. After I gather myself, Diane fills me in on the few details she knows.

My mother and her husband of thirty years, Kenneth Andrews, were in New York where they had gone to see a revival of *Oklahoma!* on Broadway. Staying at the Harvard Club, Ken had awakened early and, seeing that she appeared to be sleeping, stepped into the bathroom to shower. On returning to the bedroom, he noticed that she had not stirred. I imagine him attempting to wake her by gently pressing against her shoulder the way one might awaken a sleeping child and then the horror when he realizes she will never wake again. Of course, I can only speculate on this, but when I saw him, the depth of Ken's grief was palpable, even as it was hidden beneath his New England stoicism.

Dead! Such an uncompromising word. Harsh in comparison to "passed away," which seems gently euphemistic with its suggestion that the person in question has merely gone somewhere else, perhaps if you are religious, to a place happier than the one left behind. I've always been comfortable with the harsher description. I'm at ease with, even spiritually inspired by, the idea that we come from the stuff of the Big Bang, which in the case of a living body is organized into this complicated collection of coherent organic matter (permit me to call this some kind of a miracle), and that at death our molecules break down and join the originating stuff of the universe from which we emerged. I like to imagine that all the dust of me will circulate, some of it bound to recombine, while other particles will drift in the wind across the ages, land who knows where and become who knows what. That's enough eternal life for me. It is my unscientific conjecture, referred to above, that the energy of our having lived circulates and occasionally intersects the living in dreams or, while fully awake, as an uncanny awareness. I'm not sure it is a belief so much as a speculation that just as trees in a forest are said to communicate through a subterranean mycorrhizal network, our energies—even after death—reverberate and from time to time brush against us.

My mother died in March 2001. The June memorial service for her at Harvard's Memorial Chapel was filled with old friends, colleagues of my father's and Ken's from the college and the Business School, and close friends of mine who had known my parents and wanted to pay respects to all three of them. Seated in the front pew, waiting for the ceremony to begin, I was close to the same spot I occupied when my father was memorialized thirty-four years earlier. The grief I felt at that age was inundating to the point that I remember little else. Now, as my mother is being eulogized, I am filled with the profound awareness that the two people who had created me through their love and had nurtured and protected me as I grew, who encouraged me when I was distraught or disappointed, who scolded me when I misbehaved, the two people who loved me unconditionally, and knew and accepted the good and the bad in me—all the dust of me—were no longer. I was set free of whatever constraints their existence imposed on me, but also free of their love that protected and gave me courage.

There are those who believe that elephants mourn the passing of herd members, or at the very least that they demonstrate behaviors suggesting awareness of a condition of incommunicative stillness in one of their own that is permanent and irrevocable. I remember watching a film on TV that showed elephants coming upon the prone body of the group's recently deceased matriarch. Rather than moving past, they circled her body, prodding at it with

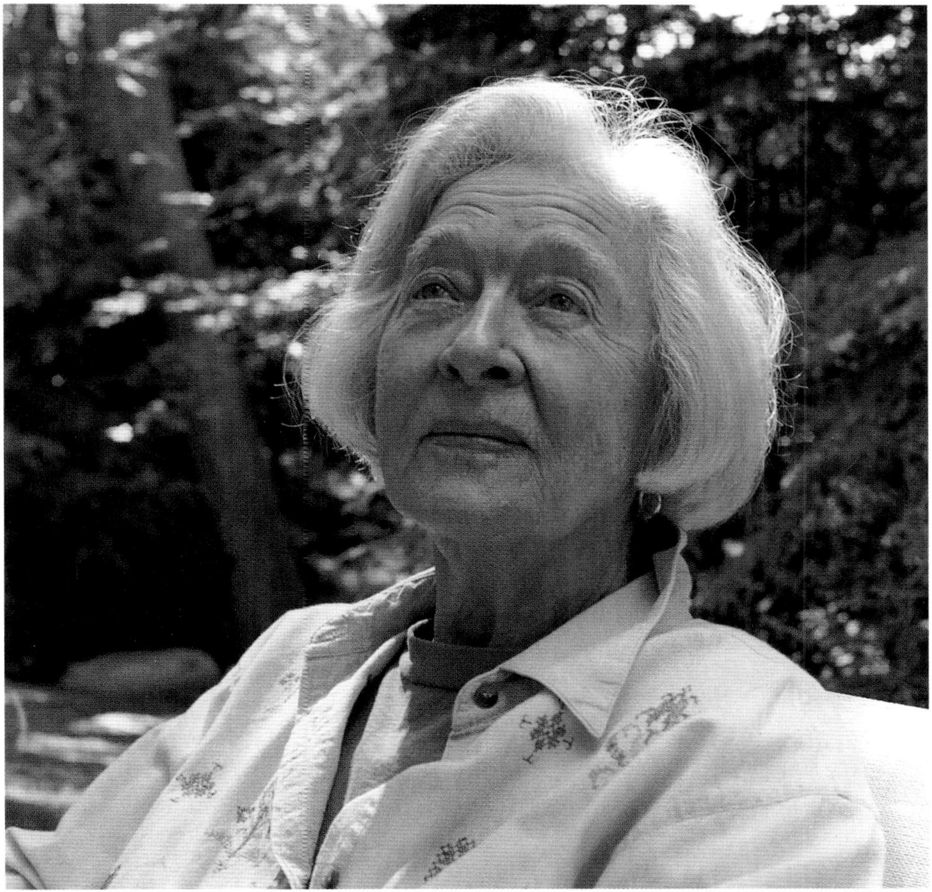

My mother, Carolyn, two years before her death in 2001
Photograph by Doug Hall

their trunks and tusks, as if trying to stir her from her slumber. This went on for some time. They would leave, return, and the behavior would start all over again. Finally, after much coming and going, they departed except for one, perhaps her progeny, a bull that stood over her, repeatedly dragging his trunk across her head and down her side or gently kneading her torso with his tusks. After several minutes, he moved away, slowly; but before disappearing, he turned for a final look and softly bellowed.

I recently read another account in which a female orca in Puget Sound, nicknamed Tahlequah by the researchers who had been studying the pod to which she belonged, refused to abandon her dead calf. For seventeen days and a thousand miles she kept the dead infant afloat by pushing it with her nose or carrying it draped across her shoulders. Finally, apparently exhausted by the effort and weak from lack of nourishment, she relinquished the corpse, circling it several times before departing to join the others who had been following her throughout the episode and vocalizing from a respectful distance. We humans, in our arrogance, assume that only we experience the sadness of death.

Leviathan

In the early 2000s, I was experiencing another kind of loss, although one far less poignant. As dedicated as I was to ideas I could work out through still images, I began to pine for the temporality of time-based media. I came to realize that the beautiful, mute, still photograph, even when presented at a grand scale, could not furnish the temporal unfolding that video provided. The sculptural, theatrical potential of video installation was sensory in ways that static images could never be. While I continued making photographs, I looked for avenues for funding and exhibition venues for expansive video projects.

As significant as the digital revolution was for photography, the opportunities it afforded video makers were even more profound. By the late nineties and early 2000s, analog video, recorded on magnetic tape that played back fuzzy images in a 3:4 aspect ratio (referred to as standard-definition video), was being overtaken by digital video (high-definition video) at a 16:9 aspect ratio that referenced cinema rather than video's progenitor, television. Expensive, cumbersome cameras were less crucial, becoming replaced by affordable, small, high-resolution versions, some looking like traditional SLR cameras and able to shoot both still photos and video. Video was no longer recorded as magnetic pulses on tape but was now stored as digital data in computers where it could be edited and manipulated with desktop applications like Apple's Final Cut Pro and Adobe Premiere Pro.

As the first decade of the twenty-first century progressed, these new technologies continued to advance. Flat-screen televisions replaced bulky CRTs with their vacuum tubes; sophisticated single lens projectors pushed aside the three-tube RGB projectors whose tubes were a nightmare to keep aligned. This was the situation in January 2012 when Cheryl Haines, executive director of FOR-SITE Foundation in San Francisco, invited me to submit a proposal for *International Orange*, a group exhibition she was organizing in celebration of the seventy-fifth birthday of the Golden Gate Bridge. It was to be sited at Fort Point, a spectacular nineteenth-century brick fort that sits beneath the southern span of the bridge. After a lot of pondering and sketching, I proposed a two-channel high-definition video projection to be installed inside the fort that would focus on the bridge and the container ships that pass beneath it. Working with talented producer and friend Starr Sutherland and sound designers Jim McKee and Jeremiah Moore, we overcame numerous technical challenges to install the work in a space on the second level of Fort Point. Framed by the brick arch of a chamber that once contained cannons positioned to protect the bay from naval attack during the Civil War and after, the videos were trained on the bridge, seen over the course of several months under differing weather conditions, and on the many immense ships that slide under it every day. Along with the sounds coming from the installation were

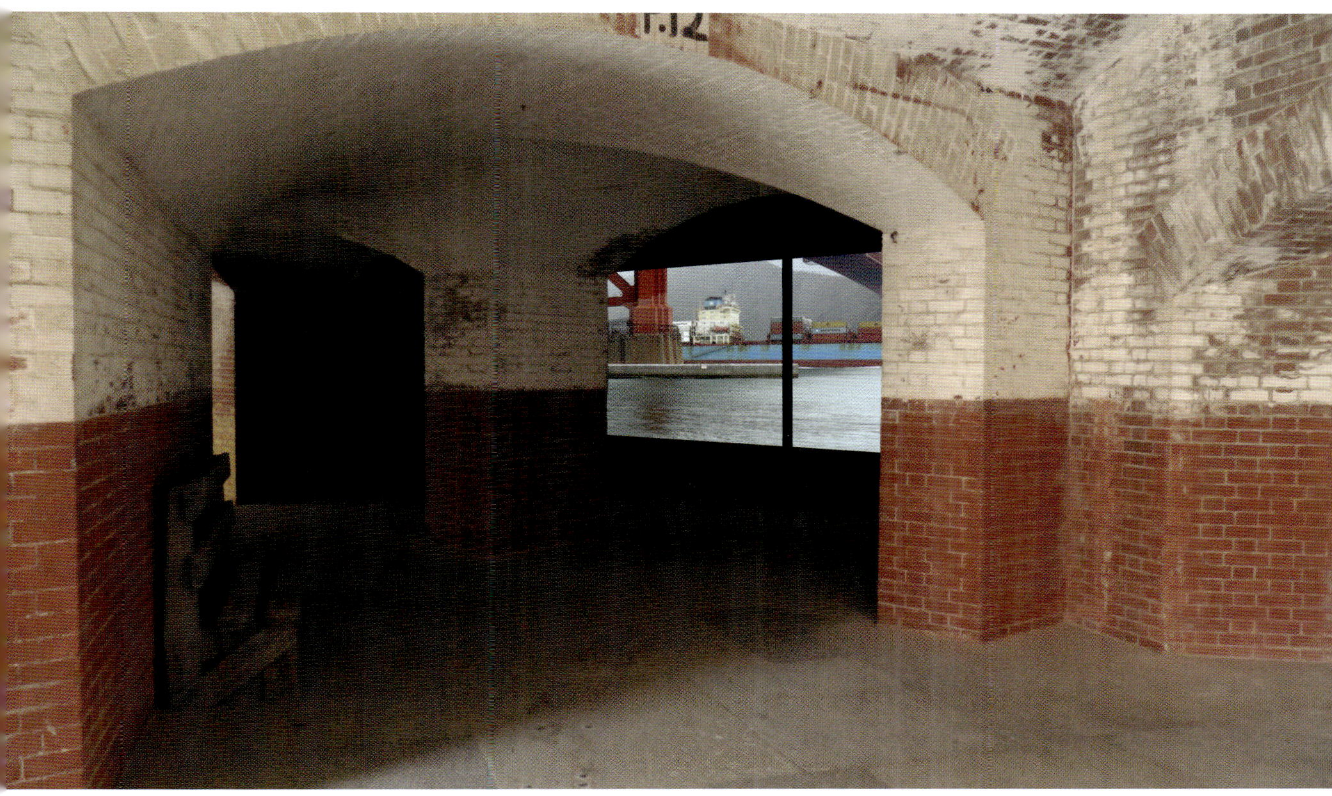

Doug Hall, *Chrysopylae*, two-channel video projection with sound, installation view, Fort Point, 2012
Photograph by Doug Hall

those arising from the surrounding bay: foghorns at the bridge, wind sweeping through the fort, and the noisy gulls circling above. Leaving the installation, one could climb a set of nearby stairs to the top of the fort and look out, in real time, at the bridge and all that surrounds it.

The thing that surprised me about this work was how emotional it felt, as if something I held within me had been let loose. For me, the ships became anthropomorphic, particularly those we shot from a small boat, expertly handled by members of the San Francisco Bar Pilots, that brought us within a few feet of them. In the video, the scraped and scarred hulls of the cargo ships look alive, like the hides of immense sea creatures. I was moved, I think, by a sense of time passing: the coming and going of the ships, the changing weather, and the soundtrack, resonating in roars and murmurs as if the ships, the bridge, the sea were calling out in a kind of mournful tone that made the experience both powerful and surprisingly intimate. Rather than intruders, bridge and ships seemed married to ocean, sky, distant hills, gulls—all were of the same world, in balance with one another, and with me. For a brief time, I found refuge in this moment of intimate tranquility, a meditative solitude that was comforting and exhilarating.

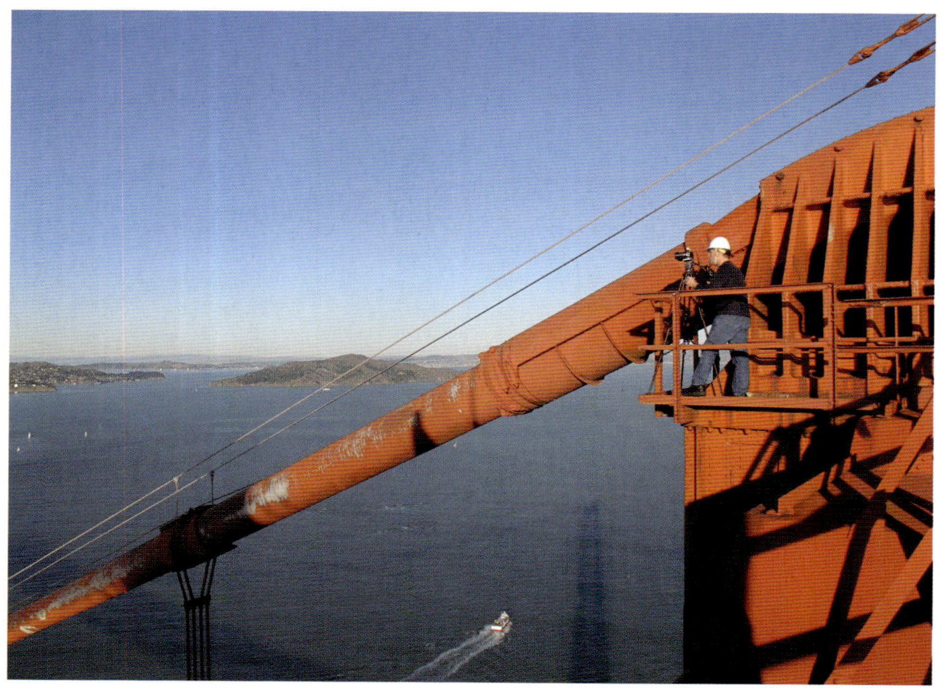

Shooting video for *Chrysopylae* from the top of the Golden Gate Bridge's south tower
Photograph by Starr Sutherland

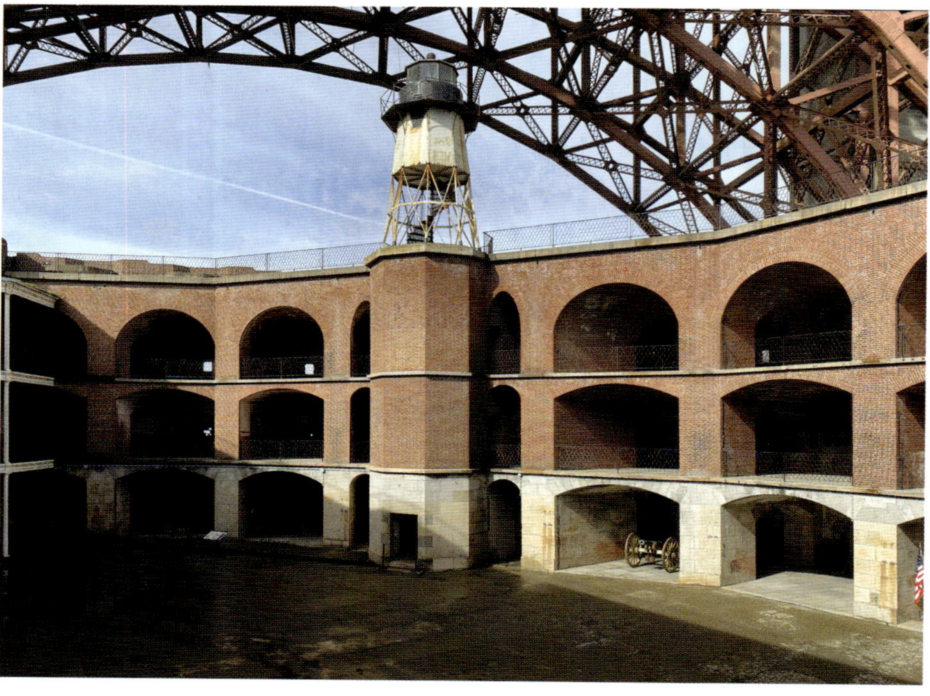

Fort Point sits beneath the southern span of the Golden Gate Bridge
Photograph by Doug Hall

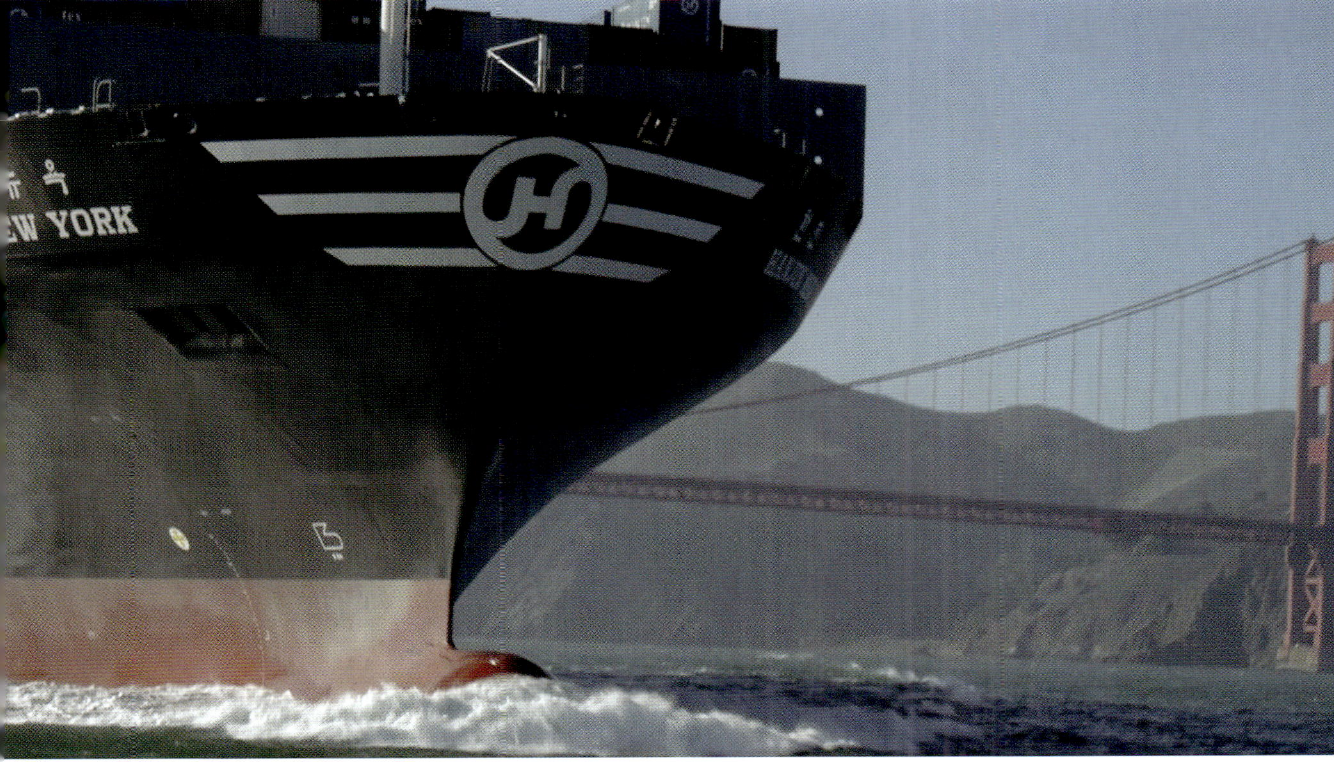

Doug Hall, *Chrysopylae*, video still of an approaching container ship, filmed from the deck of the pilot ship operated by the San Francisco Bar Pilots

I titled the work *Chrysopylae*, in recognition of the appellation given by John C. Frémont, who, upon entering San Francisco Bay on July 1, 1846, wrote, "To this gate I gave the name of 'Chrysopylae' or 'Golden Gate'; for the same reasons that the harbor of Byzantium was called Chrysoceras or 'Golden Horn.'" He added that the strait would become "a golden gate for trade with the Orient."[1]

1. "What's in a Name—The Golden Gate Bridge?" Golden Gate Bridge Highway and Transportation District, goldengate.org.

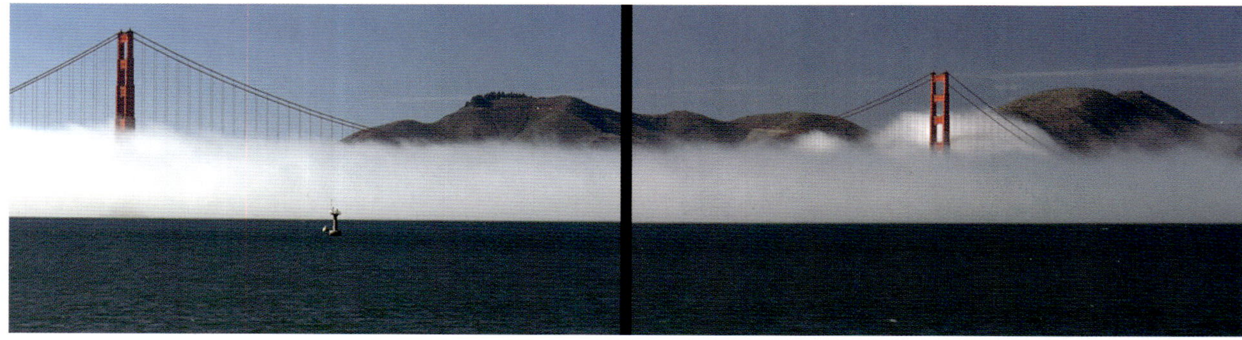

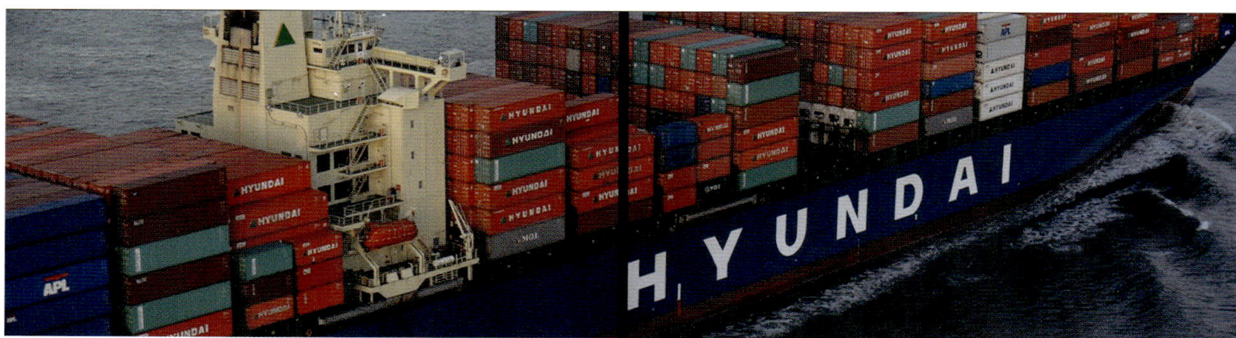

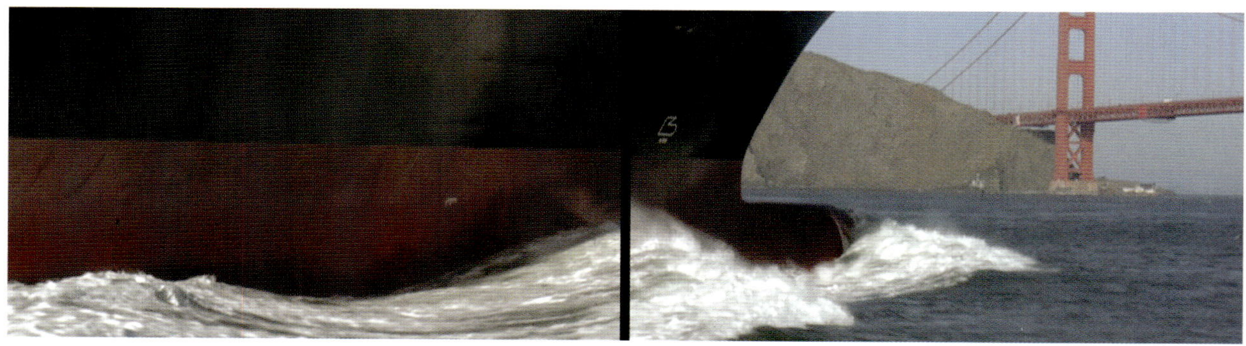

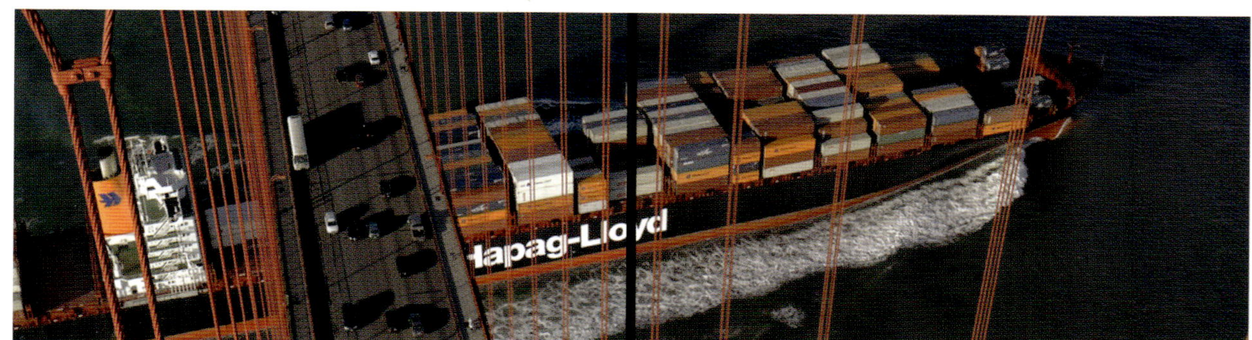

Doug Hall, *Chrysopylae*, two-screen video stills

From Roar to Whisper

We live in a world that is, I fear, headed in a direction that will make its current condition seem like utopia in comparison. I recognize this. At the same time, it's all so fascinating that I can't turn my eyes away any more than I can stop imagining another world—one that opposes the cynicism and cruelty of this one, so poignantly felt by David Wojnarowicz:

> First there is the world. Then there is the Other World. The other world is where I sometimes lose my footing. In its calendar turnings, in its preinvented existence. The barrage of twists and turns where I sometimes get weary trying to keep up with it, minute by minute adapt: the world of the stoplight, the no smoking signs, the rental world, the split-rail fencing shielding hundreds of miles of barren wilderness from the human step. A place where by virtue of having been born centuries late one is denied access to earth, choice, or movement. The bought-up world; the owned world. The world of coded sounds: the world of language, the world of lies.

And yet, it is this same world that fuels our imaginations and provides relief, perhaps even insight, not through escape but through creativity:

> But there is the World where one adapts and stretches the boundaries of the Other World through keys of the imagination.[2]

During my life as an artist, as the world and my sense of myself in it have changed, I suppose it is not surprising that there would be a shift in what I wanted to say and how I wanted to say it. Realizing the obvious dangers of over-defining the motivations behind one's art, I do feel that the person who made work in the 1970s and eighties is different from the person writing these words in 2023. Summarizing this difference, I would say that most of the earlier work, perhaps up to *Chrysopylae*, was directed toward understanding how power (corporate, political, personal) and the structures of western capitalism are expressed through gesture, language, and edifice. Of course, throughout my career there have been diversions, but this has been the main thrust, and certainly what I am best known for. Over the last decade, these issues have become less urgent to me. Instead of the roar of the capitalist sublime, I seek the more private and intimate whisper of contemplation. Perhaps the shift is ascribable to nothing more than the psychological and emotional changes that occur when one becomes certifiably old. I do think age—or rather the experiences that come with having been around for a while—has allowed the inner

2. David Wojnarowicz, *Close to the Knives* (New York: Vintage Books, 1991), 87, 88.

agitation that I consciously fueled earlier in my life to give way to an emotional state that at least approaches serenity. The fact is that, although I feel I have a lot of life left in me, I am much closer to life's exit than its entrance. Events and thoughts that seemed important even a decade ago are now trivial. And I suppose the converse is also true: the momentary trivialities of daily life supersede any grand narrative.

How recognition of mortality affects an artist's work is the subject of Edward Said's book *On Late Style*. In his introduction, Michael Wood explains how proximity to one's death inspires change. He writes, "[D]eath does sometimes wait for us, and it is possible to become deeply aware of its waiting. The quality of time alters then, like a change in the light, because the present is so thoroughly shadowed by other seasons: the revived or receding past, the newly unmeasurable future, the unimaginable time beyond time."[3] I would describe this as a shift in consciousness. In my case, it arrived gradually and anonymously, meaning that there was no eureka moment but a slow drift of my sentiments toward an awareness of my mortality. Rather than stoking fear, it has me yearning for that which is humane, intimate, and perhaps more private.

Such was my state of mind in 2015 when I traveled to Prague, where my son, Gannon, his wife, Erin, and their infant son, Atticus, had relocated so he could take a position as chief product officer at an international media company. In addition to seeing family, my visit provided the opportunity to pursue a project I'd been thinking about off and on for years—one based on a collection of letters by Franz Kafka to Milena Jesenská that were published after Kafka's death as *Letters to Milena*. Collected, edited, and first published in 1952, the letters contain Kafka's side of an intimate correspondence with Jesenská from July through November 1920. During this period, Milena, a twenty-three-year-old Czech-speaking Gentile, was living in Vienna under very difficult financial circumstances while in a strained marriage to Ernst Pollak, an important Jewish literary critic and notorious womanizer. Even as a teenager, Milena displayed a rebellious streak that dismayed her conservative father, Jan Jesenská, a prosperous oral surgeon, professor of medicine at Prague's Charles University, ardent nationalist, and virulent anti-Semite. In his introduction to the English translation of the letters, Philip Boehm describes Milena: "She experimented with drugs stolen from her father's practice. She became involved with men. She spent her father's money lavishly on clothes, presents, flowers. She was emancipated, rebellious, extravagant, decadent, daring, and very much in love with beauty."[4]

Milena's interests gravitated toward literature; she was particularly drawn to the Jewish literati who frequented the city's bohemian cafes. It was through

3. Michael Wood, introduction to *On Late Style: Music and Literature Against the Grain*, by Edward W. Said (New York: Vintage Books, 2007), xi.
4. Philip Boehm, introduction to *Letters to Milena*, by Franz Kafka, trans. Boehm (New York: Schocken Books, 1990), xi.

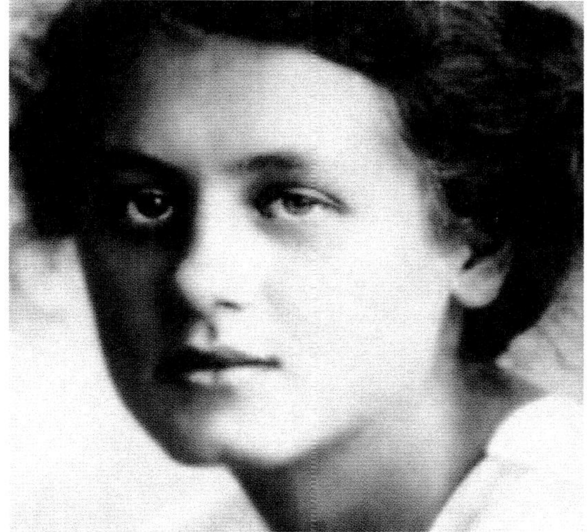 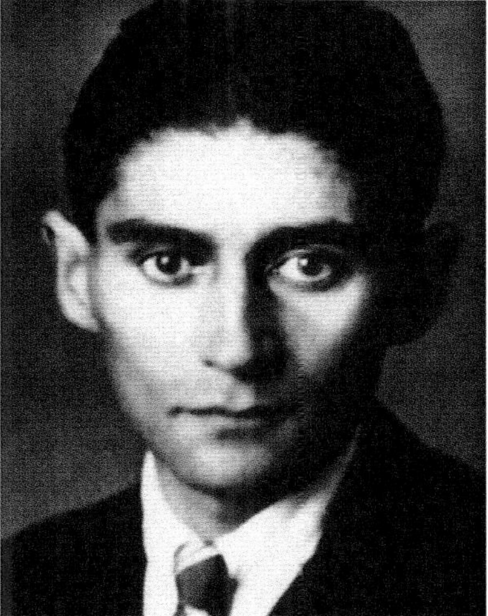

Doug Hall, *Letters in the Dark: Franz Kafka and Milena Jesenská*, 2016. Video stills, Kafka and Jesenská as they looked around the time they met in 1920

these connections that she had a passing acquaintance with Kafka and where she met, and in 1918 married, Pollak, infuriating her tyrannical father who was outraged that his daughter would marry a Jew. In part to flee her father's wrath, the couple moved to Vienna, where they lived in postwar poverty. To make ends meet, Milena worked various jobs, including as a baggage handler at the train station and, more compatible with her talents, as a translator and newspaper essayist. Kafka, thirteen years older and Jewish, was living modestly in Prague and engaged to be married. Not yet famous as a writer, he made his living as an insurance adjuster, a job whose demand for orderliness and precision suited his nature. Milena first contacted Franz about translating some of his short stories from German into Czech. Their correspondence, which began as a professional exchange, soon evolved into something much more intimate that, at its zenith, had Kafka expressing passionate love for Milena as well as confessing profound anxiety; this he refers to repeatedly, and somewhat mysteriously, throughout the letters but particularly toward the end, as "the great fear." The great fear is in a very real sense the third character in the letters—the presence that dooms their relationship, making any lasting intimacy impossible for Kafka.

Franz and Milena met only twice during the period of their correspondence. The first time took place over five days in July 1920 in Vienna, and from all indications was a happy time for both. A second, lasting two days, occurred several months later in Gmünd, a small town on the Czech-Austrian border, and was a disaster. Their intimate correspondence ceased shortly thereafter, although they did maintain a less personal and sporadic exchange until 1922. It is unclear if their affair ever became physical, although there is evidence that unsuccessful attempts were made during the second short visit. By all

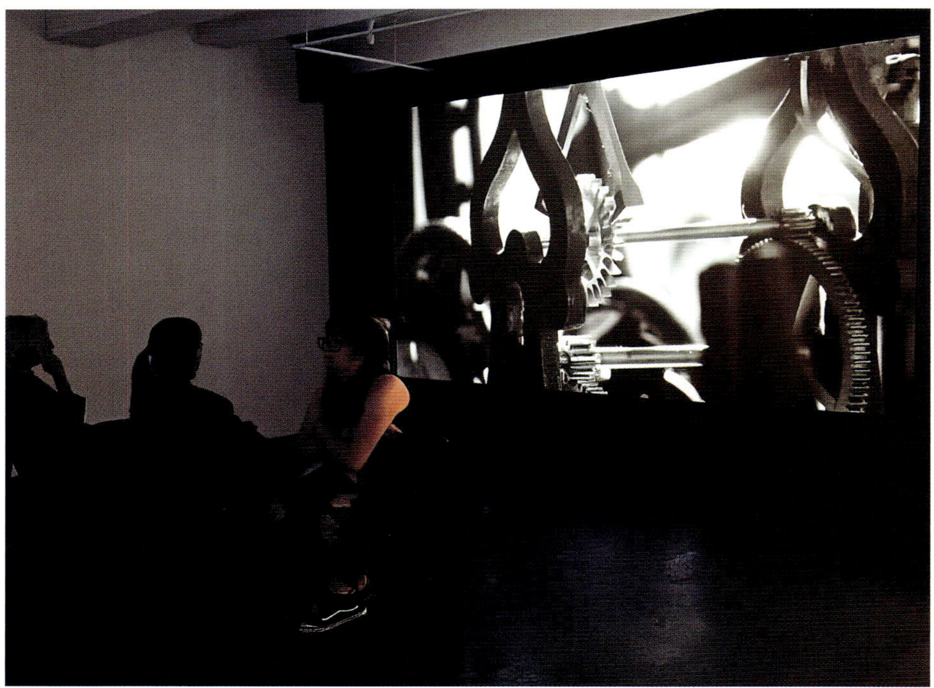

Doug Hall, *Letters in the Dark*, 2016. Detail, installation view, showing one of the two video projections, Benrubi Gallery

accounts, Kafka was made uncomfortable by human touch. In a diary entry from 1922, reflecting on those two days in Gmünd, Kafka writes, "What have I done with the gift of sex? It's been a failure, in the end that is all they will say. No doubt about that. But it might easily have succeeded. . . . M. is right: fear means unhappiness."[5] Kafka died on June 3,1924, of tuberculosis at a sanatorium in Kierling, near Vienna.

Following her epistolary affair with Kafka, Jesenská went on to have a successful career as a journalist. She divorced Pollak and returned to Prague where she became a Communist and, following her disillusionment with Stalinism and the beginning of conflict with Germany, an active member of the anti-Nazi resistance. She was married several times and had numerous affairs. She was arrested by the Nazis in 1939 and incarcerated at Ravensbrück, where she died of kidney failure in 1944, three weeks before D-Day.

Kafka's letters to Milena, when read in their entirety, follow a predictable narrative arc, beginning with the early letters, which are mostly about the business of translation, to the passionate middle letters following their Vienna rendezvous, and ending with those written after their two days in Gmünd in which Kafka insists on terminating the relationship. He writes, "You were right. Fear is wholly to blame. Do not write, Milena, and let us not see each other.

5. Franz Kafka, *The Diaries, 1910–1923*, ed. Max Brod (New York: Schocken Books, 1976), 399.

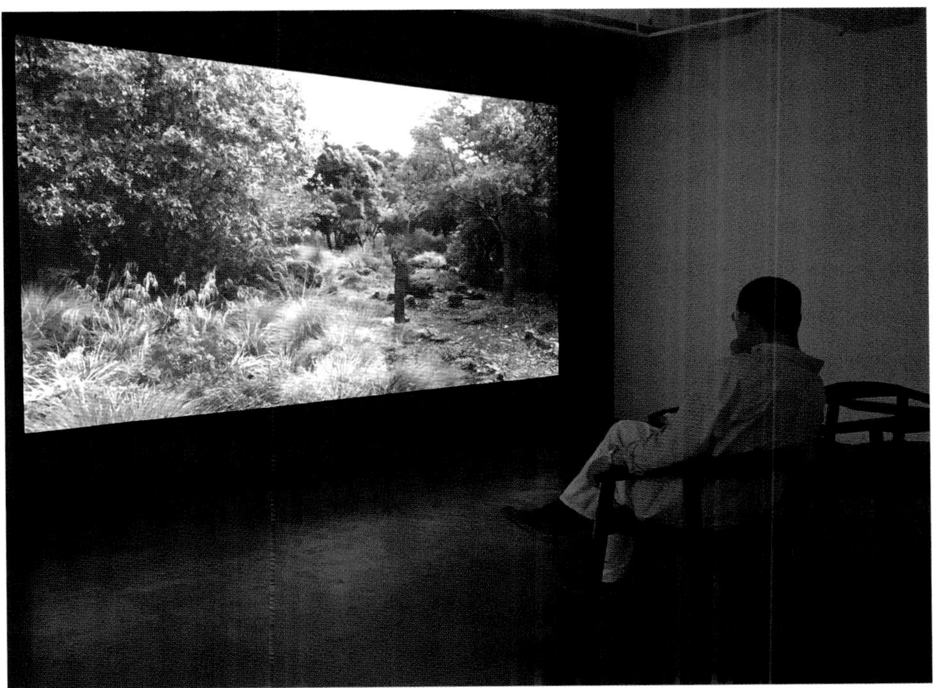

Doug Hall, *Letters in the Dark*, 2016. Detail, installation view, showing one of the two video projections, Benrubi Gallery

Only on those conditions is survival possible for me; everything else continues the process of destruction." Their brief love affair, lasting no more than five months, was a virtual relationship based on fantasies and imaginings that were partially fueled by memories of the spring days they shared in Vienna "when the chestnut trees were in bloom."[6]

Although we can get a vague sense of Milena's strong character and intelligence through Kafka's references to her letters, she is for the most part silent. The correspondence is very much a one-way conversation—Kafka's. One of the interesting challenges of the project I envisioned was to see if I could write Milena's missing letters in a way that was convincing and reflected her strong, independent character; no longer a phantom, but a woman with a strong voice, who could be seen as the full equal of Kafka. I exhibited *Letters in the Dark: Franz Kafka and Milena Jesenská* in 2016 at the Benrubi Gallery, New York. It was an installation of two projected videos in one room and photographs in another. As described in the gallery's press release, "Central to the video installation is Hall's recreation of Jesenská's letters, which he fashioned from fragments of her other writing, as well as stylistic and tonal cues in Kafka's letters to her. Kafka's letters issue from one projection, while

6. Margarete Buber-Neumann, *Milena: The Tragic Story of Kafka's Great Love*, trans. Ralph Manheim (New York: Arcade Publishing, 1977), 60.

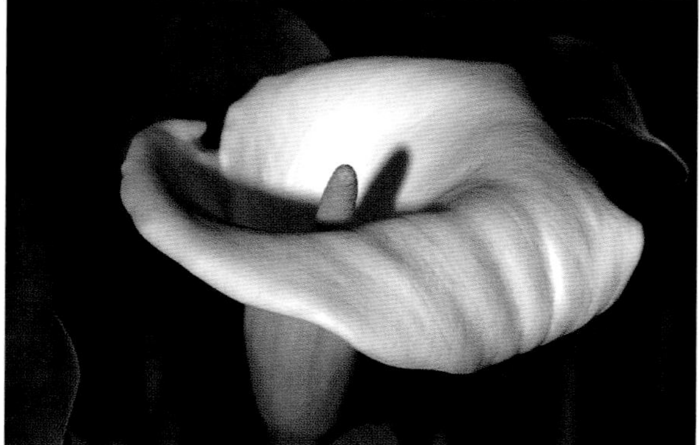

Doug Hall, *Letters in the Dark*, 2016. Two-channel video projection (still)

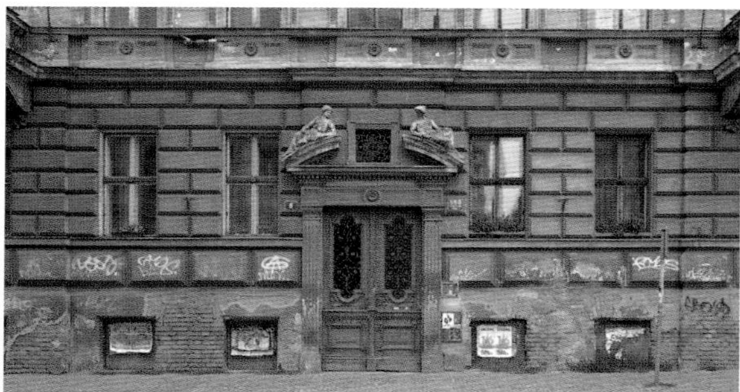
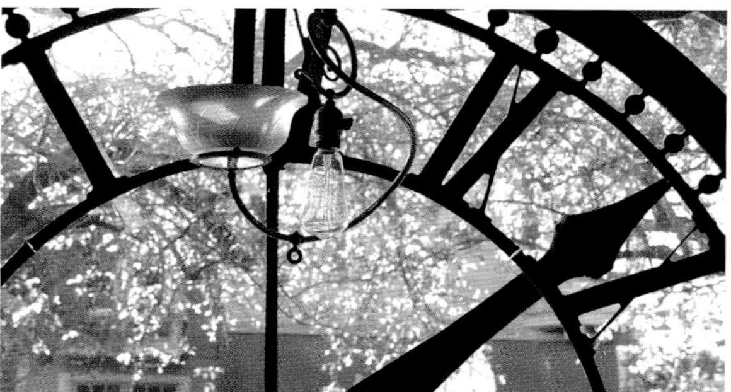

Doug Hall, *Letters in the Dark*, 2016. Two-channel video projection (still)

Jesenská's come from a second projection on the opposite wall. The spoken texts are accompanied by images of doorways, hallways, facades, gardens, and domestic interiors. The images hint at lives felt but not seen, and, as with the texts, some depict actual locations where Kafka lived and worked, while others were taken in Moscow and San Francisco, and act as proxies for Kafka and Jesenská."

The photographs in the adjoining gallery depict or represent locations that Franz, and to a lesser extent Milena, frequented in Prague, such as the Kafka family residence in Old Town Square; his father's clothing store; the Hermann Asbestos Works, his brother-in-law's "wretched" factory where Kafka worked for a year in order to appease his father; the Worker's Accident Insurance Institute, where he was employed for most of his adult life; and the Jesenská family residence on Dittrichova Street. Those photos not set in Prague refer to Kafka's novel *The Castle*, which critics have noted has parallels to the love triangle that developed between Kafka, Jesenská, and her husband Pollak. In the novel, K., the central character, needs the assistance of Klamm, amanuensis to the castle's owner, Count Westwest, to arrange a meeting so that he can get the count's permission to conduct his work as a surveyor. At the same time K. con-

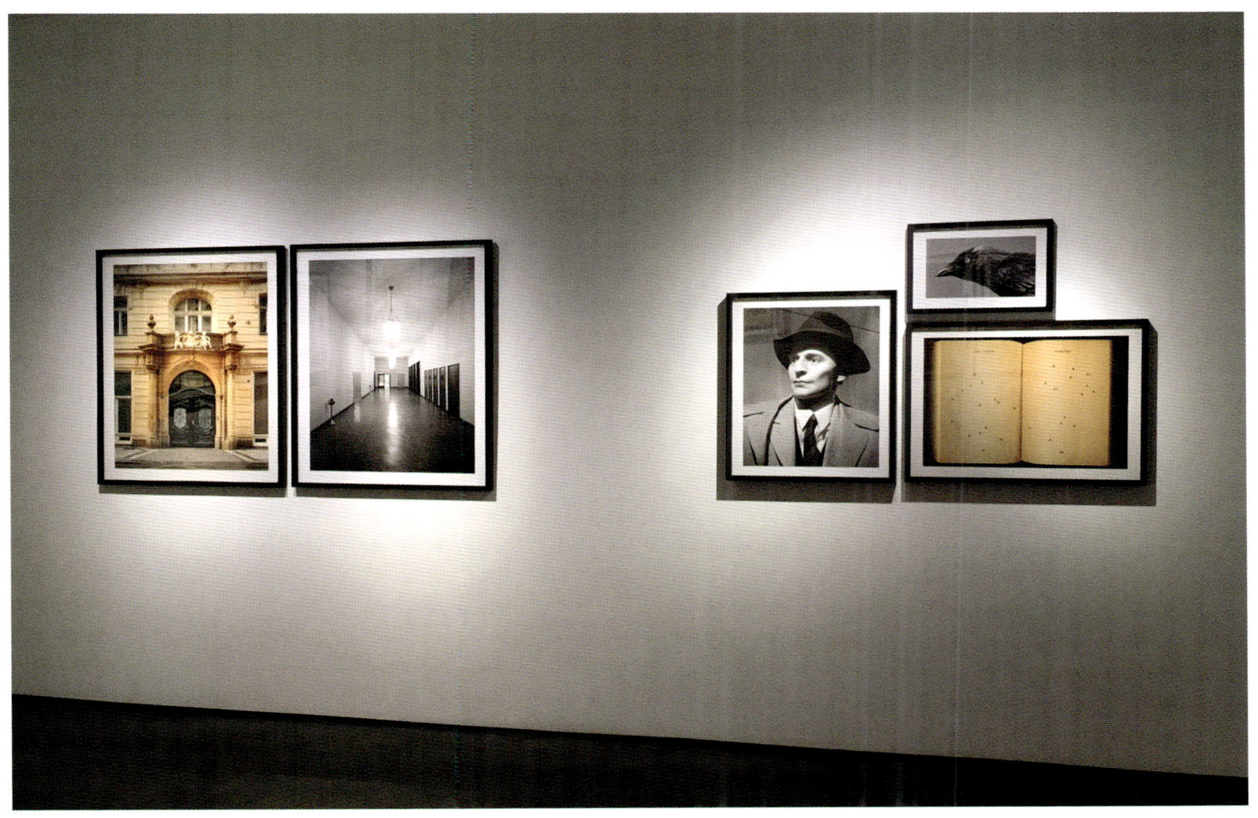

Doug Hall, *Letters in the Dark*, 2016. Detail, installation view of photographs, Benrubi Gallery

flicts with the elusive Klamm over the attentions of Frieda, who seduces K.—or does K. seduce her?—while being engaged to Klamm. As is the case with the letters, the central theme of *The Castle* is the protagonist's inability to reach his goals—inability to arrive at the castle; inability to communicate with the two assistants who purposely or inadvertently sabotage everything; inability to resolve or even understand his relationship with Frieda, or to understand how Klamm fits into it. This is the "poetics of non-arrival" in Kafka that Judith Butler refers to;[7] in the novel, it verges on slapstick—albeit dark slapstick experienced as if in the midst of a nightmare—while in the letters the condition rises to poetry, overflowing with longing. But it is a kind of rapture, at least from Kafka, that seems desperate and perhaps even narcissistic—more akin to that of a lovelorn youth pining over an impossible liaison than a grown man expressing genuine, reciprocal emotion. In the letters, one senses that Kafka has created a situation that can only end in frustration, a self-fulfilling prophecy that dooms any happy resolution and, by so doing, validates his misery.

7. Judith Butler, The European Graduate School Video Lectures, February 10 & 11, 2012, YouTube.

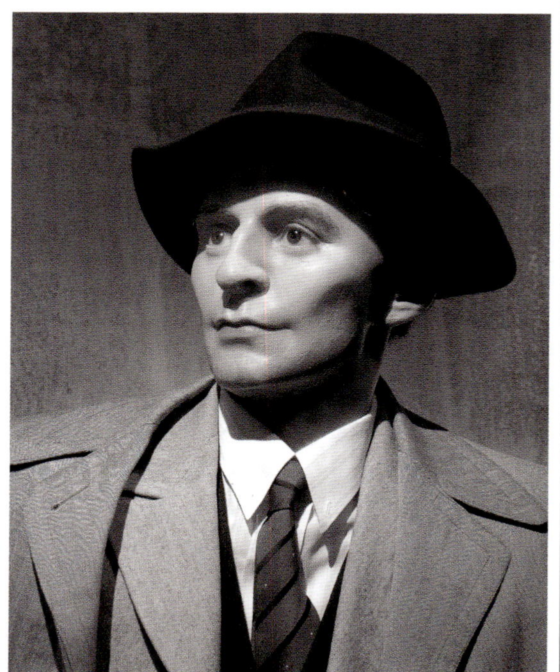

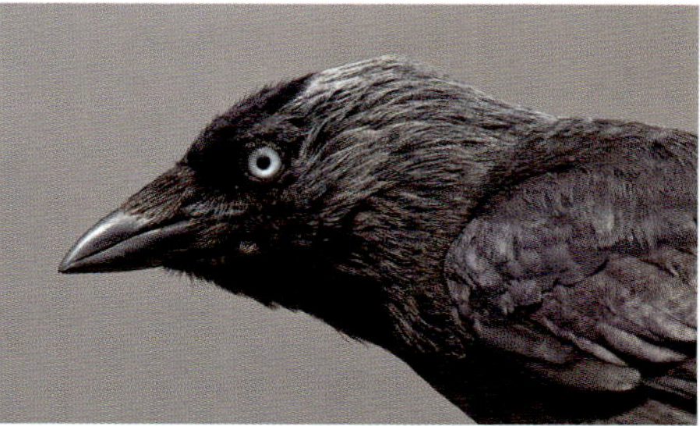

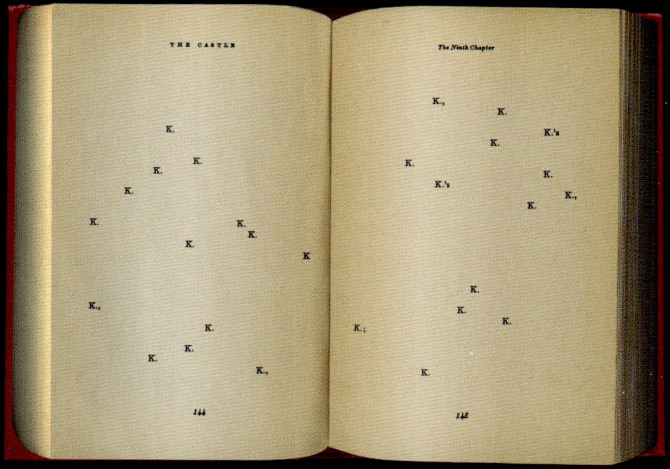

Doug Hall, *K*, from *Letters in the Dark*, 2016, triptych. Chromogenic prints, 35 × 53½ in. overall (88.9 × 133.4 cm)

My final letter from Milena to Franz from *Letters in the Dark* reads:

Dear Franz,

I've tried to act, live, think, feel rightly, guided by my conscience; but somewhere there is a fault. I want to know whether I am the kind of person who has made you suffer the way you have suffered from every other woman, so that your sickness has grown worse, so that you have had to flee from me, too, in your fear, and so that I too must get out of your life—whether I am at fault or it is a consequence of your own nature. Answer if you can. I shall be so grateful and respect your wishes from here on in. If you grant me the simple, naked truth as you know it, this will provide me with a needed point of departure.

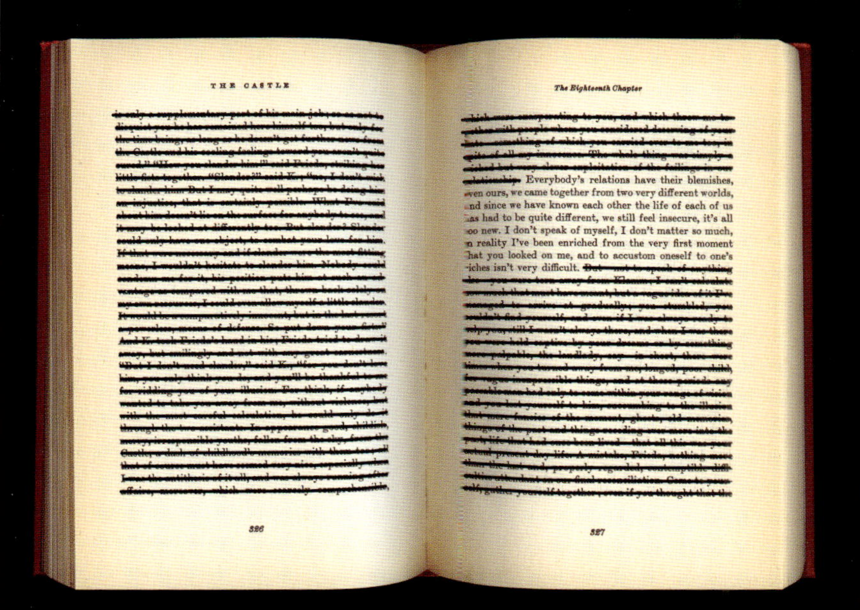

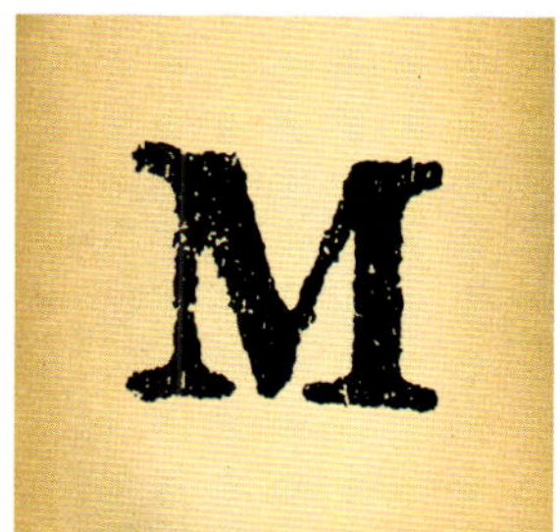

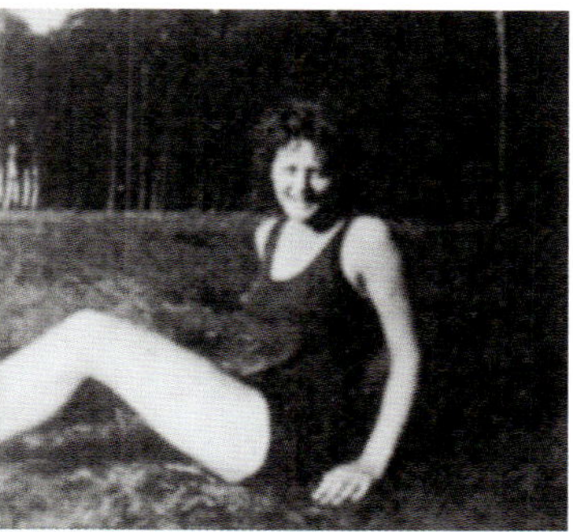

Doug Hall, *M*, from *Letters in the Dark*, 2016, triptych. Chromogenic prints, 27 × 43¾ in. overall (68.6 × 134 cm)

And Franz's last letter to Milena:
Dear Milena,
I am so ashamed of my letters I scarcely dare open your replies. I keep trying to convey something that cannot be conveyed, to explain something that cannot be explained, something in my bones, which can only be experienced in these same bones. In essence it may be nothing more than that fear we have already discussed so often, but extended to everything, fear of the greatest things as well as the smallest, fear, convulsive fear of pronouncing a single word. On the other hand, maybe this fear isn't simply fear, but also longing for something greater than anything that can inspire fear. Milena, only I am at fault because there was too little truth on my part, still far too little truth, still mostly lies, lies told out of fear of myself and fear of people. This pitcher was broken long before it went to the well. And now I'm keeping my mouth shut in order to stick with the truth a little. Lying is horrible, there's no worse mental agony. Therefore, I beg you: let me be silent, now in my letters, in Vienna, in words.

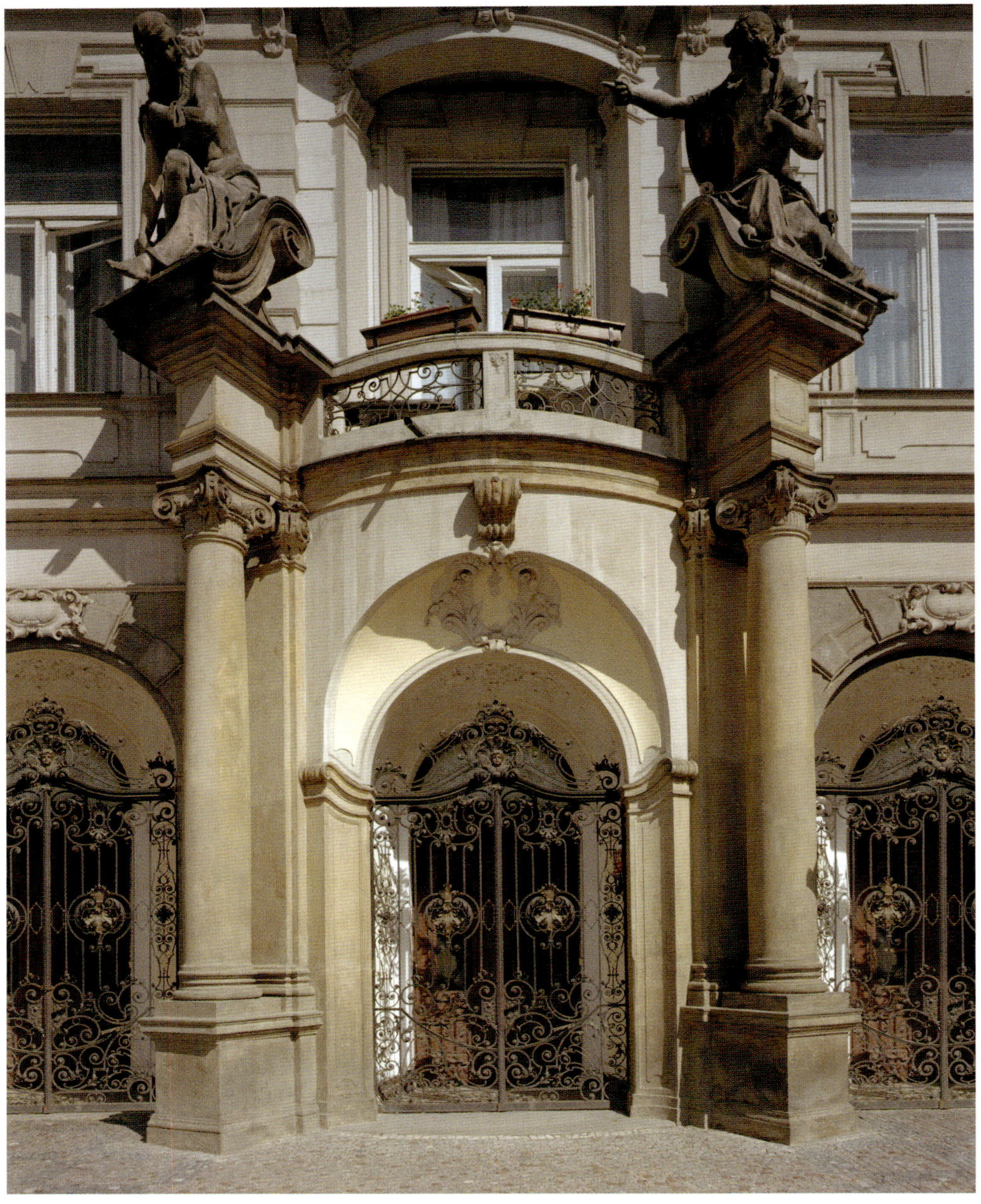

Doug Hall, *Kafka Family Residence, Old Town Square, Prague*, 2016. Chromogenic print, 37 × 30 in. (94 × 76.2 cm)

Kafka maintained a little room on the top floor of his parents' house. Together with the simple, almost miserly furnishing of the room: a bed, a wardrobe, the little, old, dark brown desk with a few books and a lot of unarranged notebooks. Although the locations changed, he seldom lived apart from the rest of the family, which was certainly not healthy for the conflicts that were inwardly consuming him.

—Max Brod, *Franz Kafka: A Biography*

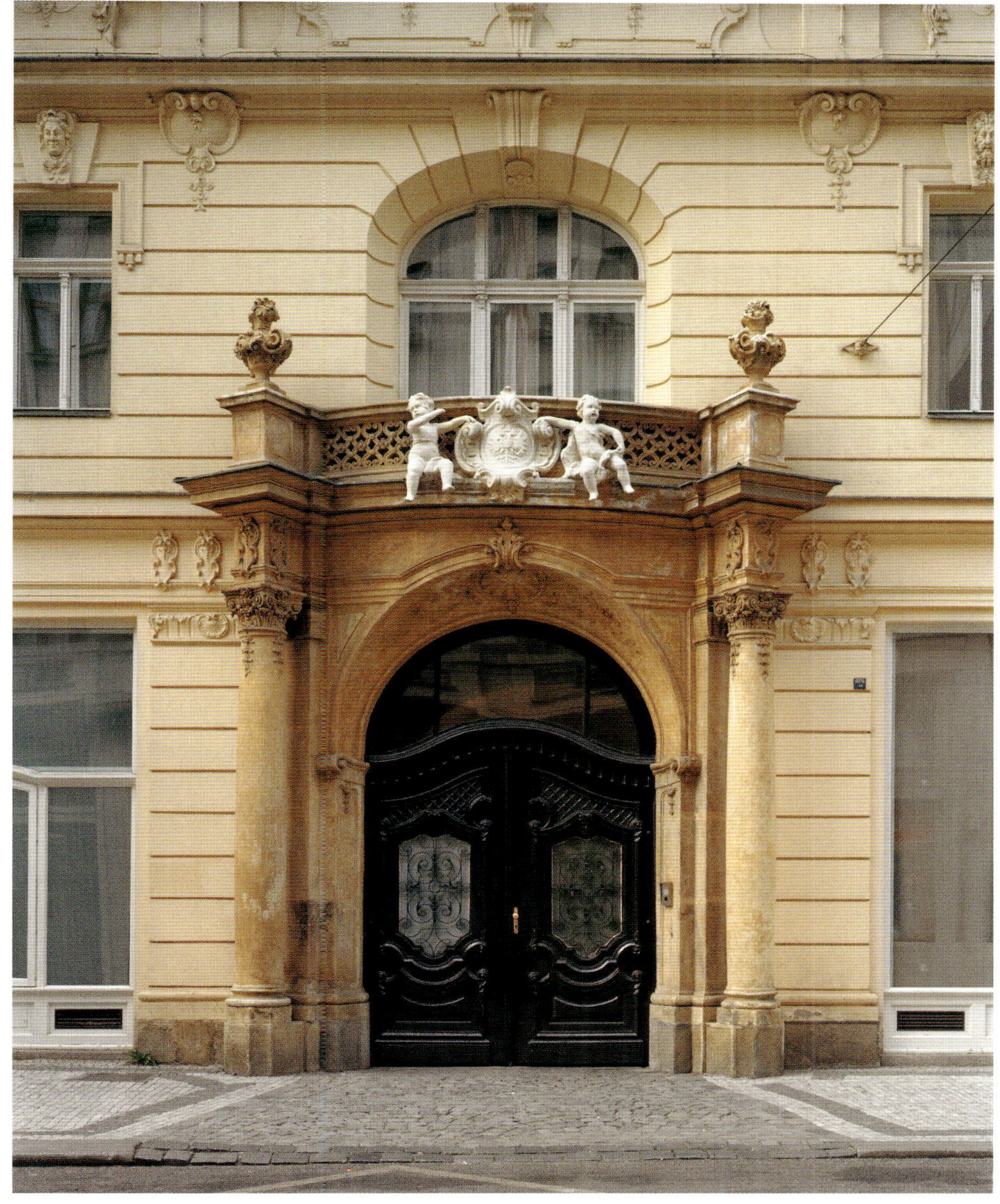

Doug Hall, *The Worker's Accident Insurance Institute, Na Poříčí 7, Prague*, 2016. Chromogenic print, 37 × 30 in. (94 × 76.2 cm)

Any official position, including his own, is something very puzzling to [Franz], very admirable, like a locomotive is for a small child. He doesn't understand the simplest things in the world.

—Milena Jesenská, letter to Max Brod

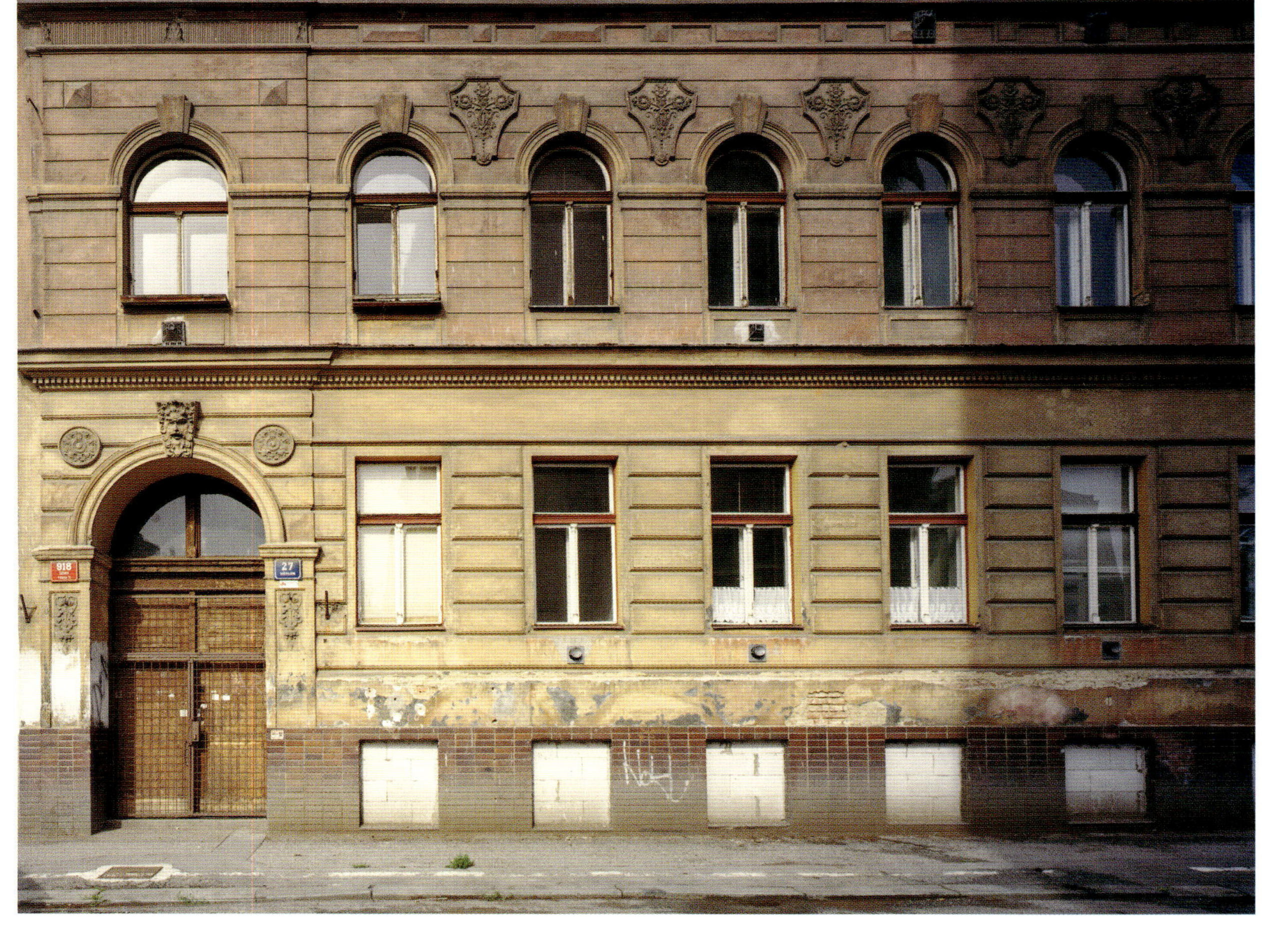

Doug Hall, *Hermann Asbestos Works, Bořivojova 27, Žižkov, Prague,* 2016. Chromogenic print, 30 × 38 in. (76.2 × 96.5 cm)

The torment that the factory causes me. Why didn't I object when they made me promise to work there in the afternoons? No one used force to make me do it, but my father compels me by his reproaches, Karl by his silence, and I by my consciousness of guilt.

—Franz Kafka, *The Diaries*, December 28, 1911

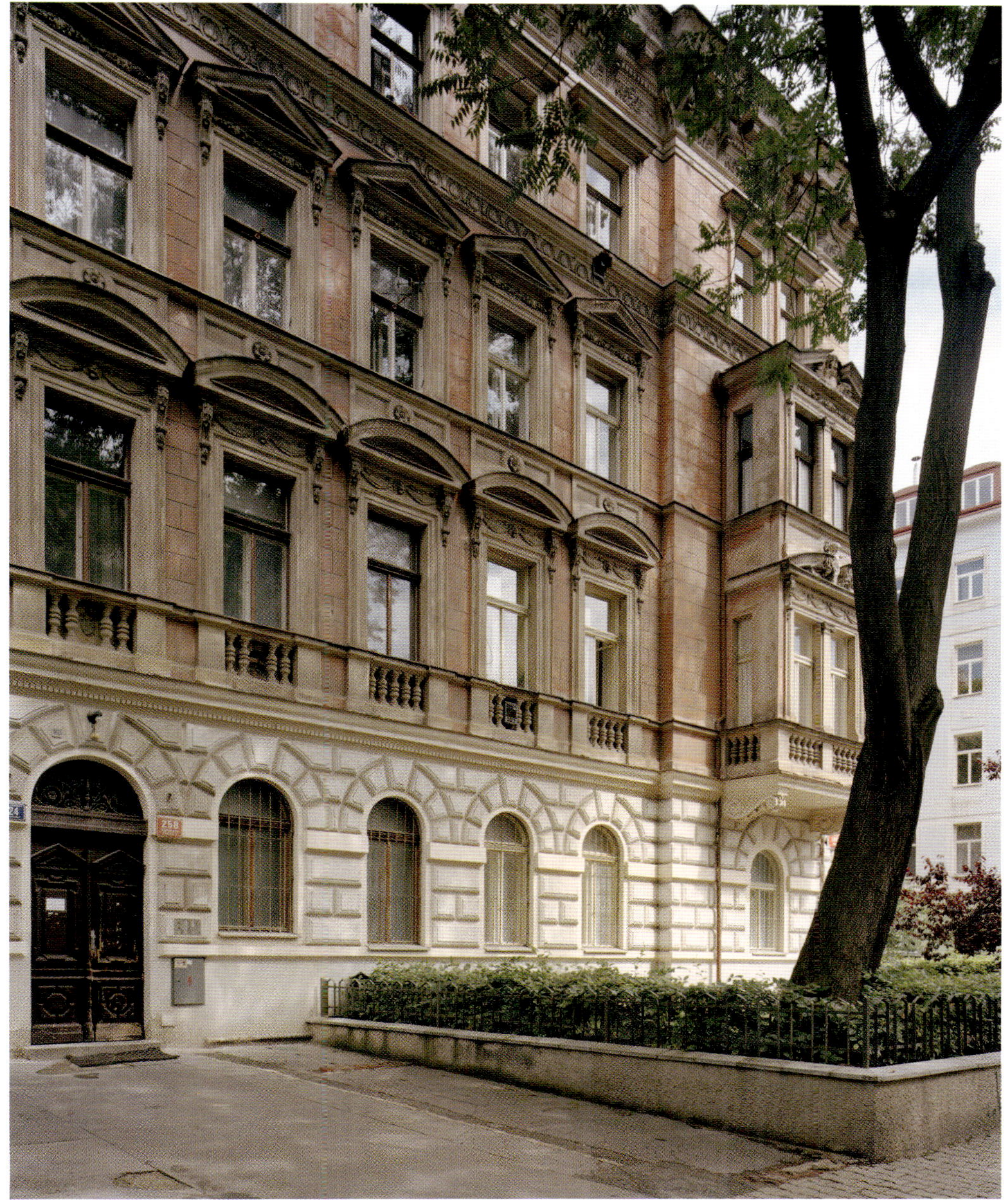

Doug Hall, *Jesenská Family Residence, Dittrichova Street, Prague*, 2016. Chromogenic print, 36½ × 30 in. (92.7 × 76.2 cm)

Milena's father, Jan, had a ferocious temper; in his frequent fits of rage, he shouted threats and obscenities. He did his tyrannical best to break Milena's spirit and force his opinions on her.

—Margarete Buber-Neumann

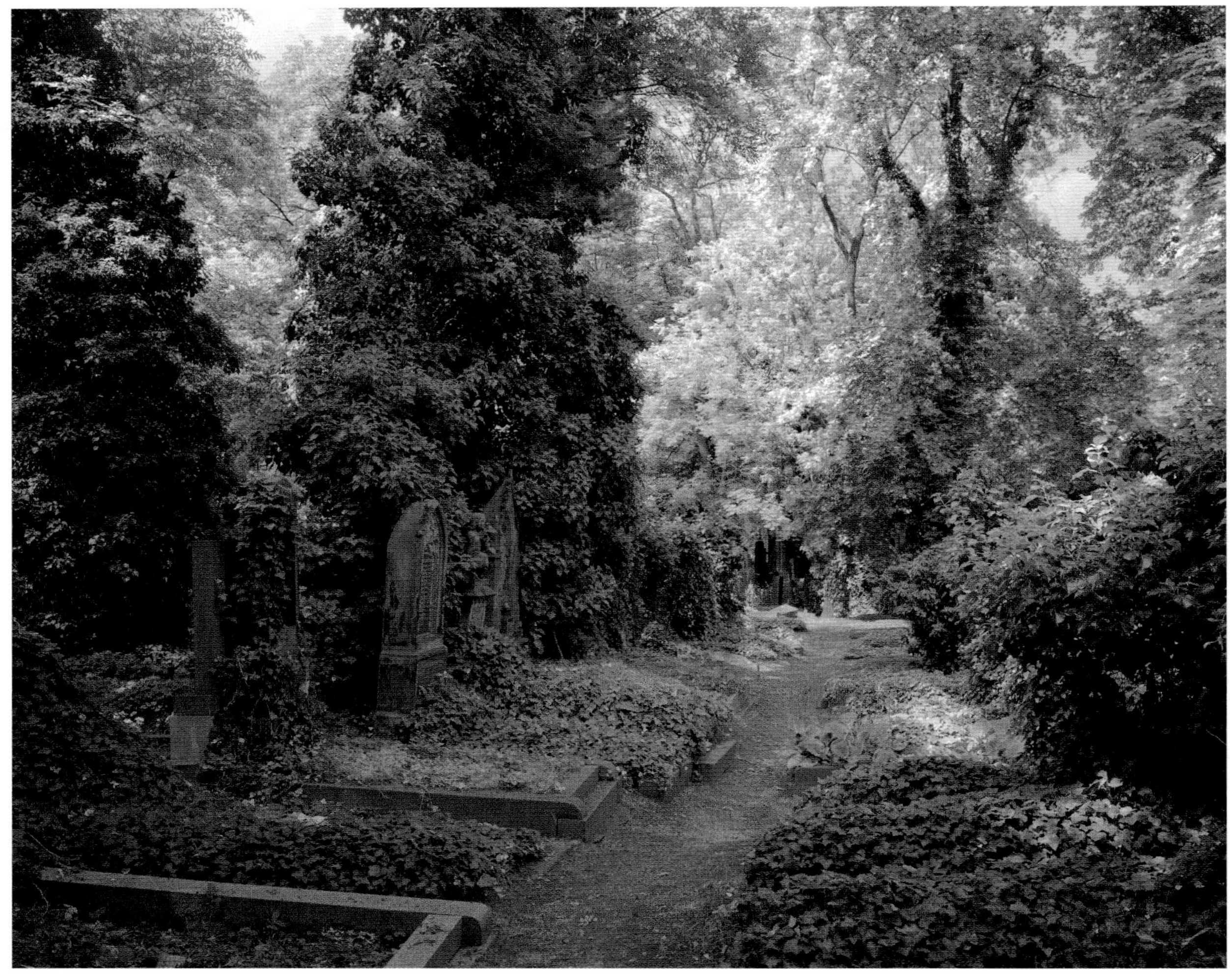

Doug Hall, *Christian Cemetery, Žižkov, Prague*, 2016. Pigment print, 43 × 49¾ in. (109.2 × 126.4 cm)

Later that afternoon someone came and told me Milena was dying. . . . Milena was in a state of euphoria. She was radiant, her dark-blue eyes were shining, and when I went up to her, she held out her arms in that beautiful gesture of hers. She was no longer able to speak. . . . Her Czech friends were surrounding her; some by her bed, others stood outside, at the window. Milena looked blissfully at them all and took her leave of life.

—Margarete Buber-Neumann on the death of Milena Jesenská at Ravensbrück

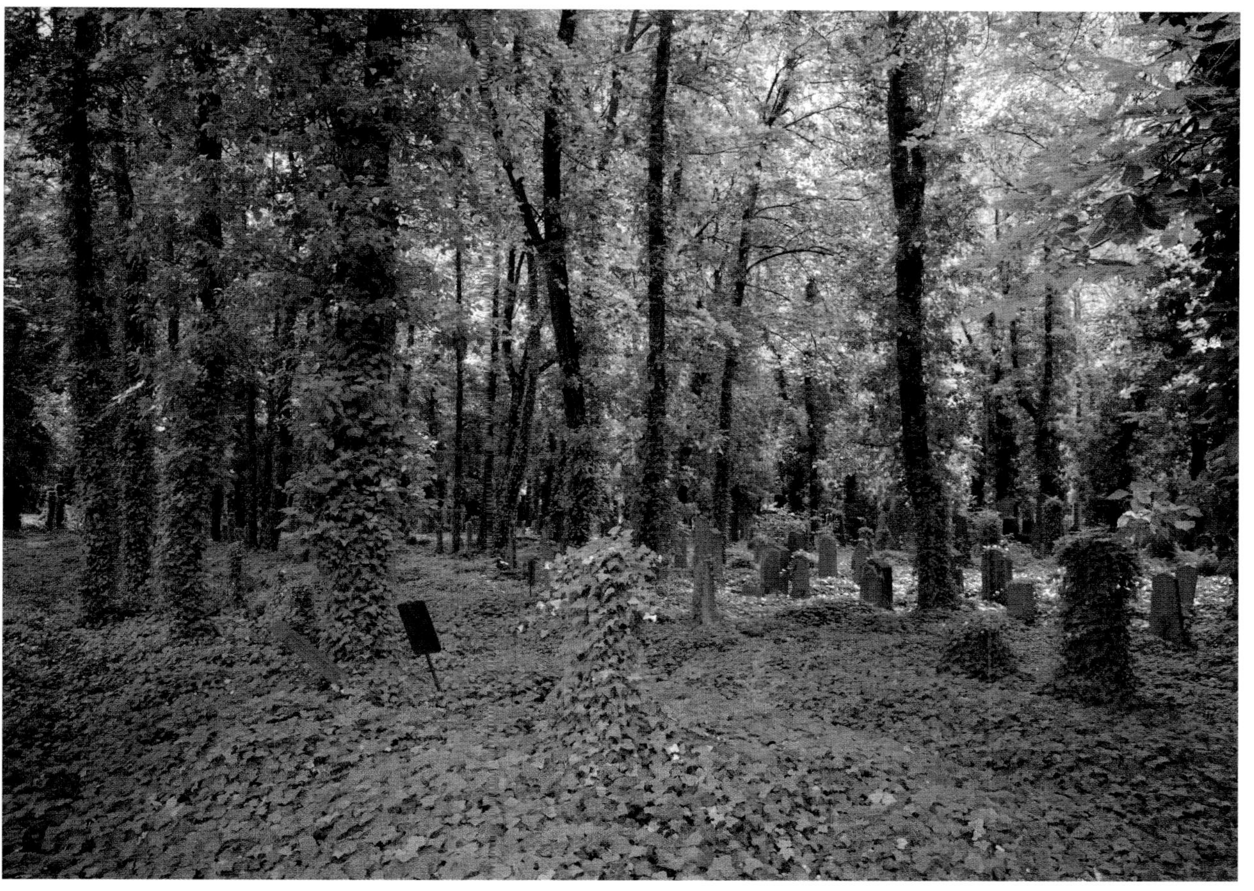

Doug Hall, *Jewish Cemetery, Žižkov, Prague*, 2016. Pigment print, 42 × 55¼ in. (106.7 × 140.3 cm)

[Franz Kafka] was shy, anxious, meek, and kind, yet the books he wrote are gruesome and painful. He saw the world as full of invisible demons, tearing apart and destroying defenseless humans. He was too clairvoyant, too intelligent to be capable of living, and too weak to fight. He was weak the way noble, beautiful people are, people incapable of struggling against their fear of misunderstanding, malice, or intellectual deceit because they recognize their own helplessness in advance; their submission only shames the victor. He understood people as only someone of great and nervous sensitivity can, someone who is alone, someone who can recognize others in a flash, almost like a prophet. His knowledge of the world was extraordinary and deep; he was himself an extraordinary and deep world.

—Milena Jesenská's obituary for Franz Kafka (an excerpt)

The Riddle Does Not Exist

It seemed certain that the fire, poised on the ridge of the grassy, oak-studded hill just east of the Oliver Ranch, would sweep down to devour everything on it, including the installation I was obsessively working on. The process that led me to this moment began two years earlier during a dinner at the California College of the Arts honoring a prominent designer. Steve Oliver, a member of the college's Board of Trustees, had invited Diane and me to join him and his wife, Nancy, at the celebration. I have known the Olivers since the late 1980s. Steve made his modest fortune in the construction business and, according to his telling, became involved with the San Francisco Museum of Modern Art to broaden his understanding of contemporary art and expand his circle of acquaintances. This, he calculated, could both benefit his business and expose him to new ideas. In the process, he became more than casually interested in the arts and started collecting contemporary works, mine included, that he accommodated in his houses. Over the course of just a few years, his interests expanded as he transitioned from collecting small works to funding and helping engineer ambitious artists' projects that are sited on his hundred-acre property in Geyserville, about seventy miles north of San Francisco. In the past twenty-five years, Steve has commissioned works by nineteen artists, including Terry Allen, Andy Goldsworthy, Ann Hamilton, Bruce Nauman, Martin Puryear, and Richard Serra.

At some point during the dinner—somewhere between the main course and dessert and probably after Steve had had a glass or two of wine—he leaned toward me and asked, "Have you ever thought about doing a project on the ranch?" I was more than slightly taken aback and don't remember how I responded. I probably stuttered something like, "No I haven't but I could." After all, it's not as if I am known for my site-specific outdoor sculptural installations. But at the same time, Steve Oliver isn't a conventional collector, and he must have had an inkling that something could come of his invitation. Over the next few days, following a couple of brief phone conversations to make sure Steve's invitation wasn't entirely wine-fueled and to get a sense of its possibilities and limitations, I started thinking about what I might do. Two potential projects began to emerge. One involved constructing a camera obscura as a way of restaging the landscape within an interior space, experienced as a projection. The other imagined treating philosopher Ludwig Wittgenstein's 1921 *Tractatus Logico-Philosophicus* as a poetic text and making it the source for a permanent sound installation at a secluded spot on the ranch. I had a vague idea that the text would be spoken by a chorus of children, but that's about as far as my thinking had evolved when Steve and I met to discuss the two options.

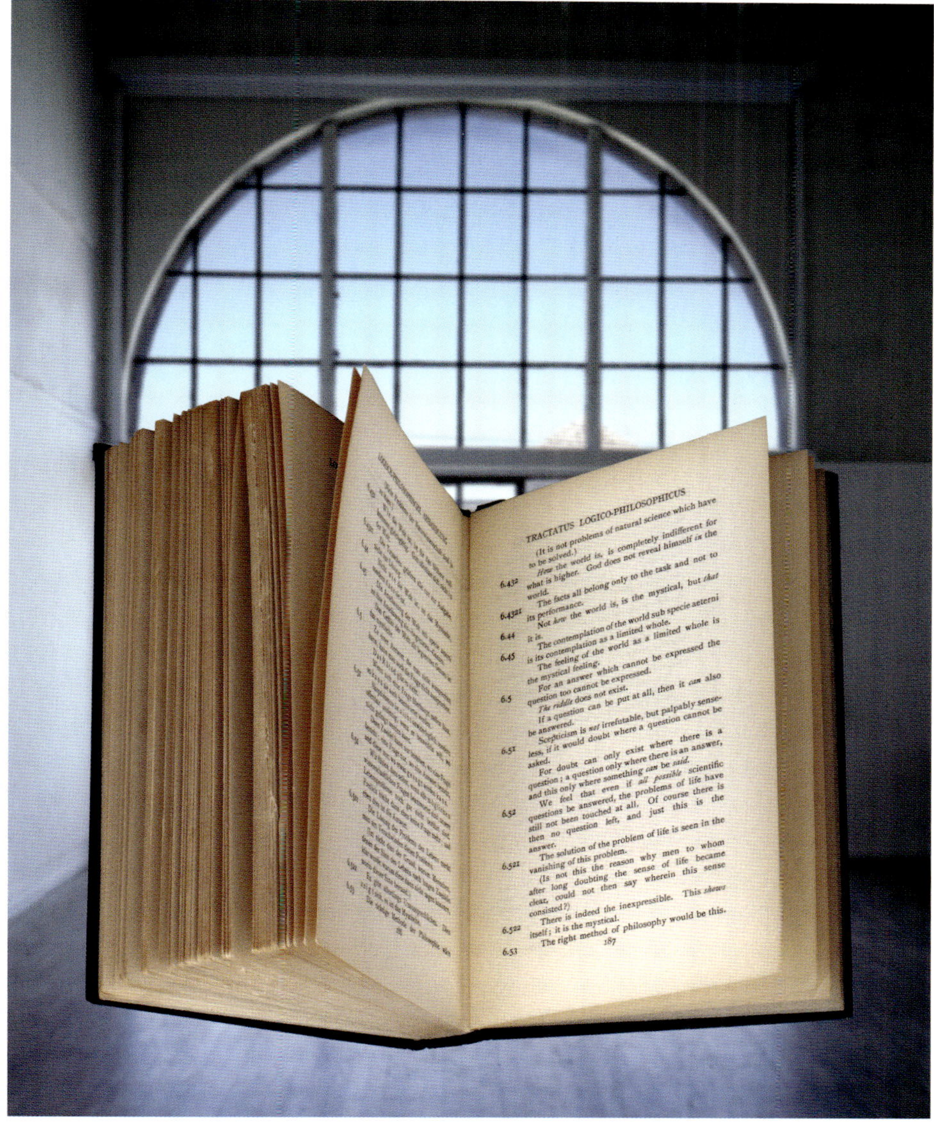

Doug Hall, *Portrait of Ludwig Wittgenstein*, 2001. Pigment print, 60¼ × 48 in. (153 × 121.9 cm)

It was with some trepidation that I presented my embryonic ideas, fearing that they were too unformed to be comprehensible. After I went through my spiel, Steve had only one question: "Which interests you the most?"

I immediately responded, "The Wittgenstein project."

"Why don't you develop that one," he said, and so it was that the project, eventually to be known as *Wittgenstein's Garden*, was born.

Tractatus Logico-Philosophicus consists of a series of short, enigmatic statements the meanings of which continue to be debated. Most philosophers will agree that it attempts to define the logical limitations of what language

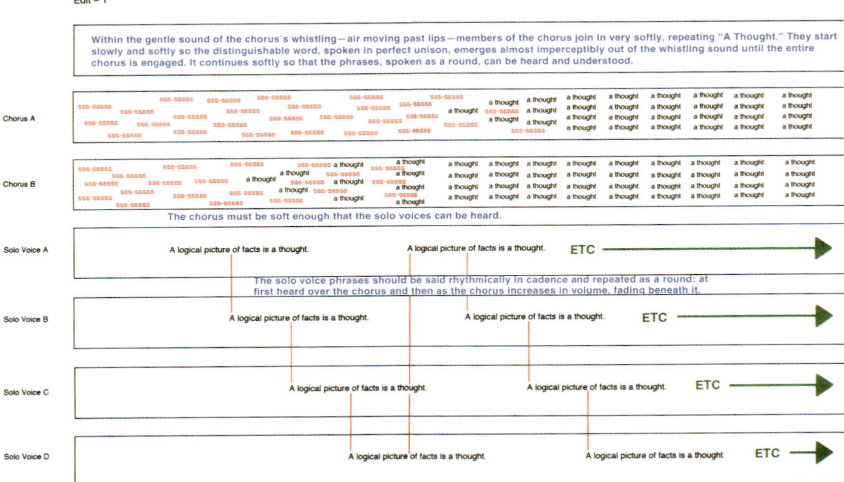

Doug Hall, "A Logical Picture of Facts Is a Thought," original graphic score for Wittgenstein's *Tractatus*

can say. Wittgenstein writes, "The limits of my language mean the limits of my world." My interpretation is that, rather than being a philosophical monument to the triumph of language, the *Tractatus* is a poignant lament to its limitations. The lament emanates from Wittgenstein's realization that our most important experiences are inexpressible through conventional language. A breeze on our cheeks, the dapple of light dancing across a landscape, the heat of the sun on our backs, the distant sound of children's voices, joy, sadness: these are feelings and experiences that transcend language's expressive possibilities. They cannot be adequately described or conveyed through mere words; they can only be shown. Wittgenstein writes, "There are indeed things that cannot be put into words. They make themselves manifest. They are what is mystical." These "mystical" things or feelings are best found or expressed through the arts, procedures that distort the conventional by showing rather than telling. Inspired by this idea of the *Tractatus* as a lament, I went into Wittgenstein's text, extracted those sections where it is best expressed, and, using a graphics program, composed it as a text that would eventually be spoken by the chorus.

Freed from the burden of understanding Wittgenstein's words—I'm not convinced anyone really can—I hoped that listeners would respond to the evocative nature of the words, allowing them to caress their imaginations, the way language can, lured by the soft voices of children while anchored to the sensations of a particular moment. This, while sitting quietly on a wooded hillside of oaks and scattered manzanitas with their thin, papery bark as red as blood.

Inspired by Oliver's encouragement and after considerable research, I reached out to Lisa Bielawa, at the time creative director of the San Francisco Girls Chorus. Immediately enthusiastic about the project, she agreed to

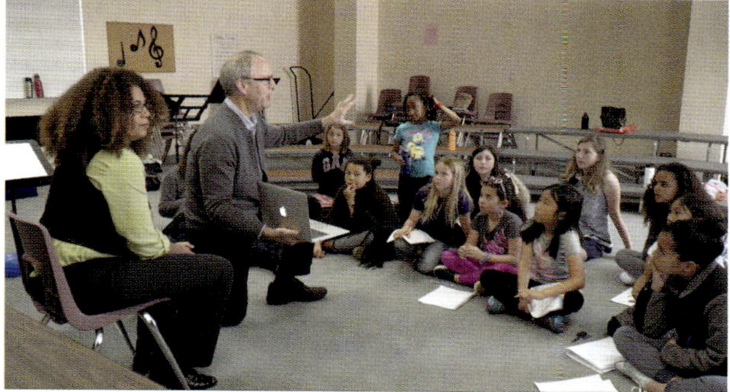

Artist trying to explain Wittgenstein to young choristers

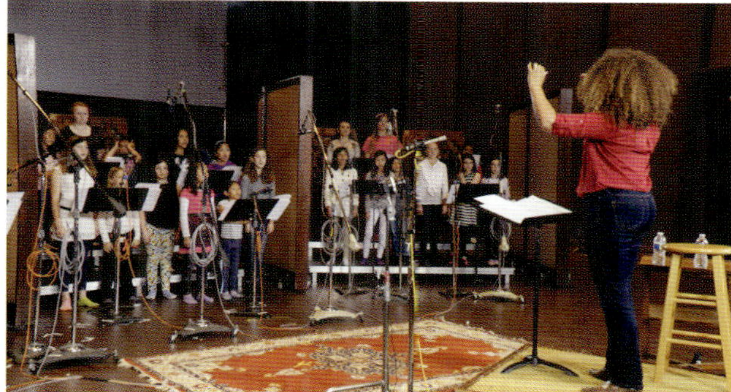

Valérie Sainte-Agathe conducting members of the San Francisco Girls Chorus during the recording at Skywalker Ranch

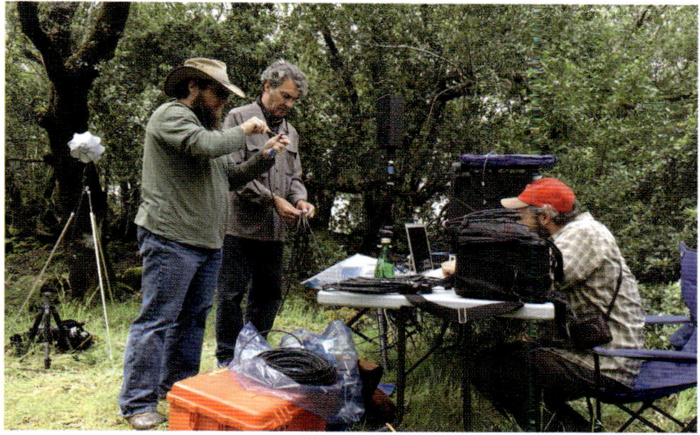

Perrin Meyer of Meyer Sound doing preliminary on-site sound study with sound designers Jim McKee and Jeremiah Moore

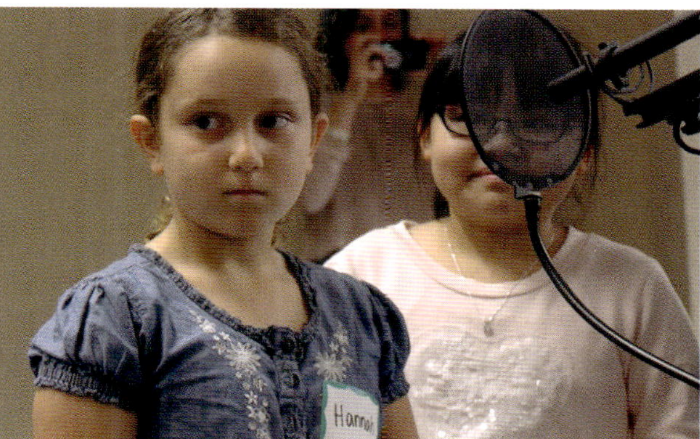

Soloists Hannah Harris and Victoria Ko from the San Francisco Girls Chorus School at an early rehearsal

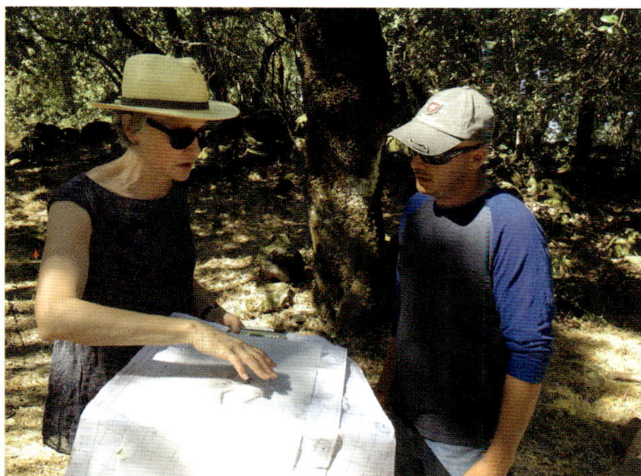

Landscape architect Andrea Cochran going over the plans with contractor Gabriel Cardenas

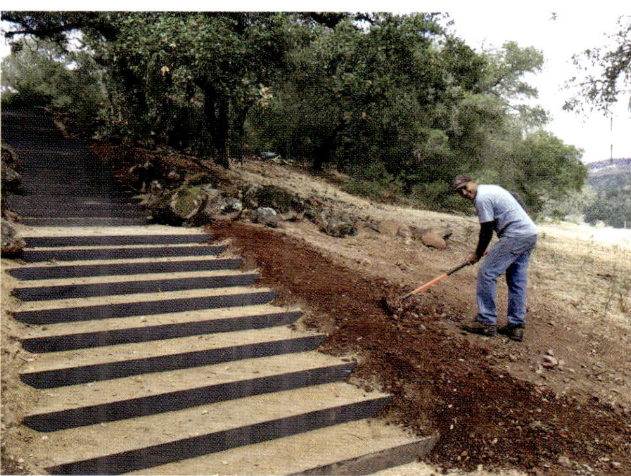

Gabriel Cardenas doing the final landscaping after completion of the stairs that lead to the listening area

assemble a group of forty young voices I would work with under the direction of choral director Valérie Sainte-Agathe. I organized the core of collaborators I'd worked with on other projects—production manager Starr Sutherland and sound designers Jim McKee and Jeremiah Moore. Lisa, a renowned composer in addition to her duties at the Girls Chorus, transcribed my graphic score into a notated one that the girls could learn. Intermittently, over several months, Valérie rehearsed the girls for the recording session that would take place at George Lucas's Skywalker Ranch. In between rehearsals and pre-production meetings, I walked the site with landscape architect Andrea Cochran, who would become instrumental in designing the listening area and the approach to it from the dirt service road below.

Over the next two years, diverted by other commitments, winter rains, and, as we neared completion in the late summer of 2017, a frightening wildfire that threatened to overcome the ranch, the surrounding fields, and Geyserville itself, we completed the project. The Pocket Fire that came within an eighth of a mile of the Oliver Ranch was one of several devastating October fires that roared through forests and communities in Marin and Sonoma Counties. The most lethal of them was the Tubbs Fire that breached Santa Rosa, killing twenty-two and destroying more than five thousand structures. The accumulated smoke and ash from all the fires was so intense that it blocked the sun as far south as San Francisco, leaving a daylong swath of darkness that looked like an apocalyptic dawn. We still refer to it as "the day without sun," which is not an exaggeration. Looking at the fire maps the morning of October 11, which included wind speeds and directions, I could see that a wall of fire was poised at the crest of the hill just east of the ranch. If things continued as they were, the fire would leap the dirt access road on the other side of the fence and rip through the ranch until it reached the Russian River just below the Oliver property. I was in despair. But just when it appeared that all was lost, the winds subsided just a bit and, more crucially, changed direction. Not radically, but enough to stop the westward rampage and turn the fire far enough south to miss the ranch. The ranch and all the projects on it were spared, although all access in and out of the area was shut down for another couple of weeks so that fire crews could move about.

In late October, when Highway 101 finally reopened, I drove through the south section of Santa Rosa that had been decimated by the fire. Great fists of flame had leaped the six-lane highway and incinerated parts of residential neighborhoods, while leaving others untouched. Houses and stores on one side of a meadow or street might be obliterated, nothing but gray ash and a few brick or stone chimneys standing, while on the other side, no damage at all. In some cases, not even the lawns adjacent to the decimated areas were singed. So arbitrary: relief for those on one side, perhaps tinged with survivor's guilt, and despair for those on the other, who lost everything.

The Oliver Ranch tours are conducted by docents, or if a group is lucky, by Steve Oliver himself, who tells his personal stories about the artists and the engineering feats that some projects required—like the massively weighty forged steel blocks that Richard Serra placed on the land that required, among other things, rebuilding the bridge across the Russian River to support them. The tours move along a dirt road and paths that circulate throughout the property, stopping at the artists' sites along the way. Mine is about the fourth stop. I situated it thinking that by the time visitors got there, they would be hot, tired, and grateful for a ten-minute rest,[8] seated on cool concrete benches on a hill shaded by trees. Visitors reach the installation by leaving the road and climbing earthen stairs, retained by Corten steel edging, that rise to the listening area situated in a lightly wooded section of the ranch. Before mounting the stairs, visitors can look up the slope to see fragments of the benches, partially obscured by the curve of the hill. As they begin their ascent, they might notice a few of the speakers on stands from which they hear voices speaking softly and intimately. Arriving at the site, where the sound becomes more distinct, visitors notice that the voices are those of children, coming from sixteen speakers situated within and around the space. The words of four soloists come from speakers set close to the benches; at a middle distance, a chorus of recorded voices joins a third group coming from speakers set far back in the woods. Meanwhile, birds flutter and chirp, light winds rustle the trees, while visitors, from their perches on the shaded rise, look out onto rolling, oak-dotted hills: green in the spring, golden in the early summer, and parched and brown by fall.

There was some critical disagreement as to the success, or even the relevance, of my staging Wittgenstein's text within a bucolic landscape. That is to be expected. However, at that moment in my life, *Wittgenstein's Garden* came as close as I ever have, or probably ever will, to evoking thoughts and feelings that had become most important to me: the reflective repose that hides within our urges to action; the thoughts that can ruminate when we are massaged by the gentle voices of children, whose complex language nurtures and reveals our hidden thoughts, sparking unexpected associations—all while looking past the dipping, weathered branches onto the sun-drenched hills and valley beyond. From a child close at hand come words, picked up in the distance as refrains that are passed about the way children might throw a ball back and forth:

8. I ended up producing two versions. The first, the artist's cut, is about twenty minutes, and it is the one I play whenever I take a group to the site. In my estimation it is the length it needs to be. However, there was a consensus among the docents that it was too long, so we edited a version that is half the duration. With a button hidden along the path, it is easy for the tour leader to select one or the other.

> The world of the happy man
> is different from that of the unhappy man.
> So too
> at death
> the world does not alter
> but comes to an end.
>
> Death is not an event in life:
> we do not live to experience death.
> If we take eternity to mean
> not infinite temporal duration
> but timelessness
> then eternal life belongs to those who live in the present.
>
> When the answer cannot be put into words
> neither can the question be put into words.
> The riddle does not exist.
>
> We feel
> that even when all possible scientific questions have been answered
> the problems of life remain completely untouched.
>
> Of course there are no questions left
> and this itself is the answer.

And the famous last statement of the *Tractatus*:

> Those things about which we cannot speak
> we must pass over in silence.

If you recall, for Kafka too, the will to language ends in silence. He writes, "Milena, only I am at fault because there was too little truth on my part. . . . And now I'm keeping my mouth shut in order to stick with the truth a little. . . . I beg you: let me be silent, now in my letters, in Vienna, in words." And it is here that I will make my own nod to silence, which, less final than Kafka's, acknowledges that while silence might close out the past, it leaves open infinite possibilities for the future and, contrary to Wittgenstein's assertion, a world that is resplendent with questions.

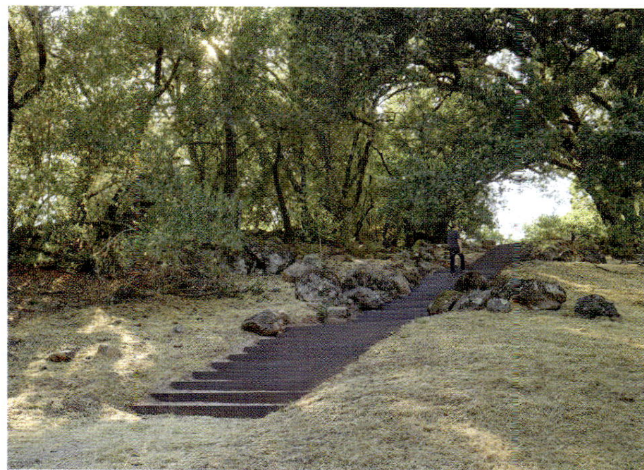

Wittgenstein's Garden, showing stairs leading to the listening area shortly after their completion and before the area was seeded with native grasses
Photograph by Marion Brenner

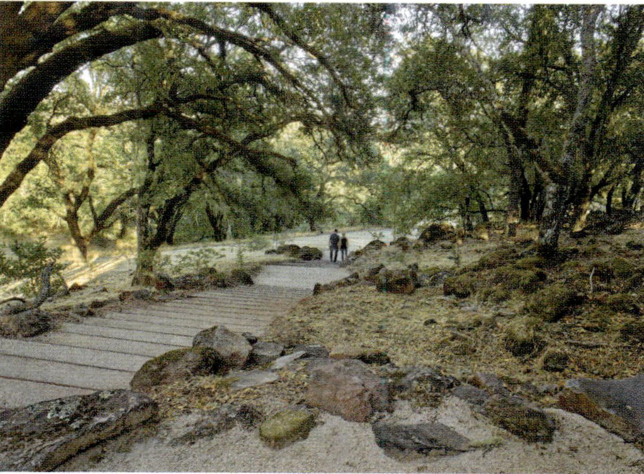

Wittgenstein's Garden, showing the stairs as seen from the listening area
Photograph by Marion Brenner

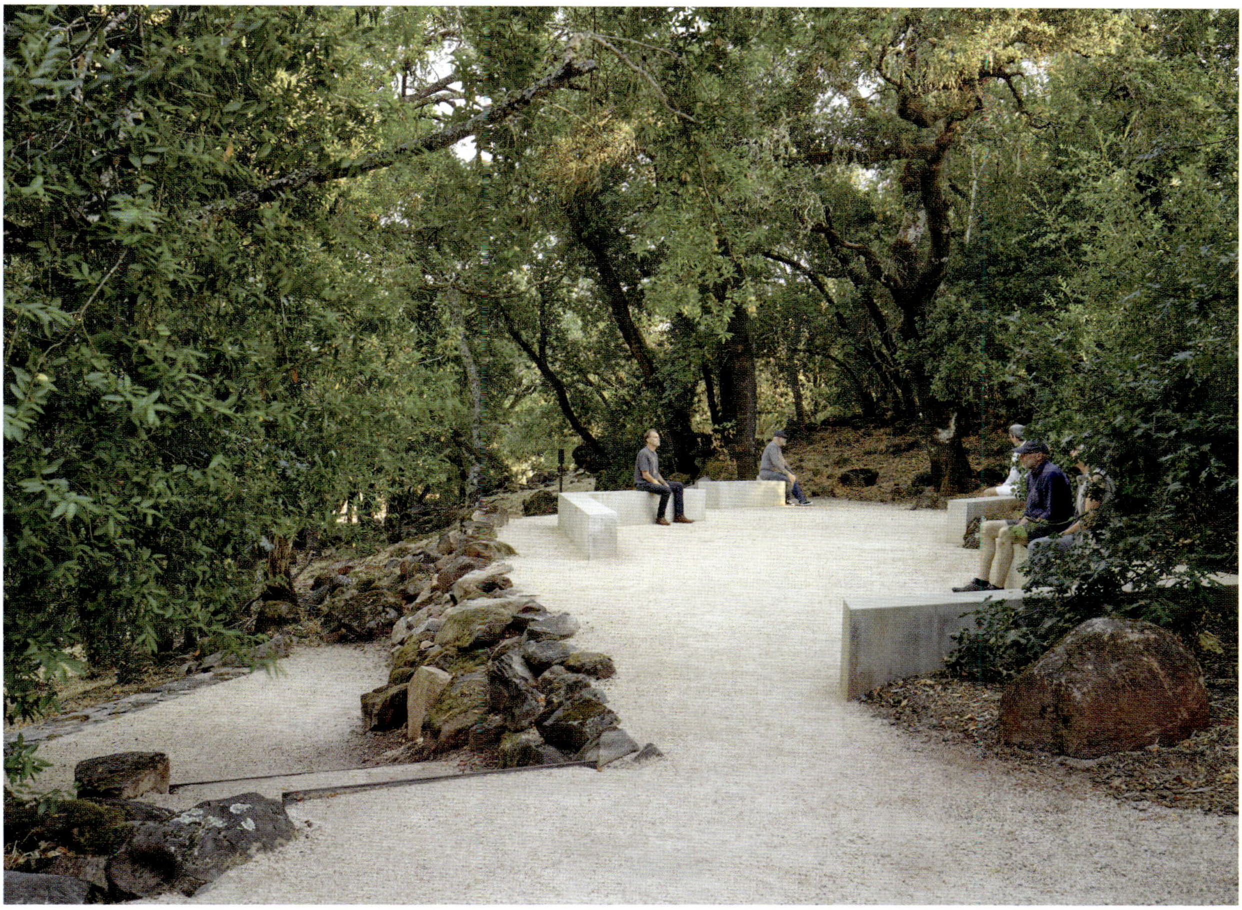

Wittgenstein's Garden, showing the listening area
Photograph by Marion Brenner

Coda

Given that we share ninety percent of our DNA with cats,
seventy percent with slugs, sixty percent with bananas,
fifty percent with trees, forty-four percent with honeybees,
and twenty-five percent with daffodils, isn't it fair to conclude
that all living things are truly connected?

—Doug Hall, *Time, Memory, and the Winter Oaks of Olompali Valley*

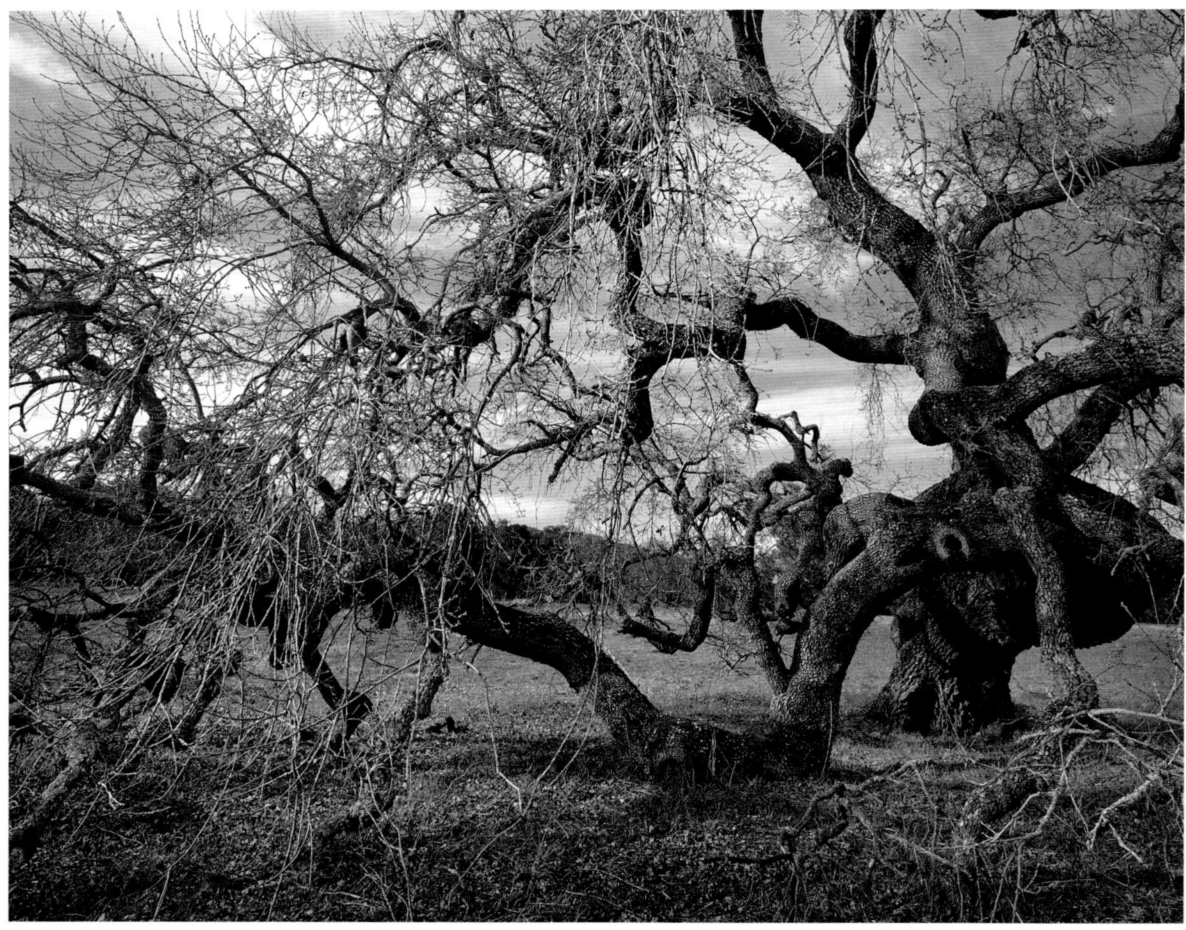

Doug Hall, *Olompali Valley Oak II*, 2023. Pigment print, 48 × 62 in. (121.9 × 157.5 cm)